GD GEW.070

A NEW
INTRODUCTION
TO
FINANCIAL ACCOUNTING

ROBERT G. MAY
University of Washington

GERHARD G. MUELLER
University of Washington

THOMAS H. WILLIAMS
University of Texas

A NEW INTRODUCTION TO FINANCIAL ACCOUNTING

PRENTICE-HALL, INC., Englewood Cliffs, New Jersey

657.4
M46n

Library of Congress Cataloging in Publication Data

MAY, ROBERT G
  A new introduction to financial accounting.

  Includes bibliographical references and index.
    1. Accounting. I. Mueller, Gerhard G., joint author.
II. Williams, Thomas Howard, joint author. III. Title.
HF5635.M454   657'.48   75-4622
ISBN 0-13-615021-7

© 1975 by Prentice-Hall, Inc., Englewood Cliffs, New Jersey

All rights reserved. No part of this book
may be reproduced in any form or by any means
without permission in writing from the publisher.

Printed in the United States of America

10 9 8 7 6 5 4 3 2 1

PRENTICE-HALL INTERNATIONAL, INC., London
PRENTICE-HALL OF AUSTRALIA, PTY. LTD., Sydney
PRENTICE-HALL OF CANADA, LTD., Toronto
PRENTICE-HALL OF INDIA PRIVATE LIMITED, New Delhi
PRENTICE-HALL OF JAPAN, INC., Tokyo

To Carol, Coralie, and Nancy
. . . and to our parents

UNIVERSITY LIBRARIES
CARNEGIE-MELLON UNIVERSITY
PITTSBURGH, PENNSYLVANIA 15213

657.4
M46n

Contents

I
ECONOMIC DECISION MAKING
AND INFORMATION

III
THE CONTEMPORARY CORPORATE
REPORTING ENVIRONMENT

Foreword

The role that accounting plays in our society today has greater significance than at any previous time. This is recognized more and more in accounting education. Considerable attention is being directed to experimentation with different approaches to the accounting curriculum. In particular, a great deal of thought has been given to finding a new and effective way to teach the introductory accounting course as evidenced by the 1971 report of the Study Group on Introductory Accounting.

This book, as an immediate outgrowth of the Study Group report, furnishes a new and relevant approach to the initial course in accounting. It is a welcome addition to the available literature.

WILLIAM R. GIFFORD, CPA
Secretary, Price Waterhouse Foundation

Preface

The title of this book implies something *new* in accounting textbook literature—an accurate description, we believe. However, the overall objective and tone of the book are a product of some longheld beliefs and attitudes of many accounting educators toward the first college-level course in accounting. Distillation of these attitudes and beliefs into the present book began in March 1968. At that time a group of four accounting educators, Paul E. Fertig, Herbert E. Miller, Gerhard G. Mueller, and Robert T. Sprouse, met in New York under the sponsorship of the Price Waterhouse Foundation to propose an exploration of a possible *new* introduction to accounting. This proposal, which eventually spawned the Study Group on Introductory Accounting, their 1971 report, and, in turn, the writing of this textbook, centered on the following statement of educational philosophy:

> The importance of accounting as a whole to a private enterprise society suggests that the first course in accounting should not be influenced by the educational needs of prospective accounting majors [alone]. Instead it should seek to convey to a general audience of college students the conceptual content of accounting, the overall scope of the accounting function, and the interpretation of accounting reports. Furthermore it should, in analytical

terms, have a primary educational objective of informed citizenship. As such, the course should be important for all college students without regard to major areas.

The notion that the first course in accounting should meet the needs of the "student citizen" rather than exclusively the needs of the student of accounting is deceptively simple. Most accounting educators are confident that some accounting education would be beneficial to all students (citizens). However, in attempting to adapt the content of the first course in accounting to this goal, we faced some difficulties (constraints). First, to convey ". . . the conceptual content of accounting, the overall scope of the accounting function, and the interpretation of accounting reports . . ." to any audience is a truly formidable task without regard to the time allowed. Second, few nonaccounting, nonbusiness majors find more than one course in accounting consistent with their many other interests and the requirements of their degrees. Third, most accounting educators, including ourselves, are skeptical about the usefulness of so-called "survey" courses in accounting. Fourth, most first-year accounting curricula are divided into financial accounting and managerial accounting segments, presented in that order. And, fifth, many educators (and students) are more satisfied with the intellectual and pedagogical character of present-day introductory managerial accounting courses than with the counterpart financial accounting courses.

The combination of a demanding objective and so many constraints led us to the realization that some compromise was unavoidable. We chose, therefore, to narrow the scope of the undertaking rather than lapse into superficiality—hence "accounting" in our title is modified by "financial." However, we feel that this concession to the "typical" curriculum and to the vastness of the territory to be covered is the only significant concession that was necessary in implementing the objectives of "A New Introduction . . ." as presented earlier. Several years of classroom experimentation with our text materials convinced us that the course we would design for a future business and/or accounting major *does not differ at the introductory level* from the ideal course for the student-at-large. This is particularly true if all three types of students enter the same first course at the sophomore level when career objectives and goals are still quite fluid.

In this book, then, we introduce the student to (1) accounting as an intellectual discipline, having a primarily utilitarian, as opposed to purely aesthetic, orientation, (2) accounting as an information specialization in society, having professional level achievement and status as one of its many manifestations, and (3) accounting as a social force, having policy implications that affect the welfare of virtually all citizens. We use the vehicle of financial accounting subject matter to accomplish these goals. At the same time our objective, in terms of specific skills, is to develop financial statement "literacy" rather than technology only.

In Part I (Chapters 1–3) we set the stage by developing certain contextual bases for later reference. Among these bases are (1) the nature of decision making, (2) the role of information in decisions, (3) conditions favorable to information specialization, (4) the role of the business enterprise, particularly the corporation, in a market economy, (5) classes of external decisions concerning the business enterprise, especially investment decisions and wealth distribution decisions (dividend policy, taxation, etc.), and (6) the demand that these decision interests create for the information specialization known as financial accounting. Necessarily, the question of what kinds of potentially useful financial accounting information about the enterprise might be produced for investment decision makers had to be addressed. Therefore the nature of the investment decision is explored in some depth, and a simplified model for investment decision making (the present value model) is fully developed. Basically in Part I the foundation is laid for developing financial accounting *in context*.

Part II consists of an exploration of the major alternative external reporting (financial accounting) models of the business enterprise. It is here that the intellectual challenge of accounting is most evident. The discussion begins with consideration of management forecasts and management-provided present values of the enterprise. It then proceeds in a logical, cohesive way to explore each of the other major alternatives in turn. Four major alternatives are treated as complete, technically feasible financial accounting models. The alternatives are (1) conventional accounting, (2) general price-level adjusted conventional accounting, (3) replacement cost accounting, and (4) market (exit) value accounting. Conventional accounting receives the greatest attention because it dominates present-day practice and can be used as a basis for introducing the others. However, the discussion is purposely even-handed, so that the reader is not encouraged to become "fixated" on *any one* of the models.

Each model is explored in the context of both the investment and wealth distribution type decisions. The central measurement principles of each are introduced and applied. Moreover, the applications are in terms of the financial accounting outputs for the entire enterprise rather than at the individual asset or liability level. This provides sufficient perspective to discuss the alternatives as possible financial reporting systems rather than only as asset valuation bases. Discussion includes strong and weak points and conditions favoring and disfavoring each model, along with interpretations of the major financial measurements (statements) produced under each.

Early in the discussion of conventional accounting the financial position framework (equation) is introduced along with transaction analysis and the accounting cycle. However, at this point we omit the traditional implements of the general journal, general ledger, and debit-credit terminology on the grounds that they are nonessential to the discussion and may be an obstacle to some students in grasping major concepts and relationships. We recognize, though, that many instructors may feel just the opposite and have developed their pedagogical techniques and styles accordingly. For their early use—*and everyone's attention at some point*—we have covered conventional financial accounting data gathering and processing requirements (including traditional bookkeeping methods) in the Appendix to the book. This placement affords maximum flexibility, since every instructor has the choice of covering the material wherever it is perceived to be most relevant (but only *after* the coverage of the basic accounting cycle in Chapter 5).

The discussion of alternative financial accounting models in Part II naturally raises the question of which is best. We therefore end Part II and begin Part III with a discussion of the dilemma of choosing a "best" financial accounting system. We point out that since a particular selection will inevitably favor some members of society and disfavor others, there will probably never be unanimity as to the best alternative. This and other dimensions of the problem make the selection of a financial accounting system a "social choice" requiring an institutional framework. That accounting information is essential to the perceived fairness and efficiency of the capital markets is still further reason for not leaving the choice of a financial accounting system in the hands of individuals who pursue only their private interests.

As an outgrowth of this transitional discussion the history of accounting policy making is briefly traced from the stockmarket crash of 1929 to the present. The influence of pre-1935 financial accounting practices and the steadfastness of the SEC preference for original transaction values (the conventional model) plus the dynamism and aggressiveness of post-World War II business activity go far in explaining present-day accounting policy-making problems. This, of course, sets the stage for an appreciation of present-day financial reporting practice and its variety of measurement rules for applying (principally) the conventional accounting model.

Throughout our coverage of present-day financial reporting practices in Part III we emphasize the duality of income recognition and related asset and/or equity valuation, rather than merely jumping from one type of asset or equity to another. We also cover certain representative areas of difficulty in applying conventional accounting where recognition or interpretation of underlying business transactions, elements of financial position involved, and/ or the entity to be accounted for are far from unambiguous (specifically, tax allocation, leases, and intercorporate investments). To reinforce major financial statement relationships we give very thorough treatment to Statements of Changes in Financial Position and the related notion of the relationship between income, working capital, and cash flows from operations. To ensure an appreciation for the totality of present-day financial reporting Part III ends with two chapters devoted to (1) the dissemination and interpretation of financial statement information, and (2) the application of the attest function to financial reporting.

Having achieved a fairly deep appreciation of accounting thought and practice in the financial accounting context as developed in this volume, we find that students can readily gain a rudimentary grasp of the counterpart dimensions of other areas of accounting activity with relatively brief exposure. For instructors who wish to achieve this additional breadth, particularly for students who take only one course, we have written a modular supplemental paperback volume entitled *A Brief Introduction to Managerial and Social Uses of Accounting*. This volume is composed of two chapters introducing managerial applications of accounting within business enterprises, one chapter covering financial and managerial applications in public sector organizations, and one chapter describing accounting applications in the management of the total economy (including income taxation, regulation, and national income accounting). It has been published separately to give instructors the option of providing more breadth without imposing a single high-priced volume on all instructors and students.

As teachers we have enjoyed the success that has come from using this book in our classrooms. We hope that others will find similar satisfaction when their students discover excitement and challenge in *A New Introduction to Financial Accounting*.

Credits

In 1967 a group of accounting educators proposed an intensive review of the collegiate introductory accounting course as it was generally taught at that time. With generous financial support from the Price Waterhouse Foundation, a Study Group organized itself to accomplish this task. The members of this group, representing a cross-section of higher education in accounting in the United States, originally included: E. H. Caplan, N. Dopuch, T. R. Dyckman, W. L. Ferrara, P. E. Fertig, J. Gray, R. H. Hermanson, C. Lawrence, H. E. Miller, G. G. Mueller, V. E. Odmark, A. Rappaport, R. T. Sprouse, J. A. Tracy, and T. H. Williams; although Professors Fertig, Hermanson, and Miller withdrew before completion of the group's work for compelling personal reasons. The Study Group published its recommendations in a 1971 report entitled *A New Introduction to Accounting,* which provided the intellectual stimulus for this book. Our debt to the work of this Study Group is substantial indeed.

After publication of the Study Group report, the Price Waterhouse Foundation supported several initial classroom applications of the Study Group's recommendations. Mr. William R. Gifford of the National Office of Price Waterhouse & Co. encouraged and nourished this project with the greatest possible foresight and determination.

We are especially grateful that at no time did the Price Waterhouse Foundation or any of the partners in Price Waterhouse & Co. attempt to influence or otherwise shape the contents of this book or the earlier Study Group report.

Fellow teachers have unselfishly provided comments on earlier drafts of this book. Some have also provided valuable problem and exercise materials for incorporation in the book. This group includes our University of Washington colleagues: D. T. DeCoster, W. L. Felix, Jr., L. C. Heath, A. Martin (now in public accounting practice), F. J. Mueller, and G. L. Sundem. It further includes D. D. Bourque of the State University of New York, F. D. S. Choi of the University of Hawaii, J. W. Deskins of the University of Illinois, C. T. Horngren of Stanford University, M. E. T. Longstaff of Highline Community College, H. E. Miller of Arthur Andersen & Co., G. B. Stenberg of San Francisco State University, R. J. Thacker of Louisiana State University, and D. J. Zulauf of Pacific Lutheran University. The help received from these colleagues provided much inspiration from draft to draft.

Billy Goetz of Florida Atlantic University, Martin L. Gosman of the University of Massachusetts, and Philip Meyers of Rochester University reviewed the manuscript in its entirety. We acknowledge with many thanks the helpful suggestions which these reviews provided.

Several graduate students at the University of Texas and at the University of Washington assisted in a number of ways in the preparation of the book. Some of them also struggled with the use of preliminary materials in actual teaching situations. We gratefully acknowledge the efforts of R. C. Burke (now at the University of Saskatchewan), J. S. Cherry, W. A. Collins (now at the University of Florida), J. S. Fuhrmann (now at the University of Illinois), E. C. Keller (now at the University of Michigan), J. D. Newton (now at the University of Alberta), H. O. Rockness (now at the University of North Carolina), D. A. Snowball (now at the University of Florida), and B. H. Spicer. A number of teaching assistants and predoctoral associates, many of whom have meanwhile completed their studies, were involved with classroom applications of preliminary text materials. All of them helped to make this book more readable and more teachable.

No book could ever be produced without capable and efficient manuscript production. Although many individuals typed portions of the manuscript, often several times in succession, we are particularly indebted to Mrs. Mary Friou, Administrative Assistant to the Department of Accounting at the University of Texas; and to Ms. Sylvia Christensen, Secretary of the Department of Accounting at the University of Washington, who in addition to production efforts, ably coordinated publication and distribution of early preliminary editions of the manuscript. We owe them both a very special vote of thanks.

The Seattle office of Price Waterhouse & Co. gave much administrative support to both the Study Group and the book production efforts. This too is gratefully acknowledged.

ROBERT G. MAY
GERHARD G. MUELLER
THOMAS H. WILLIAMS

A NEW
INTRODUCTION
TO
FINANCIAL ACCOUNTING

I

ECONOMIC DECISION MAKING
AND INFORMATION

1

The Nature and
Environment of
Accounting

WHAT IS ACCOUNTING?

Accounting is a language. It is used to communicate financial and other information to people, organizations, governments, and some technical information processing and storage devices.

Accounting information is used when one applies for a mortgage loan at a bank or when a candidate for political office wishes to make public some formal statements about his or her* financial situation. Business enterprises use accounting to plan and control their business activities and to report the results of these activities to stockholders, creditors, labor unions, and governmental agencies. Organizations not organized for profit—for example, churches and private hospitals—also use accounting for planning, conducting, and finally reporting their activities.

Governmental units do likewise. Local school districts or fire districts must organize their financial affairs as efficiently as possible, and account-

---

* In general "he" and "his" are used alone throughout this book rather than "he or she," "he/she," "person," or any other "balanced" pronoun configuration. This is done for the sake of *convenience* and *readability* only.

ing helps to do this. Larger governmental units like the Department of Health, Education, and Welfare have the same problem. In fact, accounting plays a vital role in international government agencies like the International Monetary Fund or the World Health Organization. Thus we can readily agree with the authoritative definition put forth by the American Institute of Certified Public Accountants (AICPA): "Accounting is a discipline which provides financial and other information essential to the efficient conduct and evaluation of the activities of any organization."

Having defined accounting very broadly in terms of the functions it serves in society, we can now take a brief look at its nature. While accounting is many things to many people, its nature is essentially threefold: (1) an intellectual discipline, (2) a profession, and (3) a social force.

An Intellectual Discipline

The totality of knowledge has grown so rapidly during the last century that an individual can no longer command even a cursory acquaintance with all of it. For purposes of convenience and specialized study, society has divided knowledge into separate fields. Among such fields are philosophy, physics, mathematics, political science, biology, and economics. These and other academic fields and specialized study areas are often called intellectual disciplines, or simply disciplines.

Boundaries between individual disciplines tend to be artificial and ill defined. Most business scholars agree that accounting is a separate discipline. As a field of knowledge, it is concerned with *measurements* and *information* that are useful for a broad range of decision making.

Other disciplines are also concerned with measurements and information. Thus the boundaries of accounting merge readily and significantly with the boundaries of economics, sociology, engineering, psychology, law, public administration, and statistics, to name but a few. When accounting is related to and combined with other disciplines, it tends to be more useful than when it stands alone.

Since we are concerned here with an introduction to accounting, we must never lose sight of accounting's sister disciplines. Much of the strength of the accounting discipline is drawn from insights gained in other disciplines and then transferred to accounting.

Logic and statistics are seldom studied purely for their intellectual content. Knowledge about these fields is useful in a variety of technical and nontechnical applications. So it is with accounting. The many practical uses to which accounting knowledge can be put serve as a primary attraction to the field. However, some education about the nature of accounting also seems desirable as a part of general higher education.

A Profession

Accounting does not exist in an academic vacuum. According to the U.S. Census Bureau, 703,546 persons held accounting jobs in the United States in 1970 (26 percent of these jobs were held by women). About 135,000 persons held certified public accountant (CPA) certificates issued by individual states under carefully controlled requirements. At least 350,000 were employed in business and commerce after obtaining bachelor's or master's degrees with concentrations in accounting, and an estimated 150,000 professional accountants were working at all levels of local, state, and federal government with appropriate credentials typically achieved through higher education. In 1974 colleges and universities graduated approximately 28,000 individuals holding degrees with concentrations in accounting. This rate of output hints at further increases in the various categories of professional accountants active in our economy.

A Social Force

The third part of accounting is its thrust as a social force. A brief reflection should convince one that large-scale modern business or public organizations would be impossible to direct and control without an adequate financial information system. There are some who believe that the modern corporation could not have grown to its present-day influence without the concurrent growth of accounting.

The separation of ownership and management found in today's corporate form of business is feasible only if reliable periodic financial reports flow from the professional managers to the owners. Accounting facilitates ownership by remote control—whether it involves an apartment building located across the continental United States or a multinational business operating around the globe. Moreover, accounting lies at the base of most tax systems.

Many public issues must be settled by heavy, though not exclusive, reliance on accounting information. This includes the price discrimination charges brought under antitrust legislation, the regulation of public securities (stocks and bonds) markets, the setting of telephone, power, and airline rates, the investigations of infringement upon competition through corporate mergers, and hosts of other similar issues.

Accounting information directly influences decisions in these areas. This influence arises from the way in which accounting captures data, classifies and transforms it, and later reports it to parties of interest.

THE RECIPROCAL INFLUENCE BETWEEN ACCOUNTING AND THE ENVIRONMENT

Webster's *Seventh New Collegiate Dictionary* defines *environment* as "surroundings—the complex of climatic, edaphic, and biotic factors that act upon an organism or an ecological community and ultimately determine its form and survival—the aggregate of social and cultural conditions that influence the life of an individual or community." Following from this definition, we can divide our environment into one complex of natural, physical, and biological factors and another complex of human and social factors. In accounting we are predominantly concerned with the latter.

Human and Social Environment

The human and social environment in which we live is a society organized through human endeavors—it is largely man-made. Societal organization seeks to make it possible for large numbers of people to live side by side in reasonable comfort and dignity. To accomplish this, society has organized subsystems like the economic subsystem, the political subsystem, the legal subsystem, and the social subsystem. In turn, each of these subsystems has within it many processes that help to change and redirect it. The general goal of these subsystems and their internal processes is to improve satisfaction of people's wants and needs, given the existing constraints of the natural, physical, and biological environment.

Whenever there is a process in which people are involved, someone has to make decisions about it. If decision makers have no information available, they must operate with complete uncertainty. Their decisions can then be made only on a trial-and-error basis. On the other hand, if they have even a small amount of information, they are better able to adapt to uncertainty and presumably make better decisions.

This is where accounting and other information disciplines enter the picture. As information-generating activities, they assist the decision processes within the environmental subsystems. As a result, such disciplines influence the environment and (assuming they are responsive to needs) are influenced by the environment.

The Influence of the Environment on Accounting

With specific reference to the United States (the situation differs in some other countries), we can generalize that direct influences on accounting have come from the environment through seven major channels: (1) certain historical developments, (2) organization of our social system, (3) nature of modern business enterprises, (4) prevailing taxation systems, (5) activities of public agencies, (6) the system of higher education, and (7) the legal system.

• *Historical developments.* When the Franciscan monk Luca Pacioli made early written records of something called double-entry bookkeeping during the fifteenth century in Italy, he responded to a need for a systematic and useful way to keep financial records for merchants operating in medieval Italian city-states. Thus was born a major tool of accounting—namely, "bookkeeping after the Italian fashion," which today is identified as double-entry bookkeeping. This system of bookkeeping is still a major accounting tool. It persists because it captures so well the essence of business transactions which were then, and still are, two-faceted events—someone selling and someone buying the same item. The inherent duality of such transactions provides the logic underlying double-entry bookkeeping.

As medieval commerce spread between nations, double-entry bookkeeping moved with it. From Italy it penetrated the Low Countries and Germany and then promptly moved on to England, France, and Spain.

Later the Industrial Revolution in England introduced specialization of labor and the use of long-term capital investments. Instead of having products like shoes or cloth produced by skilled craftsmen, the new order of the day became mass production of related products. This created the need to know the separate cost of each item produced, since now many *different* products could be manufactured from the same raw materials in the *same* plant. Cost accounting evolved to answer these environmentally generated needs.

Then came the formation of the British joint-stock company, which eventually evolved into today's corporate form of business organization. In the joint-stock company the owners were not necessarily managers, and the need arose for reliable periodic financial reports to the absentee business owners. Again, accounting responded by providing periodic financial reports which summarized the results the business had achieved during a specified time period. To make these reports more credible, independent examiners (auditors) began to express professional opinions about their reliability. Scotland was the home of the first group of professionally organized independent auditors, who were the forerunners of today's CPAs in the United States.

These historical illustrations provide evidence that accounting has responded to the changing needs of its environment. It continues to do so today. Consider, for instance, the views (reported by Robert Metz in a financial editorial in the *New York Times,* May 9, 1972) of David Linowes, a partner in the CPA firm Laventhol Krekstein Horwath & Horwath and professor of management at New York University. Linowes describes possible socioeconomic operating statements published by individual companies in the following terms:

> A company would get recognition for substituting lead-free paint for a poisonous compound, for voluntarily installing smoke-control equipment and for a minority hiring program. . . . And a company would get demerits for neglecting to install a safety device on its power lathes, for refusing to properly landscape strip mining sites and for neglecting to neutralize poisonous wastes before dumping them into streams.

● *The social system.* Our social system is organized around a number of constitutionally guaranteed rights which, among other things, provide freedom to speak openly, assemble in groups or organizations, own property, and be assured of due process of law.

Most influential perhaps is the right to own private property. This right gives extrinsic economic values to private property. The right to ownership of property makes it susceptible to exchange between entities. Since property exchanges take place at agreed-upon prices, we have the foundation of a financial measuring system based on the observed exchange prices. Moreover, private properties have values which, if measured appropriately, give indications of the economic wealth of individuals, groups, or organizations holding title to the property. Accountants pay close attention to what society recognizes as values, particularly exchange values.

● *The enterprise system.* The influence upon accounting emanating from the nature of business enterprise has already been suggested. Today's large-scale commercial and industrial firms control billions of dollars worth of wealth, and the largest of them conduct their business in as many as 150 different countries. Some of them are highly diversified. FMC Corporation, for instance, produces phosphorus and chlorine as well as lawn mowers and fire trucks. Its viscose division manufactures fabrics for high-fashion apparel, while its food-packaging machinery might package oranges in Israel and table fruits and vegetables in Australia. Planning the economic activities of these highly complex business enterprises and later evaluating and controlling their activities impose significant demands on the accounting information systems they use.

No elaboration seems needed to state that the scope and nature of financial information required for the conduct of a corner grocery store or an automobile service station are significantly different from those pertaining to a giant worldwide business enterprise. Similarly, differences are found elsewhere, for instance in accounting requirements between developing and developed countries. To be most useful, accounting must adapt itself closely to the specific enterprise it serves.

• *The taxation system.* Taxation systems are also a major influence upon accounting. So long as taxes are systematically assessed and collected in the form of money, an accounting information system is the essential basis of the entire process. Since tax collection is oriented toward entirely different purposes than, let us say, managerial decision making or reporting to creditors and stockholders, it follows that the same information should not necessarily be used for all three purposes. Nevertheless, and particularly in smaller firms, accounting information prepared for tax purposes is often used for various financial purposes as well. But even without the dual use of essentially tax-oriented information, tax laws broadly influence the records that people and organizations keep and the way they perceive accountable events, such as how much property tax will have to be paid when merchandise is stocked for a store, or what level of death taxes is likely to apply to an estate.

• *The regulatory system.* The sphere of influence from public agencies is widely evident. For instance, the Interstate Commerce Commission regulates accounting for several branches of the transportation industry. The Civil Aeronautics Board sets routes and fares for air transport, and various utility commissions determine electric power, natural gas, and telephone rates. More important still is the Securities Exchange Commission (SEC). It regulates securities markets throughout the country and determines the financial information that companies must disclose, both before and periodically after the sale of securities to the public. Since the SEC has the power to prohibit the sale of securities to the public if certain circumstances prevail (some of which concern financial reporting), and since it may stop the public trading of securities already issued (again, only under certain specified circumstances), it represents the greatest single influence upon the financial information provided by large corporations that reaches the public.

Still other public agencies wield considerable influence. Additional examples include the offices of state corporation commissioners, municipal business-licensing bureaus, and local planning and zoning committees.

• *The higher-education system.* The system of higher education influences accounting directly. Almost all individuals entering professional accounting today hold college degrees and have therefore been influenced by various educational programs at institutions of higher learning. Approximately seven hundred colleges and universities throughout the United States grant baccalaureates with a major or concentration in accounting. Probably four thousand to five thousand accounting faculty teach at these colleges and universities. Faculty have responsibilities for the creation of teaching materials and research activities, in addition to the classes they teach. Their research tends to influence the concepts and practices of accounting as new generations of students learn and apply new techniques. The evolutionary process that starts in the classroom eventually yields the latest authoritative professional accounting pronouncements.

• *The legal system.* The last major influence upon accounting is exerted through the legal system. Many legal contracts contain accounting provisions —from contracts for the purchase of an entire company to smaller licensing or dealership agreements. Once contractually specified, parties to an agreement usually seek to comply with the requirements.

While contractual relationships clearly influence what happens in accounting, court cases and decisions often establish accounting concepts and practices directly. For instance, several cases of major financial swindles have reached the courts, and the courts' decisions have significantly altered the accounting practices that directly or indirectly allowed the swindles to happen in the first place. Suits settled on behalf of parties who suffered damages from fallacious or misleading accounting information have likewise clearly influenced various dimensions of accounting.

The Influence of Accounting on the Environment

As is true of many of the tools that are essential to our modern economic and social systems, it is easy to take accounting for granted. Its influence is subtle; its role in even the most significant decision situations is often unobtrusive. Like many another modern convenience, its importance to us is most evident when it malfunctions or breaks down. Perhaps some examples (based on hindsight) of cases where accounting has seemingly let us down will demonstrate its influence most clearly.

• *Public regulation.* A specific example of accounting's influence upon its human and social environment is found in accounting for railroad companies. Railroad accounting is specified by requirements of the Interstate Commerce Commission. So-called uniform accounting for railroads is deemed essential for regulating the operations of railroads in the public interest and for administratively setting reasonable rates that railroads may charge for the transportation of passengers and freight.

Nineteenth-century railroad operations in the United States were heavily subsidized by federal and state governments when vast quantities of free land were donated to some railroad companies. Since "uniform" railroad accounting generally does not require specific accountability for these donations, they were treated as cost-free items. In turn this enabled railroads to show accounting profit margins considerably larger than the real economic profit they earned (i.e., value created in excess of *all* value used up). Thus widespread impressions arose that the railroad industry was a very profitable industry. The consequence of this misleading information was an overinvestment in the railroads resulting in a misallocation of economic resources. Ultimately, the overinvestment created large financial woes for railroad companies and helped to produce major calamities. Perhaps the 1971 financial collapse of Penn Central was among them.

• *Pollution costs.* A further example is the apparent widespread lack of appropriate accounting for the costs of water and air pollution. Until the late 1960s and early 1970s society was more concerned with industrialization and ever-increasing levels of economic output than with the effects of industrialization upon the social and natural environments. Consequently, arguments for the inclusion of pollution cost measurements among other items of industrial accountability were not very popular, and accounting systems generally did not include these cost estimates. Today evidence exists that this caused misallocations of economic resources, since the prices charged for many chemical and paper products, for example, were too low in relation to their "full" economic costs, that is, they excluded costs of clean air and water. In turn this led to a relative overuse of these products, and an adverse environmental effect emerged as a by-product.

WHO USES ACCOUNTING?

The preceding discussion should make it quite clear that accounting information is used at all levels of organized society. To underscore this theme, a brief comment is offered on those who use accounting information about (1) individuals, (2) business enterprises, (3) nonbusiness organizations, (4) social programs, and (5) units of government.

Information about Individuals

Accounting information about individuals is used by other individuals. This occurs, for example, when individuals plan to organize partnerships or small corporations. Individual credit is typically extended only after the prospective borrower has furnished a reasonable accounting of his private financial affairs. In recent political history there are examples of candidates for major office making public various accounting statements about their respective income and wealth positions.

Organizations are also interested in the summarized accounts of individuals. This applies to income tax collectors, since the largest share of annual income taxes collected by state and federal governments comes from individuals. It also applies to banks evaluating applications for home mortgages or for other forms of consumer credit. It even applies to scholarship committees of colleges and universities when they seek to evaluate the financial need of a student applicant!

Information about Business Enterprises*

Those who have or contemplate having a direct economic interest in business enterprises presumably benefit from having accounting information about

---

* Based on the AICPA's *Statement of the Accounting Principles Board No. 4,* "Basic Concepts and Accounting Principles Underlying Financial Statements of Business Enterprises," 1970.

those enterprises. This group of users includes (1) owners, (2) creditors, (3) suppliers, (4) management, (5) taxing authorities, (6) employees, and (7) customers.

In addition, those with indirect concerns about business enterprises include (1) financial analysts and advisers, (2) stock exchanges, (3) lawyers, (4) regulatory and registration authorities, (5) financial press and reporting agencies, (6) trade associations, (7) labor unions, and (8) the public at large.

These parties continually evaluate business firms and make decisions about them or on their behalf. This includes the entire range of the life span of an enterprise—from raising funds and other resources necessary to organize it to steps leading to voluntary or involuntary dissolution.

Information about Nonbusiness Organizations

Nonbusiness organizations like churches, hospitals, the March of Dimes, the Boy Scouts of America, the YWCA, the Red Cross, a political party, and trade or professional associations cannot get along without preparing accurate accounting information about themselves. Users of their accounting information are similar to those listed for business enterprises.

As a special party at interest, the general public wants to know enough about the financial status of such organizations to determine whether it should make private contributions to them and, if so, in what amount. One major foundation, when seeking public contributions, learned that public support for it was dwindling rapidly. Its most recent financial statements had shown that more than 50 percent of all the funds collected were spent on administration!

Information about Social Programs

The conduct of massive social programs is a relatively recent phenomenon in our society. Program administrators face the challenge of adequately reporting on the success or nonsuccess of entire programs or separate program components. This is still a frontier area in accounting.

The information needed is generally referred to as cost-benefit information, that is, the systematic assessment in terms of dollars or other measurements of the relationship between resources expended and program benefits achieved. Public agencies are a major user group. Congressional committees and elected, as well as appointed, officials are also potential users. There are even instances where official delegations from other countries are eagerly studying reports about the cost-effectiveness of certain social programs now in force in the United States.

Information about Units of Government

The leaders of virtually every governmental unit use a wide variety of accounting information. A local property assessor cannot assess and collect property taxes without statements about property value and ownership. Sales tax collections cannot take place without appropriate records of sales, and income tax collection certainly depends completely on adequate accounting for income tax purposes. Moreover, tax policy at all levels of government cannot be evolved reasonably without good accounting information about present and potential tax bases within the particular jurisdiction. For instance, the probable impact of a certain tax structure on property ownership, business formation, or employment levels cannot be estimated without underlying accounting data.

National income and gross national product accounts are needed to measure the productivity of the total economy and the distribution of economic resources that exist or become available. This type of information supports the formulation of national economic policies, the stimulation or curtailment of a nation's money supply, and most certainly its foreign trade and investment policies. Government officials use accounting information to administer sweeping price and wage control programs or less-sweeping direct foreign investment control programs. More importantly, on the same type of information, individual citizens (voters) may ultimately base their judgment of the ability of certain public officials (at all levels) to discharge their responsibilities.

A Caveat

Let us conclude this section with a caveat. It appears that the widespread and often intensive use of accounting information throughout society cannot be denied. Nonetheless, accounting information is typically only a part of all the information that decision makers use. Few decisions are or should be made on the basis of accounting information alone. At the same time, most decisions with financial or economic implications can presumably be improved with the use of accounting information.

WHY STUDY ACCOUNTING?

Nearing the conclusion of this introductory chapter, it seems well to reflect upon the purpose of studying accounting before we delve deeper into the subject matter. Why not leave the whole affair to those who like to dabble in figures, measure and talk about things in terms of dollars, and eventually become professional accountants in professional accounting service firms, industry, or government?

Basic Education

The most important reason why one should acquire some introductory acquaintance with accounting is that it seems a matter of basic higher education and good citizenship. As pointed out earlier, nearly everyone has to use accounting information more or less frequently in the "garden-variety" affairs of daily living. It is difficult to believe that intelligent decisions about personal finance, investment of one's properties, choice of one's occupation, and certainly the election of public officials cannot be improved with some introduction to the nature of accounting information and a nontechnical understanding of how this information is generated. In this sense, an introduction to accounting takes a place with many other courses comprising, in total, a broad social orientation and liberal education.

Industrialization

The second reason for learning about accounting is that our society is becoming superindustrialized. This means there will be less economic reliance on basic production and a growing importance of technical research and development activities, management know-how, and large-scale accumulations of funds for investment. While the role of accounting is important, for example, in discovering iron-ore deposits, extracting the ore, and shipping it to a steel mill, it may be even more important in making cash investments in unproved ventures or faraway places and then periodically evaluating and controlling these investments. From an accounting perspective, superindustrialization means an ever-growing reliance on organization and financial affairs and a corresponding increase of needs for all types of accounting information.

Social Concerns

We have already noted that environmental preoccupations are assuming growing importance. A great variety of social programs have not only come to stay but seem certain to increase in scope and importance. Experts of the National Conference Board predict that the major business and social changes in the next two decades will have more to do with political, economic, legal, and social processes than with new technological advances.

Accounting can contribute to measuring the effectiveness of social programs and possibly even the amount and availability of human resources (though more research is needed to develop accounting in both directions). Accounting can help to evaluate the types of tax bases needed to build new schools or hospitals, or the economic feasibility of a new mass-transportation system. With its traditional business applications, it may also help cope with new developments like public pension funds or problems of more leisure and early retirement. Furthermore, according to DR Scott, a leader of accounting thought early in our century, large and complex business organizations "internalize" otherwise open-market-based price and allocation decisions. Accounting helps to disclose such internalizations. Scott saw this as a major social benefit.

Coping with the Future

Finally, what about "future shock"? Kenneth Boulding, the widely recognized economist and social critic, observed that "as far as any statistical series related to activities of mankind are concerned, the date that divides human history into two equal parts is well within living memory." Alvin Toffler, a former associate editor of *Fortune* and now widely acclaimed social author, pointed out that man's existence might conveniently be divided into eight hundred lifetimes and that

only during the last six lifetimes did masses of men ever see a printed word. Only during the last four has it been possible to measure time with any precision. Only in the last two has anyone anywhere used an electric motor. And the overwhelming majority of all the material goods we use in daily life today has been developed within the present, the 800th lifetime.

Change used to take place mostly between generations. Now individuals must change repeatedly within their own life spans. Therefore we need as much reliable information as we can get to cushion the impact of change and to reduce uncertainty. Accounting can contribute—modestly and in concert with other information systems. Whether mundane or esoteric, individual-oriented or society-wide, business-directed or concerned with the public interest, we believe that accounting is now making, and will continue to make, positive contributions to mankind's welfare.

PLAN FOR THE BOOK

Accounting in an industrialized economy is characterized by complexity and diversity. Therefore accountants have specialized within their field, just as other professions have become specialized. The most common distinction of specialization among accountants concerns whether accounting information is intended for use by decision makers *outside* organizations or those *inside* organizational units or firms. This dichotomy is usually referred to as "external" and "internal" accounting. It is further elaborated toward the end of Chapter 2.

This book is oriented to the external users of accounting information. This group is by far the numerically larger user group. Moreover, it is typically a group much more diverse in interests and backgrounds than the internal user group. It represents more of a nontechnical and common everyday use of accounting, whereas accounting with an internal or firm focus has a more professionalized, managerial use as its objective. Students continuing the study of accounting will find a number of specialized courses in college and university curricula devoted to internal, or managerial, accounting topics as well as those devoted to the further study of external accounting requirements.

Basic Organization

The book encompasses three modular parts:

1. Introduction to accounting, decision making, the economic environment, business enterprises, and the nature of investment decisions (Chapters 1 through 3)
2. Development and comparison of alternative financial accounting models of the business enterprise which can be used to measure enterprise status and activities (Chapters 4 through 9)
3. Fundamentals of the conventional financial accounting and reporting system now generally applied within the United States (Chapters 10 through 17)

An appendix entitled "Financial Accounting Data-Gathering and Processing Requirements" explains the fundamentals of double-entry bookkeeping and the typical record-keeping cycle encountered in business firms. The material in the Appendix is not essential to the understanding of other parts of the book. Depending on the nature of a given curriculum, this material may not be taught at all, or may be covered either after Chapter 17 or as an adjunct to Chapters 5 or 6—or at several points between those extremes.

The book's organization flows from the general to the specific. Each step is carefully arranged to be internally consistent and complete at the introductory level. To provide a logical sequence, the rationale of the material in the early chapters is integrated throughout the discussion. The authors have made every effort to elaborate upon the environment in which accounting operates, to state the reasons for present accounting practice, to explore the major feasible accounting alternatives, and to examine accounting's role in special decision problem areas.

Note to Students

This book utilizes several examples that one might encounter in daily life. While the examples are hypothetical, they illustrate the fundamental practical processes with which accountants are concerned.

The book's discussion often touches upon accounting's sister disciplines—especially finance and economics, sociology, information sciences, and quantitative methods. These excursions simply underscore the point made earlier that accounting is not now, and can never be an isolated discipline if it is to achieve social usefulness.

Nonetheless, no special prerequisites or other areas of study are assumed. Freshman-level mathematics will help, as will an introduction to economics. These are not essential, however. Anyone with a fair grasp of current economic affairs, as portrayed in the daily newspapers and general information periodicals, should have no difficulty with the materials presented.

As a general introduction to accounting, the book was written with a general audience of college and university students, future business administration students, and later "majors" in accounting in mind. Long years of experience and careful analysis have convinced the authors that all three groups of students are best served by the single approach upon which the pedagogy inherent in this book is built.

Questions for Review and Discussion

1-1. Distinguish between a national idiom, a computer language, an intelligence code, and accounting. List points of similarity and dissimilarity.

1-2. What makes something an intellectual discipline? Does accounting qualify as a separate discipline? Why or why not?

1-3. Name several professions you are aware of. What characterizes a profession? Would you include accounting among the professions?

1-4. In which ways can accounting be thought of as a social science?

1-5. Systems of law are entirely man-made. What other systems fall into this same category? What do all of them have in common?

1-6. How does accounting influence its environment? Can accounting assist with ecological concerns and decisions?

1-7.   Why is accounting susceptible to influence by the environment? What aspects of the environment are most influential? Least influential?

1-8.   Accounting and bookkeeping are often thought to be synonymous. Can you suggest what the distinction between them is?

1-9.   Identify three major events in the historical evolution of accounting.

1-10.   Name seven important channels of outside influence upon accounting in the United States. What is the nature of the influence of each?

1-11.   Who might use accounting information about individual persons and for what purpose?

1-12.   List ten different parties who benefit from having accounting information about business and public organizations. Also specify individual benefits as you perceive them.

1-13.   Why are governments in so-called free-enterprise economies heavy users of accounting information? Express your thoughts in a short essay.

1-14.   Do you agree with the statement that the only justification for accounting is found in its widespread use? Explain in a short essay.

1-15.   What is the possible connection between accounting and "future shock"?

Exercises   **1-1.   When Does Accounting Begin?**   Lauren Berg, a college professor, has always wanted a small apartment house. He has never had any excess funds to invest but for years has studied building costs, maintenance costs, rental rates, and many other economic and legal factors pertaining to apartment house ownership.

In 1973 an uncle he had never met bequeathed to him the sum of $24,000. Even before these funds were transferred to him, Mr. Berg consummated an earnest money agreement in the amount of $500 from his savings for the purchase of a lot suitable for construction of a small apartment house. An architect friend prepared, cost-free, six preliminary sketches of a building that might be erected on the property selected. Armed with this preliminary information, Mr. Berg began tentative negotiations with a construction company. He had estimated that he would be able to finance a building project at a total cost of $250,000.

After the construction company assured Mr. Berg that his building project was feasible, he commissioned the architect to prepare blueprints. At the same time, Mr. Berg contacted two commercial banks, three savings and loan associations, and several insurance companies to obtain financing for his project. He also signed a conditional purchase contract for the building site in the amount of $22,000.

After the blueprints were finished, and three competitive construction contract bids obtained, it became clear that Mr. Berg's credit was insufficient for financing the contemplated apartment project. Two weeks later he received his uncle's legacy and compensated the architect for his services. He then bought himself a new automobile and made a down payment of $15,000 on a duplex building which he intended to offer for rent. At what point should the accounting process start for Mr. Berg's real estate investment project? Defend your opinion in a short essay.

1-2.   Accounting Measurement Problem.   Green Lake is a large lake in Queen City. Its beautiful beaches and parklike setting make the surrounding residential area very attractive. After much negotiation, the Urban Development Company obtained a building permit from the City Planning Commission to erect a six-unit apartment building directly adjacent to and partly protruding out over Green Lake.

Construction began immediately. At this time, a lawsuit was filed by several neighborhood residential associations and environmental groups to have the building permit declared void because the planned structure would obstruct views of existing property owners and generally deface the immediate environs of the lake.

After the Urban Development Company had invested about $300,000 in the Green Lake apartment project, a court held with the plaintiffs and ordered demolition of the construction project as well as restoration of the site to its original condition. Demolition and restoration would cost approximately $100,000. On appeal, a higher court upheld the lower court's decision.

How might accountants measure the economic worth of this project on the day before the legal decision? What difficulties do you foresee in making such measurements? Who sustained the loss in the situation described?

1-3. Accounting Information Effects.   Select three large corporations whose stock is traded on the New York Stock Exchange. From information sources available in your Business Administration Library, list the high and low price quotes for these stocks for each of the last three years. Has the average quoted price increased, decreased, or stayed the same for each stock?

Would you expect accounting information made available to stockholders to have influenced the quoted prices? If so, what do you think is the nature of this influence? Attempt to support your answer with facts as best you can.

1-4. Units to Be Accounted For.   Sears, Roebuck and Company is head-quartered in Chicago. It operates many retail stores, a large mail-order business, and scores of warehouses and certain production facilities. Also, many manufacturers produce merchandise under a Sears label through various licensed production contract arrangements.

In several metropolitan areas, Sears has as many as a dozen retail stores. Its sales territories are divided into regions, and the company operates subsidiary companies in Canada, Mexico, and South America.

List three parties each of whom would benefit from accounting for (1) each individual store, (2) all stores in a metropolitan area, (3) all stores in a region, (4) all stores in the United States, (5) the mail-order segment of the business in the United States, (6) production and licensing activities in the United States separated from all other operations, (7) all business in the United States combined, and (8) total combined worldwide business. What is the most appropriate unit of accounting for Sears, Roebuck and Company?

1-5. Duality in Bookkeeping.   Keeping track of items of wealth is the first step in the bookkeeping process which serves as a major tool of accounting. List ten items that you feel might comprise the property (or resources) of a small manufacturing company. Also list ten claims (or obligations) that various parties might have against the company. (Hint: Machines and cash-in-bank are examples of property; sales taxes payable and stocks sold to the public are claims.)

1-6. Limitation of Short Periods.   The Northern Smelting Corporation operates a large phosphorus smelter in Poca, Idaho. During 19X4 several scrubbing towers and other pollution control equipment are installed to reduce the phosphorus content of emissions from the smelter's smokestacks. The equipment costs $5.4 million; the installation and test costs amount to $0.6 million. Engineers estimate that the new equipment will have to be replaced twelve years later.

The management of Northern Smelting prepares an annual accounting information report for its shareholders. Should the entire $6 million expenditure be allocated somehow over the next twelve years? If so, how? State five reasons why *annual* business reports seem desirable, and also five reasons why they might be undesirable.

2

Decision Making,
the Economic Environment,
and the Business Enterprise

In Chapter 1 we described accounting as a field of knowledge concerned with information that is useful for a broad range of decision making. Much of the Chapter 1 discussion was devoted to giving the reader an appreciation of the breadth of accounting's role in society. With that accomplished, the task at hand is to introduce the reader to the ways and means by which accounting and accountants perform that role.

• *External accounting.* In beginning this task, however, it is necessary to acknowledge a limitation. We simply cannot deal with the full range of accounting activity and, at the same time, achieve any depth of understanding. So we are prepared to confine discussion initially to one avenue of the broader topic of accounting in society. That avenue is the concern with providing information about various kinds of accounting entities for use by external parties. To be precise, the two groups we are interested in may be defined as follows:

Accounting Entity. An accounting entity is any individual or organization that (1) is involved in using economic resources to achieve a purpose, (2)

19

has an identity of its own, and (3) is of interest to one or more individuals for decision-making purposes.

External Users of Information. External users of information concerning an accounting entity are those interested parties whose decisions relate to the entity, but who are not employed by the entity to direct its activities or utilize its resources.

• *Accounting entities.* The concept of an accounting entity is purposely encompassing, again expressing the breadth of applicability of accounting in man's activity. Individuals, governmental units, corporations, a charity fund drive, and a household are all obvious examples of accounting entities. But there are other, more subtle forms of accounting entities as well. If a man or woman is in business, if a housewife does ironing for neighbors, if a corporation administers its employees' pension fund, these *segments* may, themselves, be considered accounting entities, as may be the larger entities that contain them. Why? Because they are of decision interest in and of themselves and because their activities can be distinguished from the activities of other segments of the larger entity for decision-making purposes.

• *Entry point: financial accounting.* Although the broad definition of an accounting entity seemingly throws the discussion wide open again, we will continue to confine ourselves by dwelling only on one major class of entities. The class of interest will be that of business enterprises.

Because of their preeminence as organizational units in the productive activities of a so-called market economy, business enterprises are of particular significance. They control the bulk of productive resources at the disposal of many of the economies of the world, including our own. For this reason we will introduce external accounting in the context of accounting for the business enterprise. In traditional accounting terms we will be dwelling on financial accounting.

Financial Accounting. Financial accounting is that branch of accounting thought and practice concerned with generating useful information about business enterprises for external decision makers.

• *Decision making and enterprise contexts.* We could proceed by describing for the reader, in catalog style, the many concepts, principles, and procedures that make up present-day financial accounting practice. But the purpose of this book is to enrich the introduction to the subject matter, insofar as possible, with a knowledge of the context in which it exists. To this end, the present chapter is devoted to three important contextual relationships: (1) the relationship between decision making, information, and information specialties like accounting, (2) the role of the business enterprise in a market economy, and (3) the decision-type interests (in business enterprises) of external decision makers. The remainder of the chapter is divided into three sections, each attending to one of these topics.

DECISION MAKING AND INFORMATION
ECONOMICS—IN BRIEF

The Resource Allocation Dilemma:
Motive for Economic Decisions

The most fundamental force leading to uses for information (like accounting information) is man's basic resource allocation dilemma. Man (collectively and individually) is faced with virtually unlimited wants and needs. But, unfortunately, the means to satisfying those wants and needs, the things we call resources, are in very limited supply indeed.

• *Unlimited wants and needs.* Although it is difficult to prove rigorously, it is intuitively obvious that man has unlimited wants and needs. We can assure ourselves that this assertion is warranted by first thinking of reasonable categories or classes of wants and needs and then asking ourselves whether all individuals or groups we can think of are entirely satisfied within each category. It is impossible to answer yes, whether the category of needs is the most sophisticated (e.g., the individual's self-realization) or the most primitive (e.g., man's physiological requirements for survival—food and protection from the elements).

• *Scarce resources.* It is equally obvious today that the resources at our command are quite limited in supply. Traditionally we classify resources available to man into the somewhat rough classes of land, labor, capital, and enterprise:

>   **Land.** The word *land* when used to refer to supplies of resources includes all of the natural resources of the planet Earth and its atmosphere.

>   **Labor.** Labor as a resource category is the capacity of man for mental and physical output.

>   **Capital.** Capital consists of any implement, technology, or learned technique that improves the output of the available supply of the primary resources, land and labor. Unlike land and labor, capital is usually considered by economists to consist of resources *produced by man* as opposed to resources provided by nature.

>   **Enterprise.** Enterprise or entrepreneurial ability is a very special resource consisting of (1) the creative and leadership capacity possessed and employed by certain individuals to organize other individuals and resources to produce products and services that satisfy individuals' wants and needs, and (2) the willingness to take the risk that the prices those products and services finally bring may not equal the cost of production plus a reward to the organizer for his or her efforts.

Incidentally, it should be noted that "cash" is purposely omitted from the list of resources. As individuals, we all count the cash we have as a resource because it represents a means of securing available land, labor, capital, and so forth, through exchange. But for an economy as a whole, cash is only a medium of exchange, not a resource *per se.*

Resolving the Dilemma—The Decision-Making Process

Faced with unlimited wants and needs and limited means to satisfy those wants, man must do something to resolve the conflict. We call the process used to resolve this conflict decision making.

> **Decision Making.** Decision making is the process of choosing from among alternative courses of action, conclusions, and so forth, according to some criterion or criteria adopted by the decision maker.

It should be stressed that according to the above definition, decision making is, above all else, a process. But the definition also implies that the decision-making process will usually comprise certain features or stages similar to those that are illustrated in Exhibit 2-1 and elaborated below.

Exhibit 2-1   Stages in the Decision-Making Process

NEED FELT	PROBLEM IDENTIFIED	INFORMATION SOUGHT ABOUT ALTERNATIVES	ALTERNATIVES EVALUATED	CONCLUSION OR ACTION SELECTED	ACTION TAKEN IF APPROPRIATE	OUTCOME REVIEWED; NEW NEEDS EMERGE

Notice that in Exhibit 2-1 the separate stages of decision making are set out across a single continuous arrow with only dotted lines separating them. The intention is to emphasize that decision making is a process and to emphasize the artificiality of describing any complex process in terms of a set of discrete stages.

The process of decision making is sufficiently important and complex to warrant extensive discussion elsewhere. But here we are only interested in producing sufficient insight to facilitate an introduction to accounting as a discipline that provides information for decision making. So it is appropriate that the elaboration of the decision-making process remain uncomplicated and evolve from a simple example.

Example 2-1   Mr. Landowner is in his early twenties and has just inherited his family's farm and all the machinery, equipment, and buildings on it. The farm is near a large city, and its soil is quite good. Thus while Mr. Landowner was growing up, it provided a good life for his family. He is now alone, though, and facing the new planting season with some trepidation. He must decide what to cultivate during the coming season. Mr. Landowner's father had always planted the same things over a crop-rotation cycle of several years, preferring familiar ways of doing things even though prices of the crops he traditionally produced had steadily declined. Mr. Landowner, who had been away at college for the last several years where he had majored in history, was not satisfied with the old ways. He wanted to make sure that this year's crops brought the best possible yield from his land.

Mr. Landowner's situation clearly fits into the mold of the resource allocation dilemma outlined earlier. After spending four years at college on a penurious budget, he has a large backlog of unfulfilled wants. He has at his disposal a limited amount of land and capital goods, plus his own labor and enterprise ability. His large backlog of unfulfilled wants, along with generous but limited resources, motivates him (causes him to feel a need) to make a conscious and systematic effort to do the best with what he has at his disposal, that is, to decide the best course of action under the circumstances.

Identifying the Problem

If simply feeling a need were all that successful decision making required, we would have scarce reason for this discussion. The felt need is really only the stimulus to decision making. The process does not start in earnest until the problem is identified.

Problem identification is an organizational step. In defining the problem, the decision maker arrives at the criteria that he must eventually have in mind in order to favor one course of action over another with the expectation of satisfying his need. One way to establish the criterion or criteria that can be used to choose between alternative courses of action is through a set of related statements commonly referred to and defined as follows:

> **Statement of Objectives.** A statement of objectives is an expression of the decision maker's preferences in terms of the consequences of potential courses of action.

> **Constraints.** Constraints are statements of the limitations within which the decision maker must work in making a choice. To be feasible, an alternative course of action may not violate the constraints faced by the decision maker.

Example 2-2   Mr. Landowner has expressed the need to make the best use of his land, labor, capital, and enterprise in the coming season. Obviously, though, he may face certain limitations, either by choice or otherwise. He may reason (1) that it is too late to order new equipment and have it delivered on time; (2) that it is too late to learn complicated agricultural techniques or hire competent help for this season; (3) that it is too late to lease additional land; (4) that he must stick to crops that are reasonably suited to the soil on his land; (5) that the cost of seed, fertilizer, labor, and other inputs cannot exceed the cash on hand plus what he can borrow from the bank, pending ultimate sale of his crops, and so forth. All of these conclusions, whether in the back of his mind (implicit) or brought to the fore (explicit), constitute constraints that any crop must meet in order to be a feasible alternative for this season.

Along with a set of constraints, Mr. Landowner can construct a statement of his objective that will indicate which alternative, among those that satisfy all of the constraints, he can expect to most satisfy his need(s). To do this, he must decompose the need into elements or characteristics that can be provided by various alternatives available. For instance, as with many farmers, the produce that Mr. Landowner grows for his own consumption is insignificant in terms of his total potential production—thus attention can be focused on all his other wants and needs. Mr. Landowner will have to purchase virtually all of the goods and services that he consumes, in exchange for cash. Therefore he is likely to want to concentrate on the cash-related aspects of each of his alternatives, concluding that the crop or crops that will bring the greatest excess of cash receipts upon sale over the cash paid out for seed, fertilizer, labor, and so forth, will most satisfy all of his wants and needs. Thus Mr. Landowner has a statement of objective that indicates the positive (cash from sales) and negative (cash paid out for production) contributions that alternative crops can make to his ultimate satisfaction, plus the condition that indicates which crop would be preferable (maximum cash inflow in excess of cash paid out).

For the decision maker, defining the problem as we have defined it in the example provides two valuable inputs to the remainder of the decision process:

1. The set of constraints and the statement of objective provide a framework for the evaluation of alternatives leading to a choice.
2. The terms of the constraints and objective statement prescribe what information will be relevant to the decision maker.

Evaluation of Alternatives

Ignoring for a moment the information-gathering stage of decision making, consider the question of exactly how defining the problem can assist in the process of evaluating alternatives. Assuming that all relevant information is in hand, the problem definition can be used in the evaluation process in two ways:

1. The objective statement and constraints tell the decision maker how to combine facts and measurements about an alternative into tests of its desirability.

Example 2-3 As stated in Example 2-2, the definition of Mr. Landowner's selection problem tells him that if the description of the soil requirements of a particular crop is out of line with the soil composition of his land, the crop must be rejected as an alternative. It also tells him that the expected cost of seed for a crop is one of the items that should be subtracted from the expected proceeds of sale in order to determine its expected overall contribution of cash, and so forth.

2. Knowledge of the stated objective and constraints can be used to devise time-and-effort-saving strategies for evaluation.

Example 2-4 In Mr. Landowner's situation, for instance, one might easily fall into the trap of choosing an overly straightforward approach to evaluation, assessing the cash contribution and conformity to all constraints *for every "cash crop"* that might be grown in the area. But this approach could lead to unnecessary time and effort spent in evaluation. A better way might be to first measure the conformity to the constraints for each crop and then measure the expected cash contribution of only those that pass the test of all constraints. A still more efficient technique might be to apply the constraints in some order, rejecting immediately any crop that fails to conform to a constraint, thereby constantly narrowing the field of alternatives undergoing continued evaluation.

Regardless of their sequence of application, the constraints and the stated objective form a basis for the most important role of evaluation—that of choosing the best alternative within the limitations faced by the decision maker.

• *A common index of merit, or "common denominator."* Although defining an objective and constraints provides the necessary guidelines for evaluating decision alternatives, it does not necessarily guarantee that the final choice will be unambiguous or easy. Indeed, one of the most perplexing dilemmas in decision making is facing two or more alternatives, each of which promises more of one desirable attribute and less of other desirable attributes than the other decision alternatives. In such cases it is often worthwhile to spend additional time, while defining the problem, looking for a single index of merit, or common denominator, into which several attributes can be translated.

Example 2-5   In the case of Mr. Landowner we have already intuitively defined his objective in terms of a common scale of merit, cash flow. Think of how difficult it would be for Mr. Landowner to decide among several crops that all satisfy the applicable constraints, if the expected sacrifices required to grow and harvest the crop and the benefits from its production could not all be measured in terms of cash paid or received. Mr. Landowner would perhaps have to mentally weigh one crop that is superior on a scale measuring labor effort, against another that is superior in its low fertilizer requirements, against still another that promises more benefits from harvest, but none of which dominates all others in every respect.

Having a common scale of merit reduces all of the relevant considerations (within the constraints of the situation) to a single score or index of merit for each alternative. The choice problem is thereby simplified to selection of the alternative with the highest score among those that satisfy all constraints.

• *Quantitative versus qualitative scales.* In searching for common scales of merit on which to evaluate decision alternatives, the characteristic of quantifiability can be of great help, and sometimes of great hindrance as well. By quantifiability we mean the ability to represent, *in the form of a numerical score,* the degree to which a particular characteristic is possessed by a decision alternative. Qualitative characteristics are those that cannot be readily expressed in terms of numbers. One great advantage of quantifiable characteristics in evaluating decision alternatives is the ability to apply our well-developed mathematical operations to manipulating numerical scores, once those scores are assigned to alternatives. This often facilitates the reduction of many measured attributes of alternatives to a single score on a common scale of merit.

Example 2-6   In Mr. Landowner's case quantification of certain crop characteristics will clearly help to arrive at the cash flow to be expected from each crop. On the positive side, for instance, Mr. Landowner will find it convenient to have estimates of the *number* of bushels of expected yield per acre from each crop and the number of dollars per bushel expected price from each. Having these two numerical inputs, he can *multiply* the separate scores of each crop on the two different scales (yield and price) to get a single score measuring expected benefit from the crop (expected cash yield per acre)—a score that is measured on the same scale (money) as many other relevant characteristics of the crop.

Although quantification of attributes of decision alternatives is a powerful tool of decision making, it presents a hazard as well. Because of our ability to manipulate quantitative scores, we may tend to place too little emphasis on relevant aspects of decision alternatives that are not easily quantified. Such a tendency can lead to disastrous results.

Example 2-7   Mr. Landowner, in dwelling on the cash-flow aspects of each crop, may ignore a relevant property of farm crops like "disease resistance" that is not readily translatable into numbers. Perhaps he could choose inadvertently the worst of his alternatives, if he does not bear this important attribute in mind, in making his choice.

Upon reflection still other advantages and hazards of quantification will occur to the reader. One additional advantage that is of importance to accountants is the increased transferability of understanding that can often be achieved when attributes are quantified. For instance, if individual A wishes to describe the intelligence of individual B to individual C, the words "highly intelligent" may give C only a vague understanding of B's intelligence. An IQ score of 155 may convey much more precise understanding in C's mind. But, again, there is a hazard related to the hoped-for increase in transferability brought about by quantification. The hazard, clearly evident in the case of IQ scores, is that a score that measures only one aspect of an abstraction like intelligence will eventually become a substitute for the abstraction itself. The reader is no doubt aware of other instances of this phenomenon.

The Role of Information

In the preceding section it was assumed, for the sake of elaborating the evaluation stage of decision making, that "all relevant information is in hand. . . ." We can now gain some perspective on the information-gathering stage of decision making by dropping that assumption.

After defining a problem, the decision maker should have some ideas as to the characteristics of alternative courses of action that might impinge upon his constraints and contribute to or detract from his objective. But usually he will not be able to predict exactly the extent to which various alternatives, if adopted, will exhibit those characteristics. This condition is known as uncertainty.

> **Uncertainty.** Uncertainty is the condition of not knowing at the time of decision precisely what the outcomes of relevant future events will be, that is, not knowing precisely the consequences of alternative courses of action.

Uncertainty can never be eliminated altogether. But its effects can be lessened by such things as keeping options open and entering into contracts to assure that others *intend* to perform certain actions. The effects of uncertainty can also be lessened by acquiring information.

> **Information.** Information is any item of intelligence that improves the decision maker's understanding and predictions of the outcomes of uncertain future events.

The decision maker is essentially interested in the results or consequences that will be forthcoming from the selection of a given decision alternative. With more and more information, in any given situation the *expected* level of satisfaction from a decision usually becomes better and better. But, interestingly, this does not mean that more information is always better for the decision maker.

The Economics of Decisions and Information

The last statement above, which implies that more information is not always better for the decision maker, is seemingly in conflict with the one that immediately precedes it, which implies that more information improves the expected outcome of a decision. But the two statements are not in conflict at all.

Defining a decision problem explicitly indicates what features and characteristics about each alternative must be known in order to make the best choice *as the problem is defined*. Thus a particular problem definition prescribes that information which is decision relevant.

> **Decision Relevance.** Information is said to be relevant with respect to a particular decision situation if it may be expected to improve predictions of outcomes of future events of concern in that decision.

But it may not be economical for the decision maker to go to the lengths prescribed to make the best choice, as a part of our earlier example, which we have ignored so far, illustrates:

Example 2-8   In Mr. Landowner's crop selection problem, the objective spelled out was to select the crop that had the expectation of contributing the most cash upon sale in excess of the cash paid out for seed, labor, and so forth, required to produce it. To make the best selection, then, Mr. Landowner would technically have to know a good deal about each crop's growing habits and cultivation requirements, such as average yields per acre and average labor hours per acre required under expected conditions. He would also have to estimate the wage rate he would have to pay, and the price per unit of output that he would get at harvest time.

Now, even after growing up on the farm, Mr. Landowner is probably ignorant of most of these decision-relevant features of each crop. Furthermore, left strictly to himself, he may not be able to come up with technical information, like the expected yields of various crops in his type soil, in time to make this season's crop selection. Without any expertise he might have to experiment with small plantings of many different crops for several seasons before he could predict expected yields. But such a strategy might also mean that he would face greatly reduced cash flow from the crops for those seasons because he would be spreading himself too thin (for example, changing cultivation techniques and implements too frequently to be efficient).

In essence, this extension of Mr. Landowner's crop selection problem into the stage of information gathering emphasizes a feature of all but the most trivial decision situations: *the decision-making process, particularly the information-gathering stage, consumes resources.* Virtually every decision situation contains a trap that most of us avoid intuitively—the possibility that spending too much of our precious time, effort, and other resources on the decision might reduce our ability to undertake desirable courses of action. This leads us to two related conclusions:

1. Successful decision making is *not* simply a matter of choosing the most desirable of several alternatives but is a much more complex process of finding the most rewarding combination of (*a*) the expected decision outcome and (*b*) the level of resources expended in making the choice.
2. Information has value (depending on its decision relevance) in that it improves the expected outcome of a decision. But information is costly, as well.

The latter conclusion is of particular significance to accountants because it is at the root of why information specialists like accountants are in demand in every economic system. To see this, reconsider Mr. Landowner's position with respect to the highly technical information about crop yields that he would like to have:

Example 2-9   If Mr. Landowner had to develop complete crop-yield data for his soil type for all crops that he might consider, the prospect of gathering the information would appear very costly. He might, therefore, justifiably conclude that he would be better off scrapping the whole business of crop selection and, instead, spend his time growing any crop that he knows from experience will be worth more than the cost to produce it. In doing so, he will sacrifice the prospects of getting the highest cash production from his land, but he will avoid the possibly prohibitively greater cost of achieving the improved productivity.

But suppose Mr. Landowner can buy information about expected crop yields for his type of soil. He will gladly do so, provided he can buy it for less than the increase in cash that he expects from selecting the best crop.

Information Specialists

Fortunately for Mr. Landowner and other decision makers facing the same type of decision, there exist sources that can produce the kinds of information Mr. Landowner wants at much less cost than he can on his own. We will call such sources *information specialists*.

> **Information Specialist.** An information specialist is an individual who devotes his resources to producing decision-relevant information for others' use.

Example 2-10   In Mr. Landowner's case one way to acquire crop-yield information for his soil would be to hire an agronomist, who specializes in field-crop production and soil management. Whereas it might take Mr. Landowner several years' experimentation to develop crop-yield information for his soil, the agronomist ought to be able to estimate expected yields after spending much less time. And, although his hourly fee may be high, his total fee to Mr. Landowner may be low because of his efficiency.

The agronomist illustrates the key reason why so many people make their living providing information to others. Division of labor, leading to specialization and the development of expertise or facility in providing a particular product or service, usually results in higher productivity and/or lower cost. Where large numbers of individuals make decisions involving the same or similar courses of action, there is room for division of labor; for example, one or more individuals may then specialize in providing information (or techniques for gathering information) for all the others. Information produced will have value to many decision makers, provided it is decision relevant. Since the specialist can provide it at a lower cost (price) than would be incurred by the others in developing their own information (or information-gathering techniques), some will willingly pay for his services. Those decision makers will be able to achieve greater expected satisfaction from their decision outcomes with more information at lower cost, and the information specialist will be able to employ his talents and other resources more fully than perhaps in any other occupation. Everyone benefits, in an economic sense, from the division of labor.

Besides the benefits of division of labor inherent in information specialization, there is sometimes an additional bonus. Many individuals may find identical information to be decision relevant. In such cases the benefits of information specialization may compound.

Example 2-11   Suppose that the land Mr. Landowner owns is similar in soil composition to the land of a dozen other farmers in the same vicinity. In addition, suppose that they are all aware of the same four crops as the set of possible cash crops for their local market. If each evaluated every crop for its yield potential, fifty-two crop evaluations would be required (thirteen decision makers times four alternatives). But if they pooled information, or more likely, if they had a common source of information (an information specialist), only four evaluations would have to be made—one for each crop.

This added bonus that comes from common or universal decision relevance of information can be particularly compelling under some circumstances. For instance, even with the greater efficiency in producing information that can be achieved by a specialist, sometimes no single individual will find an item of information of sufficient value to pay for its production. Only if a number of decision makers share in its cost can it be economically produced—whereupon all will benefit from its availability. Examples include such things as weather maps and predictions, handbooks of all kinds, mathematical and statistical tables, and census reports.

In considering the multiperson (or "social") benefits of information, however, one must always be aware of the possibility of falling into the trap known as the "fallacy of composition." That is, in many cases it is not true that what is good for one is good for all. This is sometimes true of information.

Example 2-12   Suppose that Mr. Landowner and his dozen neighbors with similar soil hired an agricultural economist to rank each of the four cash crops traditionally grown in their region in terms of its expected cash yield per acre. It would be natural to expect each farmer to then select the number one crop. Although this makes sense individually, it could lead to unfortunate results for the group. Such a drastic increase in the local supply of that one crop could cause a sharp decrease in price—possibly bringing financial disaster on everyone.

On the other hand, there is no reason to conclude that the fallacy of composition obviates any potential for information to have value to many users. But it is obvious that information suited to given individuals' objectives *will not always* be similarly valuable to many individuals—even if they have similar objectives. Although the design of information for use by the many may begin at the individual level, ultimately its desirability for the many must be assessed according to its consequences *for the many*.

Accounting—An Information Specialization

Accountants, like agronomists, journalists, advertising copywriters, financial analysts, attorneys, and many others, are information specialists. *Accounting is above all else an information specialization.* Our discussion of decision making and information specialization to this point indicates that the existence of any information specialization like accounting depends on several conditions—

1. that there exist classes of decision makers with common decision problems;
2. that there are identifiable kinds of decision-relevant information of value in solving the common class or classes of problems; and

3. that to efficiently and effectively produce information relevant to the common class or classes of problems, one must become expert in applying a specialized body of knowledge or expertise.

In the remainder of this chapter and in Chapter 3 (as well as at intervals throughout the book) we will explore the first two of these conditions as the threshold to understanding accounting. That the third condition applies to accounting will be obvious as our discussion leads us into an intellectually challenging exploration of the kinds of information that are relevant for the classes of decisions served by accounting.

THE BUSINESS ENTERPRISE IN A MARKET ECONOMY—IN BRIEF

The major emphasis of this book will be the role of accounting in supplying information to several of the classes of decision makers concerned with the business enterprise. To clearly establish (1) the identity of these classes of decision makers, (2) their common decision problems, and (3) the information that they might regard as decision relevant, we will briefly review the role of the business enterprise in the context of a so-called free-enterprise, or "market," system. For the reader who has not recently reviewed the basic features of a market-type economy, a capsule review is contained in the Appendix to this chapter.

The Business Enterprise and the Enterprise Function

Given the aggregate demand for goods and services in a market economy, certain individuals, called entrepreneurs or enterprisers, in the aggregate determine what products and services will be produced and in what quantities. Enterprisers respond to the aggregate demand in the economy for various products and services by (1) organizing factors of production in order to produce specific goods and services and (2) taking the risk that the price of the goods or services sold may not exceed the cost of factors of production used. Presumably, enterprisers are motivated by the expectation that sales prices will exceed factor costs by a sufficient amount (profit) to justify the effort expended and the risk taken.

In performing their dual role of organizing and risk taking, enterprisers usually work within the facilitating framework of a business enterprise.

Business Enterprise. A business enterprise is an organization composed of one or more individuals, capital goods, and other resources, directed toward the purpose of producing specific products or services for sale.

As organizational units, businesses have a significant impact on our economic life. The business enterprise facilitates the enterpriser's activities in a number of ways:

1. The business enterprise is a means of separating the production activities of individuals from their consumption activities. In this sense an enterprise structure benefits even the individual in business for himself.

2. The business enterprise is a means of coordinating the activities of individuals engaged in (*a*) complex production processes and (*b*) large-scale production with a high degree of division of labor and specialization.

3. The business enterprise is a means of dividing or sharing, among many individuals, the enterprise function itself.

The first of these contributions needs no explanation. The second, though not so obvious, is characteristic of human activity under any economic system. Each individual can, in theory, work independently—supplying completed products or services to others. But few complex products or services can be produced efficiently "from the ground up" by a single individual. To become proficient in a highly technical process one must narrow the scope of the undertaking, that is, specialize. In most cases, however, it does not pay to have hundreds or thousands of individuals—each specializing in very limited tasks—buying thousands of partially completed products, performing one or two specialized tasks on each, and then selling them to someone who performs the next specialized production step. Transfers and exchanges would consume too much of everyone's time and resources. A single organization coordinating the efforts of specialists in all stages of production is usually the most efficient answer. Essentially it is a means of breaking down a large and complex opportunity for production into coordinated individual opportunities.

Example 2-13   The automobile industry started out in the United States with many individuals and small groups "custom" building cars. But few really prospered, since they produced at such a high cost that only a few wealthy people could afford their products. The industry did not really prosper until many of the smaller manufacturers were consolidated into a few large organizations. And, of course, the price of the automobile was finally put within reach of large numbers of people through the efficiencies of the assembly line, introduced by Henry Ford. The assembly line was as much an organizational innovation as it was a technological innovation.

• *Sharing the enterprise function.* The third contribution of the business enterprise, that of facilitating the division of the enterprise function, is really a special case of the second contribution. But because of the importance of the enterprise function, it deserves separate consideration. When an enterpriser sees an opportunity for profit in the efficient production of a particular product or service, he must do two things to exploit the opportunity. First, he has to secure the necessary factors of production. Second, he must organize them and set them in motion producing and selling the product or service to others.

To accomplish these two steps, the enterpriser must have considerable resources at his disposal initially. The reason is that before the sale of products or services starts to bring in cash, the enterpriser may have to pay for buildings, equipment, and other capital goods, as well as for material and wages. Furthermore, long after starting in a particular line of business, the enterpriser will still find it necessary to acquire and pay for factors of production before or at the time they are committed to production, with some time lag before the sale of products and services brings in cash. Virtually every production venture involves risk, that is, it requires the ongoing commitment of money capital.

> **Money Capital.** Money capital is the cash committed (or the cash equivalent of other resources committed in lieu of cash) to a business enterprise or other venture in order that it may procure and meet its obligations to pay for capital goods, labor, material, and so forth, as needed.

The provision of money capital and the acceptance of the attendant risk that the proceeds of sales may not cover the outlays for factors of production are an integral part of the enterprise function.

But individual enterprisers may not possess adequate money capital to complement their ability to identify opportunities for profit and organize production. Faced with an imbalance, enterprisers may (1) borrow money, if they can, in exchange for fixed interest payments, or (2) arrange for others to share the enterprise function with them as owners or part owners of a business, contributing money capital in exchange for a share in profits earned. In either case, the business organization is a means of breaking down a large opportunity for profit that the individual cannot exploit by himself into a number of smaller individual opportunities.

Kinds of Business Enterprises

There are three traditional kinds of business enterprises—proprietorships, partnerships, and corporations—all of which are recognized by accountants as economic units or entities separate from their owners. But they differ in a number of respects that influence the extent to which they offer the advantages described in the preceding section. In particular, they differ in legal status, arrangements for ownership and management, extent of risk or liability associated with ownership, duration of life and dissolution, and transferability of ownership interest. The differences between the three types of business enterprises with respect to these features are summarized in Exhibit 2-2 and briefly elaborated below.

• *Proprietorships.* A proprietorship is an inherently personal business. It is formed unilaterally by a single individual. It serves as an organizational identity for his production activities, to separate those activities and the resources that he devotes to them from his private life. Legally, however, a proprietorship is not a separate entity; it is identical with the owner and, therefore, cannot be involved in any legal relationship or action except in the name of the owner. If, in the conduct of the business, some person or his property is harmed, the proprietor may be held responsible (liable) not only to the extent of the resources committed to the business but for everything else he owns as well. A proprietorship may be dissolved by the proprietor more or less at will. It will, however, dissolve upon his death if he does not dissolve it sometime earlier.

Exhibit 2-2   COMPARATIVE FEATURES OF TYPES OF BUSINESS ENTERPRISES

Type of Business Enterprise	Legal Status of Business Entity	Owner-Management Relationship	Risk of Ownership	Duration of Life	Transferability of Ownership Interest
Proprietorship	Not a separate legal entity	Separation of ownership and management only by owner choice	Owner's personal fortune at stake	Expires by owner choice or death of owner	If proprietor sells his interest, the business is reconstituted under new ownership
Partnership	Not a separate legal entity	Separation only by partnership agreement	At least one partner's personal fortune at stake	Expires by choice or withdrawal of partners	Partnership share cannot be sold without agreement of other partners; new partnership is formed
Corporation	Separate legal entity	Separation of ownership and management; owners influence management indirectly	Limited to loss of interest in benefits of ownership	Indefinite life span; possibly unlimited	Usually transferable

• *Partnerships.* Partnerships are similar to corporations in one respect. They involve more than one owner. In other respects they usually resemble proprietorships. A partnership is an association of individuals, not a separate legal entity. Like a proprietorship, a partnership cannot engage in legal activity separately. Instead it enters into legal relationships or actions in the names of the partners, usually jointly. Unless otherwise agreed, each partner is entitled to a voice in the conduct of the business and the use of its resources. Each partner can usually legally bind the partnership by his own actions. Furthermore, although some partners may be able to legally limit their liability for damages to others brought about by the partnership, one or more partners are always liable to the full limit of their personal fortunes.

A partnership is formed when two or more individuals implicitly or explicitly agree to combine their efforts or other resources in an activity aimed at generating profits, and to share the resulting profits between them. A partnership dissolves upon the death, withdrawal, or bankruptcy of any partner. A partner cannot usually transfer his interest in a partnership without consent of the other partners.

• *Corporations.* Corporations, in contrast to proprietorships and partnerships, are legal entities separate from their owners. Legal actions can be conducted by or against the corporation in its own name. The owners, called stockholders or shareholders, do not have a direct voice in the conduct of the business, cannot directly use or possess its resources, and cannot bind it legally by their actions. Rather, the stockholders have the right to vote in the election of the directors who manage the corporation and to share in the profits generated by its activities.

In exchange for limited involvement or power over the resources of the business or its management, owners of corporations have a certain flexibility and immunity not enjoyed by partners and proprietors. First of all, since shareholders do not enter into personal arrangements with or become dependent on each other with respect to the business (as partners do), their shares are usually transferable without the consent of other shareholders. Thus the corporation can have a perpetual existence, with ownership (and management) passing from person to person. Second, shareholders cannot be held liable for the actions of the corporation, except to the extent of their share in the resources of the corporation and the profits derived therefrom.

These latter features of limited liability and transferability of ownership are ideal for serving the purpose of division of the enterprise function between those who recognize production opportunities and direct activities (management) and those who take the risk associated with supplying money or physical capital (owners). Why? Because those who contribute money capital but not management talent to a business are limited in the degree to which they can protect their own interests in the business's activities. They would be much less willing to back enterprising and creative managers if they could be held liable for the results to the extent of all that they possess. Furthermore, if some owners disagree with courses of action taken by management but are in the minority among all owners, it is better for everyone if they can liquidate their interest by selling it, rather than calling for dissolution of the whole business and distribution of the proceeds. The greater amounts of money capital that can be raised to complement management skill, as a result of the appealing features of corporate ownership, have made the corporate form of business preeminent in organizing large-scale production in modern market economies.

DECISION MAKERS AND DECISIONS RELATED TO THE BUSINESS ENTERPRISE

In Chapter 1 we mentioned a number of types of users of information about the business enterprise. The list included (1) owners, (2) creditors, (3) suppliers, (4) management, (5) taxing authorities, (6) employees, and (7) customers. Early in this chapter we noted that information specializations like accounting spring up where such groups exist, if they have common decision problems, demanding identifiable information that can be prepared more efficiently for them by experts or specialists. In this section, with the brief background in the preceding section about the role of the business enterprise in society, we can begin to identify some common classes of decisions shared by members of the above groups. At the outset, however, we will recognize a distinction that separates two major classes of decisions concerning the business enterprise.

Internal and External Decision Makers

We can separate all decision makers concerned with the business enterprise into two groups, internal and external, according to how their individual decisions relate to the enterprise. To distinguish internal users of information from external users (defined earlier), we have the following definition:

> **Internal Users of Information.** Internal users of information concerning the enterprise are those individuals who are employed to direct the activities of the enterprise (managers) or to utilize its resources to fulfill the goals of the enterprise (other employees).

Unlike internal users, external users generally are not employed by the enterprise to directly affect its activities or the deployment of its resources.

The relationship to the enterprise of the employee group known as management is entirely made up of decisions that affect the direction and activities of the enterprise and the deployment of its resources. Therefore, management is clearly in the internal group. Other employees may also be classified as internal users of information when they are making decisions about the conduct of their respective tasks within the enterprise. But employees may be external users of information about the enterprise as well.

When an employee is trying to make decisions about such things as his long-run job security with his employer, or whether he should change employments, he is really an external user of information considering features and characteristics of the enterprise that are of interest to him but which he probably is not employed to alter by his actions alone. Similarly, present and potential owners and creditors of large businesses (particularly corporations), taxing authorities, government regulatory authorities, suppliers, and customers, all may have an influence on the conduct of a business as groups, but they are not employed within the enterprise to affect its operations directly. Instead, they are usually concerned with whether or not to enter into some exchange or other relationship with the business entity as a whole, or to ensure its compliance with government policy or the provisions of a contract.

We can draw a definite distinction between the decision interests of internal and external users. The former are interested in choosing among decision alternatives or opportunities available to the business enterprise itself, while the latter view the business enterprise as a source of decision alternatives or opportunities available to them. With this strong distinction in decision interest between the two groups, it is easy to see why a distinct subdivision of accounting thought and activity has responded to the needs of each—managerial accounting for the internal group, financial accounting for the external group. Although many of the accounting concepts, tools, and approaches applied to problems of the two groups are the same, the differences in the decision interests mean that quite different information outputs usually result. Thus for purposes of study, as well as accounting practice, it is often useful to deal with these two branches of accounting separately—a custom we follow in this book. *The focus of the book is accounting for the business enterprise for external decision makers.*

Classes of External Decisions

The decision interests of external users of information about the enterprise can be further subdivided into two fundamental classes. One class of decisions consists of investment decisions. The other class includes quite a variety of decisions that have to do with the distribution of the current benefits from the enterprise's operations.

• *Investment decisions.* Roughly, we can define investment decisions as those involving exchanges of present resources for rights to resources in the future. Present and prospective owners and creditors have a common investment-decision interest in the business enterprise. For this reason we typically refer to present and prospective owners and creditors of a business, together, as "investors." Two avenues are available to investors to acquire the rights of creditors or owners. They may either (1) contribute money capital (or other goods and services) directly to the business or (2) buy the *transferable* rights of present creditors or owners.

Either way the *creditor* receives an implicit or explicit contractual obligation on the part of the business to (1) pay a specified amount of money, called the principal amount, after some interval, along with (2) a specified amount or rate of interest on the principal amount. The *owner* receives the right to share in proportion to his ownership interest in (1) the distributed profits of the business (e.g., dividends from corporations), and (2) the proceeds remaining after sale of the business's resources and discharge of the obligations, in case of dissolution.

In addition to acquiring rights as creditors and owners, present owners and creditors may view the reverse process as an economic opportunity. That is, they may decide to sell their rights in the business for cash or other consideration, provided the rights are transferable. In the case of nontransferable ownership interests in partnerships, the same thing can be accomplished by dissolution of the partnership and settlement with the withdrawing partner.

Both the acquisition and the sale of creditor and ownership rights in a business may properly be called investment alternatives, since they always involve an exchange of present resources (the capital contribution or price paid or received) for rights to future benefits—interest and principal payments for creditors, dividends or withdrawals for owners. *Together, present and prospective investors in businesses constitute an important class of external users of information about businesses.* And their decision problems are sufficiently interesting and challenging that we will devote the next chapter to a model for making investment decisions. The model will then serve as a basis for later discussion of the types of information about a business enterprise that are thought to be decision-relevant to investors.

• *Distributions of enterprise benefits.* At the time of deciding or reconsidering an investment in a business, present and prospective owners will be concerned with the future benefits expected from ownership. As time passes, though, owners will be interested in receiving some of those expected benefits. Since owners are residual beneficiaries of the business, they will have a natural interest in a periodic assessment of the achievements or accomplishments of the enterprise, as well as its ability to distribute money or other resources to them.

Interestingly, other groups will share the owners' interest in the accomplishments of the enterprise and its residual benefits. These groups include:

1. Management
2. Taxing authorities
3. Regulatory authorities
4. Employees

In one sense these "other interested groups" compete with owners—they share or hope to share in the residual benefits of the enterprise. But in the sense that all benefit from increases in those benefits, their interests and the interests of the owners are complementary.

Management's interest in measuring the accomplishment of the enterprise stems largely from its sharing the enterprise function with owners. Owners take the risk associated with supplying money capital to the enterprise, which is then deployed by management in pursuit of profit opportunities. To safeguard their interests, while not interfering with the management of the enterprise, owners will often find it useful to reward management with a share of profits. In pursuing their own reward, the managers will therefore presumably do what is best for the owners as well.

Where the federal, state, or local government has deemed it desirable to grant exclusive rights (monopolies) to a single enterprise to provide vital products or services (like electrical power), regulation is usually considered necessary to ensure that both the public interest and the interests of the enterprise are served. Regulation of this type of enterprise often takes the form of limiting the prices or rates charged by the regulated monopoly to the minimum level necessary to provide a "fair" reward to all suppliers of the resources required to provide the product or service to consumers. Thus regulatory commissions are almost always interested in the profits generated by the regulated enterprise at a given level of rates or prices (along with other information, such as the quality of service provided).

The currently pervasive income tax is intended to be a nonconfiscatory tax in which government simply shares in residual benefits with owners and management. That is, by only applying to profits, the tax authority never takes away from an economic unit the stock of resources with which it operates. The income tax has been likened, in this respect, to harvesting fruit from an orchard. Only the fruit is picked; the trees are left intact to produce another crop. The income tax authority is clearly interested in periodic assessments that separate the new growth (profits) from the original stock of resources of an enterprise.

Finally, whereas employees other than management are not usually compensated on the basis of profits or growth of the enterprise, they collectively often have an interest in assessment of profit and accomplishment. Their interest is often one of determining whether the benefits of production are equitably divided between labor, management, and capital contributors to the enterprise.

Thus it is clear that a number of the external groups share a common decision interest in the assessment and distribution of the residual benefits of the enterprise. After we have discussed the nature of the investment decision in the next chapter, and begin to introduce the decision-relevant accounting information for that purpose, we will come back to a concurrent consideration of information relating to the current distribution of residual benefits of the business.

APPENDIX: MARKET ECONOMIES—IN BRIEF

Distinguishing Characteristics of Free Enterprise

What distinguishes a modern free-enterprise system from other modern economies? Three characteristics seem to dominate. First, the bulk of the available *resources are privately owned* in a free-enterprise system, whereas in a socialistic economy resources are held in trust for the people by the state. One thing to recognize immediately, however, is that no economy exists today in pure form. In most economies some resources are privately owned and some are held in trust by the state. So when we refer to a particular economy as a free-enterprise, or market, economy, we are really designating a "mixed" ownership economy as being dominated by private ownership.

A second distinguishing characteristic of a free-enterprise system is *freedom of choice* in the employment and consumption of resources on the part of private citizens. This contrasts to the so-called planned economies in which a central authority makes significant decisions regarding how resources are employed and who will benefit from the resulting production. Again, most economies are not pure form; most are a mixture of individual decisions, with greater or lesser involvement of governmental authority.

The third distinguishing feature of a free-enterprise system is *market determination of prices along with the levels of production* of most goods and services. This is really an offshoot of the first and second characteristics mentioned above. With private ownership of resources and a relative absence of economic orchestration emanating from central authority, there has to be some connective tissue that accounts for the organization of all the resources in the economy to produce the specific mix of goods and services produced and enjoyed by the economy. That connective tissue is the market mechanism or price system, which we will discuss below.

Organization of a Market Economy

Whereas the market mechanism, or price system, is the connective tissue of a market economy, the structural members are the various types of economic units and the markets in which they interact.

For descriptive purposes we can separate economic units into two broad classes based on economic activity:

Consumption Units. Consumption units are individuals, families, households, and so forth, that consume basic resources, products, and services for the satisfaction of human wants and needs.

Production Units. Production units are business enterprises, government, and other organizations that exist for the purpose of producing goods and services for other economic units.

Clearly, in virtually all cases an individual can qualify as both a consumption unit and a production unit. But that need not bother us overly in this discussion, because the purpose of the consumption-production dichotomy is mainly to highlight the broad categories of interaction of units that we will refer to as markets.

Markets. Markets are sets of exchanges between economic units in which one unit gives up a resource, good, or service in exchange for some other consideration, usually money.

Note that markets are not the same as marketplaces necessarily. Rather, markets are sets of exchanges of resources, goods, or services that have something in common. The common characteristic may be the place of exchange, like the "farmers market" in many cities. Or the common characteristic may be the nature of the things exchanged, as with a "livestock market" or the local "labor market."

It is in this latter sense that we can describe the three broad markets of a free-enterprise system—the factor market, the consumer goods market, and the capital and intermediate goods market. These three markets and the way they relate to consumption and production units of the economy are represented in Exhibit 2-3.

In the factor market, individuals exchange their labor, the use of their land and buildings, and other resources, for various kinds of cash "factor payments," including wages, rent, interest, and so forth, from the production units in the economy. To be consistent we would also include in this market an imputed or hypothetical wage for the individual who operates his own business in exchange for his labor and enterprise ability.

Exhibit 2-3   Organization of a Market Economy

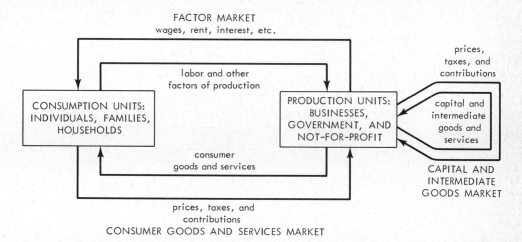

Having hired out their factors of production to businesses, government, or other production units, individuals then have the cash factor payments they receive in exchange to spend on goods and services to satisfy their wants and needs. The goods and services that are produced for direct use in satisfying human wants and needs are called consumer goods and services. The consumer goods and services market consists of all exchanges in which consumption units acquire consumer goods and services from the businesses, government, and not-for-profit units that produce them. The consideration given, usually in the form of cash, may be either a price or a fee paid to a business, taxes assessed by government, or donations made to not-for-profit organizations.

It is important to recognize that the acquisition of consumer goods and services produced by government and not-for-profit organizations is not quite the same as acquisition of goods and services from businesses. Usually, the individual who consumes a good or service produced by a business also pays the price or fee in exchange for it. With government and not-for-profit organizations, of course, such direct one-for-one relationships need not exist. Those who pay taxes, fees, and donations need not be the recipients of the goods or services provided. But in the aggregate, we can think of individuals as a group paying for, and receiving from governmental and not-for-profit organizations, goods and services that satisfy their human wants and needs.

In the capital and intermediate goods markets, business, government, and not-for-profit production units acquire goods that are (1) intended exclusively for use in producing other goods and services (capital goods), or (2) components of final consumer goods and services that are as yet incomplete (intermediate goods), or (3) services required to produce other goods and services of all kinds (intermediate services). For example, a factory building is a capital good, the component parts of a television set are intermediate goods, and the machining of parts for a new automobile by a machine shop constitutes an intermediate service.

The Market or Price System

Whereas identifying types of economic units and the broad markets in which they interact is descriptive of the structural components of a market economy, it does not convey its operating characteristics. In particular, identifying units and broad markets does not answer the following questions:

1. What products should be produced?
2. For whom should they be produced?
3. By whom should they be produced?
4. In what quantities should they be produced?

The specific answers to these questions are determined in large part by the forces of supply and demand in the market for each product and service.

• *The demand for products and services.* Each individual, acting independently, presumably has an influence on the questions of what is produced in a free economy and for whom. The degree of influence that particular individuals will have on the production of each product or service will depend on two factors: (1) the cash endowments of the individuals (or consumption units) in the economy and (2) their tastes and preferences. The set of conditioning influences on production that these factors combine to produce consists of the "aggregate demand" for each product or service that the economy can produce.

• *The supply of products and services.* During any short period of time, there will be only a limited supply of each product or service produced by the economy. The limited supply will be determined by (1) the limited resources that are at the time devoted to the production of each product, and (2) the fact that many of those resources, such as specialized plant and equipment, cannot be switched from production of one product to another on short notice. The limited supply will be offered for sale in the market for that product, and together with aggregate demand, the level of supply will determine an equilibrium price.

Equilibrium Price. The equilibrium price of a product is that price at which buyers will want to buy a quantity equal to the available supply.

• *Price, profits, and the role of the enterpriser.* Price has a special meaning to those individuals in the economy whom we will call enterprisers. The role of the enterpriser is twofold:

1. The enterpriser organizes factors of production to produce those products and services whose expected prices most exceed the costs of the factors of production.
2. In organizing factors of production, the enterpriser takes certain risks, along with his other efforts. In exchange for control over factors of production, he pays or promises to pay many factor payments, like wages, taking the chance that the value of the product or service produced will actually exceed those factor payments.

The enterpriser's economic reward is a residual. He receives the prices paid by buyers for his product and meets his obligations for all factor payments. What is left over is his, as a reward for playing his role. That residual or excess of the prices received for products over the factor costs required to produce them is called profit by some economists. Others prefer to call the residual "implicit wages" to the enterpriser, so long as it does not exceed a genuinely competitive reward for his entrepreneurial services. Only to the extent that it exceeds a competitive wage would they refer to it as profit. We follow the practice of referring to the whole residual as profit.

In their pursuit of profits, enterprisers have two valuable effects on the economy:

1. Given the tastes and preferences of all the individuals in the economy which determine the demand for each product and service, the enterprisers determine the level of available supply by responding to opportunities for profits.
2. *Under competitive conditions,* the free pursuit of profits ensures that only the most efficient producers in each industry survive and thus provide the product or service to the economy at the lowest possible cost.

Questions for Review and Discussion

2-1.   Define:

a. Statement of objectives

b. Constraints

c. Uncertainty

d. Information

e. Decision relevance

f. Information specialist

g. Business enterprise

h. Money capital

i. Internal users of information

j. External users of information

k. Accounting entity

l. Financial accounting

2-2.   What motivates the production of goods and services in a market economy?

2-3.   What is the role of the enterpriser in a market economy? Why would an enterpriser undertake this role? What methods or devices does an enterpriser employ to raise sufficient money capital for his business endeavors?

2-4.   What is an information specialist? Why do information specialists exist, that is, what function do they serve? List five types of information specialists and indicate some justification for the existence of each.

2-5.   What is the role of a business enterprise in a market economy?

2-6.   Describe the three traditional forms of business enterprise. Why is the corporation the dominant form of business enterprise (in terms of resources controlled) in a modern market economy?

2-7.   Distinguish between internal and external decision makers. How do their individual decisions relate to the business enterprise? What are the two major classes of decisions about the enterprise made by external parties?

2-8.   In general, what is the advantage of quantification in producing or using information for decisions? What are the disadvantages?

2-9.   Various governmental agencies have an interest in business enterprises (as external users of information). Describe some of these interests and the kinds of information that might be relevant to them.

2-10.   Give an example in which a particular kind of information is valuable (worth its cost) to an individual *and* to a group or class of individuals. Give an example in which a particular kind of information is valuable to an individual but not necessarily to a group. Give an example of information that is valuable to a group but not worth its cost to an individual.

2-11.   *Decision making* is defined as the process of choosing among competing alternative courses of action according to some criteria adopted by the decision maker.

1. Given that a decision maker is faced with a problem, can the decision maker elect to not make a decision regarding the problem?

2. Must the decision maker always obtain information before he makes his decision?

3. Should the decision maker always obtain information prior to making a decision?

2-12.   Is the traditional grade-point scale used in most educational institutions an example of a common scale of merit? A quantitative scale? How are grade-point averages used? What do they measure?

2-13.   Give three examples of quantified scales of merit that are often used in society today but which omit significant nonquantified information.

2-14.   Decision makers *need* good information to make economic decisions. Do you agree or disagree? Defend your position.

2-15.   More information is always better than less. Do you agree or disagree? Defend your position.

Exercises   **2-1. Cost and Value of Information.**   The Department of Accounting at State University has received two scholarship grants. Either one of the grants can be awarded this year, with the other to be awarded next year. The first grant provides that the recipient is to receive $1,500. The second grant is in the form of securities and other valuables to be sold by the trustees of a deceased benefactor's estate. If the proceeds exceed a certain amount, then the scholarship will be $2,000. If the proceeds fall short of the minimum, the scholarship will be only $1,000.

The Scholarship Committee of the Department of Accounting has selected

Student A, who ranked first among all applicants, to receive this year's award. Since one of the fellowships is uncertain in amount, the committee further decided to give Student A a choice as to which scholarship she would like best. Unfortunately, it must award the scholarship before the trustees are scheduled to sell off the property of the deceased benefactor's estate.

The committee has informed Student A of its decision and allowed one week for Student A to make a choice. In addition, it has informed Student A that the trustees of the deceased benefactor's estate (who are experts in handling estates) have estimated that there is a fifty-fifty chance that the estate's property will sell for more than the minimum amount. They indicated that they could say definitely one way or the other, but only after making a complete appraisal of the estate. Since such an appraisal was not called for in the will, however, they would have to charge the appraisal fee to whoever requested the information. The committee did not request the appraisal because the fee would then have to be paid out of the scholarship proceeds, making less available to the recipient.

Required:

Put yourself in Student A's position and satisfy the following requirements:

1. Without any additional information, can you decide between the two scholarships? If so, which would you choose? What factors make you prefer your choice?

2. Might you be willing to request an appraisal of the value of the estate's property? If not, why not? If so, what is the maximum you would be willing to pay?

2-2. Quantitative Scales.   The Pratfall Chair Company produces two lines of office chairs, standard and deluxe, both of which have been selling very well in recent years. This led the company to undertake a factory expansion and the employment and training of additional workers. Previously the factory had capacity for 100 workers (in three shifts), each of whom put in 2,000 hours per year. With the factory expansion 20 more workers have been added to the work force. All workers are paid at the same rate of $5 per hour.

A standard chair, which sells for $65, can be made in 3 hours. A deluxe chair takes 5 hours to make and sells for $100. The other costs of production associated with each type of chair are as follows:

	Standard	Deluxe
Materials	$20	$22
Hardware	5	8
Other costs	5	5

Now that the factory expansion is complete, Pratfall management is trying to decide how much of each kind of chair to produce. It has been producing and selling 30,000 standard chairs and 22,000 deluxe chairs. Management intends to produce at least as many as before of each chair so as not to disappoint faithful customers of either line. It also feels that at present prices it cannot sell more than 10,000 additional deluxe chairs or more than 20,000 additional standard chairs. Beyond these levels, prices would have to be drastically reduced.

Required:

1. On what common scale of merit should additional production of the two products be compared?

2. How much of each product should Pratfall produce? Support your answer with appropriate calculations.

2-3. Quantitative versus Qualitative Factors.   Harold Highpump is the owner and manager of a filling station. His operations have been greatly complicated by a recent (presumably temporary) gasoline shortage. He has been receiving 20,000 gallons of gasoline per month from the refinery—only about two-thirds of what he normally sells. When the gasoline is delivered each month, he must decide how much to allocate to his "regular" storage tank and how much to "premium." There is no difference between the gasoline pumped from the delivery truck. Instead, Harold pours certain "additives" into the premium tank after each delivery. During the shortage, Harold has been allocating 10,000 gallons of his monthly supply to each of the tanks.

This month, just before his monthly delivery, Harold received word from the refinery that he could have 5,000 additional gallons of gas in his next delivery provided he agrees to certain conditions: (1) he must allocate at least as much gas as last month to each tank (regular and premium), and (2) the amount of one grade of gas that he sells may not exceed 130 percent of the amount of the other grade.

Harold knows that he can sell all he wants of both grades at the present government-controlled prices of $.60 per gallon of regular and $.70 per gallon of premium. However, he has tried to maintain some fairness among his customers who demand about equal amounts of premium and regular gas. So far, no one has been able to have all the gas he has wanted.

Required:

Assuming that Harold pays $.50 per gallon for gasoline and that the additives cost $7.00 per pound and are added to the basic gasoline to get premium in a ratio of one pound per 100 gallons, how should Harold allocate his next delivery? Restrict your answer first to only quantifiable factors. Defend your answer. Are there any nonquantified factors that Harold should consider? Describe them.

2-4. Cost and Value of Information.   Mr. Landowner, described in this chapter, has asked you to help him with his decision. After talking with him and consulting with his neighbors, you determine that—

a. The best crop to plant would be either corn, wheat or green beans.

b. Growing more than a single crop on his 100 acres at this time is not feasible because of higher cultivation costs.

c. Measured in bushels per acre, the expected yield from corn ranges from 60 to 120 bushels; from wheat, 90 to 100 bushels; and from green beans, 80 to 200 bushels.

d. The yield depends largely on the composition of the soil. However, you do not know the actual composition of Landowner's soil, and the soil of the neighboring farms varies from farm to farm.

Required:

1. Given the above information only, can a decision be reached? Explain the basis of your answer.

2. What choice would you recommend if you expected that the net price per bushel (selling price minus production costs) for the three crops was approximately $.75 for corn, $1.00 for wheat, and $.50 for green beans? Support your answer.

3. At this point what kind of additional information might change your answer to number 2?

4. A local consulting firm will examine soil samples for a fee of $500. Its past record indicates that it can provide an extremely exact projection of the yield per acre for any crop.

   a. Could the more exact information alter Landowner's choice of crop?

   b. Can you categorically recommend that he buy the information from the consulting firm?

5. Suppose now that you have reliable information that only one of two soil conditions exists in the region of Landowner's farm and the chances are fifty-fifty that Landowner's farm could have either condition. One condition would mean a definite wheat yield of 100 bushels per acre and a bean yield of 180 bushels. The other condition would mean a wheat yield of 90 bushels and a bean yield of 200. Should Landowner pay for a consulting report costing $600 that will indicate exactly which condition exists in his soil? If the report would only cost $300?

2-5. The Tale of the Ancient Taxpayers.   (Adapted from the "Sheepherder's Game" by Warren Higgins, University of Connecticut.) Once upon a time there was a tiny mountain kingdom of Cascadia, ruled by a fierce but well-loved king, Tamalpias III. Cascadia had a strictly pastoral (barter) economy, with no money ever changing hands. Instead, the principal products of the kingdom were cattle, cheese, and hides, which the residents traded among themselves and with the surrounding lowland kingdoms in exchange for produce, clothing, building materials, and so forth.

Taxes were assessed each year by the royal tax collector. According to royal decree, each person's tax was to be proportionate to how well off he was, relative to everyone else in the kingdom—in the royal tax collector's judgment, that is. Unfortunately, the royal tax collector was corrupt and accepted occasional bribes from a few, instead of their just contribution to the Royal Treasury. When King Tamalpias discovered this, he stripped the man of his position and all of his possessions and had him thrown into the dungeon for life.

In place of the royal tax collector, King Tamalpias III decreed that henceforth each of his subjects was to assess and pay his own *just* tax, based on how well off he was. The tax rate was set at 5 percent to be applied as of New Year's Day each year.

Of course, the king was no fool. He knew that not all of his subjects could be counted upon to fairly assess and pay their own tax. Some penalties for failure to comply were necessary. But most of his subjects were simple people, and the king himself abhorred complicated laws. So, being an accomplished poet (in his own opinion, at least), he penned the following limerick and had it read publicly and posted throughout the kingdom:

> There once was a citizen, Faber,
> Who was twice as well off as his neighbor,
> But he paid much less tax
> For which he was lax,
> Now he's making it up at hard labor.

Well, the limerick had the desired effect. It struck fear (and a modicum of honesty) into the hearts of most subjects. But it also caused much puzzlement among the citizenry as to how to assess the tax. As the new year approached following the decree, two old friends, Roland and Buford, were "sharing a cup" in their village pub and comparing notes. Buford was a tanner and very good at his trade. His only source of dissatisfaction in life was due to the tanning process, which gives off an obnoxious odor. Because the odor clung to him and permeated his cottage, none of the kingdom's eligible maidens would think of marrying him and moving into his cottage. Roland was a dairyman, happily married. He enjoyed his dairying very much. In past years, Roland and Buford often argued (boastfully) about which one was better off. Now they were worried about how much tax each should pay and how they should pay for it.

Buford owned mostly hides, since they were his stock in trade. For the hides on hand, 200 in all, he gave a total of 2,000 "rounds" of cheese. All of the hides were in the process of being cured, however, and when finished would bring roughly 3,000 rounds of cheese upon sale. Buford also owned 5 cows, a cottage with a beautiful view of a neighboring lowland kingdom that he enjoyed very much, and a donkey cart for taking his finished hides to market. For each of the cows, he had given 50 finished hides over the last several years. The cottage was inherited from his father, who originally gave 5 cows for it. The donkey and cart were acquired two years ago (from the time the king's latest tax decree went into effect) in exchange for a cow plus 10 finished hides.

Roland owned 20 cows. Ten were inherited from his father, who gave 600 rounds of cheese for each over a number of years. The others were acquired by Roland for an average of 700 rounds of cheese each. In addition to his cows, Roland owned 50 rounds of cheese, a cottage, and a horse-drawn wagon. The cottage was built by Roland's father about the same time Buford's father acquired his cottage. Roland's father gave 3 cows for all of the materials. The horse and wagon were acquired by Roland for a cow plus a donkey-and-cart combination (both in good shape) that no longer served the needs of Roland's dairy operation.

Required:

Let us suppose that you lived in this kingdom at this time and that you formed a tax-consulting service for the kingdom of Cascadia. Calculate the amount of tax that Roland and Buford should pay, and indicate how they should pay it.

2-6. Problem Definition—A Highly Structured Decision. Suppose IDRA, an international disaster relief agency, has as its primary goal to be prepared to deliver all the food (needed for a balanced survival diet), clothing, and temporary shelter required by disaster victims anywhere in the world at any time. The agency can count on air transport for goods and personnel at the time of disaster from the nation concerned or sympathetic neighbors. The agency has always received ample storage space free or at minimal fees from various governments and private individuals. Its mission, therefore, is mainly to maximize the amounts of food, clothing, and shelter at the ready in its storage locations around the world. Unfortunately, it operates on a limited budget. Each year IDRA undertakes a fundraising drive and then allocates the total amount received to the three categories of food, clothing, and temporary shelter. Then its procurement directors for each category take over from there. Assume that *you* are the procurement director for food. Assume further that no single food commodity is optimal, so the problem involves selecting an optimal mix of several basic food commodities.

Required:

1. Satisfy the following two questions as an integrated set, that is, each should be answered in relationship to the other. (See the hints below.)

   (a) What statement of objective(s) would you use to guide your choice of how much of each basic food commodity to buy?

   (b) What constraints are present and how would you state them in relationship to (in the same terms as) the objective function?
   Hint #1: The decision alternatives in question are alternative mixes, proportions, or sets of total purchases of each of several food commodities.
   Hint #2: A major hurdle in the problem is to find a common scale of merit for incorporation in the statement of objective(s).

2. Can you suggest some procedure for efficiently evaluating alternatives and coming to a solution?

3. Indicate some nonquantifiable aspects of the problem. How do they complicate the problem definition or solution?

4. Suppose that IDRA cannot get unlimited storage space. Does this complicate the problem definition or solution? If so, how?

3

Investment Decisions:
A Simplified Model

In Chapter 2 we noted that the investment decision is one of two major categories of decisions made by external parties who have an economic interest in the business enterprise. Starting with Chapter 4 we will face the challenge of specifying some alternate kinds of information about business enterprises that accountants can produce for investment decision makers. In this chapter we intend to give the reader some general understanding of the nature of investment decisions and how one might go about making them—to which later discussion will relate.

The chapter is divided into three major sections. The first describes more fully investment decisions and some of their general characteristics. The second section develops the simplified model for choosing between investment decision alternatives. And the third section is an elaboration, to bring out some more subtle but important aspects of the simplified model.

THE INVESTMENT DECISION PROBLEM

The Objective of Investment Decisions and Its Implications

All economic decisions are presumably made for the ultimate purpose of enhancing the individual's well-being, that is, the satisfaction of wants and needs that the individual experiences. Investment decisions are no exception. But investment alternatives usually do not directly offer satisfaction of wants and needs. Instead, like many other production-oriented (as opposed to consumption-oriented) activities, investment decisions usually deal with the material or physical means to human satisfaction that we refer to as wealth.

> **Wealth.** Wealth is the command over present and future goods and services owned or controlled by an economic unit as of a point in time.

Wealth is clearly not identical with well-being or satisfaction. Satisfaction may be derived from all kinds of nonmaterial, noneconomic things like friendship, esteem, and self-confidence. But, in general, economists have assumed that, other things being equal, more wealth means more well-being for the individual, since the term *wealth* embraces all *economic sources* of present and future want satisfaction.

• *The objective of investment decisions.* In Chapter 2 we defined *investment decisions* as those decisions involving exchanges of present goods and services for rights to goods and services in the future. Thus investment decisions can be thought of as exchanges of wealth in one form (usually rights to present goods and services) for wealth in another form (rights to future goods and services). It is generally assumed in economics and accounting that investment decisions are made *with the objective* of maximizing wealth.

• *Implication of wealth maximization.* The implication of this objective is that the investment decision maker must be able to assess or measure the wealth that he is expected to give up, and the wealth he expects in return, in some comparable way. Accomplishing this, he will maximize his wealth by choosing the alternative with the maximum excess of wealth return over wealth given up. The central purpose of this chapter is to develop the methodology for making the necessary measurements. A useful first step in that direction is to be more specific (albeit briefly) about the wealth-related features of investment alternatives.

Features of Investment Decisions with Some Simplifying Assumptions

In order to be explicit about how individuals ought to go about choosing between investment alternatives, we will make some simplifying assumptions. First, we will assume that all wealth given up or returned in each investment alternative is in the form of cash, rather than dealing with investment alternatives in the general terms of rights to goods and services incorporated in the definition of investment decisions above. Second, we will ignore constraints on the decision maker and concentrate instead on methodology for determining the amount that a given investment alternative will contribute to the wealth of the decision maker. Finally, for the present, we will assume that all future cash flows, whether to be paid out or received, are known with certainty at the time of decision. Each of these assumptions is discussed briefly below.

• *Cash-flow orientation.* Although it is a narrowing assumption that invest-ment alternatives are composed exclusively of cash flows, it is not a particu-larly damaging one in view of the environment. In a modern economy vir-tually no one produces goods and services exclusively to directly satisfy his own wants and needs. Nearly every individual (1) specializes to a degree in producing some specific good or service, (2) exchanges quantities of that good or service for cash, and (3) uses the cash proceeds to purchase other goods and services to directly satisfy his wants and needs. Like other pro-duction-oriented activities, most investments offer *primarily* cash returns in the future in exchange for present cash commitments or outlays.

Nevertheless, some investment decisions hinge on the more qualitative (noncash) aspects of the alternatives. So it must be remembered that the importance of cash in our discussion of investment decisions is not that it is the *only* relevant aspect of investment decisions but that it is a relevant and quantifiable feature of practically all investment decisions.

• *Constraints ignored.* In Chapter 2 we mentioned that a decision maker faced with a decision situation will want to define his choice problem by spe-cifying both a statement of objectives and constraints. But in our discussion of investment decisions we will ignore constraints for two reasons. First, con-straints are not usually properties of investment decisions *per se* but rather are limitations that are imposed on the decision maker, for example, having a limited budget. Whereas the constraints faced by the individual may be unique to him, the objective of wealth maximization seems to apply widely across decision makers and investment alternatives.

Second, as was pointed out in Chapter 2, constraints can be applied in sequence before or after the decision maker has considered an alternative's promised contribution to his decision objective. Whatever choice or ranking we make between investment alternatives, based on their contribution to the objective of wealth maximization alone, it may later be altered when the con-straints faced by the decision maker are brought to bear.

• *Certain cash flows.* In Chapter 2 we defined *uncertainty* as the condition of not knowing at the time of decision precisely what the outcomes of rele-vant future events will be. Because investment decisions involve future flows of resources (usually cash), they are complicated by uncertainty. But pre-cisely because uncertainty complicates investment decision making, we will ignore it for the present. However, we will return to the matter of uncertainty in a later section of the chapter because it is an important aspect of most in-vestment decisions.

Investment Decisions under Certainty

Having made the foregoing simplifying assumptions, we can be specific about the features of investment decisions with which the decision maker must come to grips. We can now describe investment decisions as those decisions involving alternatives consisting of cash flows that may differ with respect to (1) magnitude and (2) the times, present and future, at which cash inflows and outflows will take place.

Example 3-1 An individual has two possible investment alternatives, investment A and investment B, each requiring an initial outlay of $100 but promising different cash inflows (returns) at the end of each of the next five years, as shown in Exhibit 3-1.

Exhibit 3-1

	Initial Outlay	Returns					Total Returns
		At the end of year:					
		1	2	3	4	5	
Investment A	−$100	$40	$35	$30	$25	$25	$155
Investment B	−$100	$25	$30	$30	$35	$40	$160

Which alternative should the individual choose? It is technically impossible to answer at a glance. We may come to the hasty conclusion (after some mental arithmetic) that investment B is better, since it promises $160 over five years in return for $100, whereas investment A promises only $155 in total. Such a conclusion implies that the $10 and $15 *greater* inflows in years four and five promised by investment B are worth more in combination than the $15 and $5 *greater* inflows in years one and two promised by investment A. But such a conclusion cannot be reached unequivocally.

One person may prefer the later, but greater, excess inflows of investment B over the earlier, but lesser, excess inflows from investment A. Another person may have the opposite preference. In either case, the individual will need to determine which of the two different sets of promised inflows will leave *him* better off.

Our simplified model of investment decision making developed in the next section will specify how an individual can make such a determination in cases where one alternative does not clearly dominate all others in every respect. But understanding the model depends on the three "building-block" concepts of (1) time preference for money, (2) compound interest, and (3) present value. These concepts are developed in turn below.

A MODEL FOR INVESTMENT DECISIONS— DEVELOPMENT

Time Preference for Money

Most individuals do not value the opportunity to have a specific amount of money now equally with the opportunity to have the same amount, no more, no less, at some future date. Most individuals would rate the opportunity to have the money now higher (in personal satisfaction) than waiting one year to have the same amount. We will call this phenomenon an individual's *time preference for money* and define it more explicitly as follows:

Time Preference for Money. An individual's preference for possession of a given amount of cash now, rather than the same amount at some future time, is called "time preference for money."

Two basic reasons account for most individuals' time preference for money. First, money is the means by which individuals acquire most goods and services. And most people prefer present consumption to future consumption of the same goods and services, either (1) because of the urgency of their present wants or (2) because of the risk of not being around to enjoy future consumption that is imposed by man's temporal condition. Second, there are usually opportunities to put present cash to work earning additional cash. For instance, an individual offered $100 now or $100 one year from now can usually take the $100 now, put it in a savings account, and withdraw that amount plus $5 or $6 interest in one year. Thus, if he wishes to maximize his wealth, the opportunity to save would lead him to prefer $100 now to $100 one year hence.

• *Time preference expressed as a rate.* Generally, an individual's time preference for money can be characterized for convenience by an interest rate, with the aid of a simple mental game. The individual merely asks himself, "If I am offered either possession of $10 today or the right to have some greater amount one year from today, at what greater amount would I be exactly indifferent between the two opportunities?" If the answer to this question is $11, for instance, it implies that $11 to be received one year from now is equivalent in value (personal satisfaction) to having $10 in hand right now. This in turn implies that the strength of the individual's time preference for money can be designated by the 10 percent per year differential (*time preference rate*) that was added to get $11. Similarly, if it would only take $10.50 to be possessed one year from now to make the individual indifferent, his *time preference rate* for money would be only 5 percent. (Note: A commonly used synonym for time preference rate is the term *discount rate.*)

• *Using the time preference rate.* How does knowledge of a specific time preference rate help the individual in his investment problems? It permits the individual to translate different amounts offered at different times of possession to amounts of *equivalent value* to him in the present, a common point of reference.

Example 3-2   Take an individual with a time preference rate of 10 percent. If someone offered him a chance to have $1,155 one year from now in exchange for giving up $1,000 of his dollars today, would he take the offer? The answer is yes. When the individual determines that his time preference rate is 10 percent, he is saying that he is indifferent between any amount today and 110 percent of that amount one year hence. He would obviously favor more than 110 percent of the amount one year from now, but if the amount offered one year from now were less than 110 percent of the immediate payment, he would retain the immediate payment. Now we can ask the question: Between what amount today and $1,155 one year from now would our investor be indifferent? The answer is that amount of which $1,155 is exactly 110 percent. Dividing $1,155 by 1.10 we get:

$$\frac{\$1,155}{1.10} = \$1,050,$$

or more than the $1,000 that the individual is asked to give up today.

This means that if the individual had been asked to give up $1,050 to get $1,155 back after one year, he would be indifferent—not really caring whether he took the offer or not. Since the actual offer calls for him to give up only $1,000 to get $1,155 back after one year, he will take it. He only has to give up $1,000 to get something that is equivalent (in value to him) to having $1,050 in his possession right now.

• *Time preference, consumption levels, and alternate opportunities.* Before leaving this introductory level of discussion about time preference for money, some additional subtleties need to be brought out. Primarily it should be noted that, at any point in time, the individual's time preference for money may be conditioned by a number of things. Among the important conditioning variables are (1) the present level of consumption enjoyed and (2) the attractiveness of opportunities available.

To see intuitively that the present consumption level enjoyed conditions time preference, consider the contrast between an individual existing at the subsistence level versus one who is very wealthy. The former is not likely to be able to think of a rate high enough to make him forgo present survival (present consumption at the subsistence level) for opulence in the future. On the other hand, the latter may be willing to forego additional present consumption at a fairly low rate, simply because he already "has everything."

To see the influence of other opportunities on the individual's time preference rate, consider a brief example.

Example 3-3   Suppose an individual is currently consuming well above the subsistence level, that is, postponement of present consumption is feasible. Also, suppose initially that he can place cash in a savings bank that will return $105 after one year for every $100 deposited. Assume that the 5 percent rate of return implied by the savings bank deal is just sufficient to make the individual decide to save some of his money. But before actually depositing the money, he becomes aware of a chance to place $450 in an investment club that guarantees $470 in return in one year. The question is: Is the investment club deal attractive to the individual? The answer is no. As long as the investor can receive $105 for each $100 of consumption forgone for a year, he can actually receive $472.50 from the saving bank at the end of a year for foregoing $450 in present consumption. He would not want to receive less in one year for the same sacrifice.

The example can be generalized to any investment alternative. An investor will be indifferent to an investment alternative if it promises a return equal to his opportunity rate.

Opportunity Rate. An investor's *opportunity rate* (of return) is the rate he can earn on his best known investment alternative.

An investor will favor any new alternatives promising returns higher than his present opportunity rate. New alternatives offering less than the opportunity rate of return will be rejected. Thus the investor's time preference rate *is his opportunity rate,* assuming he has passed the threshold of deciding to forego present for future consumption.

The Rationale for Compound Interest

So far, we have only worked out sufficient logic for deciding between cash inflows and outflows that are separated by one period, such as one year. What about more complicated investment opportunities of more than one period's duration, like the unresolved choice between investments A and B in Example 3-1? We need to extend the logic developed above and thereby make it more flexible.

Let us continue to work with an individual who has determined that it takes a 10 percent premium to make him indifferent to inflows or outflows of cash one year apart. The question now before us is, How should he arrive at comparative values of inflows and outflows two, three, or any number of years apart?

Once an individual has determined his personal time preference for money for any single period of time (like one year), we can determine the relative difference in amounts that he would require for postponing possession of cash for any longer period. If an individual has determined that his time preference rate is 10 percent, for instance, he would insist on receiving at least $1.10 after one year, or 110 percent in return for an original sacrifice of $1 today. Now, if we asked him to give up $1 for two years, would he accept $1.20, or 100 percent + 10 percent + 10 percent, at the end of two years in return? The answer is no.

A two-year period, after all, is nothing more than two successive one-year periods. If the individual first agreed to give up $1 for one year, he would have $1.10 back at the end of that year in exchange for the original $1. If he recommitted the whole amount for an additional year, he would demand 110 percent of the whole amount, or $1.21 ($1 $\times$ 1.10 $\times$ 1.10) at the end of the second year. Notice that for any time after the first year he will insist on receiving a premium on the first-year premium as well as a premium on the original amount. When the premiums are called interest rates, this concept is described as *compound interest*.

The same reasoning can be extended to a third year. We now know that an individual with a time preference of 10 percent would be indifferent between $1 today and $1.21 ($1 $\times$ 1.10 $\times$ 1.10) at the end of two years. And, having $1.21 at the end of the second year, he would be indifferent between holding it or giving it up for one more year for a return of $1.21 $\times$ 110 percent, or approximately $1.33 ($1 $\times$ 1.10 $\times$ 1.10 $\times$ 1.10). In other words, he is really indifferent between $1 now and $1.33 to be received at the end of three years. We could continue to work out amounts for four years, five years, six years, and so forth, but it has already become awkward to continue verbally. Besides, a formula can be used to symbolically represent the amount that an individual would demand after any number of years in return for $1 given up initially at any rate of interest.

• *The future value of one dollar.* Let r represent the decimal equivalent of the individual's time preference rate for one period (0.10 per year in the above discussion). And let n be the number of years before payoff. Then the future value (amount of cash) an individual would require in return for $1 given up for n years at r rate, represented as $FV_{(n,r)}$, is equal to:

$$FV_{(n,r)} = \$1 \times (1.0 + r)^n$$

Example 3-4   To show that this is so, consider the example used in the discussion above; r is 0.10, so the term in parentheses would be 1.10. To represent the inflow from a sacrifice of \$1 for three years, we raise 1.10 to the power $n = 3$:

$$FV_{(3, 0.10)} = \$1 \times (1.10)^3$$
$$= \$1 \times (1.10)(1.10)(1.10)$$
$$= \$1.33$$

We get the same amount that was computed earlier using verbal rather than symbolic logic. The advantage of the formula is that it characterizes all of our logic for any interest rate and any number of years.

• *The future value of any amount.* As a final comment on the generality of the logic embodied in the above formula, it should be pointed out that what we calculate as future value for a sacrifice of \$1 for some number of years can easily be used to determine the future value for any number of dollars initially sacrificed.

Example 3-5   The inflow for a sacrifice of \$9 for three years at 10 percent is simply nine times the inflow for \$1, or:

$$9 \times \$1(1.10)^3$$
$$\$9 \times 1.33 = \$11.97$$

Symbolically, if the number of dollars to be sacrificed for n years is represented by S, then the inflow at the end of n years can be represented by

$$S \times FV_{(n,r)}$$

Or,

$$S \times (1.0 + r)^n$$

Recalling the original motivation for this discussion, it may now be observed that we have the power in the concept of compound interest to compare cash inflows and outflows that are separated *by more than one period,* given an individual's time preference rate *per period.*

Example 3-6   If an individual with a time preference rate of 10 percent per year were offered an opportunity to pay out \$55 now for a return of \$68 after two years, should he take the offer? The answer is yes, because he would be exactly indifferent between having \$55 now and having $\$55 (1.10)^2$, or $\$55 \times 1.21$, two years from now. Since the latter amount, \$66.55, is less than the payoff offered, \$68, we know that the individual would willingly give up \$55 now to get the return of \$68 two years from now.

Present Value

Although our analytical power over investment opportunities is considerably expanded with the introduction of compound interest, we still lack something. Whereas we now can translate any amount of present cash into an amount of cash of equivalent value to be received at the end of any number of future periods, it is convenient in investment decisions to be able to work in the other direction. In this section the discussion will turn to the appropriate technique for working from future cash flows to their present values.

> **Present Value.** The present value of a future cash inflow or outflow is the amount of current cash that is of equivalent desirability, to the decision maker, to a specified amount of cash to be received or paid at a future date.

Once we have concluded that our individual with a time preference rate of r per year is indifferent between \$1 now and $(1.0+ r)$ one year from now, or $(1.0 + r)^2$ after two years, or $(1.0 + r)^3$ after three years, and so forth, we can ask a set of related questions. How much would the same individual give up now to get a payoff of \$1 at the end of one, two, *or* three years? The answer in each case is a matter of proportionality.

Consider the one-year case. Assuming a time preference rate of 10 percent, the *present value* of one dollar to be received at the end of one year must bear the same relationship to the \$1 inflow as a \$1 sacrifice bears to an inflow of \$1.10 after one year. We can represent this logic algebraically as a set of related ratios with the symbol $PV_{(1,0.10)}$ representing the present value of \$1 to be received in one year at a 10 percent time preference rate:

$$\frac{PV_{(1,0.10)}}{\$1} = \frac{\$1}{\$1.10}$$

Or, solving for the present value:

$$PV_{(1,0.10)} = \frac{\$1}{\$1.10} = \$.909$$

This means that assuming a time preference rate of 10 percent, the present value of \$1 to be received after one year is equivalent to 90.9 cents now. To see that this is consistent with the individual's expressed time preference, we only need to note that one dollar (the promised inflow) is 110 percent of 90.9 cents.

The present values of one dollar inflows at the end of two- and three-year waiting periods can be worked out similarly. Since the individual with a time preference rate of 10 percent is indifferent between \$1 now and \$1.21 after two years, he is also indifferent between 82.6 cents now and \$1 after two years:

$$\frac{PV_{(2,0.10)}}{\$1} = \frac{\$1}{\$1.21}$$

$$PV_{(2,0.10)} = \frac{\$1}{\$1.21} = \$.826$$

The same individual, indifferent between $1 now and $1.33 three years from now, must also be indifferent between 75.1 cents now and $1 three years from now:

$$\frac{PV_{(3,0.10)}}{\$1} = \frac{\$1}{\$1.33}$$

$$PV_{(3,0.10)} = \frac{\$1}{\$1.33} = \$.751$$

Naturally, the same type of calculations can be worked out for any individual for any number of years and any time preference rate.

• *The present value of one dollar.* The general form of the foregoing present value calculation technique can be represented symbolically as follows:

$$PV_{(n,r)} = \frac{1}{FV_{(n,r)}} = \frac{1}{(1.0 + r)^n}$$

Notice that the present value of $1 to be received at the end of n years at r rate is simply the reciprocal of the future value to be received from investing $1 for n years at r interest rate.

• *The present value of any amount.* The advantage of knowing the present value of $1 by applying the formula above is that the present value of an inflow of any number of dollars, represented by P, can be found by simply multiplying the present value of $1 by P. Symbolically this can be represented as follows for a given time preference rate, r, and number of years, n:

$$P \times PV_{(n,r)} = P \times \frac{1}{(1.0 + r)^n}$$

This formula tells us how much current cash we would consider to be equivalent in value to, say, $100 to be received three years from now ($n = 3$) if our time preference rate (r) were 10 percent. The term $PV_{(n,r)}$ tells us that the present value of each of those dollars is:

$$\frac{1}{(1.0 + 0.10)^3} = 0.751.$$

Therefore the total is worth 100 times that amount (100×0.751), or $75.10.

• *Present value and future value tables.* Once the above notion is understood, a good deal of efficiency can be achieved in finding the present value (to an individual with a given time preference rate) of any amount of dollars promised at the end of any number of years. How? The formula that determines the present value will lead to the same conclusion for a given n, r, and P, regardless of who does the calculation. Thus it has been found convenient to have precalculated tables of present values of $1 to be received at the end of any reasonable number of years (say, one to thirty) at any reasonable interest rate (say, 1 percent to as much as 20 percent). Table 3-1, in Appendix A to this chapter, is just such a table. To use Table 3-1, one need only read off the present value of one dollar to be received at the end of *n* years at *r* rate as the number at the intersection of the *n*th row and the column labeled *r* rate in the table. To confirm this, recall that earlier we computed the present value of $1 to be received at the end of one, two, and three years for a time preference rate of 10 percent. The amounts computed earlier were $.909, $.826, and $.751, respectively. The same amounts are shown at the intersections of the .10 column of Table 3-1 and the first row (one year), second row (two years), and third row (three years), respectively. The same convenience is available in Table 3-2 (also in Appendix A), which is organized in the same way for future values of one dollar at the end of *n* years at *r* rate of interest. In taking advantage of the convenience of the table, however, one must never lose track of the logic behind the numbers that appear there.

One additional convenience of precalculated valuation factors, available in special cases of so-called annuities, is described in Appendix B to this chapter—along with the related table of annuity values.

Net Present Value: A Model for Investment Choice

With the aid of present value tables like Table 3-1, an individual who can specify his time preference rate for money can determine the amount of dollars today that would be of equivalent value to him of any given future cash inflow or outflow. We will see below that with very little more effort, these individual present values can be combined to get a single total present value for each investment opportunity.

Example 3-7   Again assume a time preference rate of 10 percent *and* recall the unresolved choice between investments A and B introduced in Example 3-1. Because a decision maker can assign a present value to any single dollar promised in any future year, he can assign total present values to all the promised annual cash flows of investments A and B, as shown in Exhibit 3-2.

• *Calculating net present values.* Looking just at investment A, the decision maker has recognized that, to him, the receipt of $40 one year from now is equivalent to receiving $36.36 today. Likewise, the receipt of $35 two years from now is "worth" the equivalent of $28.91 today. Similarly for the other three years' payoffs of $30, $25, and $25, respectively. But if the $40 at the end of year one is worth $36.36 today and the $35 at the end of year two is worth $28.91 today, it is sensible to conclude that any opportunity combining $40 at the end of the first year *and* $35 at the end of the second would be worth $36.36 plus $28.91, or $65.27 in total today. For each of the two promised cash flows has been measured on the same numerical scale—present dollar value. Thus we can generalize that *the total present value of a set of promised future cash flows is the sum of the present values of all of the individual periodic cash flows.* When an investment opportunity promises both

Exhibit 3-2

	Initial Outlay	Returns				
		At the end of year:				
		1	2	3	4	5
Investment A:						
1. Promised cash flows	−$100	$40	$35	$30	$25	$25
2. Present value of one dollar at 10%	1.00	0.909	0.826	0.751	0.683	0.621
3. Present value of promised cash flows (line 1 × line 2)	−$100	$36.36	$28.91	$22.53	$17.08	$15.53
Investment B:						
1. Promised cash flows	−$100	$25	$30	$30	$35	$40
2. Present value of one dollar at 10%	1.00	0.909	0.826	0.751	0.683	0.621
3. Present value of promised cash flows (line 1 × line 2)	−$100	$22.73	$24.78	$22.53	$23.91	$24.84

future cash inflows and outflows (as in any case requiring an initial outlay), we can sum the present values of the inflows and the outflows separately and find the difference between the sums.

Net present value. The sum of the present values of the future cash inflows minus the sum of the present values of the present and future cash outflows is called the *net present value* of an investment opportunity.

Example 3-8 Returning to investment A, we can conclude that the total present value of the inflows is:

$$\$36.36 + \$28.91 + \$22.53 + \$17.08 + \$15.53 = \$120.41$$

The total present value of the outflows is obviously $100, the present value of the solitary (initial) outlay. The net present value of investment A is therefore $120.41 − $100.00 = $20.41.

• *Interpreting net present values.* The interpretation of this net present value number is very useful for decision-making purposes. The present cash value of the outlays required to enter upon investment A as a course of action is $100. The present value of the benefits (cash inflows) from doing so is $120.41. Therefore the act of paying out $100 to enter upon investment A is *equivalent* to paying $100 and immediately receiving $120.41 in return. The gain is $20.41, the net present value of investment A. The investor would obviously find this an attractive course of action unless some other course of action, like investment B, promises an even greater net present value (or cash-equivalent gain). To find out if B is more attractive, we follow the same procedure as with the calculation of the net present value of investment A.

Example 3-9   The present value of the outflows for investment B is equal to the $100 initial outlay, as with A. The total present value of all of the inflows from B equals:

$$\$22.73 + \$24.78 + \$22.53 + \$23.91 + \$24.84 = \$118.79$$

The net present value of B is therefore $118.79 − $100.00 = $18.79. To undertake investment B *is equivalent,* to the decision maker, to receiving an immediate cash gain of $18.79.

We now know, of course, that the decision maker would prefer investment A to investment B, since we can be reasonably sure that he would prefer an immediate cash gain of $20.41 to a gain of $18.79, the net present values of investments A and B, respectively. In other words, calculating and comparing net present values provides a basis—a decision model—for choosing between complex investment alternatives.

• *Summary of the net present value model.* In summary, any individual who can specify his time preference rate for money can specify a present value or amount of current cash that is of equivalent value to him of any specified (certain) amount of cash to be received or paid at the end of any future period. From there it is a matter of only three additional arithmetic steps to comparing *net present values* of complex investment alternatives. The total sequence of steps in the process is:

1. Specify the cash inflows and outflows in each period associated with each investment alternative.
2. Calculate the present value of each individual cash inflow and outflow associated with each investment alternative.
3. Aggregate (sum) the present values of all the positive and all the negative cash flows for each alternative.
4. *Find the net present value* of each alternative by calculating the difference between the total present value of the positive cash flows and the total present value of the negative cash flows.
5. Finally, choose that alternative or combination of alternatives with the largest net present value.

These five steps, represented schematically in Exhibit 3-3, constitute our simplified model for investment decisions. They have been illustrated by Examples 3-7, 3-8, and 3-9. Now it remains for us to show that the net present value technique is a means for choosing between investment alternatives in a way that satisfies the assumed objective of wealth maximization.

Present Value and the Concept of Wealth

At the beginning of this chapter *wealth* was defined as the command over present and future goods and services owned or controlled by an economic unit as of a point in time. *Investment decisions* were described as those decisions involving alternative commitments or sacrifices of current forms of

Exhibit 3-3   Net Present Value Model

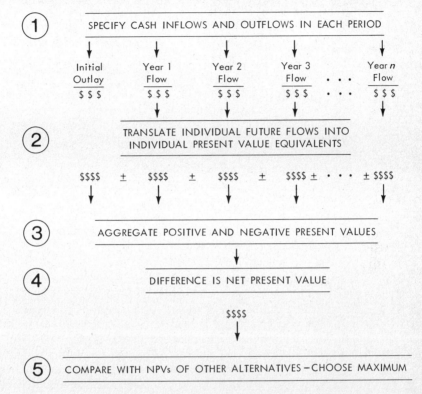

wealth that are expected to lead to greater quantities of goods or services in the future, that is, greater wealth. The discussion then proceeded to the development of a decision model that called for choosing from among all investment alternatives the alternative (or set of alternatives) whose net present value is greatest. In adopting this criterion we implicitly accepted present value as a means of measuring the abstract concept, wealth. To see this clearly, consider the individual choosing between investments A and B.

The individual, whose time preference rate was 10 percent, would choose investment A over investment B because A has a *net* present value of $20.41 as opposed to B's net present value of only $18.79.

Prior to selecting investment A or B, the individual presumably has wealth in the form of $100 in cash. After selecting investment A and paying the $100 initial outlay, investment A replaces the $100 cash. But how do we assess the meaning to the individual of his wealth prior to and subsequent to his decision? Technically we cannot. Only the individual can "feel" the satisfaction that he gets from owning $100 in cash or the "feeling" he gets from owning the rights to investment A.

But because cash is the medium by which an individual in a modern economy acquires goods and services (the components of wealth), we can make an inference about the individual's feelings of wealth from holding cash. For instance, we can say that when our individual has $100 cash he feels as wealthy as the goods and services he can command with $100 cash can make him feel. More cash will always make him feel more wealthy (because he can command more goods and services), and less cash will always make him feel less wealthy. So we say that an individual with $100 cash has $100 of wealth. Now what about possession of an item like investment A? How wealthy does that make the individual? We have already answered that question.

In assessing the present value of A, we were saying that an individual with a specified time preference of 10 percent per year would value investment A exactly as he would value $120.41 *in cash* today. Thus we can conclude that possessing investment A makes him feel as wealthy as possessing $120.41 in cash, the (total) present value of A. Hence, the wealth of an individual can, in a sense, be measured (quantified) as his current cash on hand *plus the present value* of the future cash inflows and outflows that he will receive from all of his noncash wealth items.

As a final thought, it should be emphasized that present values are not wealth *per se* but rather are valuations of wealth (or wealth items).

> **Valuation.** Valuation is the measurement (quantification) of wealth (or wealth items) in money terms.

Therefore, any valuation (like present value) may be used interchangeably with wealth, only with qualification. The qualification is necessary because the individual can use present value (for instance) as a means of quantifying his wealth only insofar as he can translate his wealth items into equivalent cash flows for which he can then calculate present values based on his time preference for money. In the case of investment A this is easy. It promises no *direct* want-satisfaction, as we have described it. Its only physical property is a stream of future cash flows. But other types of wealth items, art objects for example, obviously possess significant noncash want-satisfying properties. Recall, however, that we have purposely excluded consideration of such items through our initial assumptions.

Net Present Value and Wealth Maximization

Having established that present values can be thought of as a means of quantifying or valuing wealth, we can reflect briefly on the relationship between the net present value decision-making criterion and the objective of investment decision making, that is, wealth maximization. This is the final step in introducing the net present value model as a simplified but plausible way of approaching investment decisions.

Returning to the example, we can look at investment A's *net* present value of $20.41 as being composed of two parts: (1) a negative component amounting to the present value of the wealth that the individual gives up, in this case $100, and (2) a positive component representing the present value of the wealth that the individual gets in return, in this case $120.41. Thus, *the net present value of a decision alternative may be thought of as the improvement in wealth (as measured in terms of present value) that will result from selecting the alternative.* Choosing investment alternatives on the basis of maximum net present value improves the wealth position of the individual to the fullest, that is, it maximizes wealth as measured in terms of present values at the time of decision.

PRESENT VALUE METHODOLOGY— SOME ELABORATION

In the preceding section we completed the development of a simplified model with which decision makers can approach investment decisions, with the objective of maximizing their wealth. This section is devoted to some features of present value methodology that are not quite as central to the problem of investment decisions as the discussion in the preceding section. But each of these additional topics will either strengthen the reader's grasp of the basic model or extend it in a direction that will be relevant to discussion in later chapters.

Sensitivity of Net Present Value to Time Preference Rate

A most important feature of the net present value model is its dependence on the time preference rate selected. Without preselecting a time preference rate, one cannot accomplish the step of translating cash flows of various future periods into cash of a single common period, the present. Furthermore, the outcome of a decision can be highly sensitive to the magnitude of the rate selected. Although we may calculate net present values of several decision alternatives based on one rate and conclude that an individual who selects that rate would unequivocally choose one alternative above all others, we cannot always conclude—without repeating all the calculations—that another individual selecting a different time preference rate would choose the same alternative. To see that this is so, consider Example 3-10.

Example 3-10   Two investors, X and Y, are considering the same investment, a corporate bond that is selling for $963. The bond has a face, or principal, value of $1,000 and will mature in one year, that is, the principal of $1,000 will be paid in exactly one year. The bond pays 5 percent interest per year on the principal, including the year of maturity. Thus in one year the bond will pay $1,000 principal plus $50 interest for the year to anyone who presents the bond for redemption at that time.

Of the two investors, X has selected a higher time preference rate, 10 percent; Y's rate is only 8 percent. X has decided not to buy the bond based on present value calculations, whereas Y has decided to buy—also based on present value calculations. At his 10 percent time preference rate, X values each dollar to be received in one year as if it were $.909 in present cash, that is, .909 is $PV_{(1,0.10)}$, according to Table 3-1. Hence the present value of $1,050 to be received in one year is $954.45 to X ($1,050 × 0.909), somewhat less than the $963 price of the bond. For Y, with a time preference rate of 8 percent, the present value of one dollar to be received in one year is $.926. The present value of $1,050 in one year to Y is therefore $972.30 ($1,050 × 0.926), or somewhat more than the $963 selling price of the bond. Thus Y finds the bond an attractive opportunity; X does not.

Although it is a special case, the example highlights a phenomenon that holds in general. It is always true that an individual who places a higher time preference rate on money will assign a lower present value to a given number of dollars promised in a given future year than will an individual with a lower time preference rate. This reasoning follows directly from the logic of present value which is embodied in the formula:

$$PV_{(n,r)} = \frac{1}{(1.0 + r)^n}$$

Since r, the time preference rate of the individual, appears in the denominator of the formula, we know that the greater r is, the less will be the present value of each dollar promised in any future period. This makes sense, of course, since an individual who expresses a high time preference rate expresses a stronger immediate demand for money, either because of the urgency with which he wants to consume or the attractiveness of his alternate investment opportunities. Naturally, such a person will be less patient about waiting any given amount of time for a given amount of money and will therefore value future money less.

The Equivalence of Net Present Value and Valuations at Future Points in Time

Since investment decisions generally involve giving up wealth in present form (cash) for wealth in future form (future cash flows), one way that we can state the goal of any investment decision is as follows: to leave the decision maker better off in the future by selecting the investment alternative that will lead to the best cash (or equivalent wealth) position at any future point in time. In our earlier discussion of net present value and wealth maximization, we implied that the net present value criterion is a means to achieving the above goal. However, by shifting the point in time at which we evaluate alternatives, we can show that when it is applied to investment alternatives, the alternative with the greatest net present value is indeed the alternative that will leave the investor better off in the future than any other alternative.

In this respect, as we developed our description of the net present value criterion, we relied on two relevant assumptions, one explicit and one implicit. We explicitly assumed that all future (and present) cash flows associated with each alternative are known with certainty. In addition, we implicitly assumed that the time preference rate for money that the individual specifies at the time of decision will continue to characterize his time preference as he proceeds through future years.

Based on these assumptions and the formula for the net present value of an investment alternative, we could rigorously show that the net present value criterion is equivalent to a valuation of the alternatives at any point in the future. But it is much simpler to proceed by example.

Example 3-11   An investor with a time preference rate of 12 percent wishes to choose between two investments, ABC and XYZ. Each offers a single cash flow at the end of the second year and again at the end of the fourth year hence. Each requires an initial outlay of $2,000. ABC will pay the investor $2,000 at the end of year two and $1,000 at the end of year four. XYZ will pay $1,000 and $2,000, respectively. The net present value calculations at 12 percent shown in Exhibit 3-4 indicate that the investor would choose ABC with a net present value of $230 over XYZ with a net present value of $69.

Exhibit 3-4   NET PRESENT VALUE @ 12%

	Investment ABC			Investment XYZ		
Year of Cash Flow	*Cash Flow*	$PV_{(n,0.12)}$	*PV of Cash Flow*	*Cash Flow*	$PV_{(n,0.12)}$	*PV of Cash Flow*
0	−$2,000	1.000	−$2,000	−$2,000	1.000	−$2,000
2	2,000	0.797	1,594	1,000	0.797	797
4	1,000	0.636	636	2,000	0.636	1,272
Net present value			$ 230			$ 69

• *Terminal cash position.* To demonstrate the equivalence of the net present value criterion and future valuations, we project the investor into the future and examine his cash (or equivalent) position. If the present value criterion is consistent with the wealth-maximizing objective, then the investor should be better off, in terms of cash (or equivalent) position, by possessing the alternative that had the greatest net present value than if he possessed any of the other alternatives. Although this should hold true at any future time, it is particularly convincing to consider the end of the lives of the investment alternatives, such as the end of year four in Example 3-11. By that time, each alternative will have run its full course, that is, will have provided all of the cash flows expected at the time of decision. Any difference in the investor's cash position associated with the various decision alternatives as of that time will presumably continue for all time.

Exhibit 3-5 is an assessment of the year-four cash position that would result from investments ABC and XYZ, assuming everything works out as was expected at the time of decision. The logic underlying Exhibit 3-5 and its implications are discussed in the next several paragraphs.

Exhibit 3-5   VALUE AT 12% OF INVESTMENTS ABC AND XYZ
                              AS OF THE END OF YEAR FOUR

	Investment ABC			Investment XYZ		
Year of Cash Flow	*Cash Flow*	$FV_{(n,0.12)}$ *Factor*	*Year-Four Cash*	*Cash Flow*	$FV_{(n,0.12)}$ *Factor*	*Year-Four Cash*
2	$2,000	1.250	$2,500	$1,000	1.250	$1,250
4	1,000	1.000	1,000	2,000	1.000	2,000
Total year-four cash			$3,500			$3,250
Initial Outlay	−2,000	1.570	−3,140	−2,000	1.570	−3,140
Net year-four cash			$ 360			$ 110

Note in Exhibit 3-5 that the total year-four cash position with respect to both ABC and XYZ is greater than the sum of the actual cash flows ($3,000 in each case). This is a manifestation of the reasoning underlying the individual's time preference rate. Referring just to investment ABC, for instance, we can draw some inferences about the effect as of year four of its cash flows on the investor who has expressed a time preference rate of 12 percent. The receipt of $2,000 at the end of year two has one of two implications for the investor's year-four position:

1. He will have reinvested the $2,000 at the time of receipt at 12 percent compounded annually for two years. This would give him $2,000 × $FV_{(2,0.12)}$ = $2,000 × 1.250 = $2,500, at the end of year four.
2. Or, he will have spent the $2,000 (plus any interest earned) sometime between the end of year two and the end of year four.

In the latter case, spending the $2,000 (plus any interest earned) would presumably have yielded as much satisfaction, at the time, as the prospect (at that time) of having $2,500 at the end of year four. So, in either case, having $2,000 at the end of year two is equivalent to having $2,500 two years later, at the end of year four. Thus in Exhibit 3-5 we show the contribution of the $2,000 year-two cash flow to the investor's year-four cash (or equivalent) position as $2,500. The same reasoning applies to the year-four effect of the $1,000 year-two cash flow promised by investment XYZ.

Now consider the effect on the investor's prospective year-four cash position of the year-four cash flows from ABC and XYZ. Since no time lapses between the receipt of the cash flows and the assessment of the investor's position (both at year-end), the year-four cash flows are shown at the amounts received.

To summarize, *the terminal (or other future) cash position* to be expected from a given investment is the sum of the future values of the promised cash flows, invested from the time of receipt to the end of the investment's life at the time preference rate. Note that the terminal cash position (total year-four cash) expected from ABC is $3,500 while XYZ will provide only $3,250. Since ABC had a greater net present value at the time of decision, does this prove our point? In this case the answer is yes. Since ABC and XYZ would have cost the investor the same initial outlay of $2,000, the one providing the greater terminal cash is the more desirable. But since investments will not, as a rule, have identical costs, we should go one step further before concluding.

• *Net terminal (or other future) value.* To compare the expected terminal benefits of investments having unequal costs, somehow the different initial costs must enter the comparison as of the terminal date. To do this we must answer the question, What is the effect on the investor's cash position, as of the terminal date, of the initial (plus any subsequent) outlay made to acquire the investment? The answer is the future value of the outlay, at the time preference rate, invested from the time it was paid to the terminal date. For instance, in the case of either ABC or XYZ, giving up $2,000 at the outset to acquire the investment meant that the investor had to forego the benefits of investing that $2,000 at 12 percent for four years in order to receive the benefits promised by either investment ABC or investment XYZ. So in Exhibit 3-5 we have subtracted from the total year-four cash positions promised by ABC and XYZ $3,140, the year-four value of the $2,000 initial outlay ($2,000 × $FV_{(4,0.12)}$ = $2,000 × 1.57 = $3,140). The result is the *year-four net value.* It represents the *additional* year-four cash or equivalent promised by each investment, over that which would be possessed if the initial outlay had been kept and reinvested at compound interest.

Notice the "net year-four cash" line of Exhibit 3-5. Taking account of the initial outlays has not upset the ranking of ABC and XYZ. The alternative that had the greatest net present value at the time of decision, ABC, has the greatest net value subsequently. One way to finally reinforce that this will always be the case is to calculate the present values *at the time of decision* of the year-four *net* cash values of the investment alternatives, as shown in Exhibit 3-6.

Exhibit 3-6	Investment ABC	Investment XYZ
Year-four *net* cash values	$360	$110
$PV_{(4,0.12)}$	.636	.636
Approximate *net* present values	$229	$ 70

Although there is considerable rounding error in present values calculated to three decimals and future values calculated to two decimals, the point of the calculations comes through. The present value of the *future net value* of ABC approximates the *net present value* of ABC ($230) at the time of decision. The same is true of XYZ (net present value of $69 at the time of decision).

Have we thus been indulging in circular reasoning? Definitely so—but in this case to good purpose. Since we set out to employ the concept of time preference for money in choosing between investment alternatives, we would indeed be disappointed if the concept did not produce the same results regardless of what point in time we choose to evaluate the alternatives. In fact, it is helpful to complete the circuit, so to speak, to assure ourselves that we have not erred in applying the concept. As an exercise the reader may wish to show that the present values of the net values of investments ABC and XYZ as of any other future year (particularly year two) also approximate the net present values of the alternatives.

Present Value and the Hicksian Concept of Income

A well-known economist, J. R. Hicks, proposed a concept that he called *income,* which is, by definition, tied to the concept of wealth. Income in the Hicksian sense is of obvious interest to all wealth holders and wealth seekers —as will be apparent from the following definition:

Income (Hicksian). In the Hicksian sense, income is the maximum amount of wealth that can be disposed of by an economic unit during a period of time without reducing its remaining wealth below the level at the beginning of the period.

Hicksian income, in the abstract, is the total increase in wealth that is experienced by the economic unit during a period of time. It is therefore a measure of accomplishment, and, as implied in the definition, it is also the maximum amount that an individual would want to consume or a business to expend if it were interested in preserving its original wealth position. For this reason we will refer to Hicksian income as *disposable wealth,* a more descriptive term and one that will not be confused with other economic and accounting uses of the term *income.*

Perhaps the definitional properties of Hicksian income are intuitively obvious. What is less obvious is the dependence of any assessment of Hicksian-type income on the prior assessment of wealth at the beginning and at the end of a period of time. Although an individual can perhaps "sense" how much his wealth position has increased or decreased over a period of time, a business cannot "feel" its wealth. And even an individual may find that he is better able to decide how much he can spend on consumption and reinvestment if he has just quantified or assessed his wealth and income.

● *Calculating income based on present values.* In later chapters of this book we will return from time to time to the dual concepts of wealth and Hicksian income (disposable wealth) to see how they may be represented using alternate valuation or assessment techniques. For now, since we have already established that the present value technique may be used to assess wealth in terms of money, we will illustrate the calculation of income using present values as the means of measuring wealth.

Example 3-12 For convenience we will again refer to the individual with a time preference rate of 10 percent and the choice between investments A and B. Assume that he has already paid $100 in exchange for investment A. His wealth at this point in time (the beginning of the first year of investment A) is $120.41—the present value of investment A recalculated in Exhibit 3-7.

Exhibit 3-7 WEALTH POSITION—BEGINNING OF YEAR ONE VALUATION

Cash flows promised:		Beginning of year one:	
At the end of year	Amount	$PV_{(n,0.10)}$	Present Value of Cash Flows
1	$40	.909	$ 36.36
2	35	.826	28.91
3	30	.751	22.53
4	25	.683	17.08
5	25	.621	15.53
Total present value			$120.41

Now suppose that the first year goes by and we are interested in assessing the individual's wealth at the end of the first year and his income during the year. Let us assume for simplicity that he continued to hold investment A and realized, as expected, the first annual cash flow of $40. His wealth items would then consist of $40 cash plus investment A with four years' cash flows remaining. His end-of-year-one wealth can be assessed using present values, as shown in Exhibit 3-8.

Exhibit 3-8   WEALTH POSITION—END OF YEAR ONE VALUATION

Cash flows promised:		End of year one:	
At the end of year	Amount	$PV_{(n,0.10)}$	Present Value of Cash Flows
1	$40	1.00	$ 40.00
2	35	.909	31.82
3	30	.826	24.78
4	25	.751	18.78
5	25	.683	17.08
Total present value			$132.46

Notice that each cash flow promised by investment A is worth more at the end of year one than at the beginning, since the individual has one year less to wait for cash. And, of course, the first promised cash flow of $40, which one year ago had a then-present value of 0.909 per dollar, or $36.36, is now actually in hand, so it has a present value of a-dollar-for-a-dollar (or $40). The $35 promised for the end of year two is now only one year away and so is worth 0.909 end-of-year-one cash equivalent per dollar promised (as opposed to 0.826 per dollar one year ago). Similarly, the $30 year-three cash flow has a present value as of the end of year one of 0.826 per dollar—and so forth through the fifth year's cash flow.

So, as can be seen from the total of the last column of Exhibit 3-8, the wealth of the individual at the end of year one is $132.46. Since these calculations have not contemplated that he disposed of any wealth during the period, calculating income is a relatively simple matter. The difference between end-of-year-one wealth ($132.46) and beginning-of-year-one wealth ($120.41) is the amount that he *could* dispose of immediately and still be as wealthy at the end of the year as at the beginning. His income, therefore, is $132.46 − $120.41 = $12.05. (Note that if for purposes of determining income we wished to include in the year the instant in which the investor purchased A, his income would be $20.41 greater, i.e., it would include the gain experienced from purchasing A. Income in that case would be the difference between the end-of-year present value of $132.46 and the prepurchase beginning-of-year value of $100.)

• *Time preference and other determinants of income.* Not surprisingly, the investor's income (excluding the initial gain) is approximately 10 percent of his beginning wealth (but for rounding error it would be exact), a reflection of his time preference for money. After all, the only thing that has happened in the one year is that he is one year closer to all the cash flows embodied in investment A and therefore values them all at 110 percent of their values at the time of decision. But we have implicitly assumed that (1) the individual's time preference rate does not change from year to year, and (2) all future cash flows will occur as expected.

Of course, in a real-world situation, neither of these assumptions will necessarily hold. By the end of the first year of investment A, any one of several unexpected changes might take place. None of the changes will alter beginning-of-year value, because as soon as the new period starts, that value becomes a matter of history. But by altering end-of-period value, the changes we are concerned about also alter the measured income for the period. Three types of changes can alter the end-of-year value from what it would be under the two assumptions mentioned above:

1. The individual's time preference for money could change during the period. If the rate of time preference increased, end-of-period value and, therefore, income would be less than otherwise; if it decreased, end-of-period value and income would be greater. (Note: To affirm the effects of different time preference rates on present value calculations, refer back to the section of this chapter entitled "Sensitivity of Net Present Value to Time Preference Rate.")

2. The actual cash flows of the current period can be more or less than the cash flows expected at the beginning of the period. If the actual cash flows are greater than expected, end-of-period value and income for the period will be greater, and conversely if actual cash flows are less than expected.

3. The individual may revise his expectations of remaining future cash flows as of the end of the year. If his revised estimates are greater than previously, end-of-year value will be greater, and conversely if end-of-year estimates are less than previous estimates.

Each of the three types of changes can take place by itself or in combination with the others.

Uncertainty and Risk Assessment in Investment Decision Making

Uncertainty was earlier defined as the condition of not knowing at the time of decision what the exact outcomes of alternative courses of action will be. Under uncertainty, the best the decision maker can do is to choose alternatives that he *expects* will provide him with the greatest future benefits. After choosing, though, he may be disappointed in that the alternative selected may perform less well than his expectation at the time of decision.

For simplicity, we have ignored the problem imposed on decision making by uncertainty as we have developed the rationale for the net present value criterion. But since uncertainty is a most compelling problem facing the decision maker, we cannot ignore it entirely. Instead we will introduce the related concept of risk and illustrate some means by which the decision maker may compensate for risk within the present value model. *The reader should recognize, however, that we are concerned only with gaining sufficient insight to recognize the structure of the investment decision problem, including uncertainty, and some of its implications.* Therefore, it is reasonable to proceed via an example.

To keep the example manageable, we will make two simplifying assumptions. First, we will assume that the individual is only interested in investing in one investment at a time. Second, we will concern ourselves only with opportunities to invest for one period at a time, meaning that we will only have to work with a single initial outlay and a single actual inflow at the end of one period for each alternative.

Example 3-13   An individual wishes to invest as much as $1,000 in a single investment opportunity for one year. His time preference rate for any *certain* cash flow is 8 percent. An opportunity, C, is available, but it does not promise a certain return at the end of a year. Instead, there are several possible returns associated with it, each having some probability of occurring. Investment C can therefore be represented by a table of possible returns like that depicted in Exhibit 3-9.

Exhibit 3-9   INVESTMENT C

Possible Cash Flows	Probability of Cash Flows
$1,250	.25
1,000	.50
750	.25

The probabilities in Exhibit 3-9 indicate that if an individual were to choose investment C time after time for a virtually unlimited number of years, he would receive $1,000 at the end of the year about 50 percent of the time, $1,250 about 25 percent of the time, and $750 about 25 percent of the time.

• *Expected cash flows.* Clearly, uncertain investments like C, which offer more than one possible cash flow at the end of a period, are more of a challenge to evaluate than those offering a single certain return. One way of dealing with the extra complexity is to use a single number as "representative" of all of the several possible cash flows from an investment. Then one can arrive at present values for uncertain investments in the same way as for certain investments by using the "representative" cash flow for each period for each investment. A single number that might be used for this purpose is the mathematical expectation from the investment, or, more simply, the expected cash flow.

Expected Cash Flow. The expected cash flow for a period from an investment is the sum of the products of (*a*) each possible cash flow, times (*b*) its probability of occurring.

In other words, the expected cash flow is the amount that an individual would receive *on the average* at the end of a year from a particular investment, if he entered into that investment over and over again.

Example 3-14   Drawing on the possible cash flows and their probabilities from Exhibit 3-9 for investment C, we can calculate its expected cash flow, designated $E[C]$ below.

$$E[C] = .25(\$1,250) + .50(\$1,000) + .25(\$750) = \$1,000$$

• *Risk associated with uncertain investments.* Now that we have arrived at a "representative" cash flow for investment C, the question is, How can the individual value that amount in terms of our present value methodology? Should he apply his 8 percent time preference rate for certain cash flows to the expected cash flow from an uncertain investment? The answer is no, because most individuals would not consider the expectation of $1,000 equivalent to the certainty of $1,000. A *risk* is associated with the $1,000 expected cash flow of uncertain investment C.

> **Risk.** With respect to investments, risk is the potential that less-than-expected cash flows will result from a particular investment.

Since, for any given investment in C, there is a 25 percent chance that the cash flow will be $250 less than $1,000, C is a risky investment. Most (but not all) people are *risk averse,* meaning that they would respond to this risk negatively, considering C to be less attractive than $1,000 certain—even though there is an equal probability that any given investment in C will yield $250 in cash flows greater than expected, as well. This is because most individuals view a dollar loss or penalty as more undesirable than an equally probable dollar of bonus is desirable. Furthermore, the greater the probability of less-than-expected cash flows and/or the more they depart from expectations, the more negatively the individual will react, other things equal.

• *Assessing risk with present values—one approach.* Although we would not want to apply a time preference rate for certain cash flows to the expected cash flows from a risky investment for the reasons given above, there are some simple and logical alternatives. One is called the *certainty equivalent approach.*

The certainty equivalent approach requires that the investor play a mental game. He must suppose that he is just about to receive the cash flow from a risky investment at the end of some future period but does not know precisely how much it will be. Then he must pose the question, If someone offered to pay me a *sum certain* in exchange for the rights to the cash flow, how much would it take to make me indifferent between the sum certain and the impending, but uncertain, cash flow? The answer is called the *certainty equivalent* of the uncertain cash flow.

The certainty equivalent is an alternate "representative" number for the uncertain cash flow. It is likely to be less than the expected cash flow for risky investments for the reasons given above, that is, the individual responds negatively to the risk associated with the expected cash flow.

Unlike the problem encountered with the expected cash flow, the individual can logically apply his *time preference rate for certain cash flows* to the certainty equivalent of an uncertain cash flow to get its present value to him as of the time of his decision.

Example 3-15   The individual considering investment C might decide that even though it has an expected cash flow of $1,000, the risk associated with the possible payoff of $750 more than offsets the good feeling he associates with the possible payoff of $1,250. Thus, he considers an investment in C to be equivalent to an investment in a sum certain of only $950. To get the present value of investment C, the individual finds the present value of $950 to be received at the end of one year at 8 percent, his time preference rate for certain cash flows.

• *Risk and present value—summary.* Although there are other methods of incorporating risk assessments into calculation of present values for risky investments, we need not enumerate and illustrate them all. Regardless of which of several recognized methods is used, the same two conclusions about the risk and the present value of uncertain cash flows (risky investments) can be drawn:

1. Risky investments will always have less net present value to the risk-averse individual than an investment in certain cash flows equal to the expected cash flows from the risky investment.

2. If any two risky investments have the same expected cash flows, the risk-averse investor will assign a lesser present value to the more risky investment.

It is important to bear in mind that to arrive at present values of risky investments in the way described above, the individual must consider how he personally feels about the risk associated with the expected cash flows promised by the risky investments. But, having made such an assessment, he can arrive at a single present value of the future cash flows from a risky investment that can be compared with the certain present outlays (using certainty equivalents or some other technique). Thus, although we developed the net present value model under the simplifying assumption of certain future cash flows, it can accommodate the problem of uncertainty inherent in most investment decisions.

APPENDIX A

Table 3-1

PRESENT VALUE OF ONE DOLLAR

	.01	.02	.03	.04	.05	.06	.07	.08	.09	.10	.12	.14	.15	.16	.18	.20
1	.990	.980	.971	.962	.952	.943	.935	.926	.917	.909	.893	.877	.870	.862	.847	.833
2	.980	.961	.943	.925	.907	.890	.873	.857	.842	.826	.797	.769	.756	.743	.718	.694
3	.971	.942	.915	.889	.864	.840	.816	.794	.772	.751	.712	.675	.658	.641	.609	.579
4	.961	.924	.888	.855	.823	.792	.763	.735	.708	.683	.636	.592	.572	.552	.516	.482
5	.951	.906	.863	.822	.784	.747	.713	.681	.650	.621	.567	.519	.497	.476	.437	.402
6	.942	.888	.837	.790	.746	.705	.666	.630	.596	.564	.507	.456	.432	.410	.370	.335
7	.933	.871	.813	.760	.711	.665	.623	.583	.547	.513	.452	.400	.376	.354	.314	.279
8	.923	.853	.789	.731	.677	.627	.582	.540	.502	.467	.404	.351	.327	.305	.266	.233
9	.914	.837	.766	.703	.645	.592	.544	.500	.460	.424	.361	.308	.284	.263	.225	.194
10	.905	.820	.744	.676	.614	.558	.508	.463	.422	.386	.322	.270	.247	.227	.191	.162
11	.896	.804	.722	.650	.585	.527	.475	.429	.388	.350	.287	.237	.215	.195	.162	.135
12	.887	.788	.701	.625	.557	.497	.444	.397	.356	.319	.257	.208	.187	.168	.137	.112
13	.879	.773	.681	.601	.530	.469	.415	.368	.326	.290	.229	.182	.163	.145	.116	.093
14	.870	.758	.661	.577	.505	.442	.388	.340	.299	.263	.205	.160	.141	.125	.099	.078
15	.861	.743	.642	.555	.481	.417	.362	.315	.275	.239	.183	.140	.123	.108	.084	.065
16	.853	.728	.623	.534	.458	.394	.339	.292	.252	.218	.163	.123	.107	.093	.071	.054
17	.844	.714	.605	.513	.436	.371	.317	.270	.231	.198	.146	.108	.093	.080	.060	.045
18	.836	.700	.587	.494	.416	.350	.296	.250	.212	.180	.130	.095	.081	.069	.051	.038
19	.828	.686	.570	.475	.396	.331	.277	.232	.194	.164	.116	.083	.070	.060	.043	.031
20	.820	.673	.554	.456	.377	.312	.258	.215	.178	.149	.104	.073	.061	.051	.037	.026
21	.811	.660	.538	.439	.359	.294	.242	.199	.164	.135	.093	.064	.053	.044	.031	.022
22	.803	.647	.522	.422	.342	.278	.226	.184	.150	.123	.083	.056	.046	.038	.026	.018
23	.795	.634	.507	.406	.326	.262	.211	.170	.138	.112	.074	.049	.040	.033	.022	.015
24	.788	.622	.492	.390	.310	.247	.197	.158	.126	.102	.066	.043	.035	.028	.019	.013
25	.780	.610	.478	.375	.295	.233	.184	.146	.116	.092	.059	.038	.030	.024	.016	.010
26	.772	.598	.464	.361	.281	.220	.172	.135	.106	.084	.053	.033	.026	.021	.014	.009
27	.764	.586	.450	.347	.268	.207	.161	.125	.098	.076	.047	.029	.023	.018	.011	.007
28	.757	.574	.437	.333	.255	.196	.150	.116	.090	.069	.042	.026	.020	.016	.010	.006
29	.749	.563	.424	.321	.243	.185	.141	.107	.082	.063	.037	.022	.017	.014	.008	.005
30	.742	.552	.412	.308	.231	.174	.131	.099	.075	.057	.033	.020	.015	.012	.007	.004

Table 3-2

FUTURE VALUE OF ONE DOLLAR

	.01	.02	.03	.04	.05	.06	.07	.08	.09	.10	.12	.14	.15	.16	.18	.20
1	1.01	1.02	1.03	1.04	1.05	1.06	1.07	1.08	1.09	1.10	1.12	1.14	1.15	1.16	1.18	1.20
2	1.02	1.04	1.06	1.08	1.10	1.12	1.14	1.17	1.19	1.21	1.25	1.30	1.32	1.35	1.39	1.44
3	1.03	1.06	1.09	1.12	1.16	1.19	1.23	1.26	1.30	1.33	1.40	1.48	1.52	1.56	1.64	1.73
4	1.04	1.08	1.13	1.17	1.22	1.26	1.31	1.36	1.41	1.46	1.57	1.69	1.75	1.81	1.94	2.07
5	1.05	1.10	1.16	1.22	1.28	1.34	1.40	1.47	1.54	1.61	1.76	1.93	2.01	2.10	2.29	2.49
6	1.06	1.13	1.19	1.27	1.34	1.42	1.50	1.59	1.68	1.77	1.97	2.19	2.31	2.44	2.70	2.99
7	1.07	1.15	1.23	1.32	1.41	1.50	1.61	1.71	1.83	1.95	2.21	2.50	2.66	2.83	3.19	3.58
8	1.08	1.17	1.27	1.37	1.48	1.59	1.72	1.85	1.99	2.14	2.48	2.85	3.06	3.28	3.76	4.30
9	1.09	1.20	1.30	1.42	1.55	1.69	1.84	2.00	2.17	2.36	2.77	3.25	3.52	3.80	4.44	5.16
10	1.10	1.22	1.34	1.48	1.63	1.79	1.97	2.16	2.37	2.59	3.11	3.71	4.05	4.41	5.23	6.19
11	1.12	1.24	1.38	1.54	1.71	1.90	2.10	2.33	2.58	2.85	3.48	4.23	4.65	5.12	6.18	7.43
12	1.13	1.27	1.43	1.60	1.80	2.01	2.25	2.52	2.81	3.14	3.90	4.82	5.35	5.94	7.29	8.92
13	1.14	1.29	1.47	1.67	1.89	2.13	2.41	2.72	3.07	3.45	4.36	5.49	6.15	6.89	8.60	10.70
14	1.15	1.32	1.51	1.73	1.98	2.26	2.58	2.94	3.34	3.80	4.89	6.26	7.08	7.99	10.15	12.84
15	1.16	1.35	1.56	1.80	2.08	2.40	2.76	3.17	3.64	4.18	5.47	7.14	8.14	9.27	11.97	15.41
16	1.17	1.37	1.60	1.87	2.18	2.54	2.95	3.43	3.97	4.59	6.13	8.14	9.36	10.75	14.13	18.49
17	1.18	1.40	1.65	1.95	2.29	2.69	3.16	3.70	4.33	5.05	6.87	9.28	10.76	12.47	16.67	22.19
18	1.20	1.43	1.70	2.03	2.41	2.85	3.38	4.00	4.72	5.56	7.69	10.58	12.38	14.46	19.67	26.62
19	1.21	1.46	1.75	2.11	2.53	3.03	3.62	4.32	5.14	6.12	8.61	12.06	14.23	16.78	23.21	31.95
20	1.22	1.49	1.81	2.19	2.65	3.21	3.87	4.66	5.60	6.73	9.65	13.74	16.37	19.46	27.39	38.34
21	1.23	1.52	1.86	2.28	2.79	3.40	4.14	5.03	6.11	7.40	10.80	15.67	18.82	22.57	32.32	46.01
22	1.24	1.55	1.92	2.37	2.93	3.60	4.43	5.44	6.66	8.14	12.10	17.86	21.64	26.19	38.14	55.21
23	1.25	1.58	1.97	2.46	3.07	3.82	4.74	5.87	7.26	8.95	13.55	20.36	24.89	30.38	45.01	66.25
24	1.27	1.61	2.03	2.56	3.23	4.05	5.07	6.34	7.91	9.65	15.18	23.21	28.63	35.24	53.11	79.50
25	1.28	1.64	2.09	2.67	3.39	4.29	5.43	6.85	8.62	10.83	17.00	26.46	32.92	40.87	62.67	95.40
26	1.30	1.67	2.16	2.77	3.56	4.55	5.81	7.40	9.40	11.92	19.04	30.17	37.86	47.41	73.95	114.48
27	1.31	1.71	2.22	2.88	3.73	4.82	6.21	7.99	10.25	13.11	21.32	34.39	43.54	55.00	87.26	137.37
28	1.32	1.74	2.29	3.00	3.92	5.11	6.65	8.63	11.17	14.42	23.88	39.20	50.07	63.80	102.97	164.84
29	1.33	1.78	2.36	3.12	4.12	5.42	7.11	9.32	12.17	15.86	26.75	44.69	57.58	74.01	121.50	197.81
30	1.35	1.81	2.43	3.24	4.32	5.74	7.61	10.06	13.27	17.45	29.96	50.95	66.21	85.85	143.37	237.38

Table 3-3

PRESENT VALUE OF AN ANNUITY OF ONE

	.01	.02	.03	.04	.05	.06	.07	.08	.09	.10	.12	.14	.15	.16	.18	.20
1	.99	.98	.97	.96	.95	.94	.93	.93	.92	.91	.89	.88	.87	.86	.85	.83
2	1.97	1.94	1.91	1.89	1.86	1.83	1.81	1.78	1.76	1.74	1.69	1.65	1.63	1.61	1.57	1.53
3	2.94	2.88	2.83	2.78	2.72	2.67	2.62	2.58	2.53	2.49	2.40	2.32	2.28	2.25	2.17	2.11
4	3.90	3.81	3.72	3.63	3.55	3.47	3.39	3.31	3.24	3.17	3.04	2.91	2.85	2.80	2.69	2.59
5	4.85	4.71	4.58	4.45	4.33	4.21	4.10	3.99	3.89	3.79	3.60	3.43	3.35	3.27	3.13	2.99
6	5.80	5.60	5.42	5.24	5.08	4.92	4.77	4.62	4.49	4.36	4.11	3.89	3.78	3.68	3.50	3.33
7	6.73	6.47	6.23	6.00	5.79	5.58	5.39	5.21	5.03	4.87	4.56	4.29	4.16	4.04	3.81	3.60
8	7.65	7.33	7.02	6.73	6.46	6.21	5.97	5.75	5.53	5.33	4.97	4.64	4.49	4.34	4.08	3.84
9	8.57	8.16	7.79	7.44	7.11	6.80	6.52	6.25	6.00	5.76	5.33	4.95	4.77	4.61	4.30	4.03
10	9.47	8.98	8.53	8.11	7.72	7.36	7.02	6.71	6.42	6.14	5.65	5.22	5.02	4.83	4.49	4.19
11	10.37	9.79	9.25	8.76	8.31	7.89	7.50	7.14	6.81	6.50	5.94	5.45	5.23	5.03	4.66	4.33
12	11.26	10.58	9.95	9.39	8.86	8.38	7.94	7.54	7.16	6.81	6.19	5.66	5.42	5.20	4.79	4.44
13	12.13	11.35	10.63	9.99	9.39	8.85	8.36	7.90	7.49	7.10	6.42	5.84	5.58	5.34	4.91	4.53
14	13.00	12.11	11.30	10.56	9.90	9.29	8.75	8.24	7.79	7.37	6.63	6.00	5.72	5.47	5.01	4.61
15	13.87	12.85	11.94	11.12	10.38	9.71	9.11	8.56	8.06	7.61	6.81	6.14	5.85	5.58	5.09	4.68
16	14.72	13.58	12.56	11.65	10.84	10.11	9.45	8.85	8.31	7.82	6.97	6.27	5.95	5.67	5.16	4.73
17	15.56	14.29	13.17	12.17	11.27	10.48	9.76	9.12	8.54	8.02	7.12	6.37	6.05	5.75	5.22	4.77
18	16.40	14.99	13.75	12.66	11.69	10.83	10.06	9.37	8.76	8.20	7.25	6.47	6.13	5.82	5.27	4.81
19	17.23	15.68	14.32	13.13	12.09	11.16	10.34	9.60	8.95	8.36	7.37	6.55	6.20	5.88	5.32	4.84
20	18.05	16.35	14.88	13.59	12.45	11.47	10.59	9.82	9.13	8.51	7.47	6.62	6.26	5.93	5.35	4.87
21	18.86	17.01	15.42	14.03	12.82	11.76	10.84	10.02	9.29	8.65	7.56	6.69	6.31	5.97	5.38	4.89
22	19.66	17.66	15.94	14.45	13.16	12.04	11.06	10.20	9.44	8.77	7.64	6.74	6.36	6.01	5.41	4.91
23	20.46	18.29	16.44	14.86	13.49	12.30	11.27	10.37	9.58	8.88	7.72	6.79	6.40	6.04	5.43	4.92
24	21.24	18.91	16.94	15.25	13.80	12.55	11.47	10.53	9.71	8.98	7.78	6.84	6.43	6.07	5.45	4.94
25	22.02	19.52	17.41	15.62	14.09	12.78	11.65	10.67	9.82	9.08	7.84	6.87	6.46	6.10	5.47	4.95
26	22.80	20.12	17.88	15.98	14.38	13.00	11.83	10.81	9.93	9.16	7.90	6.91	6.49	6.12	5.48	4.96
27	23.56	20.71	18.33	16.33	14.64	13.21	11.99	10.94	10.03	9.24	7.94	6.94	6.51	6.14	5.49	4.96
28	24.32	21.28	18.76	16.66	14.90	13.41	12.14	11.05	10.12	9.31	7.98	6.96	6.53	6.15	5.50	4.97
29	25.07	21.84	19.19	16.98	15.14	13.59	12.28	11.16	10.20	9.37	8.02	6.98	6.55	6.17	5.51	4.97
30	25.81	22.40	19.60	17.29	15.37	13.76	12.41	11.26	10.27	9.43	8.06	7.00	6.57	6.18	5.52	4.98

APPENDIX B: PRESENT VALUE OF AN ANNUITY

Situations are frequently encountered in which it is desirable to determine the present value of a series of identical cash flows. Such series, called annuities, can be valued in a straightforward fashion in the sense that the present values of each of the individual flows can be determined as described in the body of this chapter, and then the present value of the series is determined by summing the present values of the individual flows. However, because an annuity consists of a stream of identical flows, a certain arithmetic convenience can be achieved in determining its present value.

Example 3-16 Suppose we wish to determine the present value of $1,000 to be received (or paid) at the end of each year for three years and that the appropriate time preference rate is 10 percent. The straightforward calculation is as follows:

Year	Cash Flow	$PV_{(n,0.10)}$	Present Values
1	$1,000	.909	$ 909
2	1,000	.826	826
3	1,000	.751	751
		2.486	$2,486

The present value of the annuity of $1,000 for three years at 10 percent is the sum of the present values of each of the $1,000 installments at 10 percent. That is, the present value of the annuity is the sum of the individual products of (1) the present value factor for a given year in the annuity and (2) the constant cash flow. But we know from elementary algebra that the *sum of the products* of a series of multiplicands and a *constant multiplier* is equal to the *product of the sum* of the multiplicands and the constant multiplier. What this means is that the present value of the annuity in Example 3-16 (and all similar streams of cash flows) can be determined by multiplying the constant cash flow by the *sum* of the present value factors for each individual year:

$$\$1,000\cdot(.909 + .826 + .751) = \$1,000 \cdot 2.486 = \$2,486$$

Furthermore, since the sum of the present value factors will be the same for any annuity involving a given number of years and a given time preference rate, annuity factor values are precalculated and made available in tables such as Table 3-3 in this Appendix. Notice, for instance, that in Table 3-3 the value of $1 to be received at the end of each of three years at 10 percent (i.e., $n = 3$, $r = 0.10$), is 2.49, approximately what we calculated in the above example (but taken to only two decimal accuracy).

Questions for Review and Discussion

3-1. Define the following terms:

a. Investment decision

b. Well-being

c. Wealth

d. Time preference rate

e. Opportunity rate

f. Compound interest

g. Future value

h. Present value

i. Net present value

j. Expected cash flow

k. Risk

3-2. How does the concept of wealth relate to the concept of well-being?

3-3. What justification is there (if any) for the assumption that investment alternatives offer strictly cash inflows and outflows as opposed to flows of wealth in other forms?

3-4. In developing the net present value model, the chapter ignores constraints on decision makers (such as limited budgets). What justification is there for ignoring such constraints, which are often present in real-world investment decisions?

3-5. Most individuals seem to exhibit a time preference for money. Give the reasons that presumably explain such a preference.

3-6. An individual's time preference for money may be expressed as a rate. Explain.

3-7. What relationship (if any) exists between an individual's time preference rate and opportunity rate?

3-8. Explain in words the economic significance to an individual of the following:

a. The present value of an amount of money to be received at a future date

b. The present value of an obligation to pay an amount in the future

c. The future value of an amount invested or consumed today

3-9. The *net* present value of an investment opportunity is the cash equivalent of the gain (loss) experienced by the investor in undertaking the opportunity. True or false? Explain.

3-10. List the five steps required to apply the net present value model.

3-11. Explain in words why investment decisions based on the net present values of alternatives may be different if different time preference rates are used.

3-12. Explain in words why income (disposable wealth) under the present value model is equal to beginning-of-period value times the time preference rate assuming everything works out as expected.

3-13. Most (but not all) people appear to be risk averse. What does this mean?

3-14. Given a future cash flow and an individual's time preference rate, what is meant by the statement that the individual is indifferent between the present value of the future cash flow and the future cash flow itself?

3-15. What must be specified before one can determine the net present value of an investment opportunity?

3-16. What is the effect on the first year's expected income if at the end of the first year of an investment—

a. the individual's time preference rate has increased?

b. the actual cash flows of the current period are greater than the cash flows expected at the beginning of the period?

c. remaining future cash flows are expected to be less than previously expected?

3-17. Present value (and therefore *net* present value) is an example of a common scale of merit. Do you agree or disagree? Explain your answer.

3-18. As an investor you are faced with an opportunity that provides an expected cash flow of $25,000 at the end of each of the next three years. You are concerned with the risk associated with these uncertain cash flows and consider these uncertain cash flows to be the equivalent of a certain cash flow of $20,000. The time preference rate you consider satisfactory for certain cash flows is 8 percent.

While you are considering your investment decision, another investor offers to purchase the investment opportunity at a much higher price than you would be willing to pay. Why should this other investor be willing to pay more for the investment than you would be willing to pay?

Exercises

3-1. Future Values of Amounts Invested. Determine the following future values utilizing an opportunity rate of 8 percent:

1. The future value of $5,000 to be invested now for a period of five years

2. The future value at the end of three years of an investment of $4,000 now and $4,000 one year from now

3. The future value at the end of eight years of an investment of $6,000 at the end of each of the first four years and a withdrawal of $5,000 per year at the end of years five through seven

3-2. Present Values of Future Cash Flows. Compute the present value of each of the following cash flows utilizing an opportunity rate of 12 percent:

1. $1,000 cash outflow immediately

2. $2,000 cash inflow one year from now

3. $2,000 cash inflow two years from now

4. $1,000 cash outflow three years from now

5. $3,000 cash inflow three years from now

6. $2,000 cash inflow four years from now

3-3. Net Present Value. Calculate the net present value of the total cash flows in problem 3-2 utilizing an opportunity rate of 12 percent.

3-4. Net Present Value of an Opportunity. Determine the net present value of a business opportunity that costs $1,000 initially and generates cash inflows of $2,000, $2,000, $3,000, and $1,000 at the end of years one through four, respectively. An additional outlay of $1,000 for maintenance will be necessary at the end of year three. The salvage value of the opportunity at the end of year four also equals $1,000. The appropriate discount rate is 12 percent.

3-5. Future Value of a Replacement Fund Program.   The William Corporation is currently using equipment that will become obsolete in five years. To provide the necessary funds for replacement of the equipment, the company plans to invest $40,000 in U.S. securities now, $50,000 at the end of each of the next two years, and $60,000 at the end of each of the two years after that. If these securities will pay an after-tax rate of return of 4 percent, compounded annually, what amount will be available at the end of the fifth year?

3-6. Future Adequacy of a Savings Fund Program.   Mr. E. K. Roarke wishes to provide for the college education of his six children. He estimates that each child will require $3,000 for each of the four years of college payable at the beginning of the school year.

   The triplets are fifteen years old and will start college in exactly three years. The twins are fourteen and will start college in four years. The youngest child is seven years old and will start college in eleven years.

   If Mr. Roarke deposits $52,000 in a savings account that pays an annual interest rate of 6 percent, will he have provided for the college educations? What is the exact amount Mr. Roarke should deposit now to provide for the college educations?

3-7. Sensitivity of a Decision to Time Preference Rate.   The Hobard Cattle Company needs grazing land for its cattle operation. It can either purchase the land outright for $160,000 or lease it for $10,000 per year on a fifteen-year lease. The rental fee is payable at the beginning of each year. In either case, the company must pay all taxes and maintenance costs. The land will be needed for fifteen years, at which time it would be salable for $200,000. If the company required a before-tax rate of return of 8 percent for this type investment, which alternative should it choose? If it requires 6 percent?

3-8. Present Value of an Investment in Common Stock.   Mr. Ronald Downs wishes to invest $10,000 for a five-year period. He is considering the purchase of Buford Company common stock, which currently pays an annual cash dividend of $2. Mr. Downs expects that this dividend will be paid each year for the next five years and that the stock at the end of the five-year period will be selling for approximately $30. If investments of comparable risk yield a before-tax rate of return of 10 percent, what is the maximum amount Mr. Downs should be willing to pay for a share of stock?

   If the stock is currently selling for $25 per share, should Mr. Downs be willing to purchase it?

3-9. Present Value of an Investment in a Promissory Note.   A promissory note is offered for sale on which the yearly payments are $45. There are ten payments still due, with the first one due one year from now. The principal amount, $1,000, is to be repaid at the end of the tenth year. What is the maximum amount an investor would pay for this note if he wished to earn at least 8 percent on this type investment? If he wished to earn 10 percent?

3-10. Present Value of a Taxicab Business.   You have an opportunity to invest in a taxicab business. The business owns one cab and has made the following estimates of future cash flows. Assume that these cash flows take place at the end of the year and that you consider them to be realistic.

a. Passengers pay $.38 per mile for cab service.

b. Gas, oil, tires, and other operating expenses are $.10 per mile.

c. The driver is paid $.08 per mile plus tips.

d. The present owner expects that the cab will carry passengers a total of 50,000 miles per year for the life of the automobile, which is three years. After three years the car will be worthless.

e. You have decided to invest if you can earn a before-tax rate of 10 percent on your investment.

Required:

What is the maximum amount you would pay to acquire the business? What is the amount of net income (disposable wealth) you expect to earn for the first year's operations? Explain.

3-11. Evaluating an Offer for the Taxicab Business. Assume you have purchased the taxicab business described in problem 3-10. At the end of the first year, after you have withdrawn the cash receipts, you are approached by an investor who offers you $17,500 for the business. Should you sell?

3-12. Effects on Income of Changes in Expectations and Preferences. Assume that you have purchased the taxicab business described in problem 3-10. Instead of paying the driver $.08 per passenger mile as originally projected, you had to pay $.10 per mile.

Required:

1. What would the first year's income have been if no change in costs had occurred?

2. What is the first year's income, given the change in cost?

3. What is the first year's income if there is also an increase in your time preference rate from 10 percent to 12 percent?

3-13. Determination of the Implicit Time Preference Rate. Mr. Curtis Driver owns a ferry service which carries workers to and from an offshore drilling rig. The rig will be operational for three years. When it is shut down, Mr. Driver plans to liquidate his business and retire. The contract under which the business operates pays a flat sum of $100,000 every year at the end of the year. Expenses amount to $75,000 per year. Mr. Driver withdraws $25,000 every year and expects to be able to sell his equipment for $30,000 when he retires. At the end of the first year, Mr. Driver is approached by an investor who offers him $68,192 for the business. Should Mr. Driver sell? (Hint: At what time preference rate would he be indifferent?)

3-14. Net Present Value: Sensitivity to Time Preference Rate. The company you work for, Starr Cutter, is a medium-size tool and die company that is interested in expanding its line of services to its customers. The company has decided to provide one new service that requires the purchase of a new machine. Two brands of the machine needed are available, brand A and brand B.

The machines differ only in the way they affect the "other" costs of providing the new service to customers, that is, they have different break-in periods, rates of physical deterioration, maintenance requirements, and so forth, but they will provide the same output capacity. As a result, the following patterns of cash flows have been estimated for the two machines:

	A	B
Initial price of machine	$20,000	$21,500

Annual net proceeds:

At the end of year

1	$10,000	$ 5,000
2	10,000	10,000
3	10,000	10,000
4	5,000	10,000
5	5,000	10,000

You are asked to choose the best machine for the company to buy. Your first impulse is to compute a net present value for each machine, but you have run into a problem. The treasurer of the company thinks the time value of money to the firm is 10 percent (compounded annually), but the president insists it is more like 15 percent.

While they are debating the question, you decide to compute net present values at both interest rates, hoping that maybe one machine will prove better regardless of which rate is used.

Does the same machine prove to be "best" for both interest rates? If not, explain.

3-15. Risk and Relative Value. An investor has two uncertain one-year investment opportunities, Y and Z. Each calls for an initial outlay now and promises possible payoffs in one year as follows:

Y		Z	
Probability	*Payoff*	*Probability*	*Payoff*
.20	$40,000	.20	$35,000
.60	50,000	.60	50,000
.20	60,000	.20	65,000

1. How would you value Z relative to Y, that is, "greater than," "equal to," or "less than"? Would you expect most people to apply the same relative ranking? Explain the rationale for your ranking.

2. Would your answer to number 1 differ if Z promised the following payoffs in one year? Why or why not?

Z	
Probability	*Payoff*
.25	$40,000
.50	50,000
.25	60,000

3-16. Comprehensive Present Value Exercise.   Tri-Cities Tours is a small business that is up for sale. The business is well known in the Tri-Cities area and has enjoyed consistent success. The company operates out of a small rented office. Its only substantial assets are *two* touring buses, each in good working condition. You are interested in buying the business and have been given access to all of its financial records for purposes of determining what you think it is worth. Based on your investigation you have made the following estimates:

a. *Each* of the buses will be operated for a total of 1,500,000 passenger miles per year.

   (1) The average cash fare per passenger mile will be about $.05.

   (2) Fuel, lubricants, and routine service will run about $.01 per passenger mile.

b. Other yearly costs of operating the business are expected to be:

Rent	$12,000
Wages and salaries	60,000
Bus overhauls	18,000
Insurance	10,000

c. The buses will no longer be suitable for the touring and charter business after three more years of operations. However, each is expected to bring $10,000 upon sale at that time.

Assume unless otherwise stated that the appropriate time preference rate is 10 percent.

Required:

1. What is the maximum amount you would be willing to pay for the company?

2. Suppose the asking price of the owner is *less* than the amount you calculated in number 1. List the factors that could each, independently, account for the difference. (Assume real-world conditions and take into account the direction of the difference between the two amounts.)

3. Assume that you bought the business at the amount you calculated in number 1.

   (a) How much income (disposable wealth) would you *expect* to report in the first year? Explain the source of this income.

   (b) Indicate, for each of the following changes in circumstance during the year, whether the effect on income would be an increase or a decrease relative to your answer to *a*. Explain your reasoning.

   (1) Fuel costs less than expected.

   (2) Your time preference rate increases.

   (3) Your assessment of the risk of the business lessens.

4. Assume that you bought the business and your time preference rate changed from 10 percent to 12 percent immediately after purchase. What would happen to (*a*) the future value of the business and (*b*) the present value of the business? Explain in words why the effects you have indicated would occur.

II

FINANCIAL ACCOUNTING MODELS OF THE ENTERPRISE

4

Conventional Accounting:
An Investment Decision
Perspective

Business enterprises, as described earlier, are organizational units that employ factors of production in producing specialized products and services for sale. Often a business organization is necessary in order to exploit certain production opportunities efficiently, particularly those that require complex production processes with a highly specialized division of labor, and those that require large-scale physical capital. To serve their purpose, often business enterprises must start out with and continue to control large blocks of money capital. Typically, in the case of large corporations, the necessary money capital is supplied by investors who, for the most part, are not directly involved in the operations of the business.

Prospective investors who supply money capital to business enterprises are presumably interested in selecting the best employment for their funds among the many opportunities available. Relevant information about alternative opportunities is presumably valuable to them in making the best choices. Considering the large numbers of business enterprises available as potential investment opportunities, however, the cost of collecting and evaluating relevant information about every alternative is probably prohibitive. Since it is possible for many potential owners and creditors to have an investment interest in any given business, there is a good deal of potential for duplication of effort. But as was pointed out in Chapter 2, such potential duplication of effort is good reason for one group, in this case accountants employed by the enterprise, to provide information about the business for use by the many interested parties. It must also be recalled, though, that to succeed in eliminating wasteful duplication in information gathering and dissemination, there must be identifiable kinds of information that are decision relevant to many of the potential decision makers. The remainder of this chapter is devoted to (1) examining more closely the decision situation faced by investors in business enterprises, and (2) introducing some alternate kinds of information about the business enterprise that might be decision relevant to present and potential investors.

Investments in Business Enterprises

Prospective owners and creditors who supply capital to a business do so in return for expected future cash inflows. For instance, a creditor (e.g., an owner of a corporate bond) acquires contractual rights to specified future payments of interest and principal amounts. A purchaser of a share of corporate stock, on the other hand, acquires the right to share proportionately with all other shareowners in the residual cash flows generated by the corporation. Therefore, the decisions of shareowners and creditors as to which of many enterprises to invest in fit into the context of the net present value model that was introduced in Chapter 3.

In order to choose to invest in a particular business, both the creditor and the owner would presumably want to assess the present value of the rights that come from investment and compare that present value with the amount they will have to pay to receive those rights. They would then compare the net present values of investments in various businesses in determining the investment or set of investments they will undertake.

• *Valuing investment opportunities.* The nature of the decision to invest in a business, as described above, is simple in principle. In practice, however, it is a formidable challenge. The process of arriving at present values, as described in Chapter 3, begins necessarily with the step of specifying the cash flows expected from an investment in future periods. Of course, other elements, such as selection of the appropriate time preference rate (opportunity rate), are necessary as well. But the valuation of a particular investment opportunity cannot proceed without a projected stream of future cash flows on which to operate.

For the prospective owner, the step of projecting or forecasting future cash flows is quite open-ended. For the prospective creditor, the step is simplified somewhat, as the expected cash flows from his investment are usually specified in a contract. On the other hand, in the real world (the world of uncertainty) both the creditor and the owner will want to assess the risk associated with expected future cash flows. The greater the risk associated with a given expected future cash flow, the less it will be valued by either a creditor or an owner, other things equal. (See the discussion in the Chapter 3 section entitled "Uncertainty and Risk Assessment in Investment Decision Making.")

But risk assessment means that in addition to forecasting potential future cash flows, some thought must be given to the likelihood that the forecast flows will (or will not) actually materialize. Thus investors face the task of looking into the future and making some fairly complex predictions or forecasts about the amounts and probabilities of the cash payments the enterprise will be able to make to them in fulfillment of their rights as owners or creditors.

• *The business enterprise as a net producer of cash.* To gain more insight into the forecasting or cash prediction problem facing investors, we can suppose that investors view the business enterprise as a generator of net cash flows. The cash-flow-generation process in a business is based on a strikingly simple operating sequence which is descriptive (in the abstract) of virtually all business enterprises in a market economy. This operating sequence comprises the following steps:

1. The enterprise usually begins its life with an initial endowment of cash contributed by owners and perhaps creditors.
2. *The enterprise acquires control or possession of the factors of production* necessary to provide a particular product or service. In exchange, it gives immediate cash payments or promises to pay cash at some future date.
3. *The factors of production are committed* as needed to the process or processes used to generate the enterprise's product or service.
4. Finally, *finished products or services are provided* as demanded by customers, in exchange for cash or promises to pay cash to the enterprise at some future date.

• *Forecasting future cash flows.* One reasonably promising way to attempt to predict future cash flows from a particular business is to approach the operating sequence described above in reverse. First, future prices and quantities demanded are estimated, with some attention given to variations that might occur due to competitive pressure, changing tastes and preferences, and so forth. Expected sales, along with probable payment terms, then lead to estimates of the amounts and timing of cash inflows. The quantities of resources required to satisfy demand are determined, based on knowledge of the ratios of inputs to outputs inherent in the production process. Finally, the prices and payment terms for various resources enter into estimates of probable amounts and timing of cash outflows to support operations. The difference between estimated cash inflows from sales and estimated cash outflows in support of operations is the estimated net cash inflow or outflow of the enterprise for a given future period (assuming no additional capital contributions from owners or dividend payments to them).

Example 4-1   Sports Equipment Sales Corporation (called S.E.S.) was founded a number of years ago to merchandise a variety of sports equipment to retail customers. There are 10,000 shares of S.E.S. stock outstanding at present, owned by approximately five hundred people. The company grew rapidly in its early years, but now management believes, on the basis of market research, that it has reached its limit as far as increased activities are concerned.

For at least the next thirty years, though, it expects to maintain an annual level of cash receipts from sales of $500,000. Costs of merchandise sold at that level of activity are expected to be $400,000 per year. The company has

a thirty-year lease on its retail store building calling for annual rental payments of $10,000. Wages, salaries, maintenance, and miscellaneous outlays
are expected to be $37,500. The company has just renovated the interior and
exterior of the store and purchased new display equipment, and so forth.
But it expects to have to repeat these outlays every ten years until it gives
up the lease on the building. This means that major outlays of $50,000 for
renovation are expected around the end of years ten and twenty, in addition to all routine outlays connected with merchandising operations in
those years. Finally, it should be added that to raise additional money capital
a few years ago, S.E.S. issued fifty corporate bonds with face values of
$1,000 each, on which it must pay a total of $2,500 interest annually. The
bonds are due to be paid off at the end of thirty years at face value, $50,000.

To summarize, the cash flows to be generated by S.E.S. Corporation over the
next thirty years are shown in Exhibit 4-1.

Exhibit 4-1

S.E.S. CORPORATION
Thirty-Year Estimated Cash Flows

Years 1 through 30

Sales receipts		$500,000
Merchandise costs	$400,000	
Rent	10,000	
Salaries, etc.	37,500	
Interest on bonds	2,500	450,000
Net *annual* cash flow		$ 50,000 *per year*

Year 10

Renovation costs	$50,000

Year 20

Renovation costs	$50,000

Year 30

Bond redemption	$50,000

• *Some impediments to investor forecasting.* Now the forecasting procedure
described above is straightforward enough. Unfortunately, to follow it is by
no means an easy or inexpensive undertaking, particularly for a prospective
investor in a large corporation. For, as described in Chapter 2, investors in
large corporations are essentially "outsiders." That is, they do not take part
directly in the operations of the enterprise. But the "outsider" status of investors is not, itself, a problem. As described earlier, it is actually desirable
that large numbers of investors be able to *delegate* the operation of large businesses to a specialized group of insiders known as "management." As a result, however, investors individually and as a group typically do not have
ready access to much of the information, particularly about production processes, factor costs, and so forth, that would facilitate the kind of forecasts
that they would probably find most useful. *This obviously creates a dilemma.*

Investors have a use for forecasts of future enterprise cash flows, but they
cannot easily, or at reasonable expense, procure the kind of detailed underlying information on which to base forecasts. This dilemma is one of several
stimuli that explain the continued presence of financial accounting as a me-

dium through which managements of enterprises provide certain financial information to investors. Before proceeding to the kind of information that currently characterizes financial accounting practice, we first consider some idealized possibilities. Although not in widespread use, these alternative reporting possibilities are receiving growing support. Furthermore, they provide a thought-provoking context in which to introduce conventional financial accounting.

Some Prospects for Information Supplied by the Enterprise

One obvious alternative to consider is that the management of each enterprise should issue public forecasts of future cash flows for everyone's use.

• *Management forecasts.* Although public issuance of forecasts of future cash flows has been the exception in recent corporate financial reporting, the idea is gaining support for a number of reasons:

1. Estimates of future cash flows are of obvious interest to investors.
2. No one is in a better position than management to assess (*a*) the demand for an enterprise's products, (*b*) the input requirements for its production processes, (*c*) the input and output prices in the industry in which it competes, etc.
3. Only management can fully assess the future implications of *its own internal decisions* regarding the course that the enterprise will follow.
4. For its own internal use, management will have projected future cash flows anyway, so that making them public involves relatively little additional effort.
5. Since internal management forecasts exist, they should be made public (at least in the case of large, publicly held corporations) lest they be "leaked out" to a privileged few who could then exploit them to special advantage.

In summary, all of these reasons add up to one conclusion: because management specializes in operating the business enterprise, it has a tremendous comparative advantage over outsiders in projecting future events and relationships on which forecasts of cash flows can be built.

• *Valuation of the enterprise—a further refinement.* Given that (1) the management of an enterprise has a comparative advantage in projecting future cash flows, and (2) the investors are interested in the value of those cash flows, it has been suggested that the ideal information to be provided to outside investors by management is the present value of the enterprise.

Example 4-2   Based on the projected cash flows in Exhibit 4-1, and assuming that the management of S.E.S. Corporation feels that 10 percent is an appropriate discount rate, the present value of S.E.S. can be calculated as in Exhibit 4-2.

Exhibit 4-2   PRESENT VALUE OF S.E.S. CORPORATION

Years	Cash Flow	$PV_{(n,\,0.10)}$	Present Value of Cash Flows
1–30	+$50,000/yr.	9.430*	$471,500
10	− 50,000	.386	− 19,300
20	− 50,000	.149	− 7,450
30	− 50,000	.057	− 2,850
Present value of S.E.S. Corporation			$441,900

*Note that since $50,000 is the annual cash flow expected for every year from year one through year thirty, we have taken the convenient computational shortcut of using the present value factor from Table 3-3 of a thirty-year annuity at 10 percent. See Appendix B to Chapter 3 for an explanation of annuities and the use of Table 3-3.

Perhaps it is intuitively appealing to have management actually provide a ready-made present value of the enterprise (as opposed to only providing cash forecasts), on the grounds that it would be a further savings of effort for investors. They would, after all, have possibly complex cash forecasts reduced to a single number. On the other hand, if management only provided its valuation of the enterprise to outsiders in place of the underlying forecasts of future cash flows, certain objections come to mind.

One reason for not substituting a present value of the enterprise for forecast future cash flows is that the value of a possible investment interest in the enterprise might not be directly inferred from the value of the enterprise as a whole. For instance, in Example 4-1 it was noted that S.E.S. Corporation has 10,000 outstanding ownership shares. In Example 4-2 the present value of S.E.S. was calculated based on an assumed 10 percent time preference rate. Does that mean that to an investor the value of one ownership share is $44.19, that is, the present value of the enterprise ($441,900) divided by the number of shares outstanding (10,000)? Not necessarily. Except in the special case where all cash inflows in excess of required outflows are paid immediately to owners, there will probably be significant differences in timing between cash flows to the enterprise and cash flows to the investor.

Another reason for not substituting a present value for a set of forecast cash flows is that individual investors may vary as to their assessments of the risk associated with management's forecast cash flows (including possible forecast error or bias). They may also differ in the way that they take this risk into account in placing a value on the cash flows. To deny them access to the actual forecast cash flows would therefore deny them certain potentially relevant inputs to their individual valuations.

• *Some problems with management forecasts.* In view of the objections raised above, it is not surprising that present-day financial reporting does not consist of public issuance of present values of the many business enterprises in the economy. But given the tremendous comparative advantage possessed by management, it is perhaps perplexing that management forecasts of future cash flows are rarely made public. In point of fact, though, there are some significant reasons that make the dearth of management forecasts more understandable, particularly from management's point of view.

One of the great advantages of management forecasts noted above is that they would reflect the latest management decisions as to competitive strategy, production method, and so forth. Unfortunately, disclosure of such forecasts not only would help investors but might inform the "competition" of management's strategies, making their success less likely.

In addition, there is another serious reason to question whether it is feasible for business enterprises to produce forecasts for present and potential investors. The estimates of future cash flows expected to be generated by the business are just that—estimates. Although the accountants working for the business may be best qualified to make such estimates, they may err. Indeed, in an uncertain environment, actual experience may depart from prior expectations by chance alone. Furthermore, the managements of business enterprises have vested interests in investors' decisions. That is, investors decide whether or not to place money capital at the disposal of managers. Therefore, there may be a temptation for management to bias estimated future cash flows in order to influence investor decisions.

One can visualize, then, what the results would be if many investors relied upon the accountants' expert opinions, in the form of forecasts of future cash flows disclosed by managements of various enterprises, only to be disappointed by later experience. It would be difficult to separate those cases in which the accountants had erred or were purposely biased and those in which uncontrollable events intervened. It is for this reason probably more than any other that in today's environment business enterprises have not provided forecasts of future cash flows for use by present and prospective investors.

• *The outlook for management forecasts.* At this writing, the role of management forecasts in the financial reporting practices of large, publicly held corporations is in a state of potential change. It is widely acknowledged that such forecasts have advantages for present and prospective investors but that they also have disadvantages as viewed by management. To date the decision to issue forecasts has been at the discretion of management. Hence it is understandable that few forecasts extending very far into the future have been issued. But the balance could shift at any time.

Perhaps managements of more and more companies will begin to see a greater advantage in satisfying the public demand for forecast-type information. More likely, however, governmental and professional authorities may see fit to impose a forecast requirement on companies whose financial affairs come within their authority. (Chapter 10 contains an extensive discussion of the role of the Securities and Exchange Commission and certain professional bodies in setting financial reporting policy.) In view of the potential for a shift from a world of virtually no management forecasts to a world of mandatory issuance of forecasts, our ensuing discussion of other information about the enterprise for investors will be consistent with both worlds.

Relevance of Past Performance in Forecasting

In moving from a discussion of management forecasts to other currently more practical information alternatives, two implications of the foregoing discussion carry over. *First, the nature of the investor's decision problem is unchanged, whether or not management issues forecasts of future cash flows.*

That is, presumably investors want to arrive at valuations of investment opportunities based on the expected future cash flows and expected risk that they associate with those opportunities. Knowledge of management forecasts simply offers some potential for arriving at better expectations with perhaps less expenditure of time and other resources in the process. *Second, whether or not management issues forecasts, some more factually based types of information about the enterprise are relevant to investors.* As was noted above, one of the major objections to management forecasts is that such forecasts may be in error or even purposely biased. To give investors some basis for acceptance, rejection, or modification, management forecasts should be accompanied by other financial information portraying the present and past operations of the enterprise, against which the forecasts can be compared. Moreover, in the absence of management forecasts, such information will serve the same function with respect to investors' own forecasts.

In considering financial reporting alternatives, either as substitutes where management forecasts are not forthcoming or as complements where they are, it follows from the preceding discussion that we want to consider alternatives that (1) are not as susceptible to bias and error in reporting as forecasts, and (2) can nevertheless be employed in forecasting uncertain future cash flows by investors. To be less susceptible to bias than management forecasts, the "other information" reported by the enterprise to investors must be based more on facts—on the actual events and activities experienced by the enterprise. To be employed by investors in forecasting, the "other information" presented must bear some discernible (logical) relationship to that which is of interest—namely, future cash flows.

Past Performance Related to Future Cash Flows

The notion that information about events and activities already experienced by an enterprise could be relevant to the estimation of future cash flows is based on an assumed continuity of events and activities engaged in by the enterprise. That is, although many aspects of an enterprise's activities (like its product lines, production processes, etc.) may change over time, many important aspects remain constant or change slowly. Thus the immediate past provides a context in which to consider future possibilities. The further various future possibilities depart from the immediate past, the less credible or probable they will seem.

The idea of continuity of events can be applied to the enterprise as a generator of cash flows. For instance, recall that earlier the enterprise was described in terms of an operating sequence that included (1) acquisition of resources for immediate or future cash flows, (2) conversion of resources into products and services, and (3) sales of products and services in exchange for immediate or future cash receipts. For most enterprises this sequence or process of generating cash flows is more or less continuous. Furthermore, an enterprise will usually tend to be engaged in all steps simultaneously.

• *Enterprise performance.* Assuming that there is some continuity in the cash-generating process, a portrayal of the enterprise's present "performance" in that process would presumably be relevant to investors who are interested in future cash flows. By "performance" we mean the rate at which the enterprise is generating cash inflows in excess of cash outflows. Such a rate can be thought of as representing the enterprise's *cash-generating ability* or *cash-generating capacity per unit of time.*

Periodic Net Cash Flow as a Measure of Performance

With the above discussion in mind, we are prepared to discuss some alternative measures of enterprise "performance," in the "cash-generating-ability" sense. An obvious first choice for a periodic performance measure is the net cash flow of an enterprise for a given period, such as a week, a month, a year.

> **Net Cash Flow.** Net cash flow may simply be defined as the excess of total cash received by the enterprise during a period of time over total cash disbursed during the same period of time (but excluding dividends or withdrawals paid to owners or contributions made by owners).

• *Advantages of net cash flow.* As a measure of performance, net cash flow has some definite advantages that make it attractive for periodic reporting to outside investors:

1. The amounts of cash taken in and paid out by an enterprise are largely factual data—not matters of estimate.
2. The computation of periodic net cash flow is identical to the computation of the cash flows of future periods that are of interest to investors.

• *Disadvantages of net cash flow.* But net cash flow has at least one distinct disadvantage as well. When measured over short periods of time (really, any period short of the full life of the enterprise), it may seriously misrepresent the *cash-generating ability* of the enterprise for several reasons:

1. Many of the larger cash expenditures in a particular period may be made to acquire resources like buildings and equipment that will be used to produce the products and services of many future periods' operations.
2. Often resources may be acquired on credit and used to produce products and services in a particular period, for which payments are not made until later periods.
3. Much of the cash received in a particular period may be payments from customers for products and services provided by the firm in earlier periods on a postponed-payment basis.

Thus there is no necessary association between the measure of effort (total cash expenditures) and the measure of accomplishment (total cash receipts) embodied in the performance measure, periodic net cash flow. With no such association, there is some reason to doubt the usefulness of net cash flow (by itself) as a measure of performance for outside investors to use in judging future cash-generating ability of the enterprise.

• *Disadvantages of net cash flow illustrated.* In a period in which the enterprise is actually very efficient in producing products and services of great value to its customers, its net cash-flow performance might look very bad simply because it makes an expenditure for a new piece of equipment that will help it continue producing efficiently for many months or years to come. Whereas the act of buying a piece of equipment may be good for future cash-generating ability, it will have an extraordinarily negative effect on the measure of the current period's performance of the enterprise. Similarly, in a period in which an enterprise's productivity declines, its net cash-flow performance may continue to look good, sustained by cash collections from customers for products and services provided in past periods. This point is illustrated in Example 4-3.

Example 4-3

Let us suppose that you have decided to enter into business for yourself and have hit upon the idea of opening an ice cream parlor. You have found a store to rent at a good location (plenty of pedestrian traffic), so you expect good demand for ice-cream cones as well as ice-cream specialties to be made to order for banquets and such.

To get the business started, you invest $7,500 cash on August 1, 19XX, pay three months' rent in advance totaling $600, and begin buying and installing equipment as well as hiring a manager and some part-time student employees. The equipment costs $6,000 but will meet the business's needs until it wears out in about five years and has to be scrapped. After installing the equipment and hiring the employees, you purchase the following additional items: (1) supplies (cones, napkins, etc.) for $200 cash and (2) ice cream, $300, with payment due at the time of the next delivery. With delivery of the latter two purchases you commence business, completing the first month's (August's) operations very smoothly. The remaining facts of operations for August are as follows:

1. You had cash ice-cream sales of $4,000 for the whole month. And, in addition, you provided ice cream for several big banquets for which payment totaling $500 will not be received until September.
2. Salaries and wages for August paid on or before August 31 totaled $1,200. In addition, $300 of salaries and wages for work done during August had not been paid as of August 31. They will be paid on the first payday in September.
3. In total, $1,650 worth of ice cream (including the first order) was purchased from the local dairy, of which $1,300 was paid in August—the other $350 not being due until the first ice-cream delivery in September.
4. Miscellaneous cash expenditures were made, totaling $100, for heat, light, and so forth, during August.
5. An additional $100 worth of supplies was ordered and received in August but will not be paid for until September.
6. At the end of August the manager noted that only about $200 worth of all the ice cream purchased during the month was still on hand along with about $150 worth of supplies.

All things considered, you are pleased with the first month's operations of the business, in fact, so much so that you want to open another store at another location. Since you do not have enough money of your own for the expansion, you must try to borrow from the local banker. This makes it necessary to convey some idea to him of how your business is going, so that he can assess your ability to pay back a loan in the future. How do you go about representing your business's operations to him? You try the net cash flow for the month of August to see if it gives a satisfactory representation of the business's cash-generating ability.

The total cash receipts of the business (excluding the initial investment) are the $4,000 of cash sales noted above. To get the *net* cash flow from the business for the month of August, you determine the difference between these total cash receipts of $4,000 and the total of the cash disbursements, as shown in Exhibit 4-3.

Exhibit 4-3

ICE CREAM PARLOR
Net Cash Flow for August 19XX

Total cash receipts		$4,000
Cash disbursements for:		
Equipment	$6,000	
Three months' rent	600	
Supplies	200	
Salaries and wages	1,200	
Ice cream	1,300	
Miscellaneous	100	
Total cash disbursements		9,400
Net cash flow		−$5,400

The net cash flow is −$5,400. In other words, the business, after being initially established, experienced a net cash outflow or drain of $5,400 in the month of August, obviously not a very satisfactory measure of "performance" in August. Why? Because there is an indiscriminant matching of dollars paid out and dollars received as if each dollar expended and received applied equally to the operations of the business during the month of August—which intuitively is not the case. The positive side of performance, the total cash receipts of $4,000, does not include $500 to be received in September for ice cream *provided to banquet customers in August*. Similarly, the negative side of the measure of August performance includes the whole $6,000 laid out for equipment that will last five years, and $600 in rent that covers not only August but September and October as well. In addition, it omits all of the $350 that will be paid in September for the last delivery of ice cream that was at least partially used in August, and the $300 that will be paid in September for work performed entirely in August.

Conventional Accounting Performance Measurement

The above discussion leads one to conclude that in searching for a measure of the periodic performance of the enterprise, the search ought to go further than the periodic net cash-flow measure. Indeed, an alternative measure of periodic performance of the enterprise is included in "conventional accounting." ("Conventional accounting" is the label that we will apply to the financial accounting model that dominates accounting practice today.) Like periodic net cash flow, the measure of performance produced by conventional accounting, called *net operating income,* is the difference between a measure of accomplishment, called *revenue,* and a measure of effort or sacrifice, called *expense.* Although the data used in conventional accounting are the same as the data used in calculating periodic net cash flow, that is, prices received for products and services and prices paid for factors of production, they are used more selectively and in different periods in the life of the enterprise to measure performance. Most of these differences are embodied in the definitions of revenue and expense under conventional accounting.

• *Revenue defined.* For all practical purposes, we can define conventional accounting revenue as follows:

> **Revenue.** Generally, revenue is the sum of the selling prices (or fees) of all products sold and services provided to customers during the current period —whether or not the sales are cash sales or "credit sales." (Credit sales are sales for which the customer promises to pay at a later time.)

Notice that revenue differs from the total cash receipts of the enterprise for the period of interest. Cash receipts may include payments made by customers in the current period for products and services received in an earlier period. Similarly, revenue will usually include the selling prices of products or services provided during the current period for which no cash will be received until a later period.

Example 4-4   In Example 4-3 above, only $4,000 was actually received by the ice cream parlor from customers during the month of August, all from purchasers of ice-cream cones. That $4,000 is the measure of total accomplishment under net cash-flow performance measurement. But there was $500 worth of ice cream sold to banquet customers who did not pay immediately, but rather promised to pay in September. Both the $500 promised to be paid and the $4,000 actually paid by customers in August are included in August revenue of $4,500. Furthermore, the $500 due from customers *will not be included* in revenue upon receipt in September as part of that month's total accomplishment.

• *The realization principle and revenue.* It should be noted that the above definition of revenue is somewhat simplified for purposes of present discussion. Measurement of revenue under conventional accounting requires the application of a somewhat more sophisticated criterion than the one implied by our definition. In the general sense, conventional accounting revenue measurement is governed by the realization principle.

> **The Realization Principle.** Accomplishment (revenue) should be recognized in the period when the prices to be received for products and services provided by the enterprise (1) become reasonably certain and (2) have been "earned" by the enterprise.

The term "earned" in the definition is generally interpreted as meaning that the enterprise does not face any substantial additional production barriers or steps before actually providing a satisfactory product or service to a customer, thus ensuring that the price of that product or service will actually be forthcoming. In a market economy, fairly strict interpretation of the word "earned" *usually implies* that a legally enforceable sale of a product or completion of a service has already taken place. Furthermore, a legally enforceable sale usually satisfies the stipulation that the price to be received from a customer be reasonably certain as well. Thus our definition of revenue in the preceding paragraph describes the result of applying the realization principle in the majority of cases in practice. We will take up discussion of the several types of special cases encountered less frequently in practice in Chapter 11.

• *Relationship between revenue and cash receipts.* Over the whole life of the enterprise, the *sum* of all periods' revenues will equal the *sum* of all periods' cash receipts from sales of products and services. The differences between the revenue and the cash receipts of individual periods will usually only be a matter of timing. The reason is that regardless of which way the enterprise recognizes accomplishment, the price paid by a customer for a given product or service will be included in the measure of accomplishment in only one period in the life of the enterprise. The price of the product will be recognized either in the period in which the customer buys the product (revenue measure of accomplishment) or in the period in which he pays for it (cash receipts measure). Furthermore, if the performance measurement period is very long (say, as long as a year), a particular customer's purchase is apt to result in a cash receipt in the same period as it would be included in revenue anyway. So why bother with the distinction? The answer is important enough to warrant some brief additional discussion.

• *Measuring periodic accomplishment.* The "real" economic accomplishment of an enterprise for a period of time is the total value that the enterprise has added to all resources (raw material, etc.) that it controls, *by all of its productive efforts.* Although this is what we would like to measure ideally, it is impossible to measure all value added in any largely objective way. For instance, if an enterprise starts raw materials into production during a period of time but does not bring them to completion during the same period, how is it to characterize what it has accomplished in any largely factual way? The partially completed goods may be worthless junk if never brought to completion. Or it may turn out that a whole batch cannot be sold upon completion because for one reason or another it does not meet acceptable quality standards.

Furthermore, in the case of many production techniques, it may be impossible to say when a certain percentage of the final conversion of raw materials to finished goods has been completed. In any case it will require a largely subjective judgment to estimate the total value added to goods and services brought to various stages of completion during the period. So even though we would like to include all "real" value added by an enterprise when measuring its accomplishments for a period, we cannot objectively do so.

• *The advantages of revenue for performance measurement.* Among the outside events that could be relied upon to affirm value added, the receipt of a customer's payment in cash leaves the enterprise more certain of the value of the products it has provided than does the customer's promise to pay. Nevertheless, conventional accounting usually recognizes the "value added" embodied in an enterprise's products in the periods in which they are sold rather than in the period of receipt of cash, for two reasons:

1. Thanks to the existence in our socioeconomic system of a stable legal environment that will enforce the customer's agreement to pay, the additional uncertainty caused by recognizing accomplishment before cash is received is minimal and can often be predicted with accuracy.
2. The period in which a product is sold is almost always earlier than (or the same as) the period in which cash is received, and hence chronologically closer to the period(s) in which most of the productive activity that added value to the product took place. Thus the measure of accomplishment (and hence the measure of performance) in conventional accounting is less likely to represent productive potential that is outdated or no longer achievable.

Thus in conventional accounting we use revenue (as described earlier) as a measure of accomplishment because it is usually sufficiently more timely to offset its slightly lesser objectivity than net cash receipts.

• *Measuring periodic effort or sacrifice.* Earlier in the chapter it was pointed out that one objection to a net cash-flow concept of performance is a general lack of association between the level of measured accomplishment and the level of measured effort for a given period. In conventional accounting that objection is largely overcome. But it must be noted that the measurement of accomplishment, revenue, is not conditioned upon the measurement of effort. In measuring revenue under the realization principle, we ignore many of the real economic efforts of a particular period by which the enterprise adds value. Instead of measuring value added as it takes place, we recognize in the period of sale cumulative efforts of the present and past periods embodied in completed products and services provided to customers.

• *Expense defined.* To achieve the hoped-for cause-and-effect association between measured effort and measured accomplishment, measurement of conventional accounting expense for a period is conditioned upon revenue recognized for the period, as indicated by the following definition:

Expense. Insofar as possible, total expense for a period includes the costs of all resources that were sacrificed to produce the revenue recognized in the current period.

Again, our definition is a simplification of a more general and sophisticated set of criteria. The implied relationship in the definition between expense recognition and revenue recognized for a given period is a simplification of *the matching principle.*

The Matching Principle. Insofar as possible, the total sacrifices made in all periods to produce and sell a particular product or service should be recognized as expense in the period in which the revenue from the same product or service is recognized.

The matching principle gives to conventional accounting performance measurement what is lacking in net cash flow—an intuitive cause (effort) and effect (accomplishment) relationship. But the matching principle as defined implies some concept for measuring the sacrifice (effort) made in producing products and services. The measure of sacrifice in conventional accounting is governed by what we will call *the original transaction cost principle,* or, more simply, *the cost principle.*

> **The Cost Principle.** The measure of sacrifice associated with the acquisition and subsequent use of any resource is the price paid for the resource, that is, its cost, in the exchange or exchanges in which it was acquired.

Clearly, our definition of expense is simply a combination of these two fundamental principles.

• *Expense recognition illustrated.* Expense recognition, according to the matching principle, calls for a selective measure of effort that is consistent with the measured accomplishment (revenue) of a given period. For any given period, the sum of the prices of the products and services provided to customers is the recognized measure of accomplishment. Then, ideally, in the same period the sum of the prices paid for resources used to produce *those* products and services is the recognized measure of effort.

Example 4-5

Again recalling the facts of the ice cream parlor situation introduced in Example 4-3, we can contrast the expenses that would be recognized during the month of August with the cash disbursements recognized earlier.

Notice that in Exhibit 4-4 there are two directions of contrast between August cash disbursements and August expenses. In the cases of equipment, rent, and supplies, the cash expenditures exceed recognized expense. In each case we are recognizing that the business paid for more of that resource in the month of August than was sacrificed to produce August's revenues of $4,500. For instance, equipment was purchased for $6,000 but was expected to supply service for five years, or sixty months. Assuming equal applicability of that service to all sixty months, the cost of the first month's use would be $1/60 \times \$6,000$, or $100.

Similarly, three months' rent was prepaid at $600, but two months' paid-up occupancy remain, indicating that only one-third, or $200 worth of occupancy, was used up. In the case of supplies, $300 worth was received, but $150 worth was still on hand at August 31, as yet to be sacrificed. Thus we infer that supplies used during August originally cost $150.

In the case of salaries and wages as well as ice cream, the expense recognized for August exceeds cash disbursements for August. In both cases we are recognizing that the sacrifice of a resource took place in connection with production of August's revenue of $4,500, regardless of when cash will actually be paid. For instance, even though we only paid salaries and wages of $1,200 during August, salaries and wages for hours actually worked (in producing August's revenue) amounted to $1,500; the additional $300 will be paid on the first payday in September. Similarly, ice cream worth $1,650 in total was received from the dairy during August. Of that amount $350 had not been paid for at August 31, but only $200 remained unsold. We therefore infer that the cost of the ice cream sold during August was $1,450.

No difference between the August cash disbursement and the expense recognized for miscellaneous heat, light, power, and so forth implies that all such items or services were used to produce the revenue of the month in which they were paid.

Exhibit 4-4

ICE CREAM PARLOR
Cash Disbursements versus Expenses
For August 19XX

	Cash Disbursed in August	Expense Recognized in August
Nature of the sacrifice:		
Equipment	$6,000	$ 100
Rent	600	200
Supplies	200	150
Salaries and wages	1,200	1,500
Ice cream	1,300	1,450
Miscellaneous	100	100
Total	$9,400	$3,500

• *Product expenses versus period expenses.* We have made quite a point of the association between revenue and expense brought about in conventional accounting through the matching principle—particularly by contrast to the lack of association between periodic cash receipts and disbursements. But some slight qualification is in order lest we mislead the reader about what can actually be expected from applying the matching principle in practice.

To be strictly applied, the matching principle requires that virtually every sacrifice of any resource used in production in a given period (1) be specifically identified with a particular product or service, (2) have its original cost (in conventional accounting) accumulated with the costs of all other sacrifices made to produce that product or service, and (3) be recognized as an expense in the period in which the particular product or service is sold or provided.

Even when possible, such specific identification of every resource sacrifice with some product or service is very costly. Furthermore, such scrupulous matching of resource sacrifices with products or services and later with revenue is often impossible. Some resource sacrifices are easily traced to the specific products sold in specific periods.

Example 4-6   In the case of the ice cream parlor, the ice cream used during August was used in the ice-cream cones and banquet desserts sold during August.

On the other hand, some resource sacrifices simply cannot be directly associated with specific products or services provided.

Example 4-7 The manager of the ice cream parlor may have spent most of his time in August making business contacts with restaurants and caterers in trying to promote future banquet business. But it would be difficult or impossible to discern which future sales, or how many, are a direct result of the manager's expenditure of time (the enterprise's expenditure of salary) during August.

Hence the matching principle is rarely followed to perfection. Instead, a rough dichotomy is usually followed in recognizing expenses for a given period.

If a resource sacrifice has been made in a particular accounting period, an accountant will consider the way in which the resource was used. If consumption of the resource can be identified or associated with a specific product or service (or batch of products and services), its original cost to the enterprise is accumulated ("attached" to the product or service) until the period in which the specific products are sold or services completed, at which time the related revenue is recognized. Product expenses are resource costs, like the cost of ice cream, that logically "attach" to products. Product expenses are recognized as expenses in the period in which the particular product is sold.

But if a resource is consumed during the period and its consumption bears no discernible relation to the production of any particular present or future product(s) or service(s), that is, it cannot be specifically identified with a unit of present or future revenue, its cost is recognized as an expense in the period in which it is consumed or sacrificed. Such costs, like the manager's salary, are called *period expenses*.

This rough dichotomy is somewhat evident in our recognition of the August expenses of the ice cream parlor above. The point of bringing up the distinction here is that while conventional accounting performance measurement is based on a cause-and-effect relationship between sacrifices made and resulting accomplishments recognized, in practice such a relationship is never perfectly achieved. But every effort within reasonable limits is usually made to match a cost with the specific revenue (product) that it helped to generate, before resorting to the expedient of merely treating the cost as an expense in the period in which the resource is used.

• *Measuring periodic performance.* The index of periodic performance in conventional accounting is called *net operating income*.

Net Operating Income. Net operating income may be defined very simply as the algebraic difference between revenues and expenses recognized in a particular period:

$$\text{Net operating income} = \text{Revenues} - \text{Expenses}$$

Example 4-8 Since we have earlier calculated the ice cream parlor's revenue ($4,500) and expense ($3,500) for the month of August, it is a simple matter to determine net operating income:

$$\text{Net operating income} = \$4,500 - \$3,500 = \$1,000$$

and to display the details in a sensible array called an income statement, illustrated in Exhibit 4-5.

As we would expect, the $1,000 net operating income measure of performance for the month of August contrasts sharply with the ice cream parlor's net cash flow of −$5,400 calculated earlier.

Exhibit 4-5

ICE CREAM PARLOR

Income Statement
For the Month of August 19XX

Revenue from sales of ice cream		$4,500
Less expenses:		
Equipment	$ 100	
Rent	200	
Supplies used	150	
Salaries and wages	1,500	
Cost of ice cream sold	1,450	
Miscellaneous heat, light, etc.	100	
Total expenses		3,500
Net operating income		$1,000

Because net operating income is simply the difference between revenues and expenses, most of its properties as a periodic performance index derive from the way that expenses and revenues are measured. Hence we have briefly summarized the properties of revenue, expense, and net operating income in Exhibit 4-6.

Exhibit 4-6   SUMMARY OF CONVENTIONAL ACCOUNTING OPERATING INCOME MEASUREMENT CONCEPTS

	Definition (What?)	Conventional Timing (When?)	Conventional Measurement (How much?)
Revenue:	Value of goods and services provided to customers during the current period	Recognized when goods have been delivered or services have been rendered	Price (fee) paid or agreed to be paid by the customer
Expense:	Value of resources consumed in the past or present (sometimes the future) to provide a product or service	Recognized in the period in which the related revenue is recognized, i.e., expense is "matched" against revenue	Cost of (original price paid for) resources consumed to provide the products or services delivered during the period
Net operating income:	Difference between revenue and expense of the period	Determined as a result of recognizing the related revenue and expense of the period	Difference between the aggregate prices (fees) from products sold and services rendered and the aggregate costs of the resources sacrificed in providing those products and services

There are still many issues not covered so far concerning income measurement and the larger conventional accounting framework or context into which income measurement fits. These issues are the subjects of Chapters 5 and 6 and several other later chapters. But it is felt that one last item of elaboration on an earlier theme is worthwhile here.

• *Net income versus net cash flow.* Assuming that the agreed-to selling prices of products provided are all collected from customers eventually, the sum of the revenues recognized in all the individual periods of an enterprise's life will equal the sum of all the cash receipts over the life of the enterprise. Similarly, since expenses are recognized in terms of the prices originally paid for resources used in the business, the sum of the expenses recognized over the enterprise's life will equal the sum of all cash disbursed for resources used in production over the same period. It is therefore also true that the sum of the income amounts calculated for all of the periods in an enterprise's life (the sum of the revenues minus the sum of the expenses) *must equal the net cash flow over the whole life* of the enterprise (excluding payments to and receipts from owners).

Thus, over the whole life of the enterprise, conventional accounting income is completely consistent with long-run net cash flow. It differs from periodic net cash flow only in the way that it represents performance or the rate of progress in the successive time periods along the way. In differing along the way from periodic net cash flow, it presumably provides *a better index of long-run net cash-flow potential* than does periodic net cash flow. The now-familiar reason is that matching is an attempt to relate the revenues and expenses of a particular period on a cause-and-effect basis, insofar as possible.

Questions for Review and Discussion

4-1. Define:

a. Net cash flow

b. Revenue

c. Expense

d. The realization principle

e. The matching principle

f. The cost principle

g. Product expense

h. Period expense

4-2. From an investment decision viewpoint, what aspects of the business enterprise are decision makers concerned about?

4-3. The cash-flow-generating process of a business enterprise is strikingly simple (in principle). Describe the steps in the cash-generating (operating) sequence of a business enterprise.

4-4. Give several reasons favoring the publication of management forecasts of future cash flows.

4-5. Although the potential relevance of management forecasts for investor decisions can be established, certain problems limit the feasibility of having management supply such forecasts to outside investors.

a. What are these limitations?

b. Does the presence or absence of management forecasts alter the investor's basic decision problem?

4-6. It has been suggested that there are some significant reasons why managers prefer not to publish cash forecasts in the present environment. Give the reasons.

4-7. The scarcity of management forecasts in present-day financial reporting (and the probable usefulness of supplemental information even if forecasts were generally available) led to our discussion of net cash flows and net operating income as possible alternatives or supplements to forecasts. What criteria were used to introduce these alternatives?

4-8. Provision of historical cash flows for use by investors in making investment decisions is considered to have both advantages and disadvantages. Discuss both.

4-9. The conventional accounting performance measure, called net operating income, is based on historical events.

a. What are the reasons for this historical orientation when investors are concerned strictly with future cash flows in valuing prospective investments?

b. How or why can historical measures of performance be used as indicators of likely future performance?

4-10. Distinguish between:

a. Cost and expense

b. Product versus period expense

4-11. Over the whole life of an enterprise, net cash flow from operations will equal net operating income. Explain why this is so.

4-12. The discussion in the chapter considered net cash flow and net operating income to be alternative performance measures (primarily for exposition purposes). Do you see any potential usefulness in viewing the two measures as complementary? Explain your position.

4-13. Net operating income is not considered to be a forecast *per se,* though it is presumably relevant to investors who wish to forecast future cash flows. Under what conditions will the current period's net operating income be an actual forecast of the next period's (or other future periods') net operating income(s)? Does knowledge of these conditions have any implications for investors?

4-14. Conventional accounting net operating income can be thought of as an attempt to simulate the net cash flow from the operations of the business *as if* (1) the business acquires all resources for cash in quantities no greater than the current period's requirements, (2) all products produced (purchased) are sold in the same period *and* all products sold are produced (purchased) in the same period, and (3) all sales are for cash. Do you basically agree or disagree? Explain your position. Do you wish to qualify your basic agreement or disagreement in any way?

4-15. The timing of recognition of revenue generally determines when many expenses will be recognized. Explain why this is so. What kinds of expenses will generally not be subject to this pattern of recognition?

Exercises

4-1. Net Cash Flow for Future Cash-Flow Predictions. John Jacobsen and Steve Block started a small delicatessen specializing in exotic sandwiches two years ago when they were both undergraduates in business administration. The business has been very successful, and what was initially viewed as a temporary venture to defray college expenses now appears to be able to provide a good permanent income for one of them. Steve is interested in remaining in the business, and John has agreed to sell his share if they can agree on a mutually satisfactory purchase price. Steve has suggested using past cash flows of the business as an indicator of likely future cash flows. John, on the other hand, believes that past cash flows are not representative due to heavy initial cash outflows for start-up costs and relatively light cash inflows while the business was building up a clientele. Actual net cash flows for the first two years of operation were −$1,000 the first year and $6,000 the second year. They each have projected annual net cash flows as follows:

	John (projected)	Steve (projected)
Year 1	$10,000	$ 6,000
2	12,000	8,000
3	14,000	8,000
4	14,000	8,000
5	16,000	8,000
6	18,000	8,000
7	20,000	10,000
8	20,000	10,000
9	20,000	10,000
10	20,000	10,000

Required:

1. Assuming the business will last for only the ten years projected, what is the PV of the business in each case if their time preference rate is 10 percent?

2. Suppose you are John. How might you go about convincing Steve that your projections are more realistic based at least in part on the actual events and transactions of the business during the first two years?

4-2. Feasibility of Future Cash-Flow Projections. The Northern Construction Corporation is engaged primarily in the construction of various government projects. Over the years it has developed a management team that is one of the best in the region when it comes to working with government agencies and knowing what government construction projects are in the offing. Three years ago the management of the firm believed that the number of government projects it would be able to undertake was likely to increase substantially. Based on this premise, it projected net cash flows that were significantly larger than in the past. In the belief that this information was important to both current and potential stockholders, it supplied the following estimates of future net cash flows:

19X0	$ 60,000
19X1	75,000
19X2	90,000
19X3	120,000
19X4	125,000
19X5–19X9	130,000

Unfortunately, in the years immediately following these projections there was a significant cutback in actual government expenditures. As a result, the company's realized cash flows stayed approximately constant at a level of $60,000. Furthermore, the company's management saw little prospect for cash flows to increase in the foreseeable future.

Required:

1. Assume that there are a total of 1,000 shares of stock in the corporation. If the shareholders' time preference rate is 10 percent, what are the present values of the shares for the two sets of circumstances? (Assume that net cash flows are distributed in full to owners in the year received.)

2. Suppose you had purchased shares based on management's first cash-flow projections (and had paid approximately their then present value). How might you react to the revised estimates? Why?

4-3. Net Cash Flow as a Performance Measurement.   The Green Thumb Nursery was started five years ago to raise and sell various kinds of decorative trees and shrubs. The varieties that it grows require from three to five years to reach a salable size. As a result, it has experienced rather heavy cash outflows in the first five years of operation while growing the shrubs, but relatively small cash inflows, since it has had few shrubs of marketable size. Net cash flows for these years were as follows:

Year 1	$(60,000)
Year 2	(40,000)
Year 3	(42,000)
Year 4	(34,000)
Year 5	(6,000)

Because of these heavy cash outflows, the firm is in need of additional capital and is currently attempting to attract new investors. It realizes that investors make investment decisions on the basis of prospective future cash flows, but it is unwilling to make such estimates public because of the potential legal liability if they are not realized as projected.

Required:

1. One alternative it has considered is simply presenting the entirely factual and objective historical cash flows, but it feels that they do not adequately represent the past performance or future potential of the firm. Comment on this alternative. Why may it be inadequate information for prospective investors?

2. How might it alternatively present largely factual information that would be more likely to give investors an indication of potential future cash flows?

3. What sort of criteria should be used for generating the information for potential investors?

4. If you were in a position to supply all of the additional capital required, what combination of information would you request? (Assume anything that you request will be forthcoming.)

4-4. Net Cash Flow as a Performance Measurement.   The Coastal Trading Company's principal activity is the sale of fishing equipment, supplies, food, and clothing to the Alaskan fishing industry. Its business, like the fishing industry, is highly seasonal. Outfitting boats during the months of June and July accounts for approximately 40 percent of its annual sales. As a result it uses these two months as an indicator of its performance for the year. During June 19XX it had sales of $172,000, of which $16,000 was paid in cash and the balance was sold on account. Also during June it received payments on account from May sales totaling $18,000. Merchandise sold during June included goods purchased in May totaling $43,000, goods purchased on account during June totaling $48,000, and goods purchased and paid for in June totaling $23,000. In addition, it paid accounts payable for merchandise received in May totaling $23,000. June salaries and wages, advertising, and miscellaneous expenses were paid as incurred and totaled $14,000.

In July, as the fishing season progressed, the company's sales declined to $82,-000, of which $61,000 was paid in cash and $21,000 was sold on account. It received payments on account during July of $156,000. Merchandise sold during July had a cost of $52,000 and was purchased in previous months. There was no new merchandise purchased during July. July cash payments included wages and salaries, advertising, and miscellaneous expenses totaling $11,000, and payments on account for June purchases totaling $40,000.

Required:

1. Construct separate cash-flow statements for June and July based on the above information.

2. Which month's indicated cash performance is better? Explain.

3. Which, if either, is the better indicator of future performance of the company? Explain.

4. What are the problems associated with use of either statement alone as an indicator of likely future performance?

5. In August sales declined further to $63,000, of which $46,000 was cash and $17,000 was sold on account. Payments received on account from May and June sales totaled $20,000. Based on this information, what is total revenue for the three months? What are total cash receipts for the same period? Discuss the reasons for their similarity despite the use of different principles in determining each.

4-5. The Maine Fish Company—Cash-Flow Performance.   The Maine Fish Company has recently set up a new operation which will own and operate a chain of fish, chip, and chowder restaurants. It has appointed a bright young employee, Jim Robinson, to manage the operation, and realizing that it is net cash flow that is important to investors, it has decided to base his salary in part on the cash flows he generates. Specifically, he is to receive 3 percent of the net cash flow in the form of an annual bonus. But Jim does not know this.

During the first year of operations, Jim was able to open a total of four new restaurants and make final plans for an additional three. He feels that this was a rather outstanding performance and as a result is looking forward to a substantial bonus. The following events summarize his activities for the year.

a. Purchased property for the four restaurants for $80,000.

b. Signed contracts for purchase of three additional pieces of property costing a total of $65,000 but has not yet paid for them.

c. Constructed the four restaurant buildings. Total cost was $143,000, and he expected they would last about twenty years each.

d. Purchased equipment for $62,000, which he expected would last ten years.

e. Hired six full- and part-time employees for each restaurant.

f. Paid for initial advertising for the four restaurants of $7,200.

g. Paid wages totaling $37,000 for the year.

h. Paid for food supplies totaling $66,000.

i. Miscellaneous expenditures for the year totaled $4,300.

j. Received cash from sales totaling $134,000. (All sales are for cash.)

In checking over his records at year-end, Jim found that he had virtually no unpaid bills outstanding but had $3,000 in wages which were earned but as yet unpaid. Similarly, he had $2,000 worth of food supplies remaining at year-end.

Required:

1. Prepare a cash-flow statement for Jim's operations for the year.

2. How much is Jim's bonus likely to amount to? Do you think it adequately rewards him for his performance?

3. Can you suggest an alternative measure of performance on which to base Jim's bonus? How much bonus would he receive for the first year under your plan?

4-6. Revenue Recognition. The National Manufacturing Corporation is currently compiling its income statement for the year immediately past. It is using the realization principle for recognition of accomplishment and has events as follows:

a. Signed a contract for sale to the Metal Stamping Company of $60,000 worth of machinery which it manufactures. Of this $60,000, $32,000 worth has been manufactured and delivered during the year. The balance is to be manufactured and delivered next year.

b. Sold $43,000 worth of machinery to the Northwest Metal Products Company, all of which has been delivered. However, it has not yet received payment for these goods.

c. Completed manufacture of $82,000 worth of machinery for which it has no buyer as yet.

d. Received a partial payment in advance of $15,000 for machinery that is to be manufactured and delivered to the Water Research Laboratory next year. The total selling price of the machinery is $37,000.

e. Manufactured and sold machinery to various customers during the year totaling $172,000. At year-end, it had received payments for this machinery totaling $155,000. The remainder is to be collected next year.

f. Received payments totaling $35,000 for machinery that had been delivered to various customers in the year preceding the past year.

Required:

1. How much revenue is attributable to the year's performance for each of the above events, using the criteria embodied in the realization principle? Explain your answer in each case.

2. For what reasons does conventional accounting use the realization principle for recognition of accomplishment?

4-7. The Matching Principle.   Jack's Gardening Service is a small sole proprietorship started by Jack Williams three years ago. The principal activity of the business is maintenance of residential and commercial landscaping. Prior to now, Jack has been measuring the success of his enterprise simply on the basis of cash flow. However, he realizes that cash flow alone is not necessarily a good measure of performance and does not take into account the need to replace resources as they are used. In particular, he is concerned with leaving enough cash in the business to replace his truck and equipment as the need arises. Thus he has decided to use conventional accounting net operating income as his measure of performance. He is presently concerned with matching efforts (expenses) with last month's accomplishments (revenues). The relevant facts are as follows:

a. At the start of his business, he purchased a truck for $4,000. He estimated at that time that it would last him six years and that he could sell it at the end of the six years for $400.

b. He also purchased mowers, a Rototiller, and other equipment at the outset, for which he paid a total of $1,400. He estimates that this equipment will have to be replaced at the end of the fourth year and that he will get a $200 trade-in allowance for the equipment at the time of replacement.

c. During the past month, he paid out $72 for gas used in his truck and mowers during the month.

d. He paid wages to employees of $800 during the month, $200 of which was for time worked in the previous month.

e. He purchased $450 worth of fertilizer and other supplies on account. At the end of the month, he had $200 worth of fertilizer and supplies remaining. He had started the month with $50 worth of fertilizer and supplies.

f. On January 1 of the current year, he had paid for various business licenses and insurance for the year totaling $600.

g. At the end of the month, he paid his bookkeeper for three months' services. This totaled $165.

h. At the end of the month, he withdrew $750 from the business to pay personal living expenses.

Required:

1. Using the matching principle, what are Jack's expenses for the month based on the above events? Explain your reasoning in each case.

2. Which of the above might be classified as product costs? Which are period costs?

4-8. Revenue Recognition.   Theodora Thimble operates a women's wear shop which produces custom-made as well as ready-to-wear women's outfits. During a recent month the events listed below took place. Indicate how much revenue should be recognized for the month in each instance (including amounts implied but not directly stated).

a. Customers were permitted to put a number of items on "layaway" for deposits totaling $200. At the end of the layaway period the customers need not buy the items, in which case they forfeit their deposits. Otherwise the deposits apply against the price.

b. A customer dropped by to try on a custom-made outfit. The outfit was satisfactory and the sale completed. The customer paid the balance of $80 between the $100 price of the dress and the deposit paid at the end of last month when she ordered the outfit.

c. Other customers were measured for custom-made outfits, with total selling prices of $3,000. At the time of measurement, when the order is accepted, customers pay 20 percent of the total price.

d. Received $2,000 for cash sales, some of which were out of layaway with deposits totaling $200 received earlier.

e. Received $3,500 in cash payments on credit sales. The beginning balances due from customers totaled $4,000, but by month-end they totaled $5,000.

4-9. Net Cash Flow and Net Operating Income Contrasted.   George Craft owns and operates a boardinghouse near a large university. He started the business two years ago when he leased a large old house for $3,600 per year payable one-half on January 1 and one-half on July 1 of each year. The house accommodates fifteen students for both room and board at a monthly rate of $100 each and provides meals only to another ten students for $60 per month each. To establish his venture, Mr. Craft had to buy both furniture and food preparation equipment. The furniture cost $3,600 two years ago, and he estimates that it will last no more than a total of six years. The food preparation equipment cost a total of $3,000, and he estimates this equipment will have to be replaced every five years.

During May of this year, he made food purchases of $970 on account and paid for April's purchases totaling $1,060. He estimated he had $240 worth of food on hand at the end of April and $190 worth of food on hand at the end of May. He employs one person who handles both cleaning and meal preparation for a salary of $650 per month. Heat, light, and other miscellaneous expenses for May totaled $73.

Mr. Craft is currently reevaluating the profitability of his investment. He is unsure whether to measure it on the basis of net cash flows or net operating income.

Required:

1. Prepare a statement of net cash flows for May for Mr. Craft's venture.

2. Prepare a conventional accounting income statement for May.

3. Which is the better performance measurement (i.e., which is a better indicator of the long-run cash-generating ability of the venture)? Explain.

4-10. Net Operating Income and Net Cash Flow Contrasted.   Diver Supply Company was recently formed by Tim Wilson to manufacture a new kind of "wet suit" for skin divers. In its first month of operation, the firm was involved in the following transactions:

April	1	Tim invested $10,000 cash in the business.
April	1	Purchased wet suit material on account for $1,700. The account must be paid by May 10.
April	1	Hired two part-time employees to assemble wet suits at a salary of $200 each per month.
April	2	Purchased equipment for manufacture of the wet suits. He paid $7,200 for the equipment.
April	5	Signed an agreement with a local sporting goods store to supply wet suits for April and May delivery (one-half delivered each month). The total selling price was $3,600, $1,000 of which was paid at the time of the order, the remainder to be paid at the end of May.
April	30	Paid employees for month of April. Counted inventory and found there was $700 worth of material still unused. Delivered one-half of the wet suit order as scheduled.

Required:

Assuming that the equipment has a three-year life with no salvage value, that no additional materials were purchased in April, and that he had no finished wet suits in inventory at the end of April:

1. Prepare a cash-flow statement for the month of April.

2. Prepare a conventional accounting income statement for the month of April.

3. Compare the two statements. Which do you think is a better performance measurement? Explain.

4-11. The Matching Principle—Small Business Transactions.   The Custom Sign Company is a sole proprietorship started by John Smythe during March of this year. The principal activity of the business is construction and painting of exterior signs for commercial establishments according to customer specifications.

When the business was started, Mr. Smythe opened a checking account in the name of the business. Until now, he has been evaluating his monthly performance by the monthly increase (decrease) in the balance of the firm's checking account. However, he realizes that net cash flow is not the only measure of performance and that net cash flow does not take into account the usage of equipment and services that were paid for in prior months. He has therefore decided to use conventional accounting operating income as a measure of monthly performance.

At the end of the current month (September), he is concerned with properly determining and measuring the expenses of the month. Since he has no credit customers, he feels that cash receipts (collected at the time signs are completed) are a fair measure of revenue.

Some of the notes that Mr. Smythe has made to himself include the following information:

a. On March 1, he purchased a used heavy-duty pickup truck for $2,700. He estimated that the pickup would last for five years and that he could sell it for $300 at the end of the fifth year.

b. Immediately after the purchase of the pickup, he purchased a portable gasoline-powered generator and installed it in the pickup for use in on-site sign construction and painting. The total cost of the generator was $1,200. He estimated the life of the generator to be eight years and the salvage value to be $240.

c. Other equipment purchases on March 1 totaled $540. The estimated life at the time of purchase was three years (no salvage value).

d. At the same time he purchased the truck (March 1), he paid for the city and state licenses required to operate a commercial business. The cost of the licenses totaled $40, and the licenses expire on October 31.

e. Mr. Smythe acquired an insurance policy (truck, fire, casualty, and liability) effective March 1. The policy is for a three-year period, with prepayments of annual premiums on March 1. The annual premium for the first year is $480.

f. Mr. Smythe rented a small building on April 1 for the storage of materials and equipment and for off-site sign construction and painting. The rental is $100 per month, with prepayments of three months' rent due every three months. He prepaid three months' rent on April 1 and July 1.

g. Gasoline for the pickup and generator is purchased using a credit card. During the current month he purchased $80 worth of gasoline using the credit card. He also paid an oil company statement (for gasoline purchased in prior months) for $120.

h. He purchased $750 worth of sign materials (lumber, paint, etc.) during the month. He estimated the cost of the materials on hand at the beginning and the end of the month to be $200 and $150, respectively.

i. He withdrew $450 at the end of August to pay for his estimated September personal expenses and withdrew $500 at the end of September for his estimated October personal expenses.

Required:

1. Using the matching principle, what are the September expenses for the Custom Sign Company? Explain your reasoning for each item included or excluded.

2. Which of the September expenses might be classified as products costs? Which are period costs?

4-12.   Cash Flows and Conventional Accounting Income.   Mary Morton owns and operates a photography shop which specializes in pictures for special occasions. She started the business last year when she leased an old house which could be converted into a studio. The rental on the house is $2,400 per year, with advance quarterly payments due on the first of January, April, July, and October. The lease is renewable on an annual basis for up to five years. At the end of five years, the lease may be canceled or renegotiated.

Before she could begin operations, Ms. Morton had to convert the interior of the house to a studio, purchase furniture and fixtures, and purchase photography equipment. The leasehold improvements (cost to convert interior to a studio) cost $1,800. If the lease is canceled at the end of the five-year lease period, the leasehold improvements belong to the owner of the house. The cost of furniture and fixtures was $4,800. Ms. Morton estimated that the useful life of the furniture and fixtures would be eight years and that the salvage value would be negligible. The photography equipment cost $2,700. The estimated life of the equipment is ten years, but Ms. Morton plans on trading in all equipment for new equipment every three years. She estimates that the trade-in value at the end of three years will be one-third of the original purchase price.

During April of this year, she purchased $600 worth of film and other photography supplies on account and paid all the outstanding statements for prior months' purchases in the amount of $400. She estimated that she had $200 and $300 worth of photography supplies on hand at the beginning and the end of the month, respectively.

Ms. Morton bills customers after they have ordered photographs from the proofs. During the current month, she billed customers in the amount of $2,800. She collected $2,700 from customers during the month.

Ms. Morton employs an assistant who aids in studio photography, acts as secretary-receptionist, and keeps books on a cash basis. Her salary is $700 per month. Miscellaneous expenses (including utilities) totaled $100 for April and were paid for in April. Ms. Morton withdrew $500 for personal expenses at the end of the month.

In prior months Ms. Morton had not tried to measure the profitability of the business, since she had no cash problems. However, she now anticipates a rise in the price of film and other photography supplies of approximately 10 percent, and she plans to raise the salary of her assistant to $750 in the near future. Therefore she is wondering how much effect the expected cost increases will have on profitability and whether or not she should revise her price schedules. She also is unsure whether to measure performance on the basis of cash flows or operating income.

Required:

1. Prepare a performance statement for April based upon net cash flow as a measure of performance.

2. Prepare a conventional accounting income statement for April.

3. Which is the better profitability measure (i.e., which is the better indicator of long-run cash-generating ability)? Why?

5

Conventional Accounting:
Framework, Recognition of
Economic Events,
and Periodic Statements

In Chapter 4 conventional accounting performance measurement was introduced. Conventional accounting also includes a well-developed framework within which periodic determination of net operating income is accomplished. There are two (perhaps more) important reasons for the development and use of such a framework.

First, periodic income determination uses data from economic events very selectively, often requiring that information about events be recorded at the time of their occurrence for use in income determination in later periods. For instance, during a particular year a significant resource like a piece of heavy equipment may be acquired by the enterprise but not put into use immediately. Hence no expense is recognized in the current period with respect to that resource. But its cost (purchase price) needs to be recorded at the time of purchase for use in later periods to recognize the expense associated with its use in production as the products it helps to produce are sold.

Second, many economic events to which the enterprise is party, but which do not affect income determination in the period in which they take place, are of economic significance themselves—quite apart from their significance in later income determination. The piece of equipment mentioned above is a good example. Its mere possession by the enterprise may be a significant clue to future productivity—a supplement to current net operating income data in projecting the future cash flows of the enterprise. Similarly, payment of cash to discharge a loan that was originally used to finance the purchase of productive resources may prove helpful in assessing the ability of the enterprise to satisfy its creditors and therefore its ability to borrow additional funds in the future. Finally, the receipt of cash from customers for sales already included in revenues of prior periods may be significant affirmative evidence that recognition of revenue at the time of sale is not unwarranted in light of experience with collections.

At any rate, conventional accounting includes a *framework* which facilitates the determination of net operating income and which, when reported along with net operating income, conveys additional information about the enterprise's status and activities. That framework is called *financial position*. It consists of several broad classes of elements known as *assets, liabilities,* and *owners' equity*.

Building the Framework—Assets and Liabilities Defined

Until now, we have avoided much of the traditional vocabulary of accounting or have used it in the very loose way that many of its terms are often used by nonaccountants. The term *asset* is one that we have largely avoided. Now we will be more precise.

Assets. Assets are resources (rights or possessions) to which an accounting entity is legally entitled and which are expected to produce future benefits.

Example 5-1　Examples of assets are easy to find, but it is important to remember that assets include nonphysical rights to benefits as well as physical possessions that can be used to produce benefits. Thus assets include such things as:

1. Cash
2. Copyrights and patents
3. Buildings
4. Equipment
5. Autos, trucks, buses
6. Amounts due from others for products sold to them

Roughly speaking, *liabilities* are the opposite of assets. But they can be more precisely defined as follows:

Liabilities. Liabilities are obligations of the accounting entity to provide cash or other benefits to some other economic unit at some future time.

Example 5-2　As with assets, examples of liabilities are easy to conceive. But, again, the less clearly defined obligations must be included along with more obvious obligations. Thus liabilities include such things as:

1. Amounts due suppliers for items delivered, for which payment has been deferred
2. Unpaid wages and salaries for work already performed
3. The services that may eventually have to be performed under terms of warranties given with products sold
4. A mortgage note on a building or equipment

Valuation of Assets and Liabilities
in Conventional Accounting

The above definitions of assets and liabilities are not strictly unique to conventional accounting. They are common to a number of possible financial accounting models of the business enterprise, including conventional accounting and several others, to be discussed in Chapters 7, 8, and 9. One of the principal things that distinguishes one accounting model from another, however, is the way that assets and liabilities are valued in each.

In the discussion in Chapter 3 entitled "Present Value and the Concept of Wealth," we defined *valuation* as the measurement (quantification) of wealth in money terms. Applying present value methodology, we value any given asset or liability by assigning to it an amount equal to the present value of the future cash flows expected to be received or paid. Under conventional accounting, assets and liabilities are also assigned money values. The basis for assigning the values, however, depends on whether the item being valued is a "monetary" or a "nonmonetary" asset or liability.

Monetary Assets and Liabilities. Monetary assets include cash plus all assets consisting of rights to *receive fixed amounts of dollars at future times*. Monetary liabilities are all obligations to pay fixed amounts of dollars at future times. Monetary assets and liabilities consist of such things as:

Monetary Assets	*Monetary Liabilities*
1. Cash	1. Amounts payable to suppliers
2. Savings deposits	2. Wages due employees
3. Amounts owing from customers for products delivered or services rendered	3. Taxes owed to government units

Nonmonetary Assets and Liabilities. Nonmonetary assets and liabilities, as the label implies, are all assets and liabilities other than monetary assets and liabilities. Nonmonetary assets and liabilities consist of such things as:

Nonmonetary Assets	*Nonmonetary Liabilities*
1. Raw materials on hand	1. Obligations to deliver products in the future (usually for which payment has been received)
2. Equipment	
3. Buildings	
4. Land	2. Obligations to perform services (for which payment has been received)
5. Copyrights, patents, etc.	

• *Valuing monetary assets and liabilities.* Because monetary assets and liabilities consist of cash and claims to specific amounts of cash, it is typically relatively easy to value them. For instance, most people would agree that a promise to pay $100 with virtual certainty tomorrow or next week is worth roughly the same as $100 possessed today. The exceptions, of course, are the monetary assets (liabilities) calling for uncertain receipt (payment) of cash in the more distant future, thereby making risk and the time value of money significant factors in their value. Such cases are discussed in some detail in the context of conventional accounting in Chapters 11 and 13. For the present, we ignore time value of money and risk in introducing conventional accounting valuation.

Thus, when we refer to monetary assets and liabilities in this discussion, we are concerned only with cash and amounts that are collectible or payable in the near future (a month or two, at most) with virtual certainty. Most such monetary assets are received in exchange for the products or services sold by the enterprise. Most such monetary liabilities are owed to suppliers of resources used in the business. *In conventional accounting most short-term monetary assets (liabilities) are valued at their nominal amounts, that is, the specified amounts to be received (paid).* In most cases of short-term monetary assets, the amount to be received (from, say, a customer) is also equal to the cash or its equivalent in products or services given in exchange for the (customer's) promise to pay. Similarly, in most transactions giving rise to a short-term monetary liability, the amount to be paid is equal to the cash or its equivalent in goods and services received in exchange for the liability.

Example 5-3 Suppose an enterprise provides services for two different customers. One pays $1,000 in cash; the other receives services worth $2,000 and pays the $2,000 before the end of the month. The enterprise would recognize the new monetary assets at the amounts received or to be received, namely, cash of $1,000 and "accounts receivable" of $2,000.

Example 5-4 Suppose an enterprise receives supplies worth $3,000 from a supplier and incurs an obligation to pay the $3,000 in thirty days. The liability "accounts payable" is valued at the amount agreed to be paid, $3,000.

• *Valuing nonmonetary assets and liabilities.* Relative to monetary assets (liabilities), nonmonetary assets (liabilities) are typically more difficult to value. The benefits to be derived from nonmonetary assets are determined by how they are used to produce future cash flows. If a nonmonetary asset is held for sale, the benefits from its possession depend on the price it will bring at the time of eventual sale. If a nonmonetary asset is held for use in the business, the benefits from its possession depend on the amounts of products and services it can be used to produce and the prices they will bring. To directly value nonmonetary assets (liabilities), therefore, requires the kind of forecasts of highly uncertain future cash flows that conventional accounting is supposed to avoid. Thus, direct valuation of nonmonetary assets is usually avoided in conventional accounting. *Under conventional accounting a nonmonetary asset is valued at an amount equal to the cash plus monetary assets (or liabilities) given in exchange for it.* This is justified on two grounds.

First, in most transactions in which the enterprise acquires nonmonetary assets, it gives up strictly cash and other monetary assets or liabilities in exchange. Second, it is presumed that if an economic entity is behaving rationally, then the value of what it receives in a given exchange transaction must be worth at least as much as the value of what it gives up in return. It is therefore both convenient and sensible to value the nonmonetary assets acquired at the amounts of monetary assets and liabilities given to acquire them.

Example 5-5   Suppose a retail business acquired merchandise for resale in its stores. In exchange for the goods delivered, it paid $500 at delivery and agreed to pay $1,500 at the end of the following month. The nonmonetary asset acquired, namely, "merchandise," is valued at $2,000, the sum of the monetary assets given (cash) plus the monetary liabilities incurred (accounts payable) in exchange for it.

The reader should be aware that most, but not all, nonmonetary assets are acquired in exchange for cash plus other monetary assets or liabilities. Some are acquired in exchange for other nonmonetary assets. Such cases present greater valuation problems for accountants. Although the additional problems are not insurmountable, they do introduce complexities that are best avoided at the outset. Hence, they too—along with the time and uncertainty dimensions in valuing monetary assets—are postponed to later chapters.

Conventional Accounting Valuation— General Comments

To summarize the above discussion of conventional accounting valuation, it can be said that assets and liabilities are initially valued at their "original transaction values."

> **Original Transaction Value.** The original transaction value of an asset or a liability is the value established in the exchange(s) in which the asset was acquired or the liability incurred. Usually such exchange values are determined by the amounts of monetary items given, promised, received, or to be received, depending on the circumstances.

This general statement, although somewhat abstract, is convenient because it embraces both nonmonetary and monetary assets and liabilities. As a result, the term *original transaction value* (or the more customary *historical value*) can be used to represent conventional accounting valuation in general. Incidentally, when the idea of original transaction value is applied only to non-monetary assets, the term *original transaction cost* (or *historical cost*) is used.

The reader should recognize that although an asset is initially valued at its original transaction value (cost) in conventional accounting, the asset may not persist in being valued at its full initial cost as time passes. In the case of a nonmonetary asset that is used in production, portions of its cost will be recognized as expense in periods in which products that it has been used to produce are sold. Each time a portion of an asset's original transaction cost is recognized as an expense, its remaining recognized value to the enterprise is reduced by that amount, as is illustrated later. Not surprisingly, a recognized expense is often described simply as an *expired cost,* referring to the idea that expenses are portions of the original costs of assets proportionate to the amount of the asset that has been used up or has expired. Similarly, the value of an asset at a point in time (and sometimes the asset itself) is often referred to as an *unexpired cost,* or a *potential expense.*

Completing the Framework—Owners' Equity; Financial Position

The owners' equity of a business enterprise is an abstraction or concept, based on the roughly opposite economic implications of assets and liabilities. This is summarized in the definition that follows:

> **Owners' Equity.** Owners' equity represents the owners' residual interest in, or rights to, the future (cash) benefits from the enterprise, in excess of what is required to satisfy the enterprise's liabilities.

• *Valuation of owners' equity.* Owners' equity is not valued or measured directly. At any given point in time, total owners' equity is valued at the amount by which the values placed on all assets exceed the values placed on all liabilities. In other words:

The value of owners' equity equals the sum of the values assigned to all the assets of the enterprise minus the sum of the values assigned to its liabilities —which is usually simplified to: Owners' equity = Assets − Liabilities.

• *Financial position defined.* Defining assets, liabilities, and owners' equity brings us to a final important definition in building the framework for conventional accounting.

> **Financial Position.** Financial position is the financial status of the enterprise, consisting of the values assigned to its assets, liabilities, and owners' equity, as of a moment in time.

• *The accounting equation.* Because of the way that owners' equity is valued, financial position always satisfies the relationship implied in the following equation, called the basic accounting equation:

$$\text{ASSETS} = \text{LIABILITIES} + \text{OWNERS' EQUITY}$$

Interestingly, this equation, in expanded form, can be used as a clerical device to represent an enterprise's status as of a point in time. It also serves as a framework within which to recognize its performance for a period of time.

Applying Conventional Accounting Concepts within the Framework

Let us now return to the case of the ice cream parlor introduced in Example 4-3. We will trace the ice cream parlor's economic status (financial position) through the first month of operations, relying on the definitions and

relations developed in the preceding discussion and using the basic accounting equation as a clerical (bookkeeping) device.

• *Original investment in an enterprise.* Recall that the first event in the
history of the ice cream parlor was the investment of cash of $7,500. The
effect of that event on the ice cream parlor's financial position can be represented as follows:

$$\text{ASSETS} = \text{LIABILITIES} + \text{OWNER'S EQUITY}$$
$$\$7,500 = \quad -0- \quad + \quad \$7,500$$

The investment has put $7,500 of monetary assets in the form of cash under
the control of the business. Since no liabilities now exist, owner's equity equals
total assets.

• *Acquiring an asset.* Let us now consider the next event in the life of the
business, the purchase of equipment for $6,000. To recognize this event we
need to take advantage of the clerical convenience of the financial position
equation. That is, we need to expand it to include more detailed elements of
financial position, or "accounts," as elements of financial position are customarily called. In this case we need only expand the assets class to handle
the event involving two kinds of assets, cash and equipment. Just before the
purchase of the equipment, we can think of the financial position of the business as follows:

$$\text{CASH} + \text{EQUIPMENT} = \text{LIABILITIES} + \text{OWNER'S EQUITY}$$
$$\$7,500 + \quad -0- \quad = \quad -0- \quad + \quad \$7,500$$

This represents no substantive change from the earlier representation, since
the amount of total assets is the sum of all the individual asset values. But
now we can represent the change in the enterprise's status that has resulted
from the purchase of equipment as shown in Exhibit 5-1.

Exhibit 5-1	Cash	+ Equipment =	Liabilities	+ Owner's Equity
ORIGINAL POSITION	$7,500 +	—0— =	—0— +	$7,500
Event: Purchase of equipment	($6,000)	$6,000		
NEW POSITION	$1,500 +	$6,000 =	—0— +	$7,500

What we have done is start with an initial position, then recognize an event
(the purchase), and finally arrive at a new position incorporating the effect
of the event. Notice that the "event" line simply indicates that the purchase
results in a decrease in cash of $6,000 (denoted by the parentheses around
the $6,000 in the Cash column) and an increase in another asset, equipment,
in the same amount. When the elements of the event line are added (algebraically) to the prior total of their respective accounts, the result is a new
financial position different from the original position and *reflecting the occurrence of the event.*

Several additional observations can be made at this time about the procedure illustrated in Exhibit 5-1. First, the "original position" satisfies the equality condition of the basic financial position equation—the total of the assets equals the total liabilities plus total owner's equity. Second, the "event" line also satisfies the equality condition—it represents offsetting plus and minus elements to only the *assets* side of the equation, which means that the equality condition is not disturbed. Third, as a result of these first two observations, the "new position" line also satisfies the equality condition. The total assets (cash of $1,500 plus equipment of $6,000) equal the sum of the liabilities (zero) and owner's equity ($7,500).

Finally, it probably seems sensible that the mere acquisition of one asset for another (cash for equipment) does not increase owner's equity. In conventional accounting this is generally the case. Remember that in conventional accounting nonmonetary assets are valued at their original transaction cost to the enterprise. Hence, in recognizing the purchase of the equipment, the value assigned to the equipment must equal the value of the assets given up (in this case $6,000 in cash). With no change in total assets (or liabilities in this case), there simply can be no change in owner's equity recognized from such an exchange.

• *Prepaying for a service or benefit.* Now consider the second event of interest in tracing the ice cream parlor through its first month of operations, the payment of three months' rent totaling $600. Before we consider how to recognize the effect of this event on financial position, a further point needs clarification. Prepaid rent conforms to the definition of an asset given earlier. Upon prepayment of rent, the enterprise has a right to occupy a building that can be used to produce goods and services and therefore contribute to future cash inflows to the enterprise. So in prepaying rent, the enterprise gives up one asset—cash—and receives another asset—the right to occupancy (customarily we call this asset "prepaid rent"). Since the prepayment of rent is an exchange of an asset for an asset, it has an effect on financial position similar to the effect of the purchase of equipment. That effect along with the purchase of equipment is represented in Exhibit 5-2.

Exhibit 5-2	Cash	+ Equipment +	Prepaid Rent	=	Liabilities	+	Owner's Equity
ORIGINAL POSITION	$7,500 +	—0—	+ —0— =		—0—	+	$7,500
Event 1: Purchase of equipment	($6,000)	$6,000					
Event 2: Prepayment of rent	($ 600)		$600				
NEW POSITION	$ 900 +	$6,000	+ $600	=	—0—	+	$7,500

Again notice that no change in liabilities has taken place and no change in owner's equity is recognized. Also notice that both the additional event line and the new position line again conform to the equality condition. In the new position, *assets* (cash of $900, equipment of $6,000, and prepaid rent of $600) add up to the same total as *liabilities* (still zero) plus *owner's equity* ($7,500).

• *Cumulative effect of events on financial position.* Finally, notice that the new position shown in Exhibit 5-1, after only the equipment purchase had taken place, has been dropped from the worksheet in Exhibit 5-2. This does not change the result from what it would be if we calculated the new financial position after the equipment purchase first, and then modified *that* position further for the prepayment of rent. Furthermore, in practice it is both tedious and unnecessary to recalculate a new financial position after each event. Thus, all of the events for a particular period of time are recorded in a manner analogous to the "events" lines we have used above. Then, at the end of a typical accounting period, each account is adjusted for the *cumulative effect* of all events affecting the account. This is illustrated in Exhibit 5-2 with respect to the cash account, the only account affected by more than one event so far. The new position of $900 results from subtracting the two reductions of $6,000 and $600 (or a total of $6,600) from the original position of $7,500.

• *Recognizing all of the events of an accounting period—a financial position worksheet.* We now shift away from the introductory practice of finding a new position after each event in the example. Instead, we will consider the effects of all events of the first month's operations on one worksheet. A new financial position is computed as of the end of the month, taking account of all the events of the month at once—as would likely be done in practice. Exhibit 5-3 represents the worksheet for the month of August. Each event line is numbered and will be discussed below with the exception of numbers 1 and 2, which are the now-familiar equipment purchase and rent prepayment events.

The reader will notice that there are a few differences in form between the expanded worksheet in Exhibit 5-3 and the earlier forms in Exhibits 5-1 and 5-2. First, there are a few more headings because as we consider more types of events, we need the greater descriptive power of a more detailed financial position equation. Second, there is a double vertical line separating the assets from the liabilities and owner's equity (the claims to assets). This is nonessential but serves as a reminder of the location of the "equals" sign in the financial position equation and also reminds us that as we recognize each event we should leave the equality condition undisturbed. Some of the other unfamiliar features of this expanded worksheet are explained as we discuss the treatment of individual events below.

Recognition of External Events, or "Transactions"

Many "events," as we have been calling them, that affect the financial status of the enterprise are exchange transactions between the enterprise and other economic entities. For obvious reasons, such events are referred to as *external events,* or *transactions*. Besides the equipment purchase and prepayment of rent, lines 3 through 10 on the worksheet also represent the effects on financial position of transactions engaged in by the ice cream parlor. Discussion of these events follows.

Exhibit 5-3

ICE CREAM PARLOR
Financial Position Worksheet

Description	Cash +	Accounts Receivable +	Prepaid Rent +	Ice Cream +	Supplies +	Equipment +	Accumulated Depreciation =	Wages and Accounts Payable +	Owner's Equity
Original Position	7,500								7,500
1. Purchase of equipment	(6,000)					6,000			
2. Prepayment of rent	(600)		600						
3. Purchase of supplies	(200)				200				
4. Purchase of ice cream				300				300	
5. Additional ice-cream purchases				1,350				1,350	
6. Payments for ice cream purchased	(1,300)							(1,300)	
7. Additional supplies purchased					100			100	
8. Sales	4,000	500							4,500 (R)
9. Miscellaneous expenses paid	(100)								(100) (E)
10. Payment of salaries and wages	(1,200)							300	(1,500) (E)
11. Cost of ice cream sold				(1,450)					(1,450) (E)
12. Cost of supplies used					(150)				(150) (E)
13. Recognition of expired rent			(200)						(200) (E)
14. Recognition of equipment depreciation							(100)		(100) (E)
New Position	2,100 +	500 +	400 +	200 +	150 +	6,000 +	(100) =	750 +	8,500

• *Purchase of supplies for cash* (*line 3*). At the beginning of its first month the enterprise purchased supplies for $200 cash. In purchasing supplies for cash, the enterprise decreased its level of cash by $200 as indicated by the "(200)" in the Cash column of line 3 and established a stock of supplies that it will value at the "original transaction cost" of $200 as indicated by the "200" in the Supplies column of line 3. Again, the effect on *total* assets is zero; one type of asset has replaced another of equal amount.

• *Purchase of merchandise on account* (*line 4*). Also as part of its starting-up activities, the enterprise purchased $300 worth of ice cream. But rather than paying cash immediately, the enterprise was able to postpone payment until delivery of the second order of ice cream. Hence the enterprise incurred a liability by exchanging a promise to pay (an obligation) for an asset, ice cream. When an enterprise promises to pay one of its regular suppliers (like the ice cream vendor) for goods delivered, we usually refer to the liability as an *account payable*. Thus line 4 contains a "300" item in the Ice Cream column and an identical "300" item in the Wages and Accounts Payable column, recognizing an increase in both assets and liabilities (again, no change in owner's equity).

• *Additional merchandise purchases* (*line 5*). The original statement of the facts in Example 4-3 indicated that the total ice cream purchases for August amounted to $1,650, including the first purchase of $300 recognized on line 4. This means that another $1,350 was purchased beyond that already recognized in Exhibit 5-3. Thus line 5 shows a *further* increase in the stock of ice cream of $1,350 and an additional increase in the obligation to pay the ice cream supplier. Here we are using a *summary event* to represent probably three additional weekly deliveries of ice cream after the initial delivery but before the end of the month. To be completely descriptive, we should recognize each of the additional purchases on a separate line in the worksheet. But the final effect on financial position of recognizing several different purchases totaling $1,350 is exactly the same as one purchase for the whole $1,350. So we take advantage here of the summary transaction to eliminate unnecessary detail.

Similarly, as each new delivery was made, presumably the prior purchase was paid for in cash, eliminating the prior liability and establishing an obligation to pay for the new delivery in its place. But none of these timing differences is important as long as we do not calculate a new financial position before we have recognized the effects of all the events or transactions that affect the account in question. Note that all the individual August cash payments for ice cream deliveries are recognized in one summary transaction on line 6 of Exhibit 5-3.

• *Payments for prior purchases* (*line 6*). Example 4-3 indicated that of all of the ice cream deliveries received in August, only the last, in the amount of $350, had not been paid for by the end of the month. Hence, $1,300 of the total $1,650 ice cream deliveries was paid during the month. Line 6 represents the effect on financial position of a summary transaction in which cash of $1,300 was paid to reduce the obligation to pay the ice cream supplier by $1,300. Notice that no change is recognized in the stock of ice cream as a result of paying the supplier for ice cream already delivered and recognized.

• *Additional supplies purchased* (*line 7*). Before the end of the month an additional $100 purchase of supplies was made "on account," that is, with a promise to pay the supplier. Hence the line 7 treatment of the second supplies purchase is the same as the purchases of ice cream "on account" recognized on lines 4 and 5. The Supplies column contains an increase of $100 with a matching increase in the liability, accounts payable.

Revenue Recognition within the Financial Position Framework

Before moving to an explanation of line 8 of Exhibit 5-3, it is appropriate that we develop for the reader the relationship between the concepts involved in conventional accounting performance measurement and the framework of financial position. The first relationship, which is illustrated on line 8 of Exhibit 5-3, is the relationship between the revenue of an enterprise and the changes in financial position that are implied by its recognition.

When an enterprise provides products and services to customers in a period, there is an infusion of new assets in the form of cash or promises to pay from customers. The reader will recall that the amount of revenue (or accomplishment) recognized for the period is the total amount of this inflow of resources, that is, the total prices paid or agreed to be paid by customers for products and services provided. Now consider the effect of sales of products and services (revenue) on financial position.

When the enterprise provides a product to a customer for cash or a promise to pay, the enterprise gains a new asset. But since no new obligation (liability) arises, the increase in assets is matched by an equal increase in owner's equity. Owner's equity is defined in such a way that this is always true. (Recall that Owner's Equity = Assets − Liabilities.) But it is also intuitively sensible. Revenue is the measure of accomplishment of the enterprise. And accomplishments should improve the owner's position or interest in the enterprise provided the enterprise is recognizing and meeting its obligations (liabilities). If products are provided and no new obligations are incurred, any increase in assets increases the owner's interests in the enterprise. So revenue is recognized as an increase in owner's equity at the same time (in the same period) that we recognize increases in cash and promises to pay (referred to as accounts receivable) from sales to customers. This is illustrated on line 8 of Exhibit 5-3.

• *Revenue recognition* (*line 8*). Example 4-3 indicated that the ice cream parlor's sales of ice cream cones for cash during its first month came to $4,000. Sales of banquet desserts on credit came to $500, none of which had been collected as of the end of the month. Thus there has been an increase in cash of $4,000 and an increase in another monetary asset, accounts receivable, valued at $500. Furthermore, according to the realization principle, all actual sales, whether made for cash or for customers' promises to pay, are recognized as revenue during the period. And, as mentioned above, revenue by itself is recognized as an increase in owner's equity. Line 8 indicates an increase in cash of $4,000, an increase in accounts receivable of $500, and a total increase in owner's equity of $4,500. The (*R*) notation on the worksheet next to the 4,500 in the Owner's Equity column is to distinguish this increase due to revenue from other possible increases in owner's equity like an additional investment of assets. No other types of increases actually take place in the first month of the ice cream parlor's operations, but the notation will later help the reader in more complicated problems.

Expense Recognition within the Financial Position Framework

If we were to draw a line below line 8 of the worksheet and compute a new financial position recognizing revenue but omitting the related expenses, the result would be nonsense. In describing revenue as the increase in owner's equity due to recognized productive accomplishment for a period, we must bear in mind that some sacrifice is always involved in providing products and services to customers. So the effect of the operating performance of a period on the financial position of the enterprise is not complete unless both revenue and expenses are recognized.

The matching principle calls for the recognition, in the period in which products are sold (and revenue is recognized), of the resource sacrifices that were made to produce the products and provide them to customers. Thus the recognition of expense means a recognition of decreases in the amounts of various kinds of assets controlled by the enterprise. Since the assets were sacrificed, not to decrease the liabilities of the enterprise but to produce products, there is no offsetting decrease in liabilities. Rather, a decrease in owner's equity in the amount of total expenses is recognized at the same time that the expense-related reductions of various types of assets are recognized. Lines 9 through 14 of Exhibit 5-3 are illustrative of expense recognition. Since the reasoning behind each item of expense of the ice cream parlor for August was covered in Chapter 4, we will mainly concern ourselves here with the changes in financial position that relate to the recognition of each expense item.

• *Miscellaneous expense (line 9).* One hundred dollars in cash was paid during August by the ice cream parlor in miscellaneous types of expenditures (heat, light, power, etc.). Thus on line 9 of the worksheet we recognize a $100 decrease in cash to recognize the expenditure of some of that resource. Since the facts of the problem as stated in Example 4-3 were silent about any association between the $100 expenditure and revenues (sales) of future periods, we consider the whole $100 an expense of the current period, August. Thus on line 9 a decrease in owner's equity of $100 is recognized and labeled (*E*) for expense.

• *Salaries and wages, paid and accrued (line 10).* The $1,200 wages and salaries actually paid to employees during August constitute resource sacrifices made during the month to provide the ice cream to customers, resulting in the month's recognized revenue. Unless some of the labor paid for during the month can be related to products or services of future periods, all of the $1,200 should be matched against current revenue, that is, all of the $1,200 should be recognized as expense in August.

In addition to the $1,200 in cash paid to employees for salaries and wages earned, another $300 was earned by employees during August but not yet paid by August 31. Unless those $300 in wages and salaries clearly relate to revenues of September or later months, the matching principle requires that they too be matched against August revenue as expense. So on line 10 of the worksheet we recognize not only a decrease in cash for wages paid of $1,200 but also an increase in a liability (as of August 31) of $300 of wages payable (in the Wages and Accounts Payable column). The total salary and wages expense recognized for the month of $1,500 appears appropriately as a decrease to owner's equity.

• *Accrual accounting.* The treatment of wages, as yet unpaid, as an expense of the period, is another example of the contrast between conventional accounting performance measurement and net cash flow. In this case, the sacrifice of a resource (labor) is recognized in a period before cash is expended, whereas in the case of such long-lived assets as plant and equipment, the cash expenditure is often made first, followed by many periods of recognized sacrifice as the resource is used up in the production of revenue. In practice, many expenditures are made in periods after the period in which resources or services are used and matched against revenue. This requires the recognition in the earlier periods of obligations to eventually pay for the services consumed, such as the wages payable in the case at hand. Such obligations are sometimes referred to as *accruals* or *accrued liabilities,* from which one of the synonyms for conventional accounting derives—*accrual accounting.*

Recognizing Internal Events

With the recognition of salaries and wages expense for August, we have exhausted the set of transactions that the ice cream parlor engaged in during its first month of operations. We are now ready to consider the effects on financial position of what we will describe as *internal events,* after which we will be in a position to view the overall effects of the enterprise's operations, particularly its net operating income, on financial position.

Unlike the first ten events (or summary events) in the first month's history of the ice cream parlor, the last four events that are recognized in Exhibit 5-3 do not come to our attention as a result of new transactions with economic units outside the enterprise. Rather they are changes in the components of financial position that are evidenced largely by observation of events within the enterprise. Most, but not necessarily all, of these internal observations have to do with the physical sacrifice of resources experienced in the production of the revenue recognized. Recall that because of the realization principle, revenue is generally recognized in connection with an external transaction of the current period, that is, a sale of a product to a customer. But only sometimes is an expense evidenced by an external transaction *of the current period,* such as the wages, salaries, and miscellaneous expenses in the ice cream parlor example. In many cases expense recognition is a matter of determining how much of an asset's original transaction cost should be recognized as an expense in a period some time after the asset was acquired in an external transaction. This is what we do, based on the facts in the ice cream parlor example, on lines 11 through 14 of Exhibit 5-3.

• *Merchandise used* (*line 11*). It was noted in Example 4-3 that, of all the ice cream purchased during the month of August, $200 worth was still in the freezers at the end of the month. Since $1,650 was purchased (received) in total, this means that $1,450 was either wasted or consumed by employees, or conveyed to customers in return for their cash and promises to pay. In any case, the internal observation that $200 worth remains tells us that a total sacrifice (expense) of ice cream worth $1,450 was made to generate the month's sales revenue of $4,500. That amount ($1,450) is therefore recognized as a reduction in the stock of ice cream with a matching reduction in owner's equity (with an expense designation) on line 11 of Exhibit 5-3.

• *Supplies used* (*line 12*). Similar reasoning applies to the recognition of the original cost of supplies used. The internal observation that, of all supplies purchased during the month, $150 worth remains to be used tells us that $150 were used up during August and their cost should be matched against August revenues as an expense. This reasoning is recognized by a decrease in supplies of $150 and a matching decrease in owner's equity of $150, on line 12.

• *Expired rent* (*line 13*). On line 2 we recognized that at the beginning of the month, upon payment of three months' rent in advance, the enterprise had exchanged one asset, cash, for another, the right to occupancy. But as of the end of the month, one-third of the total occupancy rights have expired. On line 13 we recognize a one-third reduction in the asset of $200, along with a concurrent $200 reduction in owner's equity for rent expense.

• *Depreciation of equipment* (*line 14*). Earlier discussion of the net cash-flow method of measuring performance brought out that the total cost of the equipment purchased at the beginning of August should not be considered a sacrifice of doing business only in August. The equipment is expected to serve the business for five years, or sixty months. But neither is it sensible to wait until the equipment is completely worn out to recognize that its service potential has been completely consumed. Rather, in conventional accounting, some of the original cost of such long-lived assets is recognized as expense in each period of the asset's life—ideally, in proportion to the "depreciation" or decline in its service potential that is actually consumed in each period.

However, it is usually difficult to perceive how much of the service potential of an asset expires in any given short segment of its life. The usual practice is to make a so-called reasonable estimate of how long the item will last and then choose some reasonable, systematic pattern of apportioning the original cost of the asset to each of the periods in its expected life. The simplest of these patterns is called the straight-line method, in which an equal share of the original transaction cost is apportioned to each period of the life of the asset. For the sake of simplicity this method has been adopted for purposes of our example. Discussion of other, perhaps more sophisticated, methods is postponed to Chapter 12.

Using the straight-line method we apportion or allocate $100 of the cost of the equipment to the first month of operations. (Based on an estimated life of five years, or sixty months, and a total original cost of $6,000, the per-month allocation is $6,000 ÷ 60 = $100.) Line 14 therefore shows a reduction of owner's equity of $100 in the month of August and a matching reduction in a column on the asset side of the worksheet—but not the Equipment column. Rather, the reduction appears in the column headed Accumulated Depreciation. Actually, the reasons for this seeming complication are rather uncomplicated and sensible.

• *Accumulated depreciation—a contra-asset account.* First, the $100 expense recognized for use of the equipment for the month of August was based on an uncertain estimate that the equipment would last exactly sixty months—no more, no less. The amount of expense recognized is also based on the assumption that the business is what is referred to as a "going concern," that is, it will continue to operate long enough to experience all of the equipment's service-in-use potential. Either the going concern assumption or the estimate of useful life could prove to be wrong, in which case the enterprise would want to modify the effects on financial position (expense) that it has recognized based on the error. If so, it will prove convenient not to have lost track permanently of the total original transaction cost of the equipment or have to comb through old records to find it.

Second, there is the matter of portraying decision-relevant information through the statement of financial position (to be discussed more fully shortly). The financial position of an enterprise does convey information, in conjunction with net income, on which investors might base their estimates of future cash flows of the enterprise. In this sense it is often relevant to preserve and convey the original cost of long-lived assets along with depreciation-to-date, because often together they better portray the operating capacity of the assets than does the unexpired cost of the assets alone.

Example 5-6 Suppose an enterprise acquired a $1 million diesel-driven electrical power generator, expected to last twenty years and having a capacity in each year of its economic life that is twice that of a $500,000 generator. After ten years the enterprise, using the straight-line method of depreciation, will have offset a total of one-half of its original cost against revenues of the ten years, leaving an unexpired value of $500,000. If only the $500,000 is reported in the enterprise's financial position, it might be interpreted that the enterprise had a generating capacity equal to that of a $500,000 generator. In fact, though, the enterprise has a generator with twice the capacity per period of a $500,000 generator, but one that has served half of its expected useful life.

Hence, as a general rule, the total original transaction costs of long-lived assets are not directly reduced by the amounts of expense recognized in connection with their use. Instead, a separate, offsetting account, called a *contra-asset account,* is set up to recognize the reduction in use. The *accumulated depreciation* account of Exhibit 5-3 is just such an account. Its always-negative balance serves to modify the equipment account's balance. The two accounts are complementary in representing a long-lived asset and are never considered separately as components of financial position. Thus we recognize depreciation expense with a *decrease* in owner's equity of $100. At the same time, we *increase* the magnitude of the negative accumulated depreciation account by $100, which is tantamount to decreasing the equipment account itself. The difference is only a clerical convenience reflecting the tentative nature of recognizing the expiration of the cost of long-lived assets, and possibly portraying a more accurate picture of the production capacity of the enterprise resulting from possession of the asset.

End-of-Period Financial Position

We have now represented in Exhibit 5-3 the effects on various elements of financial position of each external or internal transaction of the enterprise for the month of August. It requires only a simple additional step to arrive at a new financial position. The new level of each account is found by adding to the original level all increases indicated in the column of that account and subtracting from that sum all decreases indicated in the same account.

Example 5-7   To illustrate, consider the cash account. Upon establishment of the business with the initial investment, the enterprise had a stock of $7,500 cash. During the month it experienced an inflow of cash from sales of $4,000 recognized on line 8 of Exhibit 5-3 in the Cash column. Thus $7,500 + $4,000 = $11,500 was the total available cash during the month. In addition, the enterprise experienced outflows of cash during the month represented by all the numbers in parentheses in the Cash column, each individually representing one expenditure or group of expenditures: Their total is $9,400 (6,000 + 600 + 200 + 1,200 + 1,300 + 100), which when subtracted from $11,500 gives the remaining stock of cash at the end of the month, $2,100, shown at the foot of the Cash column.

Applying the same logic to other columns gives the amounts shown as the new (or end-of-month) levels in all the other accounts as well.

Example 5-8   Starting with the initial position of zero in the stock of ice cream, we add $300 for the initial purchase from line 4 and $1,350 in additional purchases from line 5 and subtract $1,450 of ice cream consumed from line 11, leaving an end-of-month balance in the ice cream account of $200.

Why bother with the new position? The answer brings us back to the overall view of conventional accounting.

• *The relevance of financial position.* First, the $200 stock of ice cream, like the remaining stock of $400 of prepaid rent, as well as the remaining stocks of all other assets, are the original costs of resources that have not yet been consumed in the production of revenues. Thus they will be recognized as expense and matched against revenue of future periods if and when the products they are used to provide are sold to customers. The ending financial position of one period is the beginning financial position of the next period and carries forward information for future use in performance measurement.

Second, since financial position is a way of characterizing the resources (and obligations) that are in the command of the enterprise at a point in time, it is considered to have potential, in and of itself, to convey additional information to external investors about the ongoing ability of the enterprise to generate cash. This of course leads to the next consideration—that of how to represent financial position of the enterprise to interested external parties.

• *The balance sheet, or statement of financial position.* One of the primary means of conveying information about an enterprise to outside investors is through the periodic publications customarily referred to as financial statements. One of the several statements published each period is a tabular presentation of financial position which (again as a matter of custom) is often referred to as a balance sheet.

A balance sheet (or statement of financial position) is merely an organized array of the names of the components of the financial position and the amounts of their levels. The balance sheet is suitably labeled to identify (1) the enterprise, (2) the nature of the statement, and (3) the *point in time* for which the financial position is being represented. Perhaps the best way to explain the statement is by illustration. Exhibit 5-4 portrays a balance sheet for the ice cream parlor as of the end of August.

Exhibit 5-4

ICE CREAM PARLOR
Statement of Financial Position
As of August 31, 19XX

Assets:		
Cash		$2,100
Accounts receivable		500
Prepaid rent		400
Ice cream		200
Supplies		150
Equipment	$6,000	
Less accumulated depreciation	(100)	5,900
Total assets		$9,250
Liabilities and Owner's Equity:		
Wages and accounts payable		$ 750
Owner's equity		8,500
Total liabilities and owner's equity		$9,250

Notice that the two sides of the financial position equation are presented separately—all assets first, then all liabilities and owner's equity following. Notice too that their totals are equal (they balance each other). Not surprisingly, this is the reason why the term *balance sheet* is often used interchangeably with *statement of financial position.*

• *Constructing a balance sheet.* To construct a balance sheet at the end of any period is a simple matter if a worksheet has been constructed recording all the changes in financial position since the last statement date. Such is the case in the ice cream parlor example. So all that is necessary, after arriving at a new position at the foot of Exhibit 5-3, is to transfer the new level of each account to its place on the face of the balance sheet in Exhibit 5-4. The reader need only glance back at the last line of Exhibit 5-3 to confirm that each number that appears at the foot of the column of one of the accounts appears opposite that account in Exhibit 5-4.

The Statement of Income, or Results of Operations

The other statement that has traditionally been a part of the periodic accounting representation of a business enterprise is the statement of results of operations, customarily referred to as the income statement. The income statement for the ice cream parlor's August operations has already been illustrated in Chapter 4, Exhibit 4-5. We have reproduced that statement in Exhibit 5-5 for the reader's convenience, to help us make several more points about income measurement and reporting.

Exhibit 5-5

ICE CREAM PARLOR
Income Statement
For the Month of August 19XX

Revenue from sales of ice cream		$4,500
Less expenses:		
Equipment depreciation	$ 100	
Rent	200	
Supplies used	150	
Salaries and wages	1,500	
Ice cream used	1,450	
Miscellaneous heat, light, etc.	100	
Total expenses		3,500
Net operating income		$1,000

• *Constructing an income statement.* The income statement is an array or presentation of recognized revenue and expenses for a period, along with the residual, net operating income (or loss). Like the balance sheet, the income statement is usually headed by suitable labels identifying (1) the enterprise, (2) the nature of the statement, and (3) the *period* in the life of the enterprise covered by the statement.

Given a financial position worksheet, complete with respect to all events affecting financial position for a period of time, construction of an income statement is a simple mechanical process. The income statement is simply an array of the changes in owner's equity due to recognized revenues and expenses during the period. Glancing back at Exhibit 5-3, the reader will see that each of the numbers (labeled *R* or *E* for *revenue* and *expense*) appearing in the Owner's Equity column appears on the income statement opposite a description of the event (or class of events) that it represents. The total expenses are then subtracted from total revenue to get net operating income, the net result from operations and the index of performance in conventional accounting.

• *The relationship between net operating income and financial position.* As we have proceeded through our line-by-line explanation of the recognized changes in financial position of the ice cream parlor during its first month, we have paused several times to explain certain important relationships and concepts. Two of these important relationships were the relationship between revenue and financial position and the relationship between expense and financial position.

In each period recognized accomplishment (revenue) increases owner's equity to reflect the increases in assets of the enterprise (cash and accounts receivable) brought about by sales of products and services. Expenses decrease owner's equity to reflect the sacrifices of assets (or increases in liabilities) made in present and past periods to produce the current period's revenue. Combined, these two effects increase (decrease) owner's equity by the amount of net operating income (net loss). Or, in other words, net operating income is the recognized net increase in the ownership interests of the enterprise that results from its productive activities—its performance. We will see later that owner's equity may increase or decrease for other reasons, for example, gains or losses (to be defined in Chapter 6) and additional investments or withdrawals of assets by the owner(s) during the period. *But net operating income (loss) is that portion of the total increase or decrease in owner's equity that is due to the recognized productive performance of the enterprise during the period.*

The reader should be aware, then, that the income statement is a descriptive statement of how and to what extent the recognized accomplishments (revenues) and efforts (expenses) of the enterprise altered the ownership interest in the business during a period of time (in the case of the ice cream parlor, the month of August).

Along with knowledge of any gains or losses and additional owner's investments or withdrawals of assets during the period, the income statement can be thought of as explaining the change between two levels of owner's equity—that at the beginning of the period and that at the end of the period. In the case of the ice cream parlor, the $1,000 net income completely explains how the ownership interest in the enterprise went from an initial level of $7,500 to $8,500 at the end of August—since there were no gains, losses, additional investments, or withdrawals during that time. Thus the income statement bears a well-defined relationship between the ending and beginning balance sheets of the period that it covers.

Other Statements of Change in Elements of Financial Position

Even though net income, and hence the change in the owner's equity element of financial position, are of special interest, the income statement *may not be the only* statement of a change in a financial position component that is of interest. The change in the stock of cash, for instance, may also be of interest. Even though we noted earlier that the change in cash in a single period (net cash flow) may be a poor index of long-run cash-generating ability, it may indicate how cash, as a facilitator of exchanges (and therefore a productive factor), is being used by the enterprise.

The income statement explains the change in one particularly important component of financial position—owner's equity. To construct a statement explaining the change in *any* component of financial position, one need only follow the basic ideas described above for the income statement. That is, after identifying the enterprise, the statement, and the period covered, array the increases and decreases that appear in the worksheet column of that component of financial position opposite brief descriptions of the events that caused them.

Example 5-9   To illustrate, a statement of cash flows for the ice cream parlor for the month of August appears in Exhibit 5-6. Again, the reader will be able to trace each item to the Cash column of Exhibit 5-3.

Exhibit 5-6

ICE CREAM PARLOR
Statement of Cash Flows
For the Month of August 19XX

Cash receipts from sales		$4,000
Cash disbursements:		
Purchase of equipment	$6,000	
Prepayment of rent	600	
Purchase of supplies	200	
Payments on account		
for ice cream purchases	1,300	
Payments of salaries and wages	1,200	
Miscellaneous payments	100	
Total cash disbursements		9,400
Net cash decrease		($5,400)

Notice that, in the same way that the net income number explains the change in owner's equity, this net cash decrease explains the change in the cash account from an initial level of $7,500 to an ending level of $2,100. At the same time, it lists or itemizes the individual causes that made up the change.

So the cash-flow and income statements are each special cases of a more general concept, that is, *statements of the flows* (increases and decreases) that describe the transition between the beginning and ending *stocks* in a component of financial position. In Chapter 15 this notion is further elaborated and still another example of a frequently reported flow statement (the Statement of Changes in Financial Position) is discussed.

The Events, or Transactions, Approach to Accounting—A Perspective

The body of this chapter has described for the reader the most fundamental concepts of conventional accounting and their applications to measuring the status and activities of a business enterprise. Many different themes have been woven into the single illustration. Because of the richness of the resulting fabric, it would perhaps be helpful to the reader to have a brief summary that will serve as a mode of operation for applying conventional accounting concepts in other situations. Such a summary appears at the end of this section. Before getting to the summary, however, it is appropriate to develop some perspective on the approach to accounting measurement underlying it.

• *The transactions approach and comparative values approach contrasted.* Two of the major periodic outputs of the present-day financial-accounting system are the balance sheet, portraying financial position or status as of the end of a period, and the income statement, portraying performance in productive activity for the period. In the illustration in this chapter we arrived at these end results by (1) starting with the beginning financial position of the enterprise and (2) recognizing all of the changes in that financial position resulting from the external and internal economic events that affected the enterprise during the period. But it was not necessary to proceed event-by-event to determine ending financial position and measure net income.

Ending financial position, in principle, can be constructed at the end of the period without recognizing all of the many events that took place individually. The employees of the enterprise can count the cash on hand and confirm the amount on deposit with the bank. They can observe the amounts of supplies and merchandise on hand at year-end and determine the prices originally paid from the purchase invoices or bills sent by the suppliers. Knowing the original cost and expected lives of the long-lived assets, they can determine the amount of depreciation-to-date on each. And they can ascertain the undischarged amounts of liabilities as of the end of the period.

Having valued all of the end-of-period assets at their unexpired costs and all of the end-of-period liabilities at their undischarged original transaction values, owner's equity would be measured by the difference between total assets and total liabilities.

Example 5-10   In the ice cream parlor example, the cash count and confirmation of cash in the bank, and the counts of ice cream and supplies on hand at the end of August, would show: cash of $2,100, ice cream of $200, and supplies of $150, all on hand at month-end. Examining copies of the unpaid sales invoices sent to banquet customers would indicate $500 in accounts receivable at the end of August. With knowledge that $600 was prepaid during August for rent through October, the $400 portion unexpired at August 31 would be determined. Similarly, with knowledge of the original cost ($6,000) and expected life (sixty months) of the equipment, after one month it would be valued at $6,000 less $100 accumulated depreciation.

Examination of the unpaid bills from suppliers and unpaid time cards of employees would lead to recognition of $750 in wages and accounts payable. Then with all assets and liabilities valued, ending owner's equity would be measured by the difference between the sum of the assets and the sum of the liabilities:

$$\text{Owner's equity} = \$9,250 - \$750 = \$8,500$$

The $8,500, of course, checks with the owner's equity figure shown earlier on our worksheet and balance sheet, as expected. But the process by which it was derived differs from the event-by-event process depicted in the worksheet.

Just as it is not necessary to recognize individual events and transactions to get end-of-period financial position, it is not necessary to explicitly measure revenues and expenses to determine net operating income for the period. If financial position is measured at the end of each successive accounting period, we can always take advantage of the relationship between net operating income and financial position to measure periodic net income.

We emphasized earlier that net operating income is the change in owner's equity from the beginning to the end of the period *that results from operations.* Thus we know that the change in owner's equity for a period equals net operating income plus (minus) any new investments (withdrawals) and plus (minus) any gains (losses).

Example 5-11 The ice cream parlor started August with owner's equity of $7,500 (equal to the owner's original contribution of cash). The August 31 owner's equity, calculated above, is $8,500. Since there were no gains or losses or investments or withdrawals by the owner during August, net income must be $8,500 − $7,500 = $1,000. That, of course, checks with the income statement figure shown earlier in our event-by-event illustration.

• *The advantage of the transactions, or events, approach.* In view of the discussion in the above paragraphs, one might question why accountants in practice bother with the event-by-event approach to accounting for the business enterprise. It appears to involve more effort for the same results. The answer is that although the transactions, or events, approach may require more effort, it provides a richer and potentially more useful fund of information. Under the comparative valuation approach illustrated above, for instance, one would know the beginning and the ending balance in owner's equity plus the net income for the period, but none of the details of revenues and expenses that are forthcoming in the transactions approach would be made available to investors. Such detail is usually considered helpful to using conventional accounting net operating income as a basis for predicting future cash flows. Thus the additional effort involved in the transactions approach is usually considered worthwhile.

• *The accounting cycle—a summary of the transactions approach.* Although more complicated than the comparative valuation approach to accounting, the transactions approach can be summarized in a few broad steps as follows:

1. Start with the ending financial position of the prior period, that is, each account in the financial position begins the new period with the ending balance of the prior period.
2. Recognize the changes in financial position brought about by transactions entered into by the enterprise during the accounting period. In most cases, as a result of applying the realization principle, the revenue of the period is recognized in this stage of the accounting cycle.
3. Before assessing the end-of-period financial position, recognize all changes in financial position believed to have taken place during the period but which were not a direct result of a current transaction between the enterprise and another economic unit. Many kinds of expenses are recognized in this stage through application of the matching principle, for example, depreciation of long-lived assets acquired in earlier periods and accrual of liabilities for services received but not paid for.
4. Assess the end-of-period financial position.
5. Report the end-of-period financial position, net income, and other relevant aspects of the change in financial position, cash flow for example, in a coordinated set of statements. Customarily the set of financial statements includes an income statement and a balance sheet at a minimum.

This outline constitutes a brief but complete statement of the process illustrated in the main body of this chapter. The next chapter continues with the discussion of conventional accounting, elaborating the concepts of income and financial position and concluding with some evaluation of conventional accounting as a financial accounting model.

Before going on with our elaboration of conventional accounting concepts, we should point out that we have resorted to a considerable degree of abstraction in this chapter to depict the essential features of the accounting cycle. The ice cream parlor example and the worksheet format are representative only "in principle" of the accounting cycle under conventional accounting. As a practical matter one would not expect to fit on a single page all of the accounts and transactions of even the simplest types of businesses for the shortest accounting periods. Clearly a more sophisticated set of tools is required for practical applications of the accounting cycle. Traditional bookkeeping offers just such a set of tools, which has evolved together with conventional accounting over several centuries.

For the interested reader the traditional bookkeeping cycle, along with both nontraditional and traditional sets of procedures and tools for implementation, is introduced in the Appendix at the end of the book. The reader may take advantage of the opportunity to become acquainted with the important process of bookkeeping at any time after covering this chapter.

Questions for Review and Discussion

5-1. Define:

a. Assets

b. Liabilities

c. Monetary assets and liabilities

d. Original transaction value

e. Owners' equity

f. Financial position

5-2. What justification is there (if any) for valuing nonmonetary assets at the amount of cash or other monetary assets (or liabilities) given in exchange for them?

5-3. Owners' equity is not valued directly. True or false? Explain your answer.

5-4. Because of the way that owners' equity is valued, the sum of the values assigned to the assets of the enterprise is equal to the sum of the values assigned to the liabilities plus owners' equity. Show that this is true.

5-5. Explain the distinction between an external event and an internal event. What is the significance of the distinction in the accounting cycle?

5-6. Strictly speaking, the value of the financial position framework is that it provides a clerical framework for processing transactions and calculating income. True or false? Explain your answer.

5-7. Explain in words why revenue is recognized as an increase in owners' equity.

5-8. Explain in words why expenses are recognized as decreases in owners' equity.

5-9.   Give some reasons why the unexpired costs of long-lived assets are accounted for with two accounts in financial position.

5-10.   Net operating income explains the difference between the beginning and the ending owners' equity of the business for a given period. True or false? Defend your position.

5-11.   Since the transactions approach to conventional accounting perhaps requires more record-keeping effort than the comparative values approach, why do accountants bother with the transactions approach in practice?

5-12.   In the ordinary course of events, the revenue for a period is recognized in connection with external events, whereas expenses are often recognized only as the result of recognizing internal events. Do you agree or disagree? Explain your position.

5-13.   In conventional accounting, when an asset is acquired it is valued at its original transaction value (cost)—the amount of cash or other assets and liabilities given in exchange for it. Does this amount represent the value of the asset to the firm? Defend your answer.

5-14.   Suppose that at the end of the business year a business immediately sold all of its assets to various buyers and paid off all of its liabilities. Would the resulting cash available for the owners be equal to the year-end owners' equity figure? Explain your position.

5-15.   One of the things that distinguishes conventional accounting from strictly cash basis accounting is the recognition of accruals. Do you agree or disagree? Explain your position.

Exercises   **5-1. Inventory Stocks and Flows.**   Arnhem Distributors commenced 1973 with 5,000 plastic boomerangs costing $2,500. It purchased 12,000 more boomerangs at $.75 per boomerang. By the end of the year, 3,000 of the boomerangs were left (all purchased during the year).

Required:

1. What was the cost of the boomerangs sold?
2. What would have been the cost of the boomerangs sold if the company had commenced the period with 5,000 boomerangs costing $.80 per unit? (The rest of the facts remain the same.)

5-2. Inventory Stocks and Flows.   Toowoomba Traders sold 1,200 Spiro Agnew candles in 1972. The cost of the candles sold was $700. If the closing inventory of 300 units cost $150, and if 1,000 units had been purchased during the period for $600:

1. What was the number of units in opening inventory?
2. What was the cost of the opening inventory?

5-3. Determining Net Income.   On July 31, 1974, Percy, who owns Pike Street Antiques, drew up a statement of financial position for his business.

Assets:			Liabilities and Owner's Equity:	
Cash		$ 4,000	Accounts payable	$ 3,500
Merchandise		8,000	Wages payable	200
Accounts receivable		1,500	Loan from finance	
Fixtures and			company	2,500
fittings	$3,000		Total liabilities	$ 6,200
Less accumulated				
depreciation	(1,000)	2,000	Owner's equity	9,600
Prepaid rent		300	Total liabilities and	
Total assets		$15,800	owner's equity	$15,800

Given:

a. Sales for August were $6,500.

b. $500 worth of those sales were returned by dissatisfied customers.

c. $700 was paid out for wages during August. Percy's shop assistants had not been paid for the last two days of August, which meant that $70 was owing to them.

d. The statement of financial position at the end of August showed that total accumulated depreciation of fixtures and fittings was $1,075.

e. By the end of August, only one week's rent ($150) was still prepaid. Percy had paid an additional $450 to his landlord during the month.

f. An additional $2,000 worth of merchandise was purchased during the period. $6,500 was still on hand at the end of the period.

g. Interest on the loan amounted to $40 for August. Percy paid the $40 on August 31.

Required:

Produce an income statement for Percy's business for the month of August 1974.

5-4. Conventional Accounting Valuation and Income Determination in Perspective. During March 1974 Ron Barassi Furniture Builders Company produced the following product lines:

Costs	*Line A*	*Line B*	*Line C*
Raw materials	$300	$250	$420
Labor costs	150	200	120
Other manufacturing costs	100	75	150
Total costs	$550	$525	$690

"Other costs" were incurred amounting to $300, but these could not be specifically identified with any of the particular products.

Beitzel Custom Builders was building competitive product lines and had the same costs, with the exception that its "other costs" amounted to $200.

By the end of March the Barassi Company had sold all of the products associated with line A and line B for a price of $850 and $800 respectively. The

Beitzel organization had, however, only sold the products of its line B for a price of $825. There appeared to be little doubt that the other projects would soon be sold, however, at prices of $850 for its line A and $925 for its line C.

Required:

1. Draw up an income statement for each of the two companies.

2. Based on conventional accounting valuation principles, calculate the difference in the recognized values of "furniture inventory" that would be shown on the statement of financial position of each company as of March 31 (you can assume that the companies are identical in every respect except where information has been given to the contrary).

3. Explain the reason for the differences between the two companies in income and furniture inventory.

4. Are the differences economically significant?

5. What justification can you give for the contrast between the accounting differences noted above?

5-5. Product versus Period Expenses.   The Big Deal Land Developers Corporation began operations on January 1, 1974, with $600,000 in cash, contributed by a number of wealthy financiers. Two projects were commenced immediately— the Mingenew Marshes scheme and the Pukapunyal project. During the first three months of 1974, the following events occurred.

January   Land at Mingenew was purchased for $100,000.
            Land at Pukapunyal was purchased for $200,000.
February   Land surveys necessary to eventual subdivision and sale of the
            properties were conducted at a cost of $10,000 ($4,000 for Mingenew,
            $6,000 for Pukapunyal).
March   Contractors cleared the land at both projects.
            Cost: Mingenew $30,000
                   Pukapunyal $25,000
            Roads and drainage were established at Mingenew at a cost of $15,000.
            On March 30 the Mingenew project was sold for $230,000.

During the three months a total of $18,000 was paid in wages and salaries for head office staff. Other general and administration expenses amounted to $30,000. All transactions in the period were cash transactions. During the period April 1 to June 30, general and administration expenses were $29,000, and head office salaries and wages were $16,000. Roads and drainage were established at Pukapunyal at a cost of $48,000. A new project (the Dongara project) was commenced during June, with the purchase of a tract of land at a cost of $70,000. A land survey was conducted at a cost of $10,000. On June 28 the Pukapunyal project was sold for $350,000.

Required:

1. Produce an income statement for Big Deal Land Developers Corporation for the three months ending March 31, 1974. List the *total* assets of the corporation as of March 31.

2. Perform the same functions that you did for requirement 1 for the period April 1 to June 30.

5-6. Applying the Accounting Cycle.

July 1   Smith and Smythe deposited $1,000 each in a bank account under the name of the Campus Record Center. They paid $1,200 for three months' rental of a shop, and after arranging a $500 loan from the bank, spent $700 on equipment such as record racks and a cash register. The partners felt this equipment would last five years and have proceeds of $100 on disposal.

July 2   Hired Sally Swinger as a salesgirl at $400 a month.

July 3   Purchased records on credit at a cost of $1,500.
Purchased general supplies for cash at a cost of $100.
Billed by the university paper for $60 for advertisements.

July 4–12   Cash sales of records $950; paid advertising bill.

July 11   Paid $20 for insurance to the end of the month. Purchased 200 records at a cost of $2 per record (credit transaction).

July 12   Paid $500 to suppliers of records.

July 12–31   Paid Sally her monthly wage.
Record sales (cash) $1,000.
Repaid the bank, including interest, with a payment of $510.
Paid $60 for insurance to October 31.
Paid $50 to a local artist for a personal appearance at the store.
Paid $250 to record suppliers.
Counted record stock and found stock costing $1,300 still on hand.
Counted general supplies and found supplies costing $80 still on hand.

Required:

Produce a worksheet and an income statement for the Record Center for the month of July 1974. Draw up a statement of financial position as of July 31, 1974.

5-7. Applying the Accounting Cycle. Five years ago several individuals got together and started a business called Copy Fast Corporation. The business consisted of several part-time employees and some high-speed dry-copying equipment. Small (several-page) copying jobs are done for cash as people walk in with them off the street. Large jobs, on the other hand, are done for regular customers and on a competitive-bid basis. The balance sheet of the business as of the end of its third year is as follows:

COPY FAST CORPORATION
Statement of Financial Position
As of the End of Year Three

Assets:			Liabilities and Owners' Equity:	
Cash		$ 4,000	Accounts payable	$ 2,500
Accounts receivable		3,000		
Supplies and paper		6,000		
Equipment	$15,000			
Less accumulated			Owners' equity	18,000
depreciation	(7,500)	7,500	Total liabilities and	
Total assets		$20,500	owners' equity	$20,500

During year four the following events were recognized:

a. Cash sales of $9,000 and credit sales of $20,000 were made.

b. Paper and supplies worth $10,000 were purchased on account.

c. Rent of $2,400 for the year was paid in cash.

d. The equipment is estimated to last five years in total and bring $2,500 upon resale at the end of that time.

e. Wages of $9,000 in total were paid all in cash.

f. At year-end $7,000 worth of supplies and paper were still on hand, and $2,000 of the total accounts receivable from customers had not been paid.

g. The business paid all but $4,000 of its total accounts payable by year-end.

h. The owners withdrew cash equal to conventional accounting net income at year-end.

Required:

Record the effects on financial position of the above events in worksheet form. Prepare an ending balance sheet and an income statement for year four as well.

5-8.   Applying the Accounting Cycle.

January 1–5 $18,000 is placed in a bank account entitled Chablis Enterprises by Harry Wreir.

Three months' rent (amounting to $1,200) was paid by Harry for a wharf-side building to be used for a restaurant. Harry bought cooking equipment at a cost of $5,000, paying $3,000 and being granted thirty days' credit for the balance. The equipment will have a life of four years and is expected to bring a price of $1,000 on its disposal.

Harry purchased supplies costing $2,000 on credit. Harry hired cooks, waitresses, and a resident band. The total payroll of $2,000 will be paid every two weeks. Harry purchased furniture costing $6,000 for cash. The furniture will last ten years and have $1,200 salvage value.

January 6   The Chablis Restaurant opened.

January 6–31   Wages were paid totaling $4,000 ($700 was owed by Harry at the end of the month). An additional $2,000 was paid by him for guest performers, and $6,000 worth of supplies of food and drink were purchased on credit. Suppliers were paid $7,000 (including the $2,000 owed for cooking equipment). Harry withdrew $500 in cash for his own personal use. Supplies costing $2,200 were still on hand at the end of the period. Revenue from meals for the month amounted to $15,500 (all paid in cash).

Required:

Produce a worksheet and an income statement for January, and a statement of financial position as of January 31, 1974.

5-9.   Levels and Changes in Owner's Equity.   Bob Menzies is the sole owner of a plumbing business—Menzies Plumbing Company. On December 31, 1971, the company's statement of financial position showed total assets to be $15,000 and total liabilities $2,000. On December 31, 1972, owner's equity was $18,000.

Required:

1. What was the owner's equity on December 31, 1971?

2. If total assets were $23,000 on December 31, 1972, what were total liabilities at that date?

3. If there were no withdrawals from the business or contributions to the business by Bob, what was the net income for 1972?

4. If Bob had contributed $2,000 in cash to the business in 1972, what would net income for 1972 have been?

5. Ignoring number 4, what would have been the net income for 1972 if Bob had withdrawn cash of $4,000 during 1972?

6. What would net income have been if, during 1972, Bob had contributed the $2,000 *and* withdrawn the $4,000?

7. Given the information in number 6, what revenue must the company have earned during 1972 if total expenses were $3,000?

5-10. Recognition of Effects of Events on Financial Position.

Required:

Indicate the row number, the account (column), and the amount of all numbers missing in Exhibit 5-7.

5-11. Relationship of Financial Position and Statements of Change.   The following statements for John Gorton Enterprises are presented to you.

JOHN GORTON ENTERPRISES
Statement of Financial Position
As of December 31, 1971

Assets:		
Cash		$5,000
Prepaid rent		100
Merchandise		400
Equipment	$2,400	
Less accumulated depreciation	(800)	1,600
Total assets		$7,100
Liabilities and Owners' Equity:		
Accounts payable		$1,000
Interest payable on bank loan		100
Bank loan		2,000
Owners' equity		4,000
Total liabilities and owners' equity		$7,100

JOHN GORTON ENTERPRISES
Income Statement
For Month Ended January 31, 1972

Revenue		$6,000
Less Expense:		
Merchandise used	$1,500	
Rent	150	
Equipment depreciation	400	
Interest on bank loan	25	
Wages	600	
Total expenses		2,675
Net income		$3,325

Exhibit 5-7

BULLA BULLA ENTERPRISES—WORKSHEET

Description	Cash	Accounts Receivable	Merchandise	Prepaid Rent	Equipment	Accumulated Depreciation	Accounts Payable	Wages Payable	Interest Payable	Mortgage Payable	Owner's Equity
1. Beginning Position	1,500	1,000	2,500	200	6,000	(1,500)	1,750	—0—	100	3,000	
2. Cash sales	1,300										2,000 (R)
3. Purchased merchandise on credit							500				
4. Credit sales											
5. Paid rent in advance				100							
6. Receipts from customers		(2,500)									
7. Payments to suppliers	(1,000)										
8. Purchased equipment with cash	(1,000)										
9. Credit sales of $1,500											
10. Paid wages	(700)										
11. Paid advertising	(300)										
12. Paid interest owing	(100)										
13. Purchased merchandise with cash	(200)										
14. Depreciation											(800) (E)
15. Merchandise used			(900)								
16. Rent expense for period											(150) (E)
17. Accrued wages								200			
18. Interest expense for period (not paid)											(80) (E)
19. Contribution by owner	2,000										
20. Ending Position											

JOHN GORTON ENTERPRISES
Statement of Cash Flows
For Month Ended January 31, 1972

Inflows:	Cash sales		$6,000
Outflows:	Accounts payable	$1,000	
	Rent	100	
	Interest	50	
	Wages	600	
	Total outflows		1,750
	Net cash inflows		$4,250

Additional information:

a. There were no contributions or withdrawals by the owners during January 1972.

b. No credit sales during January 1972.

c. All merchandise was bought on credit. During January, merchandise costing $1,600 was purchased.

Required:

Prepare a statement of financial position as of January 31, 1972. *Hint:* The income statement and statement of cash flows are both "change" statements. They provide information on the month's increases to and the decreases from items in the December 31 statement of financial position given above. For example:

Cash balance, December 31, 1971	$5,000	(from beginning statement of financial position)
Additions	6,000	(from statement of cash flows)
	$11,000	
Subtractions	1,750	(from statement of cash flows)
Cash balance as of January 31, 1972	$ 9,250	

5-12. Net Income and Owners' Equity.   You are at the monthly meeting of the Muckinhudin Investors' Club. The club's investment in McMahon Corporation is shortly to be discussed. The club has a 10 percent interest in the corporation and receives 10 percent of any dividends that the corporation pays to its stockholders. You were responsible for bringing the 1972 financial reports of McMahon Corporation to the meeting but have discovered that you have neglected to do so. By a stroke of good fortune you discover that today's newspaper has a brief article on the McMahon Corporation, from which you can glean the following information:

	1971	*1972*
Sales	60,000	65,000
Total assets	120,000	125,000
Total liabilities	90,000	80,000

Sales are the only form of revenue for McMahon Corporation.

Required (each question is independent unless otherwise stated):

1. Assuming there were no dividends paid and no contributions made by stockholders to the corporation during 1972, calculate the corporation's 1972 net income figure.

2. Assuming that there were no dividends paid but that the corporation's stockholders contributed an additional $10,000 (in proportion to their previous holdings) in cash during 1972, what would be the corporation's net income for 1972?

3. Now assume the same facts as in number 2, except that you now recall that the Muckinbudin Investors' Club received a cash dividend of $2,000 during 1972. What would be the 1972 net income for the corporation now?

4. Using the conventional accounting net income figure derived in number 3, what would be McMahon Corporation's total expenses for 1972?

5. You have a sneaking suspicion that the sales figure given for 1972 is wrong. You are also satisfied that the figure for net income that you derived in number 3 is correct. If the total expenses incurred by McMahon Corporation for 1972 were $60,000, what should the sales figure have been?

5-13. Recognizing Accounting Principles. Three important principles of conventional accounting have been discussed in the chapter: the realization principle, the matching principle, and the original transaction value (cost) principle. Identify the principle that is most relevant to each of the following events. (Note: More than one principle may be involved.)

a. Purchased a used truck at a cost of $3,000. The asset "truck" was increased by $3,000 in the worksheet.

b. Supplies originally costing $1,500, which had been used to produce goods sold during the period, were recorded as an expense.

c. Prepaid rent was reduced by $500, representing the amount expired for the period.

d. No entry was made to record an order received for 100 of the power tools manufactured by the company (total price, $3,000).

e. Through a friend, you purchase for $450 a piece of equipment that normally costs $500. You record an increase of $450 in equipment held by you.

f. Depreciation of equipment is recorded as $600 for the period.

g. Marketable securities costing $3,000 increase in value to $5,000. No entry is made to record the increase.

h. $500 is paid in advance to you for services to be performed by you next year. Your recognized net income for the current period is unaffected by the event.

i. Wages accrued at the end of 1969 are recorded in the 1969 worksheet.

j. Interest earned, but not received, on a loan made by you to an associate is recorded as income of the period.

5-14. Internal-External Events Recognition. Indicate whether the following events result from internal events (*I*) or external transactions (*T*).

a. Recorded purchase of $500 worth of supplies on credit.

b. From a count of supplies, calculated and recorded the cost of merchandise used as $400.

c. Recorded $700 depreciation of machinery.

d. Recorded the expiration of $200 of prepaid rent.

e. Recorded payment of advertising bill of $25.

f. Recorded withdrawal of $300 cash by a partner in the business.

g. Recorded $300 as wages owed by business at end of period.

h. Cash dividends earned by the business were recorded as revenue.

5-15. Recognizing Effects of Events on Financial Position. For each of the following events relating to the Wonthaggi Weavers Company, indicate the effect upon the individual accounts in the company's financial position. Treat each event *independently*, and do *not* do a worksheet. Indicate in each case whether the event is a transaction (*T*) or an internal event (*I*). Expenses and revenues are to be identified as such. For example:

> Incurred and paid advertising of $200
> (T) Assets (cash)—decrease of $200
>   Owners' equity (advertising expense)––decrease of $200

Events:

a. Purchased wool from suppliers on credit for $1,000.

b. Purchased weaving machine for $5,000, paying $2,500 in cash with the bank paying the balance.

c. Placed advertisements in the local paper at a cost of $180—payment has not yet been made.

d. Paid rent for the next eighteen months—$1,800.

e. Paid wages owed for work done in the preceding period—$800.

f. Paid $500 to bank in repayment of a loan.

g. Made sales of $3,000 to a major retailer who paid cash of $1,500 and promised payment of the balance within thirty days.

h. One of the owners contributed a delivery van (market value $2,000) to the company.

i. Depreciation of equipment for the period—$150.

j. The retailer (in g above) returned some goods, claiming he was overstocked. Wonthaggi Weavers gave him a credit note for $500 (i.e., reduction in the amount payable).

k. Discovered at the end of the period:

 (1) Wool supplies used during period cost $300.

 (2) Amount of prepaid rent that expired during the period was $500.

 (3) Wages owing at end of period were $250.

 (4) Interest owing at the end of the period was $80.

l. Paid a $500 cash dividend to owners.

5-16. Recognition of Internal Events. The Custom Sign Company's financial position worksheets (Exhibits 5-8 and 5-9) contain the external cash transactions

Exhibit 5-8

CUSTOM SIGN COMPANY
Financial Position Worksheet

Description	Cash	Materials	Prepaid Expenses	Long-lived Assets	Accumulated Depreciation	Accounts Payable	Owners' Equity
1. Original investment	10,000						10,000
2. Purchase of pickup	(2,700)			2,700			
3. Purchase of generator	(1,200)			1,200			
4. Purchase of other equipment	(540)			540			
5. City and state licenses	(40)		40				
6. Insurance premium	(480)		480				
7. Quarterly rental—4/1/74	(300)		300				
8. Quarterly rental—7/1/74	(300)		300				
9. Purchases of material	(3,000)	3,000					
10. Withdrawals through 7/31/74	(1,000)						(1,000) (W)
11. Payment of gasoline credit card statements	(300)						(300) (E)
12. Cash receipts from customers	6,200						6,200 (R)
13. Withdrawal at end of August	(450)						(450) (W)
Position after *cash* events through 8/31/74	5,890	3,000	1,120	4,440	—0—	—0—	14,450

Exhibit 5-9

CUSTOM SIGN COMPANY
Financial Position Worksheet

Description	Cash	Materials	Prepaid Expenses	Long-lived Assets	Accumulated Depreciation	Accounts Payable	Owners' Equity
Beginning Position—9/1/74	?	?	?	?	?	?	?
a. Purchase of materials (paid by check)	(750)	750					
b. Payment of gasoline credit card statement	(120)					(120)	
c. Withdrawal at end of September	(500)						(500) (W)
d. Cash receipts from customers	1,800						1,800 (R)

based on information available in Problem 4-11. Also, the worksheets contain external cash transactions based on the additional information below.

a. Materials purchased through 8/31/74 (paid for by check)—$3,000.

b. Cash withdrawals for personal expenses through 7/31/74—$1,000.

c. Total of gasoline credit card statements paid by check through 8/31/74 (treated as an expense when paid)—$300.

d. Cash received from customers through 8/31/74—$6,200.

e. Cash received from customers during September—$1,800.

f. Original investment—$10,000 cash.

For purposes of convenience, prepaid licenses, prepaid rent, and prepaid insurance have been grouped into one account—prepaid expenses. The long-lived assets account includes the pickup, generator, and other equipment. The accumulated depreciation account may be used for depreciation on all long-lived assets.

Required:

1. Complete the financial position worksheet as of 8/31/74 by:

    (a) Recognition of external transactions not involving cash up through 8/31/74 (if any).

    (b) Recognition of internal events for the period 4/1/74 through 8/31/74.

2. Complete the financial position worksheet as of 9/30/74 by:

    (a) Recognition of external transactions not involving cash in September (if any).

    (b) Recognition of internal events in September.

3. Prepare a statement of financial position as of 9/30/74. What is the net income for September?

(Note: *You must refer to Problem 4-11 in order to complete this problem.*)

5-17.   Recognition of Internal Events.   The financial position worksheets (Exhibits 5-10 and 5-11) contain the external cash transactions based on information available in Problem 4-12. Also, the worksheets contain external cash transactions based on the additional information below.

a. The photography studio was opened on October 1, 1973. At that time the lease officially began, and Ms. Morton paid for the leasehold improvements, furniture and fixtures, and photography equipment.

b. Ms. Morton hired her assistant on November 1, 1973. Her salary is paid by check on the last working day of each month.

c. Payments on account for film and photography supplies from 10/1/73 to 3/31/74—$2,000.

d. Receipts on account from customers from 10/1/73 to 3/31/74—$10,000.

e. Payments for miscellaneous expenses totaled $800 for the period 10/1/73– 3/31/74.

f. Cash withdrawals totaled $2,400 for the period.

g. Original investment—$15,000 cash.

Exhibit 5-10

MARY MORTON PHOTOGRAPHY STUDIO
Financial Position Worksheet

Description	Cash	Accounts Receivable	Film and Supplies	Prepaid Rent	Long-lived Assets	Accumulated Depreciation	Accounts Payable	Owner's Equity
1. Original investment	15,000							15,000
2. Leasehold improvements	(1,800)				1,800			
3. Furniture and fixtures	(4,800)				4,800			
4. Photography equipment	(2,700)				2,700			
5. Quarterly rental on 10/1/73	(600)			600				
6. Quarterly rental on 1/1/74	(600)			600				
7. Salary of assistant for 11/1/73–3/31/74	(3,500)							(3,500) (E)
8. Payments on account for film and photography supplies	(2,000)						(2,000)	
9. Receipts on account from customers	10,000	(10,000)						
10. Miscellaneous expenses	(800)							(800) (E)
11. Cash withdrawals	(2,400)							(2,400) (W)
Position on 3/31/74 before recognition of external events not involving cash and internal events	5,800	(10,000)	—0—	1,200	9,300	—0—	(2,000)	8,300

155

Exhibit 5-11

MARY MORTON PHOTOGRAPHY STUDIO
Financial Position Worksheet

Description	Cash	Accounts Receivable	Film and Supplies	Prepaid Rent	Long-lived Assets	Accumulated Depreciation	Accounts Payable	Owner's Equity
Beginning Position—4/1/74	?	?	?	?	?	?	?	?
a. Quarterly rental on 4/1/74	(600)			600				
b. Payments on account for film	(400)						(400)	
c. Salary of assistant	(700)							(700) (E)
d. Miscellaneous expenses	(100)							(100) (E)
e. Cash withdrawal	(500)							(500) (W)
f. Receipts on account	2,700	(2,700)						

h. Unpaid amounts due from customers were $700 and $800 at the beginning and the end of April, respectively.

For convenience, leasehold improvements, furniture and fixtures, and photography equipment have been lumped into one account—long-lived assets. The accumulated depreciation account may be used for depreciation on all long-lived assets.

Required:

1. Complete the financial position worksheet as of 3/31/74 by:
   (a) Recognition of external transactions not involving cash up through 3/31/74.
   (b) Recognition of internal events for the period 10/1/73–3/31/74.
2. Complete the financial position worksheet as of 4/30/74 by:
   (a) Recognition of external transactions not involving cash in April.
   (b) Recognition of internal events in April.
3. Prepare a statement of financial position as of 4/30/74.

(Note: *You must refer to Problem 4-12 in order to complete this problem.*)

6

Conventional Accounting:
Some Elaboration

In the preceding two chapters we introduced some fundamental accounting definitions and concepts—assets, liabilities, owners' equity, revenue, expense, financial position, and results of operations. In addition, we introduced the basic principles that govern the way in which the concepts and definitions are applied—realization, matching, and recording of assets and liabilities at original transaction values. Finally, we applied the basic definitions, the concepts, and the principles of conventional accounting to an illustrative example. For the sake of simplicity, however, Chapters 4 and 5 were limited to the most fundamental level, exposing only the most basic (and distinctive) characteristics of conventional accounting.

In this chapter we (1) look at conventional accounting from a point of view different from the performance-measurement orientation that was used to introduce it and (2) discuss some of the strengths and weaknesses of conventional accounting in both practical and theoretical terms. To the extent possible, some additional features of conventional accounting are also introduced.

INFORMATION FOR DISTRIBUTION
OF ENTERPRISE BENEFITS

Assessing the "Disposable" Wealth
of the Enterprise

In Chapter 2 we noted that besides investment decisions there is another class of decisions, involving parties outside the business enterprise, with which accountants might concern themselves. That class of decisions has to do with periodically distributing the residual benefits generated by the enterprise between (1) owners (in the form of withdrawals or dividends), (2) management (in the form of bonuses or other incentives), and (3) government (in the form of income taxes). As has been pointed out several times in earlier discussion, an investment decision is a personal decision. It requires that the individual determine the value *to him* of the future cash flows that he estimates will be forthcoming from an investment in the enterprise. If the value to him is greater than the price he has to pay, he will find the opportunity attractive; otherwise he will not. On the other hand, decisions as to the distribution of residual benefits of the enterprise generally are not personal in nature. They have to do with rights of different groups that have an interest in the enterprise. Furthermore, the interests involved are often competing interests. Thus there is some potential that different information will be relevant for decisions involving distributions of enterprise benefits than that which is relevant for investment decisions.

• *The relevance of disposable wealth.* All interests in the distribution of residual benefits of the enterprise have one thing in common: the determination or measurement of the amount of wealth of the enterprise that is actually residual or disposable at a given point in time. But *residual* and *disposable* are relative terms—they imply measurement relative to some criterion. Specifically, they imply that it is desirable to preserve some identifiable level of wealth, a "criterion level" against which disposability can be gauged. If, at the end of a period, the measured wealth of the enterprise exceeds that level, the excess may be considered disposable or expendable.

• *The Hicksian concept of income (disposable wealth).* One "criterion level" that has some relevance for virtually all purposes is the level embodied in the so-called Hicksian concept of income defined in Chapter 3. Recall that Hicksian income (disposable wealth) is the amount of wealth that may be disposed of (distributed) by an economic unit during a period of time, without reducing the remaining wealth *below the level at the beginning of the period.*

• *The Hicksian criterion and owners' interests.* The Hicksian criterion for measuring disposable wealth is of obvious interest to owners. Dividends or withdrawals in excess of Hicksian-type income, period after period, imply a shrinkage in the wealth that remains in control of the enterprise and, concurrently, a shrinking in the interests of the owners. If it is desired that the enterprise retain its economic stature, Hicksian-type income is the maximum level of consistent distributions that should be made to owners.

- *The Hicksian criterion and management rewards.* With the separation of ownership and management, owners who do not control the enterprise directly often share the residual benefits of the enterprise (in the form of profit sharing) with the managers who do control its destiny. To motivate management to act in the interest of the owners, it is often considered important to tie its rewards to a basis that reflects the interests of the owners. Since management starts each period with a stock of wealth that was the result of all prior management actions (its own and its predecessors), it therefore seems reasonable to measure *management's* performance from that initial level.

- *Income taxation and the Hicksian criterion.* The philosophy of income taxation is to take a portion of the new wealth generated by an economic unit each period, always leaving untouched the wealth base that produced the increment. To tax the disposable wealth of the enterprise measured on a basis other than against its beginning-of-period wealth might tend to confiscate some of the wealth base with which the enterprise operated throughout the period. Hence, the Hicksian criterion of beginning-of-period wealth as the basis for measuring disposability is consistent also with the philosophy underlying income taxation.

We should hasten to add, however, that tax policy often departs from the simplistic philosophy described above, when serving many of its special purposes, for example, as an economic incentive system. We will devote part of Chapter 14 to the way that income taxes are treated in present-day financial reporting practice. In the meantime we will assume that there is no income tax in most of our discussion in order to avoid unnecessary complication.

Conventional Accounting Measurement of Wealth

The concept of disposable wealth requires that some measurement or assessment of wealth be made. In Chapter 3 we called the process of measuring wealth items, and expressing (quantifying) their magnitudes in terms of numbers of dollars, the process of *valuation*. We noted then that present value is one approach to valuation.

Conventional accounting may also be thought of as an approach to valuation and wealth assessment. The basis of valuation in conventional accounting is the original transaction value (cost) of an item of wealth. It should be emphasized, however, that as with present value, *the original transaction value of a wealth item is not synonymous with wealth.* At best, since it was a price willingly paid for an asset by the enterprise at the time the asset was acquired, the original transaction value is evidence that the future benefits that were *then expected* from its possession were worth as much or more than the amount paid. Presumably the enterprise would not have acquired the asset otherwise.

Since, by definition, an asset is a positive item of wealth and a liability is a negative item of wealth, the financial position (equation) of an enterprise is, in a sense, a wealth assessment. At any moment in time it includes the unexpired original transaction values of each of the assets then possessed and the undischarged original transaction values of each of the liabilities as yet unsatisfied. Intuitively, to assess the wealth of the enterprise, one would sum the original transaction values assigned to the liabilities and subtract the total from the sum of the values assigned to the assets. But this is precisely the conventional accounting definition of owners' equity (also referred to in this sense as "net assets" or "net worth"). Total owners' equity (total assets minus total liabilities), therefore, can be thought of as representing the wealth of the enterprise as of a point in time, *based upon valuation at original transaction values.*

• *Conventional accounting net operating income and the Hicksian criterion.* Having seen that in conventional accounting the owners' equity portion of the enterprise's financial position may be thought of as an assessment of its wealth, it follows that conventional accounting *net operating income* is the measure of disposable wealth in the Hicksian sense (in the absence of gains and losses, which are discussed in a later section). We originally introduced net operating income from a performance-measurement point of view. But we went to some length in the preceding chapter to point out that *net operating income is synonymous with an advance in owners' equity,* barring any gains or losses and additional contributions or withdrawals of assets by the owners. In fact, the reader will recall that the income statement was described as an explanation of the change in owners' equity due to operations between the beginning and the ending financial position of a period.

• *Net operating income as a measure of disposable wealth—an illustration.* In the absence of gains or losses or owners' investments or withdrawals, the net operating income for a period is equal to the increase in owners' equity and thus is matched by an increase in the excess of assets over liabilities. Subsequent distribution of assets to the owners in an amount equal to net income will therefore set owners' equity back to its level at the beginning of the period. Thus conventional accounting net income conforms to the Hicksian definition of income or disposable wealth given earlier, *based on valuation of assets and liabilities at original transaction values.* But perhaps the point can best be seen by example.

Example 6-1 Suppose that an individual starts a merchandising business with an initial investment of $6,500 in cash. At the outset he buys equipment that will last three years for $6,000 cash and an initial stock of merchandise for $1,000 on account. With these initial outlays he commences business and operates for three years, each year withdrawing cash at the end of the year equal in amount to the net income for that year. Exhibit 6-1 gives summary facts

Exhibit 6-1

MERCHANDISING BUSINESS
Facts of Operations

	Year 1	Year 2	Year 3
Sales (all in cash)	$4,500	$5,000	$5,000
Merchandise purchases on account (not including initial purchase)	500	2,000	600
Payments on account	1,000	1,800	1,300
Merchandise on hand at year-end	500	1,000	—0—
Labor expense (all paid in cash)	300	300	300

concerning the business's operations for the first three years (assuming that there is no income tax). At the end of the third year the equipment is completely worn out, and a junk dealer has agreed to haul it away for whatever salvage value he can get for it.

By using the convenient clerical device of the three-year financial position worksheet in Exhibit 6-2, we will be able to assess the recognized effect of these facts on the accounts of the enterprise.

Many aspects of Exhibit 6-2, such as the treatment of individual summary transactions, should already be familiar to the reader, so we will restrict ourselves to the few additional observations necessary to make the point at hand. First, notice that the financial position as of the end of each year is the beginning position from which we work for the next year. Once we add or subtract the effects of a period's events on the various accounts and arrive at a new financial position, we need not reconsider those events in the next period.

More important, notice the relationship between net operating income for each year and the amount of the owner's withdrawal in the same year.

Example 6-2   If we constructed income statements for each year, we would get the results shown in comparative form in Exhibit 6-3.

In each year, the owner has withdrawn an amount equal to the net operating income for that year. (Note that the last event line for each year in Exhibit 6-2 shows a decrease in cash and a decrease in owner's equity designated with a W for withdrawal.)

Now in order for net operating income to conform to the Hicksian concept of income, the business must be left as well off at the end of a period in which a withdrawal equal to net operating income was made as it was at the beginning of such a period. A glance at Exhibit 6-2 (the owner's equity balance in beginning and ending "position lines" for each year) confirms that this is indeed the case.

The business starts its first year with wealth (owner's equity) of $6,500, all held in the form of cash. It proceeds with its operations and "earns" net operating income of $1,200. If the owner withdraws nothing (and invests nothing additional) from the business in the first year, the net operating income of $1,200 means that owner's equity, and therefore the net assets of the business, would be greater by that amount at the end of the year than at the beginning of the year. Therefore, net operating income is the amount of cash or other assets that can be removed from the business without reducing the net assets at the end of the year below the level at the beginning of the year. Thus in year one, after a withdrawal of $1,200 cash, the business ends the year with an excess of the unexpired original transaction costs of assets over the undischarged original transaction values of liabilities of exactly $6,500, the amount of *net assets* (assets minus liabilities) with which the year was started. However, the composition of the financial position has changed from the all-cash composition of assets at the beginning of the year to the mixed composition at year-end. The same reasoning also applies to the second and third years.

However, by the end of the third year when (1) the equipment has be-

Exhibit 6-2   MERCHANDISING BUSINESS
                              Three-Year Financial Position Worksheet

Description	Cash	Merchandise	Equipment	Accumulated Depreciation	Accounts Payable	Owner's Equity
Beginning Position	6,500					6,500
Year 1:						
Equipment purchased	(6,000)		6,000			
Merchandise purchased		1,000			1,000	
Merchandise purchased		500			500	
Sales	4,500					4,500 (R)
Payments for merchandise	(1,000)				(1,000)	
Labor expense	(300)					(300) (E)
Merchandise used		(1,000)				(1,000) (E)
Equipment depreciation				(2,000)		(2,000) (E)
Owner's withdrawal	(1,200)*					(1,200) (W)*
Ending (Beginning) Position	2,500	500	6,000	(2,000)	500	6,500
Year 2:						
Merchandise purchased		2,000			2,000	
Sales	5,000					5,000 (R)
Payments for merchandise	(1,800)				(1,800)	
Labor expense	(300)					(300) (E)
Merchandise used		(1,500)				(1,500) (E)
Equipment depreciation				(2,000)		(2,000) (E)
Owner's withdrawal	(1,200)*					(1,200) (W)*
Ending (Beginning) Position	4,200	1,000	6,000	(4,000)	700	6,500
Year 3:						
Merchandise purchased		600			600	
Sales	5,000					5,000 (R)
Payments for merchandise	(1,300)				(1,300)	
Labor expense	(300)					(300) (E)
Merchandise used		(1,600)				(1,600) (E)
Equipment depreciation				(2,000)		(2,000) (E)
Owner's withdrawal	(1,100)*					(1,100) (W)*
Ending (Beginning) Position	6,500	—0—	6,000	(6,000)	—0—	6,500

* See the "Three-Year Comparative Income Statements" in Exhibit 6-3 for the determination of withdrawal amounts for each year.

Exhibit 6-3

MERCHANDISING BUSINESS
Three-Year Comparative Income Statements

	Year 1	Year 2	Year 3
Revenues from sales	$4,500	$5,000	$5,000
Less expenses:			
Labor expense	300	300	300
Merchandise used	1,000	1,500	1,600
Equipment depreciation	2,000	2,000	2,000
Total expenses	$3,300	$3,800	$3,900
Net Operating Income	$1,200	$1,200	$1,100

come completely worn out (the negative "accumulated depreciation" balance then offsets entirely the original transaction cost) and (2) the business has not replaced the stock of merchandise sold during the year, the wealth position of the enterprise not only equals but is identical in composition to the position with which it started its short economic life—$6,500 cash and $6,500 owner's equity. Of course, we have made the unusual assumption in the example that the enterprise has a very short life cycle. But this somewhat unrealistic assumption serves to illustrate that in using conventional accounting net operating income as a measure of "disposable wealth," *the concept of wealth involved is the money capital invested in the enterprise.*

Disposable Wealth Measurement— Some Additional Features

• *The legal criterion for disposable wealth.* So far, we have only considered the Hicksian criterion for measuring disposable wealth and the way that conventional accounting net operating income conforms to that criterion. The Hicksian criterion seems relevant for most purposes, but in the corporate form of business another criterion is relevant for a purpose not yet discussed —determining the legality of dividends.

Corporations would not exist legally were it not for permissive legislation on the part of state governments allowing for the chartering of corporations. One of the desirable attributes of the corporate form of business is the limitation of the liability (potential losses) of the owners of the corporation to the amount of their current interest in the corporation. To protect other parties, however, the state laws governing corporations usually restrict dividends paid to owners, so that the original capital contributed to the corporation by owners remains intact (in the form of recognized net assets) to satisfy the rightful claims of other parties. That is, dividends may only be distributed to the extent that net assets exceed the money capital of the enterprise contributed by owners in exchange for shares of stock. Thus, for legal purposes, some measure of the extent to which the recognized net assets of a corporation currently exceed the capital paid in by owners is usually relevant for dividend-distribution decisions.

In the paragraphs that follow we will show how conventional accounting has traditionally adapted to the legal concept of disposable wealth as well as the Hicksian concept. One word of caution, however. The economic and accounting interpretations of the original contributions by owners to the enterprise may differ from the interpretation called for by statute or handed down in court decisions. Rather than get into the complexities involved, we will assume for illustrative purposes that no such differences exist. In any case, we must recognize that *in practice legal pronouncements prevail over accounting theory in determining the legality of dividends.*

• *Two criteria for disposability; one measurement system.* We have noted above that there are two criterion levels of wealth for decisions concerning distributions of dividends to owners: (1) the original capital contributed by owners (paid-in capital)—the criterion level relevant for legal purposes, and (2) the beginning-of-period net assets or owners' equity—the criterion level relevant for most other purposes. Both of these criterion levels are usually handled simultaneously in conventional accounting through the recognition that the owners' equity component of financial position can be split into two separate parts or accounts called *paid-in capital* and *retained earnings*—just as the category *assets* is broken down into *cash, accounts receivable, supplies,* and so forth.

> **Paid-in Capital.** Paid-in capital is that part of total owners' equity equal to the amount of money or other capital contributed by owners to the enterprise in exchange for ownership interests.

> **Retained Earnings.** Retained earnings is that part of owners' equity equal to the cumulative excess of net income over dividend distributions to owners from the inception of the business.

Example 6-3   Reconsider the merchandising business introduced in Example 6-1. Suppose that instead of distributing cash equal to net income ($1,200) in year one, it distributed only $600, retaining $600. Assuming that all other facts remain the same except that the subdivision of owner's equity into paid-in capital and retained earnings is recognized, the first year's operations are represented in Exhibit 6-4.

Notice the several changes from the earlier worksheet in Exhibit 6-2. First, of course, there are two accounts that together represent total owner's equity: paid-in capital and retained earnings. Second, all revenue, expense, and withdrawal amounts are shown as increases or decreases to the retained earnings account. The paid-in capital account is only increased when new ownership contributions are received in exchange for new shares in the business, and decreased when old ownership interests are liquidated or retired. The retained earnings account is increased to the extent of net operating income (revenues minus expenses) and decreased to the extent of dividends paid to the owner. The balance of the retained earnings account at the end of any period is the amount by which cumulative net operating income exceeds cumulative dividends.

Finally, note that since only $600 was withdrawn by the owner instead of $1,200, the full amount of net operating income for year one, there is a $600 balance of retained earnings at the end of year one. This, of course, is matched by $600 more assets (cash) than the enterprise would have had if $1,200 had been withdrawn. Thus the $600 represents a growth in the money capital of the enterprise over the $6,500 originally invested by the owner. Total

Exhibit 6-4

MERCHANDISING BUSINESS
Year One Financial Position Worksheet

Description	Cash	Merchandise	Equipment	Accumulated Depreciation	Accounts Payable	Paid-in Capital	Retained Earnings
						Owner's Equity	
Beginning Position	6,500					6,500	
Equipment purchased	(6,000)		6,000				
Merchandise purchased		1,000			1,000		
Merchandise purchased		500			500		
Sales	4,500						4,500 (R)
Payments on account	(1,000)				(1,000)		
Labor expense	(300)						(300) (E)
Merchandise used		(1,000)					(1,000) (E)
Equipment depreciation				(2,000)			(2,000) (E)
Withdrawal	(600)						(600) (W)
Ending (Beginning) Position	3,100	500	6,000	(2,000)	500	6,500	600

owner's equity of $7,100 ($6,500 paid-in capital plus $600 retained earnings) reflects the growth in net assets.

In year two, recognized net operating income (in the original example, $1,200) will measure the advance in recognized net assets (resulting from operations) beyond this new level of $7,100. Net operating income will again represent the amount of cash or other assets that can be withdrawn without reducing the enterprise net asset position *below its beginning-of-year level.* On the other hand, at the end of year two, year-two net operating income ($1,200) *plus* the beginning balance in retained earnings ($600) is the total amount ($1,800) that can be withdrawn *without reducing the net assets of the enterprise below the level of paid-in capital of $6,500.* The reader may find it a useful exercise to show that this is true, working from the year-one ending position in Exhibit 6-4, using the facts of operations from Exhibit 6-1, and varying the withdrawal policy appropriately.

Thus, within the conventional accounting framework, *net operating income for a period, alone or in combination* with the beginning balance of retained earnings, provides the information that we have concluded is relevant for wealth distribution purposes. Having made this point, we will not continue to separate the paid-in capital and retained earnings portions of owners' equity in our examples until later chapters. The distinction is irrelevant for most of the additional points we will be illustrating in the meantime, and the extra detail may therefore be avoided. It should be noted, however, that in practice retained earnings are customarily separated from the paid-in capital of an enterprise.

• *Net operating income—performance or disposable wealth measure?* In the paragraphs above we have shown that for most purposes, net operating income (the measure of performance in conventional accounting) also serves as the measure of disposable wealth. This dual role of net operating income seems inherently sensible in that the recognized advance in wealth (net assets) of an enterprise ought to be related to its performance in productive activity.

The duality occurs because, as a result of the way that revenues and expenses are defined, net operating income usually represents the overall change in net assets (owners' equity) from all sources other than additional contributions and withdrawals by owners. But we must recognize that this relationship, and hence the duality of net operating income, does not always hold fast. There are some changes in net assets (owners' equity) other than owners' contributions and withdrawals that are clearly not a part of the enterprise's performance in the long-run cash-generating sense. Generally, such changes are referred to as extraordinary gains and losses.

> **Extraordinary Gains (Losses).** Extraordinary gains (losses) are changes in owners' equity due to clearly abnormal events or transactions. By "clearly abnormal" is generally meant that (1) such events are not a normal part of the operations of the business in the long run *and* (2) such events occur infrequently in the environment in which the enterprise operates.

Extraordinary gains and losses usually arise out of such unusual events as theft (except shoplifting and other forms of "normal" pilferage), fire, expropriation of assets by a foreign government, or condemnation by a domestic government unit. When an extraordinary gain or loss has taken place, the insurance proceeds or other compensation (in rare cases the sale price) received in connection with the gain or loss is considered *roughly analogous* to the price received for one of the enterprise's products or services (revenue). The unexpired cost of the asset lost or given up is the measure of sacrifice in giving it up (or losing it), *roughly analogous* to the expense incurred in providing products and services. But there is an important difference. Revenue and expense apply to the regular productive activities of the enterprise— meaning the provision of products and services to customers on a regular and recurring basis; extraordinary gains and losses, on the other hand, are not due to regular productive activity.

• *Recognizing gains and losses.* When an asset held by the business as part of its operations is lost, we offset the insurance proceeds or other compensation received against the unexpired cost of the resource given up (lost), recognizing only the difference as a net increase (gain) or decrease (loss) in owners' equity.

Example 6-4   Weather Sealing Incorporated is a small company that waterproofs basements, roofs, patios, and so forth. Its status and activities for the current year, 19XX, are represented on the worksheet in Exhibit 6-5. The first event recognized for the year is the total loss in a hurricane of a truck with an original transaction cost of $5,000 and accumulated depreciation of $2,000 that had been used in the business through last year. Insurance proceeds were $2,500. A new truck has been leased (rather than purchased) in its place.

Exhibit 6-5

Description	Cash	Accounts Receivable	Supplies	Equipment and Truck	Accumulated Depreciation	Accounts Payable	Owners' Equity
Beginning Position	200	1,000	2,000	10,000	(5,200)	1,000	7,000
Loss of truck	2,500			(5,000)	2,000		(500) (L)
Purchased supplies			8,000			8,000	
Fees earned		50,000					50,000 (R)
Collections	50,000	(50,000)					
Salaries and wages	(35,000)						(35,000) (E)
Payments on account	(7,000)					(7,000)	
Supplies used			(9,000)				(9,000) (E)
Depreciation					(800)		(800) (E)
Ending Position	10,700	1,000	1,000	5,000	(4,000)	2,000	11,700

The reasoning that underlies the treatment in Exhibit 6-5 of the loss of the truck starts with recognition, in the cash account, of the insurance proceeds received, $2,500. Then, along with recognizing the infusion of cash resulting from the loss of the truck, there is concurrent recognition that an asset, the truck, was lost. Prior to the loss, the truck was represented in the financial position of the business in two accounts. Its original cost of $5,000 was included in the equipment and truck account up to the time of loss. Depreciation-to-date on the truck of $2,000 was also included in the accumulated depreciation account. The loss of the truck, in the amount of its $3,000 unexpired cost, was therefore recognized by a $5,000 decrease in the equipment and truck account, offset by a $2,000 decrease in the negative balance of the accumulated depreciation account.

Offsetting the net decrease in assets of $3,000 for the previously unexpired cost of the truck against the $2,500 insurance proceeds gives a $500 overall decrease in assets—a loss. The overall decrease in assets is matched by a $500 decrease in owners' equity designated with an L for loss. Although gains and losses are, by definition, not a part of normal operations and therefore are usually not thought of as part of the performance of the enterprise, they must be reckoned with in measuring disposable wealth at the end of a period.

Example 6-5   From Exhibit 6-5 it can be seen that income from operations for the period in question was $5,200, that is, revenue of $50,000 minus total expenses of $44,800 ($35,000 wages, plus $9,000 supplies, plus $800 depreciation). But if $5,200 cash had been distributed to owners as dividends at the end of the year, end-of-year cash would have been reduced to $5,500, and end-of-year owners' equity would have been reduced to $6,500.

The fact that a dividend of $5,200 would reduce owners' equity to $6,500, an amount less than the recognized owners' equity at the beginning of the period, is important. It means that net income from operations, still the measure of enterprise performance, does not in this case qualify as a measure of disposable wealth in the Hicksian sense. Rather, the disposable wealth amount in this case consists of the $5,200 net income from operations minus the $500 loss from the truck, or $4,700. The reader can confirm, by looking back at Exhibit 6-5, that an end-of-year cash dividend of $4,700 would reduce the business's net assets (owners' equity) only to the $7,000 level of the beginning of the year.

• *Two income measures.* To accommodate the notion that gains and losses are significant for disposable wealth measurement but not necessarily for performance measurement, accountants usually report two income numbers in any period in which gains and losses occur. They can be distinguished as follows:

Net Operating Income. Net operating income (loss) is the excess (deficiency) of revenues from operations over related expenses.

Net Income. Net income (loss) is defined as net operating income (loss) of the period, plus or minus any recognized gains or losses, respectively. Net income equals net operating income when there are no gains and losses. It is in this sense that the two are often used synonymously in uncomplicated or simplified situations.

Example 6-6

Again return to Example 6-4—Weather Sealing Incorporated. To portray both the performance of the enterprise for the year 19XX and the disposable wealth, the accountants would prepare an income statement as shown in Exhibit 6-6.

Notice that since the net income figure is more inclusive, the statement works down to it after first showing the more selective (excluding gains and losses) net operating income figure. By reporting both net operating income and net income on the same statement, the statement presumably serves both types of decision needs of outside groups (investment decisions and wealth distribution decisions).

Exhibit 6-6

WEATHER SEALING INCORPORATED
Income Statement for the Year 19XX

Revenue		$50,000
Less expenses:		
Salaries and wages	$35,000	
Supplies used	9,000	
Depreciation	800	
Total expenses		44,800
Net operating income		$ 5,200
Less loss on truck		500
Net income		$ 4,700

• *Disposable wealth versus available cash.* Before leaving our discussion of disposable wealth measurement, one final important point needs to be emphasized. The point is this: the net income (disposable wealth) of the enterprise for a period may be large, but the enterprise may not be able to distribute cash dividends to owners equal to net income. The reason may already have occurred to the reader. As a disposable wealth index, net income measures the advance in assets (*of all kinds*) in excess of liabilities. Net income may be substantial, but the net assets of the enterprise may not be in readily distributable form. So most wealth distribution decisions are based on two considerations, net income and the availability of cash.

Example 6-7   Interior Designs Incorporated is a quality retailer of furniture, specializing in complete decoration of business and residential interiors. The company buys only floor samples of its furniture line. When it sells furniture, the items are delivered direct to the company's customers from the manufacturer, and Interior Designs is billed for their cost at that time. The company has just completed a very profitable year, as is evidenced on the worksheet in Exhibit 6-7.

Exhibit 6-7

Description	Cash	Accounts Receivable	Floor Samples	Equipment	Accumulated Depreciation	Accounts Payable	Owners' Equity
Beginning Position	10,000	50,000	5,000	20,000	(10,000)	25,000	50,000
Sales		250,000					250,000 (R)
Collections	220,000	(220,000)					
Cost of furniture						120,000	(120,000) (E)
Salaries and wages	(70,000)						(70,000) (E)
Rent	(15,000)						(15,000) (E)
Floor samples purchased	(20,000)		20,000				
Payments on account	(120,000)					(120,000)	
Depreciation					(5,000)		(5,000) (E)
Ending Position	5,000	80,000	25,000	20,000	(15,000)	25,000	90,000

Notice that net income was substantial; revenues of $250,000 less expenses totaling $210,000 equals income of $40,000. This of course is matched by an increase in the excess of recognized assets over liabilities. But at the end of the period the stock of cash is far too low to pay dividends to owners equal to net income. This is due in part (1) to the purchase of $20,000 in new floor samples, and (2) to the apparent buildup in the stock of accounts receivable during the period, probably because of some large sales toward the end of the year on which payments are not yet due. Assuming that the enterprise required a minimum cash balance of, say, $3,000 to conduct its transactions, the maximum end-of-year dividend that it could pay to owners would be $2,000 ($5,000 cash balance minus $3,000 minimum cash requirement).

Example 6-7 serves to illustrate an entirely predictable phenomenon. Although net income may be the measure of disposable wealth in the abstract, the stock of available cash of the enterprise is a practical constraint on the distribution of dividends at any point in time.

CONVENTIONAL ACCOUNTING: SOME QUALIFICATIONS

Uncertainty in Conventional Accounting Measurements

Although conventional accounting net income is largely factually based, that is, based on values established in actual exchange transactions, it is not wholly "factual." Conventional accounting does not require the kind of estimation of future events that forecasts or present values of enterprises would require. It nonetheless requires more estimation and is therefore more subject to uncertainty than appears to be the case at first glance. Two significant areas in conventional accounting measurement that require estimates are (1) the apportionment of the cost of long-lived assets to various periods in which their service potential is used, and (2) the collectibility of prices to be paid in the future by customers for products and services provided.

• *Uncertainty and long-lived assets.* Estimation is required in determining how many periods the enterprise will benefit from the use of each of its long-lived assets. The total amount that can be recognized as expense over the whole useful life of any one of the enterprise's long-lived assets is limited to the original transaction cost of the asset. However, the amount that is recognized as expense in a given period depends on the estimate at that time of how long the asset will continue to provide service. If the enterprise overestimates or underestimates the useful life of the asset, it will tend to recognize too little depreciation expense or too much, respectively. As a result of the error in depreciation expense, net income will be overstated or understated, respectively, depending on which way the enterprise errs in estimating the useful lives of its long-lived assets.

• *Uncertainty from the realization principle.* Besides the allocation of the cost of long-lived assets to individual periods, conventional accounting net income is subject to possible overstatement or understatement from other sources. One such source is application of the *realization principle.* Generally speaking, revenue is recognized in the period of sale of products and services to customers rather than the period in which customers finally pay. Although for most businesses a *bona fide* sale gives sufficient certainty of collection to warrant revenue recognition in the period of sale, some accounts will undoubtedly not be collected even from the best clientele. Merchandise will no doubt have to be repossessed or perhaps will be lost altogether. Any business that makes "credit sales" faces these "facts of life." Hence, revenue is usually recognized in the period of sale, but only in the amount of the total credit sales that are then *expected* to actually be collected.

If, in the period of sales, the enterprise fails to accurately estimate the amount or percentage of the total prices promised to be paid by customers that will actually be paid, then later experience with collections will lead to unexpected increases or decreases in accounts receivable recognized in connection with the original sales. Revenue and net income will therefore originally be too high if many accounts turn out to be uncollectible, or too low if fewer defaults by customers take place than expected. In either case the effect will be the same as when a period's net income is inflated or deflated because of understatement or overestimate of depreciation expense. The specific techniques for recognizing initial estimates of uncollectible customer accounts and later recognition of actual customer defaults is covered in Chapter 11.

Some Implications of and Adaptations to Uncertainty

What are the implications of an actual overstatement or understatement of income? Presumably, the many decisions that were influenced by reported income might have turned out differently if the overstatement or understatement had not occurred. Investors who decided to buy, sell, or hold the stocks or bonds of the company may have pursued other courses of action. Similarly, in the case of a significant overstatement, the propriety or legality of dividend distributions might have been challenged if income had been stated differently at the time. Hence, in extreme cases, when significant overstatements or understatements of income later come to light, their disclosure can result in legal actions on behalf of present and former owners and creditors for damages allegedly caused by reliance on the earlier misleading information.

• *Adaptation in dividend policy to uncertainty.* One of the most obvious and simple adaptations that enterprises have made to uncertainty in income determination is that they rarely distribute assets to owners in amounts equal to net income period after period. They almost always distribute less—thereby hedging against the possibility that when new and better information is available, it may appear that the enterprise earned less than originally recognized. (Also, the owners may prefer to have the enterprise grow by reinvesting part of each period's earnings in the business.)

• *Conservatism in applying conventional accounting.* Still another adaptation to the uncertainty involved in income measurement is a tendency in practice toward so-called conservatism in applying conventional accounting principles. *Conservatism* refers to the inclination to overestimate expenses or losses of a period so as to consciously reduce the probability that income will be inadvertently overstated.

Revenue is recognized in the period in which a product is actually sold. Theoretically, total expense for a period is supposed to include the original transaction cost of the resources sacrificed to produce and distribute the products that were sold during the period. But as we noted earlier, a perfectly scrupulous matching of the original costs of resources with the products they served to produce is rarely fully achieved in practice. Instead, in each period, each significant resource sacrifice is scrutinized by the accountant. If the sacrifice bears some discernible relationship to the production of a particular product, it is recognized as an expense in the period (possibly a later period) in which that product is sold. On the other hand, if the sacrifice does not bear a discernible relationship to the production of a particular product or group of products, it is recognized as an expense in the period in which the resource is consumed. Hence, there may be a tendency in practice to err on the "early side" in recognition of expenses.

It may have occurred to the reader that this kind of conservatism is good in the sense that when expense tends to be overstated and income tends to be understated, lesser amounts of assets will tend to be distributed to owners than otherwise. This, of course, tends to conserve the assets of the enterprise. But from other points of view, there is an element of nonconservatism when this type of biasing of net income occurs. When certain types of expenses are recognized early to depress the current period's income, the income will be equally overstated in the later period in which the expense should have been recognized. Furthermore, an investor may pass up an opportunity to invest in (or a present owner may sell) what will ultimately prove to be a very successful enterprise simply because at the time the enterprise may have been painting an unnecessarily glum picture of itself by stating income too conservatively.

If conservatism is carried too far, it can undermine the usefulness of accounting outputs, particularly operating income (as a performance measure). Excessive conservatism negates the supposed cause-and-effect relationship between revenues and expenses—the feature that presumably makes net operating income representative of current productive ability.

Conventional Accounting Income—Relevance in Times of Changing Prices

• *Income measurement summarized.* Net operating income, being the difference between revenues and expenses, measures the recognized increase in net assets from the operations during the period over and above the original costs of the assets sacrificed in connection with those operations. If net assets are reduced by distributing to owners amounts equal to net operating income (net income if gains or losses are experienced) period after period, the recognized net assets (owners' equity) of the enterprise at the end of a period will equal the level at the beginning of the period. If this policy is followed from the inception of the business, net assets at the end of each period will always equal the original capital paid in by the owners. At the same time, net operating income presumably represents the ability of the enterprise to convert the productive resources it acquires into products and services of greater value than the cost or sacrifice made to acquire the resources.

Net operating income as a disposable wealth measure was illustrated in Example 6-1 (the merchandising business). The owner invested $6,500 cash at the outset. Part of the cash ($6,000) was then converted into equipment that lasted three years. The business then proceeded with three years of operations. Each year, net operating income was calculated and cash was withdrawn in that amount. When the cycle of asset replacement was interrupted at the end of year three, that is, the used-up equipment and merchandise inventories were not replaced, the enterprise actually started year four in exactly the same position as at the beginning of year one—with $6,500 cash and no other assets or liabilities (see Exhibit 6-2).

The reason for returning to this example is that by looking at some of the options available to the enterprise at the beginning of year four, we can re-examine the relevancy in the preceding three years of conventional accounting net operating income as a measure of performance and as a measure of disposable wealth.

• *The relevance of conventional accounting income measurement.* As it enters year four with exactly $6,500 cash and $6,500 owner's equity, the merchandising enterprise has two options that are of particular interest to us. First, the business can return all of the $6,500 cash to the owner and go out of existence. Or, second, it can replace the worn-out equipment and exhausted merchandise inventory, much as it did at the beginning of year one, and continue in business. A good test of the relevance of conventional accounting is (1) whether, upon returning the $6,500 *wealth preserved in the enterprise,* the owner would be as well off in possessing that amount as when he first invested it in the enterprise, and (2) whether, upon replacing its equipment and stock of merchandise, the enterprise can continue to carry on business in succeeding years as well as it did in earlier years, *as reflected in net income of those years.* If economic conditions are static, the answer to both questions is yes. By *static* we mean that nothing in the environment changes (including the prices, the tastes, preferences, and values of the owner, the efficiency of the enterprise, etc.). But if certain economic conditions change (prices in particular), then some problems arise with conventional accounting income measurement. The problems introduced by changing prices are described below.

• *Changes in general purchasing power.* Because of the relationship between cash and wealth, the owner would be as well off upon return of his $6,500 as he was with the same amount at the start of business only if the prices of goods and services have not increased or decreased significantly in the meantime. The $6,500 cash preserved in the business has no intrinsic value itself. Rather, it is the medium of exchange by which goods and services are acquired to satisfy an individual's wants and needs. Hence we can say that upon receiving $6,500 cash at the end of three years, the owner will be as well off as he was at the outset if he can command the same kinds of goods and services with that cash in the same quantities as he could at the outset.

But suppose that prices generally rose during the three years from the time of the original investment to the time of the final withdrawal. That would mean that the owner generally could not purchase as many goods and services upon receiving his $6,500 cash back at the end of three years as he could have purchased with the same amount at the time that he made his investment. If that is the case, then in the intervening three years conventional accounting net income did not faithfully represent to him the maximum amounts he could safely withdraw from the business and spend each year *and still preserve his initial investment economically intact.* Furthermore, one would also tend to question the extent to which conventional accounting net operating income (which equals net income in the absence of gains and losses) characterizes "performance" in the sense of the enterprise's ability to generate cash (purchasing power) for distribution to owners over the long run.

• *Changing replacement costs.* Technically, it must be assumed that an enterprise cannot exactly duplicate its past performance in the future. Too many variables in production processes cannot be controlled with absolute precision. But if conditions exist that make it *unlikely* that the "performance" represented in the net operating income of one year (or several years) could ever be matched in subsequent years, then the relevance of net operating income as an index of long-run cash-generating ability would be subject to some doubt. Such is the case when the cost to replace a productive asset changes substantially before the end of the asset's useful life.

Suppose, for instance, that after the first three years had lapsed, the cost of new equipment capable of another three years of the same service as the old equipment has risen to $7,000 from the $6,000 paid at the beginning of year one. At the start of year four the enterprise, with its original money investment of $6,500 intact, would not be able to replace the worn-out equipment without borrowing or additional investment from the owner. Thus, in the sense that the enterprise cannot continue to operate as before on its original capital, it is not as well off (as wealthy) as it was originally. In retrospect, then, net income did not turn out to be a faithful index of the amount of assets that could be withdrawn by the owner in the first three years of operations and still preserve the enterprise's ability to continue its operations thereafter.

Furthermore, under the circumstances, net operating income for the first three years may not be a very representative index of the longer-run cash-generating ability of the enterprise. After all, if it replaces the equipment at $7,000 and the equipment lasts only three years, as did the original equipment, the enterprise will have sacrificed $1,000 more for the same productive ability as it had in the first three years of its life. It will therefore somehow have to sell merchandise for $1,000 more in the following three years without increasing the cost of the merchandise it sells or its labor expense. Otherwise it will not do as well as the performance in its first three years of operations.

• *Price changes and the relevance of conventional accounting.* It was pointed out above that for conventional accounting net income to be thought of as a clear and unambiguous performance measure and index of disposable wealth, economic conditions, particularly prices, must be unchanging. When prices are changing significantly, the relevance of conventional accounting is somewhat open to question. It should be noted, however, that there are suggested accounting techniques (models) that reflect changing prices as they take place. Although these alternative financial accounting models are rarely used in present-day financial reporting, they are worthy of discussion, if only because price changes have become an increasingly significant economic phenomenon. Hence, several alternative models will be introduced, along with some of their apparent advantages and disadvantages, in Chapters 7 and 8.

Some Advantages of Conventional Accounting

• *Why conventional accounting?* In Chapter 4, when we introduced conventional accounting, we noted that it is the accounting model that is most evident in actual practice. In the preceding discussion, however, we have introduced some limitations on conventional accounting induced by changing prices. Perhaps it would be helpful, therefore, if we summarized the features of conventional accounting that make it so appealing in practice before looking at the alternatives designed to compensate for its limitations.

Conventional accounting lies between the two extreme possibilities that we have discussed so far for providing information about a business enterprise to outsiders. It does not provide information as objective as cash receipts and disbursements, alone, nor as potentially relevant to the needs of outside investors as would provision of management forecasts of expected future cash flows. But we must also point out that conventional accounting nevertheless possesses certain perceived advantages.

• *Objectivity.* Several of the relative advantages that many accountants attribute to conventional accounting can be summarized in the term *objectivity*. Accountants usually think of conventional accounting as being more objective than alternative models (other than the cash receipts and disbursements model). Typically, what they mean is that conventional accounting information is based on largely factual data, and that the original transaction values that are the basis of conventional accounting representations (statements) are relatively more verifiable than the valuations under alternative models.

The basic data used in conventional accounting are restricted to prices arrived at in the actual exchange transactions of the enterprise that have already taken place with outside, independent economic units, that is, the original transaction values from purchase and sales transactions. Hence, the data base is relatively factual (unlike the projections of future events, e.g., future cash flows required for management forecasts).

We acknowledged earlier that there is uncertainty in connection with asset and liability valuation and related revenue and expense recognition in conventional accounting. But, generally, any consistent overstatement or understatement of assets, liabilities, expense, or revenue will eventually be corrected as long as valuations are restricted to (unexpired) original transaction values. For instance, if an expense (say, depreciation) is understated in a given year, then the value of the related asset (say, equipment) is overstated (accumulated depreciation is insufficient). This means that in later years additional depreciation will be recognized equal to the deficiency in earlier years. Although compensating errors are not themselves desirable, the point is that within conventional accounting there are some limitations to errors (and manipulations), both as to amount and duration.

Furthermore, provided evidence of original transactions, such as sales slips and invoices, is not lost or destroyed, a skillful observer (usually a professional auditor) can *verify* that what the business enterprise represents on its financial statements is indeed a reasonable (fair) representation, within the conventional framework, of the status and activities of the enterprise. This verification process (called auditing) is such an important feature of present-day financial reporting by business enterprises to outside investors that it is discussed much more fully in Chapter 17. For now, it is sufficient to say that conventional accounting representations are considered to be relatively *amenable to verification,* which provides an additional deterrent (although not perfect protection, as we shall see later) against dishonesty and a safeguard against persistent error or personal bias.

Summary

The discussion in this chapter has been devoted to filling out the reader's understanding of conventional accounting. It included the disposable wealth measurement aspects of conventional accounting, along with a number of major qualifications as to conventional accounting's operational characteristics, such as implications of uncertainty and price changes. The discussion, however, is by no means complete. It would be impossible to cover all the details of conventional accounting in several volumes—to say nothing of several chapters! Instead, the discussion has been devoted only to significant aspects of the way that conventional accounting represents business enterprises and their activities *as a whole.* Other aspects of conventional accounting are discussed in the course of the next several chapters—as they are brought out by the contrasts between conventional accounting and the alternative models that will be introduced there.

Questions for Review and Discussion

6-1.   Define:

a. Paid-in capital

b. Retained earnings

c. Extraordinary gains (losses)

d. Net operating income

e. Net income

6-2.   Describe the Hicksian concept of disposable wealth. Of what relevance to parties external to the enterprise is the Hicksian concept?

6-3.   Explain in your own words why conventional accounting net operating income conforms to the Hicksian concept of disposable wealth (in the absence of any extraordinary gains and losses).

6-4.   The measurement of disposable wealth is potentially relevant to interested external parties besides owners who are concerned about dividends or withdrawals. Elaborate.

6-5.   If an enterprise distributes cash dividends equal to net income each period from its inception, what minimum amount of recognized net assets will always be retained by the enterprise? Why?

6-6.   What is the legal criterion for measuring disposable wealth? What is its significance? In general, how is the legal criterion accommodated within conventional accounting?

6-7.   Why are extraordinary gains and losses excluded from the conventional accounting measure of performance?

6-8.   List three reasons that an enterprise might have for not distributing dividends equal to disposable wealth.

6-9.   What is *conservatism* in conventional accounting? What apparently motivates conservatism among accountants or managers?

6-10.   One advantage of conventional accounting is its objectivity. Is it entirely objective? Explain.

6-11.   Conventional accounting *assumes* that prices are static. True or false? Defend your position.

6-12.   Suppose a company distributed cash dividends to owners equal to only one-half of its net income for a period. What are the implications of such a dividend policy for investors interested in the business? How would you describe the effect of such a policy on the business to someone who knows nothing about accounting (i.e., nothing about net income)?

6-13.   In this chapter it was noted that conventional accounting is subject to uncertainty. What are some of the sources of uncertainty in conventional accounting? How is uncertainty dealt with in conventional accounting? If you could redesign conventional accounting to deal more effectively with uncertainty, how would you alter it?

6-14.   Suppose that each year for the last several years Corporation X recognized a significant extraordinary loss in its income statement entitled "Loss on uncollectible customer accounts." What would you conclude about (a) the losses and (b) the management of the corporation?

Exercises   **6-1. Identifying Changes in Owners' Equity and Income Measures.**   For each of the following events, indicate its individual effect upon (a) the wealth (net assets) position, (b) the disposable wealth for the period, and (c) the performance of the company for the period.

  a. The company pays off a bank loan.

  b. Wages for the period are paid by the company.

  c. One of the owners contributes cash to the company.

  d. The company makes cash sales.

  e. One of the *owners* uses up company supplies.

  f. The *company* buys stocks in X Corporation.

  g. The company receives cash dividends from X Corporation.

  h. Depreciation of equipment (amounting to $300 of the total original cost of the equipment) is recorded.

  i. Rent expense is $500 for the period.

  j. Owner contributes a motor vehicle to the company.

  k. Advertising expense for the period is $100—it is not yet paid.

  l. The *company* pays cash dividends.

  m. Three years' insurance is paid in advance.

  n. Sales on credit are made.

  o. Supplies are used up by the company.

6-2.   Identifying Changes in Owners' Equity and Income Measures.   Owners' equity is affected by each of the following transactions. Construct a table showing the ultimate effect of each upon retained earnings, paid-in capital, net income, and net operating income. (Note: (1) Many of the items will have an effect upon more than one of the concepts, (2) the kind of business under consideration may be different from item to item, as indicated, and (3) it is assumed that the balances in paid-in capital and retained earnings are sufficient to absorb any appropriate decreases.)

Example:	Paid-in Capital	Retained Earnings	Net Income	Net Operating Income
Wages Expense of $300	None	(300)	(300)	(300)

a. Sales revenue of $600.

b. Gain of $100 from sales of machinery (not purchased for resale).

c. Owners were paid dividends of $1,000.

d. Sales returns by customers of $80.

e. Additional new owners contributed $5,000 to business.

f. Loss from destruction of merchandise by fire ($200).

g. Depreciation expense of $1,000.

h. Newspaper company is forced to pay $5,000 damages in libel suit (not covered by insurance).

i. Partner signs over the title of his car (market value $3,000) to the business (no consideration given by business).

j. Investors' club earns $500 in cash dividends.

k. Land speculation company earns $400 profit on sale of land.

l. Manufacturing company earns $1,000 profit on the condemnation of land for a freeway.

m. Partner is paid a $600 salary as the actual manager of the business.

n. A machine that had not been fully depreciated was unexpectedly determined to be completely worn out. It originally cost $5,000; depreciation to date is $4,000.

6-3.   Cash and Disposable Wealth.   Albany Rentals is a car rental firm which has been operating for several years. The owner, Algernon Albany, has followed the practice of withdrawing cash equal to the net income of each period. The beginning of 1973 balances in the accounts of the business are as follows:

Assets:			Liabilities and Owner's Equity:	
Cash		$ 1,000	Accounts payable	$ 2,000
Accounts receivable		2,500		
Gas and oil supplies		500		
Motor vehicles	$16,000			
Accumulated			Owner's equity	15,000
depreciation	(3,000)	13,000	Total liabilities and	
Total assets		$17,000	owner's equity	$17,000

During 1973 the following events were recorded:

Cash rentals earned	$4,000
Credit rentals earned	4,000
Purchases of gas and oil supplies (credit)	1,500
Rent paid for 1973	2,000
Depreciation expense for 1973	2,500
Supplies on hand at end of year	250
Repairs expense (all paid)	700
Payments on accounts payable	2,750
Receipts from accounts receivable	1,000

Required:

1. Record the information for 1973 on a financial position worksheet.

2. Produce an income statement for 1973.

3. Discuss whether Algernon is able to follow his usual withdrawal policy. Explain your reasoning.

6-4. Uncertainty and Disposable Wealth Measurement.   Max decides to go into business operating a charter bus at tourist resorts. He commences the business on January 1, 1972, by placing $10,000 in a bank account, out of which he purchases a bus for $7,500. *He decides that each year he will withdraw all the disposable wealth* that the business earns. The bus is expected to have a life of five years, at the end of which Max expects to sell it for $1,500. The other bus company transactions for 1972 and 1973 were:

	1972	1973
Cash fares	$12,000	$13,000
Charter fares (credit)	5,000	3,500
Insurance paid	1,500	700
Wages paid	7,500	7,000
Payments from customers	2,000	3,500
Gas and oil supplies purchased on credit	2,000	1,600
Payments to suppliers	500	3,100
Gas and oil on hand at end	400	—0—
Repairs and maintenance (all paid)	1,800	1,900
Insurance cost unexpired at year-end	500	—0—

All events for 1972 are recorded on the financial position worksheet in Exhibit 6-8. At the end of 1973 Max discovers to his horror that he will never collect the $3,000 that had been owing from 1972 and the debt must be considered a total loss. He decides to sell his bus, thinking that he can start the business afresh in 1974. He receives only $3,100 for the bus.

Required:

1. Record all the facts as they took place in worksheet form for 1973. (Do not forget the depreciation of the bus.)

2. Draw up an income statement for each of the two years.

3. In drawing up the income statement, did you show the losses on the customer's bad debt and from the sale of the bus as extraordinary losses? Why or why not?

Exhibit 6-8

MAX'S BUS COMPANY—1972

Description	Cash	Bus	Accumulated Depreciation	Accounts Receivable	Prepaid Insurance	Supplies	Accounts Payable	Owner's Equity
Balances, Jan. 1, 1972	10,000							10,000
Bus	(7,500)	7,500						
Cash fares	12,000							12,000 (R)
Credit fares				5,000				5,000 (R)
Insurance	(1,500)				500			(1,000) (E)
Wages	(7,500)							(7,500) (E)
Customer payments	2,000			(2,000)				
Supplies						2,000	2,000	
Payments to suppliers	(500)						(500)	
Supplies used						(1,600)		(1,600) (E)
Repairs and maintenance	(1,800)							(1,800) (E)
Depreciation expense			(1,200)					(1,200) (E)
Withdrawal	(3,900)							(3,900) (W)
Balances, Dec. 31, 1972	1,300	7,500	(1,200)	3,000	500	400	1,500	10,000

4. Give brief answers to the following: Is it likely that Max is in a position to "start the business afresh in 1974"? If not, why not? How could he have reduced the chances of ending up in such a position?

6-5. Gains, Losses, Disposable Wealth, and Performance.   On January 1, 1974, Maude, Mabel, Molly, and Mildred went into partnership, each contributing $15,000 in cash. The aim of the partnership, M, M, M & M Partners, was to provide a reliable income for the ladies, through the renting of apartments. A block of land was purchased for $20,000 in cash, and a small apartment building was built on it at a cost of $24,000, again paid in cash. The partners purchased a van for $5,000 cash. At a loss as to what to do with the remaining funds, they left $1,000 in the bank and invested the remainder in marketable securities. They intended to purchase additional marketable securities from time to time and finally convert them into cash as soon as they could afford more apartments. The apartments were considered to have a life of twenty years, with no salvage value; and the van to have a life of eight years, with expected proceeds of $200 on its disposal.

The following cash transactions occurred up to December 1, 1974:

Collections of rent	$11,000
Maintenance expense	1,500
Property tax paid	400
Wages expense	3,300
Motor vehicle expense	500
Insurance paid	1,000

On December 1, the apartment building was destroyed by a fire as a result of a tenant's smoking in bed. The insurance company reimbursed the partnership to the extent of $20,000. The land was sold for $24,000 in cash. The marketable securities were sold for $11,000 on December 30. With the cash now available, the partners paid $50,000 on December 31, 1974, for a new and larger apartment building. The apartment building was valued at $35,000, and the land on which it stood was assessed at $15,000. No operating revenue was earned during December, but miscellaneous expenses ($300) and motor vehicle expenses ($100) were incurred and paid.

The above information for 1974 appears in worksheet form in Exhibit 6-9.

Required:

1. Prepare a 1974 income statement for the partnership. (Note: Reread sections on recognizing gains and losses, pp. 167 to 169.)

2. What amount do you consider to be the appropriate measure of performance for the period? The measure of disposable wealth?

6-6. Uncertainty, Gains and Losses, and Disposable Wealth.   You and a friend, Zeke Zonker, pooled your resources of $1,000 each in cash and entered the business of selling lecture notes at the beginning of the autumn quarter, 1974. You intend to operate the business, Zapper and Zonker Enterprises, at least until the end of spring, 1975. You purchased a printing press at a cost of $2,500 (the bank lent you $1,000—interest free), which you expect will be sold for $1,900 at the

Exhibit 6-9

M, M, M & M PARTNERS

Description	Cash	Land	Buildings	Accumulated Depreciation	Motor Vehicle	Accumulated Depreciation	Marketable Securities	Owners' Equity
Contribution by partners	60,000							60,000
Purchase of land	(20,000)	20,000						
Purchase of apartments	(24,000)		24,000					
Purchase of van	(5,000)				5,000			
Purchase of marketable securities	(10,000)						10,000	
Revenue earned	11,000							11,000
Maintenance expense	(1,500)							(1,500)
Property tax expense	(400)							(400)
Wages expense	(3,300)							(3,300)
Motor vehicle expense	(500)							(500)
Insurance expense	(1,000)							(1,000)
Depreciation on apartments				(1,100)				(1,100)
Loss of apartments	20,000		(24,000)	1,100				(2,900)
Sale of land	24,000	(20,000)						4,000
Sale of marketable securities	11,000						(10,000)	1,000
Purchase of apartments	(50,000)	15,000	35,000					
Depreciation on motor vehicle						(600)		(600)
Miscellaneous expenses	(300)							(300)
Motor vehicle expense	(100)							(100)
Ending Position	9,900	15,000	35,000	—0—	5,000	(600)	—0—	64,300

end of spring, 1975, or $1,100 at the end of spring, 1976. You will depreciate the equipment at a rate of $200 a quarter. Your method of operation is simple— you and Zonker collect the materials and print the lecture notes which you sell to three distributors. The distributors are given until the end of each quarter to pay Zapper and Zonker Enterprises.

At the commencement of business you and Zonker have an argument. Zonker considers that at the end of each quarter you and he should receive a cash dividend equal to the income earned for the period. "It's disposable wealth, isn't it?" is his argument. You assert that "to be on the safe side" only 50 percent of the income should be withdrawn each quarter. You win.

At the end of the autumn quarter, things have gone well. You earned $800 profit and withdrew $200 each. The balances of the Zapper and Zonker Enterprises balance sheet were as follows:

ZAPPER AND ZONKER ENTERPRISES
Balance Sheet
As of the End of Autumn Quarter, 1974

Cash	$1,200	Accounts payable	$ 200
Supplies	100	Bank loan	1,000
Equipment	2,500	Total liabilities	$1,200
Accumulated depreciation	(200)	Owners' equity	2,400
Total assets	$3,600	Total	$3,600

In the next two quarters the following events occurred:

	Winter	Spring
Credit sales to distributors	$2,200	$1,800
Receipts from distributors	1,800	1,550
Wages paid	550	600
Advertising and insurance paid	50	100
Supplies purchased on credit	600	250
Repaid part of bank loan	500	500
Payments to accounts payable	700	350
Supplies on hand at end of winter	250	—0—

Additional information:

a. At the end of winter, one of the distributors, named Ripoff, owed $400. No action was taken as he promised to pay early in the spring quarter, which he did. During the winter $500 of the bank loan was repaid.

b. At the end of spring, Ripoff owed $650. The amount was written off as a bad debt, for a telegram was received from him saying that he was in Tahiti with a cocktail waitress from the Pink Pussycat Tavern. Just at the end of spring quarter classes, vandals broke in and destroyed the printing press. The insurance company paid insurance proceeds of $1,650.

c. The policy that the cash dividend could not exceed 50 percent of net income was adhered to in both winter and spring.

d. A worksheet for winter appears in Exhibit 6-10.

Exhibit 6-10

ZAPPER AND ZONKER ENTERPRISES

Description	Cash	Supplies	Equipment	Accumulated Depreciation	Accounts Receivable	Accounts Payable	Bank Loan	Owners' Equity
Opening Balances (beginning of winter)	1,200	100	2,500	(200)		200	1,000	2,400 (R)
Credit sales					2,200			2,200 (R)
Receipts on account	1,800				(1,800)			
Wages	(550)							(550) (E)
Advertising and insurance	(50)							(50) (E)
Supplies purchased		600				600		
Payments to suppliers	(700)					(700)		
Supplies used		(450)						(450) (E)
Bank repayment	(500)						(500)	
Depreciation				(200)				(200) (E)
Withdrawal	(475)							(475) (W)
Balances (end of winter)	725	250	2,500	(400)	400	100	500	2,875

Required:

1. Complete a worksheet for spring.

2. Produce an income statement for winter and for spring.

3. How did you classify the losses on bad debts and the printing press? Justify your treatment.

4. At the end of spring, have Zonker and Zapper at least maintained their original investment of $2,000? What would have been the position if Ripoff had not failed to pay the money he owed and if the equipment had been sold for $1,900 as expected?

5. Explain the justification for not paying out all disposable wealth at the end of a period.

6. If Zapper and Zonker Enterprises had continued in business, do you think that their winter quarter income was representative at the time of their long-run cash-generating ability? Why or why not?

6-7.   Detecting Misapplications of Conventional Accounting.   The owner-president of the Gidgiegannup Electrical Contractors Company was elated, but at the same time concerned, by the financial results of his firm for the month of May. Knowing you to be a particularly astute student of accounting, he confides in you. "This business has lost money over the last few years. I was seriously considering going into another line of business, but look at the worksheet for May. It indicates our best month ever! One thing worries me though—at the end of April my accountant retired, and I replaced him with a new fellow. Now I don't know whether my previous accountant was dishonest or just making us look bad, or whether the new fellow has made mistakes favorable to us. Can you look into it?" He hands you the worksheet shown in Exhibit 6-11.

With typical determination you conduct a thorough investigation of the accounting records of the Gidgiegannup Electrical Contractors Company and discover the following:

a. That the equipment bought at the end of April 1974 has a life of only five years, at the end of which it will have no salvage value.

b. That the prepaid insurance (paid on May 1) represented insurance for the period May 1, 1974, to April 30, 1975.

c. That the rent (which was paid on May 1) represented rent for the period May 1, 1974, to June 30, 1974.

d. That interest on the bank loan is 1½ percent per month, payable quarterly. The last quarterly payment was on April 30.

e. That advertising amounting to $150 had been billed by the local newspaper. Only $100 of that bill had been paid and duly recorded as an expense.

f. That the employees are paid at the end of the week following work performed and are thus owed wages for the last week of May amounting to $380. None of the wages paid this period related to work performed in previous periods.

g. That Fred Nurk, who owed the company $400, had skipped to Argentina.

h. That work had been completed and delivered to a customer at a price of $200 but had not been recorded in any way. No payment has been made by the customer.

Exhibit 6-11

GIDGIEGANNUP ELECTRICAL CONTRACTORS COMPANY

Description	Cash	Accounts Receivable	Electrical Supplies	Prepaid Insurance	Prepaid Rent	Equipment	Accumulated Depreciation	Insurance Payable	Rent Payable	Wages Payable	Interest on Loan	Accounts Payable	Bank Loan	Owner's Equity
Opening Balances	6,000	2,000	500			6,000						5,000	3,000	6,500
Revenue earned		8,000												8,000 (R)
Receipts from customers	5,000	(5,000)												
Supplies purchased			1,000									1,000		
Payments to suppliers	(800)											(800)		
Wages paid	(1,600)													(1,600) (E)
Advertising paid	(100)													(100) (E)
Insurance paid	(600)			600										
Rent expense paid	(800)													(800) (E)
Supplies used			(700)											(700) (E)
Balances (end of May)	7,100	5,000	800	600		6,000						5,200	3,000	11,300

187

i. That an electricity bill for $300 had been received at the end of May but was not reflected in the accounts.

Required:

1. Present an income statement for May 1974 as it would have been had you not examined the records.
2. Starting with the May 31 balances as shown, make the necessary entries on a worksheet to record the facts that you have unearthed.
3. Draw up a revised income statement.

6-8. Conventional Accounting Transaction Interpretation.   Following are a set of transactions and events for a hypothetical corporation for the year just ended. Interpret each according to the conventional accounting model and, in a table, (1) indicate the accounts or elements of the corporation's financial position that are affected by each item, giving the account name, amount, and direction of change (distinguish between paid-in capital and retained earnings), and (2) indicate the amount and direction of the effect of each item on net operating income and net income. (The first item is used as an example below.) If you feel you have to make any significant assumptions in order to interpret an item, show it as a footnote to your answer table.

a. The company had a combined beginning supplies inventory and purchases for the year with a total cost of $20,000. The supplies remaining at year-end originally cost $1,000.

b. Rent for the year amounted to $2,400. However, it had been paid in a two-year rent payment prior to the beginning of the year.

c. Equipment originally costing $20,000 and depreciated-to-date in the amount of $12,500 was lost due to an accident at the beginning of the year. Insurance proceeds were $9,000.

d. Sales for cash amounted to $15,000. New credit sales equaled $75,000. Goods were delivered to customers who had advanced the full selling prices of $10,000 last year.

e. At the beginning of the period the *accumulated depreciation* on assets employed in the business was $225,000. At the end of the period it was $250,000.

f. New owners contributed $90,000 cash to the corporation.

g. Wage and salary payments made during the year equaled $55,000. However, wages of $5,000 were owed to employees at year-end for work already performed. No wages were owed at the beginning of the year.

h. Dividends of $20,000 were declared and paid to owners during the year.

Example:

	Income Measures Affected	
Accounts Affected	*Net Operating Income*	*Net Income*
a. Supplies inventory (19,000) Retained earnings (19,000)	(19,000)	(19,000)

6-9. Financial Statement Relationships. The statement of financial position for the Larson Electronics Corporation, which was based on the conventional accounting model, reflected the following information:

	12/31/73	12/31/74
Total assets	$5,200,000	$5,800,000
Total liabilities	1,200,000	1,000,000

During 1974 the total revenue generated by normal business operations was $10 million. In addition, the company sold a parcel of land it had owned for several years at a gain of $200,000. The corporation declared and paid cash dividends to its shareholders amounting to $500,000 in 1974.

1. What was the value of owners' equity on December 31, 1974?

2. What was Larson's net income (disposable wealth) for 1974?

3. What was Larson's net operating income (measure of performance) for 1974?

4. What was the amount of the expenses associated with normal business operations recognized by Larson Electronics Corporation during 1974?

7

Modifications for
General Price-Level Changes

In Chapter 6 it was shown that in times of changing prices, conventional accounting loses some of its intuitive appeal as a means of measuring enterprise performance and disposable wealth. The purpose of this and the next chapter is to introduce three of the more frequently suggested modifications and departures from conventional accounting designed to accommodate changing prices.

The implications of changing prices can be assessed at two levels. First, there is general inflation or deflation. Inflation or deflation refers to the general drift upward or downward in prices, the exchange rates at which money is traded for all goods and services. Second, the prices of some goods or services rise (rise more rapidly) or fall (fall more rapidly) relative to the prices of other goods and services whether or not prices are generally rising or falling. This chapter will approach the problem of changing prices at the former (general) level; the next chapter will approach the problem at the latter (specific) level.

Incidentally, the reader may note a contrast between the way that we introduced conventional accounting in earlier chapters and the way that we approach alternative models of the enterprise in these two chapters. Conventional accounting was introduced first with performance measurement in mind and was then followed by an elaboration of the disposable wealth measurement aspects of the model. In introducing alternative models, disposable wealth measurement is dealt with first, followed by discussion of performance measurement. However, there is no substantive reason for the reversal of order, other than convenience in exposition.

The Relevance of Changes in General Purchasing Power

What we are about to describe in this chapter is the basic technical methodology and the underlying rationale for adapting conventional accounting to the phenomenon of general inflation or deflation. The result of the adaptation will be a modified conventional accounting model that includes measures of performance and disposable wealth *that have the same characteristics in times of generally changing prices that conventional accounting measures have in times of static prices.* Before proceeding, however, some attention to our motivation is in order.

Generally, the prices of all goods and services do not rise and fall together. Some rise or fall faster than others; and the prices of some goods may actually move in the opposite direction to the general inflationary trend. Furthermore, all economic units—businesses as well as individuals—tend to have unique spending patterns. As a result, inflation or deflation will have a different impact on each economic unit depending on the relative price changes of the goods and services it prefers. But if inflation or deflation has a unique impact on each business and individual, why attempt to modify conventional accounting on the basis of the general trend in prices? The answer lies in the rationale for using money values as a *common unit* of expression under any circumstances (i.e., static prices or not).

Since the prices of some goods and services go down while others go up (or they change at different rates), it is certainly true that some people will derive relatively more or less *satisfaction* from money than others as prices change. However, the satisfaction we get from spending is not a basis on which we can defend using money as a common unit of expression in the first place—even in times of perfectly stable prices. The mere fact that individuals' tastes and preferences change over time means that satisfaction from spending will change *even though no prices change.* The basis for using money as a unit of measure is its meaning as an index or unit of command over quantities (and varieties) of goods and services. The power of money generally to command goods and services is a function of the quantities of the various goods and services available and the prices of those goods and services. When prices generally go up or down, that power changes proportionately for everyone, quite apart from individual tastes and preferences. That is, in exercising individual purchasing preferences at any point in time, each individual sacrifices or foregoes just what everyone else foregoes in alternative goods and services for every dollar spent on a particular item.

When prices generally rise or fall, it alters the *sacrifice* of alternate goods and services embodied in spending any given dollar on any given item. This is why the original transaction costs employed (recognized) in conventional accounting gradually become less relevant over time when prices generally rise or fall. An amount of dollars actually spent in the past to acquire a resource ceases to represent currently the *original* sacrifice of alternate goods and services to possess that particular resource. *In adjusting original transaction values for changes in general purchasing power, the purpose is to express the original sacrifice in terms of the number of current (or recent) dollars that, if spent today, would mean the foregoing of the same alternate real goods and services.*

With this rationale established, we will proceed by (1) describing briefly some tools for recognizing and adjusting for changes in purchasing power, (2) developing an easily calculated measure of disposable wealth that takes into account generally rising or falling prices, and (3) showing finally that this measure of disposable wealth is composed of two parts, each of which measures an aspect of enterprise performance in times of changing prices.

Price-Level Indexes and Comparative Purchasing Power in Constant Dollars

In Chapter 6 we referred to changes in purchasing power without describing how changes in purchasing power are measured, or even how purchasing power itself is measured. As a rule, purchasing power and purchasing power changes are characterized by means of price-level indexes.

> **Price-Level Index.** A price-level index is a numerical score representing the cost of a particular bundle of goods and services as of one point in time (some year) *relative to* the cost of the same bundle of goods at some reference point in time (usually called a "base" year).

The hypothetical bundle of goods is usually constructed so as to contain typical or representative proportions of the goods and services purchased by a class of economic units whose purchasing power is of interest, such as households, businesses, unmarried college students, or all economic units in the economy.

• *Constructing index numbers.* Suppose that the typical or average bundle of goods for some particular class of economic units has the costs shown in the second column of Exhibit 7-1 in the years 1965–70—the total costs being derived by (1) determining how much of each product or service was included in the typical bundle, (2) multiplying each product's quantity by its price, and (3) totaling the amounts calculated in (2).

Exhibit 7-1   COST OF GOODS AND PRICE-LEVEL INDEX

Year	Cost	Index Value
1965	$1,980	90
1966	1,870	85
1967	2,090	95
1968	2,200	100
1969	2,420	110
1970	2,310	105

As is the usual custom, let us choose one year, say 1968, as the base year and set its index value to 100 (we could use any convenient number and still gain the manipulative advantages of an index). We are saying that $2,200 on the money scale is equivalent to 100 on *our* price-level index scale. Using proportions, we can then work out index values for all the other years relative to the base year. For instance, to get an index value for 1969 we need only pose the question, $2,420 is to $2,200 as *what* index value is to 100? Letting i represent the unknown value, the answer may be worked out as follows:

$$\frac{\$2,420}{\$2,200} = \frac{i}{100}$$

$$i \cdot \$2,200 = \$2,420 \cdot 100$$

$$i = \frac{2,420}{2,200} \cdot 100$$

$$i = 110$$

Posing similar questions for the other years fills out the price-level index column of Exhibit 7-1.

• *Using price-level index numbers.* Now we can conveniently make some statements about the purchasing power of the hypothetical class of economic units of interest. For instance, we can say that in 1970 it took $105, on the average, for that class of economic units to buy what it could buy in 1968 for $100. In other words, prices for this group had risen on the average to 1.05 of what they were in 1968 (105/100). Or in still other words, a dollar in 1970 was worth only 95.24 percent of what it was worth to this group in 1968, on the average (i.e., it would buy only 100/105 as many goods and services).

Similar comparisons can be made for other years—and we are not restricted to comparisons between the base year and nonbase years. For instance, since 1967 has an index value of 95 and 1966 has a value of 85, we know that prices for the group rose 11.76 percent on the average between 1966 and 1967, i.e., 1967 prices were 95/85, or 1.1176 of 1966 prices on the average.

Finally, and most important for our purposes, if we have a set of price-level index values and the price paid for a particular good purchased in a particular year, we can translate the price paid into an equivalent money sacrifice in the dollars of any other year. For instance, if an item purchased by our hypothetical group cost $240 in 1968 (when the index was 100), we can say that it would have required $264 to make the same sacrifice of alternate goods and services in 1969 (when the index was 110), that is, $240 \cdot 110/100 = $264. This type of translation will be the bulwark of the techniques introduced in later sections of the chapter.

Selecting an Appropriate Index

Before leaving the topic of price-level indexes and their applications, an additional point relevant to the purpose of this chapter ought to be made.

Our interest in this chapter is to preserve, in times of generally changing prices, the meaning that the original transaction values employed in conventional accounting have in times of static prices. That is, we are interested not in changing, but in correcting the values used in conventional accounting for a change in the size (purchasing power) of the unit of measure (the dollar) used to express those values.

To accomplish this purpose, the price-level index that we use to characterize general purchasing power must possess certain ideal properties. It must be as broadly based as possible—it should include quantities and prices of as many of the available goods and services in the economy as possible. In addition, it should include correction factors for changes in the quality of the goods and services available. Changes in quality are a major confounding force in attempts to characterize changes in the size of the dollar (general purchasing power) over time. If prices generally rise so that a dollar purchases less on the average, the sacrifice in quantity of goods and services foregone in spending a dollar goes down. However, if products improve in quality, the sacrifice of real economic service of those products foregone does not go down in proportion to the quantity reduction. So some qualitative correction is certainly in order if a price-level index is to express changes in general purchasing power accurately in an economy characterized by rapidly changing technology.

Needless to say, no one now prepares an ideal price-level index for the U.S. economy, but several reasonably good indexes are provided by certain government agencies. The Gross National Product Implicit Price Deflator produced by the U.S. Department of Commerce is broadly based. But some authors find it objectionable because it is not corrected for changes in quality of goods and services. On the other hand, the Bureau of Labor Statistics' Consumer Price Index is widely accepted as a measure of general price levels and is not as greatly affected by changes in quality of products as some indexes. However, it is not our purpose to go into great detail about the suitability of various available indexes.

Conventional Accounting in Times of Generally Changing Prices

To review again briefly the problems encountered in conventional accounting in times of inflation or deflation and to suggest the means to their solution, let us consider an extremely simple example. Example 7-1 is easily followed through to a complete solution. Yet it can be used to illustrate all of the necessary technical skill involved in adjusting conventional accounting for changes in the general level of prices.

Example 7-1   Our hypothetical case will be the Trading Corporation founded by Mr. Speculator a year ago to buy and sell various products on a strictly cash basis. Mr. Speculator started Trading Corporation with an investment of $8,000 of his own money plus $2,000 borrowed from a friend at 5 percent interest per year. The friend agreed that the interest was to be accrued continuously in each year but need not be paid each year. Rather, it could be added to the loan balance, accumulated, and paid at the end of the five-year loan period.

At the beginning of the year Trading Corporation made several large purchases of surplus commodities and retail products at going-out-of-business auctions, spending $9,000 of its cash. No other purchases were made during the year. Instead, the goods purchased at the beginning of the year were gradually sold off throughout the year until only $900 worth of the original inventory remained at year-end. Total cash sales, though, amounted to $12,000 during the year.

The conventional accounting treatment of these facts is represented in the financial worksheet in Exhibit 7-2. With one exception, the worksheet is the same as all others we have used before. The exception is that the last line is not labeled "Ending Position." Instead, it bears the label "Preliminary Balances." This label implies that something remains to be recognized. That is indeed the case. Mr. Speculator has not made his annual withdrawal of cash from the business. The purpose of arriving at what we have labeled Preliminary Balances is to give Mr. Speculator an idea of what ending financial position would be if no withdrawal were made. The "preliminary balance" numbers in each element of financial position are calculated as if they were the amounts in the enterprise's ending position.

Exhibit 7-2

TRADING CORPORATION
Financial Position Worksheet
For the Year 19X1

Description	Cash	Inventory	Loan	Owner's Equity
Beginning Position	10,000		2,000	8,000
Purchases	(9,000)	9,000		
Sales (throughout year)	12,000			12,000 (R)
Cost of sales		(8,100)		(8,100)(E)
Interest			100	(100)(E)
Preliminary Balances	13,000	900	2,100	11,800

Exhibit 7-2 points up a dilemma faced by Mr. Speculator. He wants to determine how much of the end-of-year cash he should withdraw from Trading Corporation for his personal use in the coming year. Mr. Speculator owns several small businesses that have generally provided him with a good living. But to ensure that this continues, he has always tried to restrict his withdrawals to amounts that do not impair his original investment in each business. That policy has been easy to follow in recent years. Prices generally have not changed (hypothetically, of course), and the yearly conventional accounting net income from each business has served as a reasonably satisfactory index of how much he could withdraw. But this year is different. Severe inflation has set in, so that the general price-level index went from 100 at the beginning of the year to 121 at the end, averaging 110 during the year.

As Exhibit 7-2 reflects, conventional accounting net operating income for Trading Corporation for its first year of operations is $3,800 ($12,000 sales revenue less $8,200 total expense). If Mr. Speculator withdraws cash in an amount equal to net operating income of $3,800, as he has done in past years with his other businesses, the effect on Trading Corporation's financial position is illustrated in Exhibit 7-3, which picks up where Exhibit 7-2 leaves off.

Exhibit 7-3

TRADING CORPORATION
Financial Position Worksheet
As of the End of 19X1

Description	Cash	Inventory	Loan	Owner's Equity
Preliminary Balances	13,000	900	2,100	11,800
Withdrawal	(3,800)			(3,800) (W)
Ending (Beginning) Position	9,200	900	2,100	8,000

A withdrawal of $3,800 in cash would leave net assets of $9,200 cash plus inventory with an original cost of $900 less a liability of $2,100, a total equal in number of dollars to Mr. Speculator's original investment of $8,000. But Mr. Speculator's original investment of $8,000 was made when the price-level index was at 100. By the end of the year, with the price-level index at 121, it would take $121/100 \cdot \$8,000$, or $9,680, to represent the same amount of general purchasing power as $8,000 represented at the beginning of the year. Thus, to withdraw $3,800 would be to shrink the asset base of the business below its original purchasing power. Conventional accounting net income (net operating income if no gains and losses are experienced) therefore does not serve at least one of its purposes—that of a reliable index of disposable wealth—in times of rising prices.

Disposable Wealth in Times of Generally Changing Prices

Now suppose Mr. Speculator wanted to withdraw only as much cash as would not impair the original purchasing power invested in Trading Corporation. How would he determine that amount? One's first impulse might be to look to the strictly conventional accounting preliminary balances shown on the worksheet and observe that before any year-end withdrawal there would be $13,000 cash plus inventory with an original cost of $900 less a liability of $2,100—a total of $11,800 of net assets possessed by the business. A hasty conclusion would then be that Mr. Speculator could withdraw cash equal to the difference between the net assets possessed prior to the withdrawal, $11,800, and the end-of-year dollar equivalent of his original $8,000 investment, or $9,680. Although it is perhaps intuitively appealing, this conclusion is logically inconsistent.

The $9,680 is the amount of end-of-year dollars equivalent in purchasing power to $8,000 at the beginning of the year, whereas the $11,800 is a mixture of dollars of different purchasing power, that is, the $11,800 is the sum of $13,000 year-end cash and $900 original cost of inventory in *beginning-of-year dollars* less the year-end liability balance of $2,100. We simply cannot subtract $9,680 *end-of-year dollars* from this mixed sum of $11,800 and get meaningful results. First, some adjustment has to be made in order to measure Trading Corporation's preliminary ending position on the same basis as the $9,680 criterion amount, that is, end-of-year dollars. In making this adjustment, we encounter an important application of the difference noted in Chapter 5 between monetary and nonmonetary assets and liabilities.

• *Adjusting ending balances in accounts.* Recall that by definition monetary assets (including cash) and monetary liabilities are rights to receive and obligations to pay fixed amounts of dollars at specified times. Although the purchasing power of a dollar may change over time, such specific amounts do not change. Monetary assets and liabilities, valued at their specified or nominal amounts, are always stated in current dollars. Hence, adjustment for changes in purchasing power of year-end balances of monetary assets or liabilities is neither necessary nor appropriate. In the case of Trading Corporation, then, no adjustment is made to the preliminary ending cash balance of $13,000 or the ending loan balance of $2,100.

However, the same is not true of nonmonetary items, which, in the case of Trading Corporation, includes only the inventory with an original cost of $900. Each of those 900 beginning-of-year dollars originally spent on the items in the ending inventory represents a purchasing power sacrifice different from a one-dollar sacrifice at the end of the year. In fact, we know that in order to have given up as much purchasing power at the end of the year as was given up at the beginning of the year for those items, it would take $121/100 \cdot \$900 = \$1,089$. To state the entire ending position of Trading Corporation in year-end dollars, it is necessary to adjust the original cost of the inventory upward from $900 to $1,089.

Although such an adjustment satisfies the purpose of measuring all assets of Trading Corporation in terms of year-end dollars, it raises some questions as well. First, how can we arbitrarily alter the amount of an asset held by the enterprise as of a point in time? Second, what does it mean when we increase the dollars of Trading Corporation's ending inventory from $900 to $1,089? Has the enterprise gained something?

The answer to both questions is that we have not altered the inventory element of financial position by making our adjustment. Rather, the whole process is like dealing with a foreign currency. By the time we get to the end of the year—the point in time at which we wish to calculate disposable wealth —beginning-of-the-year dollars are no longer the dollars we deal in. Because of inflation, we deal in a new currency—no matter that we call it by the same name, dollars.

Now suppose that all of the purchases at the beginning of the year had been conducted in a foreign currency, but at the end of the year Trading Corporation switched to dollars. Would it alter financial position to restate in terms of the new currency the costs of the nonmonetary assets purchased with the old currency? No, it would just be stating the same facts in terms of the new currency. Essentially that is what we do when we state the original purchasing power cost of Trading Corporation's ending inventory in end-of-year dollars. Furthermore, since the end-of-year assets of the enterprise are unaltered by the conversion to a new currency, no change in the wealth of the enterprise (gain or loss) occurs. The larger "adjusted" inventory of $1,089 is simply the same wealth item (inventory) valued at the same value, the original purchasing power given in exchange for it. But, inasmuch as prices have generally risen during the year, it requires more dollars (each of lesser purchasing power) than at the time of the purchase *to represent the sacrifice made in the original transaction.*

• *Calculating disposable wealth—summary.* Now, in summary, we can conclude that (1) prior to any withdrawal by Mr. Speculator, Trading Corporation has net assets expressed in end-of-year dollars of $11,989 ($13,000 in cash plus ending inventory having an original purchasing power cost in *end-of-year dollars* of $1,089 less a liability of $2,100), (2) it is necessary to have only $9,680 net assets in end-of-year dollars to have an end-of-year purchasing power equivalent of the original $8,000 invested in the business, and (3) therefore, $2,309 of cash ($11,989 − $9,680) can be withdrawn from the business at year-end without reducing the recognized purchasing power of the recognized net assets (owner's equity) below the level at the beginning of the year.

The latter conclusion is just what Mr. Speculator wants to know, that is, he can withdraw $2,309 from Trading Corporation at the end of its first year of operations without impairing the purchasing power that he originally invested in the business. Furthermore, the steps required to arrive at this amount are straightforward and few in number, even for the most complicated business enterprise. The steps are listed below and illustrated with reference to Trading Corporation in Exhibit 7-4.

1. The end-of-year balances in all nonmonetary elements of financial position must be adjusted to their equivalent purchasing power in end-of-year dollars. (In the example the $900 original cost of the ending inventory was adjusted to end-of-year dollars of equivalent purchasing power, $1,089 —lines 7 and 8 of Exhibit 7-4.)

2. The net (or sum) of all monetary and adjusted nonmonetary assets and liabilities must be calculated to get a price-level-adjusted end-of-period net asset figure. (In the example, we added the end-of-year cash balance of $13,000 to the adjusted ending inventory figure of $1,089 and subtracted the liability balance of $2,100 to get the adjusted net asset figure of $11,989—line 8 of Exhibit 7-4.)

3. The end-of-year dollar equivalents must be calculated for the net assets (assets minus liabilities) *at the beginning of the period* plus any additional investments of assets during the period. (In the example there were net assets of $8,000 at the beginning of the year; the end-of-year dollar equivalent of the $8,000 was $9,680—line 9 of Exhibit 7-4.)

4. Subtract the amount described in number 3 above from the adjusted net asset figure in number 2 to get the amount, if any, of withdrawable assets, i.e., disposable wealth. *We will call this amount price-level-adjusted net income.* (In the example, we subtracted $9,680 from $11,989 to get $2,309—lines 8, 9, and 10 of Exhibit 7-4.)

The effect of a cash withdrawal of $2,309 on Trading Corporation's ending financial position is illustrated in Exhibits 7-5 and 7-6. Notice particularly that (1) the financial position worksheet in Exhibit 7-5 starts with the price-level-adjusted preliminary balances from Exhibit 7-4 (line 8), and (2) the after-withdrawal owner's equity equals the criterion amount of $9,680 in both Exhibits 7-5 and 7-6.

Exhibit 7-4

TRADING CORPORATION
Price-Level-Adjusted Net Income
(Disposable Wealth)
For the Year 19X1

Description	Cash	Inventory	Loan	Owner's Equity
1. Beginning Position	10,000		2,000	8,000
2. Purchases	(9,000)	9,000		
3. Sales	12,000			12,000 (R)
4. Cost of sales		(8,100)		(8,100) (E)
5. Interest			100	(100) (E)
6. Preliminary balances	13,000	900	2,100	11,800
7. Adjustment factor		121/100		

8. Price-level-adjusted
   balances   13,000 +   1,089   − 2,100 = $11,989
9. P-L-A beginning net assets (owner's equity) $8,000 × 121/100 = 9,680
10. P-L-A net income (disposable wealth) $ 2,309

Exhibit 7-5

TRADING CORPORATION
Financial Position Worksheet
19X1

Description	Cash	Inventory	Loan	Owner's Equity
P-L-A preliminary balances	13,000	1,089	2,100	11,989
Withdrawal	(2,309)			(2,309) (W)
Ending Position	10,691	1,089	2,100	9,680

Exhibit 7-6

TRADING CORPORATION
Balance Sheet
As of the End of 19X1

Assets:		Liabilities and Owner's Equity:	
Cash	$10,691	Loan	$ 2,100
Inventory	1,089	Owner's equity	9,680
		Total liabilities and	
Total assets	$11,780	owner's equity	$11,780

As a final observation, the reader should be aware that the method of calculating disposable wealth worked out in this section is a direct application of the Hicksian definition of income (disposable wealth) discussed in Chapters 3 and 6. That definition states that disposable wealth is the amount of wealth that an economic unit can dispose of during a period without leaving itself worse off at the end of the period than at the beginning. Direct application of the definition therefore implies that beginning and ending wealth (net assets) are measured (allowing for owner investments and withdrawals) and that the difference between the two figures is disposable wealth for the period. That is precisely what the technique described in this section does—

with the addition that both beginning and ending net assets are measured in terms of the same units, end-of-year dollars.

Thus we can say with confidence that regardless of the complexity of the business, we can find the amount of disposable wealth in times of rising or falling prices that, if distributed by the business, will leave its initial purchasing power intact. This amount (price-level-adjusted net income) thus serves as a reliable index of disposable wealth in times of changing prices in the same sense that conventional accounting net income serves that purpose in times of stable prices.

Price-Level Changes and Performance Measurement

It should be recalled, however, that in times of stable prices, at least, conventional accounting income measures have another desirable property as well as measuring disposable wealth. Net operating income measures the performance of the enterprise. That is, net operating income characterizes the enterprise's recognized current ability to produce products whose values to customers (revenues) exceed the costs of resources sacrificed to produce them (expenses). And to the extent that current performance is sustainable, or a measure of the business's continuing capability, net income presumably can provide owner-investors and creditors with valuable information about the kind of future cash-generating ability to expect from the enterprise.

Therefore, even though we now have a way of determining a reliable index of disposable wealth in times of changing prices, we ought to go further and ask the question, Is there also a way of characterizing performance in times of changing prices, comparable to conventional accounting net income in times of stable prices? The answer is yes. But it will take some additional analysis of our example to see that this is so.

• *Conventional accounting performance measurement and changing prices.* One logical place to start in arriving at a performance measure in times of changing prices is the logic of conventional accounting performance measurement. The appeal of conventional accounting net income as a performance measure is the matching principle—according to which revenues are offset by *causally related* expenses to get the index of performance, net operating income. So as a first step we might ask, Does conventional accounting net operating income have the same appeal as a performance measure in times of changing prices that it has when prices are stable? If not, why not?

The answer to the first question is no. The reason is apparent when we analyze the conventional accounting net operating income for Trading Corporation's first year, shown in Exhibit 7-7.

Exhibit 7-7

TRADING CORPORATION
Income Statement
For the Year 19X1

Sales revenue		$12,000
Less expenses:		
Cost of sales	$8,100	
Interest	100	8,200
Net operating income		$ 3,800

Why is the $3,800 conventional accounting net operating income figure unsuitable as a performance measure under the hypothetical circumstances of our example? We noted above that it was unacceptable to add the $13,000 preliminary end-of-year cash balance to the $900 beginning-of-year cost of the ending inventory. Each dollar included in one of the figures represents a different amount of purchasing power than each dollar in the other figure. Hence to add them gave a result that was meaningless in conveying a total purchasing power consistent with the parts. Similarly, the revenue figure of $12,000 and the expense (cost of sales) figure of $8,100 and the interest expense figure of $100 in Exhibit 7-7 *do not* represent total accomplishments (values provided to customers) and total sacrifices (cost of resources provided), respectively, in equal-sized purchasing-power units, that is, on the same measurement scale.

• *Price-level-adjusted operating income.* The $8,100 originally paid for the goods sold was paid (sacrificed) at the beginning of the year when the price level was at 100, whereas the $12,000 received from customers was received throughout the year as the price-level index averaged 110. By year-end, when all the interest had been accrued, the index had reached 121, and none of the amounts continued to convey the purchasing power given or received at the times of the original transactions. Because the meaning of one dollar continued to change throughout the year, original numbers of dollars exchanged lost their ability to convey the significance of the original economic events. But the situation is not without remedy. Just as we adjusted the 900 original dollars paid for the ending inventory to 1,089 equivalent end-of-year dollars in an earlier section, we can adjust both conventional accounting revenues and expenses of the period to their end-of-year dollar equivalents. The appropriate translations appear in Exhibit 7-8.

Exhibit 7-8

TRADING CORPORATION
Statement of Price-Level-Adjusted Operating Income
For the Year 19X1

	Original Transaction Value	Adjustment Factor	Price-Level-Adjusted Value
Sales revenue	$12,000	121/110	$13,200
Less expenses:			
Cost of sales	8,100	121/100	$ 9,801
Interest expense	100	121/110	110
Total expense			$ 9,911
Price-level-adjusted operating income			$ 3,289

The reasoning behind the translations in Exhibit 7-8 is basically the same as that used earlier. Since the price level averaged 110 as sales revenues were received throughout the year and since the price level had reached 121 by year-end, we can conclude that on the average for every $110 received from customers during the year, Trading Corporation would have had to receive $121 at year-end to receive the same amount of purchasing power. Hence 13,200 end-of-year dollars ($12,000 · 121/110) shown in the Price-Level-

Adjusted Value column equals the *purchasing power equivalent of the 12,000 actual revenue dollars received* during the year shown in the Original Transaction Value column. The item in the Adjustment Factor column, 121/110, is the ratio of end-of-year dollars to average-of-year dollars of equivalent purchasing power. It is used to get the adjusted figure from the actual dollar total. Note again that the purpose of the adjustments is not to alter the original transaction value basis, but rather to express all revenues and expense amounts in equal-sized units, namely, end-of-year dollars. Perhaps it is also best recognized at this point that the above method for price-level adjusting total revenue for the period is purely an expedient method. A more precise way for price-level adjusting an aggregate of many individual exchange prices, like total revenue for a period, is to first adjust the price received (or paid) in each individual transaction, according to the price level at the time that the individual exchanges took place. Then the individually adjusted prices can be summed to arrive at an adjusted aggregate.

However, such a method involves considerably more effort than the use of the average index method employed above. Furthermore, provided the set of sales or other individual transactions is fairly evenly distributed over the period, relatively little difference in the results of applying the two methods is to be expected. In practice, the selection of a method would involve a trade-off between precision and clerical cost and effort. But since nothing is gained by greater precision for purely expositional purposes, we will continue to use the more convenient average index method in the present discussion.

The reasoning underlying the adjustment of expenses (cost of sales and interest) is similar to that for revenues. Since the cost of the goods sold to customers during the period was expended at the beginning of the year when the price-level index was 100, we know that it would take 121 end-of-year dollars for every \$100 actually spent to represent the original purchasing power sacrificed. Thus the cost of sales in end-of-year dollars is \$9,801 (121/100 · \$8,100). Since the interest was accrued continuously over the period, it is adjusted like the revenue.

When we subtract the \$9,911 adjusted total expense from the \$13,200 adjusted sales revenues we get \$3,289, the amount labeled *price-level-adjusted operating income* in Exhibit 7-8.

> **Price-Level-Adjusted Operating Income.** Price-level-adjusted operating income equals price-level-adjusted revenue minus price-level-adjusted expense for the period.

Notice that the amount is different from (in this case, less than) the \$3,800 net income calculated earlier according to conventional accounting. This, of course, is a result of the adjustments to take account of changes in purchasing power in measuring revenue and expense—but it is only a result of the adjustments. With respect to matching revenues and expenses based on original transaction values, the price-level-adjusted calculation agrees with the unadjusted version. One might expect then that price-level-adjusted operating income would have *all* of the characteristics in times of changing prices that conventional accounting net operating income has in times of stable prices. But the \$3,289 price-level-adjusted operating income calculated above hardly agrees with the amount of disposable wealth of \$2,309 calculated in

Exhibit 7-4—which brings us to the final major issue in our discussion of performance measurement in times of changing prices.

Relationship between Performance and Disposable Wealth in Times of Changing Prices

In Chapter 6 we noted that in the absence of gains and losses, conventional accounting net operating income served the dual role of both a performance index and a disposable wealth index. The duality was entirely sensible. After all, disposable wealth is the advance in net assets of the enterprise over and above what it would take to simply retain its initial position. But in the long run one would expect such advances (apart from extraordinary gains and losses) to result from the productive efforts, that is, performance, of the enterprise. Indeed the question can be asked, What is performance if it is not the generation of disposable wealth? So, in the normal course of events, we would think that a good measure of "performance" should also be a good measure of disposable wealth as well—barring extraordinary events.

Of what interest is the duality notion to our discussion of price-level-adjusted operating income? Price-level-adjusted operating income is analogous to conventional accounting net operating income in the aspect of "performance" that it measures, that is, it characterizes the enterprise's efficiency and effectiveness in producing products or services. But price-level-adjusted operating income does not, by itself, measure disposable wealth (even in the absence of extraordinary gains and losses). This suggests that perhaps in times of changing prices there is an additional aspect of wealth change (and possibly performance change) besides the enterprise's active efforts to produce products and services. Indeed there is! In times of rising or falling prices there is a real, though subtle, *additional* source of increases and decreases in enterprise wealth—quite apart from the so-called productive activity engaged in by the enterprise. Interestingly, we will see that the distinction between monetary and nonmonetary assets again becomes important in explaining this "additional source."

• *Monetary assets and liabilities in times of changing prices.* If you have ever heard the expression "Go in debt and let inflation bail you out," you have some idea of what happens to debtors and creditors as prices rise. A liability usually specifies that a particular number of dollars be paid by the debtor to the creditor at specific future times. If prices rise between the time the debt is incurred and the time it is paid off, the debtor benefits by paying back less in purchasing power than agreed to at the time the debt was incurred—and vice versa if prices fall. Conversely, the creditor gets back less purchasing power than bargained for during a period of rising prices and more when prices are falling.

True, the debtor may pay and the creditor may receive compensating interest payments. But then the interest paid may not all be disposable if the creditor wishes to maintain his purchasing power intact. Furthermore, most individuals and businesses find it necessary to hold cash in hand (or in "checking" accounts) where it earns no compensatory interest, simply to facilitate the payment of debts when due and to acquire assets directly for cash when necessary. Holders of cash balances are affected in the same way as creditors in times of rising and falling prices. If a business holds a specific, fixed amount of dollars as prices rise, it is losing purchasing power. The longer it waits, the fewer goods and services it will be able to command with the given amount of dollars—and vice versa when prices are falling.

Perhaps these basic facts about the effect of inflation or deflation are already familiar to the reader. What may not be so familiar is that virtually every business holds some monetary or fixed-dollar assets (typically including at least some cash and accounts receivable), and at least some monetary liabilities as well. Depending on the balance between monetary assets and liabilities, the enterprise will have the advantage (or disadvantage) of being either a "net" debtor or creditor in times of changing prices.

• *Monetary gains and losses.* Why are we interested in the net debtor-creditor characteristics of the firm? Because the *monetary gains and losses* experienced by the enterprise are the additional explanatory factors linking price-level-adjusted operating income to disposable wealth in times of inflation or deflation.

> **Monetary Gains and Losses.** Monetary gains (losses) are increases (decreases) in purchasing power that result from holding monetary assets and/or carrying monetary liabilities during a period of changing prices.

• *Calculating monetary gains and losses.* To see the relationship between (1) net monetary gain or loss, (2) price-level-adjusted operating income, and (3) price-level-adjusted net income (disposable wealth), reconsider the Trading Corporation example. Trading Corporation had only two monetary items, cash and a loan. That greatly simplifies our exposition of the relationship. Rather than losing from the simplicity, discussion will benefit. Although we will only deal directly with a single monetary asset (cash) and a single liability (the loan) and a period of rising prices, our reasoning and techniques apply with only minor modification to any business situation in times of falling as well as rising prices.

Example 7-2   Recall Trading Corporation's cash position and the changes that took place in that position during its first year of operations (see Exhibit 7-2). The company started its existence when the price-level index was at 100 with $10,000 of cash. It immediately expended $9,000 of its cash for inventory while the price-level index was still at 100. Throughout the year, however, it received a total of $12,000 from sales to customers as the price-level index went from 100 to 121, averaging 110. The company ended the period with $13,000 actual cash on hand. Since the company held cash, a monetary asset, as prices rose during the year it was losing purchasing power. The only question is, How much purchasing power did it lose as a result of its cash holdings? To answer this question we have to pose several other questions.

Suppose that Trading Corporation had done nothing more than hold its original $10,000 throughout the year, neither spending any of it nor receiving any additional cash. It would have lost purchasing power. It would still only have $10,000 at year-end, but prices generally rose, that is, the index went from 100 to 121. One way of assessing the loss of purchasing power is to ask the question, How much cash would Trading Corporation have to have at the end of the year to have as much purchasing power then as it had at the beginning of the year with $10,000? The answer is that it would take $121/100 \cdot \$10,000$, or approximately $12,100 at year-end, *to have no loss in purchasing power*. So, if Trading Corporation had done nothing more than hold its $10,000, it would have lost purchasing power equivalent to 2,100 end-of-year dollars—the difference between the no-loss amount of $12,100 and the amount it would actually have possessed, $10,000.

But Trading Corporation did not just hold its $10,000 in cash. For one thing, it spent $9,000 of its original cash on inventory right at the start of the year when the index was still at 100. Assuming for the sake of argument that the corporation had *no* cash receipts, the expenditure on inventory would have reduced the actual cash balance by $9,000 to $1,000. In addition, since the purchasing power of the $9,000 of cash was actually utilized when the index was at 100, it also reduces the no-loss, end-of-year cash requirement as well, by $121/100 \cdot \$9,000$, or $10,890. So the expenditure of $9,000 (of the original $10,000) at the beginning of the year means that the corporation would not need $12,100 at year-end, but rather $12,100 − $10,890, or $1,210. The net amount of $1,210, of course, equals the $1,000 balance remaining at the beginning of the year after the inventory purchase times the factor $121/100$.

Now we can take account of the effect of the gradual cash receipts of $12,000 from sales during the year. The receipts from sales increased the actual balance of cash from $1,000, right after the inventory expenditure, to $13,000 by year-end. But because these cash receipts were received as the price level was rising, they increase the no-loss end-of-year cash requirements even more. Since the price level averaged 110 as the $12,000 was gradually received, but had reached 121 by year-end, the corporation would have to have $121/110 \cdot \$12,000$, or $13,200, included in its end-of-year cash to not have lost purchasing power from holding the additional $12,000 of cash receipts. Adding this to the no-loss requirement of $1,210 for the $1,000 balance (after the expenditure) gives a total no-loss requirement of $14,410.

We now have the information required to assess the total loss of purchasing power experienced by Trading Corporation from holding cash during a year of rising prices. Since it would take a total year-end cash balance of $14,410 to experience no loss from holding cash, whereas Trading Corporation only had an actual balance of $13,000, its monetary loss from holding cash for the year was $1,410. The steps in arriving at this conclusion are summarized in Exhibit 7-9.

The similar reasoning that applies to monetary liabilities is illustrated in Exhibit 7-10 with respect to the loan made to Trading Corporation by a friend of the owner. At the beginning of 19X1 when the price-level index was at 100, the friend loaned $2,000 to the corporation, none of which was paid off. In addition, $100 in interest became due during 19X1, but rather than being paid, that amount was added to the balance of the loan (with the agreement of the lender) to be subject to future interest. As Exhibit 7-10 shows, the end-of-period dollar equivalent of the loan received plus the interest due at year-end equals more than the actual year-end balance of the loan. Thus Trading Corporation experienced a monetary gain during 19X1 with respect to the loan.

Exhibit 7-9
TRADING CORPORATION
Monetary Loss from Holding Cash
For the Year 19X1

	Cash Account	Adjusting Factor	Price-Level-Adjusted Amounts
Beginning balance	$10,000	121/100	$12,100
Inventory purchase	(9,000)	121/100	(10,890)
Sales revenue	12,000	121/110	13,200
Ending balance	$13,000		$14,410
Less actual balance			13,000
Monetary loss			$ 1,410

Exhibit 7-10
TRADING CORPORATION
Monetary Gain from Loan
For the Year 19X1

	Loan Account	Adjusting Factor	Price-Level-Adjusted Amounts
Beginning balance	$2,000	121/100	$2,420
Interest	100	121/110	110
Ending balance	$2,100		$2,530
Less actual balance			2,100
Monetary gain			$ 430

• *Calculation of monetary gains and losses—summary.* Although the logic underlying the calculation of monetary gains and losses is somewhat abstract and perhaps difficult to understand, Exhibits 7-9 and 7-10 illustrate that such calculations can nevertheless be reduced to just five simple mechanical steps for any monetary element of financial position:

1. Array the beginning balance and all increases and decreases in the monetary item in tabular form and calculate the ending position (or balance).
2. Translate the beginning balance and all increases and decreases to the number of end-of-year dollars of equivalent purchasing power to the actual amount at the time the transaction took place (at the beginning of the period for the beginning balance).
3. Calculate the price-level-adjusted ending balance in the same way the actual balance is calculated, but using the price-level-adjusted figures.
4. Find the difference between the actual ending balance and the price-level-adjusted (no-monetary-gain-or-loss) ending balance.
5. Interpret the difference.

With the exception of step 5, the process is illustrated by Exhibits 7-9 and 7-10. Since step 5 is the only nonmechanical step remaining after we have systematized the process, we now briefly consider this interpretation step.

• *Interpreting monetary gains and losses.* Interpretation of the difference between the actual and the price-level-adjusted ending balance for a monetary item depends on two things: (1) the direction of the difference and (2) whether the monetary item is an asset or a liability. If, for instance, the monetary item is an asset and the price-level-adjusted balance is greater than the actual balance (this happens when prices rise), it means that the enterprise actually *has less* of that asset at the end of the period than would be required to *not* have a loss of purchasing power. Thus the difference constitutes a monetary loss. On the other hand, if the actual ending balance of a monetary asset is greater than the price-level-adjusted balance (this happens when prices fall), the difference is interpreted as a gain.

Contrary reasoning applies to monetary liabilities. The price-level-adjusted balance of a monetary liability is the amount that the enterprise would have to owe its creditor(s) to owe the same purchasing power as it received at the time it incurred the debt. Hence if the actual balance is *less* (as it would be if prices have risen), the enterprise will have gained—will owe less purchasing power than originally promised. The opposite is true if the actual balance of the liability is more than the price-level-adjusted balance (prices have fallen), that is, a monetary loss has been sustained.

• *Price-level-adjusted net income.* Recall now that when we earlier calculated Trading Corporation's price-level-adjusted operating income for 19X1, we knew that we had not finished the task of measuring total performance in a manner consistent with measured disposable wealth in times of changing prices. After all, price-level-adjusted operating income was $3,289 —considerably more than the $2,309 we had already determined would lead to nonexcessive withdrawals. The discrepancy between these two figures indicated that there must have been some identifiable loss in purchasing power that resulted from some source other than the productive activity of the year.

As we have since shown, there was indeed a *monetary* loss of $1,410 and a monetary gain of $430 experienced by Trading Corporation in 19X1. Together they make up a *net* monetary loss of $980. With this net monetary loss, we can now reconcile the $3,289 price-level-adjusted operating income with the $2,309 disposable wealth figure that we earlier labeled *price-level-adjusted net income.*

> **Price-Level-Adjusted Net Income.** Price-level-adjusted net income is composed of price-level-adjusted operating income plus or minus the net monetary gain or loss experienced by the enterprise.

The identity relationship implied by this definition is illustrated with the Trading Corporation example in Exhibit 7-11.

Notice that the price-level-adjusted net income is identical in amount to the $2,309 determined earlier to be the amount of disposable wealth produced during the year. It is in fact the same number, simply calculated in a different, perhaps more meaningful, way. Thus we not only have a reliable measure of disposable wealth (price-level-adjusted net income), we have it broken down by source. Price-level-adjusted operating income (in this case $3,289) is the advance in wealth (net assets) measured in end-of-year dollars, recognized in connection with the productive activities of the enterprise.

Exhibit 7-11
TRADING CORPORATION
Statement of Price-Level-Adjusted Net Income
For the Year 19X1

Year-end Dollars

Sales revenue		$13,200
Less expenses:		
Cost of sales	$9,801	
Interest	110	9,911
P-L-A operating income		$ 3,289
Less net monetary loss:		
Monetary gain from loan	$ 430	
Monetary loss from cash	(1,410)	(980)
P-L-A net income		$ 2,309

It would all be disposable wealth were it not for the net monetary loss (in this case $980) due to the effect of inflation on the purchasing power of the enterprise's holdings of monetary items.

Unlike our Trading Corporation example, in actual practice even relatively small businesses are likely to have several monetary assets and liabilities. To arrive at the net monetary gain or loss directly in such cases involves the two-step process illustrated above, consisting of (1) determining the monetary gain or loss from each monetary asset or liability and (2) determining the net monetary gain or loss by finding the difference between the sum of the individual monetary gains and the sum of the individual monetary losses.

Clearly, the direct approach to finding the net monetary gain or loss could involve extensive calculations in the case of large businesses. But fortunately the direct approach can be avoided by taking advantage of the identity relationship:

P-L-A net income = P-L-A operating income ± net monetary gain (loss)

By calculating any two of the three amounts indicated in a given case, the identity can be solved for the third. Thus direct calculation can be avoided for whichever of the three figures would be most burdensome to calculate directly.

Price-Level-Adjusted Income Measurement—
Interpretation

Considerable effort has now been devoted in this chapter to developing techniques to compensate for general price-level changes in arriving at measures of performance and disposable wealth for an enterprise in times of changing prices. The effort led first to a description of an easily calculated measure of disposable wealth. We called that disposable wealth measure *price-level-adjusted net income*. Then, in seeking to satisfy the intuitive idea that disposable wealth produced by the enterprise ought to be the result of identifiable types of performance, we determined that price-level-adjusted net income could be broken down into two parts. One of these parts, *price-level-*

adjusted operating income, clearly relates in concept to the conventional accounting measure of performance. It agrees item for item (all revenues and expenses) in calculation with conventional accounting net operating income, but each item is adjusted to its original purchasing power equivalent in end-of-period dollars.

The other part of total disposable wealth for a period is the subtle (but real) change in purchasing power experienced by the enterprise from holding monetary assets and having monetary liabilities in times of changing prices. When we add the *net monetary gain* or subtract the *net monetary loss* experienced by the enterprise to its price-level-adjusted operating income, we get price-level-adjusted net income, the amount of disposable wealth generated by the enterprise for the period. At this point a final question of interpretation remains.

Is price-level-adjusted net income or net operating income an index (in times of changing prices) of long-run ability to produce products with values in excess of the costs of resources used to produce them—at least in the same sense that conventional accounting net income constitutes such an index in times of static prices? The answer is generally no. Conventional accounting operating income has a high degree of intuitive appeal as a performance measure *under static prices* for a good reason. If in a future period the enterprise provides the same quantity and quality of products to customers as in the current period, using the same quantity and quality input resources with the same efficiency, it will have the *same operating income* (assuming no price changes). This will generally not be true of price-level-adjusted income measures in times of generally rising or falling prices *unless* the prices charged for products and the prices paid for input resources by the enterprise have *changed in proportion* to the general trend in prices. If this condition is not met, then adjustments for changes in the prices of the specific products sold and resources used by the enterprise are necessary to replicate in times of changing prices the properties of conventional accounting operating income (under static conditions). Such adjustments are the subject of Chapter 8.

Assuming, however, that the prices received and paid by the enterprise do change in approximate proportion to the general trend, the appropriateness of the price-level-adjusted income measures as measures of performance is still subject to some further qualification. Whether the price-level-adjusted operating income or the net income measure best characterizes "performance" depends on the kind of inflation experienced during the accounting period. If the economy experienced a short-lived, once-and-for-all burst of inflation during the accounting period, there is some question about the long-run performance relevance of the net income measure, since it incorporates net monetary gains and losses. Although net monetary gains or losses do indeed represent current period gains or losses in purchasing power, the forces that give rise to them are not forces that originate within the firm. If the forces of inflation or deflation that contributed to the current period's monetary gains or losses are known to have ceased, the enterprise will not experience continued monetary gains or losses. Under such circumstances, price-level-adjusted *operating income,* rather than price-level-adjusted net income, is the current period's manifestation of the enterprise's ongoing productive ability.

In the case of ongoing inflation or deflation, monetary gains and losses become an ongoing part of an enterprise's economic activities. The measure of efficient management, even in times of stable prices, is the excess of the value of products and services that it can produce over costs of resources consumed, with a given level of investment in both nonmonetary *and monetary* assets. But in times of ongoing inflation or deflation, another dimension is added to the management of a business enterprise—that being to regulate or manage its mix of monetary items in such a way as to accomplish its production objectives at the minimum monetary loss or maximum monetary gain due to inflation or deflation. Thus, in times of ongoing inflation or deflation, price-level-adjusted net income, which includes monetary gains and losses, is a better index of long-run productive ability of the enterprise than is price-level-adjusted operating income.

• *The present status of general price-level accounting.* At the present time only one or two major U.S. companies have issued financial statements adjusted for changes in general purchasing power. Although financial reporting authorities (principally the Accounting Principles Board of the American Institute of Certified Public Accountants) favor the publication of such statements, they have endorsed them only as supplements to, not as substitutes for, conventional financial statements. However, a different situation prevails outside the United States. For instance, several high-inflation countries in South America and the Far East generally require financial reporting on a price-level-adjusted basis.

Questions for Review and Discussion

7-1.   Define:

a. Price-level index

b. Price-level-adjusted net income

c. Price-level-adjusted operating income

d. Monetary gain (loss)

e. *Net* monetary gain (loss)

7-2.   Given that all economic units have unique preferences for different kinds of goods and services, how can we justify adjusting original transaction values for changes in the general purchasing power of the dollar?

7-3.   Briefly explain how a price-level index is constructed. In what way does technological change enter into the construction and use of a general price-level index?

7-4.   Suppose you have been asked to construct a price-level index for the U.S. consumer.

a. How would you go about constructing such an index?

b. What characteristics would you like it to have?

c. Would you use the same index for the Northwest Computer Manufacturing Company? Explain.

7-5.   For purposes of general price-level adjustments of financial statements, what properties should the price-level index selected possess?

7-6.   Price-level-adjusted net income measurement is an example of an application of the Hicksian definition of income. Do you agree or disagree? Explain your position.

7-7. In arriving at price-level-adjusted expenses, the original costs of resources used to produce the revenue of the period should be adjusted for changes in the general level of prices between the time the resources are used and year end. True or false? Defend your position.

7-8. Explain why debtors gain and creditors lose in times of general inflation.

7-9. a. How do we distinguish monetary assets (liabilities) from nonmonetary assets (liabilities)?

b. Classify each of the following as to whether it is a monetary or a nonmonetary item. Explain, in each case, why you chose the classification you did.

> Cash
> Merchandise inventory
> Marketable securities
> Note payable
> Obligation to deliver goods in the future
> Accounts receivable
> Goods purchased but not yet paid for
> A note payable secured by a mortgage
> U.S. government bonds held by the firm
> Taxes owed to the federal government
> A parcel of land owned

7-10. Assuming that the prices paid and received by the enterprise change in approximate proportion to the general trend, which price-level-adjusted income measure is the most appropriate measure of enterprise performance? Explain.

7-11. When prices generally increase, owners of monetary assets lose while owners of nonmonetary assets gain. True or false? Defend your position.

7-12. When prices generally rise, conventional accounting operating income is clearly irrelevant as a measure of enterprise performance in the long-run cash-generating-ability sense. Do you agree or disagree? Defend your position.

7-13. In measuring price-level-adjusted net income, beginning net assets (owners' equity) is adjusted as a single figure, whereas ending net assets (owners' equity) is a composite of the adjusted and unadjusted assets and liabilities of the entity as of the end of the period. Is this an inconsistency? Explain your position.

7-14. Price-level-adjusted operating income has all of the properties in times of changing prices that conventional accounting operating income has if prices are static. Do you agree or disagree? Defend your position.

Exercises   **7-1. Present Value and the Price Level.** Mrs. Ann Smith, in looking forward to retirement, invested $10,000 on January 1, 1963, in U.S. government bonds. The bonds paid interest at a rate of 10 percent per year, compounded, with repayment of principal and interest on January 1, 1973. In effect, she postponed consumption in 1963 in favor of consumption during her retirement. At the time she invested, her time preference rate between current and future consumption was 10 percent and she expected no inflation. However, during the 1963 to 1973 time period, the price level moved from a beginning level of 100 to a 1973 level of 140.

Required:

1. In retrospect (i.e., on January 1, 1973), how do you suppose she felt about her investment? Explain.

2. If she had anticipated the inflation, what is the maximum amount she would have paid for the investment in 1963?

7-2.   Present Value and the Price Level.   Mr. Al Johnson is considering purchase of a bond with a face value of $5,000 which is to be repaid in six years. It has a coupon interest rate of 6 percent. He realizes that the price level has been rising at an average rate of 3 percent per year during the last two years and expects inflation to continue at that rate for the life of the bond.

Required:

1. How might he recognize this in considering the investment?

2. What is the maximum amount he would be willing to pay for this bond under these circumstances if his time preference rate is 4 percent for cash flows of constant purchasing power?

7-3   Computation of Price-Level Indexes.   Suppose the U.S. Bureau of Labor Statistics had been buying what it considered to be a representative "basket" of consumer goods over the last six years with year-end costs as follows:

1969	$2,400
1970	2,700
1971	2,500
1972	3,000
1973	3,300
1974	3,200

Required:

Construct a price-level index based on these figures, using 1971 as the base year. What is the rate of inflation (deflation) in each of the years?

7-4.   Computation of Monetary Gains (Losses).   The Ace Novelty Company has experienced the following changes in its accounts receivable during the past year:

Beginning balance	$ 23,000
Sales on account January through March	46,000
Sales on account April through June	41,000
Sales on account July through September	33,000
Sales on account October through December	52,000
Payments received (uniformly during year)	160,000

The beginning price-level index was at 100. Average quarterly indexes were 105, 110, 115, and 120, respectively, with an ending price-level index of 125. The average index during the year was 112.5. Compute the monetary gain (loss) from accounts receivable during the year. Is it a gain or a loss? Why?

7-5.   Price-Level-Adjusted Net Income.   The Rainbow Distributing Company acts as a wholesaler of various leisure time products including boats, swimming gear, ski equipment, and all-terrain vehicles. As a part of its operations, it performs final assembly of much of the equipment from component parts. Thus its principal assets are the land, buildings, and some machinery required in its assembly lines. It also carries a large inventory from which it satisfies the seasonal demands of its customers. The worksheet shown in Exhibit 7-12 represents its beginning position on January 1, 197X. Transactions for the current operating year are also included in the worksheet.

Required:

1. Based on the figures provided, what is conventional accounting net income or disposable wealth for the year?

2. Suppose prices during the current year have risen from a January 1 level of 200 to a year-end level of 220, averaging 210 during the year. Assume revenues, purchases, accounts receivable, wages, miscellaneous expenses, and advertising were generally received or paid uniformly throughout the year, and beginning inventory was all sold during the year. The interest on the note, however, was paid at year-end. The management is concerned about the impact of the price changes on the company's disposable wealth. You, as its accountant, are asked to compute price-level-adjusted disposable wealth (net income) for the year. (Calculate adjustment factors to only two-decimal accuracy.)

3. Discuss the reasons for the difference between income computed in number 1 and that computed in number 2.

4. If management pays dividends equal to the net income computed in number 2 above, can it be sure that it will retain enough capital in the firm to always be able to repurchase its operating resources as required and continue to carry on the business? Explain.

7-6. Price-Level-Adjusted Operating Income. The accountant for the Northern Equipment Corporation, a small manufacturer of camping equipment, has just completed his worksheet summarizing 197X events for the firm. He has noted that the firm has experienced serious inflation for the first time during the previous year and is concerned about its impact on operating performance. Prior to this year, prices had been stable but had risen steadily during the year and had reached a level 15 percent higher by year-end. The worksheet for the year is shown in Exhibit 7-13.

Price-level indexes for the year were as follows:

> January 1, 197X—87
>
> December 31, 197X—100
>
> Average index during 197X—91

All transactions for the firm occur uniformly throughout the year with the exception of interest expense which is paid December 31. All beginning inventory was sold.

Required:

1. Compute conventional accounting net income for the year.

2. Compute price-level-adjusted operating income for the year. (Carry calculation of adjustment factors to two decimals only.)

214

Exhibit 7-12

RAINBOW DISTRIBUTING COMPANY
Financial Position Worksheet

Description	Cash	Accounts Receivable	Merchandise Inventory	Machinery and Equipment*	Buildings*	Land	Accounts Payable	Notes Payable	Owners' Equity
Beginning Position	20,000	63,000	56,000	79,000	93,000	35,000	47,000	25,000	274,000
Purchase of inventory for sale			121,000				121,000		
Revenue from sales	26,000	265,000							291,000 (R)
Wages paid	(86,000)								(86,000) (E)
Collections of accounts receivable	256,000	(256,000)							
Payments of accounts payable	(136,000)						(136,000)		
Miscellaneous expenses (heat, light, taxes, etc.)	(29,000)								(29,000) (E)
Equipment depreciation				(14,000)					(14,000) (E)
Buildings depreciation					(7,000)				(7,000) (E)
Advertising	(18,000)								(18,000) (E)
Cost of goods sold			(116,000)						(116,000) (E)
Paid interest on note payable	(1,500)								(1,500) (E)
Ending Position	31,500	72,000	61,000	65,000	86,000	35,000	32,000	25,000	293,500

* Balances are net of accumulated depreciation.

Exhibit 7-13

NORTHERN EQUIPMENT CORPORATION
Financial Position Worksheet

Description	Cash	Accounts Receivable	Inventory	Equipment	Accumulated Depreciation—Equipment	Buildings	Accumulated Depreciation—Buildings	Land	Accounts Payable	Notes Payable	Owners' Equity
Beginning Position	24,000	40,000	70,000	36,000	(8,000)	52,000	(16,000)	17,000	20,000	28,000	167,000
Revenue from sales	16,000	300,000									316,000 (R)
Inventory purchases			200,000						200,000		
Payments received on accounts receivable	310,000	(310,000)									
Payments on accounts payable	(190,000)								(190,000)		
Wages and salaries	(90,000)										(90,000) (E)
Heat, light, etc.	(4,000)										(4,000) (E)
Miscellaneous expenses	(12,000)										(12,000) (E)
Interest expense	(1,400)										(1,400) (E)
Inventory sold			(180,000)								(180,000) (E)
Equipment depreciation					(4,000)						(4,000) (E)
Buildings depreciation							(4,000)				(4,000) (E)
Preliminary Ending Position	52,600	30,000	90,000	36,000	(12,000)	52,000	(20,000)	17,000	30,000	28,000	187,600

3. How are the two income numbers you have computed conceptually different?

7-7. Monetary Gains (Losses).

1. Using the information and worksheet found in Exercise 7-6, compute the monetary gain or loss for the year from holding cash. Is it a gain or a loss?

2. What is the meaning of the price-level-adjusted cash amount that you have computed?

7-8. Monetary Gains (Losses)—Annual versus Quarterly Data.   Suppose you have the following information concerning the changes in accounts receivable for the Ace Novelty Company during the past year.

Beginning balance	$ 23,000
Sales on account	172,000
Payments received on account	160,000

The beginning price-level index was 100. During the year, the price-level index averaged 112.5 and was at a level of 125 at year-end.

Required:

1. Assuming sales and payments on account occurred uniformly during the year, what is the monetary gain (loss) on accounts receivable?

2. Compare this with your answer in Exercise 7-4 above. Explain the differences.

7-9. Price-Level-Adjusted Operating Income.   Following is the conventional accounting income statement of the Fullmer Sales Company for the year ending December 31, 1973.

FULLMER SALES COMPANY
Income Statement
For the Year Ending December 31, 1973

Revenue from sales		$1,750,000
Less expenses:		
Cost of goods sold	$1,400,000	
Wages and sales commissions	175,000	
Interest expense	22,000	
Equipment depreciation	43,000	
Total expenses		1,640,000
Net income		$ 110,000

Prior to 1973, prices had been stable at a price level of 75. However, during 1973 the economy experienced rapid inflation. By the end of 1973 the price-level index was at 90. The average index during the year was 82. Merchandise sold was purchased uniformly throughout the year, and wages and commissions were paid as earned, also uniformly throughout the year. Interest was accrued continuously. No new equipment purchases were made during the year.

Required:

1. What is price-level-adjusted operating income for 1973? (Carry calculation of adjustment factors to only two decimals.)

2. In what way does price-level-adjusted operating income differ conceptually from conventional accounting operating income? Is the price-level-adjusted figure a better measure of performance? Explain.

7-10.   Price-Level Changes and Disposable Wealth.   The president of the Mid-eastern Transportation Company has become concerned about the impact of inflation on the financial position of his company. He has presented you with the worksheet shown in Exhibit 7-14 in which beginning balances have been restated for all prior changes in purchasing power. Recorded transactions occurred uniformly throughout the year.

In addition, the president has told you that the beginning-of-year price level was 120, the end-of-year price level is 132, and the average level during the year was 126.

Required:

1. Based on the information he has supplied, what is the price-level-adjusted change in owners' equity for the year? (Calculation of adjustment factors required to two-decimal accuracy only.)

2. Can the president pay out this amount as a dividend to stockholders and rest assured that the firm is retaining enough resources to replace assets as they wear out? Explain.

3. The president is also interested in the impact of inflation on operating performance. Compute both conventional accounting operating income and price-level-adjusted operating income for the year.

7-11.   Disposable Wealth with Price-Level Movements.   The University Student Services Company had the following financial position as of January 1, 197X.

UNIVERSITY STUDENT SERVICES COMPANY
Balance Sheet
As of January 1, 197X

Assets:			Liabilities and Owners' Equity:	
Cash		$ 900	Note payable	$2,000
Inventory		3,500		
Office equipment	$2,500		Owners' equity	4,400
Less accumulated				
depreciation	500	2,000	Total liabilities and	
Total assets		$6,400	owners' equity	$6,400

During 197X, its second year of operation, the company entered into the following transactions:

a. Sold merchandise for a total of $14,000.

b. Purchased additional merchandise for $8,200.

c. All of the beginning inventory was sold.

d. $2,800 worth of the merchandise purchased remained at year-end.

e. Paid wages to employees totaling $3,000.

f. Recorded depreciation on office equipment for the year totaling $500.

g. Made an annual payment on the note payable totaling $500, of which $100 was interest charges.

Exhibit 7-14

THE MIDEASTERN TRANSPORTATION COMPANY
Financial Position Worksheet

Description	Cash	Accounts Receivable	Trucks	Accumulated Depreciation—Trucks	Buildings	Accumulated Depreciation—Buildings	Land	Notes Payable	Owners' Equity
Beginning Position*	16,000	8,000	24,000	(12,000)	52,000	(16,000)	40,000	7,000	105,000
Revenue from sales	42,000	14,000							56,000 (R)
Payment on accounts receivable	12,000	(12,000)							
Miscellaneous expense	(16,000)								(16,000) (E)
Wages	(24,000)								(24,000) (E)
Truck depreciation				(4,000)					(4,000) (E)
Buildings depreciation						(2,000)			(2,000) (E)
Ending Position	30,000	10,000	24,000	(16,000)	52,000	(18,000)	40,000	7,000	115,000

* All balances stated in beginning-of-year dollars (index of 120).

All merchandise was sold uniformly throughout the year for cash. Likewise, purchases occurred throughout the year and were paid for with cash. Wages were paid as earned.

Required:

1. Record the above in worksheet form.

2. The company is operated as a student cooperative, with all profits distributed to students at the end of each year. During 197X the price level, after remaining stable for several years, has moved from a January 1 level of 240 to a December 31 level of 264, averaging 251 during the year. The members of the cooperative suspect that the inflation has had an impact on the amount they should distribute to students. They have come to you for help.

   (a) Compute their price-level-adjusted net income for 197X. (Carry calculation of adjustment factors to only two decimals.)

   (b) Is the answer in (a) above the amount you would recommend distributing in 197X? Why or why not?

7-12. Relationship between Price-Level-Adjusted Income Measures.   The conventional accounting income statement of Planetary Gears Corporation for 19X3 follows. The revenues earned during the year, the wages paid, and the miscellaneous expenses all resulted from transactions taking place throughout the year. The rent was all prepaid at the end of the prior year. The steel used was purchased in part ($300,000) prior to the beginning of the year and in part ($500,000) at regular intervals throughout the year. However, it was used at a fairly even rate during the year. Interest was accrued continuously. No equipment was purchased during the year. During 19X3 the price-level index rose from 120 to 135, averaging 125 for the year as a whole. All beginning balances in nonmonetary assets had been previously adjusted to beginning-of-year dollars.

PLANETARY GEARS CORPORATION
Results of Operations (in thousands of dollars)
For the Year Ended December 31, 19X3

Revenues		$3,000
Less expenses:		
Steel used	$ 800	
Rent	30	
Wages	1,000	
Depreciation	500	
Interest	70	
Miscellaneous	100	2,500
Net operating income		$ 500

Required:

1. Determine price-level-adjusted operating income. (For convenience round adjustment factors to two decimals.)

2. Assume that price-level-adjusted net income was $400,000. Was there a net monetary gain or a net loss for the period? What amount?

3. Assuming that the company started 19X3 with equal amounts of monetary assets and liabilities, what does your answer to number 2 imply about the mix of monetary assets and liabilities during the year? Explain your answer.

7-13. Relationship between Price-Level-Adjusted Net Income, Operating Income, and Net Monetary Gain or Loss. The Regina Stamping Company has been in business for three years. Its operations and other changes in financial position during year three are reflected in the conventional accounting worksheet shown in Exhibit 7-15. For both of the first two years of operations, the general price-level index remained steady at 200. But during year three, the index went from 200 to 242, averaging 220 for the year as a whole.

Required:

1. Determine price-level-adjusted *net* income for the period. The steel was all purchased (line 1) at the beginning of the year, whereas all other external transactions were made at intervals throughout the year. Show your computations.

2. Determine price-level-adjusted *operating income*. Show your computations.

3. Calculate the monetary gains and losses from each monetary asset and liability and the *net* monetary gain or loss for the period. Be sure to note whether it is a net gain or a net loss amount.

Exhibit 7-15

REGINA STAMPING COMPANY
Financial Position Worksheet—Year Three

Description	Cash	Accounts Receivable	Sheet Steel	Net Equipment	Accounts Payable	Owners' Equity
Beginning Position	3,000	3,000	6,000	20,000	2,000	30,000
1. Purchased steel			16,000		16,000	
2. Rent and wages paid	(11,000)					(11,000) (E)
3. Sales		43,000				43,000 (R)
4. Payments on account	(15,000)				(15,000)	
5. Receipts on account	41,000	(41,000)				
6. Steel used			(17,000)			(17,000) (E)
7. Equipment depreciation				(2,000)		(2,000) (E)
Preliminary Balances	18,000	5,000	5,000	18,000	3,000	43,000

7-14. Price-Level-Adjusted Financial Statements. Ms. Barbara Smith, a stockholder in the Midwestern Packing Corporation, has just received the firm's annual report for 197X. Introductory comments to the financial statements included in the report explain that the company has provided two sets of financial statements for the year. One set has been prepared using conventional accounting. The other set has been adjusted for the inflation that has occurred during the year. The company explains that it has elected to include both sets of statements due to the inflation in the current year which occurred for the first time in the company's history. It notes that it feels that the 10 percent inflation experienced during the year has had a significant impact, and it believes that the price-level-adjusted statements will provide significant additional information to the investor. Ms. Smith does not understand the difference between the statements and has come to you for an explanation. She presents you with the following.

MIDWESTERN PACKING COMPANY
Conventional Accounting Balance Sheet
As of December 31, 197X

Assets:			Liabilities:	
Cash		$ 50,000	Accounts payable	$ 64,000
Accounts receivable		170,000	Notes payable	17,000
Inventory		83,000	Mortgage on building	52,000
Equipment	$120,000		Total liabilities	$133,000
Less accumulated depreciation	44,000	76,000		
Buildings	$ 96,000		Owners' equity	350,000
Less accumulated depreciation	24,000	72,000		
Land		32,000	Total liabilities and owners'	
Total assets		$483,000	equity	$483,000

MIDWESTERN PACKING COMPANY
Conventional Accounting Income Statement
For the Period Ending December 31, 197X

Revenue from sales		$680,000
Less expenses:		
Cost of goods sold	$479,500	
Wages and salaries	90,000	
Heat, light, etc.	15,000	
Property taxes	5,000	
Interest expense	4,500	
Equipment depreciation	12,000	
Buildings depreciation	4,000	
Total expenses		610,000
Net income		$ 70,000

MIDWESTERN PACKING COMPANY
Price-Level-Adjusted Balance Sheet
As of December 31, 197X

Assets:			Liabilities and Owners' Equity:	
Cash		$ 50,000	Liabilities:	
Accounts receivable		170,000	Accounts payable	$ 64,000
Inventory		87,150	Notes payable	17,000
Equipment	$132,000		Mortgage on building	52,000
Less accumulated depreciation	48,400	83,600	Total liabilities	$133,000
Buildings	$105,600			
Less accumulated depreciation	26,400	79,200	Owners' equity	372,150
Land		35,200	Total liabilities and owners'	
Total assets		$505,150	equity	$505,150

MIDWESTERN PACKING COMPANY
Price-Level-Adjusted Income Statement
For the Period Ending December 31, 197X

Revenue from sales		$714,000
Less expenses:		
Cost of goods sold	$503,475	
Wages and salaries	94,500	
Heat, light, etc.	15,750	
Property taxes	5,250	
Interest expense	4,725	
Equipment depreciation	13,200	
Buildings depreciation	4,400	
Total P-L-A expenses		641,300
Price-level-adjusted operating income		$ 72,700
Less monetary loss		8,550
Price-level-adjusted net income		$ 64,150

In addition, the annual report provides the following information:

a. Although prices in general were up a total of 10 percent for the year, prices were up an average of 5 percent during the year.

b. The company began the year with no inventory and made inventory purchases uniformly throughout the year.

c. No new buildings or equipment were acquired during the year.

d. Taxes and interest are accrued throughout the year.

e. Wages and salaries, as well as heat, light, etc., were paid as incurred uniformly throughout the year. Sales revenue and collections of accounts receivable similarly occurred uniformly during the year.

Required:

1. Reconcile the differences, that is, show the calculations involved in computing the price-level-adjusted statements. (Note: For convenience, calculate adjustment factors to only two decimal places.)

2. Explain the meaning of the monetary gains (losses) that you compute.

7-15. Relationship between Price-Level-Adjusted Income Measures. The Walker Book Company has been in business for two years. Its operations and other changes in financial position during year two are reflected in the conventional accounting worksheet shown in Exhibit 7-16. For the first year of operations, the general price-level index remained steady at 90. But during year two the index went from 90 to 120, averaging 100 for the year as a whole.

The purchase of new books (line 1) was made at the beginning of the year (when the general price-level index was still 90), whereas all other external transactions were made at intervals throughout the year.

Required:

1. Determine price-level-adjusted *net* income for the period. Show your computations.

2. Determine price-level-adjusted *operating income*. Show your computations.

3. From your answers in numbers 1 and 2, calculate the net monetary gain or loss for the period. Be sure to note whether it is a net gain or a net loss amount.

Exhibit 7-16

WALKER BOOK COMPANY
Financial Position Worksheet—Year Two

Description	Cash	Accounts Receivable	Book Inventory	Fixtures	Accumulated Depreciation— Fixtures	Accounts Payable	Owners' Equity
Beginning Position	6,000	3,000	12,000	9,000	(900)	3,000	26,100
1. Purchased books			18,000			18,000	
2. Rent and wages paid	(10,000)						(10,000) (*E*)
3. Sales		50,000					50,000 (*R*)
4. Payments on account	(15,000)					(15,000)	
5. Receipts on account	45,000	(45,000)					
6. Cost of books sold			(24,000)				(24,000) (*E*)
7. Depreciation of fixtures					(900)		(900) (*E*)
Preliminary Balances	26,000	8,000	6,000	9,000	(1,800)	6,000	41,200

8

Current Exchange Price
Financial Accounting Models

In Chapters 4 through 7 we considered the characteristics and implications of conventional accounting and general price-level-adjusted accounting for the enterprise. Price-level-adjusted accounting differs from conventional accounting only in that it adjusts the dollar amounts used to represent original transaction values for changes in the purchasing power of the dollar. The purpose of the adjustments, however, is to capture with a new number the *original* value (in purchasing power) given or received in a past transaction.

In this chapter we consider for the first time genuine departures, *in principle,* from conventional accounting concepts. We introduce two additional financial accounting models, the replacement-cost model and the market-value model, each significantly different from conventional accounting. Both of the models are motivated by a desire to achieve a presumably more relevant representation of enterprise status and activities in times of changing prices than either the conventional model or the price-level-adjusted model produces. In both cases, the purpose of gaining a different representation of enterprise status and activities is achieved through use of a valuation base different from original transaction values.

Both the replacement-cost and market-value models are implemented using current exchange prices. For this reason we give some attention to the general notion of current exchange prices before introducing each of the models in turn.

Current Exchange Prices

An *exchange price* is the amount of cash (or equivalent) paid, received, or promised *in exchange* for some right or possession.

> **Current Exchange Price.** As the term implies, current exchange prices are prices that are being paid or received in exchange for particular rights or possessions at the present time.

Current exchange prices are therefore of obvious significance for all economic units. They reflect current conditions of supply and demand in the markets in which individuals and business enterprises buy resources for use in production and sell resulting products and services. Thus, current exchange prices provide information to individuals and enterprises as to their exchange options. As mentioned above, current exchange prices may also be used for valuation purposes to reflect desired concepts of enterprise wealth and income.

• *Entry and exit prices.* A distinction between current exchange prices (which will become significant in our later discussion) has to do with which side of the exchange transaction the economic unit is on.

> **Current Entry Price (Replacement Cost).** When taking the point of view of the buyer of a product or service, we usually refer to the current exchange price as the *entry* or *input* price. The terms *entry* and *input* express the notion that the exchange price is the amount required to "enter" the item into the control of the buyer. Among accountants, the current entry price of a resource is usually referred to as its current *replacement cost*.

> **Current Exit Price (Market Value).** The obvious counterpart terminology, when we take the point of view of the seller, is *exit* or *output* price, expressing the notion that for the seller the exchange price is the amount received as one of his products or services is given up. Among accountants, the current exit price of a resource is usually referred to as its current *market value*.

Although this distinction between entry and exit prices may seem trivial at first glance, in many cases it can be significant. Often the current exit and entry prices of a given asset are different when we take the point of view of the same economic unit buying and selling that asset.

Example 8-1   Take the position of a used-car dealer with respect to the purchase or sale of a particular used-car model. The current entry price for the dealer is likely to be the local wholesale price for the particular model, whereas the dealer's current exit price is probably the local retail price of the same model. There may be several hundred dollars difference between the two prices.

Now consider the individual interested in buying or selling the same used-car model. Unless the individual has time to locate another individual buying or selling the used-car model that he wishes to sell or purchase (respectively), he will have to go to a dealer. Thus the dealer's current exit price is the individual's current entry price, and vice versa. For both the individual and the dealer, there is a difference between the current entry price and the current exit price of the given used-car model (although the relationship between the two amounts is reversed).

Even when we are considering both sides of the same exchange, the entry price for the buyer may differ from the exit price of the seller, and both may differ from what we will call the nominal selling price in the exchange.

Example 8-2   Suppose that Mr. Homeowner puts his house up for sale. Mr. Renter comes along and makes Mr. Homeowner an offer of $30,000 for the house. Mr. Homeowner accepts. The nominal selling price is $30,000. But Mr. Renter will actually pay more than $30,000 and Mr. Homeowner will receive less because of certain additional costs of the transaction. The most obvious additional cost of the transaction is usually a sales or excise tax levied against either the buyer or the seller according to the law of the state in which the sale takes place. Other transaction costs in this case include the real estate commission (seller), the title search and insurance (buyer and/or seller), and the cost of securing a mortgage (buyer usually; seller in some instances).

RECOGNITION OF CURRENT RESOURCE ENTRY PRICES (REPLACEMENT COSTS)

Conventional Accounting—A Point of Departure

Now that we have some idea as to what is meant by current exchange prices, we are ready to apply them to the problem of accounting for the business enterprise. To set up the motivation for recognition of current replacement costs of resources, we start by contrasting the basic concept of the enterprise underlying conventional accounting with the enterprise concept that underlies recognition of replacement costs. We refer to the two concepts as the *money capital* and *physical capital* points of view, respectively.

• *The money capital point of view.* When we introduced conventional accounting performance measurement in Chapter 4, we alluded to an operating sequence or cycle as the backbone of our model of the enterprise. For present purposes, we can paraphrase the stages in that sequence as follows: (1) the enterprise starts with invested cash, (2) it converts the cash into physical factors of production, (3) it commits its factors to production of products and services, (4) it provides the products and services to customers, and (5) it thereby converts them back into cash. Thus we can think of the business enterprise as a reservoir of cash which is continuously converted into productive resources and back into cash of greater quantity. This is the basic philosophy or concept of the enterprise that is implicit in the use of conventional accounting net income as a performance measure and as a measure of disposable wealth. In performance measurement, the measure of the sacrifice or effort expended in using a resource in production is the money committed to acquire it for use. The measure of accomplishment is the money received or to be received for products or services provided. In disposable wealth measurement, the essential thing in preserving the economic essence of the enterprise is the preservation of assets equal to its cash or money endowment. This may be referred to as the money capital point of view of the enterprise. We earlier illustrated the way that conventional accounting fulfills the money capital or cash reservoir concept of the enterprise (Examples 6-1 and 7-1). However, introduction of another example at this point will aid in illustrating the way that replacement cost accounting, in contrast, fulfills the physical capital point of view.

Example 8-3   The Shirttail Store is a small retail store dealing exclusively in men's and women's shirts (blouses). Prior to January 1, 19X1, the date the store opened for business, the owners invested $80,000 in cash. Immediately thereafter interior fixtures for the store were ordered at a cost of $10,000. The fixtures had an expected useful life of two years and would probably not be worth more than the cost of removal after that period ended. In addition, a full year's supply of shirts was ordered, 12,000 in all, at a cost of $5.00 per shirt. These two important purchases used up all but $10,000 of the original money capital. However, the $10,000 was considered just adequate to meet the payroll and other expenditure requirements between the time of the major purchases of inventory and fixtures and the time that sales began to provide a steady inflow of new cash. Hence the owners considered the $10,000 to be as much a permanent investment in the business as the investment in fixtures and inventory.

The first year of operations, 19X1, lived up to expectations exactly. All 12,000 shirts were sold. The sales of shirts were quite seasonal, however, and sales from month to month fluctuated considerably. The actual sales volumes by two-month periods are shown in Exhibit 8-1 (column 1).

Exhibit 8-1

SHIRTTAIL STORE
Schedule of Sales Volume and Wholesale and Retail Prices
For 19X1

Two-Month Period:	(1) Shirts Sold	(2) Wholesale Price	(3) Shirttail's Price
Jan.–Feb.	1,000	$5.00	$10.00
Mar.–Apr.	1,000	5.10	10.00
May–June	2,000	5.20	10.00
July–Aug.	1,000	5.30	10.50
Sept.–Oct.	3,000	5.40	10.50
Nov.–Dec.	4,000	5.50	10.50

Column 2 of Exhibit 8-1 shows the prices being charged during the year by wholesale suppliers of shirts. Although Shirttail Store had purchased a full year's supply at $5.00, it was very clear by midyear that the next year's supply would cost more. In anticipation of higher costs, the manager raised the store's retail price (column 3) from $10.00 to $10.50. He justified this change to the owners at the time on two grounds: (1) his competitors had already raised their retail prices because they were already paying the higher wholesale prices, and (2) he expected to have to charge $10.70 in 19X2 (based on an expected wholesale price of $5.50), and the earlier price change would make the transition from $10.00 to $10.70 seem more gradual to customers.

During 19X1 expenses other than cost of shirts sold and depreciation of fixtures amounted to $50,000. This information and the information given above are reflected in the worksheet in Exhibit 8-2, based on conventional accounting concepts.

Exhibit 8-2

SHIRTTAIL STORE
Financial Position Worksheet
For 19X1

Description	Cash	Inventory	Fixtures	Accumulated Depreciation	Owners' Equity
Beginning Position	80,000				80,000
Bought fixtures	(10,000)		10,000		
Purchases	(60,000)	60,000			
Sales	124,000				124,000 (R)
Other expenses	(50,000)				(50,000) (E)
Cost of sales		(60,000)			(60,000) (E)
Depreciation				(5,000)	(5,000) (E)
Preliminary Balances	84,000	—0—	10,000	(5,000)	89,000

The owners of Shirttail Store agreed at the outset to withdraw an amount of cash equal to net income at the end of each year. Notice that if they followed that policy at the end of 19X1 they would withdraw $9,000 in cash, leaving ending owners' equity equal to beginning owners' equity of $80,000, *which in turn equals the initial money capital invested in the business.*

As we have illustrated above and in earlier examples, if the enterprise continues to distribute cash to owners equal to net income period after period, it will continue to retain net assets (owners' equity) equal to the initial money capital contributed by the owners. Furthermore, if and when an enterprise that follows such a policy finally ceases to operate (assuming no losses on final disposition of its assets), it will end its life with cash equal to the original investment of the owners.

● *The physical capital point of view.* However, there are ways of viewing the business enterprise under which preservation of its original cash endowment is not the really essential factor in preserving its economic essence. One such view is the physical capital (as opposed to money capital) point of view. The physical capital approach does not view the business enterprise as a reservoir of cash that is converted into productive resources and then back into cash via the sale of products or services. Rather, it takes the point of view that enterprises are formed and continue to operate in a market economy for purposes of providing specific products and services efficiently. And they are able to stay in business only so long as they maintain at least a long-run capability to provide some product or service that is valued more highly by customers than its resource costs.

The essence of the enterprise that must be preserved, therefore, is not an arbitrary amount of cash, but a more abstract "capability to produce." More specifically, the enterprise is viewed as (1) a reservoir of physical resources, (2) which, when combined efficiently, are capable of providing products and services of value, (3) which in turn can be sold to customers, (4) producing infusions of cash into the enterprise, (5) to be used to replace the productive capacity of resources used up in providing the products and services.

Thus the relevant test of effort in measuring the ongoing cash-generating capability of the enterprise (performance) is the cost to replace resources used up in the production of revenues earned. And the relevant test for preserving the economic muscle of an enterprise at a particular point in time is whether or not it has the capability to replace its productive resources (or the services they perform) as they are consumed. Of course, as long as economic conditions remain static (prices do not change), the amount of original money capital contributed to the enterprise continues to be adequate to replace any resources purchased and used in the business as they wear out. Thus, under static conditions, original money capital would be equivalent to the original physical capital requirement. (Similarly, if *all prices* in the economy change by the *same percentage* over a period of time, ability to replace the assets employed in the business can be maintained so long as the original purchasing power of the money capital invested in the business is maintained —by using price-level-adjusted net income as the measure of disposable wealth.) A problem arises, though, when the prices of the productive resources of a particular enterprise rise disproportionately relative to all other prices in the economy.

Example 8-4   At the 19X1 year-end meeting between the owners and the manager of Shirttail Store, the owners were given the worksheet shown in Exhibit 8-2. All were in favor of total withdrawals equal to the net income of $9,000. But the manager objected. He pointed out that if $9,000 were withdrawn from the business, there would be only $75,000 remaining cash. After allowing for the $10,000 cash balance required to meet "other expenses," only $65,000 would be left for purchasing 19X2's inventory of shirts. That was $1,000 less than the $66,000 required to buy a full year's supply of 12,000 shirts at the expected price of $5.50. Furthermore, the manager pointed out that the prices of the fixtures had risen in several jumps during 19X1, so that comparable fixtures would cost $1,000 more if replaced immediately at the end of 19X1. He conceded that the fixtures would not have to be replaced until the end of 19X2, but he wondered where the extra cash would come from if he was already short $1,000 for replacing inventory at the end of 19X1.

Under the circumstances depicted in Example 8-4, it can hardly be concluded that preservation of the original money capital of the enterprise (and therefore the use of conventional accounting net income as a measure of disposable wealth) is a means of preserving its economic strength. Upon reflection, the same must be concluded about conventional accounting net income as a measure of performance in the sense of characterizing the Shirttail Store's long-run cash-generating ability. For at the end of 19X1 it is known that even if in the next year the business provides the same number of shirts to customers with precisely the same efficiency as in its first year of operations, the costs of the shirts sold (and in a sense fixtures used) will definitely be higher than their past transaction costs. Thus when prices have risen, the total amount of expense recognized under conventional accounting is *biased downward* with respect to the enterprise's *ongoing* ability to acquire the resources necessary to continue to provide the same quality of merchandise to its customers as before. Thus, *other things being equal,* conventional accounting net income is *biased upward* (when prices have risen) relative to the enterprise's ongoing ability to provide products whose values to customers exceed their costs.

Now we should pose the question whether there is any systematic way of accounting for the enterprise's status and performance that avoids the bias. The answer is, Yes and no. *No* if prices change precipitously so that, for instance, the manager of the Shirttail Store could not have known, prior to all 19X1 distributions to owners, that the business would have to pay substantially higher prices in 19X2 for new shirts than it originally paid in 19X1.

If such changes in prices are not known until resources are actually replaced, then no specific provision can be made for them. Perhaps the only adaptation possible is a general reluctance on the part of management to distribute cash from the enterprise to its owners, lest the distribution turn out to be excessive in retrospect. But provided the changes in prices of individual resources are less precipitous, we can arrive at (1) an index of disposable wealth that is more reliable than conventional accounting net income in preserving the enterprise's ability to replace its productive resources, and (2) some measures of performance that avoid the obvious bias of conventional accounting net income when replacement costs of resources have changed. The modifications to conventional accounting that are required to achieve these purposes are described in the remainder of this section.

Current Replacement Costs and Disposable Wealth Measurement

Although the motivation differs, the measurement of disposable wealth on a replacement-cost basis involves roughly the same set of steps as those used in measuring disposable wealth on a general price-level-adjusted basis. The reason for the similarity is that in both cases we are striving for an application of the Hicksian definition of income that is consistent with a particular view of enterprise "well-offness." The direct measurement of Hicksian income involves comparing the before-withdrawal level of wealth at the end of a period with a criterion level—that of the beginning of the period. The difference is disposable wealth. (Refer back to Exhibit 7-4 and the related discussion to recall how the application with respect to general price-level changes was made.)

One problem encountered in Chapter 7 in developing a general price-level-adjusted disposable wealth measure was the requirement that both ending wealth and beginning wealth (net assets) of the enterprise must be measured on the same basis in order for their difference to be meaningful. The same problem is encountered in replacement-cost applications. Let us first consider beginning net assets.

- *Adjusting beginning net assets.* Under conventional accounting, the amount of beginning net assets (owners' equity) represents the amount of money capital committed to the enterprise by the owners as of the beginning of the year. According to the money capital point of view, preserving that original money capital commitment is sufficient to maintain intact the economic essence of the enterprise. Under the physical capital point of view, it is sufficient *only if prices do not change.* That is, if prices do not change, the amount formerly available to invest in the resources (assets) employed by the enterprise will continue to command the same quantities of those resources.

If prices of resources employed by the enterprise increase, on the other hand, it is necessary to retain additional money capital in the enterprise (through lesser withdrawals or even additional cash investments) in order for the enterprise to have the ability to acquire all of the same resources in the same quantities. Thus from the physical capital point of view, we wish to add allowances to the original beginning-of-period owners' equity for the changes in the costs of resources employed by the enterprise during the period. By adding such allowances *we set a higher "criterion level"* of net assets against which to compare the net asset level at the end of the period.

Example 8-5   In the case of the Shirttail Store, price increases were experienced in 19X1 for two of the resources employed in the business, inventory and fixtures. In Example 8-4 the manager exhibited concern that the original money capital of the enterprise was inadequate to carry on, in view of the price increases. He was right. At the beginning of 19X1 the $80,000 of original money capital was adequate to purchase fixtures at $10,000 plus 12,000 shirts for $60,000 ($5.00 each), leaving the necessary $10,000 cash balance to cover other costs until sales "caught up" with the major purchases. At the new prices it would take $1,000 more to buy the same fixtures at the end of 19X1 and $6,000 more for the same quantity of shirts, 12,000 × ($5.50 − $5.00), or $87,000 total money capital to command the same resources—as shown in Exhibit 8-3.

Exhibit 8-3   SHIRTTAIL STORE
Replacement-Cost-Adjusted Beginning Owners' Equity
As of the End of 19X1

Owners' equity as of the beginning of 19X1		$80,000
Add:		
Increase in replacement cost of fixtures	$1,000	
Increase in maximum commitment of money capital		
to inventory (12,000 shirts @ $.50)	6,000	
Total additional capital requirements		7,000
Replacement-cost-adjusted beginning owners' equity		$87,000

The $87,000 shown in Exhibit 8-3 is the criterion level of net assets below which the enterprise may not fall if it is to carry on its operations as before, *at the new level of prices.* In arriving at the amounts of the adjustments in Exhibit 8-3, we applied the following rule: Each adjustment is the difference between the replacement cost and the original cost of the particular resource at *the maximum level of investment by the enterprise in that type of resource.*

In the case of Shirttail Store's inventory purchases, the maximum investment is one year's supply (12,000 shirts). In the case of the fixtures, the maximum investment was presumed to be the same number and types of items that cost $10,000 at the beginning of 19X1. Hence, after the adjustments have been made, the resulting adjusted level of owners' equity ($87,000) may be interpreted as the amount of money capital required at the beginning of 19X1 if the enterprise had had to carry on all the activities that it did carry on during 19X1, *but at end-of-period prices.*

• *Adjusting end-of-year balances.* In adjusting ending net assets to a replacement-cost basis, we again encounter the distinction between monetary and nonmonetary assets. The distinction has the same implication in replacement-cost accounting as in general price-level accounting. Hence, we have only to adjust the end-of-19X1 balances in the *nonmonetary* accounts of the Shirttail Store to an end-of-19X1 replacement-cost basis. Referring back to Exhibit 8-2, we note that there are only two nonmonetary accounts with nonzero balances at the end of 19X1, the fixtures account and the related accumulated depreciation account.

The fixtures account has a balance of $10,000 (the original cost of the fixtures)—thus requiring a $1,000 upward adjustment to the $11,000 end-of-19X1 replacement cost of the fixtures. The accumulated depreciation account shows a negative balance equal to one-half the original cost of the fixtures, or $5,000. On a replacement-cost basis, the depreciation should be one-half the replacement cost of the fixtures, or $5,500—implying a further (negative) adjustment of $500 to the account. These adjustments are shown along with the conventional accounting worksheet for Shirttail Store's 19X1 operations (from Exhibit 8-2) on lines 1–9 of Exhibit 8-4. The justification for the combined adjustments is this: (1) the adjusted beginning owners' equity was measured *as if* the enterprise originally had sufficient money capital to purchase the resources it employed during the period at their end-of-period replacement costs, (2) so if those resources *had originally been purchased* at their replacement costs, they would appear in the ending financial position *at their unexpired replacement costs.* Hence the adjustment of the ending balances in all nonmonetary accounts to their unexpired replacement-cost levels is consistent with the supposition underlying the measurement of replacement-cost-adjusted *beginning* net assets.

After the ending balances of the nonmonetary assets and liabilities (if any) are adjusted, the adjusted ending *net asset* figure is arrived at in the usual way —the sum of all liabilities is subtracted from the sum of all assets (see line 10 of Exhibit 8-4). And having arrived at replacement-cost-adjusted beginning and ending owners' equity figures, the disposable wealth (net income) for the period is, of course, derived by subtracting the beginning figure from the ending figure. When this final operation is performed in our example as illustrated in Exhibit 8-4 (lines 10, 11, and 12), the $2,500 replacement-cost-based net income figure presents quite a contrast to the conventional accounting net income of $9,000.

• *Replacement-cost-based disposable wealth—summary.* The steps discussed in the preceding several paragraphs and illustrated in Exhibit 8-4 can be summarized as follows:

1. *Beginning owners' equity is adjusted* for the difference between the end-of-year replacement costs of resources used in the business and the amounts at which they could have been acquired at the beginning of the year (see Exhibit 8-3 and line 11 of Exhibit 8-4).

2. *The end-of-year balances* (before owner withdrawals) in all nonmonetary elements of financial position *are adjusted* from their unexpired original transaction costs to their unexpired current replacement costs (line 9 of Exhibit 8-4).

3. The amount of end-of-year adjusted net assets (owners' equity) based on current replacement cost is determined by finding the difference between the sum of the assets and the sum of the liabilities, after adjustments (line 10 of Exhibit 8-4).

4. The amount described in step 1 is subtracted from the adjusted net assets found in step 3 to arrive at the amount, if any, of withdrawable assets, that is, disposable wealth.

Exhibit 8-4

SHIRTTAIL STORE
Replacement-Cost-Based Net Income
For 19X1

Description	Cash	Inventory	Fixtures	Accumulated Depreciation	Owners' Equity
1. Beginning Position	80,000				80,000
2. Bought fixtures	(10,000)		10,000		
3. Purchases	(60,000)	60,000			
4. Sales	124,000				124,000 (R)
5. Other expenses	(50,000)				(50,000) (E)
6. Cost of sales		(60,000)			(60,000) (E)
7. Depreciation				(5,000)	(5,000) (E)
8. Preliminary balances	84,000	—0—	10,000	(5,000)	89,000
9. Adjustments to replacement cost	—0—	—0—	1,000	(500)	

10. Replacement-cost-adjusted preliminary balances $\quad$ 84,000 + —0— + 11,000 + (5,500) = $89,500

11. Replacement-cost-adjusted beginning owners' equity (see Exhibit 8-3 and related discussion) $\quad$ 87,000

12. Replacement-cost-based net income (disposable wealth) $\quad$ $ 2,500

As a rough test of whether the $2,500 replacement-cost-based net income (disposable wealth) figure in Exhibit 8-4 (and, therefore, the steps underlying its calculation) has the appropriate characteristics, consider the following further example.

Example 8-6   Suppose that (1) the owners of Shirttail Store were persuaded, on the basis of Exhibit 8-4, to withdraw only $2,500 from the business at the end of 19X1, and (2) everything worked out in 19X2 as expected by the manager, that is, the store bought 12,000 shirts at $5.50 each and sold them at $10.70 each and there were no further changes during 19X2 in the replacement costs of the resources used by the business.

In the absence of any further replacement-cost changes, additional replacement-cost adjustments are unnecessary and we may revert to conventional accounting for 19X2 (*starting from the replacement-cost-adjusted preliminary balances at the end of 19X1, of course*). Exhibit 8-5 illustrates the results for Shirttail Store for 19X2. Notice that a withdrawal *equal to 19X2 conventional accounting income* of $6,900 leaves exactly $87,000 of owners' equity, all in the form of cash. The $87,000 is precisely the amount still required to replace the fixtures at $11,000, the one year's supply of 12,000 shirts at $66,000, and leave $10,000 for the required minimum cash balance. This implies that our replacement-cost-based measure of disposable wealth for 19X1 adequately compensated for the changes in replacement costs that took place up to the end of 19X1 (the time at which the measurement presumably was made)—in the sense that restricting the 19X1 withdrawals to that figure ($2,500) ensured that the ability of the enterprise to acquire the resources it uses in production was not impaired.

Exhibit 8-5

SHIRTTAIL STORE
Financial Position Worksheet
For 19X2

Description	Cash	Inventory	Fixtures	Accumulated Depreciation	Owners' Equity
Replacement-cost-adjusted preliminary balances, end of 19X1	84,000	—0—	11,000	(5,500)	89,500
Withdrawal	(2,500)				(2,500)
19X2 Beginning Balances	81,500	—0—	11,000	(5,500)	87,000
Purchases	(66,000)	66,000			
Sales	128,400				128,400 (R)
Other expenses	(50,000)				(50,000) (E)
Cost of sales		(66,000)			(66,000) (E)
Depreciation				(5,500)	(5,500) (E)
Fixtures scrapped			(11,000)	11,000	
Withdrawal	(6,900)				(6,900) (W)
Ending Balances	87,000	—0—	—0—	—0—	87,000

Replacement-Cost-Based Performance Measurement

We noted earlier that when replacement costs of resources increase through time, conventional accounting net operating income (based on expenses measured in terms of the lower original transaction costs) is biased upward relative to the ongoing cash-generating ability of the enterprise. Why? Because if the same productive activities are replicated in future periods with exactly the same efficiency, income (and cash flow) would be less, *other things being equal*, because more would be paid for the (same) resources used. In this section we are going to explore some operating income measures that, hopefully, are not biased due to changing replacement costs, but which nevertheless maintain an orientation to actual (past and present) productive activities.

Why try to maintain an orientation to past and present activities? The answer takes us back to our original motivation in Chapter 4 for introducing measures of performance (operating income) as basic financial accounting outputs. In making investment decisions, investors presumably use some estimates of the future cash flows and attendant risk associated with an investment in a business. Whether management provides forecasts of future enterprise cash flows or investors produce their own forecasts, measures of the enterprise's demonstrated ability to generate cash in the immediate past should be useful in testing the credibility of such forecasts. This is an objective that conventional accounting performance measurement (net operating income) is intended to serve.

Conventional accounting net operating income focuses on a particular set of products or services (the ones that were sold or provided in the current period) and the set of productive activities that produced them. By matching the prices received for the products sold against the prices paid for the resources consumed, net operating income attempts to measure the contribution *of that set of activities* to the long-run cash flow of the enterprise. Presumably, then, if the enterprise were to engage in an identical set of activities in the future, with the same efficiency as demonstrated in the past, the same contribution to long-run cash flows would result.

We recognize, of course, that sets of activities will virtually never repeat themselves exactly. But that does not mean that measurement of past performance is futile. It simply means that a measure of past performance is not a forecast *per se*. Instead, it may only provide a starting point for forecasting (assuming that the forecaster attempts to predict first the ways that future activities will differ from past activities, and then the amounts by which the resulting future performance will depart from past performance).

• *Relevance of operating income based on replacement costs.* With this motivation in mind, we now turn to a consideration of the relevance of current replacement costs in measuring *past* performance. When replacement prices at the end of a period differ from the prices paid for resources that expired during the period, we are put on notice of an almost certain difference between the cash-flow implications of past and future activities. Assuming that the activities of the current period are repeated exactly in the future, the current (end-of-period) replacement costs of the resources used in the current period presumably are better estimates of the costs to be incurred in the future period than are the past transactions costs of the same resources. Thus, by restating current period performance in terms of the end-of-period replacement costs of resources used, we take into account the expected difference, due to price changes to date, between present and future performance. We do not, however, preempt the function of forecasting *per se, since we still reflect the same past productive activities (but in terms of a more current set of prices)*.

In measuring performance using replacement costs, we are interested only in measuring the total flow of resources that actually took place during the period in terms of their replacement costs. Presumably, by expressing the actual resources consumed in producing revenues in terms of their end-of-period replacement costs, the replacement-cost-based measure of expense simulates the expenses that we would have recognized under conventional accounting, *assuming* that all resources used during the period had actually been acquired at their replacement costs. The reason for the full adjustment to end-of-period replacement cost is that if the same resources are acquired and used in future periods, they will all be acquired for the new prices (assuming no further price changes). However, in attempting to apply this notion (by measuring actual resource sacrifices (expenses) of the period in terms of end-of-period replacement costs), a substantial question immediately comes to mind. Is it reasonable to adjust expenses to end-of-year replacement costs while measuring revenue on the basis of prices actually received during the period? The answer is no.

Unless the future prices charged to customers remain the same as they were in the current period, adjusting *only* expenses is perhaps no better than no adjustment at all. Without an adjustment for replacement costs, net operating income is biased with respect to probable changes in future costs. But with no concurrent adjustment to revenue, replacement-cost-based operating income is the result of matching current replacement costs of resources against possibly obsolete selling prices. Thus it is questionable whether such a measure of performance constitutes a better measure than conventional accounting net income. Furthermore, the problem would probably be encountered frequently in practice, since, historically, selling price increases have typically followed resource cost increases.

• *Replacement-cost-based operating income.* Assuming that we wish to retain the relevance of the most current replacement-cost information (i.e., end-of-period costs), an obvious solution is to define replacement-cost-based operating income as follows:

> **Replacement-Cost-Based Operating Income.**   Replacement-cost-based operating income equals revenue, measured at end-of-period selling prices, minus related expenses, measured in terms of the end-of-period replacement costs of *the resources actually consumed* in producing the revenue of the period.

Example 8-7   In Example 8-3 it was noted that Shirttail Store sold 12,000 shirts during 19X1 and that the end-of-19X1 replacement cost and selling price of one shirt were $5.50 and $10.70, respectively. It was further noted in Example 8-4 that fixtures like those in use during 19X1, which originally cost $10,000, would have cost $11,000 to replace at the end of 19X1. Based on these cost (and price) changes and assuming no change in the costs of "other" resources used in the business, the Shirttail Store's replacement-cost operating income is contrasted with its conventional accounting income for 19X1 in Exhibit 8-6.

The figures in the Conventional Accounting column are identical to the revenue and expense figures appearing in the owners' equity column of the conventional worksheet in Exhibit 8-2. The sales figure and cost of sales figure in the Replacement-Cost column are the result of multiplying the 12,000 shirts sold during 19X1 by the end-of-19X1 price of $10.70 and replacement cost of $5.50, respectively. The depreciation of $5,500 is the result of dividing the end-of-year replacement cost of the fixtures in use during

19X1 ($11,000) by their expected useful life of two years. The "other" expenses are shown at the same $50,000 in both columns because we have assumed that the prices of "other" resources used in the business have not changed during the year.

Exhibit 8-6

SHIRTTAIL STORE
Comparative Operating Income Statements
For 19X1

	Conventional Accounting	Replacement-Cost Accounting
Sales revenue	$124,000	$128,400
Less expenses:		
Cost of sales	$ 60,000	$ 66,000
Depreciation	5,000	5,500
Other	50,000	50,000
Total expenses	$115,000	$121,500
Net operating income	$ 9,000	$ 6,900

A most important feature of replacement-cost operating income based on end-of-period prices is that it bears the same relationship to future operating income, after replacement costs have changed, that conventional operating income bears to future operating income under static conditions. In the case of Shirttail Store, for instance, if (1) 12,000 shirts are again purchased and sold in 19X2, (2) with the same operating efficiency as in 19X1, and (3) with *no further* change in replacement costs or selling prices, the operating income in 19X2 will again be $6,900, the same as the *replacement-cost* operating income for 19X1 shown in Exhibit 8-6. Note that Exhibit 8-5 already demonstrates in worksheet form that this will be the case under precisely the same set of assumptions as those listed above. Thus we have now shown that (1) we can construct a replacement-cost-based disposable wealth measure that will tend to preserve the physical capital of the enterprise in times of changing prices, and (2) we can construct a performance measure based on replacement costs that bears the same relationship to future cash-generating ability in times of changing prices as conventional operating income does under static conditions.

Having illustrated and noted the special relevance of replacement-cost operating income *based on end-of-period prices,* we hasten to add an important qualification. Measuring operating income based on end-of-period prices takes advantage of the most current price information, but it is also susceptible to the question of whether the current period's sales volume could have been achieved (or can be in the future) at end-of-period prices. If it is unlikely that current sales volume can be replicated in the future, our discussion above of the special relevance of replacement-cost operating income measured in terms of year-end prices loses some of its persuasiveness.

An alternative approach is to adjust the costs of resources used to their replacement costs at some time during the period, such that expenses are measured on a more or less comparable basis with the actual prices charged to customers during the period (i.e., the actual revenue of the period). However, we must recognize that this alternative, too, has some drawbacks. For one, although it may use more current price information than conventional accounting, it does not make use of the most current cost information (as of the time statements are prepared). For another, although it may be intuitively obvious that an expense like cost of goods sold should be measured at replacement costs prevailing at the time the goods were sold, the best way to measure such expenses as depreciation on a replacement-cost basis that is consistent with actual revenue is not so obvious. Should replacement costs of long-lived assets be estimated (as a basis for depreciation expense) as of the middle of the period? Or should some kind of average of replacement costs prevailing during the period be used?

Clearly, the circumstances in individual cases may favor one or the other of the alternatives for measuring replacement-cost operating income. The authors, however, have illustrated only the first alternative (replacement-cost operating income based on end-of-period prices) because of its potentially greater decision relevance. On the other hand, measuring replacement-cost operating income at within-period replacement costs is probably the most likely to be acceptable as a practical matter simply because it relies on prices actually received by the company (in the case of revenue) and prices at which resources *could* actually have been bought (in the case of expense) rather than current exchange prices at which the company has not yet bought and sold. Unfortunately, for this same reason this alternative does not represent as potentially great an improvement over conventional accounting in times of changing prices as the end-of-year pricing alternative. Interestingly, a rough approximation of the within-year pricing alternative is actually widely used in accounting practice. It is called the *Lifo* inventory method and is described in some detail in Chapter 12.

Relationship between Replacement-Cost-Based Performance and Disposable Wealth Measures

At the point in Chapter 7 when we had arrived at a general price-level-based disposable wealth measure, we set out to reconcile that measure to enterprise performance. We were able to complete the reconcilement primarily because of a very important property of price-level-adjusted accounting—it is restricted in all of its measurements to original transaction data. The only departure from conventional accounting is that certain price-level ratios are used to translate original transaction values into their equivalent values in the purchasing power units of a later point in time. In replacement-cost-based accounting we are purposely trying to go beyond the kinds of measurements that can be made using only original transaction data. Once we are outside the bounds of a single data base, we seek to employ the outside data (in this case, current replacement costs and selling prices) in the way most appropriate to the purpose at hand.

Unfortunately, however, the more we exercise this freedom of selection in pursuing an appropriate replacement-cost-based performance measure, the further it will depart from an easily recognized relationship with the measure of disposable wealth described earlier. The fact that in replacement-cost accounting unique adjustments are made for each type of resource employed in the business further complicates the problem of reconcilement—compared to general-price-level accounting, where the same ratio of price levels applies to the amounts exchanged in all transactions of a given date, regardless of the resource purchased or sold.

Because of the complications involved we do not attempt to reconcile replacement-cost-based net income and net operating income at this point in our discussion. However, for the interested reader, a reconcilement of the two income measures based on the Shirttail Store example is contained in the Appendix to this chapter.

Alternate Concepts of the Enterprise and Alternate Valuation Bases

In the preceding pages we have been exploring some ways to give expression in financial accounting to a different concept of the enterprise than is implied in conventional accounting. The enterprise is viewed as a reservoir of physical wealth rather than money wealth. Indexes of disposable wealth and performance measurement based on this concept were shown to be feasible through the recognition of current replacement costs of assets. This constitutes a departure from the principle of recognizing assets at their unexpired original transactions costs under conventional accounting. But most of the other principles introduced in our earlier discussion of conventional accounting were still employed in the same way, for example, the realization and matching principles. And, in particular, we still retain the definitional identity *Assets = Liabilities + Owners' equity*.

What differs is the way that we represent assets in terms of money. We simply use a different *valuation basis,* current replacement cost, for each individual kind of asset. However, by making this single change, we achieve a different way of representing enterprise status and performance, thought to be more relevant under conditions of rising replacement costs than conventional accounting outputs.

Some Limitations Associated with Recognizing Replacement Costs

Before leaving the subject of replacement-cost accounting, we must recognize that there are some significant limitations to applications of replacement costs. For instance, in practice it may sometimes be difficult to associate a specific replacement cost with a specific asset. One important reason for this difficulty is the very reason that original transaction costs become obsolete. Changing technology and changing forces of supply and demand may greatly alter the forms and service characteristics of resources available to the enterprise. It may be physically impossible to replace a specific asset with an identical asset at any price. If this is the case, no current replacement costs for such assets will be readily available. Instead, it may be necessary to substitute current replacement costs of assets or services that will provide roughly the *same production or service potential* as the assets employed in the business in their present form. In extreme cases, however, increasing replacement costs of productive resources may mean that the enterprise will actually change its line of business or its production methods in the future and, therefore, cease to employ the kind of assets in question altogether.

Example 8-8   Axle Forging Company owns an XR-1 stamping machine purchased ten years ago for $100,000. Its capacity of 3,000 stampings per hour is still adequate for the company's needs. But it will have to be replaced in another two years. Unfortunately, the XR-1 model is no longer produced. Virtually all available substitutes are faster and much more expensive. The nearest thing to an XR-1 available at present is another manufacturer's XX-4. It has a capacity of 4,000 stampings per hour and costs $200,000. After some thought, company management has concluded that if the XR-1 were presently worn out, it would be replaced by an XX-4. The current replacement cost of the XR-1 is therefore $200,000. However, management has concluded that if the price of an XX-4 rises to as much as $250,000 in the next two years, it will not replace the XR-1. Instead, it will buy stampings from an outside supplier.

Of course, in situations where assets cannot be literally replaced or where it is uneconomical to do so, the replacement costs of such assets may be no more useful in arriving at relevant measures of enterprise performance and disposable wealth than are long outdated original transaction values.

Present Status of Replacement-Cost Accounting

With the exception of a few companies that have in the past reported approximate replacement-cost depreciation figures (usually with techniques similar to general price-level adjustments), the authors know of no major U.S. companies that apply replacement-cost accounting for external reporting purposes. There are, however, a number of European examples of replacement-cost-based financial statements among significant enterprises (principally companies based in the Netherlands). Replacement-cost statements presently are not required by any authority in the United States. The reason that they are probably not forthcoming from U.S. companies *voluntarily* is that applying replacement-cost accounting would require additional efforts (costs) on the part of the enterprise beyond the costs of producing presently required conventional accounting statements, and, as will be elaborated in Chapter 9, there is no way to tell clearly whether the benefits to various users of the statements would justify the additional cost.

RECOGNITION OF CURRENT EXIT PRICES (MARKET VALUES)

Another Point of Departure—Conventional Accounting Recognition of Accomplishment

In the replacement-cost section of this chapter, we began by reviewing some of the distinctive features of conventional accounting income measurement. That review brought out some limitations of the conventional accounting model, setting up the motivation for recognition of current replacement costs. In this section we will again review a very important aspect of conventional accounting: the recognition of accomplishment of the enterprise in productive activities and its measurement. Again, a limitation of the conventional model will be exposed, this time motivating the recognition of still another alternate valuation base: current market value.

• *The realization principle reconsidered.* When we first introduced conventional accounting net income as a measure of enterprise performance in Chapter 4, we described it as the difference between recognized revenues and expenses. *Revenue* is the money representation of the recognized accomplishment of the enterprise for an accounting period; *expense* is the money representation of the *related* sacrifice. Because of the desirability of relative objectivity in measuring performance for the benefit of outside investors, conventional accounting is very selective in the way that it recognizes accomplishment. The realization principle generally restricts our measure of the accomplishment of an enterprise to the prices agreed to be paid by customers for the completed products *actually sold* and services *actually performed* during the period. But, of course, the value of those completed products and services *sold* during the current accounting period may be the result of the actual production activity of some past accounting period (or perhaps many past periods). Furthermore, current period production activity may go unrecognized, at least in part, during the current accounting period because the products and services produced will not all be brought to completion and sold until a future accounting period.

This does not necessarily mean that the recognition of efforts and accomplishment is not synchronized. On the contrary, the matching principle requires that insofar as possible the efforts expended (assets expired) in production activity be recognized as expenses in the period in which the total related accomplishment is recognized—usually the period of sale. But because the recognition of accomplishment and effort is postponed until the period of sale, the "performance" embodied in conventional accounting net income may be out of synchronization with the real productive activities that took place during the current period.

Perhaps in the many manufacturing and service operations where there is a relatively short lag from the beginning of production or service to completion and sale, the potential for measured performance to be greatly out of synchronization with the bulk of current productive activity is slight. But in some types of business enterprises where production-to-sales lags are long or sales are infrequent or sporadic due to the nature of the business, conventional accounting revenue based on the realization principle may be a very untimely measure of periodic accomplishment of the enterprise. This point can be illustrated as follows.

Example 8-9   Suppose several friends pooled their cash to form an investment company several years ago. Five individuals each contributed $2,000 for a total of $10,000. The whole amount was immediately invested in common stocks of some large publicly held corporations whose stocks are traded on a major securities exchange. These investments were expected to pay regular dividends and appreciate in value as well.

The common stocks were held for three years and then sold for $15,000. In the meantime $500 in total dividends was received throughout each year, including year three. Furthermore, the prices at which the stocks could have been sold went up to $11,000 by the end of year one and $13,500 by the end of year two. As the cash from the dividends was received at the end of each year, it was put into a savings account at 4 percent annual interest pending the accumulation of a sufficient amount to purchase another substantial block of common stock. After sale of the initial block of securities and receipt of dividends and interest for year three, $16,000 was reinvested in common stocks right at the end of the year. The conventional accounting treatment of these facts appears in Exhibit 8-7.

Notice that interest and dividend income is recognized as received in the year earned and that the original common stock investments are recognized at their original transaction cost of $10,000 right up to the time of their sale, the point at which a higher value is actually "realized." This conventional accounting treatment of the facts results in the net income figures for the first three years of Investment Company's operations shown in Exhibit 8-8.

Exhibit 8-7

INVESTMENT COMPANY
Financial Position Worksheet—Conventional Accounting Basis
For the First Three Years of Operations

Description	Cash	Stock Investments	Owners' Equity
Original Investment	10,000		10,000
Year 1			
Bought stock	(10,000)	10,000	
Received dividends	500		500(R)
Ending (Beginning) Position	500	10,000	10,500
Year 2			
Received dividends	500		500(R)
Received interest (4% × $500)	20		20(R)
Ending (Beginning) Position	1,020	10,000	11,020
Year 3			
Received dividends	500		500(R)
Received interest (4% × $1,020)	41		41(R)
Sold stock	15,000	(10,000)	5,000(R)
Bought stock	(16,000)	16,000	
Ending (Beginning) Position	561	16,000	16,561

Exhibit 8-8

INVESTMENT COMPANY
Comparative Statements of Net Income
For the First Three Years of Operations

	Year 1	Year 2	Year 3
Dividend income	$500	$500	$ 500
Interest income		20	41
Gain from sale of stock			5,000
Net Income	$500	$520	$5,541

- *The realization principle and performance.* Although this accounting treatment is a strict application of the realization principle as it is traditionally interpreted, there is something troubling about the pattern of the amounts of net income recognized for the first three years. Using net income as an index of performance implies that the year three performance of the Investment Company was more than ten times "better" than either year one or year two. But the principal difference between year three and years one and two is the single transaction that took place in which the company gave up one asset, common stock, in exchange for another asset, cash. The question is whether the transaction event itself was of sufficient economic significance that all the difference between the final selling price and the original transaction cost of the common stock ($5,000) should be assigned as income to the period in which that event took place. A traditional interpretation of the realization principle implies that the answer is yes, since the period of actual sale is the first time period in which the increase in value of the common stock was affirmed in an actual transaction with an independent economic unit (the purchaser). The third year is, furthermore, the first time in which the increase in value was "realized" in the form of a flow of new cash or claim to cash (the selling price).

The Value-Added, or Accretion, Concept of Accomplishment

There is reason to object to the traditional view that a sale transaction is the dominant or "critical" event in determining the period in which the accomplishment embodied in a particular asset is recognized. The purpose of net income as a performance measure is to characterize the results of the productive activity of the enterprise for a period of time. But the productive activity of the enterprise includes all activity within the enterprise that advances or adds to the value of the goods or services that the company produces or holds for sale. To measure actual performance for a period, then, it is necessary to measure the advance toward ultimate sale value of all assets of the enterprise during a period, not just those that were actually brought to completion and sale. This is known as the value-added, or accretion, concept of income.

Typically, the problem in applying the value-added concept of income is to measure objectively the advances in asset values that were created during a period. This is particularly difficult in the case of partially complete manufactured goods, which are sufficiently specialized that they are not very usable or salable in any but final or complete form. It would be a matter of judgment on the part of management as to how much increase in value should be ascribed to such an asset (say, an automobile) at the end of a period in which it was brought from zero to only 50 percent completion. Less difficulty is encountered in applying the value-added concept of income when the principal economic activity of the enterprise is the production of products that are readily salable in all stages of completion, or merely the holding of readily marketable final goods for sale—provided the relevant market values (current exchange exit values) are available.

- *Market values and the value-added concept.* The Investment Company example fits into the latter category. One of the enterprise's principal activities is the holding of marketable securities not only for regular dividend returns but also on the expectation that they will increase in value. Furthermore, since the common stocks bought and sold by Investment Company are traded on a well-organized securities exchange, their exit values at virtually any time can be determined from the prices at which those stocks are then selling on the exchange. Thus the Investment Company is a good case for illustrating how current market values can be used to implement the value-added concept of income.

Example 8-10   The worksheet in Exhibit 8-9 showing year-by-year recognition of current market values contrasts with the conventional accounting treatment of Investment Company's first three years of operations illustrated earlier (Exhibit 8-7).

Exhibit 8-9

INVESTMENT COMPANY
Financial Position Worksheet—Current Market Value Basis
For the First Three Years of Operations

Description	Cash	Stock Investments	Owners' Equity
Original Investment	10,000		10,000
Year 1			
Bought stock	(10,000)	10,000	
Received dividends	500		500(R)
Increase in market value of stock		1,000	1,000(G)
Ending (Beginning) Position	500	11,000	11,500
Year 2			
Received dividends	500		500(R)
Received interest (4% of $500)	20		20(R)
Increase in market value of stock		2,500	2,500(G)
Ending (Beginning) Position	1,020	13,500	14,520
Year 3			
Received dividends	500		500(R)
Received interest (4% of $1,020)	41		41(R)
Increase in market value		1,500	1,500(G)
Sold stock	15,000	(15,000)	
Bought stock	(16,000)	16,000	
Ending (Beginning) Position	561	16,000	16,561

• *Unrealized gains and losses—interpretation.* The first departure from conventional accounting in Exhibit 8-9 appears at the end of year one when the then-current market values of the common stock are recognized. The line on the worksheet labeled "Increase in market value of stock" shows a $1,000 increase in Stock Investments and a concurrent $1,000 increase in Owners' Equity, labeled *G* for *gain*. This gain or income is recognized at the end of year one, even though it has *not yet been realized* in the form of cash or claims to cash. The reasoning is as follows:

The process or activity of holding securities in anticipation of an increase in their value was carried on throughout year one. If the securities had been sold at the end of year one, their sale would have yielded approximately $11,000, or $1,000 in excess of their original transaction costs. Therefore, $1,000 is the increase in value brought about by the first year's holding activity. In the event that the securities had actually been sold at the end of year one, the $1,000 income or gain would have actually been "realized" in the conventional sense. That the enterprise did not actually sell at the $11,000 price should not alter our view of the first year's holding activity. It only indicates that the enterprise expected additional gains from additional years' holding activities.

The same reasoning applies to the recognition of the additional increase in value to $13,500 during year two, a further gain of $2,500. Finally, in year three, before the securities were sold, the additional gain recognized is only $1,500, the excess of the $15,000 then-current market value (selling price) over the end-of-year-two market value of $13,500.

• *Recognition of market values and the timing of income.* Now the importance of this exercise shows up best for this example when we compare in Exhibit 8-10 the *pattern* of recognized net income that accompanies recognition of the current market value of the securities with the conventional accounting pattern depicted earlier.

Exhibit 8-10

INVESTMENT COMPANY
Comparative Income Statements
For the First Three Years of Operations

	Year 1	Year 2	Year 3	Total
Conventional Accounting				
Dividend income	$ 500	$ 500	$ 500	$1,500
Interest income		20	41	61
Gain from sale of stock			5,000	5,000
Total net income	$ 500	$ 520	$5,541	$6,561
Current Market Values Recognized				
Securities gains	$1,000	$2,500	$1,500	$5,000
Interest income		20	41	61
Dividend income	500	500	500	1,500
Total net income	$1,500	$3,020	$2,041	$6,561

Period-by-period recognition of the current market value of the securities leads to a more even spread of the total gain from holding the securities over all three years that they were held. But the smoothness or evenness of the pattern is not the important difference. That simply follows our contrived facts which specified that the price of the securities rose in each year of the total holding period. We could have just as readily supposed that after rising to $11,000 by the end of year one, the prices of the securities fell to $9,000 by the end of year two but recovered and rose to $15,000 by the end of year three when they were sold.

The conventional accounting treatment of this alternate set of facts would be Identical to the conventional accounting treatment of the original set of facts, since all market prices or price changes would be ignored until the securities were sold at the end of year three. But recognizing current market values of the securities year by year gives quite a different picture.

Exhibit 8-11

INVESTMENT COMPANY
Comparative Income Statements
For the First Three Years of Operations

	Year 1	Year 2	Year 3	Total
Current Market Values Recognized				
Securities gains (losses)	$1,000	($2,000)	$6,000	$5,000
Interest income		20	41	61
Dividend income	500	500	500	1,500
Total net income	$1,500	($1,480)	$6,541	$6,561

The picture in Exhibit 8-11 is very uneven—but so are the facts. That is the important point. The recognition of current market values permits us to recognize changes in value between the point (in time) of entry of resources into the enterprise and the point of their final exit in a sale transaction.

Incidentally, it is important to note one common feature of both conventional accounting and the recognition of current market values. Notice in the comparative statements in Exhibit 8-10 that the total net income for all three years is the same amount, $6,561, for both conventional and market-value accounting. This is no coincidence. The total advance in value of the enterprise from the investment in the securities is ultimately governed by the difference between the price paid originally to acquire the securities and the price finally received from the sale (plus dividends received). But the recognition of current market values of the securities in the periods between purchase and sale assigns portions of that total to accounting periods between the point of purchase and the point of sale. Conventional accounting recognizes the total change between the actual entry and exit prices of the securities in the period of sale.

Market Values of Assets Not Held for Eventual Sale

Our use of the Investment Company example above made it easier to develop one important rationale for market-value accounting. However, we should recognize that such a simple example leaves untouched some important issues in applying market-value accounting. In particular, the example purposely omitted consideration of the valuation and related income effects of assets held for use in a business (as opposed to assets like marketable securities held for sale) and of the problems of matching efforts and accomplishments in measuring performance. The application of exit prices to assets held for use in production raises a problem. Here, rather than using depreciation based on (1) original transaction cost, or (2) price-level-adjusted cost, or (3) replacement cost as a measure of services consumed, the change in the market value of assets used in production is the measure of sacrifice (expense) for a period. Because enterprises generally do not engage in regularly trading the kinds of assets they use in production, they typically must buy such assets at higher (retail) prices than they can sell the same assets for (whole-sale). Hence there is usually a significant drop immediately after acquisition in the value of such assets. If the acquisition of a productive asset involves a large expenditure, as is often the case when a firm acquires plant and equipment, this dual-market phenomenon may in fact produce a distortion in the measure of performance for the first period of use. For this reason (as well as some others), current market exit prices are frequently not advocated for use by firms with large investments in productive plant and equipment (assets not held for sale); the Investment Company represents the type of situation that is most amenable to this valuation methodology.

A Format for Reporting Market-Value-Based Operating Income

Even though market-value accounting relies on a valuation base different from that of conventional accounting (and replacement-cost accounting), the attempt to match efforts and accomplishments in measuring performance is still relevant. This is based on the assumption that investors interested in the long-run cash-generating ability of the enterprise are interested not just in the final operating income figure but also in the significant positive and negative components that make it up. However, since we wish to recognize increases in values of assets as income in the period in which they take place rather than the period in which revenue is realized, the conventional revenue-expense in-come statement format is inappropriate. An alternative format is suggested in Exhibit 8-12.

Exhibit 8-12
MARKET-VALUE-BASED INCOME STATEMENT FORMAT

Net increase (or decrease) in market values of assets produced (or held) for sale
Plus other income:
    Dividends
    Interest
    Increases in market values of assets held for use in the business
Less expenses:
    Wages and salaries
    Selling and administrative expense
    Interest
    Decreases in market values of assets held for use in the business
    Other expense
Operating income

Notice that the format recognizes that the primary positive component of income, in the long-run sense, is the increase in the value of assets that the enterprise produces (or buys and holds) for sale to customers. Although in any given period the enterprise may experience income from other sources, in the long run its "stock-in-trade" will presumably be the most important source of cash flows. Thus the format begins with the increase (or decrease) in value of "stock-in-trade" assets (rather than revenue) and then continues with much the same organization as a conventional income statement.

The only other exception is the treatment accorded assets held *for use in the business* rather than for sale. Besides the conceptual problem (noted in the preceding section) with the often dramatic decline in value when such assets are placed in use, they present another problem in reporting income. Although they are held for consumption in operating the business, in some periods their market values may increase (appreciate) rather than decrease (depreciate). When the values of such assets increase, they contribute to the income of the period, though they are not primary sources of income. When the values decrease (as would be expected in the long run of all such assets other than land), the decreases are expenses. The format recognizes these possibilities with a heading for possible increases in the values of such assets under "other income" and one for decreases under "expenses."

Example 8-11 Wilderness Tents, Inc., is a retail tent store. It buys a single tent model made to its specifications for $250 each and sells all it can handle (about 1,000 per year) at $500 each. Its status and operations for a recent year, 19X3, are shown in the worksheet in Exhibit 8-13. The income statement in Exhibit 8-14 is prepared from the information in the worksheet according to the format shown in Exhibit 8-12.

Exhibit 8-13

WILDERNESS TENTS, INC.
Financial Position Worksheet—Current Market Value Basis
For the Year 19X3

Description	Cash	Tents	Equip-ment	Build-ings	Land	Owners' Equity
Beginning Position	5,000	15,000	16,000	24,000	20,000	80,000
Purchased tents	(250,000)	250,000				
Increase in market value of tents		250,000				250,000 (G)
Tent sales	500,000	(500,000)				
Wages and salaries	(100,000)					(100,000) (E)
Other expenses	(50,000)					(50,000) (E)
Decrease in market value of equipment and buildings			(4,000)	(6,000)		(10,000) (E)
Increase in market value of land					5,000	5,000 (G)
Ending Position	105,000	15,000	12,000	18,000	25,000	175,000

Exhibit 8-14

WILDERNESS TENTS, INC.
Market-Value-Based Income Statement
For 19X3

Increase in value of tents held for sale		$250,000
Plus increase in value of land		5,000
		$255,000
Less expenses:		
Wages and salaries	$100,000	
Decrease in market value of buildings	6,000	
Decrease in market value of equipment	4,000	
Other expense	50,000	160,000
Net operating income		$ 95,000

Recognition of Market Values and Measurement
of Disposable Wealth

As in the case of recognition of current replacement cost, recognition of market prices results in a concept of disposable wealth that contrasts period by period with disposable wealth measured under conventional accounting. Under conventional accounting, periodic net income is the difference between ending owners' equity (net assets), adjusted for additional investments or withdrawals, and beginning owners' equity (net assets). Thus net income is equal to the advance in recognized net assets of the enterprise over the unexpired original transaction's costs (original money invested) of assets as of the beginning of the period. Disposing of assets equal to conventional accounting net income therefore sets the enterprise back to a position of having recognized net assets equal in amount to the unexpired original cost of assets as of the beginning of the period.

When assets are valued at their current market prices, on the other hand, something different happens. Of course, net income still equals the difference between beginning and ending owners' equity for the period (adjusted appropriately for additional investments or withdrawals). But with the individual assets valued at their beginning and end-of-period market values, *owners' equity has a different interpretation* than under conventional accounting. Essentially, it is the amount of cash that can be realized by the enterprise or its owners as of a given point in time through immediate disposal of its net assets. Thus, beginning owners' equity is the amount of cash proceeds from sale of net assets that the owners could have enjoyed at the beginning of the period, and ending owners' equity represents the amount of cash value that could be realized at the end of the period. The difference between the two figures is therefore the amount of cash (or other assets) that can be distributed to owners without setting the enterprise back below the beginning-of-year cash value of its net assets.

It is important to note, however, that in order for the above interpretation of market-value-based owners' equity to be completely valid, the enterprise's liabilities must be valued not at their original transaction values, but at the amount that would be accepted in full payment as of the given balance sheet date. Only if the liabilities are so valued will the excess of (1) the sum of the asset values over (2) the sum of the liability values actually represent the net proceeds from disposal of the enterprise's assets and discharge of its liabilities.

It is also noteworthy that in market-value-based disposable wealth measurement we are again concerned (as we were in conventional accounting) with a purely money-oriented concept of enterprise wealth. That is, the criterion level of wealth is the beginning cash equivalent (upon sale) of the enterprise's net assets. This is in contrast to replacement-cost disposable wealth measurement where the criterion level is measured in money terms but is the amount of money capital necessary *to maintain a given physical operating capability*. One significant implication of this money-wealth orientation is that if the enterprise consistently distributes assets to owners equal to market-value-based net income in every period from the inception of the business, the enterprise will retain net assets equal to the original money capital contributed by the owners—the same result as obtained under conventional accounting (though at any point the net asset composition would differ between the two models).

Another significant implication of the money-wealth orientation of market-value accounting is that in times of generally changing prices, general price-level adjustments are as applicable to market-value accounting measures as they are to conventional accounting. (Recall from our Chapter 7 discussion that general price-level adjustments do not change the values used to represent the enterprise and its activities but are simply a means of expressing those values in the purchasing power units in existence at year-end.) As in conventional accounting, when market-value accounting is adjusted for changes in the general price level, a difference (net monetary gain or loss) emerges between (adjusted) market-value net income and net operating income.

Example 8-12   Refer back to the case of the Investment Company whose activities for its first three years of operations are depicted according to market-value accounting in Exhibit 8-9. Suppose that during years one and two no change in the general level of prices took place, but during year three the price level rose uniformly from 100 to 110. Suppose further that the interest and dividends were received throughout the year and that the transactions in common stock took place at year-end. Exhibit 8-15 shows the general price-level-adjusted, market-value-based income calculations for year three. Notice that, as in the case of conventional accounting adjusted for changes in general purchasing power, the difference between the price-level-adjusted operating income and the monetary loss equals the net income figure.

The Special Relevance of Market-Value-Based Net Assets

One question that the present owners of an enterprise should ask themselves from time to time is whether the enterprise should stay in business at all. To resolve this question, the market value of the net assets of the enterprise is one of the relevant bits of information.

The question essentially boils down to this, Does the value of the enterprise as a going concern (i.e., a generator of future cash flows through production of valuable products and services) exceed the value of the enterprise upon cessation of operation? The latter value quite clearly is the sum of the market values, at the time, of the assets of the enterprise less the sum of the discharge values of the liabilities—or what we have called the market value of the net assets of the enterprise (owners' equity, under market-value accounting).

Since every business should be able to justify its existence to its owners, the market value of the enterprise's net assets is one alternative accounting output that is, *at least in principle,* clearly relevant to investor-owners. However, there are some limitations to market-value accounting that deserve mention as well.

Some Limitations Associated with Recognizing Market Values

As was true of recognition of replacement costs, recognition of market output values is subject to some significant limitations. Whereas our primary example, Investment Company, dealt with readily marketable securities for

Exhibit 8-15

INVESTMENT COMPANY
Income Calculations
Year Three

Net Income:

Ending owners' equity from Exhibit 8-9 (all elements of ending financial position are already stated in end-of-year dollars)		$16,561
Beginning owners' equity from Exhibit 8-9 adjusted for price-level change $14,520 \times \dfrac{110}{100}$		15,972
Price-level-adjusted, market-value-based net income		$ 589

Operating Income:

Increase in value of securities held:		
End-of-year value	$15,000	
Less adjusted beginning-of-year value $13,500 \times \dfrac{110}{100}$	14,850	$ 150
Dividends and interest $541 \times \dfrac{110}{105}$		567
Price-level-adjusted, market-value-based operating income		$ 717

Monetary Loss from Holding Cash:

	Actual		Adjusted
Beginning balance	$ 1,020	$\times \dfrac{110}{100}$	$ 1,122
Dividends and interest	541	$\times \dfrac{110}{105}$	567
Sale of stock	15,000		15,000
Purchase of stock	(16,000)		(16,000)
Ending balance	$ 561		$ 689
			561
Monetary loss			$ 128

Reconcilement:

Price-level-adjusted operating income	$ 717
Less monetary loss	(128)
Price-level-adjusted net income	$ 589

which "realizable" current prices existed, many firms' assets may not have well-established and accessible markets. It may not be clear at all that a particular enterprise can actually realize the current prices if it decides to enter the market and sell. If the firm produces a unique or "differentiated" product, it may be difficult to accurately estimate what price a particular quantity or supply of that product will bring without actually selling it. Furthermore, it may take considerable time before it can be sold, or there may be additional operations required before the product is in condition for sale. In the former case, it may be necessary to arrive at a present value of the more distant future proceeds of sale as a means of recognizing the current value of assets of the enterprise. In the latter case, it is necessary to estimate the costs of completion and sale of the asset and deduct that from what it would currently sell for if complete and ready for sale. A current market value reduced for estimated costs of completion and sale is usually referred to by accountants as the *net realizable value* of the asset.

What all these reservations mean is that the decision relevance that can be achieved potentially by recognition of current market values is accompanied by a whole range of problems that have something in common. There is an element of subjective judgment required that is not present in the same form in conventional accounting (though we recognize that there are areas of judgment in conventional accounting). And since subjective judgments are less susceptible to verification by outside independent parties, they open up opportunities for personal bias or manipulation that might not be present otherwise.

Present Status of Market-Value Accounting

At the present time, as one might expect, the primary examples of applications of market-value accounting in practice are the mutual funds (investment companies) and insurance companies, which have large amounts of marketable securities among their assets. The authors know of no major U.S. manufacturing companies that now provide such information (except for supplementary disclosure of the market values of readily marketable securities held by such companies). Perhaps this is a reflection that such information (1) is not presently required by authorities, (2) is costly to prepare, and (3) is subject to the limitations noted above.

APPENDIX: RECONCILEMENT OF REPLACEMENT-COST MEASURES OF PERFORMANCE AND DISPOSABLE WEALTH

In spite of the complicating factors described in the body of this chapter, in very simple cases we can see the relationship between replacement-cost-based performance and disposable wealth measures. Furthermore, a simple case can be used to show why the complications arise in more realistic cases. The Shirttail Store example will serve these purposes well.

In conventional accounting the measure of performance (net operating income) equals the measure of disposable wealth (net income)—in the absence of any extraordinary gains and losses. By definition (the Hicksian definition), net income is the difference between ending and beginning owners' equity (adjusted for additional owner investments or withdrawals). On the other hand, net operating income is by definition the difference between total revenue and total expense. It just happens that revenues increase ending owners' equity relative to beginning owners' equity, and expenses decrease the difference. Thus in the absence of gains and losses, the difference between the two owners' equity figures (net income) equals the difference between revenues and expenses. We will now show that a similar (though not identical) kind of relationship holds in simple cases under replacement-cost accounting.

Consider Exhibit 8-16. We have depicted the calculation of net operating income and net income under both conventional and replacement-cost accounting concepts, based on the facts of the Shirttail Store's 19X1 operations. The figures in the Replacement Cost column are equal to the corresponding conventional accounting figures *plus* (*or minus*) the appropriate adjustments shown in the Adjustments column. (We have numbered the adjustments to facilitate later discussion.) The Conventional column should be self-explanatory, given the facts of the example and the worksheet that appeared in Exhibit 8-2. Note, however, that in this case conventional accounting operating income and net income *are equal* (i.e., there are no extraordinary gains or losses). The adjustments made to beginning and ending owners' equity to get replacement-cost-based net income should also be self-explanatory, based on earlier discussion and Exhibits 8-3 and 8-4. We are simply depicting those adjustments in a different format.

Exhibit 8-16

SHIRTTAIL STORE
Conventional and Replacement-Cost-Based
Net Income and Net Operating Income
19X1

	Conventional	Add (Deduct) Adjustments	Replacement Cost
Net Income			
Ending owners' equity:	$ 89,000		
Adjustments for current replacement cost for:			
Fixtures		$1,000 (3)	
Accumulated depreciation		(500)(3)	$ 89,500
Less beginning owners' equity:	80,000		
Adjustments for additional replacement cost of:			
Fixtures		1,000 (3)	
Inventory		6,000 (2)	87,000
Net income	$ 9,000		$ 2,500
Net Operating Income			
Revenue	$124,000	4,400 (1)	$128,400
Less expenses:			
Cost of sales	60,000	6,000 (2)	66,000
Depreciation	5,000	500 (3)	5,500
Other	50,000		50,000
Total	$115,000		$121,500
Net operating income	$ 9,000		$ 6,900

Now consider the replacement-cost-based operating income statement in Exhibit 8-16. It repeats the replacement-cost-based operating income calculation that appeared in Exhibit 8-6 (i.e., all revenue and expense figures are stated at end-of-year prices). The lower Adjustments column contains the differences or adjustments that would have to be made to the corresponding conventional accounting figure to state each revenue and expense item at end-of-year prices. Note in particular that unlike the conventional accounting figures, replacement-cost operating income does not equal replacement-cost net income.

Since (1) the conventional accounting figures are equal, and (2) the replacement-cost figures are arrived at by adjusting the conventional accounting figures, the difference between the replacement-cost net income figure and the operating income figure must be explainable in terms of the adjustments. To facilitate such an explanation we have identically numbered the adjustments made in measuring replacement-cost net income *that correspond to* adjustments made in measuring replacement-cost operating income.

The first thing to note is that the $4,400 adjustment (labeled (1)), made to arrive at replacement-cost revenue, equals the difference between replacement-cost operating income of $6,900 and net income of $2,500. This is not surprising, since the $4,400 adjustment is the only adjustment that does not have a counterpart in the calculation of net income as well as operating income calculation. Having made this observation, it is necessary to further show that this result is not a coincidence.

The fact that the $4,400 adjustment appears in the replacement-cost operating income calculation but not the net income calculation is entirely consistent with the purposes of the two kinds of income measurement involved. In measuring performance (in the future cash-generating sense), it seems logical to assign end-of-year prices to the actual sales quantities of the period—the rationale being that the resulting revenue figure better represents future periods' revenues, assuming other things (e.g., sales volume) remain equal. However, since end-of-year prices were not actually received on all sales during the period, they did not become a part of the wealth possessed by the enterprise during the period and, therefore, should not influence the assessment of disposable wealth generated during the period.

Now let us recognize that if the $4,400 adjustment of revenue to year-end prices were omitted from Exhibit 8-16, replacement-cost operating income and replacement-cost net income *would both equal* $2,500. To complete our analysis we will show that this equality can also be explained (i.e., it is not a coincidence). If we can establish this, we will have shown that there is an underlying systematic relationship between replacement-cost net income and operating income, however obscured it may be in more complex situations.

To measure net income on a replacement-cost basis, we added $6,000 (labeled (2)) to beginning owners' equity for the increased cost of one year's supply of inventory. Adjustments of this sort by themselves lower replacement-cost-based net income relative to conventional accounting net income by raising the criterion level of net assets (beginning owners' equity). Notice also that *in measuring replacement-cost-based operating income* we added the identical figure to cost of sales—thus identically reducing replacement-cost-based operating income relative to the conventional accounting figure. On the one hand, we are saying that because the cost of shirts has increased, more capital must be retained in the business, making disposable wealth less. On the other hand, we are also saying that because of the same cost increase, future cash generated from sales each year will tend to be less, other things being equal.

Although the rationale is the same, the consistency between the adjustments to replacement-cost operating income and net income for the change in cost of the fixtures is more complicated. Looking first at the operating income calculation, the $500 adjustment (labeled (3)) to one year's depreciation is easy to understand. Since it represents an increase in expense over the conventional accounting figure, it induces a decrease in replacement-cost operating income relative to conventional accounting operating income. However, in the net income calculation there are three adjustments labeled (3). The key is to see that they accomplish the same thing (an overall decrease in net income of $500).

Note that beginning owners' equity is increased by the full difference ($1,000—labeled (3)) between original cost ($10,000) and replacement cost ($11,000) of the fixtures. That, by itself, would tend to *decrease* replacement-cost net income by a full $1,000, whereas we reduced replacement-cost operating income by only $500, the amount of one year's additional depreciation. But since the fixtures still have one year of useful life remaining as of the end of 19X1, they appear in ending financial position as two accounts, the fixtures and the related depreciation account. The fixtures' net value is therefore included in ending owners' equity. Hence we adjust ending owners' equity for the replacement cost of the fixtures (a positive adjustment of $1,000) *and* for the additional replacement-cost accumulated depreciation to date (a negative amount of $500).

The effect of these two adjustments is to add back to net income an overall amount of $500 to offset the negative effect of the full $1,000 adjustment to beginning owners' equity. This establishes the arithmetic consistency between the adjustments made to measure disposable wealth (net income) and performance (operating income) on a replacement-cost basis.

In the net income calculation, the adjustment to beginning owners' equity for the full increase in the cost of long-lived assets like the fixtures is based on the notion that the enterprise will eventually have to have that full amount of additional capital to replace the fixtures. Then by adjusting the end-of-year balance of the fixtures account *and accumulated depreciation to date* for the change in cost, we implicitly recognize that not all of the difference must be retained (through lower cash distributions to, or additional investment by, owners) *in the period in which the cost increase took place.* Part of the additional retainage can be achieved over the remaining life of the assets by valuing them at the new replacement cost and depreciating them at accordingly higher levels in subsequent periods.

Before leaving the topic of the relationship between replacement-cost-based operating income and net income, an important point requires reemphasis. As was pointed out in the body of this chapter, in most cases replacement-cost net income and operating income will not only not be equal, the relationship between them will also be much more obscure than in our simple example. The point can now be put more strongly by comparison to conventional accounting. In conventional accounting, the only condition for net income to equal net operating income is that there be no extraordinary gains or losses. In replacement-cost accounting all of the following conditions must be met:

1. No extraordinary gains or losses.
2. In measuring performance, expenses must be adjusted to year-end prices, but no adjustment to revenues of the period may be made. (Note: None will be necessary where no changes in selling prices have taken place by year-end.)

3. All resources must be purchased in quantities equal to *at least* one period's usage or sales requirements.

4. All resources purchased in greater-than-one-year's supplies (long-lived assets) must be in their first period of use.

Since conditions 3 and 4 above will almost never be met as a practical matter, it is easy to see why we must consider separate measurement of replacement-cost-based net income and net operating income. (Several of the problems at the end of the chapter require application of replacement-cost accounting in situations where conditions 2, 3, and 4 are not met.)

Questions for Review and Discussion

8-1. Define:

a. Current exchange price

b. Current entry price (replacement cost)

c. Current exit price (market value)

d. Replacement-cost-based operating income

8-2. General price-level accounting as described in Chapter 7 does not depart from conventional accounting (in principle), whereas replacement-cost and market-value accounting do depart significantly from conventional accounting. Do you agree or disagree? Defend your position.

8-3. Explain the distinction between the money capital and the physical capital point of view. How do the two views differ with respect to the selection of an appropriate valuation base for the net assets of the enterprise?

8-4. In measuring replacement-cost-based net income, beginning owners' equity is increased by the difference between beginning-of-period and end-of-period replacement costs of resources employed in the business. Explain how this adjustment relates to the objective of preserving the physical capital of the enterprise.

8-5. When the replacement costs of resources used in a business increase over time, conventional accounting operating income may become an upward-biased index of long-run cash-generating ability. Comment.

8-6. Under certain assumptions, replacement-cost-based operating income possesses the same properties in times of changing prices that conventional accounting operating income possesses in times of static prices. Explain.

8-7. Recognition of current market values is a means of avoiding a limitation imposed by a strict application of the realization principle. Describe the limitation and how recognition of market values may overcome it.

8-8. In applying the market-value model, assets held for use in the business present some conceptual difficulties. Describe the difficulties.

8-9. The market-value model, like the conventional accounting model, is oriented toward a money capital concept. True or false? Defend your position.

8-10. There is a special decision relevance to market-value-based net assets (owners' equity) as of the end of a period. Describe this special relevance.

8-11. In this chapter alternative valuation bases (current-exchange values) have been used to illustrate financial accounting models of the enterprise that are potentially more decision relevant than the conventional model. Does this mean that the replacement-cost and market-value models are clearly superior to the conventional accounting model? Support your answer.

8-12. Teachers Pension Fund is an independent investment company owned by teachers all across the country. It is designed so that the teachers and their employers can make contributions to one ongoing retirement plan, regardless of where or for what school the teacher works. When contributions are made, they are used to purchase shares in the company in the name of the teacher on whose behalf they are made. The company invests contributed funds in securities of various kinds. When a teacher retires, the company buys an annuity policy (a set of monthly payments) with an insurance company for an amount equal to the teacher's share in the net assets of the company at the time of retirement. What accounting valuation basis should be used for measuring the net assets of the company—original transaction values, replacement cost, or market value? Defend your choice.

8-13. For purposes of measuring net income (disposable wealth), the chapter discussion points out that adjustments for general price-level changes are appropriate under the market-value model (as under conventional accounting). However, no mention of general price-level adjustments was made in connection with the replacement-cost model. Do you consider such adjustments (general price-level adjustments) to be appropriate under replacement-cost accounting as described in this chapter? If so, why? If not, why not?

8-14. Discussion in this chapter noted that recognition of market values of assets is one means of implementing the value-added concept of income. However, recognizing market values will approximate the value-added concept *more or less* depending on the circumstances faced by the individual enterprise. What circumstances are particularly important in this respect?

Exercises   **8-1. Replacement-Cost Operating Income.** Bernie Bedazzled purchased a large lawn mower at the beginning of 1973 for $600 in cash. The lawn mower was expected to last for five years with no salvage value.

During 1973 Bernie paid a thirteen-year-old boy a total of $200 to mow lawns for customers on weekends. Fuel costing Bernie $100 was purchased for cash, and none was left at the end of 1973. Bernie provided his lawn-mowing services on a strictly cash basis, and by the end of 1973 he had received $700 from customers.

No price changes occurred during 1973, with one exception. If Bernie were to purchase the same lawn mower (new) at the end of 1973, it would cost him $700. Bernie does not expect to raise his fees, however, because competition in the lawn-mowing business is very rigorous.

Required:

1. If Bernie were to use the current *replacement-cost model* for accounting purposes, what would be the net operating income that would be reported for 1973?

2. At what amount would the lawn mower be shown in the balance sheet at December 31, 1973, using the above model?

8-2. Replacement-Cost Income Measures.   The Terry Towrope Tugboat Company provides tugboat services in and around the port of Toowong. Its financial statements for the year ended December 31, 1974, are as follows:

TERRY TOWROPE TUGBOAT COMPANY
Balance Sheet
As of December 31, 1974

Assets:			Liabilities and Owners' Equity:		
Cash		$ 320,000	Accounts payable		$ 200,000
Accounts receivable		400,000			
Fuel		10,000			
Supplies		10,000			
Tugboat and					
equipment*	$2,000,000				
Less accumulated depreciation	(200,000)	1,800,000	Owners' equity		2,340,000
			Total liabilities and owners'		
Total assets		$2,540,000	equity		$2,540,000

* These assets when purchased in January 1974 had an expected useful life of ten years and an expected salvage value of zero.

TERRY TOWROPE TUGBOAT COMPANY
Income Statement
For the Year Ended December 31, 1974

Revenue (towing fees)		$800,000
Less expenses:		
Fuel	$100,000	
Wages and salaries	110,000	
Supplies	60,000	
General administrative	30,000	
Depreciation of tugboat and equipment	200,000	500,000
Net income		$300,000

During 1974 there has been *no* change in the general level of prices; however, the replacement cost of tugboats and equipment has risen to $2,400,000. The prices of the fuel and supplies used in the business remained the same at year-end as during the year. The port authority has approved an increase of 15 percent in towing fees for the coming year. The port of Toowong is very busy, and hence no decrease in traffic is expected at the new rates.

Required:

Calculate replacement-cost-based net income and net operating income for 1974. (Hint: In finding beginning owners' equity, assume that there were no investments or withdrawals by owners during 1974.)

8-3. Replacement Cost Accounting.   Capital Computer Corporation is engaged in providing computer services to small businesses that do not have computers of their own. CCC, as it is called, has been in business for three years. Its very simple balance sheet at the end of year three and its income statement depicting results of year three's operations follow.

CAPITAL COMPUTER CORPORATION
Balance Sheet
As of the End of Year Three

Assets:			Liabilities and Owners' Equity:	
Cash		$ 900,000	Accounts payable	$ 50,000
Accounts receivable		300,000		
Supplies		50,000		
Computer equip-ment	$1,500,000			
Less accumu-lated depre-ciation	(900,000)	600,000	Owners' equity	1,800,000
			Total liabilities and owners'	
Total assets		$1,850,000	equity	$1,850,000

CAPITAL COMPUTER CORPORATION
Income Statement
For Third Year of Operations

Revenue (service fees)		$1,200,000
Less expenses:		
Wages and salaries	$400,000	
Supplies	50,000	
Rent (office and equipment)	10,000	
Depreciation of computers	300,000	760,000
Net income		$ 440,000

Through the end of year two no changes in the replacement cost of computer equipment took place. But during year three it became known that the replacement cost of the computer equipment increased to $2 million. When the equipment was purchased three years ago, it was expected to last five years and have no salvage value. The firm had the same expectations at the end of year three. The firm had more customers than it could handle during year three, so it felt safe in increasing its fees as of year-end by 8 percent.

Required:

1. Based on the information given, prepare a replacement-cost-based operating income statement for year three.

2. Based on the information given, in what sense does the replacement-cost-based operating income figure better represent the enterprise's cash-generating ability than the conventional accounting net income figure?

3. Determine replacement-cost-based net income. (Hint: In finding beginning owners' equity, assume that there were no investments or withdrawals by owners during the year.)

4. Explain in your own words any difference that you find between replacement-cost-based net income and net operating income.

8-4. Replacement-Cost Performance Measurement. Desk Lighting Company assembles and distributes a single fluorescent desk lamp model that is popular with department stores and office equipment dealers. The company consistently assembles 3,000 lamps per month from standardized parts. Parts are ordered at the end of each month in amounts equal to the parts used. The supplier is informed of each part used and the quantity required for one lamp, plus the number of lamps for which the company wants parts. The supplier then delivers the right quantity of each type of part, billing the company at a single "per lamp" price for the parts. When an order is received, the stock on hand is rotated so that the older parts are used first.

The company started 19X1 with 6,000 sets of lamp parts, all purchased at $4.00 per lamp set. During the year, 3,000 lamps were assembled and sold each month, and 3,000 part sets were ordered to replace those used. Selling prices and parts costs for the year (by quarter) were as follows:

	Jan.–Mar.	Apr.–June	July–Sept.	Oct.–Dec.
Selling price	$9.00	$9.50	$10.00	$10.50
Parts cost	4.00	4.25	4.75	5.00

The replacement cost of a set of parts as of December 31, 19X1, is $5.20. The company anticipates raising its price to customers to $10.75 as of January 1, 19X2.

In addition to the parts used in the lamps, certain tools and equipment are used in the assembly operation. The tools and equipment presently in use were purchased three years ago for $200,000. They are expected to last five years in all and have a zero net salvage value. During 19X1 the cost of replacing the tools and equipment started at about $230,000 and reached $260,000 by year-end. The average of month-end price quotations for the year was $240,000.

During 19X1 rent, wages, and other expenses amounted to $50,000. There was no increase in these expenses during the year, and none is anticipated for the foreseeable future.

Required:

1. Prepare comparative operating income statements with columns for:
   (a) Conventional accounting
   (b) End-of-year replacement-cost accounting
   (c) Within-year replacement-cost accounting (average prices)
2. Contrast the statements in terms of the way that they represent performance in the long-run cash-generating sense.

8-5. Replacement Cost: Comprehensive Problem. Rod Reel has developed a revolutionary new design for a side cast fishing reel. He set up a new company with two well-heeled friends, each making an investment of $75,000 and Rod investing $50,000. Rod rented factory space and purchased the necessary tools and equipment. The primary raw materials needed to make the reels are stainless steel sheeting and a plastic preparation which is to be shaped by compression into the proper form. It was determined, after careful study, that production could continue smoothly if orders for raw materials were made as follows:

1. 2,000 square feet of stainless steel is ordered when the inventory on hand falls to 1,000 square feet (which is generally all used up by the time the new delivery is received).

2. 3,000 pounds of plastic preparation when the inventory on hand falls to 1,000 pounds (which is generally all used up by the time the new delivery is received).

During the first year of operations the following transactions took place:

Item	Amount
a. Purchase of tools and equipment with an expected useful life of ten years and zero salvage value	$ 80,000
b. Rent	$ 10,000
c. Raw materials purchased all for cash	
(1) Stainless steel	6,000 sq. ft.
(2) Plastic preparation	6,000 lbs.
d. Sales (all on account)	$180,000
e. Receipts from customers	$170,000
f. Wages and salaries paid	$ 60,000
g. Raw materials in inventory at the end of the year	
(1) Stainless steel	2,000 sq. ft.
(2) Plastic preparation	3,000 lbs.
(3) Other	—

By year-end the prices of the tools and equipment had risen to $100,000. Based on averages, however, they could have been replaced during the year at $90,000.

The steel purchased during the year was purchased at an average price of $10 per square foot. However, the price of steel went from $9.50 per square foot at the beginning of the year to $11 at year-end. The steel actually used had been purchased at an average price of $9.75 (the steel on hand at year-end had all been purchased at $10.50). Similarly, the price of plastic went from $4.75 per pound to $5.50 by year-end. However, the plastic purchased during the year was purchased in two 3,000-pound orders at $4.75 and $5.25. All of the first order and none of the second order had been used by year-end. As a result of these price increases, the company expects to raise prices 10 percent on the average after the first of the year.

The conventional accounting treatment of these facts appears in the worksheet on the following page.

Required:

1. Determine the amount of replacement-cost-based net income.

2. Draw up a comparative replacement-cost-based operating income statement on the basis of

   (a) Average prices

   (b) End-of-year prices

Description	Cash	Accounts Receiv- able	Steel	Plastic	Tools and Equip- ment	Accumu- lated Depreci- ation	Owners' Equity
Beginning Position	200,000						200,000
Purchased tools, etc.	(80,000)				80,000		
Paid rent	(10,000)						(10,000) (E)
Purchased materials	(90,000)		60,000	30,000			
Sales		180,000					180,000 (R)
Receipts	170,000	(170,000)					
Wages and salaries	(60,000)						(60,000) (E)
Materials used			(39,000)	(14,250)			(53,250) (E)
Depreciation						(8,000)	(8,000) (E)
Ending Position	130,000	10,000	21,000	15,750	80,000	(8,000)	248,750

8-6. Replacement Cost: Speculative Gains. The Peter Pulley Boat Fitting Company specializes in making brass fixtures and fittings for all types of sailboats and pleasure craft. The company has been in operation for a number of years. Its latest balance sheet is as follows.

PETER PULLEY BOAT FITTING COMPANY
Balance Sheet
As of December 31, 1973

Assets:			Liabilities and Owner's Equity:	
Cash		$140,000	Accounts payable	$ 35,000
Accounts receivable		15,000		
Brass inventory		10,000		
Supplies		5,000		
Tools and equipment*	$90,000			
Less accumu- lated depre- ciation	(45,000)	45,000	Owner's equity	180,000
			Total liabilities and	
Total assets		$215,000	owner's equity	$215,000

* Tools and equipment are depreciated on the basis of an expected useful life of six years and a zero salvage value.

The transactions taking place in 1974 were as follows:

a. *Additional* equipment identical to that making up the tools and equipment figure in the 1973 balance sheet has been acquired for $120,000. The additional equipment has an expected useful life of six years and a zero salvage value.

b. Sales on account—$300,000.

c. Collections of $180,000 were received from customers by year-end.

d. Rent paid—$15,000.

e. Wages and salaries paid—$35,000.

f. Purchase of supplies—$15,000 on account. Supplies worth $6,000 were on hand at the end of 1974.

g. While there had been no change in the price of brass in 1973, at the beginning of 1974 Pulley expected that the price of brass would rise substantially. He therefore abandoned his policy of placing a new order for $20,000 worth of brass when inventory on hand was down to $10,000 and, instead, immediately purchased brass for $100,000 at the beginning of the year. In retrospect, it was clear that his action was wise, as the price of brass rose 20 percent soon after this purchase. There was $20,000 worth of brass (at original cost) on hand at the end of the year.

h. At year-end Pulley was able to raise his prices 5 percent without expecting any loss of business.

Required:

Draw up a replacement-cost-based operating income statement for the year ended December 31, 1974, based on year-end prices. Does this statement better represent "performance" than a conventional statement? In what way (if any)? Is there any aspect of Pulley's performance not represented in replacement-cost-based operating income? Comment.

8-7. Market Value and General Price-Level Changes. New Deal Leases is in the business of buying, selling, and leasing land. Its financial position on January 1, 1972, was:

Cash	Accounts Receivable	Land	Owners' Equity
5,000	2,000	35,000 ‖	42,000

During the first six months of 1972 the following events occurred:

a. The amount due from customers at the beginning of the period was received.

b. Lease rentals earned throughout the period (all of which have been collected) amounted to $3,000.

c. Wages incurred and paid throughout the period, $1,800.

d. Advertising expense (paid on January 2, 1972), $400.

e. On June 30 a number of buyers made firm offers to buy the land for a price of $38,000. The land was not sold, however.

Required:

1. Show the income statement for the period ended June 30, 1972, according to (a) the conventional accounting model and (b) the market-value model.

2. In your judgment, which income figure better represents the company's performance? Explain.

3. Repeat number 1, assuming that the price level went up by 8 percent for the whole six-month period, but the ending price level was up only 5 percent over

the average for the six-month period. Assume further that no changes in prices have taken place in prior years.

8-8. Market Value and Conventional Accounting Contrasted.   The chairman of Razzle-Dazzle Investment Corporation has just attended a professional development course run by the Sharftville Chamber of Commerce and has learned that conventional accounting has certain limitations for financial reporting by investment companies.

He sends you a memorandum asking for a report on the conventional accounting model versus the current-exchange-output accounting model. He specifically asks you to include in your report a discussion of the effect a change from the conventional model to the current-exchange-output model would have on the reported profit of Razzle-Dazzle Investment Corporation. From the accounting records and external sources, you gather the following information about the years 1969, 1970, and 1971:

a. Razzle-Dazzle Investment Corporation was set up in 1969 with an investment by the owners of $100,000 in exchange for stock in Razzle-Dazzle.

b. Early in January 1969, and immediately after the corporation was set up, $70,000 was invested by Razzle-Dazzle in common stocks and $20,000 in bonds (paying 10 percent interest per annum). The stocks and bonds purchased are listed on the Sharftville Exchange.

c. Administrative expenses were as follows:

1969	$5,000
1970	1,250
1971	2,000

d. Toward the end of December 1969, dividends on the common stocks totaling $4,000 as well as the interest on the bonds was received.

e. There were *no* transactions in 1970 other than the receipt toward the end of December of dividends on the common stock totaling $4,500 and the interest on the bonds.

f. Early in July 1971, before any dividends or interest had been received, the common stocks were sold for $90,000 and the bonds for $18,000. No further transactions took place in 1971.

g. From stock exchange records you find that the market values of the common stocks and bonds held were as follows:

December 31, 1969:	Common stock	$82,000
	Bonds	19,000
December 31, 1970:	Common stock	89,000
	Bonds	18,000

Closing notes:

1. Assume for the sake of simplicity that no interest was earned on the balance of cash held at any time by the corporation.

2. No withdrawals were made over the three years. You should, however, include in your report an explanation of the amount technically disposable each year

from an accounting viewpoint and any financial constraints that might hamper such a withdrawal.

3. Append worksheets to your report.

8-9. Market Value and Conventional Accounting Contrasted. Speculation Corporation is an investment company formed by members of several well-acquainted families who together own all outstanding common stock. The company has been in existence for only three years. It started with a total cash investment by all the shareholders of $100,000. The elected officers immediately purchased a plot of land for $40,000 in cash, and marketable securities for $40,000. The remaining $20,000 was invested for the first year in savings certificates at 6 percent. The $20,000 plus interest was returned to the business just before the end of the first year. At the start of each subsequent year any cash remaining in the business after dividend payments (withdrawals) was again invested in one-year savings certificates at 6 percent. There was general agreement among the shareholders right from the beginning that cash dividends to the shareholders (withdrawals) *would equal income each year*. The shareholder-elected officers have accounted for the company from the start according to conventional accounting. Each year they have reported conventional accounting income and financial position, made the appropriate payments of cash dividends to the shareholders, and, for the information of other shareholders, have obtained appraisals and market prices on the land and securities held at the end of each year.

This latter practice has caused some dissent among the shareholders, particularly the younger ones. They agree with the policy of distributing cash dividends only to the extent of net income. But they also feel that increases in the market values of the land and securities ought to be included in net income.

The following facts relate to the first three years of operations of Speculation Corporation:

| | Dividends Earned on Securities | Rent from Land | Year-end Market or Appraisal Values | |
			Securities	Land
Year 1	$4,000	$5,000	$39,000	$45,000
Year 2	4,000	6,000	38,000	55,000
Year 3	3,700	6,500		

Just before the end of year three, the land purchased at the outset was sold for $54,000, and the marketable securities for $41,000.

Required:

1. In worksheet form, record the effects on financial position of Speculation Corporation of all of the above facts for each of the first three years *as if* current market and appraisal values had been used by the company. Assume that dividends to owners were based on market-value-based income. (Do not forget the interest on the savings certificate that will be received at the end of each year.)

2. Make up a comparative schedule of net income for each of the three years and in total according to:

(a) Conventional accounting

(b) Recognition of market and appraisal values

3. Repeat number 2, assuming that there were no cash dividends to shareholders of Speculation Corporation in any of the years. Explain the differences between your answer under this assumption and your earlier answers.

4. Comment on what you feel are the pros and cons of the two systems in terms of how well they measure the performance of Speculation Corporation for the long and short runs and in terms of which system provides the "best" measure of disposable wealth in your estimation.

8-10. Unrealized Gains and Disposable Wealth.   The Ayers Rock Land Corporation was formed two years ago for the primary purposes of real estate development and land speculation. The principals of the corporation are N. Kelly and R. Hood. N. Kelly contributed the assets of his business, N. Kelly and Associates, which had an appraised value of $300,000 made up as follows:

Cash	$230,000	
Land	50,000	(1,000 acres in the vicinity of Ayers Rock)
Office buildings	20,000	

R. Hood contributed his substantial land holdings of 30,000 acres with an appraised market value of $300,000.

During 19X0, the first year of operation, the following events took place:

a. The 30,000 acres contributed by R. Hood were leased to a rancher for $.60 per acre per annum.

b. Some 4,000 acres were purchased in the vicinity of Muckawilla Springs for speculative purposes at $20 per acre.

c. Plans were drawn up for a motel and dude ranch on the 1,000 acres near Ayers Rock. Construction had been completed by the end of the year at a cost of $75,000.

d. Administrative expenses amounted to $4,000 for the year, and office salaries to $6,000.

e. At the end of the year the market value of the 30,000 acres leased to the rancher remained unchanged; however, several offers had been received for the 4,000 acres at Muckawilla Springs. The highest of these offers was $130,000. An appraiser estimated the market value of the motel and dude ranch, together with the 1,000 acres, at $150,000. The market value of the office buildings was $20,000.

During 19X1, the following events took place:

a. Early in 19X1 the rancher made an offer to purchase the 30,000 acres he was currently leasing for $13 per acre. This offer was accepted, and a check for the full amount was received by Ayers Rock Land Corporation.

b. Of the 4,000 acres at Muckawilla Springs, 2,000 acres were sold at $40 per acre. Interest in the remaining 2,000 acres was high, and the partners were confident that they could at this time realize at least $40 per acre.

c. The motel and dude ranch proved to be a successful undertaking. Revenues (all in cash) totaled $80,000 for the year; operating expenses (all of which had been paid by year-end) came to $50,000. An offer of $200,000 was received for the motel and dude ranch but was declined.

d. In June N. Kelly heard rumors that a large mining company had discovered a significant reserve of nickel on a nearby property. On the basis of this rumor the partners bought up $100,000 of the company's common stocks.

The market value of the shares rose rapidly as other investors reacted to the rumors, but a report from the company's directors toward the end of 19X1 indicated that the find was not as extensive as rumored and the market value of the common stock fell rapidly. At year-end the market value of the partners' holding was $70,000.

e. Administrative expenses and office salaries were the same as in 19X0.

f. There was no change in the market value of the office buildings.

Required:

Using the current exchange *output* model

1. Draw up worksheets for each of the two years.

2. Draw up income statements for 19X0 and for 19X1.

3. Discuss any difficulties that might be encountered in distributing, in cash, the full amount of net income to owners each year.

8-11. Market Value Net Income and General Price-Level Changes. The Low-Turnover Investment Company was formed at the beginning of 1972 with $20,000 cash contributed by the partners. Immediately thereafter, the company purchased 5,000 shares of Eastern Central Railroad for $8,000, and 100 shares of Western Satellite Corporation for $12,000. The partners believed this constituted a balanced portfolio and decided to ignore the day-by-day fluctuations in market prices and hold on to the stock for long-term growth. On December 31, 1974, the stock was sold: Eastern Central for $10,000, and Western Satellite for $15,000.

The market value of the stock at the end of each of the previous two years follows:

	December 31, 1972	December 31, 1973
Eastern Central Railroad	$ 6,000	$ 9,000
Western Satellite Corporation	10,000	25,000

Required:

1. What will be the net income for each of the three years and in total under (a) conventional accounting and (b) market-value-based accounting.

2. The partners took issue with the income measures you came up with under the market-value-based model. They argued that the numbers were "merely paper profits or losses," and for that reason they intended to ignore the numbers in a retrospective assessment of their performance as investment fund managers. Assuming that you were one of the advocates for market-value-based accounting, indicate *briefly* how you would reply to this argument.

3. If the general price level was at 100 on January 1, 1972, but had reached 120 by December 31, 1974, what would *total* price-level-adjusted net income be for the three-year period?

9

Financial Accounting Models
in Perspective

Our consideration of several alternative financial accounting models of the enterprise in Chapters 4 through 8 has been a challenging task. Each model in turn has received our full attention. But the models are significant only in the environmental context developed earlier. Thus, to put them in perspective in this chapter, we first turn to briefly outlining the role of accounting in that context. Next, we focus on the characteristics of several alternative models by means of a simple illustration to which each of the models is applied for contrast. Finally, we confront the problem of choosing the "best" model, which we point out is a problem of social choice and therefore not easily resolved even in principle.

REVIEW OF BASIC CONCEPTS

The Basic Premise: Information for Decision Making

Accounting is a field of knowledge that is concerned with *information* that is presumably useful for a broad spectrum of decision making. The usefulness of information of various types, including accounting information, stems basically from the existence of scarce resources. In order to allocate these resources to achieve his goals, the decision maker (whether a business manager, a government official, or someone acting on his behalf) seeks information that will enable him to understand and better predict the possible outcomes of various alternative courses of action (and the likelihood of their occurrence).

Accounting as an Information Specialization

The character of the information required for a particular decision is obviously a function of the type of decision problem confronting the decision maker. Where a group of decision makers with similar decision problems exists in society, information specialists tend to appear. Information specialists are individuals who devote their resources to producing (or providing others with the means to produce) decision-relevant information for others' use. Three conditions are necessary for specialization in information: (1) there must exist a class (or classes) of decision makers with common decision problems; (2) there must be identifiable kinds of decision-relevant information of value in solving these problems; and (3) to efficiently and effectively produce information relevant to the common class (or classes) of problems, one must become proficient in applying a specialized body of knowledge or expertise. Recognizing the way in which these conditions are satisfied for accounting as an information specialization serving decision makers external to the enterprise provides an important perspective on financial accounting.

Decision Problems Concerning the Business Enterprise

One way of identifying common classes of decision makers with common decision problems is to focus on particular types of organizational entities. Although accounting information has a role in decision problems revolving around many different types of organizations, as was pointed out in Chapter 1, we have chosen to place our major emphasis in this book on the role of accounting in supplying information to several of the classes of decision makers concerned with the *business enterprise*.

A number of types of users of information about the business enterprise are identified in Chapter 1, including owners, creditors, suppliers, management, taxing authorities, employees, and customers. While each of these groups has special decision problems that benefit from accounting information, it is useful in the study of accounting to combine them into two groups, internal and external, according to how their individual decisions relate to the business enterprise. The emphasis of this book is on *accounting for the business enterprise for external parties*.

● *Classes of external decisions.* The decision interests of external users of information about the business enterprise can be divided into two important classes: (1) investment decisions and (2) decisions concerning the distribution of the current benefits from the operations of the enterprise.

Investment decisions involve selecting opportunities to exchange present resources (wealth) for rights to resources in the future (also wealth)—generally with the objective of maximizing wealth. The external parties who are concerned with business enterprises as investment alternatives (principally present and prospective owners and creditors) are called *investors*.

Decisions concerning the *distribution of the current benefits* from the operations of the enterprise focus on the ability of the firm to distribute money or other resources to parties with an interest in it, and the equitability of the distributions that are made. Included in the class of interested parties are present owners, creditors, taxing authorities, and employees (particularly collective groups of employees).

Decision-Relevant Accounting Information

The kinds of decision-relevant information that accountants might provide are defined by the class of decision makers under consideration (external decision makers) and the classes of decision problems of interest to them. We introduced the net present value model in Chapter 3 as a means of describing the nature of investment decisions and as a simplified model for choosing among investment alternatives.

• *Financial accounting information for investment decisions.* From the possession of goods and the use of services, individuals derive satisfactions that are multidimensional and unique to each individual. However, it is characteristic of investment decisions that the money equivalent of goods and services serves as a substitute for other forms of satisfactions. This follows from the role of money in a market economy as a general means of acquiring the goods and services one desires. Given this role of money, it follows that the information for investment decisions can be structured in terms of the *money flows* that are expected to result from various decision alternatives.

Because an amount of money possessed today is typically more valuable to the individual than possession of an equal amount of funds at some later date, it is necessary to develop a mechanism that takes into account timing differences in money flows. The present value model serves as the means of making such adjustments. Through the use of present value methodology, the decision maker (in a hypothetical world of certainty) can choose between two or more alternative courses of action involving cash flows that differ in amount and timing.

However, in an uncertain world the valuation of alternate cash flows involves more than adjustments for their differential timing alone. Most individuals are not indifferent to different levels of risk (i.e., the potential that less-than-expected cash flows will actually be forthcoming from an investment opportunity). For the typical risk-averse individual a more risky alternative has less value per unit of *expected* cash flow than a less risky alternative. This principle can be incorporated in the simplified present value model by using certainty equivalents to represent uncertain future cash flows (which is one of several risk-adjustment techniques compatible with the simplified present value model).

While our earlier discussion of these *simplified* approaches to investment decisions is definitely only intended to brush the surface, it does permit us to infer that individuals faced with investment decisions are likely to be interested in the amount, timing, and riskiness of future cash flows.

• *Management-provided forecasts or present values.* Having established the probable investment decision relevance of the amount, timing, and risk associated with future cash flows, the next question is, What kind of (accounting) information should the management of a business enterprise provide to external investors? An obvious first choice is management's own forecasts of future cash flows expected to be generated by the enterprise. This alternative has been receiving more and more favorable support recently for several reasons. For instance, management usually prepares such forecasts for its own planning purposes. Furthermore, management is "closer" to the business than any external party and is thus in a better position to assess most internal factors (including its own plans) that have implications for future cash flows.

However, in spite of managements' probable comparative advantage in forecasting, and the urging of businesses by authorities (notably the Securities and Exchange Commission) to publish forecasts on an experimental basis, up to now such forecasts have rarely been made public. Some apparent reasons for the present dearth of management forecasts are (1) that they might disclose strategic information to competitors, and (2) that managements feel that they would be unduly exposed to accusations of intentional manipulation if their forecasts turn out to be substantially in error.

Incidentally, since a management-provided present value of the enterprise would presumably be based on management's forecast of future cash flows, all the above arguments (pro and con) apply to management-provided present values, as well as to the underlying forecasts. But, in addition, if a single present value is provided *in place of* the underlying forecasts, investors might be denied opportunities to make (and take into account) their unique assessments of the risk (and possible error or bias) characteristics of management's forecasts of cash flows.

• *Alternate information for investment decisions.* Although management forecasts are not widely available at present, it is important to remember that the *investor's decision problem is unaltered* by the infeasibility of receiving ready-made forecasts from the enterprise. He must still arrive at forecasts if he wishes to base his decisions on present values (or some analogous measure of benefits) for each of his investment opportunities. To be decision relevant, accounting information must therefore contribute to an investor's ability to estimate the future cash flows that will be forthcoming from a given enterprise. On the other hand, lest they be infeasible for the same reasons that management-provided forecasts (and present values) presently are, alternate forms of information must be more grounded in fact (i.e., be less susceptible to management manipulation and bias).

Any largely factual representation of the enterprise that is supposed to give clues to future cash flows must of course be based on some assumed cause-and-effect relationship between what can be observed as fact today and what will materialize as cash flows tomorrow and in the more distant future. Financial accounting typically applies this notion by attempting to characterize the enterprise's long-run cash-generating ability as evidenced by its current period's *performance* (*operating income*).

• *Distribution-of-benefits decisions.* The purpose of financial accounting information for distribution decisions is to facilitate the equitable distribution of residual benefits of the enterprise (which includes preservation of the wealth employed in the enterprise). In contrast to investment decisions, distribution decisions are not made by individuals strictly for their own benefit. They have to do with rights of different groups that have an interest in the enterprise.

However, all interests in the distribution of residual benefits of the enterprise have one thing in common: the determination or measurement of the amount of wealth of the enterprise that is actually residual or disposable at any point in time when a distribution of wealth is being considered. Generally, the criterion against which we measure disposability is the wealth at the beginning of the period, and from this (Hicksian) criterion we develop the second major type of accounting information for external decisions—the *measure of disposable wealth* (*net income*).

• *Comparing* (*and selecting?*) *accounting models.* Each of the models provides different wealth assessments and measures of performance and disposable wealth. A summary of the alternative model characteristics is presented in Exhibit 9-1. Final judgment on the appropriateness of a particular model for a particular class of decisions must of course be ultimately based on the costs and benefits associated with its use in those decisions. This raises the question of whether the models can, in general, be ranked in some kind of "order of preference" so that a choice of the "best" model can be made.

Before considering the issue of choosing between the alternative financial accounting models, we complete our review of their characteristics by considering a single integrated example. By means of a single set of facts to which each model is applied in turn, the contrast between the basic objectives and measurement characteristics of the various models is highlighted. We do not include management forecasts (or present values), but only consider the alternative models that might be used as the basis for financial accounting outputs *whether or not management* forecasts are provided.

COMPARATIVE ACCOUNTING MODELS:
AN ILLUSTRATION

The purpose of the following illustration is to highlight and contrast the alternative financial models of the business enterprise. Therefore, the situation constructed for our example is deliberately as simple as possible in order to avoid obscuring the basic characteristics of the models with unnecessary computational complexity. Additionally, we have chosen a situation that begins with an initial investment of cash and after two periods of operations is back to a "cash only" condition. This allows us to contrast the *periodic* measures of performance and disposable wealth in a clearcut way, because we are thus able to achieve a "total life" perspective on the operations of the firm. While the more realistic case of a business engaged in continuing operations tends to mask some of the numerical differences between the models that are created in this example, the conceptual differences between the models none-theless remain.

Basic Case Data

Example 9-1   Bill Flicker had operated a marina in Corpus Christi, Texas, for a number of years, but he had not engaged in the business of selling sailboats because of the large investment that was required in each boat. In view of a sub-stantial increase in interest among the population in the immediate area in sailboats in the 25- to 35-foot range, Bill decided late in 19X1 that he would enter this business. On December 31, 19X1, Bill formed Blue Water Yacht Sales, Inc., and entered the sailboat business as a distributor for PW-30s.

Bill did not want to get too heavily committed to this area immediately, and thus he decided to start the business with a $20,000 investment. With a cur-rent wholesale cost of $10,000 for each PW-30, Bill was restricted to an inventory of two boats. He then made the decision that he would not replace his inventory until he had sold both boats—a policy that somewhat inhibited his sales potential but at the same time provided, in Bill's opinion, less financial risk.

The operations of the company were only moderately successful. It took two years for Bill to sell both boats. (The PW-30 was a popular yacht, but it seemed that every serious customer wanted a color that Bill did not have in stock.) The activities of Blue Water Yacht Sales, and related environmental events, can be summarized as follows:

19X2

Purchased two PW-30s at start of year for $20,000
Sold one PW-30 in middle of year for $15,000

Relevant price and price-index data at end of year:
   Estimated cost of acquiring new PW-30—$12,000
   Estimated immediate-sale price for PW-30—$13,000
   Estimated 19X3 selling price for PW-30—$15,000
   General price-level index increased uniformly over the period from 140 to
     160

19X3

Sold second PW-30 at end of year for $15,000
General price-level index remained stable at 160 throughout the period, and the replacement cost of a PW-30 remained at $12,000

We will assume that Blue Water Yacht Sales, Inc., did not have other op-erating expenses during the two years, as the marina operation provided the necessary selling environment without charge.

Because Bill wished to maintain the operations at the same level until he made an explicit decision to expand (or contract) them, he had the policy of withdrawing cash at the end of each year equal in amount to the net in-come for the year.

Exhibit 9-1

SUMMARY OF CHARACTERISTICS OF VALUATION ALTERNATIVES

	Conventional Accounting	Conventional Accounting Adjusted for General Price-Level Changes	Replacement Costs (Entry Prices)	Current Market Values (Exit Prices)
WEALTH PRESERVATION (CAPITAL MAINTENANCE) CONCEPT	BEGINNING-OF-PERIOD (OR ORIGINAL) NET ASSETS (MONEY CAPITAL)*	BEGINNING-OF-PERIOD NET ASSETS ADJUSTED FOR CHANGES IN PURCHASING POWER OF THE MONETARY UNIT	BEGINNING-OF-PERIOD PHYSICAL CAPITAL (OPERATING CAPABILITY)	REALIZABLE VALUE OF BEGINNING NET ASSETS*
VALUATION PRINCIPLE	ORIGINAL TRANSACTION VALUE	PURCHASING POWER OF ORIGINAL TRANSACTION VALUES STATED IN CURRENT MONETARY UNITS	CURRENT ENTRY PRICES (REPLACEMENT COSTS)	CURRENT EXIT PRICES (MARKET VALUE)§
INCOME FLOWS Components of measures: (1) Accomplishment (revenue)	Revenue realized from sales	Price-level-adjusted conventional accounting revenue	Revenue actually realized from sales (adjusted to year-end prices)	Primarily increases in value of all assets held for sale (may also include increases in value of assets held for use)§
(2) Effort (expense)	Expenses measured by original transaction cost of resources used to produce revenue	Price-level-adjusted conventional accounting expense	Expenses measured by year-end replacement costs of resources used to produce revenue	Expenses measured by original transaction costs (wages, etc.) or changes in recognized market value of resources used to produce revenue§

(3) Other	Extraordinary gains and losses	a. Extraordinary gains and losses b. Net monetary gain or loss	Extraordinary gains and losses	a. Extraordinary gains and losses b. See footnote §
Measure of: Performance	Net operating income (1) − (2)	Price-level-adjusted operating income (1) − (2)†	Replacement-cost-based operating income (1) − (2)	Market-value-based operating income (1) − (2)§
Disposable wealth	Net income: Difference between ending and beginning net assets, allowing for distributions to and investments by owners Also: (1) − (2) ± (3), as defined above	Price-level-adjusted net income: Difference between ending and beginning net assets (owners' equity),‡ adjusted for changes in general purchasing power Also: (1) − (2) ± (3a and b), as defined above	Replacement-cost-based net income: Difference between ending and beginning net assets,‡ adjusted to a replacement-cost basis	Market-value-based net income: Difference between ending net assets‡ at end-of-period market value and beginning net assets at beginning-of-period market value§ Also: (1) − (2) ± (3a and b), as defined above

* If a policy of withdrawals equal to net income is consistently followed, beginning-of-period net assets will consistently equal original money capital contributed by the owners.
† The net monetary gain or loss is excluded from performance measurement if price changes giving rise to the current period's gains or losses are strictly transitory, i.e., it is unlikely that the enterprise will repeat such gains or losses in future periods.
‡ Adjustment to ending net assets would be made to allow for distribution to, or investments by, owners during the period, as well as for the appropriate price changes. Also, disposable wealth measurement under all models is affected by extraordinary gains and losses in the same way that such items affect conventional accounting net income.
§ Modifications may be appropriate for changes in general purchasing power, in which case the resulting price-level-adjusted, market-value-based model has all of the same additional characteristics as price-level-adjusted conventional accounting—but with a different valuation base.

Conventional Accounting Analysis

The effect of these events on the financial position of Blue Water Yacht Sales, Inc., from its inception through the end of 19X3 based on conventional accounting is summarized in Exhibit 9-2.

Exhibit 9-2

BLUE WATER YACHT SALES, INC.
Financial Position Worksheet—Conventional Accounting

Description	Cash	Inventory	Owner's Equity
Initial Investment	20,000		20,000
19X2			
Purchased two sailboats	(20,000)	20,000	
Sold one sailboat	15,000		15,000 (R)
Cost of sailboat sold		(10,000)	(10,000)(E)
Withdrawal by owner	(5,000)		(5,000)(W)
Ending (Beginning) Position	10,000	10,000	20,000
19X3			
Sold one sailboat	15,000		15,000 (R)
Cost of sailboat sold		(10,000)	(10,000)(E)
Withdrawal by owner	(5,000)		(5,000)(W)
Ending (Beginning) Position	20,000	—0—	20,000

It is immediately apparent from the financial position worksheet that the owner's equity is the same amount at the end of each of the two years as it was at the inception of the business—$20,000. This illustrates a particular consequence of valuing assets and measuring expenses (expired assets) in terms of the assets' original transaction costs. When net income is used as a measure of disposable wealth, *and* assets are withdrawn by the owner(s) in amounts equal to net income period after period, then net assets equal to the *total amount of money invested* in the business are retained at the end of each period. If, on the other hand, less than the total net income is withdrawn each period, the amount of net assets retained (and thus the balance of the owner's equity) will be equal to the amount originally invested plus the excess of net income over withdrawals. However, it is obvious from an examination of the 19X2 ending balances (even for this simple situation) that the *composition* of the net assets does not remain invariant even though the total investment or owner's equity does not change. At the end of 19X2, the $20,000 invested in the business is now held in the form of two assets— cash and inventory. At the end of 19X3, the initial investment is again solely in the form of cash only because of our "total life" assumption. Under normal operating circumstances, the *composition of net assets* will be continually changing. A systematic accounting analysis of these period-by-period fluctuations is reflected in a Statement of Changes in Financial Position—a topic covered in Chapter 15.

Net Operating Income and Cash Flow

The differences between net operating income and net cash flow for a given period result from different underlying concepts. Net operating income under conventional accounting is a measure of performance that attempts to match the efforts and accomplishments of an enterprise for a period of time. The presumption is that this measure reflects (at least for that particular period) the ability of the enterprise to generate additional economic value through its productive activities. Extrapolating from this and prior periods' net accomplishments, the investor is presumed to have an indicator of the demonstrated long-run cash-generating ability of the enterprise. When extraordinary gains and losses occur, they must be added to, or subtracted from, net operating income to get a measure of disposable wealth, net income. In the absence of such gains or losses, net operating income and net income are identical.

On the other hand, the cash flow for a period reflects the activities (excluding investments and withdrawals by the owner) that had an immediate impact on the cash balance. To the extent that the productive activities of the firm for that period have not yet generated cash, or if cash expenditures of the period were made to acquire benefits in future periods, the short-run fluctuations in cash (as reflected in the cash-flow statement) may be a poor indicator of the firm's long-run cash-generating ability. Cash flow does serve as an adequate measure of disposable wealth *if* the objective is to maintain a stock of cash equal to the original cash investment; however, there are few situations where such an objective would represent sound management or investor behavior.

The differences between conventional accounting and net cash flow measures for the Blue Water Yacht illustration are reflected in Exhibit 9-3. Since sales were assumed to be for cash, there is no difference in either year be-

Exhibit 9-3

BLUE WATER YACHT SALES, INC.
Income Statement
For the First Two Years of Operations

	19X3	19X2
Revenue from sales	$15,000	$15,000
Cost of sales	10,000	10,000
Net income	$ 5,000	$ 5,000

BLUE WATER YACHT SALES, INC.
Cash-Flow Statement
For the First Two Years of Operations

	19X3	19X2
Cash receipts from sales	$15,000	$15,000
Cash disbursements—Purchase of sailboats	—0—	20,000
Net cash inflow (outflow)	$15,000	$(5,000)

tween revenue and cash receipts—although of course in general there would be a difference. Thus, under this particular fact situation, the difference each year between the two measures (net income and cash flow) results from the different concepts underlying expenses and cash disbursements.

Recall that expenses for a period represent the original transaction cost of resources consumed in the production of the revenue of that period. Under conventional operating income measurement the purchase cost of each sailboat is recognized as an expense in the period in which the boat is sold. In the cash-flow calculation, however, the cash disbursement in 19X2 of $20,000 to acquire the two boats is reflected in that year, even though one of the boats is not sold until the following year.

Based upon our understanding of the relationship (or lack of relationship) between net income and net cash flow, we can observe a possible constraint on a withdrawal policy that is otherwise tied to conventional accounting net income. In this case, the owner was able to withdraw cash each period in an amount equal to net income *because sufficient cash was on hand*. However, because we have seen that the existence of income in any particular period does not necessarily imply a positive cash flow (indeed we had a $5,000 cash *outflow* in 19X2 at the same time that we had *net income* of $5,000), it may well be the case that the business will not have sufficient cash on hand to permit the withdrawal. This phenomenon often occurs in small or growing business organizations, and satisfactory explanation of it to the owner depends upon an understanding of the different concepts underlying net income and net cash flow. It is true, however, that the existence of net income implies an increase in net assets (measured in terms of original transaction values), and thus the owner might anticipate the availability of cash for withdrawal at some future date (assuming the business continues to operate in much the same manner in the future).

Effects of General Price-Level Changes

The concepts of disposable wealth and performance in the conventional accounting model are intuitively appealing—but the strength of the appeal depends on a price environment that is static. Essentially, the conventional accounting view (implicitly) is that the business enterprise is a reservoir of money capital. Hence, so long as net assets equal in amount to the money investment in the business are preserved, it is assumed that the wealth of the enterprise will not have been diminished. Under static price conditions, this assumption has some validity. However, in times of generally changing prices, original dollar amounts cease to have the power to represent the original economic "meaning" of the original money capital. Hence, the objective underlying general price-level adjustments of amounts otherwise determined in accordance with the conventional accounting model is clear. Original transaction values are adjusted to the current dollar equivalent of their general purchasing power at the date they were given recognition—in an attempt to recapture and preserve the economic significance (meaning) of the various original transactions.

The data for the Blue Water Yacht case reveal an assumed general price index that increases uniformly over 19X2 from 140 to 160 and then remains stable during 19X3. For transactions that took place in the middle of 19X2, the applicable index is therefore the average index level, or 150.

The general price-level-adjusted statement of financial position for Blue Water at the end of 19X2 can be obtained by applying the appropriate index values to the account balances reflected in Exhibit 9-2 *before the cash withdrawal for 19X2*. Since the owner's policy is to withdraw cash in an amount equal to net income (the measure of disposable wealth) for the year, we must first calculate the new measure of disposable wealth before the amount of the cash to be withdrawn can be determined.

Exhibit 9-4

BLUE WATER YACHT SALES, INC.
General Price-Level-Adjusted Financial Position

Description	Cash	Inventory	Owner's Equity
19X2			
Ending Position (before withdrawal)	15,000	10,000	(not used)
Adjustment Factor		160/140	
(A) Adjusted Ending Position (before cash withdrawal)	15,000	11,429	26,429
(B) Cash withdrawal *	(3,572)		(3,572) (W)
Adjusted Ending Position	11,428	11,429	22,857
19X3			
Sales	15,000		15,000 (R)
Cost of sales		(11,429)	(11,429) (E)
Cash withdrawal	(3,571)		(3,571) (W)
(C) Adjusted Ending Position	22,857	—0—	22,857

* Adjusted ending net assets	$26,429
Adjusted beginning net assets ($20,000 × 160/140)	22,857
Price-level-adjusted net income—19X2	$ 3,572

Row *A* of Exhibit 9-4 reflects the general price-level-adjusted financial position at the end of 19X2 before the cash withdrawal. Recall that the owner's equity is determined as a residual balance, that is, the excess of the sum of the adjusted asset balances over the liabilities; a specific index factor is not applied to the unadjusted figure to determine this amount.

Net income can now be computed by comparing the owner's equity balance (before any cash withdrawals) at the end of 19X2, that is, $26,429, with the balance of this account at the start of the year *restated in terms of end-of-year dollars* (see footnote in Exhibit 9-4).

Given this new measure of disposable wealth, the cash withdrawal is reflected in row *B* of Exhibit 9-4. A cash withdrawal equal to price-level-adjusted net income enables the business to retain net assets whose recognized value in end-of-year dollars is equal to the purchasing power of the net assets at the beginning of the year.

Price-level-adjusted net income can also be determined by applying the appropriate indexes to the revenue and expense items expressed in terms of their original transaction costs and to the transactions and balances of the monetary accounts. The result is two component measures: (1) price-level-adjusted operating income and (2) net monetary gain or loss, as Exhibit 9-5 illustrates.

Exhibit 9-5

BLUE WATER YACHT SALES, INC.
Price-Level-Adjusted Net Income—19X2

	Original Transaction Amount	Translation Factor	Purchasing Power in End-of-Year Dollars
Price-Level-Adjusted Operating Income:			
Sales	$15,000	160/150	$16,000
Cost of sales	10,000	160/140	11,429
Net operating income	$ 5,000		
Price-level-adjusted operating income			$ 4,571
Monetary Loss from Cash:			
Beginning cash balance	$20,000	160/140	$22,857
Purchase of inventory	(20,000)	160/140	(22,857)
Receipts from sales	15,000	160/150	16,000
Ending balance (before withdrawal)	$15,000		$16,000
			15,000
Monetary Loss			$ 1,000
Price-Level-Adjusted Net Income:			
Price-level-adjusted operating income			$ 4,571
Monetary loss			(1,000)
Price-level-adjusted net income (index of disposable wealth)*			$ 3,571

* The one-dollar difference (see Exhibit 9-4) is due to rounding.

Although the price level was assumed to remain stable during 19X3, price-level-adjusted net income nonetheless differs from that produced under conventional accounting because of the prior year effects. It is possible to analyze 19X3 in the same way that we did 19X2, and in general such an approach would be necessary. However, because the price-level index remained constant over the year, we can merely continue the financial position worksheet in Exhibit 9-4 *starting 19X3 from the price-level-adjusted financial position at the end of 19X2.* Row C of Exhibit 9-4 reflects the adjusted ending financial position at the end of 19X3.

Net income differs from the original transaction cost-based net income for 19X3 because the inventory (one remaining boat) was adjusted at the end of 19X2 to reflect changes in price levels from the time it was acquired to the end of 19X2. Thus, when this resource was sold in 19X3, the measure of the sacrifice (expense) was the original transaction cost adjusted for the price-level change during 19X2. As a result, the end-of-19X2 dollar equivalent of the original purchasing power invested in the business continued to be preserved through 19X3 ($22,857)—as opposed to the original money investment of $20,000. This is evidenced by the after-withdrawal cash and owner's equity balances of $22,857 in the ending financial position. Note, however, that the cash itself was not explicitly adjusted. The reason the cash balance is higher relative to the conventional accounting model is that the owner withdrew *less* in order to maintain the same purchasing power that existed at the inception of the business.

Recognition of Current Replacement Costs (Entry Prices)

Since the valuation alternative reviewed above is concerned with "correcting" conventional accounting valuations for changes in the general purchasing power (i.e., the size) of the monetary unit, it focuses on changes in the general level of prices. In view of the concern only with the size of the monetary unit, general price-level-adjusted conventional accounting quite properly ignores the differences between price changes for specific assets and the change in the general price-level index. We now turn our attention to the valuation methodology that focuses on one form of *specific price changes* of assets held—current replacement costs.

The concept of the business enterprise that underlies the recognition of replacement costs is that of a reservoir of physical resources which provide a given level of capability to produce products and services. Thus in determining, for example, how much disposable wealth is generated during a period of operations, the test is whether sufficient recognized net assets will remain to *replace the productive capacity* of resources used up in producing the products and services during the period, rather than simply the original money (or general purchasing power) invested in those resources. The latter criterion is the test derived from the concept of the enterprise in conventional accounting (general price-level accounting)—that the enterprise is a repository of money capital. This same test also largely applies when we correct the conventional model for changes in general purchasing power, that is, correcting to a constant scale for measuring the purchasing power of a pool of money capital.

In applying the replacement-cost model to our example, we take note of the fact that the replacement cost of inventory (sailboats) increased during 19X2 from $10,000 to $12,000. During 19X3, however, we have assumed that there were no further changes in prices.

Exhibit 9-6 traces the financial position of Blue Water Yacht Sales through the two years of operations, making appropriate adjustments for the change in replacement cost as it took place (in 19X2). The amount of the withdrawal in 19X2 ($3,000) is determined by replacement-cost-based net income, which is calculated in Exhibit 9-7. Exhibit 9-7 also shows the calculation of replacement-cost-based operating income. In this case, by coincidence, the latter figure is also $3,000. It differs from conventional accounting net (operating) income ($5,000) only in that the cost of the sailboat sold has been adjusted upward from its original cost of $10,000 to its end-of-year replacement cost of $12,000.

Exhibit 9-6

BLUE WATER YACHT SALES, INC.
Financial Position Worksheet—Replacement-Cost Valuation

Description	Cash	Inventory	Owner's Equity
Initial Investment	20,000		20,000
19X2			
Purchased two sailboats	(20,000)	20,000	
Sold one sailboat	15,000		15,000 *(R)*
Cost of sailboat sold		(10,000)	(10,000) *(E)*
Preliminary ending position	15,000	10,000	25,000
Replacement cost adjustment		2,000	
Adjusted ending position	15,000	12,000	27,000
Withdrawal	(3,000)		(3,000) *(W)*
Ending (Beginning) Position	12,000	12,000	24,000
19X3			
Sold one sailboat	15,000		15,000 *(R)*
Cost of sailboat sold		(12,000)	(12,000) *(E)*
Withdrawal	(3,000)		(3,000) *(W)*
Ending (Beginning) Position	24,000	—0—	24,000

Exhibit 9-7

BLUE WATER YACHT SALES, INC.
Replacement-Cost-Based Income Measures
19X2

Replacement-Cost-Based Net Income:

Adjusted ending owner's equity (before withdrawals)		$27,000
Less adjusted beginning owner's equity:		
Beginning owner's equity	$20,000	
Add additional cost of two sailboats	4,000	24,000
Replacement-cost-based net income		$ 3,000

Replacement-Cost-Based Operating Income:

Revenue	$15,000
Less replacement cost of sales	12,000
Replacement-cost-based operating income	$ 3,000

Conventional accounting net income is of course an adequate basis for withdrawals if the purpose is to preserve recognized net assets equal to original money capital committed. However, in replacement-cost accounting we are interested in preserving in addition the difference between the original cost and the replacement costs of assets that were in service during the period. Thus for Blue Water we add $4,000, the additional cost of the maximum inventory of two sailboats, to the original capital of $20,000. This gives us a greater criterion level of wealth to be preserved ($24,000).

But we also adjust any assets on hand at year-end to their replacement costs in arriving at prewithdrawal ending net assets (owner's equity). In the case of Blue Water Yacht Sales, the adjustment amounted to $2,000 added to the original cost of the one sailboat still on hand at the end of 19X2.

Thus replacement-cost-based net income dictates a maximum current-period withdrawal equal to conventional accounting net income (the recognized change in net assets during the period before any adjustments) *less* any additional total capital required for replacement of assets, except to the extent that those assets are presently held in the financial position of the enterprise. This is sensible, since by recognizing the replacement costs of assets held at the end of the period, the greater costs will be carried forward and matched against the revenues of future periods. Thus future periods' net income (and presumably withdrawals) will be appropriately less than if conventional accounting is consistently applied. This "chain of events" phenomenon is evident in the Blue Water Yacht Sales case. Note in Exhibit 9-6 that the $12,000 replacement cost of the second sailboat is recognized in the adjusted ending position of 19X2. That amount is carried forward and matched against the $15,000 proceeds from its sale in 19X3, leading to net income and withdrawals again equal to $3,000. After the 19X3 withdrawal the enterprise ends the year with $24,000 in cash (and owner's equity), just the amount required to renew its maximum commitment of capital to the acquisition of inventory (two sailboats at $12,000 apiece).

Recognition of Current Market (Exit) Values

The second form of current exchange price that is used as the basis of a valuation model alternative is the current exit price (market value) of an asset. Use of this model is largely motivated by a dissatisfaction with the conventional model view that a sale transaction is the "critical event" in determining the period in which the value produced by the enterprise is recognized. Advocates of the market-value model argue that to measure actual performance for a period it is necessary to measure *all increases* (*or decreases*) in the value of a firm's assets—evidenced by current market values of those assets—not just those that were confirmed by a sale to outside parties. When applied to assets held for sale or for investment purposes, like the sailboats held by Blue Water Yacht Sales, this notion of performance is appealing.

For the Blue Water case, the financial position worksheet under the current market-value alternative is given in Exhibit 9-8. Although the total net income, $10,000, for the two years is equal in amount to that calculated under the conventional accounting model, the net income for each period is quite different. These periodic differences result from the recognition in 19X2 of the increase in value of the inventory on hand (one sailboat), calculated on the basis of the estimated selling price prevailing at the end of the year, in addition to the realized profit from the sale of one boat during 19X2. Disposable wealth for 19X2 is $8,000. Then, in 19X3, the sale for $15,000 of the second boat that had a previous market value of $13,000 represents further income of only $2,000. The further cash withdrawal for 19X3 is therefore only $2,000.

Exhibit 9-8   BLUE WATER YACHT SALES, INC.
                     Financial Position Worksheet—Current Market (Exit) Values

Description	Cash	Inventory	Owner's Equity
Initial Investment	20,000		20,000
19X2			
Purchased two sailboats	(20,000)	20,000	
Sold one sailboat	15,000		15,000 (R)
Cost of sailboat sold		(10,000)	(10,000)(E)
Recognition of current market value of assets held at the end of the period		3,000	3,000 (G)
Cash withdrawal	(8,000)		(8,000)(W)
Ending (Beginning) Position	7,000	13,000	20,000
19X3			
Sold one sailboat	15,000		15,000 (R)
Cost of sailboat sold		(13,000)	(13,000)(E)
Cash withdrawal	(2,000)		(2,000)(W)
Ending (Beginning) Position	20,000	—0—	20,000

Note that the withdrawals in each year, equal to market-value-based net income, leave net assets at the end of the year with a market value equal in amount to the market value (cash value in this case) of the original investment.

Under market-value accounting the measures of performance for this case are the same as the measures of disposable wealth: $8,000 in 19X2, and $2,000 in 19X3. However, we should observe that we have so far ignored the change in the general level of prices. When we take general price levels into account, as illustrated in Exhibits 9-9 and 9-10, price-level-adjusted, market-value-based net income differs from operating income for 19X2 (the year in which the price level changed), but not for 19X3.

Without price-level adjustments, 19X2 market-valued-based net income and operating income were both $8,000. But with price-level adjustments, the figures are $5,143 and $6,142, respectively (see Exhibits 9-9 and 9-10 for the respective calculations).

Since the end-of-19X2 (beginning-of-19X3) financial position is already stated in end-of-year dollars under market-value accounting, and since no price-level changes took place during 19X3, 19X3 market-value-based net income of $2,000 is not affected by general price-level changes (not even those taking place in 19X2, since they do not affect the beginning-of-19X3 financial position). For the same reasons, neither is market-value-based operating income for 19X3 (also $2,000) affected by price-level changes (see the 19X3 portion of Exhibit 9-9).

As an additional observation on market-value accounting, we should note that the application to a retail business like Blue Water Yacht Sales implies that the underlying criterion of performance for such businesses under the current exit value model is the acquisition of goods for sale. Yet

Exhibit 9-9
BLUE WATER YACHT SALES, INC.
General Price-Level-Adjusted, Market-Value-Based
Financial Position Worksheet

Description	Cash	Inventory	Owner's Equity
Initial Investment	20,000		20,000
19X2			
Purchased two sailboats	(20,000)	20,000	
Sold one sailboat	15,000		15,000 (R)
Cost of sailboat sold		(10,000)	(10,000)(E)
Recognition of current market value of assets held at year-end		3,000	3,000 (G)
(A) Ending Position (before withdrawal)	15,000	13,000	28,000
(B) Withdrawal *	(5,143)		(5,143)(W)
Ending (Beginning) Position	9,857	13,000	22,857
19X3			
Sold one sailboat	15,000		15,000 (R)
Value of sailboat sold		(13,000)	(13,000)(E)
Withdrawal	(2,000)		(2,000)(W)
(C) Adjusted Ending Position	22,857	—0—	22,857

* 19X2 Ending net assets (from row *A* above) $28,000
Adjusted beginning net assets: ($20,000 × 160/140)   22,857
Price-level-adjusted, market-value-based net income $ 5,143

it could be argued that the principal productive activity of such a firm is *selling.* The value increase we recognized in the example stems from the displacement of the merchandise from the wholesale market into the retail market and the expectation that a sale will be consummated. Note the difference between this business environment and that of an investment company, where a given asset (security) may be bought and sold in the same market by the same entity. Additionally, the merchandising situation differs from that of a manufacturing company. In manufacturing, use of current market values for inventory, particularly completed units of inventory, recognizes value added in fabricating or construction of the items, which are often the principal productive activities of such a firm. All of these observations suggest that the nature of the business is an important consideration in deciding whether or not to use current market values for asset valuation.

One feature of using current market value as a valuation basis is that the total market values of all the firm's assets reflect its ability to generate cash in the event that it decides to dispose of its assets. While this is frequently a relevant decision alternative for the management of the firm to consider, it generally is not a course of action that will be followed—particularly for a firm engaged in production activities of some type. Additionally, it is unlikely that investors will often be concerned with this essentially short-term,

Exhibit 9-10

BLUE WATER YACHT SALES, INC.
General Price-Level-Adjusted, Market-Value-Based
Income Statement, 19X2

Operating Income:

Revenue from sales ($15,000 × 160/150)			$16,000
Adjusted cost of sales ($10,000 × 160/140)			11,429
			4,571
Add unrealized gain on sailboat held at 12/31/X2:			
Market value as of 12/31/X2:		$13,000	
Adjusted prior value (cost) as of 12/31/X2 ($10,000 × 160/140)		11,429	1,571
Price-level-adjusted, market-value-based operating income			$ 6,142

Monetary Loss from Cash:

Beginning cash balance	$20,000	160/140	$22,857
Purchase of inventory	(20,000)	160/140	(22,857)
Receipts from sales	15,000	160/150	16,000
Ending balance (before withdrawal)	$15,000		$16,000
			15,000
Monetary loss			$ 1,000

Reconcilement:

Operating income	$6,142
Less monetary loss	1,000
Price-level-adjusted, market-value-based net income*	$ 5,142

* The one-dollar difference (see Exhibit 9-9) is due to rounding.

liquidation-oriented form of a business enterprise's cash-generating potential. For these reasons, it is understandable why the application of this model is generally limited at present to firms whose assets are principally in the form of investments.

Recap of Measures of Performance and Disposable Wealth

The measures of performance and disposable wealth produced for this illustration under the six valuation alternatives are summarized in Exhibit 9-11. The summary highlights the variation that can result, both for the individual years and in the total for the two years, depending upon which valuation model is chosen. It should be observed that even where the *totals for the two years* are equal (comparing conventional and market-value accounting, with and without general price-level adjustments), this is a consequence of the particular circumstances of the case (in particular, conversion of all assets back into cash at the end of 19X3). It would not occur in most situations. Additionally, the relative size of the net income measure under the various alternatives is also a consequence of the price-change assumptions of the case; under a different set of facts a valuation methodology that produced lower measures of net income in this illustration might generate higher measures.

Exhibit 9-11   BLUE WATER YACHT SALES, INC.
Summary of Measures of Performance and Disposable Wealth

Alternative Models	Measure of Performance			Measure of Disposable Wealth		
	19X2	*19X3*	*Total*	*19X2*	*19X3*	*Total*
Cash flow	$(5,000)	$15,000	$10,000	$(5,000)	$15,000	$10,000
Conventional accounting	5,000	5,000	10,000	5,000	5,000	10,000
General price-level-adjusted conventional accounting	4,571	3,571	8,142	3,571	3,571	7,142
Replacement-cost accounting	3,000	3,000	6,000	3,000	3,000	6,000
Current market (exit) values	8,000	2,000	10,000	8,000	2,000	10,000
General price-level-adjusted market-value accounting	6,142	2,000	8,142	5,142	2,000	7,142

How do we select the "right" valuation alternative in order to obtain "correct" measures of disposable wealth and performance? Although a simple answer to this question is not possible, we will explore the dimensions of the problem in the following section.

CHOICE AMONG ACCOUNTING ALTERNATIVES

The foregoing review of the several financial accounting models introduced in earlier chapters perhaps leaves one particularly significant question unanswered. Which model or combination of models of the enterprise represents the best basis for financial reporting? This question is the most difficult to answer for anyone interested in financial accounting. The reason for the difficulty is that the selection from among financial accounting alternatives has consequences that transcend the use of information by individuals.

A Problem of Social Choice

At the individual level, the selection of a financial accounting model of the enterprise is a simple matter—at least in principle. We know from Chapter 2 that the individual should seek all information for which the expected benefit (from improved expected decision outcomes) exceeds the expected cost. As long as a particular individual is the exclusive producer (or buyer) and consumer of information about the business enterprise, the choice is his (or hers). We have no interest in preempting such individual choice here.

However, one of the most important features of financial accounting (also noted in Chapter 2) is that it goes beyond the level of strictly individual production and consumption of information. As a result, financial accounting involves a number of complications. Because the enterprise management has a comparative advantage in observing, recording, and determining the effects of enterprise activities, resources, obligations, and so forth, there is a clear benefit in having the enterprise be the primary producer of accounting information about itself. But to exploit this advantage means that many individuals may experience benefits from the information while not necessarily bearing any of the cost of its production. The costs of production are borne by the enterprise—and, through it, by its present shareholders.

In addition to *uneven* distribution among many individuals of the costs and benefits from the production of information by a given enterprise, financial accounting is thought by many to have potential for producing certain "externalities." Externalities occur in general when a number of individuals (or other entities), acting independently, create a positive or a negative *joint effect* of their actions as well as the expected individual consequences. Currently, the most familiar examples of externalities are the negative effects on the environment of various forms of pollution. No single individual produces so many pollutants that these cannot be readily absorbed by the biosphere. But together the effect can be devastating.

In financial accounting the potential for positive (and perhaps negative) externalities is usually thought to arise because decision makers are interested in making choices among investments in a number of different enterprises. This obviously involves interfirm comparisons of expected future returns (cash flows) and risk. Thus, if a particular type of accounting is selected for just one enterprise, it may not be as helpful (valuable) to decision makers as it would be if it were used by all enterprises—thus facilitating comparisons between enterprises.

We have noted above three complications in the financial accounting information choice situation not present in strictly individual information choice problems: (1) multiple users of information, (2) uneven distribution of costs and benefits, and (3) positive (and perhaps negative) external effects of financial accounting information. The implication of these three complications is that the choice of financial accounting alternative(s) is a social choice. Although the actual selection of accounting alternatives may be made by one or at most a few individuals, the outcome affects the flow of costs and benefits to many. The important questions, then, are, How should such choices be made (how should the alternatives be ranked)? and By whom? Unfortunately, no one in accounting can answer these questions unequivocally. However, we will attempt below to describe how accountants have traditionally tried to rank the alternatives, and some of the problems with the traditional criteria.

Traditional Criteria for the Financial Accounting Choice Problem

Perhaps the one widely accepted assumption about the selection of accounting alternatives is that it is probably not optimal to have business enterprises report according to *all feasible* financial accounting alternatives. The assumption is very likely to be true in the extreme, that is, the number of information alternatives could be expanded almost indefinitely (at a cost), and further benefits of additional information would eventually be exhausted. There is some question, of course, as to whether sufficient financial accounting alternatives have been suggested to date so that the costs of reporting under all the alternatives would clearly outweigh the benefits. However, there seems to be a pervasive belief to this effect.

• *Usefulness of information for decisions.* If we cannot simultaneously have accounting information based on all feasible financial accounting models of the enterprise, how do we choose a more limited ideal or optimal set? In recent years a single primary criterion has been more and more widely acknowledged as very important in ranking alternative models. That criterion is the usefulness *to decision makers* of the information produced. However, since financial accounting goes beyond the individual level, usefulness is usually translated into a number of criteria or characteristics that may be possessed to varying degrees by the information produced under each model. The most important (and perhaps the most widely acknowledged) of the criteria is decision relevance.

• *Decision relevance.* Decision relevance is, in a general sense, the obvious requirement that an individual user would impose on any information request: Does it enable him, in some measure, to better predict the outcomes that would result from various courses of action?

Example 9-2   If you were considering a career in either the legal profession or the accounting profession, the receipt of the information that the probability of rain that day is 60 percent would probably not be conceived of as decision-relevant information. On the other hand, if from another source you received information that reflected the average salaries of lawyers and accountants at various points in their career, this very likely would be considered highly decision relevant to the question at hand.

To date, the assessment by accounting researchers of the decision relevance of the various financial accounting models has taken one of two general forms:

1. The use of logic and examples to explore structural relationships between accounting information and the information requirements implied by specified decision situations
2. Empirical tests of either (*a*) the ability of accounting information to predict future phenomena (like future earnings or cash flows) of interest in the same types of decision situations or (*b*) the association between accounting information and the apparent risk and return characteristics of firms' securities as reflected by the market values of those securities

It is beyond the scope of this book to exhaustively review each of these methods. Of course, the first method (using logic and examples) has actually been used in our own earlier discussion, but the authors have not gone so far as to attempt to show logically which model is most relevant for investment and wealth distribution decisions. Rather, our purpose has been to introduce each model by showing (primarily through example) how its outputs relate to certain classes of decision situations. We have used this method only because it is the more efficient and flexible for introducing students to some of the important characteristics of each model.

Unfortunately, neither of the two relevance-assessment methods has proved particularly conclusive in ranking the alternative models in the past.

Often a logical argument (or empirical evidence) that one model produces more relevant (predictive) information than another is countered by arguments that it possesses less of another "useful" characteristic. The most frequently mentioned of these other useful characteristics is objectivity.

• *Objectivity.* In our discussion in earlier chapters, the criterion of objectivity was introduced as the intuitive notion that financial accounting information should be largely based on fact. While this notion is reflective of the general thrust of the criterion, some elaboration may be helpful.

It is sometimes suggested that the objectivity criterion be applied in accounting in the form of a degree-of-precision measure (degree-of-precision being the amount of variation that one might reasonably expect if a number of accountants made independent measurements of the same phenomenon). Accordingly, an accounting measure that is high on this aspect of objectivity would be one that does not exhibit much variation in the values assigned by different accountants to the same set of observations. Presumably, if an accounting measurement is low in precision, it is also apt to be low in terms of the expectation that users of the accounting measurement will gain the same perception from it that the preparer had in mind when making the measurement. This latter characteristic, called "shared meaning" or "transferability" of information, is what accountants are really concerned about when they talk about objectivity.

Problems with the Traditional Criteria

Although more than one characteristic (e.g., relevance and objectivity) is thought to have a bearing on the usefulness of accounting information to various classes of decision makers, this is not, in and of itself, a barrier to ranking accounting information models. For instance, one model could conceivably be acknowledged by everyone to be better than any other model with respect to every characteristic. Unfortunately, however, none of the financial accounting models put forth to date clearly dominates the others in this way. In the absence of a clearly dominant alternative, it is necessary to measure the extent to which each characteristic is possessed by each alternative, and then to be able to combine the scores on each measurement scale into a single score for each information model.

Needless to say, we have not (and cannot at present) formally specify scales on which to measure the extent to which a particular valuation model possesses each characteristic. In the case of the objectivity criterion, the degree-of-precision notion provides a good deal of guidance of this type; even here, however, precision is but part of the larger question of how much shared meaning (and thus potential transferability) exists. Furthermore, even if we could specify scales measuring relevance and objectivity, we would still lack a common scale on which to combine the separate measures (according to some trade-off system). Because of the absence of these bases for comparison, it is impossible to make direct assessments of the relative usefulness of the alternative valuation models.

Furthermore, financial accounting is concerned with information produced by one group of economic units (business enterprises) for use by other groups (external decision makers). As a result, decisions as to how to go about the financial accounting process (including the choice among accounting models) inevitably affect the distribution of costs and benefits (and therefore wealth) among the individuals in the economy. Unfortunately, few social choices involve one alternative under which everyone would clearly be better off (or at least not worse off) than under the other alternatives. This means that there will seldom be unanimous agreement to a particular social choice among all the individuals affected. Thus, since whatever choice is made will tend to favor some and be unfavorable to others, the question of what is "equitable" or fair inevitably becomes an issue. Traditionally, accounting researchers, theoreticians, and practitioners have not addressed themselves to this issue directly. As a result, relatively little is known about the possible effects of different financial accounting models on the distribution of wealth (and the fairness of the distribution) among the members of society.

The Present Social Choice Mechanism

If traditional approaches to ranking alternate financial accounting models are not capable of producing a satisfactory social ranking, how then do accountants make choices between valuation alternatives for the broad class of decision makers characterized as investors? The answer (which is elaborated in Chapter 10) is that institutional forces play a significant, perhaps dominant, role in deciding how the financial accounting function is carried out.

Questions for Review and Discussion

9-1. Accounting has been described as a field of knowledge that is concerned with information that is useful for decision-making purposes. Outline the three general conditions that must be satisfied for an information specialization such as accounting to exist, and explain briefly why they are necessary.

9-2. We have to this point limited our discussion to accounting for the business enterprise for external investors. What classes of decision makers have been excluded by this limitation? Within the scope of our analysis, what are the two general classes of decision problems identified?

9-3. In examining the kinds of accounting information that might be appropriate for investment decisions, money flows are assigned a prominent role. Explain the justification for the use of money instead of the more fundamental element of individual satisfactions. Then explain the reason why the present value model is introduced.

9-4. What are the reasons why management forecasts and ready-made present values of business enterprises are not now generally available to investors? Are these reasons equally valid when such information is to be supplied to internal decision makers?

9-5. Although management-provided forecasts and present values are not now generally available, the investor's decision problem is unaltered. How does this influence the general character of information (other than forecasts or present values) that may be useful to investors?

9-6. The alternative financial models that are considered in this book reflect different approaches to the task of representing a business enterprise and its activities to external decision makers. But each must produce measurements that are oriented to the decision problem of the external decision maker. For each of the two broad classes of external decisions, explain briefly the purpose of the related accounting measurements (regardless of the model selected).

9-7. The measures of performance and disposable wealth produced by each of the six alternative valuation models (see Exhibit 9-11) are dependent for their meaning on the wealth preservation and valuation concepts embodied in the model. For each model, describe the wealth preservation and valuation concepts and explain in your own words what the measures of performance and disposable wealth are seeking to reflect.

9-8. The revenue realization concept adopted in the conventional accounting model is an important feature of that model. What is the justification for the selection of this particular concept? In which model(s) is accomplishment recognized at an earlier stage of business activity? In which model(s) is it generally recognized later?

9-9. What aspect of business activity is represented by an expense? When are expenses recognized? How are they measured?

9-10. Explain the nature and treatment of the following items:

1. Monetary gains or losses
2. Holding gains or losses from changes in market (exit) values of resources held for use in a business

9-11. The choice among alternative financial accounting models is a social choice problem. Explain what this means. What are the implications for choosing the optimum alternative (or set of alternatives)?

9-12. In attempting to select one of the valuation models for a particular application, the usefulness criterion has often been invoked. Explain briefly the problems associated with this approach.

9-13. For each alternative valuation model, try to construct one simple, hypothetical business circumstance for which that model would seem to be poorly suited to investment decisions based on the decision-relevance criterion. For each of these circumstances, which of the valuation models seems to be most decision relevant? How would the objectivity criterion influence your choice?

9-14. Under the logical approach to selecting an optimum financial accounting model, the concepts underlying the production of information under the model presumably have to be in harmony, to some degree at least, with the specific needs of specific decision problems. Some people believe that this requirement precludes accountants from producing aggregate information that is applicable to a broad general class of decision problems. By aggregating or summarizing the results of individual transactions under a particular set of concepts, the accountant does not give the user the opportunity to "reassemble" the data under a different set of concepts. One possible alternative is, of course, to communicate a large volume of less highly summarized transaction data (the extreme form of which is sometimes disparagingly referred to as a "memory dump"). Evaluate this alternative in the context of the "choice among accounting alternatives" dilemma.

9-15.   This chapter discusses the problem of choice among financial accounting models but does not resolve the problem. Do you see any social advantages or disadvantages of simply *not* resolving the problem in favor of one model or set of models under which all similar businesses must report?

Exercises   **9-1. Multiperiod Effects of Replacement Cost Changes.**   In the Blue Water Yacht Sales illustration in this chapter, it was assumed that the replacement cost of sailboats increased at the end of 19X2 from $10,000 to $12,000, and then remained at $12,000 throughout 19X3. Now assume that this price change did not occur until early in 19X3 (and was not anticipated in 19X2).

1. What effect would this change in assumptions have on the measures of performance and disposable wealth in 19X2 under replacement-cost accounting?

2. What would be the effect in 19X3?

3. Does this situation seem typical of what you would expect in applying replacement-cost adjustments to inventory?

9-2. Relationship between Replacement-Cost Changes and Selling-Price Changes. In the Blue Water Yacht Sales illustration in this chapter, the replacement cost of sailboats increased from $10,000 to $12,000, but the 19X3 expected selling price remained at $15,000. This reduced the retailer's potential gross margin (excess of selling price over acquisition cost) on the PW-30 from $5,000 to $3,000. Assume now, however, that market conditions were such that the retailers were able to pass along this cost increase (together with their usual profit increment on each dollar of cost) to the customer, and the selling price was raised to $18,000 concurrent with the cost increase (end of 19X2).

1. What effect would this have on the replacement-cost measure of performance in 19X2?

2. What effect would this have on the measure of disposable wealth in 19X2?

9-3. Replacement-Cost, Market-Value, and Hybrid Accounting.   Food Store, Incorporated, is a local chain of small neighborhood gourmet food stores that has been operating in Coast City for six years. Its operations for the sixth year are depicted on the following worksheet according to conventional accounting. Until

FOOD STORE, INCORPORATED
Financial Position Worksheet, 19X6
(numbers in thousands)

Description	Cash	Merchandise Inventory	Net Equipment	Accounts Payable	Owners' Equity
Beginning Position	500	200	100	100	700
Purchases		520		520	
Sales	780				780 (R)
Wages and salaries	(150)				(150)(E)
Rent	(25)				(25)(E)
Advertising	(45)				(45)(E)
Payments on account	(530)			(530)	
Depreciation			(10)		(10)(E)
Cost of sales		(480)			(480)(E)
Preliminary Balances	530	240	90	90	770

the sixth year, inflation has been negligible, and the management and owners of Food Store, Incorporated, have been satisfied with conventional accounting. However, this year at the annual meeting, when management presented the conventional financial statements and announced the board of directors' intent to declare dividends equal to conventional accounting income, there was some dissent and discussion.

Both wholesale and retail food prices had increased by 20 percent during 19X6 in the area around Coast City—though general inflation was only 10 percent for the year. Food Store, Incorporated, had made both its purchases and its sales at the various prices prevailing over the course of the year, however, so its purchase costs and selling prices during the year were up by 10 percent over 19X5 (in which food prices remained steady).

One faction at the annual meeting claimed that it would be negligent of the board to declare a dividend equal to conventional net income. Since it was going to cost more to replace the merchandise in inventory at year-end, they argued that the dividend should be reduced appropriately—or even eliminated. Another faction felt just the opposite. They argued that since the merchandise on hand was worth much more than it cost, the income calculations should take this "hidden value" into account and the dividend should be increased accordingly.

The board and management agreed that there was some merit to both arguments and promised a revised analysis after the morning recess in the meeting. They turn to you to prepare the revised report. They inform you of the following additional facts:

a. The built-in equipment in use in the various stores originally cost $150,000 and is still expected to last fifteen years in total (nine more). At the end of this year and last year, it could be bought or sold at the following prices:

	Replacement Cost	Market Value
End of 19X5	$150,000	$90,000
End of 19X6	$180,000	$75,000

b. The inventory stock is always rotated so that all merchandise on hand at the beginning of the year is all sold and the inventory on hand at year-end was all purchased at approximate year-end prices.

c. The markup on inventory is consistently about 50 percent of cost.

d. The maximum investment in inventory that the company has ever made is $250,000 at beginning-of-year costs, which is equivalent to $300,000 at year-end costs.

e. No changes are expected in payroll, rent, or advertising costs during 19X7.

Required:

Prepare an analysis of the alternate ways to calculate net income for the shareholders. Include replacement-cost and market-value bases for sure. Also consider any hybrid methods that might satisfy both factions at the meeting as to the proper amount of dividends. Comment on the rationale for and the strengths and weaknesses of each income measure in the given situation.

9-4. Price-Level Depreciation.   The income statement from Indiana Telephone Corporation's 1971 annual report appears on page 296. The "Column B" figures on the statement constitute historical cost (original transaction cost) figures adjusted for changes in the purchasing power of the dollar, stated in end-of-year dollars. Below is Note 2 to the financial statements from the same annual report.

2. RECOVERY OF CAPITAL AND RETURN ON CAPITAL

Under the law of Indiana, the Corporation is entitled to recover the fair value of its property used and useful in public service by accruing depreciation based on the "fair value" thereof and is entitled to earn a fair return on such "fair value." The amount shown in Column B for telephone plant approximates the fair value of the property as determined based on the principles followed by the Public Service Commission of Indiana in an order dated September 1, 1967, authorizing the Corporation to increase its subscriber rates.

In the accompanying financial statements, Column A includes depreciation expense based on historical cost and Column B includes depreciation expense, as well as other expenses, on the basis of historical cost repriced in current dollars to reflect the changes in the purchasing power of the dollar. Also, the annual reports to the Indiana Commission are in the same basic form shown herein.

It must be kept in mind that this determination of depreciation expense is a year-to-year estimate and there are involved the questions of obsolescence, foresight, and judgment giving due consideration to maintenance but the regulatory process does not adjust even to this accurately.

If use of property, obsolescence and current denominators (in the case of monetary inflation) are used accurately by way of keeping the allowable expense of depreciation current and rates sufficient to return it along with a fair return, and the proceeds are immediately invested in property used and useful in the public service, there more likely will be a real return of capital and a fair return thereon. However, if monetary inflation continues, as it usually does, purchasing power of capital is unlikely ever to be truly returned. It must be observed there is a substantial lag in the regulatory process. In rate making there is no guarantee of recovery of capital or of an adequate rate of return to the Corporation. This is an added risk which should be considered in estimating a fair return.

Since the present Internal Revenue Code does not recognize the costs measured in current dollars, they are not deductible for computing Federal income tax payments, and the Corporation in fact pays taxes on alleged earnings which do not exist in true purchasing power. If they were deductible, as they should be, reductions in Federal income taxes as shown in Column B of $266,000 in 1971 and $252,000 in 1970 would result. By requiring the use of the Uniform System of Accounts for utility accounting and by virtue of the Internal Revenue Code, the Government has condemned and confiscated during the last 7 years over $1 million (in terms of the dollars of the years in which they were paid) of the assets of this Corporation through taxation of overstated earnings. This is true to a greater or lesser extent in each case where we have been able to ascertain the facts. We do not understand why this is currently concealed by management and accountants—to their detriment.

Statement of Income

	Column A Historical Cost		Column B Historical Cost Restated for Changes in Purchasing Power of Dollar	
	1971	1970	1971	1970
OPERATING REVENUES:				
Local service	$ 5,744,356	$5,384,154	$ 5,788,990	$ 5,695,270
Toll service	4,852,156	4,350,496	4,889,858	4,601,883
Miscellaneous	304,522	234,979	306,888	248,557
Total operating revenues	10,901,034	9,969,629	10,985,736	10,545,710
OPERATING EXPENSES:				
Depreciation provision, Note 2	1,943,551	1,541,560	2,497,078	2,026,211
Maintenance	1,486,495	1,427,487	1,505,457	1,523,311
Traffic	1,226,906	1,157,565	1,237,139	1,224,453
Commercial	511,661	449,104	515,637	475,054
General and administrative	1,055,318	1,170,198	1,068,682	1,278,407
State, local and miscellaneous Federal taxes	912,601	648,996	919,692	686,497
Federal income taxes, Note 2				
Currently payable	1,132,500	1,127,087	1,141,300	1,192,215
Deferred until future years	315,800	295,000	318,254	312,047
Deferred investment tax credit (net)	9,708	(14,997)	3,262	(21,018)
Total operating expenses	8,594,540	7,802,000	9,206,501	8,697,177
OPERATING INCOME	2,306,494	2,167,629	1,779,235	1,848,533
INCOME DEDUCTIONS:				
Interest on funded debt	651,195	659,567	656,255	697,679
Other deductions	36,828	21,355	40,229	24,583
Interest charged to construction (credit)	(63,905)	(30,442)	(64,402)	(32,201)
Other income (credit)	(95,974)	(98,759)	(96,720)	(104,466)
Gain from retirement of long-term debt through operation of sinking fund (credit)	(15,192)	(15,865)	(15,310)	(16,781)
Price level gain from retirement of long-term debt (credit)	—	—	(61,137)	(55,175)
Gain from retirement of preferred stock through operation of sinking fund (credit)	(5,055)	(5,515)	(5,094)	(5,834)
Price level gain from retirement of preferred stock (credit)	—	—	(12,908)	(12,029)
Price level loss from other monetary items	—	—	87,508	118,125
Total income deductions	507,897	530,341	526,421	613,901
NET INCOME	1,796,597	1,637,288	1,250,814	1,234,632
Preferred stock dividends applicable to the period	96,209	97,541	96,957	103,178
EARNINGS APPLICABLE TO COMMON STOCK	$ 1,702,388	$1,539,747	$ 1,153,857	$ 1,131,454
EARNINGS PER COMMON SHARE	$ 3.49	$ 3.16	$ 2.37	$ 2.32
BOOK VALUE PER SHARE	$ 21.45	$ 18.29	$ 20.19	$ 18.14
Stations in service at end of year	75,015	72,569	75,015	72,569

For book and financial reporting purposes, the Corporation provides for depreciation on a straight-line basis over the average service lives of the various classes of depreciable plant. In 1971, the overall rate was 6.3%. For Federal income tax purposes, beginning in 1967, an accelerated depreciation method is used and a provision is made in the Statement of Income for the taxes deferred as a result thereof.

Assume you are attending the annual meeting of Indiana Telephone and several shareholders, completely unfamiliar with accounting, ask you the following questions. Answer these questions as clearly as you can.

1. Briefly, what is management trying to say in Note 2 to the financial statements?
2. The bulk of the assets of ITC consists of telephone plant and equipment. Assume that the Column B figures were used consistently for such things as the basis for income tax assessment and dividend policy. Under such circumstances, would recognition of the depreciation expense figures appearing in Column B generally ensure that the telephone plant and equipment can be replaced when they wear out? Explain (defend) your answer.

9-5. Replacement Cost versus Market Value.   Phil McCavity graduated from dental school two years ago. After one year of working for another dentist, he decided to set up his own practice. His transactions during the first year of his practice are as follows:

a. Opened a bank account for his practice and deposited $5,000. At the same time he negotiated a loan of $5,000 to be repaid over the next two years at $2,500 at year-end each year. Interest on the loan is 10 percent per annum on the beginning-of-year balance, payable as of the end of each year.
b. Purchased dental tools and equipment with an expected useful life of ten years and zero salvage value for $5,000.
c. Purchased office furniture with an expected useful life of ten years and zero salvage for $1,000.
d. Paid rent monthly at $150 per month.
e. Paid receptionist $400 per month.
f. Purchased general dental supplies for $600, all of which were used during the year.
g. Billed patients $30,000. Of this amount, $2,000 was outstanding (i.e., unpaid) at year-end.
h. Repaid $2,500 on loan, together with the interest due.

No general price change occurred throughout the year. McCavity expects to retain his present fee structure, which is set by the local dental association. However, if McCavity wished to replace his tools and equipment and his office furniture at year-end, it would cost him $6,000 and $1,200, respectively, to do so. On the other hand, if he wished to sell his tools and equipment and his office furniture at year-end, he could expect to realize $4,400 and $950, respectively.

Required:

1. (a) If McCavity were to use the current replacement-cost model for accounting purposes, at what amount would the dental tools and equipment and the office furniture be shown in the ending balance sheet?

(b) Calculate his disposable wealth and draw up his operating income statement for the year.

2. (a) If McCavity were to use the current market-value model for accounting purposes, at what amount would the dental tools and equipment and the office furniture be shown in the ending balance sheet?

(b) Draw up his income statement for the year. (Hint: Base depreciation on decline in market values.)

9-6. Replacement Cost versus Market Value. Harry Flash owns a car showroom in Los Angeles. He deals in one type of imported sports car—the Thunderclap. Demand for the car has always been steady, but supply has been rationed due to import quotas.

Harry purchases each car at the factory price of $4,000. Other costs to get each car into his showroom in salable condition include transportation, $500; import duties, 5 percent of factory price; and predelivery costs, $100. Harry passes all these costs along to his customers in his selling price, together with his usual markup at 50 percent on the factory price. Harry never cuts his prices regardless of how hard a customer bargains. However, if Harry ever wished to sell off his entire inventory on short notice, he would have to discount each car by 20 percent.

Harry employs two salesmen who are paid a 10 percent commission on the selling price of each car after deducting transportation costs, import duties, and predelivery costs. Harry has ten cars on hand at the end of the year, *the minimum acceptable stock level.* His salesmen sold eighty cars throughout the year. Harry places an order for twenty vehicles when he has only twenty left in stock. Harry is required by the manufacturer to pay cash at delivery. The only other cost of operating the dealership is $20,000 annually for general administrative expenses. All sales are for cash, and all expenses are paid as they are incurred.

The showroom owned by Harry was constructed two years ago at a cost of $100,000 and is expected to last twenty years and have a zero salvage value. Its replacement cost at year-end is estimated to be equal to its original cost of $100,-000. The showroom can also be sold for this amount less a 6 percent broker's commission. The same was true at the beginning of the year.

Just before the end of the year Harry receives a letter from the sales manager of the foreign car factory indicating that due to a rise in labor costs the factory price of the Thunderclap would, in the future, be $4,500. All other costs will probably remain the same.

Harry's beginning balance sheet for the year, based on conventional accounting, is as follows.

Assets:			Liabilities and Owner's Equity:	
Cash		$107,000	Liabilities	—0—
Car inventory (10 @ cost)		48,000		
Showroom	$100,000			
Less accumulated depreciation	(5,000)	95,000	Owner's equity	$250,000
		$250,000		$250,000

Required:

1. Draw up a statement of operating income and an ending balance sheet under the replacement-cost model. Adjust sales revenues to end-of-year prices. Also indicate the amount of disposable wealth for the period.

2. Calculate income on a market-value basis. (Hint: Adjust both beginning and ending net assets to the then-current market values and then calculate income.)

9-7. Comprehensive Comparative Accounting Exercise. During her first year of practice, Wilma Jones, M.D., prepared the following conventional accounting worksheet.

Date		Cash	Supplies Inven- tory	Equip- ment	Accumu- lated Depreci- ation	Owner's Equity
1/1	Original investment	100,000				100,000
1/1	Purchased equipment	(60,000)		60,000		
1/1	Purchased initial stock of medical supplies	(20,000)	20,000			
1/1– 12/31	Fees for medical services received uniformly throughout year	90,000				90,000 (R)
1/1– 12/31	Paid employee wages uniformly throughout year	(27,000)				(27,000) (E)
12/31	Cost of supplies used		(12,000)			(12,000) (E)
12/31	Depreciation expense				(12,000)	(12,000) (E)
	Balances	83,000	8,000	60,000	(12,000)	139,000

Required:

1. What is the conventional accounting net income for Dr. Jones's first year of operations?

2. The general price-level index was 80 at the start of the year and 100 at the end of the year, and the average index for the year was 90.
   (a) What is the price-level-adjusted net income for the year?
   (b) What is the price-level-adjusted operating income for the year?
   (c) What is the amount of monetary gain or loss for the year?
       Indicate whether it is a gain or a loss.

3. On December 31 the replacement cost for the equipment was $90,000, and there was no change in the price of the medical supplies. What is the replacement-cost-based operating income for the year? (Assume that the fee structure recommended by the local medical society is unchanged.)

4. On December 31 the estimated realizable values (i.e., exit prices) were $5,000 for the inventory of medical supplies and $30,000 for the equipment. What is the current market-value-based net income for the year (including general price-level effects)?

5. Which of the two current exchange-price valuation models do you believe provides the more useful and relevant measure of net income for the doctor's first year of operations? Why?

9-8. Comprehensive Comparative Accounting Exercise. Sam Shovel is the sole owner of Shovel Leasing, which specializes in the leasing of construction equipment to local contractors. It has been in operation since January 1, 19X0, and its balance sheet at the end of the first year of operations is as follows.

SHOVEL LEASING
Balance Sheet
As of December 31, 19X0

Assets:			Liabilities and Owner's Equity:	
Cash		$ 50,000	Accounts payable	$ 30,000
Accounts receivable		30,000		
Fuel		15,000		
Parts		20,000		
Supplies		5,000		
Equipment for lease*	$200,000			
Less accumulated depreciation	(40,000)	160,000	Owner's equity	250,000
			Total liabilities and owner's equity	
Total assets		$280,000	equity	$280,000

* Information on equipment available for lease is as follows:

Item	No.	Date of Purchase	Expected Useful Life (in years)	Original Cost per Unit	Expected Salvage Value	Replacement Cost as of Dec. 31, 19X1, per Unit	Current Market Value as of Dec. 31, 19X1, per Unit
Bulldozer	4	1/1/X0	5	$20,000	—0—	$25,000	$13,000
Compressor	4	1/1/X0	5	7,500	—0—	7,500	4,000
Pneumatic drill	10	1/1/X0	5	1,000	—0—	1,000	700
Mechanized ditchdigger	5	1/1/X0	5	10,000	—0—	11,000	7,500
Mobile crane	2	1/1/X0	5	15,000	—0—	17,500	10,000

The enterprise's transactions for the year ended December 31, 19X1, were as follows:

a. Rental payments on business location, $5,000. Paid at the beginning of the year.

b. Wages and salaries paid throughout the year, $14,000.

c. Purchased on account *at the beginning of the year*—fuel, $55,000; parts, $30,000; and supplies, $15,000.

d. Payments made on accounts payable throughout the year, $80,000.

e. Billed customers $200,000 throughout the year, and by year-end had received $190,000 from customers.

f. Inventory was taken at year-end. On hand was fuel, $20,000; parts, $10,000; and supplies, $5,000.

Additional information:

a. There has been no movement in the cost of fuel, parts, and supplies.

b. It is estimated by Sam that if he should attempt to sell the fuel, parts, and supplies on hand at December 31, 19X1, their current market values would be as follows:

Fuel	$20,000
Parts	9,000
Supplies	4,500

c. The general price index has risen from 100 at the beginning of the year to 120 at the end of the year. The price index averaged about 110 for the year. There had been no movement in the general price index in 19X0. Furthermore, it is expected that the general inflation will *not* continue.

d. Market values and replacement costs of the equipment, fuel, parts, and supplies all equaled unexpired cost at the beginning of 19X1.

e. No increase in lease rates charged by Sam has occurred during 19X1, and none is anticipated in the near future.

Required:

1. Show comparative performance and disposable wealth measures for each of the following models:
   (a) Conventional accounting
   (b) Conventional accounting adjusted for general price-level changes
   (c) Current replacement-cost accounting
   (d) Current market-value accounting (including general price-level effects)

2. Show comparative net values of Equipment for Lease under each of the above models.

9-9. Comprehensive Comparative Accounting Exercise.   During her first year of business, Joan Smith, who repairs jewelry and watches, prepared the conventional accounting worksheet on the following page.

Required:

1. What is the conventional accounting net income for Ms. Smith's first year of operations?

2. The general price-level index was 90 at the start of the year and 120 at the end of the year, and the average index for the year was 100. Assume the ending inventory of supplies consists of supplies purchased at the average index for the year. (Hint: This means that the cost of supplies used consists of a *mixture* of beginning-of-year index dollars *and* average index dollars.)

Date		Cash	Supplies Inventory	Equipment	Accumulated Depreciation	Owner's Equity
1/1	Original investment	100,000				100,000
1/1	Purchased equipment	(60,000)		60,000		
1/1	Purchased initial stock of supplies	(20,000)	20,000			
1/1–12/31	Fees for repair services received uniformly throughout year	135,000				135,000 (R)
1/1–12/31	Purchased supplies uniformly throughout year	(40,000)	40,000			
1/1–12/31	Paid employee wages uniformly throughout year	(27,000)				(27,000) (E)
12/31	Cost of supplies used		(51,000)			(51,000) (E)
12/31	Depreciation expense				(12,000)	(12,000) (E)
	Balances	88,000	9,000	60,000	(12,000)	145,000

(a) What is the price-level-adjusted net income for the year?

(b) What is the price-level-adjusted operating income for the year?

(c) What is the amount of monetary gain or loss for the year? Indicate whether it is a gain or a loss.

3. On December 31 the replacement cost for the equipment was $70,000, and on that date a 10 percent increase in the price of the supplies was announced. The maximum investment at any one time in supplies (at old prices) was $20,000. However, Ms. Smith did not anticipate raising her fees.

(a) What is the replacement-cost-based operating income for the year?

(b) What is the replacement-cost-based net income for the year?

4. On December 31 the estimated realizable values (i.e., exit prices) were $6,000 for the inventory of supplies and $30,000 for the equipment. What is the current market-value-based net income for the year (including general price-level effects)?

5. Which of the two current-exchange-price valuation models do you believe provides the more useful and relevant measure of net income for Ms. Smith's first year of operations? Why?

9-10. Comprehensive Comparative Accounting Exercise. On January 1, 19X0, Peter Buckle and Sam Strap decide to invest in a leather goods store, which will produce and sell such items as leather belts, shoulder bags, and leather vests. Each invests $3,000, and they hire a leather worker who will use his own tools. A summary of their transactions during the first two years of operations is as follows:

Year 1

a. Paid rent on shop totaling $1,200 ($100 per month).

b. Purchased the following assets:

	Original Cost	Expected Useful Life	Expected Salvage Value
Sign for shop front	$400	2 years	—0—
Fixtures and fittings	$600	2 years	—0—

c. During the course of year 1, 2,200 square feet of leather was purchased at a cost of $2 per square foot. *The maximum amount of leather purchased or on hand at any given time was 600 square feet.* Thread, buckles, and other items costing $550 were also purchased. At year-end 200 square feet of leather was on hand, as well as thread, buckles, and other items which had originally cost $50.

d. Cash sales totaling $20,000 were made throughout the year.

e. The leather worker received $7,000 in wages throughout the year.

Year 2

a. Paid rent on shop totaling $1,200 ($100 per month).

b. During the course of year 2, 1,800 square feet of leather was purchased at a cost of $2.50 per square foot. Thread, buckles, and other items costing $450 were purchased. At year-end all inventory of leather, thread, buckles, and other items had been used.

c. Cash sales totaling $22,000 were made throughout the year.

d. The leather worker received $7,000 in wages throughout the year.

Additional information:

a. There was no change in the general level of prices in year 1, but in year 2 the general price index rose from 100 to 120. The average change in the general level was 10 percent for the year. The general inflation was *not* expected to continue.

b. (1) At the end of year 1 (but before preparation of the financial statements), Peter and Sam were aware that the wholesale price of leather would be $2.50 per square foot in year 2; and at the end of year 2 (but before preparation of the financial statements), they were aware that the wholesale price of leather would be $3.00 per square foot in year 3. To compensate, Peter and Sam raised their own retail prices for the coming year 10 percent across-the-board as of the end of both years 1 and 2.

   (2) The current market value to Peter and Sam of leather on hand at the end of year 1 was estimated to be $1.80 per square foot.

   (3) There was no change in the replacement cost of thread, buckles, and other items in years 1 or 2, but the current market value of these items on hand at the end of year 1 was estimated to be $40.

   (4) The replacement costs of the sign for the shop front and the fixtures and fittings are $500 and $700, respectively, at the end of year 1 and $500 and $800, respectively, at the end of year 2.

   (5) The current market values of the sign for the shop front and the fixtures and fittings are estimated to be $220 and $280, respectively, at the end of year 1 and zero at the end of year 2.

Exhibit 9-12

LEATHER GOODS STORE
Conventional Worksheet

Description	Cash	Leather	Thread, Buckles, etc.	Sign	Accumulated Depreciation	Fixtures and Fittings	Accumulated Depreciation	Owners' Equity
Original Investment	6,000							6,000
Year 1								
Purchase of sign	(400)			400				
Purchase of fixtures and fittings	(600)					600		
Purchase of leather	(4,400)	4,400						
Purchase of thread	(550)		550					
Sales	20,000							20,000 (R)
Wages	(7,000)							(7,000) (E)
Rent	(1,200)							(1,200) (E)
Leather, thread, etc., used		(4,000)	(500)					(4,500) (E)
Depreciation					(200)		(300)	(500) (E)
Withdrawal	(6,800)							(6,800) (W)
Ending (Beginning) Balance	5,050	400	50	400	(200)	600	(300)	6,000
Year 2								
Purchase of leather	(4,500)	4,500						
Purchase of thread	(450)		450					
Sales	22,000							22,000 (R)
Wages	(7,000)							(7,000) (E)
Rent	(1,200)							(1,200) (E)
Leather, thread, etc., used		(4,900)	(500)					(5,400) (E)
Depreciation					(200)		(300)	(500) (E)
Withdrawal	(7,900)							(7,900) (W)
	6,000	—0—	—0—	400	(400)	600	(600)	6,000

c. Peter and Sam follow a policy of withdrawing cash equal to net income each year.

Required:

Prepare a table of comparative performance and disposable wealth measures and ending balances in cash and owners' equity for years 1 and 2 based on the above facts and the application of:

(a) conventional accounting

(b) conventional accounting adjusted for general price-level changes

(c) replacement-cost accounting

(d) market-value accounting (including general price-level effects).

Show appropriate calculations and support. Be prepared to discuss the amounts and reasons for differences between the figures for the several models.

III

THE CONTEMPORARY CORPORATE REPORTING ENVIRONMENT

10

Capital Market Institutions and the Accounting Policy-Making Process

RESOLVING THE COMPETING CONSTRUCTS DILEMMA: ACCOUNTING POLICY

As was pointed out in Chapter 9, we have confronted the reader in Chapters 4 through 8 with several alternative financial accounting models, each having certain alleged advantages and disadvantages. It was observed that the choice between these (and still other) alternatives is complicated by a number of factors not present in simple, individual problems of choosing the most desirable information alternative. The complicating factors include the following: (1) there are multiple users of financial accounting information, (2) the costs of producing financial accounting information may be borne by entities (enterprises) other than those who experience the benefits (external users), and (3) the possibility exists for external effects of financial accounting information when all reporting entities are considered together.

The fact that different economic entities are affected by the financial reporting process in different ways and to different degrees (in terms of costs and benefits) means that a choice of one or another financial accounting model can lead to different distributions of wealth among the various entities (including individuals) in the economy. Furthermore, since different entities may be better or worse off under one model than another, there is no unanimity as to which is the best model on which to base present-day financial reporting practice.

Unfortunately, even if there were unanimity as to which financial accounting model (or combination of models) is most appropriate, there need not be agreement as to how to solve all of the measurement problems that arise in applying it to various situations arising in practice. That is, there would be (and is) disagreement over appropriate *measurement rules* to be employed at the operational level to apply any given financial accounting model. For instance, consider the measurement of depreciation under the conventional accounting model that we illustrated in our examples in earlier chapters. In particular, the total cost (less expected salvage value) of a depreciable asset expected to yield benefits over a number of accounting periods was *allocated equally* to each of the periods. It is often argued, however, that the benefits from a long-lived asset are not derived equally over its life, but that most of the value is obtained during the early years of its useful life. Acceptance of such an argument would imply that the cost should then be allocated to expense in larger amounts in earlier periods than in later periods.

Thus, a "depreciation method" might be formulated that systematically allocates the cost of an asset over its life such as to reflect nonconstant benefit patterns. (In Chapter 12 some depreciation methods of this type are illustrated.) But are such nonconstant depreciation patterns consistent with the conventional accounting model? Indeed, is the "equal amounts" method consistent with this model? As some readers may already know, the answer is yes to both questions. Both methods (and others as well) spread the original cost of the asset over all the periods it is thought to benefit and hence are applications of the cost principle for measuring expense (which is a major conceptual element of conventional accounting). In a given case, however, depending on the actual underlying pattern of (uncertain) economic benefits, one or the other pattern of depreciation may be more consistent with the matching principle. Since people will, in good faith, often disagree as to the underlying pattern of benefits, they will also often disagree as to the appropriate pattern of depreciation.

Because of (1) the lack of unanimity as to the most appropriate financial accounting model and measurement rules and (2) the implication that different alternatives may lead to different distributions of wealth in the economy, the question of what is the optimum *financial accounting policy* (the set of acceptable measurement concepts and rules at any point in time) is a socioeconomic question rather than a question of accounting theory *per se*. All such questions are, of course, ultimately decided, directly or indirectly, within some type of political mechanism.

Understandably, then, accounting policy is the result of many economic, social, and political influences, past and present. These influences are exerted by individuals and organizations of two types: (1) those stimulated by an interest in the outcomes of the decision-making process and (2) those legally vested with the power to determine the outcomes. With respect to the former type of influence, as new financial accounting concepts or measurement rules come up for consideration, many individuals and organizations, reflecting varying points of view and degrees of economic interest in the particular issues, try to bring their points of view to bear on the decision-making process. Such individuals and organizations include, among others, industry associations, professional accountants, the major stock exchanges, and financial analysts.

Our political and economic system being what it is, one might expect that the final determination of what financial accounting concepts and measurement rules are adopted by particular firms would be left to purely economic forces (i.e., the "market mechanism" would shape accounting practice). But this is not the case. As in so many areas of modern market-based economies, a government agency has been established to regulate an activity that is thought to involve elements of public interest not adequately handled by a completely free market mechanism. This agency, the Securities and Exchange Commission (SEC), has had (federal) statutory authority over financial accounting practice for most business enterprises of any size in the United States ever since the mid-1930s.

The Securities and Exchange Commission was established by the Securities Exchange Act of 1934. This act and the Securities Act of 1933 are the major sources of the SEC's authority over accounting for business enterprises. But the SEC derives additional authority under five other statutes. The full list of this statutory authority is as follows:

1. The Securities Act of 1933 (originally administered by the Federal Trade Commission)
2. The Securities Exchange Act of 1934 (established the Securities and Exchange Commission, along with vesting it with authority to regulate securities exchanges and trading of securities)
3. The Public Utility Holding Company Act of 1934
4. The Trust Indenture Act of 1939
5. The Investment Company Act of 1940
6. The Investment Advisors Act of 1940
7. The National Bankruptcy Act of 1938, Chapter X (advisory capacity to the federal courts)

None of the above legislation is devoted exclusively to corporate financial reporting. But all of the above statutes are concerned with interrelated elements of the same focal point of public interest: the process of capital formation by business enterprises and the capital markets that facilitate that process. That the public has an interest in corporate financial reporting and accounting policy making is, however, an integral part of this larger interest. To understand why and how institutions (particularly the SEC) are so influential in present-day accounting policy, we need to examine a set of related topics:

1. Capital formation in a market economy (including why the process is vested with the public interest)
2. The social demands on the corporate securities markets
3. The historical and economic reasons that stimulated government regulation which embraced accounting matters as well as other aspects of corporate capital formation

4. The evolution of accounting policy-making institutions from 1935 to the present (including the relationship between the SEC and the policy-making bodies of the accounting profession)

5. Some important environmental influences on the formulation of accounting policy

This chapter deals with each of these topics in turn.

Capital Formation in a Market Economy

The *material* standard of living of an individual or a whole society is dependent on how many goods and services can be produced in any period of time with the available supply of resources. The only way to improve the standard of living of a given population without increasing the hours of labor required is to improve the level of output of the given supply of labor hours. The efficiency of labor is improved by augmenting it with physical, technical, and human capital. In order for a high standard of living to be sustained, a high level of capital must be built up and maintained whether on an individual or a societal level.

• *Consumption postponement.* The prerequisite to capital formation is a sacrifice of current consumption. Hence, to form capital, some of the currently available supply of productive resources must be diverted from current production of final consumer goods and services to the production of capital.

For primitive man the transfer was direct and simple. The hunter, for instance, could simply pause in the middle of an expedition to fashion a weapon, thereby sacrificing the immediate bounty that he might have secured for improved performance later. But in a modern market economy the relationship between sacrificed consumption and capital formation is not so simple and direct. Here consumption is postponed through the direct or indirect savings of consumption units. Direct saving takes place when an individual, a family, or some other consumption unit does not spend all of the funds it currently receives from employment of its factors of production. Indirect saving takes place when business enterprises distribute cash to their owners in amounts less than the current income of the enterprises. In either case, some of the cash flow from production of goods and services is not spent for current consumption.

• *Demand for capital.* By itself, however, direct or indirect savings is enough. The funds not spent on current consumption by savers must be sp on something. In particular, some of it must be spent on new capital or placements for capital exhausted in current production.

Savings not spent by a given economic unit represent a lack of demand consumer goods and services, perhaps leading to unemployment of some the resources previously committed to their production (and, in the extrei possible economic recession). This is what is known as the "paradox thrift." The constituents of a society, by being frugal and not spending la amounts of their incomes, can save themselves into unemployment and e nomic recession. Savings devoted to capital formation, however, result in e ployment of some of the productive resources of the economy in the prod tion of goods and services for nonconsumption purposes.

But a balance is important. Just as an excess of savings can lead to unemployment, an excess in the other direction means that the combined demand for both consumer and capital goods and services will exceed the productive capacity of the economy, leading to inflation. The balance not only is important but also can be very delicate, as there is a somewhat natural imbalancing force at work. This imbalancing force is explained below.

• *Transfer of funds between economic units.* A particular consumer unit that has saved part of its income may dispose of its excess funds by investing directly in some form of capital, such as buildings, implements, or education. But this need not always be so, and most often it is not. Another economic unit may wish to buy something now for which it currently has insufficient funds, such as a house or a car for a consumer, or a factory or equipment for a business. Thus there is a tendency toward imbalance in the saving-spending desires of individual economic units.

If a market economy is to avoid serious unemployment or inflation, it is necessary that there be some systematic way of transferring funds from savers to those interested in using those funds currently. Furthermore, if the economy is to maintain (or increase) its standard of living, a sufficient amount of the funds saved must be spent to replace that amount of capital currently exhausted in production (or more). In a market economy the capital market serves these purposes.

> **Capital Market.** The capital market consists of all the individuals and institutions that together accomplish the transfer of funds from savers to economic units that wish to spend additional funds on capital goods and services.

• *Capital market participants and transactions.* The capital market of an economy like that of the United States is a very broad economic phenomenon, having many participants and many types of transactions and places of exchange. In general, the relationship between participants is represented in Exhibit 10-1.

Exhibit 10-1   Capital Market Relationships in New Capital Formation

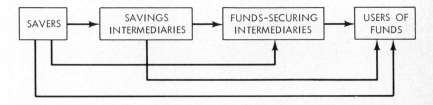

Economic units that wish to save may place their funds directly in the possession of an economic unit that will put them to use. The saver will receive some claim in return, ranging from (1) an unconditional promise on the part of the user to return the funds with interest, such as a mortgage note of a borrower who wants to purchase a home, to (2) a share of common stock in a corporation or a partnership interest, promising only a share in any earnings that are generated thereafter.

• *Capital market intermediaries.* Direct transfers would satisfy the needs of only a small fraction of the total savers and users of funds. Thus there are many types of capital market intermediaries working to satisfy demand initiated by either savers or users of funds.

On the savings side, there exist commercial banks, savings banks, savings and loan associations, mutual funds, insurance companies, and pension funds. All of these types of savings intermediaries exist as outlets or opportunities for vast numbers of consumers to put their funds to work as they save, without worrying about who will actually use the funds and for what purpose. In exchange for control over their savings, the financial intermediaries pay interest, dividends, or deferred payments (in the case of insurance companies and pension funds) to savers. The savings intermediaries, in turn, loan large blocks of pooled savings or invest them in ownership shares in various kinds of users of funds, in return for interest or dividends, presumably in excess of what they are obligated to pay their creditors (the savers).

From the other side, a potential user of funds, such as a large corporation (or a governmental unit) whose management wants to expand its operations with new plant and equipment that will cost several hundred million dollars, may find it difficult, time consuming, and costly to seek out the savings of individuals. But, fortunately, it can call upon the services of a funds-securing intermediary, usually an investment banker. The investment banker will form a syndicate with other investment bankers, and together they will buy all the securities that the corporation needs to issue in order to carry out its capital expansion. The investment bankers, in turn, sell the securities, often in much smaller blocks, to savers and savings intermediaries. The amount the investment bankers pay to the user of funds will be somewhat less than they estimate they will collect from the savers and/or the various savings intermediaries for the securities.

• *Sources of funds for business enterprises—the corporate securities markets.* The foregoing description of participants and relationships holds for the capital market in general. But since our area of interest is society's regulatory interest in accounting for business enterprises, we need only be concerned hereafter with that portion of the total capital market in which significant numbers of business enterprises (mainly corporations) raise the funds with which they acquire capital goods and services. We call this segment "the markets for corporate securities." From this point on we will ignore other segments of the capital market, such as the market for mortgage loans and the government securities markets.

**Social Demands on the Corporate
Securities Markets**

In a market economy, the public interest embraces all segments of the capital market, including the markets for corporate securities. Why? Because a healthy market economy requires a capital market that performs the functions and exhibits the characteristics that are listed below and discussed in the paragraphs that follow.

1. As mentioned earlier, for economic stability it is necessary that the supply of funds from savers be matched against the demand for funds of potential users.

2. If society is to maintain a high and growing standard of living, there must be a sufficient supply of funds at a low enough cost to business enterprises to ensure that it will be worthwhile to replace worn-out capital and add new capital to the total stock of capital in the economy. This in turn is dependent on two additional requirements:

   a. The markets must be operationally efficient.

   b. The markets must be reasonably fair, meaning free from fraud, deception, and manipulation by any participants. (This requirement is the principal motivation for a public interest in and related regulation of corporate financial reporting.)

• *Matching supply and demand for funds in the corporate securities markets.* The two major aspects of matching supply and demand for funds in the corporate securities markets are size and time. Businesses are often interested in investing in capital goods that cost enormous amounts and last many years. Savers, on the other hand, are usually interested in committing relatively small amounts and maintaining flexibility with respect to when they may recover funds committed.

The problem of size is, of course, partly solved when corporations issue large numbers of securities in small denominations in exchange for savings funds. Furthermore, savings intermediaries make available opportunities for savers to save in small amounts, completely unrelated to the denominations of securities purchased with the funds pooled from many individuals by the bank or other intermediary.

Savings intermediaries also serve as a buffer with respect to the duration of savings relative to the duration of investment in capital goods on the part of users of savings funds. An individual saver may make deposits and withdrawals from his savings or mutual fund account usually on demand, independent of the duration of investment in capital assets made by a corporation with funds received from the savings intermediary. The intermediary is in a position to match the deposits of an individual against the withdrawals of others. But what about individual savers who prefer not to save through savings intermediaries, and what about the savings intermediaries themselves? Will they not want to commit funds for intervals less than the duration of business enterprises' investments in capital goods? The answer is clearly yes. For them there exist the opportunities provided by the *secondary* market in corporate securities.

• *Primary and secondary securities markets.* The markets for corporate securities may be separated into two kinds, based on the effects that transactions in those markets have on the money capital or funds of business enterprises. The two kinds of corporate securities markets are called primary and secondary.

Primary Corporate Securities Market. The primary corporate securities market consists of all transactions in which the money capital of business enterprises is expanded through the issue of new securities or contracted through the redemption, retirement, or liquidation of previously outstanding securities of the enterprises.

Secondary Corporate Securities Market. The secondary corporate securities market consists of all exchanges involving corporate securities *except* those in which a business enterprise is selling (issuing) or buying (redeeming, retiring, or liquidating) its own securities.

Clearly, it is only in the primary market that business enterprises can acquire the necessary new funds for capital formation. This does not mean that the secondary market (including national securities exchanges like the New York Stock Exchange) is unimportant merely because the secondary market does not *directly* affect the flow of new funds to business enterprises. On the contrary, were it not for the ability to buy and sell corporate securities independent of the lives of capital assets, the securities would be less attractive at the time of issue, and thus it would be more difficult for enterprises to raise new funds.

• *Adequacy of the supply of funds for capital formation.* Savers forgo consumption because, by investing in some form of saving opportunity, they expect to have a greater ability to consume in the future. Such opportunities exist, however, only because someone will put the saved funds to use in acquiring real capital goods and services with which they can earn sufficient amounts to reward savers adequately for supplying their funds, as well as provide a return for their own efforts. But the opportunities are really reciprocal. The investor needs savers willing to supply funds for returns that are not so large as to deny him an attractive residual return on his investment and production efforts. Two things discourage the level of reciprocal opportunities generated by savers and capital formers: (1) intermediaries that require too large a share of the funds that flow into both the primary and secondary markets and (2) fraud, deception, and manipulation by primary or secondary market participants.

• *The operational efficiency of the securities markets.* In order for the economy to generate a high level of reciprocal opportunities between savers and capital formers, and so enjoy a high and growing standard of living, the securities markets must be operationally efficient.

Operational Efficiency. A securities market is operationally efficient when all of the intermediaries and others who participate in the transfer of funds from savers to users earn no more than is necessary to induce them to provide their services.

• *Primary market efficiency.* The level of operational efficiency of both the primary and secondary capital markets can greatly influence the volume of funds that flow from savers to users and hence the level of capital formation. In the primary securities market the influence is quite direct, as the following hypothetical example illustrates:

Example 10-1 MMW Corporation's management has an opportunity to invest in new capital equipment, which, after labor and other operating costs, will return, through sales of products and services, enough to recover the invested funds in twenty years, plus 10 percent per year on the original investment in the meantime. To raise the necessary funds, the company is planning to offer twenty-year, $1,000 bonds on which it will pay 6 percent, or $60 per year, to savers in addition to $1,000 at the end of the twentieth year. It is looking forward to the deal, since it only needs to make for itself $35 per $1,000 borrowed to justify its efforts in organizing the necessary resources and taking the risk that things might not work out as well as expected. But upon talking to investment bankers the company managers are disappointed.

The bankers are convinced that savers will pay $1,000 each for the bonds. But, since the investment bankers will have to incur various promotional expenses and some risk in underwriting and "floating" a large issue of the bonds, they will remit only $930 per bond to MMW Corporation, taking an estimated $70 per bond for themselves. Unfortunately, if they went ahead with the deal the management would be faced with having to pay $60 per year plus $1,000 principal after twenty years to each bondholder, while the company would earn only $93 (10 percent of $930) per year on the proceeds of each bond, plus recovering the investment of only $930 by the end of twenty years. This would leave it less than the $35 annual, residual return that it requires to justify its efforts in the expansion. Additionally, the company would need to make up the $70 difference between its recovery of $930 and the $1,000 that it will have to return to the bondholders at the end of twenty years.

Thus management may decide to forgo the contemplated expansion. But this need not have been the case if the demands of the underwriters had not been so great. If the underwriters had agreed to remit, say, $970 per bond instead of $930, the expansion might have remained attractive to management. New capital would have been formed, additional employees might have been hired, and the total production of products and services of the economy possibly expanded.

• *Secondary market efficiency.* Inefficiency in the secondary market for securities can also discourage capital formation, but in a different way.

Example 10-2   Suppose that MMW Corporation found underwriters that were highly efficient and willing to "float" MMW's bonds for a fee of only $30 per bond, or 3 percent of face value. In spite of the reasonable efficiency of the primary market, the level of efficiency in the secondary market for securities might still discourage MMW from making its capital expansion.

For instance, suppose that brokers who actually place the buy-and-sell orders and complete the exchanges of securities in the secondary market charge exorbitant brokerage fees—say 3 percent of the selling price in a given transaction. Many savers who are willing to buy an MMW bond at the time it is issued, but who are not necessarily willing to hold it twenty years to maturity, would have to sell through brokers. If they thought that in the future, when they wanted to sell, the bonds would sell for $1,000, they would expect to receive only $970 after the broker's fee. Faced with this prospect, they might not value the bonds at their principal or face value of $1,000 at the time of issue. So if they will only pay, say, $985 per bond at

the time of issue because of high broker's fees for resale, then, even with
low underwriting fees of $30 per bond, MMW will only receive $955 per
bond from the underwriters ($985 − $30). This, again, may be too little to
make the capital expansion worthwhile to the management of MMW Corporation.

In both examples, the key issue is not that any particular level of fees is too
high. But, if the level of fees prevailing at any time is higher than necessary to
induce the participants to perform their services, it will unnecessarily inhibit
the flow of funds between savers and capital formers, and thereby unnecessarily inhibit the formation of capital.

Presumably, the best insurance against excessive fees for intermediaries in
either the primary or the secondary market is the rigor of competition. Provided no intermediary or group of intermediaries can bar entry of competitors
or otherwise monopolize a part of the market, fees will be competitively low.
But in the absence of rigorous competition, on the other hand, there is a
definite societal interest in regulating or supervising the activities and fee
structures of intermediaries.

• *Fairness of markets—the source of the public interest in corporate financial reporting.* Savers invest their funds in corporate securities directly or
through intermediaries, in the expectation that the value of the returns they
will receive in the future will exceed the value of the funds they give up. The
actual returns that savers receive and/or the risks actually associated with
those returns depend upon the performance of the user of the funds—the
business enterprise. Hence the values, and therefore the prices, of corporate
securities at the time of issue or in later trading in the secondary market are
dependent on expectations of the returns the corporation will generate and
the perceived risk associated with the expected returns. It is through influence
on investors' expectations and risk perceptions that fraud, deception, and
manipulation by market participants can seriously retard the flow of funds to
business enterprises (capital formers).

Fraud, deception, and manipulation by some market participants increase
the general level of risk associated with investment in corporate securities.
Along with the potential for less-than-expected returns inherent in the economic pursuits of any business enterprise, each investor faces the additional
possibility that his expectations will turn out to be completely unrealistic because he has been deceived in some manner. This addition to the risk associated with investing in corporate securities means that the values placed
on those securities by investors will be less than they would be without the
threat of fraud or deception. (Recall the discussion in Chapter 3 of the relationship between risk and the present value of an investment.) But if the
expected prices that securities will bring from investors at time of issue are
too low, it may discourage corporations from securing the necessary funds
for capital formation—as was pointed out in the earlier examples concerning
the fees charged by market intermediaries.

Thus, in order for society to enjoy a high and growing standard of living,
it may be essential to minimize deceptive and manipulative practices on the
part of market participants. This objective is achieved, to a significant extent,
through requirements for fair and accurate reporting of all material facts—a
major source of which is the corporate financial report.

Historical Perspective on Government Regulation
of Accounting Practice

Today the corporate securities markets appear to be characterized by a reasonably high level of operational efficiency (although some brokerage fees and the administrative costs of some mutual funds have received critical public scrutiny recently). They are also characterized by a reasonably low level of fraud, deception, and manipulation. But this has not always been the case. The excesses of the decade preceding the stock market debacle in 1929 contrast sharply with today's securities markets. In the October 1959 *George Washington Law Review,* the chairman of the SEC recalled this observation from a 1938 congressional report:

> During the post-war (W.W. I) decade some $50 billion of new securities were floated in the United States. Fully half or $25 billion worth of securities floated during this period have been proven to be worthless. These cold figures spell tragedy in the lives of thousands of individuals who invested their life savings, accumulated after years of effort, in these worthless securities. The flotation of such a mass of worthless securities was made possible because of the complete abandonment by many underwriters and dealers in securities of those standards of fair, honest, and prudent dealing that should be basic to the encouragement of investment in any enterprise. Alluring promises of easy wealth were freely made with little or no attempt to bring to the investors' attention those facts essential to estimating the worth of any security.

Often based on the kind of promotion implied in the observation above, prices of corporate stocks rose in meteoric fashion during the middle and late 1920s. The *New York Times* simple average of the prices of the common stocks of twenty-five industrial corporations rose from 106 at the end of May 1924 to 449 at the end of August 1929. But in 1929 the Great Crash began, dashing the hopes and fortunes of so many who were victims of manipulation, or were denied access to sound information about the corporations whose securities they bought, or were just caught up in the atmosphere of greed and self-delusion encouraged by the dearth of such information. Between the end of August and November 13, 1929, the *Times* average fell from 449 to 224, or roughly 50 percent. The ensuing, relentless fall in securities prices that ushered in the Great Depression left the *Times* average at only 58 on July 8, 1932, or a total fall of more than 87 percent from the August 1929 level of 449.

In the aftermath of the Crash, during the economic doldrums of the Great Depression, many investigations were conducted to discover the causes of both the Crash and the Depression. No completely conclusive findings were possible, but several forms of actions were highly suspect, and public support to put an end to them was running high. Among the suspect actions were various manipulations and acts of fraud by both market intermediaries and corporate executives and promoters. Perhaps one of the most conspicuous was the lack of any consistent "hard" information on the financial standing and results of operations of many public corporations. This fact was lamented in print as early as 1927 by William Z. Ripley, a Harvard University professor of political economy and critic of American corporate reporting practices. In his book *Main Street and Wall Street,* Ripley describes his review of corporate annual reports of the time:

> Confronted with a great pile of recent corporate pamphlets on my table, the first impression is of their extraordinary diversity, in appearance, size, content, and intent. One premier concern, the Royal Baking Powder Company, fails to register any fiscal information at all, in as much as it has never issued a balance sheet or financial statement of any kind whatsoever for more than a quarter of a century. . . . Akin to it is the Singer Manufacturing Company, which handles 80 percent of the world's output of sewing machines. Neither hide nor hair of financial data for this firm is discoverable in the usual sources of information. The dance-card, bald balance-sheet, or picture book variety of corporation report follows hard upon these examples of complete reticence. . . . Yet colored pictures of factories, brightly lighted at night,—as some of these must well have been in view of their extraordinary success,—tell no tales. . . .
>
> Then there is the leaflet type, done on a single folded sheet of paper. This "tuppence ha' penny" variety, once common, is happily by way of passing out. Cotton mills are still in this stage, again with nothing but a balance sheet, and no income statement at all. . . . Or there is the pompous but empty type, suggestive of President Wilson's pithy distinction between men who grow and those who merely swell with the advance of years. . . . Other reports may well be designated the "business condition" type, devoting much attention to things in general and but little to their own affairs in particular. . . . And then there are the reports . . ., "all obfuscated and darkened over with fuliginous [sooty] matter." *

The two events that did more than any others to bring about fuller corporate financial disclosure occurred some six years after Ripley's book was published. They were passage of the Securities Act of 1933 and the Securities Exchange Act of 1934.

• *The Securities Act of 1933.* The two principal objectives of the Securities Act of 1933 are (1) to require adequate and accurate disclosure of material data, financial or otherwise, concerning securities to be sold in interstate commerce or through the mail and (2) to specifically outlaw fraud in the sale of securities whether or not newly issued, and to provide criminal penalties for offending parties, and remedies for injured parties. The law clearly stops short of directly rationing the flow of funds in the corporate securities market, that is, determining which enterprises are worthy of funds and/or the prices at which their securities may be fairly and equitably issued. Instead, the 1933 act is premised on full disclosure of all material facts about the issuer, leaving to a "free" market the determination of worth.

The principal means by which the first objective of the act is pursued is the requirement that before any security is sold or delivered across state lines

---

* William Z. Ripley, *Main Street and Wall Street* (Lawrence, Kansas: Scholars Book Co., 1972), pp. 162–64.

or through the mail, the management of the issuing enterprise must file the following:

1. All notices to be used to publicly announce the intent to sell securities
2. A registration statement
3. Circulars to be used to offer the securities for sale
4. Prospectuses to be used to describe the securities and the enterprise to prospective buyers
5. Advertising and promotional material

Both the registration statement and the prospectus required under the act must contain a recent balance sheet and several years' comparative income statements, audited by independent certified public accountants, ". . . in such detail and in such form as the Commission shall prescribe. . . ." It is this latter clause that gave first the Federal Trade Commission and later the Securities and Exchange Commission sweeping power over accounting principles and procedures.

For if the commission finds any part of the filings for a particular security objectionable, including any accounting practice incorporated in the statements, it may issue a "stop order" rendering the registration ineffective and the sale of the securities illegal.

• *The Securities Exchange Act of 1934.* The Securities Exchange Act of 1934 established the Securities and Exchange Commission and gave it authority to regulate trading in securities, securities exchanges, and the conduct and financial affairs of members of national securities exchanges along with other brokers and dealers. To accomplish its major objective of regulating trading in securities, however, the 1934 act extends the power of the commission over the accounting practices of business enterprises.

Along with requiring that trading on national securities exchanges be limited to securities registered with the commission, certain other provisions are directed toward the issues of securities "listed" (traded) on a national securities exchange. Among other things, the act requires that the issuers of listed securities file with the commission such annual reports (to be audited by independent certified public accountants if required by the commission) and such quarterly reports as the commission may prescribe. Furthermore, ". . . the Commission may prescribe, in regard to reports made pursuant to this title [law], the form or forms in which the required information shall be set forth, the items or details to be shown in the balance sheet and the earnings statement, and the methods to be followed in the preparation of reports. . . ."

Thus, as a matter of law, any business enterprise that wishes to have its securities traded on a national exchange is subject to the prescriptions of the SEC in accounting for its financial status and activities, both at the time of first listing on the exchange (registration) and thereafter. Any issuer of securities listed on a national exchange that violates the requirements of the 1934 act may have trading in its securities summarily suspended for up to ten days by the commission or up to ninety days with the approval of the president. Or, after appropriate notice and hearing, the commission may suspend for

up to twelve months, or withdraw altogether, the registration of the enterprise's securities.

Evolution of Accounting Policy-Making Institutions

Although the 1933 and 1934 Securities Acts clearly gave the SEC the
power to prescribe acceptable measurement concepts and rules right down
to the last detail, the SEC has never directly done so. Some of the original
commissioners favored an SEC-prescribed set of accepted accounting policies,
but others were unconvinced as to the desirability of that approach. Instead,
the commission has historically exercised a kind of veto power over objectionable accounting practice, otherwise accepting practices that have substantial authoritative support from the accounting profession. To facilitate
this approach, there has been an informal working relationship ever since the
late 1930s between the SEC and the American Institute of Certified Public
Accountants (AICPA). The AICPA, which represents about two-thirds of
the CPAs in the United States, has from time to time made authoritative
statements as to the acceptability of various aspects of accounting for business
enterprises; for the most part these have been understood by all concerned
parties to be supported by or acceptable to the SEC.

This informal working arrangement seemed to be advantageous to both
groups over the years from 1938 to 1973. The SEC has had the advantage of
the combined expertise of many of the most successful members of the accounting profession, who have served at no cost on either the AICPA's Committee on Accounting Procedure (1938–59) or its successor body, the Accounting Principles Board (1959–73). In addition, the SEC has automati-
cally had the official backing, in most accounting matters, of the major
national organization of the professionals who perform the audits (required
under the Securities Acts) of listed companies' financial statements. And, for
its part, the accounting profession has enjoyed the greater stature of being a
self-regulating profession, presumably mature enough to not require governmental codification of acceptable accounting practices.

In response to growing pressure from other interested organizations, however, the AICPA in 1972 approved a plan to place its traditional role of making authoritative pronouncements on the acceptability of accounting principles and procedures under the authority of a new organization, the Financial
Accounting Foundation (FAF). The foundation is separate from all existing
professional bodies and is governed by nine trustees (four practicing CPAs,
two financial executives of large corporations, one professional financial
analyst, one accounting educator, and the AICPA president serving ex
officio). The trustees of the foundation have among their principal tasks the
appointment and financial support of the newest accounting policy-making
body, the Financial Accounting Standards Board (FASB). This board, which
began operations in 1973, makes authoritative pronouncements on financial
accounting matters. As with the FAF trustees, who appoint the members of
the FASB, board membership is broadly representative. It includes four
practicing CPAs and three other individuals with extensive experience in
financial reporting. Presumably, this move away from near exclusion of non-
CPAs in generating authoritative pronouncements concerning accounting

practice will promote wider support in the financial community than had been enjoyed by the predecessor Accounting Principles Board.

Some Important Environmental Influences on the Formulation of Accounting Policy

Three major influences on the development, *by authority,* of acceptable accounting policy have been (1) the state of accounting practice prior to 1935, (2) the dynamic change in the business environment since World War II, and (3) the increasing "intervention" of (often conflicting) special interest groups.

• *Effect of pre-1935 accounting practices.* Accounting practice prior to 1935 was marked by two compelling features. First, the procedures and practices followed by business enterprises in representing their status and activities through financial statements varied greatly from enterprise to enterprise. This great diversity was uncovered early in 1935 when some twenty-five hundred enterprises listed on twenty national securities exchanges registered their securities for the first time under the 1933 and 1934 acts. The impression created was described in an accounting symposium at the University of California, Berkeley, in 1967 by Carman G. Blough, chief accountant for the SEC during those critical early years:

> Never before had so much information regarding the accounting principles, methods and procedures of business concerns been made known as that which became public during the first six months of 1935.

> For the first time it was possible to know of the many areas of differences that actually existed among the accounting practices followed by well known business enterprises. These differences soon became the subject of discussion, criticism, defense and analysis.

The second compelling feature of pre-1935 accounting practice was what seemed, in retrospect, widespread abuse by management of the rather liberal latitude it had in selecting and disclosing its accounting policy. Dissatisfaction with this degree of latitude was expressed as early as 1927 by William Z. Ripley in *Main Street and Wall Street*:

> . . . one turns in vain to many otherwise excellent statements for light as to whether the appraisal is based upon prices paid, upon the market value, upon reproduction cost, "prudent investment," or what not. The great packing concerns, now so largely publicly owned, have always been cryptic in their statements. The Federal Trade Commission in 1920 squarely criticised their inventories as invariably appraised on a market basis when sound accounting principles required basis of cost. This criticism concludes with the broadside condemnation that this accounting practice "casts doubt upon all the public statements and advertisements of the great packers." Nor may there be question that the virtual theft by bankers and the dominant stockholders from the public shareholders of the entire increment in value of their real-estate holdings in the stockyard district over a number of years,

by misuse of the holding company device in 1911, was due to a deliberate and willful failure to reflect the true state of affairs in the balance sheet. Whether such misrepresentation be understatement, as in this instance, or an overestimate, is immaterial for the purposes of this presentment. The wrong worked upon the shareholders and the public is as great one way as the other.*

The development of accounting principles after the inception of the SEC was marked by two responses to the state of prior accounting practice. An immediate but long-lasting response to management's latitude and apparent abuse of selection of a valuation basis for assets was recalled by Carman Blough as follows:

> One of the first members of the newly formed SEC to be appointed was a former General Counsel for the Federal Trade Commission who had been in charge of that Commission's very comprehensive investigation of the public utility holding companies. During that study the flagrant write-up policies of the holding companies and their subsidiaries and the havoc they caused when the crash came in 1929 and 1930 kept impressing themselves on the chief investigator to the point that their end became almost an obsession with him. It was only logical to expect that when he had an opportunity to outlaw write-ups he would do so. So strong were his convictions and so convincing were his arguments against write-ups that all of the other members of the Commission were persuaded to take a positive stand against them from the very first case in which the question arose.

Thus the principle that assets must never be valued at more than their original transaction cost became firmly established as acceptable accounting practice in SEC-related matters. Partly due to this early entrenchment, the conventional accounting model has dominated accounting policy to the present. As a result, the vast majority of present corporate financial reports are largely based on this measurement model. But the acceptance of this model is not without exception. For instance, due to the nature of their business and the character of the assets they hold, it is accepted accounting practice for mutual funds to value assets at current market (selling) prices. Nor is the conventional model accepted without challenge. That exceptions and debate exist is understandable, since no single model can be expected to apply equally well to all circumstances, nor to appeal equally to all interested parties.

An alternative to selecting a single model for all corporate reporting (one that seems to be increasingly important) is the specification of different models (measurement concepts) for different types of resources and/or obligations. Sometimes the use of different measurement concepts is prompted by the nature of the resource or obligation and thus applies to all business enterprises. In other instances, the differences are the result of situations experienced by particular firms, in which case they will only be evident on the financial statements of those firms. For example, it has been proposed that

---

* Ripley, *Main Street and Wall Street,* pp. 191–92.

inventories held for sale be valued at current market (selling) prices, and that inventories held for use in production be valued at current replacement costs.

Many other illustrations of this *eclectic approach* to accounting policy exist, and the trend in the past few years in the formulation of accounting policy seems to be in this direction. Such an approach has the positive feature of associating measurement concepts with particular economic resources and obligations which correspond fairly closely to the assumptions and objectives of the particular conceptual model. By focusing on more homogeneous clusters of items, the analysis of the appropriate model is clearly enhanced. However, the financial model of the firm (at least in current practice) requires that these individual valuations be summed, and income for the period determined. While no difficulty is encountered in generating a "number," what can such a single aggregate value represent? It is an amalgam of all the concepts underlying the individual valuations and thus may itself defy explanation. Whether this deficiency is a more serious one than the problem of attempting to associate a single measurement concept with all items within financial statements is something that future experience may reveal. In any event, eclecticism seems to be in fashion at the moment.

Another variation that has been proposed by some policy-setting bodies, but has not yet been incorporated into many corporate reports, is the presentation of a financial model of the firm prepared under one measurement concept side by side with the presentation of a financial model of the same firm prepared under a different measurement concept. For example, one proposal urges the presentation of financial statements based on the conventional accounting model side by side with a set of statements that incorporate general price-level adjustments (see Exercise 9-4 for an example of this type of reporting). Another proposal is to present two corresponding sets of statements, one using the conventional model and the other using current replacement costs. Obviously, this variation from the choice of a single measurement concept, or more precisely the presentation of one set of statements using a single measurement concept, could be extended to more than two measurement concepts presented side by side. Whether this type of variation will become accounting policy is yet to be seen. It does seem fairly clear that it is itself merely a variation of the eclecticism theme mentioned above. Thus we can characterize the current status of this type of accounting policy choice (i.e., choice of the appropriate financial accounting model, or measurement concept) as being one of "mixing and matching" different concepts with different types of situations and/or resources and obligations.

In the years immediately following 1935, the diversity and abuses in pre-1935 accounting practice created still another response whose influence is also still with us. From the first registration of so many companies' securities in 1935 and the discovery of tremendous diversity in accounting methods, the pressure was felt by the SEC and later, through the SEC, by the AICPA Committee on Accounting Procedure, to determine which methods (measurement rules) were acceptable and which were not. As a result, early in its life the Committee on Accounting Procedure decided to devote its attention to pressing current problems, reluctantly sidelining any immediate effort to develop a comprehensive and cohesive statement of broader measurement issues. The effect of this decision was (and continues to be) to limit, but not eliminate, management discretion in the choice of accounting alternatives.

• *Effect of changes in the business environment.* If the backlog of diversity and abuse originally distracted the Committee on Accounting Procedure from a broad and comprehensive approach, matters did not get better as time passed. After World War II, the tremendous growth in the economy and the change in many business practices put new pressure on certain areas of accepted accounting practice, and new and pressing problems were continually raised. Thus neither the Committee on Accounting Procedure nor its successor, the Accounting Principles Board, was able to devote much attention to a broad foundation for accounting for business enterprises—though the resolution to do so was renewed from time to time.

• *Effect of special interest groups.* We have seen that the development of accounting policy up to 1960 was largely a product of forces coming out of the Depression and the related federal and state legislation. While disagreements over proper accounting policy existed among accountants, regulatory officials, and businessmen, they were largely resolved in a low-key manner. The period after 1960, however, was as turbulent for the accounting policy process as it was for the nation. Disputes over permissible accounting procedures and methods burst onto the public scene as various interest groups pleaded their cases through whatever avenues seemed most promising, and the news media reacted in response to this purported exploitation of the investing public.

The power and influence of various interest groups within the business community created strong, and some argue inhibiting, pressure on the Accounting Principles Board. At the time the new Financial Accounting Standards Board was proposed, the following assessment of the climate surrounding the development of accounting policy was made:

> In several areas in which it [APB] proposed substantial changes . . . the Board bit off more than it could chew. It had to back down from ambitious preliminary positions.
>
> If an industry really got its back up, the Board proved unwilling or unable to override it. In oil-and-gas accounting, for instance, the major oil companies were already following the financial reporting the Board preferred. But a proposal to eliminate something called "full cost" accounting was regarded by newer and smaller companies as a life-or-death threat. *Their bitter opposition prevailed.*
>
> With industry assured a role in the proposed . . . [FASB], it's doubtful that panel would lightly regard the practical impact of its pronouncements. It would probably draw some lessons from the current Board's woes. "We have found compromise is the only way out of many of these things, and perhaps the only way to make progress," Mr. Defliese [Chairman of the APB] declares. "The Board can't opt for high theory and come out with answers totally unacceptable to business and government."
>
> Lately, the accountants have new worries from Washington. Last November, Congress stunned accounting authorities by denying them the power to decide how companies must account for the investment tax credit. The Principles Board had embarked on a course opposed by most of industry and many ac-

countants. Urged on by industry lobbyists, *Congress passed a law allowing taxpayers to account for the credit as they preferred.*

The accountants are fearful other interests will continue to appeal over their heads to Washington. One reason the oil companies prevailed is that they are known to have powerful friends. Already some opponents of proposed stiffer rules on leasing have prompted at least 30 Congressmen and Senators to write inquiries to the Principles Board.

Typically, those who intervene from Washington aren't concerned with the niceties of accounting theory. One letter-writer was Rep. Chet Holifield, an influential member of the Joint Committee on Atomic Energy. He was upset about the impact on nuclear-fuel leasing. Similarly, the Federal Power Commission recently preempted the Principles Board by specifically requiring of natural-gas companies a liberal accounting treatment the Board was moving to prohibit. *The regulatory commission apparently intended to encourage exploration for natural gas.*

This problem is bound to afflict the proposed Standards Board. . . . [The report creating it] urged that the private standards body become "more actively and intimately involved" with the needs of federal agencies capable of overriding it. The idea, the [report] said, was to educate the regulatory agencies about the importance of good accounting. But the federal agencies, with distinct priorities of their own, may prove difficult to "educate." *

The apparent success of special interest groups can only encourage them and others to continue their pressure on the accounting policy process. Thus the APB in the past, and now the Financial Accounting Standards Board, seem to function as a quasi-legislative, quasi-judicial body. The needs of various groups are acknowledged, and the board attempts to formulate propositions that are acceptable (and, it is hoped, equitable) to private individuals and the public as a whole.

But who speaks for the public? There is no question that the organized interest groups make their needs and concerns known. In a sense the APB, and now the FASB, have tried to assume the role of spokesman for the public. The members of these boards have been and are aware of the possible inequities that could be wrought upon the investing public, as well as the allocation of resources within the nation, if inappropriate accounting procedures are permitted to exist. Also, by law, the various regulatory commissions (including importantly the SEC) are charged with responsibility for the "public interest." This responsibility is, however, a formidable task for both groups.

Whether the Financial Accounting Standards Board will be successful in convincing the public that it is giving proper attention to the public interest remains to be seen. The board will apparently continue to operate under increasing pressures from a variety of sources, including more intense public scrutiny of its efforts. A system of countervailing powers seems to be taking shape in the accounting policy process. Whether the "power" of the public

* "Overhaul of Accounting Rule-Making Unit, Expected Today, Is Seen Reducing Conflicts," *Wall Street Journal,* May 2, 1972. Reprinted with the permission of The Wall Street Journal, © Dow Jones & Company, Inc., 1972. Emphasis supplied.

will become sufficiently strong to adequately represent this important, yet highly diffused, interest is as yet uncertain.

Review of Contemporary Corporate Financial Reporting

In the remainder of Part III (Chapters 11–17), we review some important areas of accounting policy and corporate reporting requirements that are necessary for understanding present-day corporate financial statements. Merely observing that the conventional accounting model has, in the main, been selected (or has evolved) as the conceptual basis underlying corporate financial reports is not sufficient. The user of financial statements must also understand the significance of alternative measurement rules *within the framework of this conceptual model*. We cannot in this introduction to accounting cover all of the areas for which alternative or controversial measurement rules exist. We have instead attempted to focus on issues that are broadly applicable to many companies' financial statements.

In our examination of alternative valuation models in Chapters 4–9, we did not distinguish between different types of business enterprises, like partnerships or corporations. Such a distinction has but few implications from the viewpoint of a general information model. However, at the level of measurement rules and institutionally imposed reporting requirements, there are some significant issues associated solely with the corporation, and particularly the *publicly held corporation*. We have elected to focus on this reporting entity for two reasons. First, financial reporting for the publicly held corporation encompasses a domain of accounting activities that has a significant impact on present-day economic and financial interests in the United States. It touches those business enterprises that control the great bulk of our economic resources, and it affects the investments (savings) of large and small investors alike. Similar importance can be attached to this area of reporting in many other countries as well. A second reason for choosing the publicly held corporation as our focus of attention is that it tends to influence and lead financial reporting in other segments of the economy. Thus, in the process of acquiring an understanding of the factors underlying corporate financial reports, one is also gaining knowledge of what is, or may soon be, the pattern of reporting practice in other parts of the business sector. Furthermore, private corporate financial reporting also affects to some degree counterpart practices in the public sector as well.

Questions for Review and Discussion

10-1.   Define:

a. Capital market

b. Primary corporate securities market

c. Secondary corporate securities market

d. Operational efficiency (of a securities market)

10-2.   Enumerate three factors that make the selection of one of the alternative financial accounting models for general use in present-day financial reporting more difficult than an individual information choice problem.

10-3.   Distinguish between financial accounting models (measurement concepts) and accounting measurement rules.

10-4.   Accounting policy is influenced by many different individuals and organizations, which for our purposes have been grouped into two broad types. Name the two types, and give an example of individuals or organizations that fall within each type.

10-5.   What are the consequences for society when there are imbalances between the level of savings and the demand for capital in the economy?

10-6.   A healthy market economy requires a capital market that performs two basic functions. Describe these functions.

10-7.   Why is regulation of corporate financial reporting—keeping it free from fraud and deception—in the public interest?

10-8.   Summarize briefly the principal objectives of the Securities Act of 1933 and the Securities Exchange Act of 1934, and describe the authority over accounting practice provided to the SEC by the acts.

10-9.   Enumerate the accounting policy-making bodies that have been set up by the accounting profession since 1935. What has been their relationship with the SEC?

10-10.   There have been three major environmental influences on the development, *by authority,* of acceptable accounting policy. Enumerate these influences.

10-11.   In the view of the authors, two features of pre-1935 accounting practice have influenced post-1935 accounting policy. What are those features and how has their influence been felt in recent years on accounting policy making?

10-12.   It has been said that the philosophy of the Securities Acts is to regulate the processes of capital formation and securities trading, but not to determine directly the allocation of money capital to firms. Explain.

10-13.   The president of a large public corporation, a prominent member of the business community, has buttonholed you at a social gathering and is complaining bitterly about SEC regulation of financial reporting. He contends that government regulation of the capital markets, or indeed any other markets, is very unhealthy for a free-enterprise system. In his opinion buyers and sellers of securities ought to be mature enough to look after their own interests without "big brother" watching over them. Furthermore, he asserts that society has no right to interfere if the individual does not want its protection. How would you rebut his contentions, assuming you chose to do so?

10-14.   Do you believe that accounting policy-making authority should be in the public or the private sector? Explain.

10-15.   As a special project, go to your library reference desk and ask for the index to the *Wall Street Journal* for a recent year. The front half of the index is a directory of companies whose names are followed by annotated lists of news items that appeared in the *Wall Street Journal* during the year covered by the index. Pick a company with only thirty to forty news items for the year.

1. How many of the news items contained accounting information?

2. Would you expect the same percentage of *accounting* news items for a company with more total news items?

3. Do you believe that some of the news events are irrelevant to external decision makers who have an investment or other interest in the company? If so, which ones? (Describe them.)

4. After seeing accounting news items in the context of the total news items for a company, what additional insight into the role of financial accounting do you feel you have?

5. Do you see some informational role for accounting outside the context of "news releases"?

6. Do you see some noninformational role for corporate financial reporting in the context of the capital formation process?

Exercises   **10-1.   The Investment Credit Controversy.**   From time to time over the last two decades Congress has included in income tax legislation a provision that permits companies making expenditures for certain kinds of capital assets (e.g., machinery and equipment) to reduce their income tax payments (usually in the year of acquisition) equal to a percentage of the cost of such assets. The intent of this particular "tax break" is, of course, to reduce the cost of capital assets relative to the expected benefits and thereby encourage companies to expand. This, in turn, presumably increases employment.

Accountants and managements have disagreed over the years as to how to account for the "investment tax credit," as it is called. Many accountants argue that the investment tax credit is a reduction in the cost of the assets acquired and should therefore be recognized as a reduction in expense (related to the use of the asset) over the asset's life. Others (including the managements of many companies), on the other hand, have argued that the credit is clearly a reduction of the income tax expense of the year in which it is recognized on the company's tax return.

In December 1962 the APB issued its Opinion No. 2 supporting the former position based on the following arguments:

> 12. In concluding that the cost reduction concept is based upon existing accounting principles we attach substantial weight to two points in particular. First, in our opinion, earnings arise from the use of facilities, not from their acquisition. Second, the ultimate realization of the credit is contingent to some degree on future developments. Where the incidence of realization of income is uncertain, as in the present circumstances, we believe the record does not support the treatment of the investment credit as income at the earliest possible point of time. In our opinion the alternative choice of spreading the income in some rational manner over a series of future accounting periods is more logical and supportable. [Copyright © 1962 by the American Institute of Certified Public Accountants, Inc.]

As the result of this reasoning, the board reached the following decision:

> 13. We conclude that the allowable investment credit should be reflected in net income over the productive life of acquired property and not in the year in which it is placed in service.

14. A number of alternative choices for recording the credit on the balance sheet has been considered. While we believe the reflection of the allowable credit as a reduction in the net amount at which the acquired property is stated (either directly or by inclusion in an offsetting account) may be preferable in many cases, we recognize as equally appropriate the treatment of the credit as deferred income, provided it is amortized over the productive life of the acquired property. [Copyright © 1962 by the American Institute of Certified Public Accountants, Inc.]

Unfortunately (for the prestige of the APB), in the months following Opinion No. 2 the SEC did not support the board, eventually announcing its official acceptance of the alternative treatment of the investment tax credit as an element of income (expense reduction) in the year in which it is applied to a company's tax bill. The APB was, therefore, forced to reconsider its position—resulting in Opinion No. 4, which was marked by dissent among members of the board but through which a majority of the board modified Opinion No. 2 as follows:

8. It is the conclusion of this Board that the Revenue Act of 1964 does not change the essential nature of the investment credit and, hence, of itself affords no basis for revising our Opinion as to the method of accounting for the investment credit.

9. However, the authority of Opinions of this Board rests upon their general acceptability. The Board, in the light of events and developments occurring since the issuance of Opinion No. 2, has determined that its conclusions as there expressed have not attained the degree of acceptability which it believes is necessary to make the Opinion effective.

10. In the circumstances the Board believes that, while the method of accounting for the investment credit recommended in paragraph 13 of Opinion No. 2 should be considered to be preferable, the alternative method of treating the credit as a reduction of Federal income taxes of the year in which the credit arises is also acceptable. [Copyright © 1964 by the American Institute of Certified Public Accountants, Inc.]

Although Opinion No. 4 represented a setback to the board's original position on the investment tax credit, some years later the board (with the composition of its members changed) revisited the issue. After conferring with SEC representatives to ensure support, the APB was about to reaffirm the basic position originally taken in Opinion No. 2 when the unprecedented action referred to in the following editorial appearing in the *Wall Street Journal* of November 23, 1971, preempted any further action by the APB or the SEC:

A VOTE FOR GIMMICKRY

Over the years, the accounting profession has had to cope with two forces that sometimes are in conflict.

On the one hand, it has professional and certain legal obligations to set and maintain acceptable and consistent standards for certifying the fairness and accuracy of corporate financial reports. On the other, it is faced with pressures from clients seeking to present their reports in ways most convenient to their own purposes.

Now, it would appear, yet another force, the United States government, is involving itself more heavily in the delicate balance of interests. From all appearances, moreover, the government is entering the lists not on the side of consistent standards but on the side of short-term convenience.

The argument is over how companies and their accountants should handle the proposed 7% tax credit on capital investment which President Nixon is pushing as an economic stimulant. The accounting profession, through its rule-making Accounting Principles Board, wants the tax-saving effect of the credit spread over the life of the capital equipment purchased, on the ground that this single method would make earnings reports consistent with each other and reduce year-to-year distortions.

The administration, on the other hand, fears that the APB approach would weaken the stimulative effect of the tax credit by preventing a quick recovery of the full 7% by companies that wanted to apply it to their earnings immediately.

Last week, the Senate sided with the administration, voting a provision into its version of the tax bill that would prohibit application of the APB rule. The APB says this could leave companies with a choice of three or more different ways of accounting for the tax credit and represents a decided step backwards "for the long, hard effort to achieve uniformity in financial reporting."

Indeed it does. And the reason all this comes about is the government's effort to make the economy, and its own record, look good through employment of a tax gimmick. In other words, the government is trying to do much the same thing responsible accountants have been trying to get corporations not to do for so many years.

The tax law still hasn't passed both houses of Congress. The APB may still win its point, but the chances don't look particularly bright. It is one thing to persuade a corporation to abide by "generally accepted accounting procedures." But it is something else again to persuade a government.*

Required:

1. Based on the above discussion and quotations, contrive a simplified example covering a two-year period in which a business enterprise acquires a long-lived asset to which the 7 percent investment credit applies. Make the following assumptions:

   (a) That all "other" revenues and expenses are alike for the two years

   (b) That income tax expense without regard to the investment tax credit is equal to 50 percent of the excess of revenue over all expenses other than income tax expense

   (c) That the new asset acquired in year one is expected to last ten years

---

* "A Vote for Gimmickry," *Wall Street Journal,* November 23, 1971. Reprinted with the permission of The Wall Street Journal, © Dow Jones & Company, Inc., 1971.

Using these assumptions, draw up income statements for the two years according to the two methods alluded to above.

2. In the *Wall Street Journal* editorial it was noted that the administration feared that the APB's position, if imposed on companies, would blunt the stimulating effect of the investment credit. Do you feel that such fears were warranted? In what sense, if any?

3. The *Wall Street Journal* editorial also expressed dismay that Congress had intervened in the process of determining accounting policy. Do you find such intervention surprising? Why or why not? Is such intervention justified in general (i.e., disregarding the facts in this particular case)?

10-2. The Oil Industry Accounting Controversy.   Below is an article from the February 16, 1972, edition of the *Wall Street Journal* describing the Accounting Principles Board's study of accounting policy for companies in the oil industry.

The accounting profession's rule-making body, already typecast as Caspar Milquetoast for repeatedly watering down stiff accounting proposals in recent years, appears ready to play the same role in a new drama.

Under heavy pressure from the oil industry, the Accounting Principles Board seems likely to reverse a tentatively proposed accounting change that would have sharply lowered the reported earnings of many oil companies, particularly smaller ones.

The board's Committee on Extractive Industries has decided to recommend to the board next month that the oil companies be allowed to continue using the controversial "full-cost" method of accounting. Insiders believe the board will concur.

The full-cost method gives a boost to current reported earnings of oil companies choosing to use the system because it permits them to stretch over a period of years such current costs as unsuccessful exploration and drilling expenses. Thus, they can report much higher earnings in the early years of an exploration program than they could if they charged off the expenses as incurred.

Most major oil companies shun the full-cost system and instead charge off these costs as they are incurred. But roughly half of the publicly held oil-exploration companies use the full-cost system, including Occidental Petroleum Corp., Tenneco Inc., Texaco Inc. and Texas Oil & Gas Corp.

Reflecting the importance of the accounting method to these companies, their stocks generally took a nosedive when the accountants' Extractive Industries Committee in November announced a "highly tentative position" withdrawing most benefits of full-cost accounting as practiced by companies operating in the U.S. and Canada.

BATTLE LINES DRAWN

Not surprisingly, these companies leapt into battle with the accountants. And not surprisingly in view of recent accounting board history, the companies apparently have succeeded in winning a reversal.

The board still bears scars from its protracted controversy over tighter rules for merger accounting. Over much of 1970, the board, badly split and under heavy pressure from industry, repeatedly weakened its proposals before reaching a compromise. (But the board has taken on a tremendous number of industries in recent years in attempts to make accounting rules more consistent. Currently keeping the board especially busy are guidelines for life insurers.)

Under regulations of the Securities and Exchange Commission and the major stock exchanges, corporate financial reports must be certified as conforming to "generally accepted accounting principles." It's the job of the 18-member Accounting Principles Board to set these principles.

Severely criticized for its sometimes bewildering and contradictory array of principles, the board in recent years has been trying to narrow the choices of accounting methods. In many cases, such as in accounting for oil-drilling expenses, the same basic costs may be reflected in shareholder reports in several different ways, to the confusion of shareholders and securities analysts. But the board's efforts, as in the current oil case, have often riled corporate treasurers, bringing reversals or compromises.

ANGUISHED OUTCRY FROM SOME

The vehemence of the attack by oil companies using the full-cost method stunned some accountants at hearings in November. Occidental called the committee proposal attacking full-cost "truly incredible." Underwriters said the proposed new rule would make it extremely difficult for smaller companies to get financing, especially in stock sales, because their earnings would be "distorted" downward.

A parade of companies using the full-cost method, their analysts, auditors and others, testified that the overall impact of adopting such restrictive proposals would be to discourage aggressive exploration just as the U.S. faces an energy crisis and just as U.S. oil and gas companies face the need to raise some $150 billion in the next decade for capital and exploratory spending.

Officials of "full-cost companies" that have already learned of the committee's reversal consider the battle won. But not all the analysts or accountants involved are happy about the reversal, and some complain that the committee caved in abysmally under pressure. "The whole thing was outrageous," fumes David Norr, a securities analyst, a committee member, and a partner in First Manhattan Co. "This was the howl of the mob determining accounting principles."

"INTERESTING EXCHANGES"

Joseph Cummings, committee chairman and a partner in Peat, Marwick, Mitchell & Co. in New York, concedes the companies using the full-cost method were quite upset and "a few interesting exchanges" took place. But he says the companies' arguments persuaded the committee to change course.

Committee members now are drafting their recommendations on oil accounting, for presentation to the Accounting Principles Board at a meeting March 8 to 10. Mr. Cummings says the recommendations will place certain restraints on full-cost accounting. But in effect the companies will be allowed to amortize, or spread out, their exploration and other costs pretty much as they have been, because they can still use an entire country or continent as a "cost center."

In accounting jargon, the "cost center" is the geographic area within which drilling and other exploratory costs may be balanced off against the income from reserves in that area. Under the present full-cost procedure, companies using the method have considered all of the U.S. and even all of North America as their "cost center"—meaning that they could capitalize all of the costs involved in a fruitless search for oil in, say, Louisiana, and balance them off against income from reserves in California over a period of years.

The harshly criticized November proposal of the Extractive Industries Committee would have narrowed the cost center down to a single producing field. Some oil analysts viewed this position as a compromise of sorts between full-cost advocates and those who favored immediate write-offs, because it did allow costs within the field to be accounted for as capital items.

SUPPORT FROM THE OPPOSITION

But to most companies using the full-cost method, the decision was clearly a death blow to their way of accounting. Even Robert Mays, comptroller of Standard Oil Co. (New Jersey), who as a mild critic of the full-cost method and whose company uses more conservative accounting, agrees that the proposal amounted to a rescission of most full-cost benefits.

"Companies frequently start out working within a broad geographic area of interest," he says, "and spend a lot of time and money identifying prospects in the area without locating a producing field. What do you do with all of the costs involved in working the whole area, the costs that can't be associated with a given field? The inference of the original (accounting panel) memorandum is that you would write them off" against current earnings rather than making them capital items to be amortized over several years.

In its review of oil industry accounting methods, the Accounting Principles Board is seeking to arrive at a set of principles to make the earnings of separate oil companies a good deal more uniform. But the uproar over the November proposals and the switch in position by the Extractive Industry Committee apparently are resulting in a continuation of two basically different ways of accounting for key expenses of oil companies.

There would, however, be some steps toward uniformity, if the committee recommendations are adopted. For example, all oil and gas companies would be required to capitalize (and therefore spread out) their costs for geological and geophysical work, property acquisition, carrying costs and several other expenses—practically all costs leading up to drilling.

Once drilling occurs, however, a company could go in either of two directions. If the well is a dry hole, a company could conservatively write off the cost of drilling it immediately, considering that field its cost center. But if a "full-cost company" drills a dry well, it will be permitted to consider the whole country its cost center, just as it does now. So it can stretch out the cost of that dry hole instead of writing it off immediately, provided it has offsetting revenues from enough proven reserves somewhere else in the country.

But critics of the plan say drilling costs generally represent a huge chunk of total expenses in exploration, and only a small percentage of wildcat wells strike oil in commercial quantities. They feel that allowing separate oil companies to treat such an important cost item in two different ways perpetuates a confusing dual system.

CHOICES IN OIL DISCOVERIES

Under the new committee proposals, a company finding oil also would have a dual choice. Under conservative accounting, companies could write off all costs, including predrilling costs, not associated with that specific find. A concern using full-cost accounting could treat that discovery exactly as it always has, capitalizing all the costs and lumping the reserves found into its total, nationwide pool.

The "full-cost companies," however, wouldn't be allowed to capitalize exploration and drilling expenses in an amount beyond the value of their existing national reserves (currently, there is no such limit). Also, under the new recommendations, oil companies would have to fully disclose expenditures on separate unsuccessful explorations, the amount of capitalization of these expenses, what reserves were discovered in given areas, and the quality of those reserves.

Richard Lemmon, adviser to the Extractive Industry Committee chairman, believes the new recommendations will bring a measure of uniformity to oil accounting. "Actually, we don't have just two accounting methods right now, but more like 200, because each method is applied with many variations," he says. "I think now we will have one accounting method, requiring the same capital expense decisions before discovery but allowing some flexibility afterward."

Others aren't so sure. Says one puzzled executive of a major oil concern, "None of it makes sense unless you've got a darn good astrologer on your staff." An accountant specializing in oil concerns says the Accounting Principles Board has "suffered through some big battles lately with the insurance industry and over investment tax credits." He adds, "So maybe they're trying some sort of compromise here. But any compromise which permits the two systems to exist is no compromise. It's simply walking away from the problem." *

Required:

1. At the time the article was written there were basically two widely practiced methods for matching the costs of unsuccessful oil and gas exploration efforts (which are presumably necessary costs of discovering oil and gas deposits) against the revenues of present and future periods. Describe the two methods as best you can, and, if possible, contrive a simple example to contrast the effects of the two methods on financial position and income.

2. The Accounting Principles Board initially favored one of the methods. Which one did it favor?

3. Some parties (entities) thought they would be penalized by limitation of ac-

---

* G. Christian Hill, "Wildcatter Wrangle," *Wall Street Journal,* February 16, 1972. Reprinted with the permission of The Wall Street Journal, © Dow Jones & Company, Inc., 1972.

ceptable accounting practice to the method initially favored by the board. Name the parties (entities), and explain why they felt as they did.

4. What benefits were alleged to be associated with limiting the acceptable alternatives for accounting for unsuccessful exploration costs?

5. The board ultimately changed its position. Did the change apparently take place exclusively because the board felt it was initially wrong on theoretical grounds? If not, what other grounds for the change are alluded to?

6. Do you feel that the board was right or that it was wrong in its decision? If you cannot decide, state "in principle" why not.

10-3. The 1974 Ponzi Caper.   Below are some excerpts from the *Wall Street Journal* of June 26, 1974, describing an investment scheme in which a number of prominent business, government, and entertainment figures might lose up to $100 million.

> Walter B. Wriston is chairman of First National City Bank, the nation's second largest. Fred J. Borch is former chairman of General Electric Co. Russell W. McFall is chairman and president of Western Union. George J. W. Goodman is the pseudonymous financial supersophisticate, "Adam Smith," who wrote "The Money Game." Murray I. Gurfein is the U.S. district judge who wrote the "Pentagon Papers" decision. You already know Jack Benny, Liza Minnelli, Walter Matthau and Barbra Streisand.
>
> Along with some 2,000 other rich and not-so-rich Americans, they appear to have fallen victim to what the Securities and Exchange Commission alleges is a classic swindle: a Ponzi scheme.
>
> This may be the biggest swindle of its kind in history. The investors, whose stakes in some cases exceed $500,000, are estimated to have put into it a total of more than $130 million. Of that, possibly $100 million or more has gone astray.
>
> It has vanished into a now-bankrupt oil-drilling operation whose cast of characters, and props, includes a persuasive Oklahoma oil lawyer, Robert S. Trippet; a California vegetable farm's irrigation piping, painted oil-field orange; an Oxford-accented salesman and his well-placed colleagues, who wined and dined prospects at places like the Twenty One Club; and a bevy of accountants and lawyers, including a partner in one of Wall Street's biggest and most prestigious old firms, Simpson Thacher & Bartlett, whose presence allegedly helped assure everybody that everything was proper.
>
> **A CRIMINAL INVESTIGATION**
>
> Persuasive, also, were handsome payouts to some early investors, who thus were encouraged to increase their stakes unaware that most of the money really was coming from their own or other investors' funds rather than from legitimate business activity. And that is what makes a Ponzi scheme. It's named after Charles Ponzi, a Boston confidence man active in 1919 and 1920, who promised $1.40 in 90 days for every $1 invested and, for a while, delivered. He took in $10 million before he was arrested, tried and imprisoned for more than five years for fraud and larceny.

The current case centers on Home-Stake Production Co., a Tulsa tax-shelter oil-drilling company, unrelated to Homestake Mining Co. of San Francisco. The Securities and Exchange Commission, which first took action against it in 1971, declared it insolvent in a little-noticed proceeding last September. The SEC is conducting an intense criminal investigation of its affairs. At least one federal grand jury is expected to convene soon, probably in Los Angeles or in New York, to hear evidence. Meanwhile, the trustee in Home-Stake's bankruptcy and four groups of Home-Stake investors have filed suits in federal and state courts in Tulsa accusing the principals of wrongdoing.

The principals generally deny having done anything wrong. Lawyer Trippet, who founded Home-Stake in 1955, took its drilling programs public in 1964 and ran it until he resigned last summer, has consented to a court injunction against securities-law violations without admitting or denying any charges by the SEC. He says he acted in "good faith" in raising money for oil drilling and warned investors that the ventures were risky. He denies charges by the SEC and others that false statements were made to investors. He notes that no court has resolved any of the factual or legal questions raised. Otherwise, he declines to discuss any specific charges on the ground that the issues are in litigation.

SOME REFUNDS

The four groups of Home-Stake investors, in their suits, have accused Harry Heller, partner in charge of Simpson Thacher's Washington office, of either knowing or failing to exercise enough care to know, that Home-Stake was engaged in illegal activities. In each year from 1964 through 1971, Mr. Heller passed upon the legality—and thus, according to the investors, lent his reputation to the veracity—of the Home-Stake circulars that offered them participations in its subsidiaries' yearly oil-drilling programs.

Mr. Heller denies any impropriety. Simpson Thacher is a defendant, too, though there's no evidence that the firm's other partners had anything to do with Home-Stake.

The story is incomplete. But investigators have turned up evidence to suggest that Home-Stake used little, of the $130 million or so it took in, for drilling. In one year, for example—1970—the Internal Revenue Service has alleged that the company used less than $3 million to drill for oil of the $23 million it raised from the sale of participation units, or shares, in its drilling program.

For that year the company did refund about $5 million to unhappy investors made wary by an SEC complaint that the offering was misleading. What happened to the rest of the money that year and other years is unclear. Royce H. Savage, Home-Stake's court-appointed trustee, has accused Mr. Trippet of diverting more than $3 million to his own use and, among other things, causing Home-Stake to provide members of his family with cars and credit cards for personal use.

Home-Stake's selling expenses clearly were very high. And some money was handed out in loans (which haven't all been repaid) and other payments to lawyers and accountants who encouraged their clients to invest in the drilling programs. This isn't necessarily illegal, but in some circumstances it can be. It also can be unethical.

Mr. Trippet, 56 years old, a graduate of the University of Oklahoma, is said to be one of the first men in the U.S. to discern the appeal of oil-drilling ventures as tax shelters for wealthy people. The total investment in them usually is tax-deductible right away. The typical investor buys in near year-end, when he gets around to tax planning. Mainly seeking a fast write-off, he doesn't necessarily expect a fast profit.

So the investor isn't especially suspicious when initial returns come slowly, and he is pleasantly surprised when big returns come fast. One group of New Yorkers invested $200,000 in Home-Stake's 1966 drilling program and $365,750 in 1967. When early returns proved better than expected, they stepped up their investment to $2.2 million in 1968 and $1.3 million in 1969. Then returns began to fall far short of projections. Some investors had been told their total return, taking tax breaks into account, might reach 700%.

There was an additional twist. The returns were distributed unequally, apparently sized to keep individual investors happy. For example, John D. Lockton, former treasurer of GE, invested $50,000 in the 1970 Home-Stake drilling program. He got a return of $2,418, or 4.8%. Western Union's Mr. McFall invested $60,000 in the same program and got a return of $6,220—or 10.4%.

Mr. McFall had made his first investment of $38,000 in 1966. His yearly outlay rose to $60,000 in 1969 and 1970, and $140,000 in 1971. By 1972, returns had dwindled and Mr. McFall kicked in only $20,000. He won't discuss his losses.

The programs were sold most intensively in Los Angeles and in New York, where early key contacts for Home-Stake Chairman Trippet were William E. Murray, a well-known tax and estate lawyer, and high GE officials. Mr. Trippet already had known a few of the GE officers; others he met through Mr. Murray, who had done legal work for some of them. Back in 1960, Mr. Borch, then a GE vice president, invested $28,000. He increased his investments to $31,360 in 1961, to $132,160 in 1964 and to $209,000 in 1965.

Eventually, at least two dozen present and former GE officials poured a total of more than $3.7 million into Home-Stake drilling programs. Mr. Lockton invested $567,000; Herman L. Weiss, now a vice chairman, invested $570,180.

Another fat New York target was the high command of First National City Bank. George S. Moore, then president and later chairman, invested $56,400 in 1964 and $256,500 in 1965, cutting back to $57,000 in 1967 and $38,000 in 1968. The current chairman, Mr. Wriston, started with an $18,800 outlay in 1964 and invested $38,000 to $40,000 in each of the next five years.

"I SHOULD HAVE LISTENED"

Home-Stake men dropped the names of GE and Citibank investors to attract others. Hoyt Ammidon, chairman of New York's U.S. Trust Co., recalls that Mr. Murray introduced Robert Trippet to him, and the two stressed that GE and Citibank officers had invested.

"Because these two organizations, including the head of the oil department at Citibank (William I. Spencer, now president), liked it, it appeared to me to have merit," Mr. Ammidon says. He invested more than $114,000 from 1966 through 1969. "The people in our own oil department were against it from the beginning," he says. "Had I been smarter I would have listened to them."

Mr. Ammidon's name helped attract still other investors: among them, Howard D. Brundage, executive vice president of J. Walter Thompson Co., the advertising agency, and Chester W. Nimitz Jr., chairman of a Connecticut scientific-instruments concern, son of the World War II Navy hero and himself a retired rear admiral. Many other major investors relied on the example of trusted peers and made little effort to investigate Home-Stake on their own.

Had they done so, however, they might have shared the experience of some investors who did look at Home-Stake's oil operations in Central California in the late 1960s. Harvey L. Garland, then operations manager, says the company had drilled five wells on a vegetable farm near the small town of Santa Maria. To make things look more impressive, he says, Home-Stake officials got permission from the farmer to paint some of his gray concrete irrigation pipes orange and code them with oil-field markings. Wells hadn't even been drilled at these locations, Mr. Garland says.

*   *   *

TARDY TAX SLEUTHS

The IRS and the SEC, both understaffed and lacking tax-shelter expertise, were slow to investigate Home-Stake and other shelters thoroughly. This was well-known among people selling them, and there's reason to believe that it encouraged shabby practices. Now that the IRS has moved, it is barred in many cases by a three-year statute of limitations from challenging deductions and collecting extra taxes for years prior to 1970. Generally, investors didn't criminally falsify their deductions, because they didn't know their money was being used questionably. Thus they aren't subject to fraud proceedings, on which the statute of limitations runs longer.

Before last April 15, however, the three-year deadline for action on 1970 returns, the IRS got waivers of the deadline from many investors, and it is moving to get waivers for later years. Taxpayers can be induced to waive the protection of the statute of limitations by an IRS threat to immediately assess whatever extra tax the IRS thinks is due.

If deductions for 1970 and later are barred by the IRS, some tax lawyers believe, investors still will be able to take theft loss deductions for their initial outlays on the ground that the investments were obtained by fraud.

In any event the Treasury is out many millions of dollars, which will eventually have to be made up by other taxpayers. The IRS and state tax men have claims against Home-Stake itself exceeding $30 million, according to Home-Stake's bankruptcy trustee. The tax claims alone far exceed the company's $18.6 million in assets estimated by a recent audit by Coopers & Lybrand, the big accounting firm.

Nobody has determined the total dimensions of the Home-Stake disaster with any real precision. Estimates have it that the company sold $3 million in common stock as well as roughly $130 million in drilling units since the late 1950s. The stock is considered by many to be practically worthless. The company is believed to have returned roughly $30 million to investors in one form or another, thus indicating a total loss of more than $100 million, excluding tax savings to investors that the IRS was too late to challenge.

Some investors now concede they should have been more careful. In 1967 Home-Stake parted company with its auditing firm, Arthur Andersen & Co., after Andersen qualified its certification of Home-Stake's 1966 annual report. "I became suspicious a couple of times, when they fired their auditors and one thing and another," says Ralph A. Hart, former chairman of Heublein Inc. "But he"—Mr. Trippet—"was such a good salesman I just kept on buying."

From 1961 through 1970 Mr. Hart put more than $322,000 into Home-Stake. He is among those suing for his losses.*

Required:

1. How did the promoters manage to lure so much money out of so many people?
2. Many of the people involved apparently did not attempt to obtain or evaluate any accounting information about the concern in question. Was that wrong or irrational on their part?
3. There are civil and criminal penalties for the kinds of wrongdoing allegedly engaged in by the promoters in this case which may be applied to satisfy (at least in part) the complaints of people who lost money. Are there any other victims besides those who invested directly in this particular case? Explain your position.
4. Besides the penalties for wrongdoers in such cases (which no doubt act as deterrents), is there any reason for society to actually prevent the wrongdoing from taking place? If so, what steps might have been taken in this case?

10-4. The Fair Market Value Controversy.   We have seen that current accounting policy embraces, in the main, the conventional accounting model as its guiding measurement concept. It was noted, however, that certain exceptions are made for specific industries or specific types of resources or obligations.

In early 1971 the Accounting Principles Board considered a possible exception. It seemed at that time tentatively inclined to recommend that investments by an enterprise in the stock of another company should be valued at current market value (selling prices) rather than at historical cost. This valuation method was to apply only where the company held investments of less than 20 percent of another company's stock; where a greater interest prevails, different (other than historical cost) accounting methods already prevail.

The treatment of the value increment that results from adopting market value and thereby adjusting the cost price of the equity investments to a larger or smaller value was not fully resolved. As indicated in our relatively brief examination of the current market-value concept in Chapter 8, the value increment may be regarded as income of the period. Indeed, this recognition of income at the time of the corresponding change in the value of the asset is a major objective of applying

---

* David McClintick, "The Big Write-off," *Wall Street Journal,* June 26, 1974. Reprinted with the permission of The Wall Street Journal, © Dow Jones & Company, Inc., 1974.

the market-value concept. However, other possible treatments of the value increment had been considered by the board.

To permit various interest groups to express their position on this proposed
change in accounting policy, the Accounting Principles Board held a public hearing in May 1971. This open hearing, which was the first such forum open to interested parties before opinions were issued, has now become a standard part of
the policy formulation process.

If any asset on the corporate balance sheet should be amenable to valuation
at current market prices, one would speculate that it would be marketable securities held by the firm. Thus one would not have expected this proposed change to
have generated much discord. However, the public hearing revealed significant
divergence in the opinions of various government and industry representatives.
Exhibit 10-2 contains selected excerpts from the testimony, both written and
oral, that was presented to the board on the subject.

Required:

1. Several different proposals for accounting for equity securities (asset valuation and related income recognition) were expressed in the public hearing.
   Based upon your review of the testimony in Exhibit 10-2, enumerate as many
   of these proposals as you can identify. For each of these positions, state briefly
   the rationale you believe supports it.

2. Summarize the general positions of the various interest groups identified in
   Exhibit 10-2.

3. If you were a member of the accounting policy-making body dealing with this
   question, what position would you support? Why?

Exhibit 10-2   SELECTED EXCERPTS FROM THE PROCEEDINGS OF THE
              "PUBLIC HEARING ON ACCOUNTING FOR EQUITY SECURITIES,"
                              MAY 25–26, 1971

1. *Position expressed by Securities and Exchange Commission:*

. . . while . . . the Commission is not unmindful of the changing nature
of the environment in which accounting is required to perform its function,
the Commission feels that the continuing weight of authority for continued
adherence to historical (acquisition) costs should not, and cannot, be lightly
disregarded. In this respect, the Commission is not yet persuaded that a convincing case for an across-the-board current value basis of presentation of
marketable securities has been made. (From SEC Position Paper, p. 354.)

2. *Position expressed by Financial Executives Institute:*

Referring back to the Committee on Corporate Reporting of the FEI, I
stated that we had a great divergence of opinion within that group on two
points. However, we were almost unanimous, first, that there was an inherent
danger in embarking on an isolated phase, such as marketable equity securities, of the broad question of fair value accounting; and second, there
does not appear to be an urgent and pressing need to concentrate on this
subject at this time, to the extent of issuing an Opinion of the Accounting
Principles Board. I must add that I have not noted anything at these hear-

ings to suggest any urgency. (From public testimony of Donald Hibbert, vice-president for finance for Kimberly-Clark Corporation and representative of the Subcommittee on Accounting for Marketable Securities of the Committee on Corporate Reporting of the Financial Executives Institute, p. 102.)

3. *Position expressed by Financial Analysts Federation:*

I will preface my remarks by describing the Federation briefly. The Financial Analysts Federation is composed of 42 societies in the United States and Canada which have an aggregate membership of some 30,000 financial analysts, and of these some 2,570 have earned the designation of Chartered Financial Analysts.

"Financial analyst" is a broad term which encompasses security analysts, portfolio managers, and executives who have responsibility for the overall direction of the investment function. Approximately two-thirds of our members are employed by institutional investors, and about one-third by brokers and investment dealers.

The position of the Federation on accounting for marketable securities has been prepared by our Financial Accounting Policy Committee, which is composed of twenty members. Mrs. Rosemarie Tevelow was Chairman of the Subcommittee on this subject and wrote the position paper, which has already been submitted. Unfortunately, Mrs. Tevelow had to be at another meeting today, or she would be here with me to present our views.

There were two dissents within the Committee on this paper. This position paper has been discussed by the Board of Directors of the Federation since its submission to the APB, but the Board has not formally approved or disapproved the paper. There has not been any opportunity to circulate the statement to the membership as a whole.

I will not read the paper, but I will summarize some of the key points. First, I think there is agreement that the conventional accounting concepts based on historical costs are not applicable to marketable securities. We feel that current values based on quotations in active markets are a far more accurate representation of worth than historical cost, which is really an incidental product of the timing of transactions. Consequently, we favor marking marketable securities to current prices, net of tax effect, as of the statement date.

While not within the purview of the present hearing, we favor also the treatment of marketable fixed income securities on the same basis as equities. Those securities are a major part of many portfolios, and are managed along with equities to achieve a maximum investment return within an acceptable limit of risk. While high quality bonds may differ from equities in their fixed return and repayment at maturity, they have, in fact, fluctuated widely in price in recent years. We consider them an inseparable aspect of total portfolio management.

Now, I should say that we have not made a study of the implications of this recommendation on life insurance companies. I think this would have to be considered, because of the substantial bond portfolios characteristic of this industry.

Our position paper favors the reporting of both realized and unrealized capital gains and losses in the income statement. The differentiation of realized and unrealized gains and losses in the income statement is meaningless when applied to securities which have liquidity and continuous quotations. An unrealized gain, sometimes referred to as a paper profit, can be realized quickly upon a call to a broker, or perhaps, if it is a very large holding, within a few days by a call to an underwriter. Furthermore, such accounting developments would be more nearly consistent with modern portfolio practice, which aims for a total return including both income and capital appreciation.

In recent years some insurance companies have begun reporting realized gains in current income, especially if they have been acquired by noninsurance holding companies. These realizations sometimes appear to be keyed to the management of total reported earnings, and therefore are not indicative of total investment performance for either the current year or for some longer period. Financial analysts have great reservations about managed earnings. I might add here that some insurance companies, possibly in trying to defend themselves against acquisition by other companies, have begun to resort to that type of reporting, presumably, in order to influence the price of their stock in the market.

We recommend that total portfolio changes, net of tax, be shown separately in the income statement. That is, they should maintain their separate character. This would mean, potentially, three segments of net income; that is, operating income, investment portfolio change, and extraordinary gains and losses. The sum of these would be net income.

We also recommend that for subsidiary companies portfolio changes in each period should keep their separate identity in consolidation at the parent company level.

The Committee could see no strong justification for industry exceptions, except for mutual funds, which are deemed to report satisfactorily on the present basis. If, however, a company which owns a few incidental securities but does not manage an investment portfolio is exempted by APB Opinion, we believe it should make disclosure of current market values nonetheless.

Two members dissent from the Committee's statement, and one statement of dissent has been submitted with the position paper. In addition, a number of our directors, who are all experienced investment men, showed some disagreement with the paper, although no formal vote was taken. I would like to summarize some of these objections.

The primary reservation was related to the significance and utility of a total net income per share figure which includes both realized and unrealized portfolio gains. It was felt that such a figure would be too volatile on a year-to-year basis to be of much use for true valuation of a company or its securities. Some expressed the view that they would have to "work around" such a figure, probably concentrating on operating earnings, as has happened with bank stocks. They believe they would be able to take care of themselves, so to speak, but wondered whether the individual with less time and knowledge could cope with the proposed reporting equally well. I think that consideration must be given to the reporting procedure in newspapers as well as in annual reports in this connection. However, the Federation has made no studies or surveys to predict the effect of portfolio change volatility on security valuation.

In general, all felt that current market value was the proper balance sheet representation, not historical cost. Also, with two exceptions, all felt that inclusion of only realized gains in net income was unsatisfactory, because of the opportunity for managing earnings. Two dissenters felt that volatility of earnings which included all portfolio changes would be too great, and favored essentially the present practice. (From public testimony of William C. Norby, executive director of the Financial Analysts Federation, pp. 108–10.)

4. *Position expressed by the insurance industry:*

Mr. Jones, the President of our Association [American Insurance Association], has just outlined our position relating to the reporting of equity securities. The philosophy and underlying reasons on which this position is based are clearly and completely described in the paper which we submitted to the Accounting Principles Board. However, there are certain aspects of this problem which are so important that I would like to take a few minutes to review them with you.

Accounting for equity securities has very significant effects for insurance companies. There are few if any other industries affected to the same extent. Insurance companies invest in equities in order to obtain favorable investment returns over a long period of time, and they do not invest—and, in fact, in some instances are prohibited from investing—in these securities for short-term speculative purposes.

Insurance companies invest large amounts in equities. For many companies the carrying value of equities in the portfolio is measured in hundreds of millions of dollars, and for some companies the amount may approach or even exceed a billion dollars. The capital gains and losses arising from these large portfolios are sizable, and fluctuate widely from year to year. The largest portion of these capital gains is unrealized.

It is apparent that this problem of accounting for equity securities cannot be viewed lightly by the insurance industry. Perhaps the most difficult portion of this accounting problem is the assignment of these capital gains and losses to the proper accounting period. A comparison of characteristics of fixed income obligations, such as bonds, with that of stocks clearly illustrates this problem.

The purchase price of a bond is determined so that the investor will achieve a certain determinable yield over the life of the investment. At the time of purchase the interest payments, or coupon amounts, are known, and there are definite commitments that such payments will be made. The period of the investment is readily determinable, and the appreciation can easily be computed by comparing the maturity value with the cost. Thus it is a simple matter to not only assign the interest payments but also the precise portion of the appreciation attributable to any one accounting period in a manner consistent with the underlying philosophy and objectives under which the investment was made.

For common stocks the situation is entirely different. There is no single rate of return which serves as the basis for determining the cost. There is no commitment that the dividend will be paid each year. The length of the investment period is indefinite, and the ultimate amount of the appreciation is not determinable. Therefore, it is impossible to accurately assign among an unknown number of accounting periods appreciation which cannot be determined, although a number of methods of accomplishing this have been suggested.

One method includes as part of net income only the realized portion of capital gains and losses attributable to equitable securities. Thus it is implied that all such gains and losses over a long period of time become part of the earned income at the instant a sale is consummated. We know this is not correct.

Another method includes the net income and both realized and unrealized capital gains and losses as they occur. This implies that the instantaneous market values at the beginning and end of the accounting period have a significant relationship to the long-term investment policy. We know this also is not correct.

Then, finally, there is the formula basis by which these capital gains and losses are included in net income. This method creates an appearance of accuracy which is more apparent than real, and tends to camouflage with mathematical detail the real problem of assigning income to the proper accounting period.

There is even some disagreement among advocates of this method. Some, in order to reflect long-term trends, favor a formula involving a long period of time—say, ten or fifteen years. Others feel that a formula involving, say, more than five years tends to obscure current trends, but they recognize that a formula involving less than five years—say, three years—encounters problems because of severe annual fluctuations.

Because of the nature of these gains and losses and the associated common difficulties, there has never been the same degree of credibility attached to capital gains and losses as has been attached to income arising from other sources. For example, financial analysts, when assessing the potential of a corporation, often give little or no weight to the appreciation in equity securities. It is apparent from the position taken by the various insurance industry associations that most managements favor a separate statement approach in reporting capital gains and losses. Regulatory authorities often require the subsequent reporting of capital gains and losses in financial statements.

These are some of the considerations which led our Association to take the position that appreciation of equity securities is a part of total gains, but the characteristics of this portion of our reports are so different from the characteristics of that portion derived from other sources that it should be reported separately, so that meaningful analysis can be made. (From public testimony of Robert McMillen, vice-president and actuary for the Travelers Insurance Companies and speaking as chairman of the Accounting Committee of the American Insurance Association, pp. 6–7.)

11

Revenue Recognition and Related Valuation Issues

Conventional accounting income measurement was originally introduced in the context of alternative forms of information that the business enterprise could provide to a broad class of external decision makers to aid them in making their investment decisions. In looking at the structure of the investment decision problem, we noticed that the investor was primarily interested in the amount and timing of future cash flows to be derived from the enterprise. Our goal, therefore, was to develop an information model that gave investors some indication of the demonstrated future cash-generating abilities of the firm. To the extent that the investor is able to estimate the future cash flows of the firm, he will have made considerable progress in estimating the cash flows that will ultimately come to him.

Although reporting directly on the historical cash flows experienced by the firm satisfied our desired criteria of factually based and objective information, we observed that these actual cash flows often produce a significantly distorted representation of the future cash-generating abilities of the firm. Consequently, we considered next a model that attempted to unscramble and rearrange the firm's experienced and anticipated cash flows in order to provide an index of the long-run cash-generating ability of the firm. This index is conventional accounting operating income.

The emphasis in the conventional accounting model is on measuring efforts and accomplishment, matching these two measurements, and associating the net amount (net operating income) with periods of time. The presumption is that income measured in this manner is in most cases a reasonable index of the firm's long-run cash-generating ability. Whether this presumption is true or not depends importantly (but not exclusively) on the manner in which we assess the efforts and accomplishments of a period of time.

We considered briefly in Chapter 4 the nature of efforts and accomplishments when the conventional accounting model was introduced. We now propose to examine more carefully the properties of these two principal components of conventional accounting income measurement. Specifically, we will examine how these general concepts are applied to some important classes of transactions, and a few of the conditions under which the concepts are modified in current corporate financial reporting. In this chapter our focus is on the measurement of accomplishments—revenue recognition and related valuation issues. In the next two chapters we turn our attention to the problems associated with the measurements of efforts—expense recognition and related valuation issues. In the process of examining the measurement of the resource flows associated with enterprise efforts and accomplishments, we will cover most of the major valuation issues associated with resources and obligations appearing on the statement of financial position. This more intensive analysis of the basic concepts of conventional accounting income measurement should enable the reader to gain a significantly greater understanding of present-day financial statements.

REVENUE—MEASUREMENT AND ASSOCIATION WITH PERIODS

The Objective of Revenue Recognition

Business activity generally takes place continuously over many time periods. The "real" economic accomplishment of an enterprise for any particular period of time, we would postulate, is the total value that the enterprise has added to all resources (raw material, labor, buildings, etc.) that it controls, *by all of its productive efforts*. Measuring the total value added for each time period for which the enterprise reports (typically quarterly, and at least annually) is the objective or goal of the revenue recognition process. But if the total process of adding value is not started and completed within the period of time for which we wish to measure the accomplishments of the enterprise, the identification of the amount of "value added" during the period is subject to a variety of assumptions about future performance and market behavior. Therefore, our measurement ideal is modified under conventional accounting by the adoption of a revenue realization principle (or convention).

The Realization Principle and Revenue

The realization principle has been previously defined as follows:

The Realization Principle. Accomplishment (revenue) should be recognized in the period when the prices to be received for products and services provided by the enterprise (1) become reasonably certain and (2) have been "earned" by the enterprise.

The realization principle posits two fundamental criteria for the *timing* of the recognition of revenue: (1) earning has taken place, and (2) the price to be received is relatively certain. The first of these criteria is largely motivated by our goal of seeking to measure the economic value added by an enterprise during a particular time interval. But the criterion is somewhat more flexible (and conceptually, therefore, less accurate). It suggests that revenue, or accomplishment, should not be recognized *before* earning has taken place, but there is no requirement that recognition track precisely with earning *as* it takes place. This compromise in our operational measurement rule from our conceptual ideal reflects the practical difficulties often encountered in attempting to identify, step by step, the creation of value. Indeed, as noted below, the most common application of the realization principle defers recognition of revenue until all, or substantially all, of the earning process has been completed.

The second criterion stems from the basic thrust of the conventional accounting model to provide objective, factually based measurements. If a high degree of uncertainty exists concerning the prices that will ultimately be received for a firm's goods or services, it is usually considered more desirable to defer recognition of revenue than to attempt to estimate these uncertain values. This position is also motivated, as is the conventional accounting model, by the desire to limit the susceptibility of the measurements to fraud and manipulation. For example, management is often rewarded, directly or indirectly, on the basis of the reported accomplishments of the enterprise. Hence, we may on occasions encounter a management that wishes to report its accomplishments in the most favorable light. If a measurement concept is overly dependent upon uncertain estimates, the accounting results may be influenced by undesirable management motives. Accordingly, revenue recognition principles (as well as other conventional accounting measurement rules) are generally constructed so as to mitigate the possibility, or the appearance of the possibility, of this type of managerial action.

Under most circumstances in current financial reporting, the realization principle is satisfied by recognizing revenue at the *time of sale*. At this point in time, title to the goods or services usually passes to the buyer, and the seller has a legally enforceable claim in the amount of the price agreed upon in the sales transaction. Additionally, there is usually no major earning effort that takes place following the sale, and it is therefore appropriate to recognize the total accomplishment reflected in the selling price.

Thus, under the "point-of-sale" interpretation of the realization principle, revenue is or may be defined under conventional accounting as follows:

> **Revenue.** Generally, revenue is the sum of the selling prices (or fees) of all products sold and services provided to customers during the current period— whether or not the sales are cash sales or credit sales (credit sales are sales for which the customer promises to pay at a later time).

Although revenue for a period may differ (often substantially) from the total cash receipts from operations of the enterprise for the same period, recall that in the long run these two measurements will be roughly equal.

The point-of-sale interpretation of the realization principle is not, however, always the most appropriate interpretation. It represents one possible trade-off, or point of balance, between the two criteria specified by the realization principle—earning has taken place, and the price to be received is relatively certain. Other possible interpretations, or trade-offs, of these criteria range from, at one extreme, estimating accomplishment, or value created, as production progresses to the other extreme of deferring recognition of accomplishment until the cash price established by the sales transaction has been collected. We will now examine some general types of business circumstances under which alternative trade-offs are considered more appropriate bases for recognizing enterprise accomplishment than the frequently used point-of-sale interpretation.

RECOGNIZING UNCERTAINTY OF COLLECTION

Upon the completion of a sale transaction, the seller either receives cash or has a legally enforceable claim against the buyer. However, a legally enforceable claim is not a guarantee that payment will be received. Whether short term or long term, all receivables (claims against customers) have a common characteristic—there is some uncertainty about their ultimate collectibility. When the uncertainty is judged to be low, or reasonably measurable, the criterion of certainty of price to be received is considered to be sufficiently satisfied to warrant recognition of the earning that has taken place at the date of sale, with concurrent recognition of the estimated losses that will be sustained from accounts that, in retrospect, turn out to be uncollectible. However, when the degree of uncertainty regarding the ultimate collection of cash is high (most frequently when the collection period extends over a long period of time), recognition of revenue is sometimes deferred beyond the point of sale. We will first cover the procedures for handling the estimated losses from bad accounts when revenue is recognized at date of sale, and then some alternative ways of deferring revenue recognition beyond the point of sale under conditions of high uncertainty.

General Uncertainty Adaptation— Estimating Bad Debts

When a customer is unable to pay his account, we call the loss suffered by the business a *bad debt loss*. Obviously, one way of handling these losses would be to recognize them as an expense of the period in which it is determined that the account is uncollectible. But is this treatment consistent with the matching principle? Generally it is not. Because of the desire to exhaust all legal remedies in attempting to collect such accounts, recognition of bad accounts often occurs in periods subsequent to the period of sale. Yet, the matching principle clearly calls for recognition of the bad debt in the same period that the sale giving rise to the account is recognized as revenue. The reason is that in most instances the extension of credit and the concomitant acceptance of the risk that some accounts will ultimately prove to be uncollectible are costs directly related to the generation of the revenue recognized.

Indeed, some view the cost of bad accounts as one form of sales promotion expense.

How can this association between *future* bad accounts and related *current* sales be accomplished? Firms generally do not make specific credit sales that they expect to prove uncollectible. But they do have historical evidence of their experience with bad accounts, and using this experience base they can *estimate* the amount of bad debts that they expect to suffer ultimately from the current period's sales. This estimate then provides the measure of the bad debt expense to be assigned to the current period. Alternatively, the estimated bad debts may be disclosed as a direct reduction from the gross amount of sales in the period to reflect the estimated "net" amount of cash that will ultimately be realized from those sales. Both of these alternatives deal only with classification *within* the income statement. Whether treated as an expense or as a reduction of revenue, the estimated bad debts method associates or matches the anticipated amount of uncollectible accounts with the related revenue.

The recognition of estimated bad debts also involves an adjustment to accounts receivable. The balance of accounts receivable is reduced from the sum of the amounts due from the individual customers to the net amount estimated to be ultimately realizable from the group of claims against customers arising out of current sales. Since the firm does not know which particular accounts will prove to be bad, the adjustment to accounts receivable is normally made using a contra-asset account similar to the accumulated depreciation account. This valuation account is typically designated "allowance for doubtful accounts." Each time that estimated bad debts are recognized as an expense, the negative balance of the account increases. When an individual account included in accounts receivable is determined to be bad, the balance of the uncollectible account is deducted from both accounts receivable and allowance for doubtful accounts, with no resulting change in the net amount estimated to be collectible. The only way that actual experienced losses will influence the net receivable value reported on the financial statement is if an end-of-period review suggests that such losses were substantially different than originally estimated, and that therefore an additional (essentially retroactive) adjustment to expense and the valuation account is required. Because of a tendency toward conservatism in setting asset values, this adjustment is triggered more quickly by experiencing greater losses than were predicted; when the converse situation is encountered (fewer losses than predicted), the allowance may remain unadjusted longer until there is more evidence that the loss rate has actually changed.

Example 11-1   Easy Sales Company makes many of its sales to customers on credit. The treasurer's staff screens the credit application of each new customer before delivery of the first order. If the customer is judged credit worthy, the goods are delivered and the customer is billed by mail. If the customer is judged not credit worthy, the goods are delivered COD. As a result of this policy, only about 2 percent of total credit sales turn out in the long run to be uncollectible.

Sales and collection data for Easy Sales for 1973 and 1974 are as follows:

Year	Sales Cash	Credit	Collections of Accounts Receivable	Accounts Determined to be Uncollectible
1973	$50,000	$300,000	$245,000	$5,000
1974	40,000	360,000	370,000	9,000

The company adheres to a practice of offsetting the *estimated* uncollectible portion of new accounts receivable against its recognized sales revenue each year for income measurement purposes. At the end of each year (as well as points in between), all unpaid customer balances are reviewed for their estimated collectibility. If the balance in the "allowance" account is deemed inadequate to absorb the estimated uncollectible accounts in the balance of accounts receivable, an additional adjustment is made.

On January 1, 1973, the balances of accounts receivable and allowance for doubtful accounts were $40,000 and $1,500, respectively. At the end of 1973, the review of open accounts indicated that the end-of-year allowance was adequate to absorb the estimated uncollectible accounts. But at the end of 1974, it was believed that the balance of the allowance was about $3,000 lower than the estimated uncollectible portion of ending accounts receivable. The cause of the inadequacy was the totally unexpected bankruptcy of a customer who owed the company $3,000 at the beginning of the year.

The facts given in Example 11-1 are analyzed in the partial financial position worksheet in Exhibit 11-1. The partial worksheet includes complete data for only two accounts—accounts receivable and allowance for doubtful accounts, because these accounts are central to our examination of the treatment of estimated and actual bad debts. Columns are provided for two other accounts (cash and owners' equity), without beginning and ending balances, to permit the disclosure of the effects of only the relevant transactions.

The estimated bad debts related to a particular year's *credit* sales are recorded in the second line of the worksheet for each year as a reduction of owners' equity and an increase in the absolute value of the negative balance in the allowance account. Each estimate is 2 percent of credit sales for the year. The effect of the first two lines, therefore, is to recognize (1) the "net" revenue of the period and (2) the value of assets received as a result of current sales *at the "expected value" of customers' promises to pay.* The expected value of the assets received is, of course, represented by the combined balances in "accounts receivable" *and* "allowance for doubtful accounts." The expected value of current revenue is represented by the *net* increase in owners' equity corresponding to the nominal amounts of the new accounts receivable of the period *less* the associated bad debts expense. The third item on the worksheet in each year reveals how the recognition of actual bad accounts is handled.

At the end of each year, the balance of the allowance for doubtful accounts is evaluated to see if it represents an adequate estimate of accounts that the firm then believes will prove to be uncollectible in the future. The credit manager or treasurer generally makes this decision after reviewing the status of each unpaid account at the end of the year. In our example, the allowance is considered adequate at the end of 1973; but at the end of 1974, the review of the accounts suggested that the balance of the allowance for

Exhibit 11-1

EASY SALES COMPANY
Partial Financial Position Worksheet—Treatment of Bad Debts

Description	Effect upon Cash	Accounts Receivable	Allowance for Doubtful Accounts	Effect upon Owners' Equity
1973				
Beginning Balances	—	40,000	(1,500)	—
1. Sales	50,000	300,000		350,000 (R)
2. Estimated bad debt expense			(6,000)	(6,000) (E)
3. Write-off of bad accounts		(5,000)	5,000	
4. Collections on account	245,000	(245,000)		
Ending (Beginning) Balances	—	90,000	(2,500)	—
1974				
1. Sales	40,000	360,000		400,000 (R)
2. Estimated bad debt expense			(7,200)	(7,200) (E)
3. Write-off of bad accounts		(9,000)	9,000	
4. Collections on account	370,000	(370,000)		
5. Adjustment to allowance for doubtful accounts			(3,000)	(3,000) (E)
Ending Balances	—	71,000	(3,700)	—

doubtful accounts was understated by $3,000. That is, the net amount estimated to be collectible from the open accounts at the end of 1974 is believed to be $3,000 less than the net recorded accounts receivable (accounts receivable less allowance for doubtful accounts). Therefore, an additional adjustment of $3,000 is required (line 5 of the 1974 worksheet). This adjustment further reduces 1974 net revenue and increases the balance of the allowance for doubtful accounts (thus reducing the net accounts receivable).

Such an adjustment might be considered to be an "extraordinary" loss item, requiring special recognition in the income statement for the period. Indeed, if the estimating procedure has been fairly accurate in the past and this adjustment is largely related to the one unexpected event, there is considerable merit in this position. However, while this type of adjustment may be given special disclosure (a separate line) in the income statement, it may not be handled as an extraordinary item (i.e., it must be recognized as a deduction in arriving at *net operating income*) under currently prevailing authoritative standards for financial reporting. The reason for this restriction is that such adjustments may be jointly caused by (1) unexpected events or conditions and (2) management's estimation errors. Thus management might make its performance look better currently by purposely underestimating bad debt expense and later recognizing the estimation error (bias) as an extraordinary loss. The fact that such adjustments are not permitted to be treated as extraordinary items means that they will inevitably show up as part of future periods' performance (operating income), which presumably reduces the incentive for manipulation.

Adaptation to High Uncertainty—Deferral of Revenue Recognition

The bad debt estimation procedure is applicable to all situations involving credit sales, regardless of the period of time over which the accounts are to be collected. Use of this method permits timely recognition of revenue when sales take place, with an allowance for the normal uncertainty associated with the extension of credit. However, there are instances, such as in the case of *some* long-term installment contracts, where the uncertainty is so great that the bad debt modification of measured accomplishment does not adequately deal with the problem. Because of the high degree of uncertainty, the point-of-sale basis for recognizing revenue may be abandoned in favor of a revenue recognition basis that is tied directly to the collection of cash. The most frequently used cash-collection-based method is known as the *installment sales method.*

- *Installment sales method.*

Example 11-2   The Funtier Land Company has been organized to develop and sell lots in West Texas. The company's objective is to create a retirement community paralleling some of those already developed in Arizona and Florida. While the owners of the company believe that the climatic conditions are suited to this type of development, they realize that many potential customers may have reservations about the viability of the project. Under these circumstances, it will be difficult to sell the lots on a cash basis, or even on credit if the terms of sale provide for full payment to be made within a fairly short period of time. Yet some lots must be sold and building initiated if this potential customer apprehension is to be alleviated. Therefore, the developers decide initially to offer the lots for sale for $99 down, and $400 at the end of each year for the next five years. If a customer fails to make a payment on his contract within a sixty-day grace period after each annual due date, title to the land reverts to the developer.

Under conditions such as those described in Example 11-2, it is difficult to determine at the time of sale the amount of cash that will ultimately be realized from any single customer. Previous experience on projects of this type and risk indicates that many customers will default, often early in the life of the contract, and therefore the unadjusted total value of sales transactions of a period may be a poor indicator of accomplishment for that period of time. If a reasonable estimate of the potential losses from the installment contracts can be made, the total revenue can be recognized in the period of sale and the estimated bad debt expense matched against it. Note that the estimate of losses on bad accounts must take into account the estimated market value (perhaps the *cash* value) of the land that reverts to the developer upon default of a contract. However, the management of

Funtier may decide that it is not possible to make a reasonably dependable estimate of the number of land contract accounts that will default or prove to be "bad." Therefore, it might elect to recognize the profit from the transaction in some relationship to actual collections of cash using the installment sales method.

If the cost of each lot to Funtier Land Company was $1,099, the total profit to be recognized when the cash is ultimately collected will be $1,000 ($2,099 − $1,099). Under the installment sales method of recognizing accomplishment, the profit to be recognized in any period is determined by multiplying the $1,000 total potential profit by the ratio of cash collections in that period to the total cash to be collected over the life of the contract. This method is illustrated in Exhibit 11-2.

At the point of sale (1) the account containing the cost of the item sold is reduced by that cost (in this case $1,099), (2) the cash account is increased by the amount of the down payment ($99), (3) the account "installment contracts receivable" is increased by the amount of the installments (in this case $2,000), (4) a *negative balance* contra-asset account, "deferred income on installment contracts," is set up equal to the portion of the estimated income on the yet to be collected installments (in this case $950), and (5) owners' equity is increased by just the portion of total estimated income applicable to the down payment (in this case $50). Thereafter, as each installment is received: (1) cash is increased and installment contracts receivable is decreased by the amount of the installment (in this case $400), and (2) the negative balance of the deferred income on installments is reduced and owners' equity is increased by the portion of the total income applicable to the installment (in this case $190 for each installment).

Exhibit 11-2   REVENUE RECOGNITION PATTERN FOR
FUNTIER LAND COMPANY UNDER INSTALLMENT SALES METHOD

Year	Cash Collection	Ratio of Cash Collected to Selling Price	Profit Recognized
1	$ 499	$499/$2,099 = 24%	$ 240 (24% × $1,000)
2	400	400/ 2,099 = 19	190 (19 × 1,000)
3	400	400/ 2,099 = 19	190 (19 × 1,000)
4	400	400/ 2,099 = 19	190 (19 × 1,000)
5	400	400/ 2,099 = 19	190 (19 × 1,000)
	$2,099	100%	$1,000

• *Cost recovery method.* An even more conservative response than the installment sales method to a high degree of uncertainty is to defer recognition of income until the cost of the product sold has been fully recovered. Thus, in our example, no income would be recognized until cash of $1,099, equal to the cost of the land, had been collected. After the total cost had been recovered, all subsequent collections would be recognized as income. This very conservative approach, which represents an extreme form of the trade-off between the two realization criteria (in favor of certainty of price), has few supporters, however, and would probably be encountered only rarely in current financial reporting. On the other hand, the installment sales method of recognizing revenue is applied in current financial reporting by some companies, and by many more in the recognition of taxable income for types of business transactions qualifying for such treatment under provisions of the federal income tax code (because it results in a deferral of tax payments).

PROVISION OF JOINT PRODUCTS (GOODS AND FUTURE SERVICES) FOR A SINGLE PRICE

In many instances, a single sales price includes goods that are delivered at the date of sale and the promise to provide future services. The additional services yet to be performed by the seller, which may be of many different types, often include the provision of financing services and the warranty of products for a specified period of time. Whatever the type of service, it is inappropriate to recognize the total sales price as revenue of the current period, because the company has not satisfied the *earning* criterion of the realization principle with respect to the future services. Rather, the single price must be broken down into the amounts of compensation received for each of the two distinct products sold to the customer, and revenue then recognized as earned. The portion of the price allocated to the goods that are delivered at the date of sale may be recognized in that period in accordance with the point-of-sale interpretation of the realization principle. The portion of the price allocated to future services will be recognized as revenue concurrently with the delivery of these services. This procedure is illustrated below for the two types of future services specifically mentioned—financing services and warranties.

Providing Credit As Well As a Product to the Customer

When we initially considered the simple investment decision model in Chapter 3, we recognized that dollars received at different points in time are of differing values to a recipient because of his time preference for money. The present value principles developed in that analysis are equally valid for the enterprise because it has a time preference rate based upon the opportunities it has to invest dollars on hand. Conceptually, therefore, all contractual obligations of customers to pay agreed-upon prices for delivered goods or services at some future time should be discounted at the time of sale to determine the cash equivalent value of the credit sale. This cash equivalent (present value) of the future amount to be paid by the customer is our best measure of the accomplishment reflected by the delivery of goods. The remaining portion of the total contract price which will eventually be collected represents compensation for a second service—financing the purchase for the customer. Since this compensation has not been earned at the date of sale, it should not be recognized at that time. Rather, the "financing revenue" is recognized over the period of time that the loan is outstanding in accordance with the present value techniques developed in Chapter 3.

We should note, however, that in many instances the period of time between the date of sale and the collection of cash is of such short duration that application of the present value methodology would not produce a material change or difference in the measurement of accomplishment and the related valuation of accounts receivable. But when the length of the collection period is substantial, the difference between the present value and the total amounts due from customers may be important, or material, to the statement user. If it is, the present value technique can be applied to allocate the total price between the goods and the financing service.

Example 11-3   Referring back to Example 11-2, the Funtier Land Company offered lots for sale for $99 down and $400 at the end of each year for five years. Under these circumstances, the total price of $2,099 represents compensation for two services: conveying land and providing financing. To measure the values attributable to each of these two different services, we must calculate the present value of the sales contract. Assuming Funtier has a time preference rate of 10 percent, and ignoring the question of the degree of uncertainty existing as to the ultimate collectibility of the contracts, we can measure the present value of a contract as illustrated in Exhibit 11-3.

The calculation of the present value of the sales contract in Exhibit 11-3 implies that the Funtier Land Company would be willing to accept $1,614 today in lieu of the contract provision of $99 down and $400 per year for five years. Thus, the measure of accomplishment to be associated with the sale of the land is more properly stated at $1,614 than at the total contract price of $2,099. The difference of $485 ($2,099 − $1,614) is the amount of revenue that will be earned from providing the financing service over the five-year life of the contract.

Exhibit 11-3   CALCULATION OF PRESENT VALUE OF A
                    FUNTIER LAND COMPANY SALES CONTRACT

Year	Cash Flow	$PV_{(n,\ 0.10)}$	Present Value of Cash Flows
0	$ 99	1.0	$ 99
1	400	0.909	364
2	400	0.826	330
3	400	0.751	300
4	400	0.683	273
5	400	0.621	248
	$2,099		$1,614

The amount of revenue to be recognized each period from the financing operation is, as mentioned above, based upon the present value principles outlined in Chapter 3. At the start of the first period, the receivable from a customer would amount to $1,515—the $1,614 present value (or cash equivalent value) of the contract less the $99 down payment. Then, in the first year, the firm earns (imputed) interest income of 10 percent on the $1,515 balance, or approximately $152. Since $400 is collected at the end of each period, the balance of the receivable at the end of the first year would be calculated as follows:

Accounts receivable, start of year 1	$1,515
Imputed interest income (10% × $1,515)	152
	$1,667
Collection of first $400 installment at end of first year	400
Accounts receivable, end of year 1	$1,267

Continuing in this fashion, the firm will recognize an increase in the balance of the receivable (and a concurrent increase in owners' equity) due to the imputed interest income on the accounts receivable balance at the start of each year, and the balance of the receivable will be reduced each time a $400 cash collection is received. At the end of the life of the contract, the balance of the receivable will be reduced to zero. The pattern of revenue from the financing service and the related value assigned to the receivable is summarized in Exhibit 11-4.

Exhibit 11-4 PATTERN OF REVENUE RECOGNITION AND RELATED VALUATION OF RECEIVABLES FOR FUNTIER LAND COMPANY'S FINANCING OPERATIONS (ONE SALES CONTRACT)

	Year 1	2	3	4	5
Accounts receivable balance, start of year	$1,515	$1,267	$994	$694	$364
Imputed interest income (10% of beginning balance)	152	127	100	70	36
	$1,667	$1,394	$1,094	$764	$400
Collection of $400 installment payment at end of year	400	400	400	400	400
Accounts receivable balance, end of year	$1,267	$994	$694	$364	—0—

It is important to note the overall modification in the measurement of revenue that results from recognizing the provision of two separate services instead of merely recognizing revenue in the amount of the face value of the contracts when a sale is made. If the total contract price of $2,099 is associated solely with the sale of the land, revenue of $2,099 would be recognized in the year the contract was signed and no accomplishment would be reflected over the remaining life of the contract. However, when it is recognized that two distinct services are sold or provided, and the present value methodology is used to measure the compensation received for each of them, a smaller amount of revenue (the cash equivalent value of the contract) is associated with the sale of land and recognized in the year of sale, and the remainder of the contract price is recognized as interest income over the five-year period. These comparative revenue recognition patterns are shown in Exhibit 11-5.

Exhibit 11-5 COMPARATIVE REVENUE PATTERNS FOR
FUNTIER LAND COMPANY'S TOTAL OPERATIONS
(ONE SALES CONTRACT)

Year	Collections	Revenue (Sales) Assigned Solely to Sale of Land	Revenue from Land Sale and Financing Operation		
			Sales	Interest Income	Total
1	$ 499	$2,099	$1,614	$152	$1,766
2	400	—0—	—0—	127	127
3	400	—0—	—0—	100	100
4	400	—0—	—0—	70	70
5	400	—0—	—0—	36	36
	$2,099	$2,099	$1,614	$485	$2,099

The total revenue recognized under both methods is equal over the five-year period—$2,099. And, as we have previously noted, total revenue recognized under the conventional accounting model will in the long run be equal to total cash receipts. But the principal objective in moving from a cash basis to the concept of revenue embodied in the conventional accounting model was to reflect the accomplishment of each period, and to this end, the recognition of the time value of money to measure what Funtier has earned each period from each of the two services it provides is clearly preferable. Although generally recognized to be conceptually superior, recognition of the time value of money in measuring accomplishment was not often used in practice until recently. However, the emergence of businesses like land development companies, with sale terms similar to those outlined in the example, made obvious the need for some type of modification. Recently, current accounting policy for financial reporting was modified to require that the present value technique be applied whenever the difference between the present value and the face value of a receivable is material. Therefore, we observe here an example in current accounting practice where the present value model is used as the valuation base for one enterprise resource (accounts receivable), with the related modification in the recognition of revenue.

One final comment about our example may be in order to avoid a possible misleading impression. The hypothetical sales contracts of the Funtier Land Company contained no explicit interest rates or charges. However, the concepts proposed and the approach developed are equally valid even when an interest rate is explicitly stated in a sales contract. For example, the contract might have specified interest payments at 4 percent on the unpaid balance, even though the seller's time preference rate was 10 percent. In this case, it would still be appropriate to calculate the present value of the future cash flows (including the cash interest payments to be received) *at the seller's opportunity rate* in arriving at the measure of accomplishment to be reported from the sale of land and the balance of accounts receivable at the start of the period. The present value of the contract will simply be less (greater) than the face amount of the contract if the opportunity rate is greater (less) than the arbitrary contract rate. Of course, if the interest rate included in a contract is equal to (or approximates) the firm's opportunity rate, the present value will be equal to (or will approximate) the face value and no allocation is required. Under these conditions, the cash interest payments will properly reflect the compensation earned from the financing operations.

Providing Warranty Services As Well As a Product to the Customer

When merchandise is sold with a warranty or service guarantee, the total selling price is again composed of two elements: (1) a price for the product itself and (2) a price for the warranty on the product. Under the realization principle, the amount of the selling price that is attributable to the product itself has been earned and should be recognized in the period of sale. However, the portion of the selling price that represents compensation to the seller (or manufacturer) for the guarantee he provides has not yet been earned. As in the case of the provision of financing services, this portion of the total sales proceeds should be deferred and recognized in some fashion over the life of the warranty.

Example 11-4   The Modern TV Company sells 21-inch color television sets at a price of $495. This includes a warranty on all parts and labor for a two-year period.

In establishing the selling price, the company assumed that the average cost per customer of servicing defective units would be approximately $45 in the first year of the warranty and $80 in the second year of the warranty. Since it wishes to earn a 20 percent return on its cost on this type of activity, it marked up the product $150 (120 percent × $125) to cover the warranty. Therefore, it would be willing to sell the TV unit without a service warranty at a price of $345.

Based upon these factors, it would seem appropriate to recognize revenue at the time of sale in the amount of $345 per unit. The additional $150 that is received at the time of sale is payment for undelivered services, and it is deferred to future periods for recognition as it is earned throughout the warranty period.

The recognition of revenue in the above example is the preferable way to handle warranty and service contracts that are attached to the sale of merchandise. Application of the method depends upon the ability to separate the total price of the product into the portion applicable to the product itself and the portion applicable to the warranty. A less preferable method of handling this type of sale is to recognize all of the revenue in the period of sale, and to accrue the expenses that it is estimated will be incurred in the future under the warranty. Based on the facts stated above, the Modern TV Company would recognize $495 revenue in the period of sale for each unit sold, and additionally accrue a warranty expense (and the related liability for future services) of $125 per unit in the same period. Although this accrual method does not assign the revenue for the warranty to the periods of time in which it is presumably earned. it does adhere to the matching principle by associating the expenses incurred or estimated to be incurred with the related revenue. The method is, therefore, superior to merely recognizing the total selling prices of the TV sets as revenue in the period they are sold, without giving any recognition in that period to the expenses that will be incurred as a result of the guarantee given to the customer—as might result if one merely applied the point-of-sale criterion to this type of sale without considering the future service yet to be rendered.

Similarly, in all types of cases involving goods *and future services* sold as a package for a single price, the critical question revolves around when the enterprise *earns* the revenue from each of the product and service components. Except in cases involving insuperable measurement problems or an immaterial level of future services, all sales that involve the provision of goods *and future services* for a single price should be separated into their component parts and the realization principle applied to each component individually.

RECEIPT OF FIRM ORDERS PRIOR TO PERFORMANCE

Although many retail businesses deliver merchandise to customers concurrent with their expression of a desire to purchase certain goods (for example, food stores), some retail firms and many other types of business enterprises receive *orders* for goods or services prior to their delivery. Sometimes the goods are in stock, and they are delivered shortly after the order is received. In many cases, however, a longer time period ensues between order and delivery. Products may have to be secured from suppliers, or perhaps even produced after the order is received. Services clearly cannot be stockpiled, and the resulting time delay in their delivery depends upon the scope of services requested and the degree of availability of the firm's staff. The important question here is whether this type of business arrangement justifies recognition of revenue at some time earlier than when the ordered goods or services are delivered to the customer. Two possible earlier time periods deserve consideration: (1) the date the order is received and (2) the period of time during which progress is achieved on the production of the ordered goods or services.

In considering first the possibility of recognizing at least some portion of the total price as revenue at the date the order is received, an argument can be made that the securing of orders is, in principle, an important part of the overall earning process (particularly in certain industries, such as magazine publishing). However, present accounting policy does not sanction recognition of revenue at this time, primarily because of the practical difficulty in associating the total price with at least two distinct earning processes: (1) securing the order and (2) producing and/or delivering the goods or services. Therefore, as a rule, no accounting recognition is given to the receipt of an order *unless* it is accompanied by an advance payment. Even when advance payment is received, the receipt of cash and the associated obligation to provide goods or services in the future are recognized—but no revenue is recognized.

Moving next to the second possible time period for earlier recognition of revenue—the period of time during which progress is achieved on the production of the ordered goods or services, we find here some situations in which revenue recognition is permitted under current accounting policy. It may be helpful to classify these conditions into two general categories: (1)

production and delivery of separable units of a total order and (2) production processes extending over an "extremely long" period of time where (usually because of the nature of the order) no partial deliveries can be made.

Production and Delivery of Separable Units

Example 11-5   The Ja Magazine Company was recently formed to sell the new magazine *Ja*. The price of the magazine on the newsstand is $1 per copy. Additionally, individuals can subscribe to the magazine for one year for a price of $10. During the first month of operations, the company secured 12,000 new annual subscriptions, accompanied by total advance payments of $120,000.

If the obtaining of orders were interpreted to satisfy our criteria for the recognition of revenue, the company would recognize $120,000 revenue in the first month of operation. But unless it can be argued that the order-getting process is the major part of the overall earning process, leaving only minor services yet to be performed, it would not be appropriate to recognize all of the revenue at this point in time. The presumption of current accounting policy is that this argument cannot be made, and that further it is not possible to allocate the total price in a sufficiently objective way between the order-getting process and the production-delivery process. But although no revenue is recognized at this time, the *advance payment* must be given accounting recognition as an obligation of the firm either to provide future services or, failing to do so, to return the money. For the Ja Magazine Company, a liability entitled "advance payments on subscriptions" would be recorded.

Since performance of production and delivery on orders can be associated in this case with identifiable and separable units (i.e., individual magazines), the realization principle is presumed to be satisfied with each partial delivery, and a proportional amount of the total price is recognized as revenue. Thus, in the first month that magazines are produced and distributed, the company would recognize revenue of $10,000 (1/12 × $120,000). This would be accomplished by reducing the liability, advance payments on subscriptions, by $10,000 and increasing owners' equity by a similar amount. This revenue recognition process would continue each month until the company had provided the subscribers with their twelve copies of the magazine and earned the total revenue of $120,000. Presumably, the pattern of revenue produced by this process is a better indicator of the firm's periodic accomplishment than would be achieved by waiting until complete performance on the order before recognizing any revenue.

Prolonged Production Processes on Firm Orders

In many manufacturing circumstances, production occurs before a sale is made, and thus some earning occurs prior to the date of sale. However, in balancing the trade-off between the two realization principle criteria, the point-of-sale interpretation of the realization principle has the effect of deferring recognition of any value added during production until an enforceable claim against the customer has been created through the delivery of the product. This trade-off is not without merit for most types of business activity. But where the lead time between the start of production and final delivery extends over a relatively long period of time, particularly when two or more accounting periods are encompassed, the propriety of waiting for the completion and delivery of the product before recognizing accomplishment becomes more questionable. Indeed, in such instances, we may elect to place more emphasis on the fact that revenue is being *earned* as the production process continues, and less emphasis on the fact that the ultimate profit on the project is somewhat uncertain. This exception is most often applied in the cases of long-term construction and research contracts where the ultimate price is specified in advance, and the customer is obligated under a contract to accept the product if it is satisfactorily completed.

• *Percentage-of-completion method versus completed contract method of recognizing revenue.* In the case of long-term production (contruction, research, etc.) contracts that extend over several accounting periods, there are two customary methods of recognizing revenue. One method, the *completed contract method,* recognizes revenue in accordance with the point-of-sale interpretation of the realization principle. That is, no revenue is recognized until the production is completed and accepted by the customer. All costs incurred in the production activity are accumulated and deferred (in a construction-in-process account) until delivery is made. At that time, the total sales price is recognized as revenue, and the accumulated costs of the resources sacrificed in production are recognized as an expense in accordance with the matching principle. By deferring the recognition of revenue until the period in which the project is completed, *the total accomplishment* (revenue and profit) is associated only with this period. No amount of accomplishment is attributed to prior periods, even though one or more of them may have been the locus of substantial productive activity on the project. Hence, if the long-term project(s) represents a significant part of the contracting firm's operations, the revenue recognition pattern produced by the completed contract method significantly distorts the performance (net income) reported by the firm over time.

Example 11-6   The Clean Water Research Group of Ecology, Inc., made a proposal to an environmental protection agency of the federal government to study some new types of waste disposal units that could be economically installed and used on pleasure boats. This proposal was accepted by the agency, and a contract for $1.5 million was signed on January 1, 1975. The research project was to extend over thirty-six months, and progress payments were to be made to the research group over the life of the contract on the basis of the number of hours of research time that was expended.

The project supervisor estimated at the time the contract was received that the firm would incur costs on the project amounting to $1 million. The contract price is fixed and is not subject to renegotiation if cost overruns are incurred. Thus, at the outset of the project, the estimated profit is $500,000.

Approximately six months after the receipt of this contract, which was a major source of revenue to the firm, Ecology decided to expand the amount of its capital. Therefore, the management was vitally concerned with the basis on which the accomplishment on the contract would be measured and reported. If the total profit on the contract were not recognized until the completion of the project, the operating results of Ecology for the past year would probably not be adequate to attract new equity capital. But if some recognition could be given to the accomplishment that had been achieved on the project, it would have a better chance of marketing its new issue of stock.

An alternative to the completed contract method is the *percentage-of-completion method*. Under this method, a portion of the total projected accomplishment on a long-term project is assigned to each period that the company works on the project. The total measure of accomplishment that is allocated to the various periods is the estimated total profit on the project (selling price less estimated costs to be incurred), and the basis for the allocation is the estimated percentage of the total work required that has been achieved in the period. In estimating the percentage-of-completion that has been achieved in a period, many different approaches are found in current practice. Two common approaches used are (1) the ratio of costs incurred by the end of the period to the estimated total cost of the project at completion and (2) an independent expert's (generally an architect or engineer) estimate of the physical percentage-of-completion that has been achieved by the end of the period.

Referring back to Example 11-6, assume that the actual experience of Ecology, Inc., on the research project was as follows:

	1975	1976	1977
Costs incurred	$400,000	$350,000	$275,000
Project supervisor's end-of-year estimate of costs yet to be incurred to complete the project	600,000	300,000	—0—

Using the ratio of costs incurred to estimated total costs as the basis for assessing achievement in a period, the accomplishment (profit) recognized each year under the percentage-of-completion method is reflected in Exhibit 11-6.

We may note from Exhibit 11-6 that the amount of income to be assigned to each period is, under this method, a function of (1) the costs incurred during the period, (2) the revised estimate of costs yet to be incurred to complete the project, (3) the estimated income earned to date, and (4) the amount of income recognized in prior periods. In the first year (1975), it is estimated that the percentage of the total work on the project that was achieved in that period was 40 percent, based on the ratio of costs incurred that year ($400,000) to the end-of-year estimate of total costs on the project ($1,000,000 = $400,000 + $600,000). Based on the presently estimated total income of $500,000, $200,000 is recognized as income in 1975. In 1976 the same procedure is applied. But in this year, the sum of the costs incurred to date and the revised (as of December 31, 1976) estimate of costs to complete produce a new estimate of total income from the project, $450,000. This new estimate of income is the basis for the allocation of projected accomplishment to past and future periods. The income to be recognized in 1976, then, is the difference between income allocated to work done to date and the amount of income from the project already recognized in 1975. Thus the income recognized in 1976 reflects both the estimate of accomplishment in

Exhibit 11-6

APPLICATION OF PERCENTAGE-OF-COMPLETION METHOD TO CLEAN WATER RESEARCH GROUP PROJECT

	1975	1976	1977
Contract price of project	$1,500,000	$1,500,000	$1,500,000
Less costs of project:			
Costs incurred to date	$400,000	$750,000	$1,025,000
Estimated costs to complete	600,000	300,000	—0—
	1,000,000	1,050,000	1,025,000
Total income on project (estimated at end of 1975 and 1976)	$ 500,000	$ 450,000	$ 475,000
Income to be recognized to date	$ 200,000*	$ 321,429†	$ 475,000
Cumulative income recognized in prior periods	—0—	200,000	321,429
Income to be recognized for year	$ 200,000	$ 121,429	$ 153,571

* ($400,000/$1,000,000) × $500,000.
† ($750,000/$1,050,000) × $450,000.

365

the period and the correction of amounts reported in prior periods that were based on a less current estimate of total income on the project. In 1977 the project is completed and the total income from it becomes known. Income recognized in 1977 is merely the difference between the actual total income and the cumulative income recognized in the two prior years.

A long-term production project accounted for under the percentage-of-completion method is reflected as an asset in the statement of financial position while still in progress. At any point in time, the value assigned to the project is the sum of the costs incurred and the income recognized, less any progress billings to the customer provided for by the terms of the contract. In our example, the research project would be valued at $600,000 ($400,000 costs incurred plus $200,000 profit recognized) at the end of 1975, and $1,071,429 ($750,000 cumulative costs incurred plus $321,429 cumulative profit recognized) at the end of 1976, assuming no progress billings had been made.

Whenever the production period is significantly long and the customer's eventual payment is provided for in a contract, the percentage-of-completion method is applied in order to better associate the recognition of revenue (and income) with the period in which it is earned. Using the data of our illustration, we have the following contrast between the completed contract method and the percentage-of-completion method:

	Accomplishment (Income) Recognized under:	
	Percentage-of-Completion Method	Completed Contract Method
1975	$200,000	—0—
1976	121,429	—0—
1977	153,571	475,000
	$475,000	$475,000

The percentage-of-completion method in this case clearly traces the productive activities of the firm better than does the completed contract method. But since the percentage-of-completion method introduces a much greater degree of uncertainty into the income measurement process, it should be used only when the estimates required can be made with an acceptable degree of accuracy. These estimates involve the price to be received when the project is completed, the costs to be incurred on the project, and periodic assessments of the percentage-of-completion that has been achieved. Where these estimates are believed to be reasonably dependable, current accounting policy expresses a preference for the use of the percentage-of-completion method. However, if the uncertainties associated with a long-term project are so great as to render the estimates of doubtful validity, the more conservative completed contract method should be used.

DISCOUNTS

Our discussion of the general issue of revenue recognition would be incomplete without some attention to two types of discounts that are often granted to customers: (1) trade discounts and (2) cash discounts.

Trade Discounts

In some industries, it is common practice to have a set of standard prices, together with a series of discounts granted to customers based on the volume of products they order. Sometimes these trade discounts are stated in terms of a single percentage reduction from the list price, say 10 percent. The cash price would then be 90 percent of the stated list price. At other times the trade discounts are stated as a *series* of percentage discounts from the list price, say 20/10/5. When a series of discounts is offered, the first discount is applied against the list price, and then succeeding discounts are applied sequentially to the price established after taking into account the previous discount.

Example 11-7 The Globe Steel Company sells a wide range of steel products. It maintains a standard set of list prices for these products, together with a series of trade discounts based on the volume each customer orders. In one instance, the Globe Steel Company sold 1,000 units of a particular product to a customer at a price of $20 per unit with trade discounts of 20/10/10. The actual cash selling price to the customer is computed as follows:

List price (1,000 units @ $20)	$20,000
Less: 20% trade discount	−4,000
	$16,000
Less: 10% trade discount	−1,600
	$14,400
Less: 10% trade discount	−1,440
	$12,960

In this instance, the selling price of the goods is not the list price of $20,000, but rather the $12,960 price the customer is committed to pay. Therefore, revenue from this transaction is recognized by the seller in the amount of $12,960.

In general, where trade discounts are made available to customers, revenue is recognized for each sale in the amount of the net cash price to the customer after trade discounts are deducted. The trade discounts are not expenses; rather, they are means of adjusting the set of list prices to prevailing or "competitive" cash prices.

Cash Discounts

In addition to trade discounts, sellers often grant a small cash discount, or reduction in the amount that the customer has to pay, if payment is received within a fairly short period of time. A buyer often has thirty days or more to settle his account without penalty, and the cash discount represents an inducement to the buyer to make payment at an earlier date. This inducement is offered by the seller because of a principle mentioned several times earlier—money has a time value, and he would prefer to receive the amount due to him from the sale as soon as possible. The discount provision may also reduce the risk of bad debt losses, to the extent it induces payment of amounts due.

The terms of credit sales where cash discounts are available are normally stated in the following form: terms 2/10, net/30. This means that under these specific terms the customer is entitled to a 2 percent cash discount if he pays his account in ten days, but if he does not elect to take this discount he must pay the balance in thirty days. If these terms were applied to a sale for $1,000 on July 1, the customer would have the option of settling his account for $980 if he made payment within the ten-day period following the sale, or by July 11; if the customer did not make payment in time to receive the cash discount, he would then have to make full payment ($1,000) by July 31.

Two different treatments of cash discounts are found in accounting practice. Under the older method, the seller would recognize the cash discount, *when taken by the buyer,* as an expense or negative revenue item of that period. The seller in the above example would report revenue of $1,000 and would then deduct the $20 cash discount taken. The $20 deduction would either be offset against revenue to determine net revenue or be reported as "cash discounts expense." When this method of treating cash discounts is used, the preferred treatment is to report the discounts taken as an offset to revenue.

A weakness in the treatment described above is that it does not recognize revenue at the cash equivalent price *when the customer fails to take the discount.* If the customer in the above example fails to take the discount, the sales revenue would be recognized in the amount of $1,000. However, the cash equivalent price of the sales transaction was $980—the amount at which the merchandise could have been purchased with a cash payment at date of sale or anytime during the next ten days. In response to this weakness, an alternative method of treating cash discounts is to record the revenue *and* the accounts receivable at the cash equivalent price at the date of sale—in our example, $980. Then, when the cash discount is taken, no further adjustments are required. However, when the customer fails to take the discount, the seller receives $1,000 and the accounts receivable is stated at $980. The $20 difference is reflected by the seller in his income statement as income from discounts allowed but not taken by the buyer—revenue from the short-term credit, or financing, service the seller has provided.

The problem of reporting cash discounts, whether taken or not, exists for the buyer as well as the seller. The two alternatives described above for the seller are equally applicable to the buyer. Under the first alternative, the buyer records his purchases of merchandise and the related accounts payable at their invoice price and then deducts all cash discounts that he takes from the cost of merchandise. The second alternative calls for all purchases of inventory and the related accounts payable to be recorded at the cash equivalent price, whether the cash discount is taken or not. If a cash discount is not taken, it is reported under this second method as an expense (discounts lost) of the period in which it was lost.

Under the traditional types of discount terms, it is generally highly desirable that a business not lose any discounts available to it. This observation stems from the high effective rate of interest that is usually implicitly imbedded in the discount terms. For example, with terms of 2/10, net/30, the seller is offering a 2 percent reduction in the amount owed to him if the buyer makes payment twenty days earlier than the final due date. That is, he can pay within ten days and still take the discount, but if he does not, he must pay the full amount within the next twenty days or his account becomes delinquent and subject to contractual or statutory interest charges. Assuming that the buyer is planning to make payment within the thirty-day credit period, failure to make the payment within ten days and take the discount means that he is merely deferring payment for up to twenty days. Given the 2 percent discount terms, this amounts to an effective annual interest rate on the use of money for these twenty days of 36 percent ($360/20 \times 2$ percent). Therefore, in most instances, the business would be much better off economically by borrowing money at normal bank rates rather than losing available cash discounts on its trade accounts.

SUMMARY

Our principal purpose in the foregoing discussion has been to outline and illustrate the general types of situations that justify an exception to our normal point-of-sale basis of reporting revenue under the conventional accounting model. Yet, how different do the conditions have to be in order to drop the point-of-sale criterion? It should be relatively clear that the circumstances described in our examples are not totally different from the typical conditions surrounding most sales transactions. All credit sales involve a lag in cash collection, and most business activities involve some production or service before or after the point of sale (or both). Circumstances that justify departure from the point-of-sale criterion are therefore a matter of the degree of disparity from "normality." Thus, in the application of the point-of-sale criterion, as well as the modifications of the criteria that we have reviewed, it should be apparent that there is need for both conventions (or practical guidelines) and professional judgment in determining whether a particular business circumstance falls within the range of acceptability for application of the point-of-sale criterion or whether it calls for one of the acceptable modifications.

Questions for Review and Discussion

11-1.   Define:

a. The realization principle

b. Revenue

c. Bad debt

d. Trade discount

e. Cash discount

11-2. What is the objective of revenue recognition? Explain why this objective has been modified under conventional accounting through the adoption of the realization principle.

11-3. Describe the two criteria for revenue recognition imposed by the realization principle, and indicate when and why this principle is generally considered to be satisfied in current financial reporting.

11-4. There is some uncertainty about the ultimate collectibility of all receivables, but the accounting treatment varies depending upon the degree of uncertainty. Describe in general terms the two alternative approaches to uncertainty, and indicate which, if either, of the two criteria of the realization principle is given more weight under each approach than it is given in the balance struck under the strict point-of-sale interpretation.

11-5. Why are bad debts that may be incurred in future periods estimated and reflected as expenses of the current period rather than merely reflected as expenses of the period in which they are determined uncollectible?

11-6. What effect does the write-off of a bad account receivable have on the net value of accounts receivable and expense of the current period?

11-7. When a single sales price includes goods that are delivered at date of sale and the promise to provide future services, describe in general terms the modification that is made to the point-of-sale interpretation of the realization principle (assuming both components are material and measurable). Indicate which criterion of the realization principle is given more weight in this modification than it is given in the balance struck under the strict point-of-sale interpretation.

11-8. Why is revenue not recognized on the date a firm order is received from a customer?

11-9. Describe the two general categories of business circumstances where revenue is recognized in relation to the progress that is achieved on the production of ordered goods or services. Indicate which criterion of the realization principle is given more weight in this modification than it is given in the balance struck under the strict point-of-sale interpretation.

11-10. When the percentage-of-completion method is used for recognizing revenue from a long-term production project, what amount is assigned to the project (inventory) on the statement of financial position?

11-11. On July 1, 1974, Local Speculation Company sold a parcel of land it had acquired ten years ago at a cost of $500,000 to Giant Manufacturing Company for $1,800,000. Local received a noninterest bearing note due July 1, 1977, in payment. Assuming 12 percent is the appropriate time preference rate for Local, indicate how Local would record the sale transaction on July 1, 1974. Also, prepare a schedule of revenue that Local would recognize for each year from 1974 through 1977, and calculate the value at which the note receivable would be carried in the statement of financial position at the end of 1974, 1975, and 1976.

11-12. The installment sales method for accounting for highly risky install-ment accounts receivable is described in the body of the chapter. An alternative to that method is one in which (1) the present value method is used to value the accounts receivable, with an appropriately high discount rate which recognizes the high opportunity cost for such risky credit granting, and (2) a substantial allowance for bad debts. Contrast the pattern of income recognition and asset valuation under this alternative with the installment sales method. Make up an example to illustrate your explanations. Which method do you prefer? Defend your position.

11-13. In a recent court case involving the propriety of the reported income of Four Seasons Nursing Centers of America, Inc., one of the issues was the method used to determine the percentage-of-completion achieved by the com-pany on the construction of nursing homes. Although the initial estimate of in-come under the percentage-of-completion method was based on architects' physical estimates of completion, the auditors tested these estimates by comparing costs incurred to total estimated costs and insisted that the percentage completion to date (and therefore income recognized) be reduced. Nevertheless, the auditors were criticized for having included approximately $2 million in costs incurred to date which, for the most part, consisted of the contract prices of special-order components and subcontract work done "off-site" toward completion of various nursing homes, but for which no deliveries had been made to the actual con-struction sites by year-end. Under what conditions, if any, do you believe that such off-site costs should be included in the calculation of percentage-of-completion achieved?

11-14. One of the booming industries in recent years was the franchising industry—partly, say some critics, because of the accounting methods employed. A franchise company has two principal sources of income: (1) sale of the initial franchise and related assets or services and (2) fees for continuing services based on the operations of the individual franchisees. A major accounting issue was how to deal with the initial franchise fee. For this fee, the franchisee is authorized to use rights (trademarks, trade names, patents, etc.) possessed by the franchisor, and to receive certain assistance in getting his operations started (e.g., assistance in site selection, assistance in construction, bookkeeping and advisory services, employee and management training, etc.). Typically, the franchisee makes a small down payment when the franchise agreement is signed, and he executes a note for the balance to be paid over a fairly long period of time (often at a favorable rate of interest). Based upon this general background, describe some alternative revenue recognition methods that might be used to account for the initial franchise fee, and indicate which method you would prefer. How would it affect your answer if large initial fees are required but continuing franchise fees are small in relation to future services?

11-15. Motion picture rights are typically sold for television exhibition under a contract that covers a package of several films and permits one or more exhibi-tions of each film during specified license periods. A representative license agree-ment might include the following terms (from *AICPA Industry Accounting Guide on Accounting for Motion Picture Films,* Copyright © 1973 by the American Institute of Certified Public Accountants, Inc.):

Contract Execution Date—July 31, 1973
Number of Films and Telecasts Permitted—4 films, 2 telecasts each
Fees, License Periods, and Print Delivery Dates:

Film	Total Fee	Stated License Periods From	Stated License Periods To*	Print Delivery
A	$ 800,000	10/1/73	9/30/75	9/1/73
B	500,000	10/1/73	9/30/75	9/1/73
C	375,000	9/1/74	8/31/76	12/1/73
D	225,000	9/1/75	8/31/77	12/1/74
	$1,900,000			

* The actual license periods expire at the earlier of (1) the second telecast or (2) the end of the stated license period.

Payment Schedule—$100,000 at contract execution date, $50,000 per month for 36 months commencing January 1, 1974.

The AICPA committee studying this subject identified four methods in use for financial reporting of revenue from the licensing of films for television:

1. *Contract method:* Total revenue recognized on date the contract is executed.
2. *Billing method:* Revenue recognized as installment payments become due.
3. *Delivery method:* Revenue recognized at date the prints are delivered to licensee.
4. *Deferral or apportionment method:* Revenue spread evenly over the period of the license.

After deliberating the problem, the committee concluded that a licensing agreement should be considered as the sale of a right, and that revenue should not be recognized prior to commencement of the license period and not until all of the following conditions have been satisfied:

1. The sales price for each film is known.
2. The cost of each film is known or reasonably determinable.
3. Collectibility of the full license fee is reasonably assured.
4. The film has been accepted by the licensee in accordance with the conditions of the license agreement.
5. The film is available; i.e., the right is deliverable by the licensor and exercisable by the licensee.

What amount of revenue would be recognized each year from 1973 to 1977 under each of the four methods in use at the time the committee studied the problem? Assuming that the first four of the five conditions promulgated by the committee are satisfied, what pattern of revenue would be recognized from 1973 to 1977 under this present accounting policy? Would you adjust the revenue computed under present accounting policy for the time value of money? Do you believe present policy is an improvement over the four methods the committee found in use?

Exercises

11-1. Completed Contract versus Percentage-of-Completion Revenue Recognition Methods. Free Form Construction Company was awarded a contract in 1973 by The Big University to build a new library. The contract price was $8 million, and Free Form expected to complete the job in 1976. At the time construction began (early in 1974), Free Form estimated that the total costs on the job would be $6 million.

During the construction period, the following financial data were compiled:

Date	Total Costs Incurred to Date	Estimated Additional Costs to Complete Project
12/31/74	$1,500,000	$4,500,000
12/31/75	3,900,000	2,600,000
12/31/76	6,600,000	—0—

Required:

Determine the net income that would be reported for each of the three years and in total under (*a*) the completed contract method and (*b*) the percentage-of-completion method.

11-2. Installment Sales Method. On June 30, 1974, Wilson Corporation sold a parcel of land adjacent to its main plant to Deakin the Developer for $4 million. Wilson received 10 percent down, and a three-year, 12 percent (per annum) note for the balance. The terms of the note provide that each three months Deakin is to pay $300,000 principal, plus interest on the unpaid balance. The land cost Wilson Corporation $1.2 million five years ago.

The officers of Wilson Corporation are not sure that Deakin will be able to meet his payment obligations on the note. However, they completed the deal because they believed that the price agreed upon was a very favorable one to them; $400,000 was received as a down payment, and if Deakin defaults title to the land reverts to Wilson.

Because of the uncertainty regarding the collectibility of the note, this transaction is recorded using the installment sales method of recognizing revenue.

Required:

Assuming that Deakin the Developer makes all payments as they come due, prepare a schedule showing the income that would be recognized by Wilson Corporation (on this transaction) each year from 1974 to 1977.

11-3. Joint Sale of Product and Financing Services. The Reliable Equipment Company buys construction equipment from heavy equipment manufacturers and in turn sells the equipment to small to medium-sized construction contractors. The contractors buy from Reliable rather than from the equipment manufacturer because Reliable sells equipment on the installment basis. All of the company's sales are made on an installment basis involving 20 percent down and the remainder in two equal annual installments.

The earnings of the company are composed of (1) trading profits from the sale of equipment and (2) the interest on installment sales contracts. The explicit rate is stated to be 12 percent in the sales contracts (explicitly stated because of the Truth-in-Lending Act). Sales prices are set so that if the required payments are discounted at 12 percent, the present value is equal to the list price the customer would have to pay if he bought directly from the manufacturer. Reliable makes a trading profit because it only pays 90 percent of the list price (due to volume discounts).

The company began operations at the start of 1973. The total contract sales price of the equipment sold each year for 1973–75 is:

Year	Contract Sales Price
1973	$1,000,000
1974	1,600,000
1975	2,000,000

Required:

1. Compute the cost to Reliable of the equipment sold for each of the three years. Assume that all purchases and sales occur at the *first* of the year and that installment payments are made at the end of the year.

2. Prepare a financial position worksheet that reflects the above sales, costs, and collection experience, assuming the point-of-sale method of recognizing income. Include the effects of the time value of money. Assume a beginning cash balance and owners' equity of $2 million.

11-4. Recognition of Bad Debts.   The Buy Now–Pay Later Department Store makes approximately one-half of its sales to customers on credit. The customer obtains credit by completing an application for a credit card. After the information on the application is checked by the credit department and the credit manager approves the application, the customer is issued a credit card which he must present when he purchases merchandise on credit.

The store sends a "balance forward" statement (showing beginning balance due, new purchases, payments, and ending balance due) to each customer with a nonzero ending balance at the end of each month. Payment is due when the customer receives the statement. An account becomes past due if the total balance due is not received before the next month's statements are prepared. A list is maintained of accounts with a balance past due for more than ninety days so that no further credit sales to those accounts will be made.

A study of collections on credit sales for 1970–74 indicated that approximately 1 percent of credit sales proved to be uncollectible. Also, a study of account balances at year-end showed that differing percentages of year-end balances were ultimately uncollectible, depending on the age of the account. The percentages were:

Current accounts	½%
Accounts past due— 1–30 days	1%
Accounts past due—31–60 days	5%
Accounts past due—61–90 days	20%
Accounts past due—over 90 days	30%

The store follows the practice of matching the estimated uncollectible portion of credit sales against recognized sales revenue (i.e., an "allowance for doubtful accounts" is used). Whenever a customer account is determined to be uncollectible, the balance of that account is "written off" against the balance of the allowance account. Also, at year-end the store applies the appropriate percentages (by age category) to customer balances to determine if the balance in the allowance account is sufficient to cover estimated losses in the year-end customer receivable balance. If not, an additional adjustment is made.

The store used the percentages developed in the 1970–74 study for its accounting adjustments in 1975–76. Sales and collection data for 1975–76 follow:

Year	Cash Sales	Credit Sales	Collections on Account	Accounts Determined to be Uncollectible
1975	$800,000	$ 800,000	$774,000	$ 6,000
1976	800,000	1,000,000	889,000	11,000

The "age distribution" of customer accounts at year-end for 1975–76 follows:

Year	Total A/R Balance	Current Accounts	1–30 Past Due	31–60 Past Due	61–90 Past Due	Over 90
1975	$140,000	$120,000	$10,000	$ 6,000	$ 2,000	$ 2,000
1976	240,000	180,000	20,000	20,000	10,000	10,000

Account balances at the end of 1974 were:

Accounts receivable	$120,000
Allowance for doubtful accounts	(4,000)

Required:

1. Prepare a financial position worksheet that shows the effect of the above sales, collections, and bad debts experience for 1975–76. Provide columns for Effect on Cash, Accounts Receivable, Allowance for Doubtful Accounts, and Effect on Owners' Equity.

2. What are the implications of the analysis of the customer balances at the end of 1976?

11-5. Income from Long-Term Construction Contracts. Tower Construction Company builds high-rise office buildings in areas of the Midwest. The company is small, however, and only has one major project going at a time. It usually places bids for new contracts during the year of completion of the current contract. Then, by completion of the current contract, the company is immediately able to shift its labor force to the next job. Usually only a few months of overlap occur as the new project is being planned and the old one is being completed.

In 1974 the company won the contract on the Life Insurance Building. The contract price of the building was $10 million. The construction of the building was to be started in July 1974 and completed in June 1976. The Life Insurance Company, the client, agreed in the contract to pay the Tower Construction Company on a limited percentage completion basis. Every six months a team of independent consulting engineers paid by Life would inspect the building and Tower's cost records to determine the percentage completion on the project. Life would then be billed by Tower for the percentage toward completion that occurred during the six-month period times the contract price, less 20 percent retainage to be due upon completion (to ensure Tower's interest in completing the building), and payment would be made within thirty days.

During the period July 1, 1974, to June 30, 1976, the engineers judged the project 15 percent complete by December 31, 1974, 35 percent complete by June 30, 1975, 65 percent complete by December 31, 1975, and complete by June 30, 1976. During that period of time, the following financial data were assembled by Tower's accountant:

Date	Costs Incurred to Date	Estimated Costs to Complete Project
12/31/74	$2,125,000	$6,375,000
6/30/75	3,825,000	4,675,000
12/31/75	6,300,000	2,700,000
6/30/76	9,100,000	—0—

In measuring income under the percentage-of-completion method, Tower Construction Company uses the cost data (costs incurred and estimated costs to complete the project) rather than the engineering estimates as an indicator of "percentage completion."

Required:

As of the end of each six-month period, determine the amounts called for below under (1) the completed contract method and (2) the percentage-of-completion method of accounting for long-term construction contracts:

(a) Cash collected to date, assuming that Life paid each billing in the thirty days following the date of billing.

(b) Income for the six-month period.

(c) Balance in construction-in-process account.

11-6. Warranty Contracts. The Waterfall Appliance Company assembles washing machines and dryers (the components are purchased from other manufacturers) and retails the appliances through its own appliance stores. To maintain a competitive position, the company offers a two-year warranty (the industry average) on parts and labor. The appliance store provides a repair service for warranty and general repairs. The repair service is considered to be a revenue-producing function.

Price-cost data for washers and dryers are given below. The data apply to 1972, 1973, and 1974.

	Washers	Dryers
Unit sales price	$225	$150
Unit total cost (includes components and labor)	110	90
Average unit cost of warranty service in the first year of warranty	10	5
Average unit cost of warranty service in the second year of warranty	30	5

Sales data for 1973 and 1974 are as follows:

	Washers		Dryers	
Year	Units	Dollars	Units	Dollars
1973	1,000	$225,000	800	$120,000
1974	1,200	270,000	1,000	150,000

Required:

1. (a) Calculate the markup percentage (on cost including average unit warranty cost) for both appliances.

   (b) Assuming that the percentages calculated above are appropriate for determining (1) revenue from sales and (2) revenue from warranty repairs, what portion of the selling price (for each appliance) should be recognized in the year of sale?

2. Prepare a financial position worksheet that shows the effects of the above sales and costs (for 1973–74), using the preferred method of deferring revenue from warranty sales until it is earned. You may assume the following:

   (a) Beginning balances are irrelevant and may be ignored.

   (b) All purchases, sales, and wages are for cash.

   (c) In a given year, the company produces only the units that it expects to sell (i.e., no year-end inventories).

   (d) If a part is required for a warranty repair, the part is purchased for cash when the repair is made.

   (e) All claims for first-year warranty service for units sold in 1973 are made in 1974, and so forth.

3. Enter the expected effects of 1975–76 warranty repair transactions (as a result of 1973–74 sales) on the financial statement worksheet. (Ignore other 1975–76 transactions.) What is the total net income for 1973–76? What is the balance of the deferred warranty revenue at the end of 1976?

4. (a) Prepare a schedule showing revenue and net income for 1973 and 1974 for the following alternative revenue-expense recognition methods:

   (1) Defer warranty revenue until earned

   (2) Recognize total selling price as revenue in period of sale, and accrue expected future warranty expenses

   (b) Under what set(s) of circumstances might each of the above alternatives be appropriate?

11-7. Subscription Contracts. The Sports Forecasting Company was formed in 1971 to sell the sports newsletter "We-Pick-Em." The newsletter, which is published weekly from August through December, is sold by subscription only, and the subscription price for one year is $50.

The newsletter predicted the results of games correctly 80 percent of the time during 1971–72. Therefore, the company expects an increase in subscriptions for 1973. To take advantage of the current "seller's market," the company is offering a three-year subscription for $135. The entire amount must be paid before the customer is placed on the mailing list.

The company received total payment for the following number of subscriptions in 1973–74. (Subscriptions fell off in 1974, since the newsletter was correct only 60 percent of the time in 1973.)

	One-Year Subscriptions	Three-Year Subscriptions
1973	5,000	3,000
1974	4,000	1,000

Required:

Prepare a financial position worksheet for 1973–74 that shows the effects of the above receipts, assuming that revenue is recognized in the year in which the service is provided. Assume that revenue is recognized at the end of each year. Ignore beginning balances.

11-8. Effect of Trade and Cash Discounts on Revenue Recognition.   The Swivel Equipment Company sells office equipment. The company maintains a catalog which contains standard list prices, product descriptions, and sales terms. Sales terms include allowance of trade discounts (depending upon dollar volume of an order) and cash discounts (for payment of an invoice within ten days).

Some transactions of the company during July and August were as follows:

a. Sold equipment having a list price of $200 to the Handy Office Supplies store. No trade discount was allowed, but cash discount terms were 2/10, net/30.

b. Sold equipment having a list price of $15,000 to the Globe Steel Company. A trade discount of 20/10 was allowed, and cash discount terms were 1/10, net/30.

c. Sold equipment having a list price of $6,000 to the Downtown Office Equipment Company. A trade discount of 20 percent was allowed, and cash discount terms were 1/10, net/30.

d. Received net payment from Handy Office Supplies after ten days. The store had deducted the cash discount, even though it was not entitled to do so.

e. Received net payment from the Globe Steel Company. All allowable discounts had been deducted.

f. Received full payment from the Downtown Office Equipment Company after ten days. The company had not deducted for the cash discount.

Required:

1. (a) What revenue would be recognized from sales for transactions *a–c*, assuming that cash discounts are recognized at the time of sale?

   (b) What additional revenue would be recognized at a later time, if any?

2. (a) What revenue would be recognized from sales for transactions *a–c*, assuming that cash discounts, if any, are recognized when payment is received?

   (b) What revenue offsets would be recognized at a later time, if any?

3. Prepare a table contrasting sales revenue, cash discounts taken, discounts allowed but not taken, and total net revenue for the two alternative methods of recognizing cash discounts.

11-9. Joint Services and Normal Uncertainty Combined. Computer Sales Company buys and sells small standardized computer systems. All of the company's sales are made on an installment plan involving one-third down, and the remainder in two equal annual installments.

Computer Sales Company's long-run earnings are composed of two major components: (1) trading profits from the sale of the computers and (2) the implicit interest on the installment sales contracts that the customer signs. No explicit interest charge is included in the installment sales contracts. But the company has designed the contract so that when the required payments are discounted at 10 percent, the present value is approximately equal to the market value of the computers in a cash sale. The 10 percent interest rate also approximates the market rate of interest on installment loans of equal risk (considering the contract terms, the class of clientele, etc.).

Computer Sales Company began operations at the beginning of 1974. Since that time, it has had the following sales and collection experience:

		Collections	
Year	Sales	Down Payments	Installment Payments
1974	$ 600,000	$200,000	—0—
1975	900,000	300,000	$200,000
1976	1,200,000	400,000	500,000

The costs of the computers sold each of these three years were:

1974	$480,000
1975	720,000
1976	960,000

Required:

1. Record, in financial position worksheet form, all of the effects of the above sales and collection experience according to the point-of-sale method of recognizing income from installment sales, taking into account the time value of money. For convenience assume—

   (a) That all sales are made and all collections received at the end of each year.

   (b) That the cost of computers sold is paid in cash by Computer Sales to the manufacturers at the time it sells the systems to its own customer (the manufacturer then delivers direct to Computer Sales' customers).

   (c) The company began business in 1974 with $1.6 million cash and $1.6 million owners' equity.

   (d) The company experiences no other expenses or revenues except as described above.

2. Suppose now that Computer Sales Company recognized income under the point-of-sale method, taking into account expected bad debts but ignoring the time value of money.

The industry experience has been that approximately 5 percent of the total value of the accounts receivable *at the time of sale* proves to be uncollectible. During the past years, the actual collection experience of the company was as follows:

	Collections		Amounts Determined to be Uncollectible	
Year	Down Payments	Installment Payments	From 1974 Sales	From 1975 Sales
1974	$200,000	—0—	—0—	—0—
1975	300,000	$192,000	$16,000	—0—
1976	400,000	467,000	5,000	$40,000

Using the income recognition method indicated above (i.e., point of sale with recognition of estimated bad debts), record in financial position worksheet form the effects of the sales, expenses, and revised collection experience for Computer Sales Company.

3. Suppose now that Computer Sales Company recognized income under the point-of-sale method, taking into account *both* time value of money and expected bad debts. Under this income recognition method, record in financial position worksheet form the effects of Computer Sales Company's transactions for the *first two years only*.

11-10.   The Case of the Disappearing Income.   This case concerns franchising, which is, in its simplest terms, an arrangement to distribute and sell goods or services within a specified area or at a given location. Involved are a franchisor who originates an idea for a product or service with the attendant trade name, packaging, and promotion and then grants to a franchisee the right to market at retail. The franchisor generally offers consultation and management advice for opening a product or service outlet and training and controlling its management. The franchisee usually agrees to pay a fee for the franchise as well as to purchase certain supplies from the franchisor.

In most cases, a franchisor will collect only a down payment when a franchise is granted, and the balance of the franchise fee becomes payable in future years. Accounting problems have arisen because franchisors have reported the entire franchise fee as income at the time of the grant, even though the down payment is inconsequentially small and the probability of collection highly uncertain.

Accounting problems related to franchising operations may be illuminated by considering an actual example. Of interest are the consolidated statements of income of Career Academy, Inc. and Subsidiaries for the year ended December 31, 1968, as reported in the 1968 annual report of the company and again reported in the 1969 report of the company.

On January 30, 1970, Career Academy announced a major change in accounting for its franchising operations. This change is described in a note to the 1969 statement and is also reproduced here.

Required:

1. Identify the accounting conventions that supported the amount recorded for 1968 sales of directorships as shown in the income statement from the 1968 annual report of Career Academy, Inc. (See page 383.)

2. Which accounting conventions support the alternative figure given for 1968 sales of directorships in the 1969 annual report? (See page 381.)

3. Identify three major balance sheet accounts affected by Career Academy's 1970 change in accounting methods.

4. Where, in the published financial statements, would one find the 1968 income that disappeared for purposes of the 1969 annual report?

CAREER ACADEMY, INC. AND SUBSIDIARIES
Consolidated Statements of Income
For the Years Ended December 31, 1969 and 1968

	1969	1968
Revenues:		
Income from students	$16,541,501	$12,613,757
Income from directorships	1,907,300	789,516
	$18,448,801	$13,403,273
Costs and Expenses:		
Instruction	$ 2,816,990	$ 2,445,820
Selling, general and administrative	10,762,006	8,033,536
Provision for doubtful accounts and student contract terminations	696,781	602,000
	$14,275,777	$11,081,356
Operating income	$ 4,173,024	$ 2,321,917
Other Income (Expense):		
Interest expense	$ (270,206)	$ (189,490)
Other income, net	301,228	211,075
	$ 31,022	$ 21,585
Income before provision for income taxes	$ 4,204,046	$ 2,343,502
Federal and State Income Taxes:		
Current	$ 300,000	$ 260,000
Deferred	1,928,000	982,000
	$ 2,228,000	$ 1,242,000
Net income	$ 1,976,046	$ 1,101,502
Earnings Per Common and Common Equivalent Share	$.43	$.25

NOTE TO 1969 STATEMENTS

ACCOUNTING METHODS CHANGE

On January 30, 1970, Career Academy announced a retroactive change in the accounting methods used to determine income from the sale of Director-ships. The following is a comprehensive explanation of this change and its effect on past and future income.

Reasons for the Change

Late in 1969 and early in 1970 a number of publications, including the *Wall Street Journal* and the *Journal of Accountancy* carried articles that discussed the accounting methods used by firms deriving a significant portion of their income from the sale of franchises. These articles suggested that the liberal attitude toward recognizing all income at the time of sale should possibly be replaced by more conservative methods. We reaffirmed, with the concurrence of our auditors, the validity of our accounting methods and that our system avoided the problem areas being pointed out in the articles.

Nevertheless, a high degree of speculation and uncertainty arose during the third and fourth weeks in January, 1970, within the financial community as to whether we would change our methods and how our income might be affected by a change. This speculation involved a number of different earnings projections, based on various accounting methods. The result was a seriously confused and uncertain condition that demanded clarification on our part.

Since we felt our existing accounting methods, and certain alternative methods were equally acceptable, we decided to adopt a more conservative method in order to end the uncertainty and speculation. Our auditors, Arthur Andersen & Co., concurred with our decision.

Accordingly, the new accounting method was retroactively instituted for 1969 and prior years.

The Substance of the Change

Our former accounting method provided that all income from a sale of a Directorship was recognized at the time a contract was signed. Under the new method, we will recognize income from the sale of Directorships on the basis of several performance criteria—the principal one being the number of students enrolled by the Directorship organization each year.

An amount equal to approximately 15% of the sale price is recorded as income over a period of one to two years. The remaining revenues will be recognized over an estimated 5 to 7 years period on the basis of the number of students enrolled by the Directorship each year.

Certain costs, directly associated with the establishment of Directorship organizations will be amortized against income on the same basis.

The Effects of the Change

Since this change in accounting methods was a retroactive one, it not only affects the present and future years, but also all prior years. The major effect of the change involves the deferral of Directorship revenue. You will find this change reflected in our December 31, 1969, balance sheet under the heading "Unearned Directorship Revenue." The indicated net deferral as of that date is $8,258,982, of which $1,049,329 is estimated to be realized within one year.

It should also be pointed out that there is a reserve of $2,070,000 for possible losses on Installment Notes Receivable from Directorships.

In 1969, the change in accounting methods resulted in a reduction of net income from 85¢ per share to 43¢ per share. In addition, the Notes to

Financial Statements in this report contain references to and further explanations of the new accounting method.

CAREER ACADEMY, INC. AND SUBSIDIARIES
Consolidated Statements of Income
For the Years Ended December 31, 1968 and 1967

	1968	1967
Revenues:		
Income from students	$11,921,474	$6,786,881
Sales of directorships	5,327,002	2,627,076
	$17,248,476	$9,413,957
Costs and Expenses:		
Instruction cost	$ 2,245,820	$1,430,422
Selling, general and administrative expenses	7,711,147	4,405,027
Provision for doubtful accounts, student contract terminations and estimated losses on installment notes receivable	1,522,000	828,790
	$11,478,967	$6,664,239
Operating income	$ 5,769,509	$2,749,718
Other Income (Expense):		
Interest expense	$ (189,489)	$ (107,875)
Other income, net	193,070	49,146
	$ 3,581	$ (58,729)
Income before provision for income taxes	$ 5,773,090	$2,690,989
Federal and State Income Taxes:		
Current	$ 260,000	$ 290,000
Deferred	2,800,000	1,004,400
	$ 3,060,000	$1,294,400
Net income for the year	$ 2,713,090	$1,396,589
Earnings per share	$.60	$.32

12

Expense Recognition and
Related Asset Valuation Issues

In the preceding chapter we examined the revenue recognition patterns, and the related set of criteria governing their use, that are found in present-day financial reporting. In that discussion, we relied on the general notions (principles) of matching and cost measurement when it was necessary to consider expenses together with revenue (as, for example, in the discussion of the installment sales method). Indeed, the development of the fundamental ideas of the conventional accounting model in Chapters 4 through 6 largely deals with these important expense-recognition principles in broad, conceptual terms. But certain additional problems associated with the measurement of expenses recur frequently in practice and cannot be resolved by simple recourse to broad statements of the principles. In response, a set of acceptable measurement rules, often with two or more acceptable alternative rules for a given problem, has evolved (or been promulgated) in accounting practice. In this and the next chapter we examine some of the more common expense measurement problems and the alternative ways they can be treated.

EXPENSE MEASUREMENT AND ASSOCIATION WITH REVENUE (PERIODS)

The Objective of Expense Recognition in Review

To achieve the hoped-for cause-and-effect association between measured effort and measured accomplishment, measurement of conventional accounting expense for a period is conditioned upon revenue recognized for the period, as reflected in the definition of expense introduced in Chapter 4:

> **Expense.** Insofar as possible, total expense for a period includes the costs of all resources that were sacrificed to produce the revenue recognized in the current period.

This concept of expense is the combination of two fundamental measurement principles of the conventional accounting model—the matching principle and the cost principle. The matching principle provides the key to the *timing* of expense recognition, and the cost principle establishes the amount, or value, at which the expense is *measured*. But these general concepts require some elaboration if one is to understand the way they are applied in an operational context.

Elaboration of the Matching Principle

Most expenditures are made for the purpose of generating future service potentials, or sources of future benefits to the firm. The basic objective embodied in the matching principle is to find satisfactory bases of association—hopefully, causal relationships—for linking efforts (expenses) with related benefits (revenue).

> **Matching Principle.** Insofar as possible, the total sacrifices made in all periods to produce and sell a particular product or service should be recognized as expense in the period in which the revenue from the same product or service is recognized.

To be strictly applied, the matching principle requires that virtually every sacrifice of any resource in a given period (1) be specifically identified with a particular product or service, (2) have its original price (cost) to the enterprise accumulated with the costs of all other sacrifices made to produce that product or service, and (3) be recognized as an expense in the period in which the particular product or service is sold or provided. This scrupulous matching of resource sacrifices with products or services is, however, often difficult or impossible to achieve. Furthermore, in many instances, identification of the desired relationships is very *costly* to achieve. Therefore, as was pointed out in Chapter 4, a rough dichotomy is usually followed in recognizing expenses for a given period.

If a resource sacrifice has been made in a particular accounting period, an accountant will consider the way in which the resource was used. If consumption of the resource can be identified or associated (at a reasonable cost) with a specific product or service, or batch of products and services, its original cost to the enterprise is accumulated ("attached" to the product or service) until the period in which the specific products or services are sold. In that period (when the related revenue is recognized), these accumulated resource costs logically attaching to the products or services are recognized as expenses. Because of their nature, these expenses are often referred to as *product expenses*.

But if a resource is consumed during a period and consumption bears no discernible relation to the production of any *particular* present or future product(s) or service(s), that is, it cannot be identified with a unit of present or future revenue, the cost is recognized as an expense in the period in which the resource is consumed or sacrificed. Such costs, like salaries of a firm's executives, are called *period expenses*.

Thus we do not attempt to contrive a causal relationship, or network, between all enterprise expenditures and related revenues. In the absence of a clearly discernible relationship, however, it is obviously desirable that the accountant be able to establish some systematic basis for matching expenditures against revenue, or at least periods of time presumably benefiting from the expenditures, in order to achieve the hoped-for association between effort and accomplishment. In most instances, the "systematic matching" of the conventional accounting model is grounded in the assumption that we are able to identify, in a general sense, *patterns of benefits* to be derived from the use of a resource.

Example 12-1   When a firm acquires a long-lived asset, say an office building with an expected life of forty years, we are usually unable to identify specific units of revenue generated from the use of the resource. Clearly, we would not want to recognize the total expenditure made to purchase the asset as an expense of the period in which it was acquired. Therefore, we might elect to spread the cost of the building equally over its estimated useful life (as depreciation expense), under the assumption that the benefits from the use of the resource will be received uniformly (or approximately so) over the same period. If we made a different assumption about the pattern of benefits to be received, we might recognize a correspondingly different pattern of expenses.

But even this systematic, albeit somewhat arbitrary, matching is not always possible to achieve in practice. For example, advertising expenditures often reflect efforts that contribute to more than one product for more than one time period. Such costs, referred to as *joint costs,* are not unusual items. They would include many, if not all, of the administrative costs of a business, and frequently a large bulk of the marketing effort. For expenditures of this type, the notion of a period cost, in its most extreme form, is often applied. The entire expenditure is "matched" against the period in which the expenditure is made, as there is not even any discernible basis for systematically matching it against more than one period (as there was in the case of the depreciation of long-lived assets). The principal justification for this treatment of such period costs is that by their nature they usually tend to be relatively uniform from one period to the next. Even if there were some pattern of benefits to be derived that could be identified with a large enough expenditure of effort, it is assumed that the amount of expense recognized in each period would not be substantially different from the actual expenditure made. Where this assumption is not valid, as is sometimes the case, a distortion of net income can result.

Elaboration of the Cost Principle

Once we have determined as best we can the resources that have been consumed in the production of the recognized revenue, either by direct association with products or services sold or through a more indirect assignment to periods, we then seek to *measure* the sacrifices. This measurement process is based upon the cost principle.

> **Cost Principle.** The measure of sacrifice associated with the acquisition and subsequent use of any resource is the price paid for the resource, that is, its cost, in the exchange or exchanges in which it was acquired.

Cost, as the term is used in accounting, refers to values (generally expressed as prices) established in *external transactions* involving the exchange of resources between entities. While the matching principle, not the transaction, controls the timing of expense recognition, the prices established by transactions provide the data base for ultimate expense recognition. In some instances, the occurrence of a transaction is coincident with the recognition of expense (for example, in the payment of wages). But in many instances, a transaction involves the acquisition of resources (nonmonetary assets) that will be used to produce revenue in the future. In the period of time elapsing between the acquisition and the utilization of nonmonetary assets, the transaction price (cost) is used as an expression of an asset's value in the statement of financial position. Thus, under the conventional accounting model, one way to interpret the values associated with nonmonetary resources that will be consumed in the production of future revenue is to view them as future expenses measured in terms of original transaction values or *unexpired costs.* Similarly, all expenses can be regarded as *expired costs.*

• *Original transaction value.* What are the "original transaction values" that are established in exchange transactions? In Chapter 5 this central notion of conventional accounting valuation was defined under the limiting condition that cash or other monetary items were involved in the transaction:

> **Original Transaction Value.** The original transaction value of an asset or a liability is the value established in the exchange(s) in which the asset was acquired or the liability incurred. Usually such exchange values are determined by the amounts of monetary items given, promised, received, or to be received, depending on the circumstances.

Although this definition is adequate for identifying the original transaction value in most exchange transactions, it must be enriched somewhat to cover all transaction forms.

The measure of the original transaction value, or cost, of acquiring nonmonetary assets is generally established by applying one of the following criteria, *in order of priority:*

1. Cash or other monetary consideration given
2. Cash or other monetary consideration paid (if any), plus the current exchange value of any *nonmonetary consideration given*
3. Current exchange value of monetary (if any) and *nonmonetary consideration received*
4. Cash or other monetary consideration paid (if any), plus the unexpired cost of nonmonetary consideration given

For any of the four criteria, it is assumed that the time value of money will be taken into account, when significant, in valuing monetary consideration given or received.

Example 12-2

The Roark Computer Service Company operates a computer service facility that processes information for businesses that do not have their own computers. At the present time, the company has a HAL 1975 Computer. The company has made a study of its future computer needs and has decided to trade in the computer on the larger HAL 2001 Computer.

The new computer, the HAL 2001, with a list price of $850,000, is acquired in exchange for the HAL 1975 plus a cash payment of $500,000. The estimated current market value of the HAL 1975 at the present time is $325,000. The unexpired cost (cost less accumulated depreciation) of the HAL 1975 is $260,000.

Applying our set of criteria to the facts of this case, we arrive at the following alternative transaction values (cost):

    I. Criterion 2: $500,000 + $325,000 = $825,000
   II. Criterion 3: $850,000
  III. Criterion 4: $500,000 + $260,000 = $760,000

Choice of the appropriate criterion in Example 12-2 depends both upon the order of priority of the criteria noted above and upon the *relative reliability* of the estimated current exchange values. In arriving at valuation alternative I, the estimated current exchange value of the HAL 1975 was used in conjunction with the cash payment of $500,000 to arrive at a transaction value (cost) of $825,000. For valuation alternative II, the estimated current exchange value of the new HAL 2001 (which for this example was the list price) was used to establish a transaction value (cost) of $850,000. Choice between these two alternative values (costs) will depend upon the facts of the particular case. In some instances, because of the wide prevalence of discounts, list prices are not good estimates of the current exchange value of an asset. If the accountant had no reason to believe that the estimated current exchange value of the consideration given (the $325,000 estimated market value of the HAL 1975) was biased, he would opt for criterion 2 in establishing the transaction value (cost) of the new HAL 2001. However, if the accountant believed that the estimated market value of the HAL 1975 was lacking in objectivity and reasonableness, he might elect to use the list price ($850,000) of the new computer as the measure of the transaction value in accordance with criterion 3—particularly if he believed that this list price was a relatively good measure of the exchange value of the asset acquired. If both of these estimated market values were suspect as to their objectivity and/or validity, the accountant would reluctantly apply criterion 4 (the last in order of priority) to arrive at a transaction value of $760,000 —the cash paid ($500,000) plus the unexpired cost ($260,000) of the asset (the old HAL 1975 computer) given in the exchange. This last method implicitly assigns proceeds of $260,000 to the disposition of the old computer and thus results in no gain or loss on the disposition. It should be noted that this "no profit or loss" method is often applied for federal income tax purposes in so-called nontaxable exchanges.

When cash and other monetary items are the only consideration given to acquire a nonmonetary asset, the original transaction value (cost) is uniquely determined under conventional accounting measurement rules. In all other cases, however, the accountant must exercise judgment in his determination of the cost of the new nonmonetary asset acquired. When this judgment has been exercised and a market value (or, in rare cases, an unexpired cost) used as a surrogate for the value of one of the nonmonetary assets exchanged in the transaction, the cost thus determined is thereafter treated in the same manner as if the transaction had been solely for cash.

• *Inclusiveness.* We have illustrated above that identification of the cost of acquiring a nonmonetary asset is a more complex measurement problem than it appears at first glance. Yet there is still an additional dimension to the problem. The cost of an asset, as the term is used in accounting, is a more inclusive concept than merely the price of the item. It includes all outlays to acquire and transform the asset for ultimate use or sale. The total cost of a nonmonetary asset would include, in addition to its purchase price, any outlays required to transport and/or install the asset. Additionally, if an asset is transformed in a manufacturing process into a different physical form, the cost of the transformed asset and all the other outlays involved in the manufacturing process would "attach" to the output of the production process. The sum of these attached costs would then constitute the cost of the "new" asset.

Example 12-3   Returning to the facts of Example 12-2, let us now assume that the Roark Computer Service Company determined that the cost of its new HAL 2001 computer was $825,000, in accordance with criterion 2—cash ($500,000) plus the current exchange value ($325,000) of the HAL 1975 that was traded in for the new computer. But in addition to this outlay, the Roark Computer Service Company also paid $5,000 to transport the new computer from the manufacturer's place of business to the Roark operating facilities and incurred a $1,000 cost to install the computer. Given these facts, the total cost of the new computer would be $831,000 ($825,000 + $5,000 + $1,000).

If Roark Computer Service Company had been required to make any outlays for the removal of the old computer that was traded in, these would generally not be treated as an additional cost of the new computer. Rather, they would normally be incorporated in the calculation of the gain or loss on the disposal of the old computer. In this case, the disposal of the old computer resulted in a gain of $65,000 (imputed proceeds of $325,000 less the unexpired cost of $260,000).

Example 12-4   Walker Art Wholesalers, Inc., assembles oil paintings for distribution in large shopping centers. Its "manufacturing" effort involves the acquisition of oil paintings from one source, the acquisition of frames from another source, and the assembly of the canvases and frames for distribution at several local shopping centers. In a particular case, assume that a canvas was acquired at a cost of $16, and the frame that was used on this canvas was purchased for $12. These two separate transaction values provide the basis for the valuation of the items in the two types of inventory—canvas inventory and frame inventory—before they are used in the assembly process. The estimated labor cost to assemble a finished painting is $3 per painting. Thus, when this particular painting has been assembled, or "manufactured," the cost of the new finished goods inventory (framed oil paintings) is $31 ($16 + $12 + $3). The transaction values (costs) of the raw material inputs from the two different inventories, plus the $3 outlay for the labor required to assemble the final product, *attach* to the third type of inventory item (framed oil paintings) to generate a new cost, or imputed transaction value, of $31. To summarize, the cost of finished products resulting from a manufacturing process is the sum of all the outlays (costs) made to acquire the raw material inputs and the outlays made to transform these resources for ultimate sale. When the finished product (the framed oil painting) is sold, and the revenue is recognized, the $31 cost would be then recognized as an expense (cost of sale) of the same period.

Duality of Asset and Liability Valuation and Related Expense Recognition

We have noted several times previously that under the conventional accounting model, there is a valuation linkage between the statement of financial position and the income statement. If a value is assigned to the ending balance of an asset or a liability in accordance with conventional accounting valuation principles, the related expense measure is merely a derivative calculation. Conversely, if an expense is measured independently, the related asset or liability value is inescapably determined by this expense measurement process. The two related values—expense and asset or liability value—are not independent calculations under the conventional accounting model.

The interdependency, or duality of valuation, follows from our retention of an original transaction data base for assigning values. For the case of asset valuation and the related expense recognition, the duality principle is expressed by the following basic relationship:

Ending asset value = Beginning asset value + Acquisitions − Expenses

or

Beginning asset value + Acquisitions = Expenses + Ending asset value

For any given accounting period, the beginning asset value was established at the end of the prior period. The new acquisitions of the period are a matter of record, that is, the result of observable business transactions. Under the conventional accounting model, the sum of these two values establishes an upper limit on the amount of expense that can be recognized in the period from the use of these assets. Indeed, over the life of the business, the total expense recognized will be equal to the total expenditures made to acquire resources. But, in the interim, the fundamental problem is to determine how to allocate, or split, the pool of costs associated with resources acquired and available for use between expense of the period and asset value at the end of the period. Once a decision is made on the expense, the ending value of the asset is produced as a residual calculation, and vice versa.

Example 12-5   Audio Dealers, Inc., had an inventory of high-fidelity equipment at the start of the year valued at $10,000. During the year, the company purchased merchandise in the amount of $80,000. Thus the total value (cost) of inventory available for sale during the period amounts to $90,000. Now if Audio Dealers determines that the value (cost) of its ending inventory is $20,000, the related expense (cost of sales) for the period is but a derivative calculation—$70,000. The duality relationship for this case is graphically depicted in Exhibit 12-1.

The same principles apply to the valuation of liabilities and related expenses.

While the basic duality relationship is a simple concept, it is at the same time important to keep in mind as we explore the alternative patterns of expense recognition and asset and liability valuation for specific classes of assets and liabilities.

Exhibit 12-1   Duality Principle for Asset and Expense Valuation

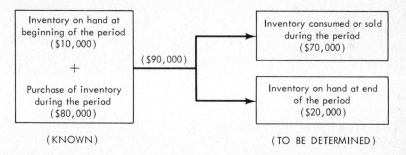

INVENTORY VALUATION AND RELATED EXPENSE RECOGNITION

In our earlier discussions of the adjustments (internal transactions) that are made at the end of each accounting period to recognize the cost of inventory sold during the period as an expense, we have assumed that we knew either the cost of the inventory on hand at the end of the period or the cost of the inventory sold or used. However, the way in which these values are determined is an important accounting issue, involving a large number of physical and clerical tasks and some important valuation assumptions. We will now explore the inventory valuation problem in greater detail, with particular emphasis on the alternative assumptions from which the accountant may choose in arriving at these measures.

The Physical Quantity Problem

Typically, the first problem in the process of assigning values to inventory "on hand" at the end of the period (and cost of sales for the period) is to determine the physical quantities applicable to these two categories. That is, we must allocate the total quantity of inventory available for sale during the period (the sum of inventory on hand at the start of the period and the purchases of inventory during the period) between (1) the quantities on hand at the end of the period and (2) the quantities that were used or sold during the period. This allocation problem can obviously be resolved by independently determining either of these two variables, and then inferring the measure of the other variable based on the total number of units to be allocated—the duality principle in operation for units as well as values.

To independently determine the quantity of units consumed or sold during the period, the firm may choose to maintain some type of record system that is continuously updated throughout the period. On the other hand, the quantity of units on hand at the end of the period can be determined by means of a physical count of the inventory. If the records and the physical counts are equally accurate, both of the methods should produce the same measures of the quantities of inventory consumed and on hand. However, in most business enterprises, either a physical count of inventory is employed in lieu of maintaining the detailed records of usage or such a count is made periodically to verify the accuracy of the records that are maintained.

The Assignment of Cost Problem

Having determined the quantity of units of inventory allocable to the two key variables—units on hand and units sold or consumed—the next task is to associate cost data (prices paid) with the quantities. The assignment is accomplished by electing one of several alternative pricing, or costing, assumptions.

• *Specific identification*. The intuitively obvious method of assigning costs to the quantities of inventory on hand or consumed is to identify the specific costs of each particular item consumed and/or on hand. Unfortunately, this method is *feasible* only under certain limited conditions. These conditions are, in general, that the inventory items be (1) uniquely identifiable and (2) of sufficient value to justify, for business as well as accounting reasons, maintaining the detailed records necessary to know the status of each separate inventory item.

Example 12-6   It is unlikely that a business that purchases, stores, and sells large quantities of wheat could identify the separate purchases (probably at varying prices) of wheat in its ending inventory because of the fungibility (interchangeability) of this type of inventory item. Therefore, in such a circumstance, it would be impossible to use the specific identification method to, say, identify with each bushel sold the price actually paid for the grain contained in it. On the other hand, for a business such as a jewelry shop, the individual inventory items are often uniquely identifiable. And because of the high value per item, the jewelry shop may maintain the necessary detailed records to aid in such activities as setting or negotiating selling prices or in providing evidence required in the event insurance claims might have to be filed. If this be the case, the specific identification method of assigning costs to units sold and on hand would be feasible.

In addition to the two constraints on the feasibility of the specific identification costing method, it is also subject to another practical limitation. We noted in Chapter 11 that one of the major considerations in the evaluation of alternative revenue methods was the degree to which any particular method was susceptible to fraud or manipulation. We are equally as concerned about this potential problem for expense recognition alternatives. And if a business elected to use the specific identification method of inventory costing, it is possible to "manage" reported income for the period by selecting the specific unit that the business chooses to sell based upon the relative costs of the items. This potentiality is present primarily when the inventory items are (1) uniquely identifiable in physical terms, (2) interchangeable in economic terms (of equal value), and (3) substantially different in terms of their acquisition costs.

Example 12-7   The Performance Investment Company invests in land and high-risk equity securities. The conventional accounting model is used to report on the firm's operations and financial position. At the present time, the company holds in its investment portfolio 1,500 shares of stock of Pacific Land Company. One block of 300 shares was acquired eight years ago at a cost of $20 per share. A second block of 800 shares was purchased three years ago at a price of $55 per share. The third block of 400 shares was acquired early this year at a cost of $100 per share. At the present time, the market price is $110 per share.

The company decides that it wishes to sell 1,000 shares from its present holding of 1,500 shares. The specific identification method of inventory valuation is feasible here, because each share can be identified by its certificate number and a specific cost associated with it. Yet, in terms of their economic value, the shares are interchangeable. If the specific identification method is elected, Performance Investment Company can affect the amount of income that will be recognized in the period by its choice of the specific shares to be sold. Thus the management of Performance Investment Company can increase its income for the period by including in the shares to be sold all the shares with a cost of $20 per share. If, on the other hand, the management were satisfied with the income that would be reported for the period and did not wish to increase it significantly with this transaction, it might elect to retain in its portfolio all of the shares with a cost of $20 per share, and to sell all of the shares with a cost of $100 per share.

• *Average cost method.* An obvious alternative to the specific identification method is to use some form of average cost. We can calculate a weighted average cost per item of inventory by adding the cost of the inventory on hand at the beginning of the period to the cost of inventory purchased during the period, and then dividing by the total number of units of inventory available for sale. The single weighted average cost calculated in this manner is then assigned both to the units of inventory sold during the period and to the units on hand at the end of the period.

Example 12-8   Using the data for the Performance Investment Company in Example 12-7, we would apply the average cost method (assuming 1,000 shares of stock were sold) as follows:

Inventory, beginning of period:		
300 shares @ $20	$ 6,000	
800 shares @ $55	44,000	$50,000
Purchases during period (400 shares @ $100)		40,000
Total cost of inventory available for sale		$90,000
Weighted average cost per share = $90,000/1,500		
= $60 per share		
Total cost of inventory available for sale allocated:		
To cost of sales (1,000 shares @ $60)		$60,000
To ending inventory (500 shares @ $60)		30,000
		$90,000

Therefore, using the average cost method, Performance Investment Company would recognize the following profit from the sale of 1,000 shares:

Sales (1,000 @ $110)	$110,000
Cost of sales	60,000
Profit on sale	$ 50,000

The average cost method of inventory valuation is generally easy to apply in practice. To use it, we need only know the total cost and total units of inventory on hand at the start of the period and acquisitions of inventory during the period—data that are generally available from the accounting system. Additionally, the method is not highly susceptible to manipulation, and it produces fairly reasonable cost allocations between inventory and cost of sales. There are, however, two other costing methods that are frequently encountered in current financial reporting, and these will now be examined.

• *First-in, first-out (Fifo) method.* In contrast to the specific identification method, which attempts to identify the costs associated with specific physical inventory flows, there is a class of costing assumptions that relies upon *assumed* flows of costs through the business enterprise. One of these methods, the Fifo method, assumes that the earliest inventory items purchased are the first inventory items sold—in measuring cost of sales, the first unit in is assumed to be the first unit out. This assumption about cost flows is in many instances justified by normal business practices. That is, the physical flow of inventory in and out of an enterprise coincides in many types of business with this assumed cost flow. This follows from the normal business objective of trying to maintain an orderly flow of its product so that it does not have old merchandise on hand.

Example 12-9   Again using the data of Example 12-7, Performance Investment Company had the following inventory acquisitions:

	Units	Unit Cost	Total
First purchase	300	$ 20	$ 6,000
Second purchase	800	55	44,000
Third purchase	400	100	40,000
	1,500		$90,000

Using these data, and the fact that 1,000 units (shares) were sold, we can assign values to either cost of sales or ending inventory in the following manner:

	Units	Unit Cost	Total
Cost of sales:	300	$ 20	$ 6,000
	700	55	38,500
	1,000		$44,500
Ending inventory:	400	$100	$40,000
	100	55	5,500
	500		$45,500

Thus the total cost of inventory available for sale ($90,000) is fully allocated between cost of sales and inventory.

In applying the first-in, first-out method to establish the value of the ending inventory, the unit cost of the latest purchase is assigned to the number of units in that purchase or in the ending inventory, whichever is smaller. If there are still more units in the ending inventory to be valued (as there are in Example 12-9), the unit cost from the next latest purchase is applied in a similar manner. We continue in this fashion until all of the units in the ending inventory have been assigned costs. If we wish to assign a value to cost of sales rather than to the ending inventory, the same procedure is followed, except that we begin with the unit cost associated with the first purchase (which is assumed to be sold first). Of course, once either one of the values (inventory or cost of sales) has been established, the other can be determined by using the duality principle illustrated earlier.

• *Last-in, first-out (Lifo) method.* An alternative costing method which is also predicated upon an assumption about the flow of costs is the last-in, first-out (Lifo) method of inventory costing. Under this method, it is assumed that items sold come from the latest acquisitions, or at least that the cost flows associated with the items sold are based upon the latest costs incurred. This method has fewer analogies in terms of physical flows of inventory units, but there are business situations where it is encountered. For example, the classic illustration of a Lifo flow of physical units is an inventory of coal, where each new acquisition is placed on top of the coal pile. In this case, the quantities used are, in the main, drawn from the latest units acquired. However, the method does not derive its principal appeal from an assumed physical analogy, but rather from the fact that it generally matches prices paid most recently for goods with current revenue.

Example 12-10   Using the Lifo method of inventory valuation for Performance Investment Company's securities, we arrive at the following allocation of costs:

	Units	Unit Cost	Total
Cost of sales:	400	$100	$40,000
	600	55	33,000
	1,000		$73,000
Ending inventory:	300	$ 20	$ 6,000
	200	55	11,000
	500		$17,000

Thus, under the Lifo cost flow assumption, the $90,000 total cost of inventory available for sale is again totally allocated between cost of sales and inventory on hand at the end of the period. But the amounts allocated to the two variables are significantly different from the allocations that were made under the Fifo method.

● *Summary of costing methods.* To recap the inventory costing methods that we have examined, Exhibit 12-2 reflects the allocation of costs under each of these methods. The hypothetical data for Performance Investment Company illustrate the potential disparity in the allocation of "costs" between cost of sales and inventory, depending upon the cost or pricing method that is adopted. In most practical applications, the disparity would not be as great as in this example, but the different inventory costing methods would nonetheless produce different values for the two variables, and thus different profit measures for the period. But where the units of inventory available for

Exhibit 12-2   PERFORMANCE INVESTMENT COMPANY
COMPARATIVE SUMMARY OF
ALTERNATIVE COSTING METHODS

Costing Method	Cost of Sales	Inventory, End of Period
Specific identification	Depends on actual physical flows	Depends on actual physical flows
Average cost	$60,000	$30,000
First-in, first-out (Fifo)	$44,500	$45,500
Last-in, first-out (Lifo)	$73,000	$17,000

sale (beginning inventory plus purchases during the period) do involve substantial differences in unit costs, the potential for variations such as those illustrated here does exist.

In this brief summary of inventory costing methods, we have implicitly assumed that the allocation of costs will be made at the end of the period. If the inventory is valued in this manner, that is, based upon the number of units on hand at the end of the period and the inferred number of units sold during the period, we refer to the approach as the *periodic method* of inventory valuation. An alternative approach is to assess the cost of sales and new inventory position throughout the period as sales are made. When this technique is used, we refer to it as the *perpetual method* of inventory valuation. The two approaches are illustrated in comparative form in the Appendix to this chapter.

Departures from Cost Basis for Valuing Inventories

Although inventories are normally valued at cost under the conventional accounting model, there are some exceptions to this general valuation rule. One exception was noted in Chapter 11 in discussing revenue recognition—those special cases where inventory is valued at net realizable value at the completion of the production process. Two other important exceptions that involve write-downs rather than write-ups of inventory are the general "lower of cost or market" test and the valuation of obsolete or damaged merchandise.

• *Lower of cost or market rule.* Inventory valuation under the conventional accounting model begins with an assessment of the cost of the inventory using one of the alternative costing methods discussed above. As a matter of general practice, the cost-based value (using individual inventory items, or categories of inventory, or the total inventory) is then compared with the current replacement cost ("market" in the terminology of inventory valuation) of the inventory. If cost exceeds market, the inventory is valued at the lower replacement cost amount. If market is in excess of the cost value, the inventory is valued at cost. This valuation approach is widely used for valuing inventories in current financial reporting and is referred to as *lower of cost or market* valuation. Lower of cost or market valuation obviously reflects an inherent conservative bias in the conventional accounting model. An implicit assumption of the method is that a drop in the replacement cost of inventory portends a drop in future selling prices, and based on this assumed market reaction, the conservative bias of the conventional accounting model is that the potential loss should be recognized as soon as possible. Note that the converse position is seldom found under conventional accounting valuation procedures; that is, potential gains are not given early recognition. As a consequence of valuing inventory at the lower of cost or market, the inventory values in the statement of financial position are also conservatively oriented. For statement users who may rely specifically on resource values for their actions (e.g., extending short-term credit), this conservatism is probably a desirable attribute of conventional accounting statements. Whether the method distorts, to some degree, the performance measure produced under conventional accounting is, however, an equally important issue to the broad class of statement users looking primarily to the firm's long-run cash-generating ability as a basis for their investment decisions. Some distortion of the performance index does seem to exist, particularly in the direction of reporting lower net income in the current period so that a more "normal" income can be reported when the goods are sold in the succeeding period.

Market is generally defined for this inventory valuation purpose as current replacement cost. But there are instances where another value may be used. In particular, the lower of cost or market test specifies that market (current replacement cost) shall not exceed net realizable value, nor be less than net realizable value reduced by a normal profit margin. If current replacement cost does exceed net realizable value, then the net realizable value becomes the "market" amount to be compared against cost. Here the reasoning is that inventory should never be valued at an amount in excess of what can be recovered upon sale. Similarly, if current replacement cost is below net realizable value less a normal profit margin, the higher figure is used because inventory need not be written down below an amount that will, upon sale, allow a normal profit when matched against revenue. Both of these tests are used in arriving at a value for "market." After this value for "market" is determined, it then is compared against cost, and the lower of the two values is used.

• *Obsolete or damaged merchandise.* When inventory items have suffered damage or obsolescence, the original costs of the items can no longer be presumed to bear any significant relationship to potential benefits (revenue). Under these circumstances, cost is abandoned as a valuation base, and the items are generally valued at their net realizable value.

Estimating Inventories from Aggregate Data

In certain situations we would like to estimate the value of inventory on hand at the end of the period without a detailed record of physical quantities on hand and/or detailed cost data for these items. For example, if a firm sustains a substantial loss to its inventory through a natural disaster, it will of course want to estimate the amount of this loss for insurance purposes. In the absence of detailed perpetual inventory records, the firm's only recourse will be to attempt to develop an estimate based on the information it does have available. Additionally, a firm may wish to test the reasonableness of the inventory value determined through the physical inventory process through the use of aggregate data. Both of these types of problems, as well as others that may arise, can be resolved by using the gross profit method of estimating inventory.

• *Gross profit method of estimating inventory.* A common method of estimating the value of inventory on hand by using aggregate data is the gross profit method. Assuming that the firm has a record of the aggregate purchases and sales for the period of time between the date the last set of financial statements was prepared and the date on which it wishes to estimate the value of the inventory, this method requires only that the firm have, or be able to estimate, the gross profit percentage—ratio of gross profit (sales − cost of sales = gross profit) to sales—that it has earned on sales of the period.

The variables we are dealing with in this measurement problem are clearly highlighted by again recalling our basic asset-expense duality relationship:

Ending inventory = Beginning inventory + Purchases of inventory − Cost of sales (to be estimated)

The accounting records of the firm will presumably reflect the inventory at the beginning of the period, based upon the physical inventory count at the end of the prior period. Additionally, these records would also generally provide the total cost of purchases made during the period. Therefore, to estimate the ending inventory, we need only estimate the cost of sales from the beginning of the period to the point in time at which we wish to estimate the ending inventory on hand (e.g., the end of the period, or the time of a natural disaster).

Can the cost of sales be reasonably estimated from the information generally available in the accounting records? The answer to this question is frequently yes! The firm may calculate from its prior income statements the gross profit percentage that it has been earning on sales. Assuming that the gross profit percentage in immediately preceding periods is relatively unchanged during the current period, or that we can otherwise estimate what the effects of current period pricing and cost changes have been on the gross profit percentage, we can apply the gross profit percentage to the recorded sales for the period to determine the estimated gross profit earned on these sales. Then, we can estimate cost of sales as follows:

Estimated cost of sales = Sales − Estimated gross profit

With this estimate of cost of sales in hand, we have value measures for the three variables needed to estimate the value of the ending inventory.

Example 12-11

The Craig Outdoors Company is engaged in the retail sales of sporting goods items. On August 7 of the current year, Craig suffered a fire which completely destroyed its stock of inventory. It did not maintain perpetual inventory records and thus had available only the financial statements of prior periods, and accounting records providing aggregate data on transactions engaged in during the current year.

The data available from the accounting records indicated that the inventory at the start of the period was valued at $20,000, purchases during the current period amounted to $60,000, and sales for the current period amounted to $75,000. Craig has earned a gross profit percentage over the last few years of approximately 40 percent, and its pricing policies (markups based on cost) were consistent in the current period with what they had been in prior periods. Therefore, the president of the company agreed that 40 percent was a reasonable estimate of the gross profit percentage earned during the current period before the fire.

Based on this information, we can estimate the value of inventory on hand at the time of the fire as follows:

Cost of goods available for sale:

Beginning inventory		$20,000
Purchases		60,000
Cost of goods available for sale		$80,000
Estimated cost of sales:		
Sales	$75,000	
Estimated gross profit (40% × $75,000)	30,000	
Estimated cost of sales		$45,000
Estimated ending inventory		$35,000

Thus, using this method of estimating ending inventory, Craig has a reasonable basis for filing a claim with its insurance company for the loss sustained in the fire.

Treatment of Manufacturing Costs

All of our examples to this point have focused on companies that purchase inventory for resale in the same form. There are, however, additional measurement problems in the valuation of the inventories of a manufacturing firm. A manufacturing firm has, in general, three basic classes of inventory:

1. Raw material inventory
2. Work-in-process inventory
3. Finished goods inventory

These categories correspond to the major forms in which the manufacturing firm holds inventory, that is, units not yet placed into the production process (raw material), partially completed units at some stage in the production process (work in process), and completed units held prior to shipment to customers (finished goods).

How do we assign costs to these various classes of inventory? Exhibit 12-3 depicts the basic inventory relationships for the three classes of inventory. We note first that no new problem is presented by the need to assign values to raw material inventories. The inventory valuation principles described previously are sufficient to value raw material inventories. Valuation of the work-in-process and finished goods inventories is, however, a more involved process. These inventories often result from the combination of several resources and the application of large amounts of labor and capital. The valuation principle we rely on for this type of measurement problem is the "costs attach" assumption.

The "costs attach" notion, which we alluded to briefly in our earlier discussion of the cost principle, assumes that the costs of inputs (material, labor, or capital) introduced into production attach to the units of production as they flow through the production process. Applying this principle to the valuation of manufacturing inventories, the cost of units in process is the sum of the costs incurred to bring the units to their present stage of completion. These costs include the cost of raw materials consumed, the cost of labor employed directly in the manufacture of the products, and a pro rata share of the general overhead costs of the factory. Thus two major additional problems involved in this measurement process are the determination of the completion status of the work in process and the identification of the costs incurred to bring units to that stage of production.

The finished goods inventory is the inventory of units that have moved completely through the production process and are on hand waiting shipment to wholesalers, dealers, or other retail customers. Valuation of this inventory class draws on the same principles that are used to value work-in-process inventories. Indeed, the measurement problem is somewhat easier because the stage of completion is not a factor to be determined.

Exhibit 12-3 **Inventory Relationships in a Manufacturing Firm**

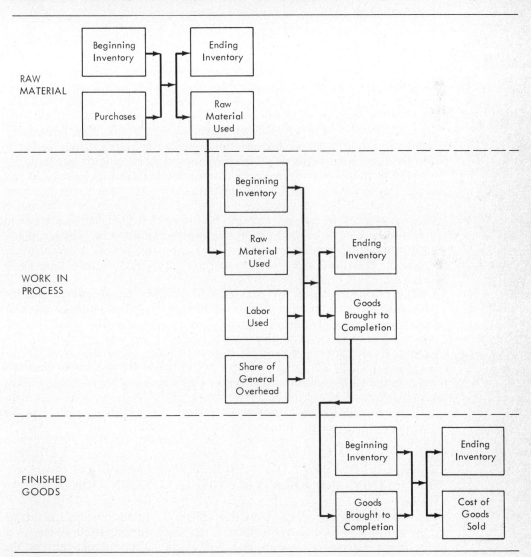

Effect of Inventory Errors on Reported Income

The determination of an inventory value at the end of an accounting period is the product of two separate tasks: (1) the determination of the physical quantity of units on hand and (2) the assignment of appropriate cost figures (depending on the cost method assumed) to these quantities of inventory. Because the determination of the actual quantity of goods on hand is a difficult task, particularly for a firm with a large and diversified inventory, we should consider what the effect of an error in this process (or, for that matter, the subsequent assignment of costs) will be on the reported income of the firm.

In assessing the impact of a possible error in inventory valuation on reported income, we return to our basic duality relationship for asset (inventory) valuation and expense (cost of sales) measurement:

$$\text{Cost of sales} = \text{Beginning inventory} + \text{Purchases} - \text{Ending inventory}$$

From this relationship, we readily observe that if the value of the ending inventory of a period is overstated, the cost of sales for the period will be understated. Conversely, if the ending inventory value is understated, the cost of sales for the period will be overstated.

Note, however, that any error in inventory valuation is then carried forward into the next period, because the beginning inventory of one period is merely the ending inventory of the prior period. Returning to our basic relationship, if the ending inventory of the current period is overstated, we noted that the cost of sales will be understated for the period, and therefore net income will be overstated. But in the succeeding period, the beginning inventory will be overstated, and thus cost of sales for the succeeding period will also be overstated, and net income will be understated. The overstatement and the understatement of net income in the two periods are of identical amounts. Therefore, over two periods, inventory errors are offsetting (self-correcting) with respect to reported net income.

The existence of this two-period, self-correction feature should not be construed to mean that the effect of an inventory error is unimportant. Our concern in formulating an index of long-run cash-generating ability is with achieving the best matching that we can of efforts and accomplishments of a period. If an inventory error (either overstatement or understatement) develops, our index will be in error for both periods. To the extent that this error in the indexes distorts the trend of earnings, as it may well do, the decision relevance of the information may be substantially reduced. Additionally, the error in the ending inventory valuation will also be reflected in the statement of financial position at the end of the period.

LONG-LIVED ASSETS (TANGIBLE AND INTANGIBLE): VALUATION AND RELATED EXPENSE RECOGNITION

A second major class of assets that creates important problems of valuation and related expense recognition is the so-called long-lived assets class. The major differences between long-lived assets and inventories are that the long-lived assets are acquired for *use* rather than sale, and the benefits to be derived from the long-lived assets generally extend over a much longer period of time than for inventories.

Long-lived assets are divided into two categories: tangible and intangible. The long-lived tangible assets class includes items such as buildings, machinery and equipment, and delivery trucks, as well as any natural resources that the firm holds, such as land and mineral rights. On the other hand, the long-lived intangible assets class, as the term is used in accounting, consists principally of rights acquired under law which do not themselves have physical substance, such as patents, copyrights, franchises, and trademarks. Because certain other assets (such as accounts receivable) also lack "physical substance," we should note that the basic test for inclusion within the intangible category is to a certain extent a matter of convention, rather than precise definitional stipulation.

The major problems in accounting for long-lived assets may be classified as follows:

1. Valuation at date of acquisition
2. Determination of the appropriate treatment of expenditures made over the life of the asset to maintain and/or improve it
3. Measurement of benefits that have been consumed in the production of revenue
4. Recognition of gain or loss on the disposal of the assets

Each of these classes of accounting problems will be considered in turn.

Valuation of Long-lived Assets at Acquisition

The valuation of long-lived assets at date of acquisition, like the valuation of any other asset, is predicated upon the basic financial model of the firm that has been selected. Thus, using the conventional accounting model, long-lived assets are valued on the basis of the outlays made to acquire them. This problem was considered at the beginning of this chapter in our discussion of the cost principle. Indeed, in Example 12-2 describing the acquisition of a new computer by the Roark Computer Service Company, we addressed the problem of the valuation of long-lived assets at date of acquisition. We need only reiterate that this valuation is based upon the application of the criteria for the determination of cost and should be construed broadly to include all expenditures made to acquire the asset and install it in position for use.

Expenditures to Maintain and/or Improve Long-lived Assets

After an asset has been acquired, additional expenditures will often be made over the life of the asset to maintain or improve its operating capability. If these expenditures do not add to, or increase, the potential benefits that can be derived from the asset, but merely maintain the asset's operating efficiency, the expenditures are generally regarded as normal repairs and maintenance and are reported as expenses of the period in which the outlays are made. On the other hand, some expenditures are made to increase the level of benefits that may be derived from the long-lived asset. Expenditures of this type are added to the unexpired cost of the asset and are then matched against revenue in future periods as the additional benefits are derived.

In many practical situations, the distinction between an expenditure that improves the asset and one that merely maintains it in proper operating order is fuzzy. In these situations, judgment must be exercised by the accountant in order to properly classify the expenditure. In making this judgment, the significance (materiality) of the expenditure is often an important consideration. If the expenditure is judged to be relatively immaterial, it will normally be treated as an expense of the period, even though it may in fact be a minor improvement. However, if the potential impact of the expenditure is material, the accountant must assess more carefully the effect of the expenditure on the services to be derived from the asset in future periods.

Measurement of Benefits Derived from Long-lived Assets

Use of long-lived assets represents a consumption of the benefits, or service potentials, inherent in the asset. Presumably, this use of resources contributes to the production of revenue of the period. In accordance with the matching principle, we wish to reflect as an expense of the current period the cost of these inherent benefits or service potentials that were consumed. Because of the indivisibility of long-lived assets, however, it is often difficult to ascertain precisely the benefits derived in a particular period.

In general, two different approaches to this problem are available. One approach is based upon the *output* of the asset. Where benefits potentially available from an asset can be expressed in terms of a maximum potential output, the total cost of the asset may under the output method be allocated to periods based upon the output produced in a period.

Example 12-12   The Jones Company acquired a machine that is expected to have a potential output of 25,000 units of the product produced on it over its life. The cost of the machine is $50,000, and Jones does not anticipate that there will be any salvage value at the end of the machine's useful life. Applying the output measure of expense assessment, we recognize as an expense of the period a cost of $2 ($50,000/25,000) for each unit produced on the machine. Therefore, if the company produced 4,000 units of product on this machine during the current period, the depreciation expense for the period would be $8,000 (4,000 × $2).

Where we can determine fairly accurately an identifiable output from a long-lived asset and also estimate the total potential output over its life, the output method produces a satisfactory matching of effort and accomplishment.

Obviously, however, we are not able to identify the specific output from a number of different types of long-lived assets—for example, an office building. In these cases, we must turn to an assessment of the service potentials consumed from the use of the asset based upon the passage of time. Such recourse to a time-based calculation is admittedly a pragmatic compromise of our matching objective. However, there are tangible assets (such as buildings) whose service potential is primarily influenced by the passage of time (forces of weather, etc.), and for which unused capacity in one period is not necessarily usable in future periods. In these cases, the time-based method of determining expense is a sensible approach to matching.

Generally, where time is used as the primary basis for determining the services derived from the use of an asset, and thus the related expense measure, we must—

1. Estimate the useful life of the asset.
2. Estimate the residual value of the asset at the end of its useful life.
3. Select a method of depreciation.

We have, in our previous discussions of the depreciation of long-lived assets, selected a depreciation method that allocated an equal portion of the depreciable cost (cost less estimated salvage value) of the asset to each period of time of its useful life. This method is called the *straight-line* method of depreciation.

There are, however, other methods or patterns of allocating the cost to be depreciated to the various periods over the useful life of a long-lived asset. Frequently, these methods produce larger measures of expense in the early years of the asset's life, and correspondingly smaller expense measurements in the later years. Two of these "accelerated expense recognition" methods which are often encountered in current practice are the sum-of-years-digits method and the declining-balance method.

• *Sum-of-years-digits depreciation method.* The sum-of-years-digits method is one of the depreciation methods that produces larger measures of depreciation expense in the early years of the life of the asset than in the later years. This pattern of depreciation expense results from applying decreasing depreciation rates to the depreciable cost (cost less the estimated salvage value).

Example 12-13   The Longhorn Manufacturing Company was formed on January 1, 1975, to manufacture various types of gift items with Longhorn emblems embossed on them. Immediately after the company was formed, embossing machinery was purchased at a cost of $16,000. It was estimated that the machinery would have a life of five years and that the residual, or salvage, value of the machinery at the end of that period of time would be $1,000. The amount of depreciation recognized under the sum-of-years-digits method is reflected in Exhibit 12-4.

The depreciation rate to be used under this method is determined by first summing the digits from 1 to n, where n is the number of years of useful life that the asset is expected to be productive. In Example 12-13, the asset has an expected useful life of five years, and the sum of the digits from one to five is fifteen ($1 + 2 + 3 + 4 + 5 = 15$). This sum is placed in the denominator in determining the depreciation rate. The numerator of the depreciation rate changes each year, starting with the largest number in the sum (i.e., 5), and decreasing by one each year until in the last year the numerator is 1. Therefore, the depreciation rate for the first year is 5/15, and when this rate is applied to the depreciable cost (cost less estimated salvage value) of

Exhibit 12-4   ILLUSTRATION OF SUM-OF-YEARS-DIGITS
                                        DEPRECIATION METHOD

Year	Asset Value, Beginning of Year	Depreciation Rate	Depreciation Expense	Asset Value, End of Year
1	$16,000	5/15	$5/15 \times \$15,000 = \$ 5,000$	$11,000
2	11,000	4/15	$4/15 \times 15,000 = 4,000$	7,000
3	7,000	3/15	$3/15 \times 15,000 = 3,000$	4,000
4	4,000	2/15	$2/15 \times 15,000 = 2,000$	2,000
5	2,000	1/15	$1/15 \times 15,000 = 1,000$	1,000
		1.00	$15,000	

$$\text{Sum-of-years-digits} = 1 + 2 + 3 + 4 + 5$$
$$= 15$$

$15,000, we obtain depreciation expense of $5,000. In the second year, the numerator of the depreciation rate is reduced by one to 4, and the rate is 4/15. Applying this rate again to the depreciable cost of $15,000, the depreciation expense for the year is $4,000. This modification of the depreciation rate continues until the last year, when the depreciation rate is 1/15. At the end of the five-year life of the asset, the asset is valued (cost less accumulated depreciation) at $1,000—the amount of the estimated salvage value.

• *Declining-balance depreciation method.* Under the declining-balance depreciation method, which also is a method that assigns larger amounts of depreciation to the earlier years, a fixed percentage is applied to the *balance of the asset* (cost less accumulated depreciation) at the start of each year to determine depreciation expense for that year. Two common percentages that are used (particularly due to their acceptability for tax purposes) are 150 percent of the straight-line rate and 200 percent of the straight-line rate. For the data of Example 12-13, the straight-line depreciation rate, given a five-year life, is 20 percent. That is, we allocate 20 percent of the depreciable cost of the asset to each year if we adopt the straight-line depreciation method. Therefore, using a 150 percent declining-balance depreciation method, our rate would be 30 percent (20 percent × 150 percent); and under the 200 percent, or double-declining-balance depreciation method, the depreciation rate is 40 percent (20 percent × 200 percent). Obviously, the double-declining-balance depreciation method will assign a larger portion of the cost of the long-lived asset to the early periods than will the 150 percent declining-balance method.

After the depreciation rate has been determined, the depreciation for the year under the declining-balance method is determined by multiplying this rate by the asset value at the beginning of each year. When this method is applied, no estimate of salvage value is used in the calculation. However, the total amount of depreciation expense recognized over the life of the asset cannot exceed the difference between cost and salvage value, that is, the book value of the asset is not reduced below its salvage value. Application of the double-declining-balance depreciation method to the facts of Example 12-13 is illustrated in Exhibit 12-5.

To briefly review the procedures followed in Exhibit 12-5, we note that in

Exhibit 12-5   ILLUSTRATION OF DOUBLE-DECLINING-BALANCE
                         DEPRECIATION METHOD

Year	Asset Value, Beginning of Year	Depreciation Rate	Depreciation Expense	Asset Value, End of Year
1	$16,000	40%	$16,000 × 40% = $ 6,400	$9,600
2	9,600	40	9,600 × 40 = 3,840	5,760
3	5,760	40	5,760 × 40 = 2,304	3,456
4	3,456	40	3,456 × 40 = 1,382	2,074
5	2,074	40	2,074 × 40 = 830	1,244
			$14,756	

the first year depreciation expense is calculated by multiplying the double-declining-balance depreciation rate (40 percent) by the original cost of the asset ($16,000), or $6,400 depreciation expense. The carrying value (unexpired cost) of the asset at the end of the year, then, is the original cost of the asset ($16,000) less the accumulated depreciation ($6,400), or $9,600. This carrying value at the end of year one is of course the asset value at the beginning of year two, and it is the base for the calculation of depreciation expense in the second year. We multiply the 40 percent rate by the $9,600 carrying value of the asset at the beginning of the second year to compute the $3,840 depreciation expense for the second year. Continuing in this fashion, at the end of year five we have an ending asset value of $1,244 (which appropriately is not less than the estimated salvage value of $1,000), and total depreciation expense for the five-year period amounts to $14,756. In general, the total depreciation expense recognized under the declining-balance depreciation method will not equal the total depreciable cost (which is the amount allocated under the straight-line and sum-of-years-digits methods), although the difference will normally be fairly small.

Discussion of Alternative Depreciation Patterns

The different amounts of depreciation expense that would be recognized each year for the data of Example 12-13 under the alternative depreciation methods we have considered are summarized in Exhibit 12-6. As noted earlier, the straight-line method allocates the depreciable cost equally over the asset's life, while the two "accelerated" methods allocate larger amounts to the early years of the asset's life. Although there exist additional alternative

Exhibit 12-6   COMPARISON OF DEPRECIATION EXPENSE DETERMINED
                       UNDER ALTERNATIVE DEPRECIATION METHODS

Year	Straight-Line	Sum-of-Years-Digits	Double-Declining-Balance
1	$ 3,000	$ 5,000	$ 6,400
2	3,000	4,000	3,840
3	3,000	3,000	2,304
4	3,000	2,000	1,382
5	3,000	1,000	830
	$15,000	$15,000	$14,756

depreciation methods, these three methods are probably selected most frequently in current practice.

The disparity of the amounts allocated to the different periods raises the question of what factors the accountant considers in choosing a depreciation method. Recall that our initial premise was that we are trying to derive a measure of effort, as reflected in the consumption of services from the long-lived asset, to match against the related revenue generated in the period. When we are selecting from depreciation methods that are related to the passage of time, however, it is difficult to apply the matching principle to uniquely identifiable revenue increments. The rationale for the selection of a particular time-based depreciation method must necessarily be related to *general* revenue and/or cost considerations. One basis that is often used to decide between alternative time-based depreciation methods is the pattern of related costs associated with the long-lived asset. A business enterprise expects some normal pattern of expenditures for repairs and maintenance over the life of a long-lived asset. If the expectation is that these costs will increase as time passes, we may conclude that a larger portion of the services inherent in the asset are consumed in the early years of its life, and thus a depreciation method should be selected that allocates a larger amount of the depreciable cost to the early years. Or the same conclusion may be reached by arguing that if repairs and maintenance expenditures are increasing over time, a combination of this expense pattern with a decreasing depreciation expense will result in a fairly uniform pattern of total expense (depreciation expense plus repairs and maintenance expense) recognized each period over the life of the asset—a condition that may be reasonably consistent with the pattern of benefits the firm expects to derive from the use of the asset.

Alternatively, the decision on the depreciation method to be selected may be based upon the expectation as to revenue patterns. For example, if the revenue to be derived from the asset is expected to remain fairly uniform over the life of the asset without any significant change in other related expenses, this may add credence to the use of the straight-line depreciation method. On the other hand, if there is an expectation of decreasing productivity over the life of the asset, this might suggest that a larger percentage of the services would be consumed in the early years of the asset's life, and thus one of the two methods that produce decreasing depreciation expense over time should be adopted.

Finally, the choice of the depreciation method is sometimes influenced by a desire to report the same depreciation expense for financial reporting purposes as is reported for income tax purposes. Present income tax law allows a company to select any of the three methods we have illustrated. In many circumstances, business enterprises opt for a depreciation method that allocates a larger portion of the expense to the early periods of the asset's life, in order to reduce their taxable income and therefore their tax liability in the early years. While the *total* income tax over the life of the asset is unaffected by the choice of any particular depreciation method (assuming no tax rate changes occur), the time preference for money concept obviously supports any action (including choice of a depreciation method) that results in the deferral of cash expenditures the firm must make. Thus, although the income tax law does not require that the same amounts be reported for tax and financial reporting purposes, many companies may wish to do so for record-keeping convenience.

Land and Natural Resources

Our discussion of the measurement of benefits received from long-lived assets has to this point concentrated on fabricated, or constructed, physical assets, such as buildings or machinery. Certain other types of long-lived tangible assets, however, have a finite reservoir of service potentials. As these benefits are consumed over time by a business enterprise, the cost of the asset must be matched against revenue in the same manner as described above.

Natural resources that are exploited by a company, such as mineral deposits or stands of timber, are examples of this class of nonconstructed assets. In many cases, the "production or output method" of recognizing the expense of consuming such resources is used. The first step is to estimate the total quantity of the resource available (e.g., number of tons of iron ore). Dividing the total cost of the asset by this estimate of total units available, we obtain a cost per unit. Then as the resources are extracted or otherwise consumed, the expense to be recognized is calculated by multiplying the cost per unit by the number of units consumed. Where it is impossible to estimate the total quantity of resources available, the measure of expense may have to be determined using a time-based exploitation pattern.

Although the recognition of the expense associated with the use of natural resources is similar to depreciation expense, a difference in terminology should be noted. The allocation of the cost of constructed, or fabricated, assets to time periods is labeled depreciation expense. The allocation of the cost of natural resources to time periods is referred to as *depletion expense*.

Land that is acquired by a company for use as a site for its manufacturing, marketing, or administrative operations represents a special case. We assume generally that the value of land for "site purposes" is unaffected by the passage of time or the intensity of use. That is, the service potential of land as a site remains unchanged over time. Accordingly, none of the cost of land used for site purposes needs to be allocated to periods or otherwise matched against revenue, and under the conventional accounting model, this asset (site land) will continue to be valued at its original cost, with no accumulated depletion. However, land held because of the natural resources it contains (including, for example, agricultural land) will be valued at original cost less accumulated depletion.

Unique Properties and Characteristics of Intangibles

Intangible assets include such resources as patents, copyrights, trademarks, franchises, and goodwill. These are real, often extremely valuable, assets, notwithstanding their lack of physical substance. The treatment of intangible assets is not in principle substantially unlike that accorded long-lived tangible assets. Intangibles are originally valued at the cost incurred to acquire them, and this cost is then allocated to expense over the expected useful life of the asset. In many cases, the life of the intangible is reasonably well defined by the legal right that the company holds (for example, the seventeen-year life of a patent).

Example 12-14   Meyer Tobacco Company, Limited, manufactures pipes. The pipes have a special finish, due largely to the unique finishing process used by the company. A patent on this process was acquired from another pipe manufacturer several years ago at a cost of $51,000. The patent is legally binding for seventeen years.

The patent is given recognition as a long-lived intangible asset in Meyer's statement of financial position. At the date of acquisition, the value of the asset would be $51,000. If the useful life of the patent were expected to be equal to its legal life, the company would then allocate a portion of its cost to expense each year. Typically, an equal amount is assigned to each year. Thus, $3,000 ($51,000/17) would be recognized as expense of each period, reflecting the estimate of the cost of the services derived from the patent during the period.

In other cases, however, the estimated useful life of an intangible is not apparent from legal or other criteria, and a more arbitrary judgment must be made.

Example 12-15   Jack Hinrichs purchases the Ford distributorship in Dime Box, Texas, from the estate of the former owner for $225,000. The business has been very successful the past fifteen years and enjoys an extremely high reputation in the community. Since the tangible assets of the firm have current market values amounting to only $150,000, it may be inferred that Jack paid $75,000 for the intangible properties of the distributorship—often referred to as "goodwill" in financial statements.

The goodwill, like the patent in Example 12-14, will be initially valued at its original cost ($75,000) in the statement of financial position. Allocation of the cost to expense is a more difficult problem, because the future periods benefiting from the firm's present reputation are somewhat indeterminate, and indeed subject to change. Thus we may have to resort to some arbitrary number of years. (Under current accounting promulgations, the $75,000 cost would be recognized as an expense over a period of time not to exceed forty years.)

Where expenditures are made to develop intangible assets (for example, research and development programs), difficult measurement problems are created. The central questions are, (1) Does an intangible asset exist? and if so, (2) What is its value? Until recently, some companies elected to capitalize their expenditures for research and development as an intangible asset (or, in some cases, in a section of the statement of financial position labeled *deferred costs*). These costs were then allocated to expense (this type of expense is often labeled *amortization* in financial statements) in future periods—often on an arbitrary basis. Where this practice was followed, the danger that the statement user had to be sensitive to was the possible overstatement of the firm's assets, that is, the recognition of the expenditures as assets when in fact assets did not exist or the values (in terms of future benefits) of the intangible assets were not sufficiently large to warrant recognition at the amount of the expenditure. Because of many observed tendencies on the part of management to capitalize research and development expenditures under questionable circumstances, accounting policy was modified in 1974 to require recognition of these expenditures as expenses of the current period. This policy is obviously conservatively biased in the measurement of net operating income of the current period. However, by eliminating all management discretion, the policy will result in the understatement of a firm's assets (and future expenses) when intangibles have been created by a research and development program.

Disposal of Long-lived Assets

At the time a long-lived asset is disposed of, which may be at the end of its previously estimated useful life or at some other earlier or later time, the gain or loss on the disposition must be recognized. This gain or loss is measured simply by comparing the carrying value of the asset (original cost less accumulated depreciation) with the sales proceeds. If there are additional expenses incurred to dispose of the asset, these expenses will also be deducted in the computation of the gain or loss from disposal of the asset. In the past, this gain or loss was treated as an "extraordinary" item in the income statement. However, accounting policy on this issue was recently changed, and now one will normally find the gain or loss on the disposal of long-lived assets as a component of net operating income (i.e., it is *not* treated as an extraordinary item). This is basically in response to the notion that gains or losses on disposal of long-lived assets are jointly a function of (1) market conditions (which determine the price received) *and* (2) *postacquisition management decisions* concerning depreciation of the assets (which determine the unexpired cost of the asset at the time of disposition). By forcing the inclusion of such gains and losses in operating income, that is, "performance," in the period of disposition, accounting policy makers have presumably removed some of the incentive that management might have had to understate depreciation on such assets during their use (and thus overstate net operating income) when the underdepreciation showed up as an extraordinary loss (and thus was excluded from operating income) in the period of disposition.

Where the disposal of a long-lived asset is in the form of a trade-in to acquire a new asset of the same kind, there is an alternative method of accounting for the transaction. This alternative, which gains much of its support due to its acceptability under the income tax law, was illustrated in Example 12-2 in our discussion of the cost of the new computer. Briefly, it involves valuing the new asset at the sum of the cash payment plus the unexpired cost of the asset traded in, with *no gain or loss* recognized on the disposition of the old asset.

APPENDIX: INVENTORY VALUATION—PERIODIC VERSUS PERPETUAL ASSESSMENT OF COSTS

In our discussion in the chapter of the pricing, or costing, methods that are available for the accountant to choose from, we assumed implicitly that the allocation of costs would be made at the end of the period. If this is the way in which the inventory is valued, that is, based upon the number of units on hand at the end of the period and the inferred number of units sold during the period, we refer to it as the *periodic method* of inventory valuation. An alternative approach is to assess the cost of sales throughout the period as sales are made. When this technique is used, we refer to it as the *perpetual method* of inventory valuation. These two methods will produce different valuations for inventory and cost of sales only if there are purchases and sales that are intermingled throughout the period, *and* only under certain of the costing methods. In particular, the specific identification and the Fifo methods produce identical results under both the periodic and the perpetual techniques. However, the average cost and the Lifo methods of inventory valuation produce different valuations depending upon whether one uses the periodic or the perpetual technique of inventory valuation. These observations are illustrated in Exhibit 12-7.

In Exhibit 12-7 we see that the Fifo method is unaffected by the application of the periodic or the perpetual techniques. Both techniques assign a value of $4,200 to the ending inventory and a value of $5,800 to cost of sales. However, the Lifo and the average cost method produce different results under these two techniques. In the average cost method, the reason for the different result is that the average cost per unit of inventory is changed each time a new purchase is made. If units sold are assigned costs at the time they are sold, as they are under the perpetual method of inventory valuation, the average cost is a function of the aggregate costs of units on hand *at that time*. Where the periodic method is applied, however, the average cost per unit is determined on the basis of *all acquisitions* during the period, and thus one weighted average cost is applied uniformly to all units sold and all units remaining in the inventory. In the Lifo method, the difference arises when some of the older acquisitions of stocks of goods are sold before new acquisitions are made. Under the perpetual method, some of these older costs will be assigned to cost of sales, and thus they cannot be later assigned to the ending inventory. Applying the periodic method, however, inventory on hand at the end of the period is based first upon units on hand at the start of the period and then upon the earliest acquisitions during the period—notwithstanding the fact that some of these units may have been sold before the acquisitions to replace them had been made.

<table>
<tr><td>Questions
for
Review
and
Discussion</td><td>

12-1. Define or *briefly* explain the following terms:

a. Expense

b. Matching principle

c. Joint cost

d. Cost principle

e. Original transaction value

f. Market (in "lower of cost or market")

g. Gross profit and gross profit percentage

h. Tangible and intangible assets

i. Depreciation, depletion, and amortization expenses

12-2. Distinguish between product expenses and period expenses. Why is the distinction necessary?

</td></tr>
</table>

Exhibit 12-7   PERIODIC VERSUS PERPETUAL INVENTORY VALUATION

BASIC DATA:	Units	Unit Cost	Total
Jan. 1—Inventory on hand	100	$10	$ 1,000
3—Sale	(100)		
5—Purchase	500	12	6,000
10—Sale	(300)		
18—Purchase	200	15	3,000
25—Sale	(100)		
On hand, end of period	300		

FIFO:

Periodic Method				Perpetual Method			
Units	Unit Cost	Total		Units	Unit Cost	Inventory	Cost of Sales
Inventory on hand:							
200	$15	$ 3,000	Jan. 1	100	$10	$1,000	
100	12	1,200	3	(100)	10	(1,000)	$1,000
300		$ 4,200		—0—		—0—	
			5	500	12	6,000	
				500	12	6,000	
Cost of sales:							
100	$10	$ 1,000	10	(300)	12	(3,600)	3,600
400	12	4,800		200	12	2,400	
			18	200	15	3,000	
500		$ 5,800		400		5,400	
Total cost allocated		$10,000	25	(100)	12	(1,200)	1,200
				300		$4,200	$5,800

LIFO:

Periodic Method				Perpetual Method			
Units	Unit Cost	Total		Units	Unit Cost	Inventory	Cost of Sales
Inventory on hand:							
100	$10	$ 1,000	Jan. 1	100	$10	$1,000	
200	12	2,400	3	(100)	10	(1,000)	$1,000
300		$ 3,400		—0—		—0—	
			5	500	12	6,000	
				500	12	6,000	
Cost of sales:							
200	$15	$ 3,000	10	(300)	12	(3,600)	3,600
300	12	3,600		200	12	2,400	
			18	200	15	3,000	
500		$ 6,600		400		5,400	
Total cost allocated		$10,000	25	(100)	15	(1,500)	1,500
				300		$3,900	$6,100

AVERAGE COST:

Periodic Method

	Units	Cost
Inventory, beginning of period	100	$ 1,000
Purchases	700	9,000
	800	$10,000
Average cost/item = $10,000/800 = $12.50		
Allocated to:		
Cost of sales (500 @ $12.50)		$ 6,250
Inventory (300 @ $12.50)		3,750
Total cost allocated		$10,000

Perpetual Method

	Units	Cost of Inventory	Average Unit Cost	Cost of Sales
Jan. 1	100	$1,000	$10	
3	(100)	(1,000)	10	$1,000
	—0—	—0—		
5	500	6,000		
	500	6,000	12	
10	(300)	(3,600)	12	3,600
	200	2,400	12	
18	200	3,000		
	400	5,400	13.50	
25	(100)	(1,350)	13.50	1,350
	300	$4,050	13.50	$5,950

12-3. What are the criteria to be applied in determining the original transaction value, or cost, of acquiring nonmonetary assets?

12-4. The *cost* of an asset, as the term is used in accounting, is a more inclusive concept than merely the price of the item. Explain what is encompassed in cost.

12-5. Express in equation form the duality of asset valuation and the related expense recognition.

12-6. Explain briefly the major inventory costing methods used under the conventional accounting model.

12-7. Identify the major exceptions to valuing inventory at cost under the conventional accounting model. What is the justification for each exception?

12-8. Since the effect of an inventory valuation error is normally "offsetting" in a succeeding time period, why should one be concerned about this type of error?

12-9. Identify the major problems in accounting for long-lived assets.

12-10. What factors should one consider when choosing a depreciation method?

12-11. In applying the "lower of cost or market" rule for valuing inventories, "market" typically refers to the current replacement cost of the inventory. What value would you choose for "replacement cost" if a series of prices was quoted, depending on the size of the order?

12-12. Many firms account for their operations on a calendar year basis; however, some adopt what is called a "natural business year." The natural business year for a firm is usually defined as a year ending on a date when operations (and usually inventory) have reached the lowest point in their annual cycle. For example, retail department stores often choose a fiscal year for accounting for their operations that ends on February 28—presumably their natural business year. How might the choice of a natural business year reduce the potential for the significant differences in net income that may result solely from firms' arbitrary choices of different (but acceptable) inventory methods?

12-13. Ozzo Corporation adopted the Lifo method for valuing its inventory of flour used in making its special brand of spaghetti when the company was formed in 1947. Since that time, the quantity of flour normally maintained in inventory has increased only slightly, because the owners decided not to expand the volume of their operations in order to maintain the quality of their product. The price of flour has increased an average of 5 percent per year since 1947. At the end of previous fiscal years, the number of tons of flour on hand has usually been within 10 percent of the normal inventory level. However, during the last few months of 1974, the corporation encountered substantial difficulties in purchasing flour, and at the end of the year, its inventory had been depleted to approximately 20 percent of its normal level. What effect would this temporary inventory reduction have on net income for 1974? Would the effect be the same if the company used Fifo? If the inventory stockout is regarded as a temporary, abnormal phenomenon, do you believe that some modification of the Lifo method might be justified? If so, what?

12-14. Each year, Chivas Walker purchases 100 cases of scotch whiskey. He stores the whiskey for eight years and then sells the aged product. In preparing his financial statements, Chivas asks you if it would be appropriate to include the interest costs he has incurred on money borrowed to finance his inventories of aging whiskey as an addition to the purchase cost of the inventory rather than as an expense of the period in which paid. How would you respond (giving specific attention to the cost and matching principles of the conventional accounting model)? Would your answer change if Chivas provided the financing from invested rather than borrowed funds?

12-15. An investor purchases a motel in Florida for $550,000. The motel is situated on land that has been leased for ten years. At the end of the ten-year period, ownership of all structures thereon reverts to the owner of the land (there is no option for renewal of the lease).

(a) What factors would you consider in deciding how to recognize the purchase price of the motel as an expense over the life of the venture?

(b) If the average occupancy rate was 80 percent from November to May, and 40 percent from June to October, would this affect your measurement of expense for annual income statements? For monthly income statements? How?

Exercises   **12-1. Comparative Inventory Valuations.**   Pryor Data Terminals compiled the following data on one of its principal products, the Datapoint 6000, for the month of August:

Date Purchased	Units	Price/Unit	Cost
Beginning inventory	20	$400	$ 8,000
8/5	40	375	15,000
8/13	50	340	17,000
8/25	40	350	14,000

At the end of August, a physical inventory indicated that Pryor had 50 units of the Datapoint 6000 on hand.

Required:

Calculate the value of the ending inventory and the cost of sales for August under each of the three inventory costing methods:

(a) Fifo

(b) Lifo

(c) Weighted average

12-2. Comparative Inventory Valuations.   Jones Electronics Wholesalers, Inc., has compiled the following data on one of its principal products, the XT-100, for the month of May:

Date Purchased	Units	Price/Unit	Cost
Beginning inventory	100	$5.00	$ 500
5/3	600	4.50	2,700
5/16	800	5.50	4,400
5/25	500	6.00	3,000

At the end of May, a physical inventory indicated that Jones had 400 units of the XT-100 on hand.

Required:

Calculate the value of the ending inventory and the cost of sales for May under each of the three costing methods:

(a) Fifo

(b) Lifo

(c) Weighted average

12-3. Inventory Valuation and Reported Income.   The following item appeared in the *Wall Street Journal,* May 2, 1974. (Reprinted with the permission of The Wall Street Journal, © Dow Jones & Company, Inc., 1974.)

> When it reported first quarter profits last week, Mobil [Oil Corporation] cited inventory gains from foreign oil as a factor in the 66% increase in overall earnings from a year earlier. Other international oil companies also had major inventory profits in the first quarter as a result of the sharp increases in prices of foreign oil posted by the producing governments at the beginning of the year.
>
> But unlike some of the other internationals, Mobil utilizes what it calls an average cost inventory accounting in its foreign operations. Income is charged with an average of current cost and historic cost. In the first quarter, Mobil said, if it had charged foreign income with current costs only, its earnings would have been lower by about $90 million.

Required:

1. What *valuation model* did Mobil use for inventory?

2. What inventory valuation *method* did Mobil use?

3. In selecting an inventory method, Mobil might also have chosen Fifo or Lifo. Indicate whether the "inventory profit" would probably have been *higher* or *lower* than $90 million if these methods had been used:

   (a) Fifo

   (b) Lifo

4. One of the alternative *valuation models* would substantially eliminate this "inventory profit" from reported income. Identify the model.

12-4. Comparative Depreciation Methods.   On January 1, 1974, Demkon Corporation acquired a new machine for producing its product at a cost of $175,000. The machine is expected to have a useful life of five years, and a salvage value at the end of the five years of $25,000.

Required:

Calculate the depreciation expense for *1975* under each of the three depreciation methods:

(a) Straight-line

(b) Sum-of-years-digits

(c) Double-declining-balance

12-5. Comparative Depreciation Methods.   The Cruse Company acquired a new machine on January 1, 1975, for $225,000. The company estimates the machine to have a useful life of six years, and a salvage value at the end of six years of $15,000.

Required:

1. Calculate the depreciation expense for each of the six years under the following alternative depreciation methods:

   (a) Straight-line

   (b) Sum-of-years-digits

   (c) Double-declining-balance

2. Assuming that Cruse Company had revenue of $800,000 and expenses (exclusive of depreciation expense) of $600,000 for each of the next six years, determine the net income that Cruse would report in the first and the sixth year under each of the three alternative depreciation methods. Assume the machine was sold for $15,000 at the end of the sixth year.

12-6. Inventory Valuation: Physical Flows and Cost Flows.   The Stanley Steel Company is a metals service center. The company buys metal sheets, bars, rolls, and so forth, in large quantities from the producers and sells in smaller quantities to local manufacturers. One of the company's most popular items is 24-by-¼ inch rolled sheet steel that it buys in 200-foot rolls and then cuts (to order) for customers in smaller lengths.

At the beginning of February 1973, the company had run out of stock of this particular rolled sheet steel. Purchases received during February were as follows:

Date Received	Number of Rolls Purchased	Price per Roll	Total Price
2/1/73	10	$100	$1,000
2/7/73	20	110	2,200
2/15/73	12	112	1,344
2/24/73	10	116	1,160
	52		$5,704

The company uses the periodic inventory method for establishing the levels of inventory and number of rolls of steel sold. At the end of February, a count showed that 15½ rolls of the 24-by-¼-inch steel were on hand.

Required:

1. Determine the value of the ending inventory and the cost of sales for February with respect to the 24-by-¼-inch steel based on each of the following cost flow alternatives:

   (a) Fifo

   (b) Lifo

   (c) Weighted average

2. Suppose that the company had kept perpetual inventory records as illustrated in the Appendix to this chapter. Indicate for each of the cost flow assumptions whether the cost of sales and inventory amounts under the perpetual inventory valuation would have been greater than, equal to, or less than the amounts recognized under the periodic method. Support your conclusion logically. You may assume that sales took place relatively evenly over the whole month. (Note: Because specific sales data are not provided, it is not possible to make actual calculations of the perpetual inventory valuations.)

12-7. Inventory Valuation: Physical Flows and Cost Flows (Perpetual Method). Refer to the data presented in Exercise 12-6. Assume that the sales of rolled sheet steel (in terms of 200-foot rolls) were made throughout February as follows:

Sale Date	Number of Rolls
2/4/73	5
2/12/73	15
2/22/73	8
2/27/73	8½
	36½

Required:

Determine the value of the ending inventory and the cost of sales in February for each of the cost flow alternatives below. Assume that the company uses the *perpetual* inventory method.

(a) Fifo

(b) Lifo

(c) Weighted average

(Note: Use of a schedule such as the following may be helpful in developing your answers.)

Date	Purchases			Sales			Balance		
	Quantity	Unit Cost	Total Cost	Quantity	Unit Cost	Total Cost	Quantity	Unit Cost	Total Cost

12-8. Effect of Inventory Errors on Reported Income.   For each of the seven independent situations below, determine the effect of the error(s) on reported net income, ending asset balance, ending liability balance, and ending owners' equity for both 1973 and 1974. Enter your answers into a table with headings as shown below. Use +'s to indicate overstatements, —'s to indicate understatements, and 0's to indicate no effect. Assume that the periodic inventory method is used for determining inventory quantities at year-end. The answers for Situation 1 have been filled in as an example. (Note: In determining the effect of an error on net income, you must first determine its effect on cost of sales.)

Situa-tion	1973				1974			
	Net Income	Assets	Liabil-ities	Owners' Equity	Net Income	Assets	Liabil-ities	Owners' Equity
1	+	+	0	+	—	0	0	0
2								
etc.								

Situations:

1. The inventory items on shelf 15-D were counted twice during the 1973 year-end physical inventory count.

2. An invoice for goods received in 1973 (and included in the physical count on 12/31/73) was not received and recorded until 1974.

3. An invoice received in 1973 was recorded as a purchase in 1973. The goods were not received until 1974 and were not included in the 12/31/73 inventory.

4. Same as Situation 3 above, except that the cost of the goods was added to the 12/31/73 inventory figure.

5. The items in inventory area 114 were not counted during the 1973 year-end physical inventory.

6. Goods received on 12/30/73 were placed in the receiving area and were not included in the physical inventory. The purchase was not recorded in the books until 1974.

7. Due to clerical multiplication errors, the cost of the 12/31/73 inventory was overstated.

12-9. Estimation of Inventories—Gross Profit Method.   The Handyman Company sells general hardware items at retail. The company uses the periodic inventory method to determine inventory quantities on hand at year-end. Interim inventory counts are not made. However, the company's accountant is responsible for preparing interim financial statements for each month throughout the year. Since a figure for cost of inventory on hand is required for each month, the accountant uses the gross profit method to estimate the interim inventory cost figures.

During 1973, total retail sales were $1 million and total cost of sales was $700,000. The cost of the 12/31/73 inventory was $150,000. The company's pricing policy for 1974 is substantially the same as the 1973 pricing policy.

For January and February 1974, total retail sales and purchases were:

	Sales	Purchases
January	$ 70,000	$60,000
February	110,000	50,000

Required:

1. What is the gross profit percentage to be used in estimating 1974 month-end inventories?

2. Determine estimated ending inventory figures and estimated cost of sales figures for January and February.

12-10. Valuation of Assets at Time of Acquisition.   The Acme Leasing Company leases passenger cars on a two-year basis. At the end of the lease period, the customer has the options of purchasing the car at a price specified in the original lease contract or returning the car to Acme. Cars returned to Acme are traded in on new cars. If necessary, Acme purchases new cars for cash to compensate for cars purchased by customers.

For 1973, the following data apply:

Number of leases expiring	20
Number of cars purchased by customers	10
Number of cars returned to Acme (and traded in on new cars)	10
Number of new cars purchased by Acme	20
List price of new cars purchased	$4,800
Trade-in allowance (on list price) per car received by Acme on cars traded in	$2,000

Total cash price per car for cars purchased for cash only by Acme	$4,700
Average wholesale price per car for cars returned by customers	$1,900
Average retail price per car for cars returned by customers	$2,300
Lease contract selling price	$2,200
Original cost of cars returned to Acme by customers	$4,400

Acme depreciates the total price of cars over an estimated five-year life (sum-of-years-digits method), even though Acme never owns the cars for more than two years.

Required:

1. What value should be recorded for the ten cars purchased for cash only? Assume that the value of the ten cars purchased for cash is independent of the value of the cars acquired by trade-in.
2. Identify several alternative approaches that might be used in determining the value of the ten cars acquired by trade-in, and determine the total value that would be assigned to the ten cars for each alternative.
3. Comment briefly on the propriety (or relative desirability) of each of the alternative approaches you developed in number 2 above.

12-11. Valuation of Copyright.   The Expensive Hardback Press published a book which luckily turned out to be a best-seller. Because of short-term cash considerations, the author and the Expensive Hardback Press sold the copyright rights to the Cheap Paperback Company for a lump sum of $130,000.

The copyright has twenty-six years remaining out of its twenty-eight-year life and can be renewed for an additional twenty-eight years. However, the Cheap Paperback Company expects to make sales of the book only during the next five years, after which the book will probably be out of print.

Required:

1. What is the expected useful life of the copyright acquired by the Cheap Paperback Company? Why?
2. What portion of the initial valuation of the copyright should be recognized as expense each year of the copyright's useful life?

12-12. Comparative Depreciation Methods.   The Skyline Construction Company purchased new construction equipment at the beginning of 1974 for $300,000. The company estimated that the useful life of the equipment would be ten years and that the net salvage value would be $25,000.

Required:

1. Prepare a depreciation schedule indicating (*a*) the annual depreciation expense and (*b*) the net asset valuation at the beginning of the year for each year of the estimated ten-year life under the following alternative depreciation methods:

   (a) Straight-line

   (b) Double-declining-balance

   (c) Sum-of-years-digits

2. Assume that the equipment is sold at the end of the eighth year for $50,000. How much gain or loss should be recognized for each alternative depreciation method?

3. Assume that the equipment is traded in on new equipment at the end of the sixth year. The net cash paid for the new equipment is $200,000. If no gain or loss is to be recorded, what initial value should be assigned to the new equipment for each alternative depreciation method?

12-13. Treatment of Repairs and Maintenance.   In December 1970 the Burp Beer Company purchased a secondhand portable conveyor line for use in loading beer trucks from various inventory areas. The conveyor line was composed of four independent sections, with each section having its own electric motor. The original (new) price of the conveyor line was $6,000, but the company paid only $4,000. At the time of purchase, the company estimated the salvage value to be $800 and the remaining useful life to be four years.

   During 1971 the company performed only routine maintenance on the conveyor line, at a total cost of $200.

   In 1972 two motors "burned up" due to overloading and had to be replaced. The cost of the motors was $600. Other maintenance expenditures in 1972 totaled $300. Also, in December 1972 the company purchased an additional section of conveyor line to serve as a backup if another section broke down and to increase the length of the conveyor line. The acquisition cost of the additional section was $1,200, and the estimated increase in salvage value was $400.

   During 1973 repairs and maintenance totaled $900 because of recurrent breakdowns. As a result, in December the company stopped using the conveyor line and reverted to manual loading of the beer trucks. The conveyor line was put up for sale, but it was not sold until April 30, 1974, for a cash price of $1,500.

   Assume that depreciation is calculated on a straight-line basis.

Required:

1. What valuation should be assigned to the conveyor line at the date of acquisition?

2. How should the acquisition of the additional section of conveyor line in 1972 be treated? Why?

3. How much depreciation should be recorded in 1974? Why?

4. Prepare a schedule showing the expense in total and by categories (depreciation expense and repairs and maintenance expense) associated with the conveyor line for each year of its life.

5. Calculate the gain or loss incurred in 1974 when the conveyor line was sold.

12-14. Calculation of Depletion.   In 19X3 the Black Gold Company acquired an option to purchase a five-year lease on a block of acreage. The option included the right to perform seismograph surveys on the land. A survey was performed and indicated the presence of strata with oil-producing potential. Therefore the company exercised its option to acquire the lease (for 19X3–X7).

A well was drilled during 19X3, and oil was found. The total recoverable barrels were estimated to be 100,000. Production was scheduled to begin in 19X4.

At the end of 19X3, the total of the expenditures made in 19X3 subject to depletion (option price, survey costs, and cost of lease) was $20,000. The total expenditures made in 19X3 subject to depreciation (tangible well costs) amounted to $30,000. The company planned to depreciate the depreciable costs over the remaining life of the lease. The salvage value of depreciable equipment was estimated to be $2,000.

Production figures for 19X4–X7 are as follows:

Year	Barrels of Oil Produced and Sold
19X4	15,000
19X5	25,000
19X6	40,000
19X7	30,000
Total	110,000

Operations were discontinued at the end of 19X7, and the lease was not renewed. The company received $2,000 for the salvageable wellhead equipment and pipe.

Required:

Prepare a schedule showing cost depletion and depreciation for each year of the well's life. Assume that the company did not change its estimate of recoverable barrels until 19X7.

12-15. Development and Start-up Costs. The accounting treatment of the costs of development and/or start-up of a major new program is a controversial issue. Late in 1974, the FASB modified accounting policy to require companies to recognize these costs as expenses of the period in which the expenditures are made—a conservative treatment that may not produce a very satisfactory matching of costs and related revenue. Prior to this time, however, the costs could be capitalized as assets and matched against (potential) revenues from the project in future periods. The hazard under this previously acceptable alternative is that the assets and net income of the early periods would be overstated if the project were not ultimately successful. This hazard was strikingly revealed in a report on the fortunes of Lockheed Aircraft Corporation (*Wall Street Journal,* June 3, 1974):

A huge write-down of its financially troubled L1011 "TriStar" commercial aircraft program, probably totaling at least $600 million, is the key element in a complex plan for a far-reaching financial restructuring of Lockheed Aircraft Corp., sources close to Lockheed said.

· · ·

Some Lockheed critics have long contended the company was engaging in "fantasy accounting" in its handling of the books for the L1011 program and doubtless will say, in the wake of one of the biggest writeoffs in American corporate history, that the company and its auditors should have "bitten the bullet" some time ago. The auditing firm . . . has regularly qualified

its opinions of the extensively footnoted Lockheed financial statements because of uncertainties over "realization of the L1011 inventories" and the
maintenance of financing arrangements.

At the end of 1973, Lockheed was carrying $1.16 billion of its total assets
of $1.85 billion (and current assets of $1.56 billion) in the form of net
inventories in the TriStar program. This unrecovered TriStar investment
comprises the plane's development costs, initial tooling and other nonrecurring costs and production costs, less payments for planes delivered to date
and customer advances on future deliveries.

Lockheed said in its latest annual report that it expected to recover this
inventory through the anticipated sale of 300 TriStars, though it cautioned
this could take into the early 1980s and was subject to certain variables and
uncertainties. Although it had delivered 56 TriStars through 1973, Lockheed
said it didn't expect to reach the point at which current production costs of
each plane will be less than the sales price of planes then being delivered
until mid-1974. It said the inventory at the end of 1974 would be only
slightly less than a year earlier and eventual recovery of about $900 million
of gross inventory depended on firm orders beyond the 129 in hand at year-
end 1973.

A write-down of the L1011 inventories of about $600 million without a new
cash infusion wouldn't drop Lockheed into a negative working-capital position but also wouldn't leave much room between current assets, which would
drop to less than $1 billion based on the year-end $1.56 billion figure, and
current liabilities, which stood at $718 million at year-end. It would, ap-
parently, wipe out the company's retained earnings, which totaled $192.8
million at year-end.

Lockheed hasn't recorded any loss (or profit) on its L1011 deliveries to
date, posting those delivered at the full sales price ($730 million in 1973
and $302 million in 1972). It has charged to income slightly over $300
million to date in general administrative expenses, however. The current
sales price of an L1011 is about $20 million.

Currently, Lockheed has firm orders, including those already delivered, for
135 TriStars and second buys, or options, for 67 more, or a total of 202.
Airline industry sources say, however, that prospects for substantial additional orders in the next few years are almost nonexistent and, except for a
few instances, airlines holding the L1011 options aren't likely to convert
options to firm orders during 1974.

.   .   .

Lockheed posted 1973 net income of $16.8 million, or $1.48 a share. This
result includes an operating profit on programs other than the TriStar and
new ship construction of $165.8 million and a loss of $69.7 million from
general and administrative costs on the TriStar program. Sales of $2.76
billion included the $730 million from TriStars, on which zero profit or loss
was recorded, as noted earlier.*

---

* *Wall Street Journal,* June 3, 1974. Reprinted with the permission of The Wall Street
Journal, © Dow Jones & Company, Inc., 1974.

Required:

1. In capitalizing the development and start-up costs of its TriStar program, do you believe that Lockheed was engaging in "fantasy accounting" as alleged by some of its critics? Would your answer have been different at the outset of the program than it is now with the benefit of hindsight?

2. Assuming it is appropriate to capitalize development and start-up costs (and many companies formerly did so):

   (a) Do you believe that the investment in the TriStar program was properly classified as a current asset—that is, inventory? Why might a corporation wish to reflect development and start-up costs as a current asset rather than some noncurrent asset such as "other assets"?

   (b) What justification might be offered for the policy of capitalizing the "net" production costs (the excess of current production costs over the sales proceeds from this production) of early production (at a minimum, at least the first 60–70 planes based on Lockheed's statement that "it didn't expect to reach the point at which current production costs of each plane will be less than the sales price of planes then being delivered until mid-1974")?

   (c) In view of the policy of capitalization adopted by Lockheed in (*b*) above, why do you suppose that it did not elect to capitalize the general administrative costs (presumably related to the program) rather than recognizing them as expenses of the period in which incurred?

   (d) After capitalizing the plane's development costs, initial tooling, and other nonrecurring costs, what system of matching these costs against future revenues was adopted by Lockheed? Do you believe this results in a proper matching of these costs with related revenue?

3. What do you suppose was the basis for the proposed $600 million write-down of an inventory carried at a "cost" of $1.16 billion (i.e., why was the proposed write-down not some larger or smaller amount)?

4. While a major program is still in the development stage, do you believe that an auditor's qualification (or caveat) that the fairness of the financial statement presentation depends upon the "ability to realize capitalized development costs" is adequate for external investors? If not, what alternative financial data and/or auditor actions would you suggest?

13

Expense Recognition and
Related Equity Valuation Issues

Having completed our examination of the expense recognition patterns associated with the two major classes of nonmonetary resources under the conventional accounting model, and the related valuation of these resources in the statement of financial position, we now turn to the valuation of liabilities and owners' equity—the claims against the assets of the business enterprise.

LIABILITIES

Basic Characteristics of Liabilities

Liabilities are obligations of the firm to external parties (individuals or other organizations) other than the owners of the firm. In general, liabilities are characterized by the following two attributes:

1. A future cash payment is required to discharge the obligation.
2. There is a time element—the time between the date the obligation is created and the date on which payment is made—that influences, implicitly or explicitly, the amount of the future cash payment(s).

On certain occasions, liabilities are discharged by some means other than a cash payment, such as the liability arising from advance payments which is discharged through the provision of products or services. The time element is, however, always present, even though it may be a very short period of time.

Obligations may be created either by acquiring resources with a provision for deferred payment (e.g., ordinary credit purchases of merchandise) or by borrowing money from some credit-granting individual or institution. In either situation, there is an input (implicitly in the case of credit purchases) of funds into the business from an outside source. Since these funds are by definition from an individual or institution other than the owners of the business, they may be characterized as a "non-owner-provided factor of production." Like all factors of production that are acquired, it is presumed that the firm can utilize this particular factor of production in a profitable manner—that is, that the output from the use of the factor of production will exceed its cost.

But what is the cost associated with the use of funds, or money resources? The *total cost* that the firm will incur from using this factor of production may be determined from the following elements of our transaction-based system:

$$\text{Total cost of money} = \text{Sum of payments} - \text{Proceeds of liability}$$

In this fundamental relationship, the *sum of payments* includes all payments labeled as interest plus the repayment of the face amount, or principal, of the obligation at its maturity date. The *proceeds of liability* refers to the value of the resources (money or other resources) received at the date that the liability was created.

Since time elapses between the acquisition of the money and the ultimate repayment, and because it is presumed that all individuals and institutions have a time preference for money, the value of the resources acquired (either cash or other resources) will be equal to the present value of the future payments that the enterprise is committed to make. In some instances, the period of time between the acquisition of resources and the ultimate repayment is very short, and there is no explicit indication of the cost of this factor of production in the exchange transaction. Nonetheless, the cost exists, even though it may perhaps be ignored for financial accounting purposes because it is not material. In other instances, the period of time between the acquisition of resources or money and the ultimate repayment is quite long. In these cases, an explicit charge for the use of the funds is normally provided for in the contract or promissory note representing the liability. This additional charge is normally expressed as a rate of interest on the balance due.

Within a transaction-based system, such as the conventional accounting model, the following measurement problems are associated with liabilities:

1. How do we allocate the total cost of using the money over the life span of a liability to appropriate periods of time within that life span?
2. How do we determine, at any point in time, the magnitude of the undischarged liability?

**A Simple Expenditure Approach to Accounting
for Liabilities**

An intuitive way to deal with the measurement problems associated with liabilities is to use a simple expenditure approach. Under this approach, all payments to creditors or lending institutions that are labeled "interest" according to the terms of the note or debt instrument are recognized as costs of using money, and these costs are assigned to the period of time in which they are paid (or accrued). The final payment to discharge the face amount of the obligation is, under this approach, not regarded as a cost of money.

Example 13-1   On January 1, 1974, Janco Corporation borrowed $10,000 from the First National Bank of Frankfort to acquire new equipment for an expansion program. The money was borrowed at an interest rate of 8 percent, and interest payments were to be made at the end of each year. The promissory note that the company signed with the bank indicated that the face amount of the liability was to be repaid on December 31, 1978. Treatment of the required payments, and the related accounting measurements, under the simple expenditure approach are illustrated in Exhibit 13-1.

Exhibit 13-1   JANCO CORPORATION
                          Simple Expenditure Approach to Bank Loan

Date	Cash Receipts	Cash Payments during Year	Interest Expense for Year	Accounting Carrying Value of Liability
1/1/74	$10,000			$10,000
12/31/74		$ 800	$ 800	10,000
12/31/75		800	800	10,000
12/31/76		800	800	10,000
12/31/77		800	800	10,000
12/31/78		10,800	800	—0—
	$10,000	$14,000	$4,000	

The simple expenditure approach produces for Example 13-1 a measure of the cost of the factor of production (use of money) that is consistent with our basic relationship:

$$\text{Cost} = \text{Sum of payments} - \text{Proceeds of liability}$$
$$= \$14,000 - \$10,000$$
$$= \$4,000$$

The allocation of this total interest cost to periods of time ($800 per year) also is an intuitively reasonable expression of the sacrifice made by the firm in order to use the funds, because there is a constant amount of creditor funds in use and constant interest expense each period. We should note, however, that if the promissory note signed by Janco had stipulated that the "interest payments" were to be made on the first day of each year (beginning January 1, 1975, rather than December 31, 1974), the matching principle would require an accrual of interest expense at the end of each year and recognition of a liability for accrued interest payable. This recognition of accrued obligations does not substantially modify the basic orientation of the expenditure approach. The recognition of interest expense for a period is still based on expenditures—paid or accrued during the period. And finally, the approach produces a valuation of the liability at the end of each period ($10,000) that generally reflects the liquidation value of the firm's economic obligation at that point in time. That is, if Janco had decided to repay its liability earlier than required, say on December 31, 1976, a $10,000 payment should (in the absence of any prepayment penalty provisions in the promissory note) fully discharge its obligation to the First National Bank of Frankfort.

While the expenditure approach produces intuitively reasonable measures of periodic interest expense and the related liability under the simple set of circumstances described in Example 13-1, transactions giving rise to the creation of a liability typically involve certain complications which tend to invalidate the method. For example, the promissory notes issued by many enterprises, particularly large corporations, are often in the form of bonds with a stated face amount and interest rate. A corporation might issue a series of bonds with a face value (principal) of $1,000 per bond and a stated interest rate of 8 percent. This means that the holder of each bond will receive $80 ($1,000 × .08) per year in interest, and $1,000 repayment of principal at the maturity date of the bond. If, however, the prevailing market rate of interest for bonds of equal risk is greater (less) than the 8 percent rate stated on the bond, the market will adjust the actual interest cost to the borrower by paying or conveying less (more) than $1,000 for each bond. If the amount paid for the bond is more than the face amount, we refer to the difference as a *premium*. If it is less than the face amount of the bond, we call it a *discount*.

Example 13-2   Holland Corporation decided to issue on January 1, 1974, 100 five-year bonds with a stated interest rate of 8 percent and a face value per bond of $1,000. The appropriate documents were prepared and offered for sale in the capital market. At the time the bonds were offered to potential buyers, the prevailing interest rate was higher than 8 percent, and the buyers compensated for the difference between the market rate and the nominal interest rate (8 percent) on the face of the bonds by paying $950 per bond. Therefore, ignoring the costs associated with marketing the bonds, Holland Corporation received $95,000 for bonds with a face value of $100,000, and it had the additional obligation of making $8,000 cash interest payments each year (interest payments are based on the face amount, not the proceeds received). If this transaction were handled under the expenditure approach, we would obtain the results illustrated in Exhibit 13-2.

The measure of the cost associated with the use of the borrowed funds in Exhibit 13-2 is again consistent with our basic relationship:

$$\text{Cost} = \text{Sum of payments} - \text{Proceeds of liability}$$
$$= \$140,000 - \$95,000$$
$$= \$45,000$$

Exhibit 13-2

HOLLAND CORPORATION
Simple Expenditure Approach to Bond Issue

Date	Cash Receipts	Cash Payments during Year	Interest Expense for Year	Accounting Carrying Value of Liability
1/1/74	$95,000			$95,000
12/31/74		$ 8,000	$ 8,000	95,000
12/31/75		8,000	8,000	95,000
12/31/76		8,000	8,000	95,000
12/31/77		8,000	8,000	95,000
12/31/78		108,000	13,000	—0—
	$95,000	$140,000	$45,000	

We may, however, question whether this cost has been properly allocated to each of the years in the five-year period that the bonds were outstanding. Specifically, should the last year bear an interest cost significantly higher than the costs recognized in each of the preceding four years merely because it is at this point in time that the difference between the $100,000 face amount of the bonds and the $95,000 original cash receipts is recognized in the form of a cash expenditure? The answer is that this allocation pattern is not justified by economic reality. We must instead devise some means of taking the $5,000 discount into account over the life of the bonds as we assess the interest cost of each period. Additionally, the value of the undischarged liability at the end of each period preceding the year of repayment is generally a poor measure of the firm's obligation. Thus the existence of premiums or discounts on the original issue of corporate bonds stimulates the need for a more refined approach to the valuation of liabilities and measurement of the related expense.

Besides the problems with the expenditure approach that are brought about by the existence of an issue premium or discount, another characteristic of some types of obligations also makes the expenditures approach unreasonable. Certain types of obligations call for periodic installment payments consisting of both principal and interest. Under such conditions, we cannot merely assess the cost of the borrowed funds in terms of the expenditure of funds during the period. We clearly must separate that portion of the payment that is made in reduction of the principal from the payment that is made for the use of money. When installment payments, or other forms of reduction of principal over the life of a liability (such as serial bonds) are combined with the existence of premiums or discounts, the weakness of the expenditure approach becomes even more evident. Therefore, we will now turn to a more refined method of dealing with the accounting problems associated with liabilities.

An Implicit Interest Approach to Accounting for Liabilities

In developing the implicit interest approach to accounting for liabilities, we will maintain the basic relationship referred to several times above relative to the *total cost* of the use of the borrowed funds over the life of the liability:

Total cost = Sum of payments − Proceeds of liability

But our objective now is to develop a better method of measuring the portion of this cost that is identifiable with any particular period of time. Such cost allocations may not be, and probably will not be, equal to the payments that are made in the same time period.

• *Measuring interest expense.* We begin our analysis by noting the basic relationship that exists between the value of a liability and the flows between parties to the borrowing transaction:

Ending value of liability = Beginning value of liability + Additional
proceeds + Interest expense − Cash payments

This relationship holds at any point in time. Therefore, at the date on which the liability is created, the value of the liability is established by the value of the proceeds received in the exchange transaction. In the first period, three types of events can change the initial value of the liability:

1. Additional proceeds can be derived from additional borrowing.
2. Interest expense is incurred.
3. Payments are made for interest and/or principal.

The values for additional proceeds and payments can be determined from the exchange transactions of these types. We need only concentrate on how to measure the proper amount of interest expense for the period.

A critical element in the calculation of interest expense is the rate of interest that was established in the market or by the lending institution at the time the liability was created. The rate the lenders wish to impose on the borrowing company is important because it is applied to the series of payments that they will receive from the company (interest payments and repayment of principal) to arrive at the present value of the liability. This present value of the liability is the amount that the lenders will be willing to pay for the bonds or other obligations of the enterprise. By accepting this price, the borrowing corporation accepts an interest cost based upon the lenders' time preference rate used in the calculation.

Example 13-3   The Escola Company issued on January 1, 1974, five-year bonds with a total face value of $50,000 and a stated interest rate of 8 percent. The market rate of interest on this date was 10 percent. Based upon the market determination of the value of the bonds at the prevailing interest rate of 10 percent illustrated in Exhibit 13-3, Escola Company received $46,210. Therefore, it had a discount on the issuance of the bonds of $3,790 ($50,000 − $46,210).

At the date of issue, the bonds are valued at the amount of the proceeds received by the borrower. On January 1, 1974, Escola would value its bond liability at $46,210. But at what amount should the company value the liability on December 31, 1974? And what is the amount of interest expense to be recognized in 1974? The answer to these measurement problems stems from a concept developed in Chapter 3, the introduction to the present value model. Under conditions of certainty, an investor expects to earn a return

Exhibit 13-3   ESCOLA COMPANY
Market Value of Bonds at Date of Issuance

	Cash Flow				
Date	Interest	Repayment of Principal	Total	Present Value Factor (10% rate)	Present Value
12/31/74	$ 4,000		$ 4,000	0.909	$ 3,636
12/31/75	4,000		4,000	0.826	3,304
12/31/76	4,000		4,000	0.751	3,004
12/31/77	4,000		4,000	0.683	2,732
12/31/78	4,000	$50,000	54,000	0.621	33,534
	$20,000	$50,000	$70,000		$46,210

equal to the product of his time preference rate and the present value of his investment at the start of the period. It seems reasonable to conclude that the issuer of the bonds would incur a cost of equal amount. And since the borrower has the legal obligation to make exactly those cash payments used in the calculation of the lender's present value of the liability, the certainty assumption is not unreasonable in accounting for the obligation.

Thus, the borrower calculates the interest expense for a period in the following manner:

Interest expense =
(Market rate of interest used in establishing the original value of the bonds) × (Recognized value of the bonds at the beginning of the period)

In our example, the market rate of interest was 10 percent, and thus we can restate the above relationship as follows:

Interest expense = 10 percent × (Recognized value of bonds at start of period)

And the recognized, or carrying, value of the bonds at the end of the period can now be determined from the general relationship between the value of a liability and the flows between parties to the transaction (ignoring here additional proceeds):

Ending value of liability = Beginning value of liability + Interest
expense − Cash payments

These relationships are applied to the data of Example 13-3 in Exhibit 13-4.

Using this implicit interest approach, the total interest expense recognized over the period of time the obligations are outstanding is equal to the excess of cash payments over the proceeds received in the loan, as our transaction-based model requires. Additionally, this expense has been allocated to the periods of time presumably benefiting from the money capital using the rate of interest (10 percent) established *implicitly* in the transaction in which the liability was originally created. Although the market rate of interest for liabilities of equal risk and stated terms may vary over time, the original loan transaction established the effective rate of interest, and the total interest cost, that Escola Company (in this case) must pay over the life of the bonds that were issued.

Exhibit 13-4

ESCOLA COMPANY
Calculation of Interest Expense and Carrying Value of Liability

Year Ended	Proceeds	(1) Carrying Value of Liability, Start of Year	(2) Interest Expense for Year—10% × (1)	(3) Cash Payment, End of Year	Carrying Value of Liability, End of Year—(1) + (2) − (3)
12/31/74	$46,210	$46,210	$ 4,621	$ 4,000	$46,831
12/31/75		46,831	4,683	4,000	47,514
12/31/76		47,514	4,751	4,000	48,265
12/31/77		48,265	4,826	4,000	49,091
12/31/78		49,091	4,909	54,000	—0—
	$46,210		$23,790	$70,000	

Note: Check on total interest expense:

Total cost (interest expense) = Sum of cash payments − Proceeds of loan
= $70,000 − $46,210
= $23,790

• *Valuing the liability.* In conventional accounting, this original transaction-based cost is used for all subsequent valuations of the liability and expense allocations, notwithstanding subsequent variability in market rates of interest. As a consequence of our expense measurement, the recognized value of the liability at any point in time reflects the present value of the remaining cash payments to be made, *at the 10 percent "original transaction" rate of interest.* If the market rate of interest also remains at 10 percent, the carrying value of the liability will equal the value at which the bonds can be traded in the market (sold by holders or redeemed by Escola). But if the prevailing market rate of interest is not equal to 10 percent, the market value of the bonds will not be the same as the value recognized under the conventional accounting model. This relationship between the conventional accounting measure of the liability and the market value of the liability is illustrated in Exhibit 13-5 for the data of our example as of December 31, 1976 (after the cash interest payments on that date). From Exhibit 13-4 we observe that the conventional accounting measure of the liability on December 31, 1976, is $48,265. This value is not changed by fluctuations in the market rate of interest. However, as is illustrated by Exhibit 13-5, the market value of the bonds is dependent upon the market rate of interest *at that time.*

Exhibit 13-5

ESCOLA COMPANY
Comparison of Present Values of Bonds
at December 31, 1976, at *Assumed* 10% and 12%
Market Rates of Interest Prevailing on That Date

A. *Assumed* market rate of interest = 10%

Remaining Cash Flows

Date	Payment of Interest	Repayment of Principal	Total	Present Value Factor (10% rate)	Present Value
12/31/77	$4,000		$ 4,000	0.909	$ 3,636
12/31/78	4,000	$50,000	54,000	0.826	44,604
	$8,000	$50,000	$58,000		$48,240

B. *Assumed* market rate of interest = 12%

Remaining Cash Flows

Date	Payment of Interest	Repayment of Principal	Total	Present Value Factor (12% rate)	Present Value
12/31/77	$4,000		$ 4,000	0.893	$ 3,572
12/31/78	4,000	$50,000	54,000	0.797	43,038
	$8,000	$50,000	$58,000		$46,610

Note: The carrying value of the bonds on December 31, 1976, under the conventional accounting model (from Exhibit 13-4) is $48,265. The difference between this carrying value and the present value of the remaining payments at 10% in *A* above is due to the rounding error present in three-place present value tables. Conceptually, the two values are equal.

Valuation of a liability using the prevailing market rate of interest would be consistent with the objectives of the *current market-value model*, because this value would reflect the amount of cash necessary to liquidate the obligation. The conventional accounting model, on the other hand, relies on original transaction values, and accordingly changes in the market rate of interest are not recognized under this model.

Retirement of Debt before Maturity

At the maturity date of a debt instrument, the carrying value of the liability is equal to the face amount of the debt. Thus, when repayment of the principal is made, there is no change in owners' equity (i.e., cash and the liability are decreased by the same amount). However, at other points in time prior to maturity, the carrying value of the liability will generally not be equal to either the face value or the current market value of the debt. Therefore, if the corporation elects to retire, or extinguish, debt prior to its maturity, either by exercising a "call" provision or by purchasing the debt securities in the open market, a difference will probably exist between the repurchase price and the carrying value of the liability. If the repurchase price is less than (exceeds) the carrying value of the liability, owners' equity will be increased (decreased). Under current accounting policy, this change in owners' equity is recognized as income (or loss) in the period in which the debt is retired.

OWNERS' EQUITY

In much of our discussion to this point, we have treated owners' equity as a *single residual calculation*—the difference between the independently valued assets and liabilities of the enterprise. And a growing number of accountants are supporting the notion that this single measure of owners' equity embodies most, if not all, of the decision-relevant information that can be provided about the equity of owners under the conventional accounting model. However, accountants have traditionally reported owners' equity for corporations by using a classification scheme that seeks to reflect the different *sources* of owners' equity. Because this classification scheme will be encountered in most contemporary corporate financial reports, it is summarized below. Additionally, several important classes of transactions between the corporation and its shareholders are briefly reviewed.

The General Distinction between Earned and Contributed Capital

Corporations would not exist legally were it not for permissive legislation on the part of state governments, allowing for the chartering of corporations. One of the desirable attributes of the corporate form is the limitation of the liability (potential losses) of the owners of the corporation to the amount of their current interest in the corporation. To protect other parties, however, the state laws governing corporations often restrict dividends paid to owners, so that the original capital contributed to the corporation by owners remains intact (in the form of recognized net assets) to satisfy the rightful claims of other parties. That is, dividends may only be distributed to the extent that net assets exceed the money capital of the enterprise contributed by owners in exchange for shares of stock. Thus, in response to the presumed decision relevance for dividend-distribution decisions of this general legal notion, the owners' equity component of financial position is usually split into two basic categories: (1) paid-in capital and (2) retained earnings.

> **Paid-in Capital.** Paid-in capital is that part of total owners' equity equal to the amount of money or other capital contributed by owners to the enterprise in exchange for ownership interests.

> **Retained Earnings.** Retained earnings is that part of owners' equity equal to the cumulative excess of net income over dividend distributions to owners since the inception of the business.

Classifications of Paid-in Capital

Paid-in capital is further broken down into additional groups or categories. One distinction is based on the type of ownership interest—the various classes of stock issued by the corporation. Another distinction evolves from the specification of "legal values" for shares of stock. Each of these is considered in turn.

• *Classes of stock.* Each share of stock of a corporation conveys certain rights to the holder. In general, holders of shares of *common stock* have the following rights:

1. Right to vote for members of the board of directors and, subject to applicable state laws, to vote on certain types of major corporation decisions (for example, merging with another corporation).
2. Right to purchase their pro rata share of any new stock issue so as to maintain the same proportionate interest in the corporation—called the preemptive right. (Many corporations have recently eliminated this right in their charters.)
3. Right to share proportionally in dividends declared by the corporation.
4. Right to share proportionally in the net assets of the firm if the corporation is liquidated.

On some occasions, a corporation will issue other classes of stock which are explicitly given preference over common stock on certain of these rights, but which may also forfeit one or more of the rights. One such general class of stock is commonly referred to as *preferred stock*. Typically, preferred shareholders are given the right to receive their share of dividends (and usually net assets on liquidation) before any distribution is made to common shareholders. Preferred stock, however, does not usually carry voting rights.

Example 13-4   Hinrichs Corporation has two classes of stock outstanding: 1,000 shares of preferred stock, which are entitled to an annual dividend of $5 per share, and 5,000 shares of common stock. Under these circumstances, no dividends can be paid to the common shareholders in any year unless the holders of the preferred stock also receive a total dividend distribution that year of $5,000 (1,000 × $5).

Another important characteristic of preferred stock is whether the dividend preference is cumulative or noncumulative. If the dividend preference is *cumulative,* any annual dividends of prior periods that the preferred shareholders were entitled to receive (if declared by the board of directors) but were not paid must be "made up" before any dividend distribution is made to common shareholders. If the preferred stock is entitled only to its annual dividend and forfeits any right to past dividends not declared and paid, it is referred to as *noncumulative* preferred stock.

Example 13-5   Referring to the facts of Example 13-4, assume that Hinrichs Corporation had paid dividends to both classes of shareholders each year since the preferred stock was issued. But in 1974 a tight cash position resulting from a significant expansion of their plant capacity caused the directors to pass the dividends for that year. In 1975 the cash position improves and the directors decide to resume dividend payments.

If the preferred stock is cumulative, a dividend distribution of $10,000 ($5,000 dividends *in arrears*—not paid—from 1974, and the current $5,000 dividend) must be paid to the preferred shareholders in order for any dividends to be paid to the common shareholders. If the preferred stock is non-cumulative, only the $5,000 current dividend need be paid to preferred shareholders in order to make a distribution to the common shareholders.

After the preferred shareholders have been paid the dividend they are entitled to, the directors may distribute whatever amount they wish to the common shareholders (subject to applicable state laws).

Obviously the cumulative provision is an important right, and most issues of preferred stock currently oustanding carry this right.

Another important preference, or special right, that has recently been attached to many issues of preferred stock is a *conversion* right. Preferred stock with this right entitles the holder, at his option, to convert each share of preferred stock into a specified number of shares of common stock. Thus, *convertible preferred stock* provides the preferred stock virtue of greater assurance of a dependable annual return, combined with the potential common stock virtue (through conversion) of sharing in the future success (large profits) of the company.

• *"Legal values" for stock.* In conformity with the objective of providing a specified capital buffer to protect the legal claims of nonowners against the corporation, the states have traditionally (at one time exclusively) provided for the specification of a value for each share of stock. This value is referred to as the *par value* of the stock. Shares of stock that carry par values are called *par-value stock.*

Par-value stock generally cannot be issued for consideration (value) less than this stated amount. In those states that permit the issuance of par-value stock at less than par value, the purchaser (shareholder) generally assumes a contingent liability to creditors and other legal claimants for the difference between the par value and the amount paid, if at some future time the net assets of the corporation are insufficient to satisfy all nonowner claims. This special contingent liability, the amount of which is fixed by the share-purchase transaction between the corporation and the shareholder, overrides the general limitation of the liability that shareholders have to their interest in the corporation.

Many states now permit the issuance of no-par stock—that is, stock without a specified par value. While no-par stock appears at first glance to compromise the notion of providing a capital buffer for nonowner interests, in reality it does not. Since the par value of stock can in most instances be of any amount, ranging down for example to $1 or less per share, the effective buffer provided by par-value stock is often negligible. The actual security for creditors is provided by the actual asset values and related earning power possessed by the corporation—not an arbitrary amount of capital specified by law. The use of no-par stock merely recognizes this fact.

In many instances, state law authorizes the board of directors to place a *stated value* on no-par stock. When this option is exercised, there is little practical difference from an accounting point of view between no-par stock with a stated value and par-value stock—although there may be some minor legal differences.

The par value or stated value of shares of stock is the basis for an additional accounting classification in the owners' equity section of the statement of financial position. The total proceeds from the sale of shares of stock are divided into two categories of paid-in capital: (1) the amount of the par (or stated) value of stock issued and (2) the excess of the paid-in proceeds over the par (or stated) value of stock issued. The legal significance of the division depends upon the state in which the corporation is chartered.

When preferred stock is issued with a par value, the dividend preference is usually stated in terms of a percentage of this par value. If the preferred stock does not carry a par value, the dividend preference is expressed in terms of a dollar amount per share.

Example 13-6   Corporation X issued 8 percent, $100 par-value preferred stock. Corporation Y issued no-par preferred stock with a dividend preference of $8 per share. Both issues of preferred stock will pay the same dividend—$8 per share. Any difference in price that investors would pay for these two stocks would therefore be solely related to the relative degrees of risk they associate with the two companies.

Dividends on Stock

The return that investors receive on their investment in a corporation is composed of two parts: (1) cash dividends and (2) changes in the market price of the stock. The market price of the stock is affected by many factors, including reinvestment of earnings and changes in the expectations of investors. Fluctuations in the market price of the stock, while of major importance to each individual shareholder, do not affect the net assets *of the corporation,* and thus they do not affect the valuation of owners' equity. Cash dividends, on the other hand, reduce the net assets of the corporation, and they must therefore be given accounting recognition.

• *Cash dividends.* Cash dividends (whether on preferred or common stock) must be formally authorized by the board of directors of a corporation. Three dates are important for cash dividends. Cash dividends are declared at some point in time (*declaration date*), payable to stockholders of record as of a second (future) date (*date of record*), and actually to be paid on a third (latest) date (*payment date*).

Example 13-7   The board of directors of Boston Corporation declared a cash dividend of $1 per share on November 28, 1974 (declaration date). The dividend is payable to shareholders registered as legal owners of the shares as of December 6, 1974 (record date), and it will be paid on December 14, 1974 (payment date).

At the date of declaration, the total dividend to be paid becomes a binding liability on the corporation. Therefore, on this date, the retained earnings of the corporation (a component of the total owners' equity) is reduced and a liability, dividends payable, recognized. Payment of the dividend at the later payment date then results in a decrease in cash and a decrease in dividends payable.

• *Stock dividends.* At times a corporation declares a dividend on a class of stock (usually common stock) payable in shares of the same stock. This type of dividend is called a *stock dividend*.

Example 13-8   Wright Corporation has 10,000 shares of common stock outstanding. The board of directors of Wright Corporation decides not to pay a cash dividend on these shares, but it does authorize a 10 percent stock dividend. This action means that Wright Corporation will issue 1,000 new shares of common stock, and each shareholder will receive 1 new share for each 10 shares he presently owns.

Many accountants and other financial experts acknowledge that a stock dividend does not by itself represent income to the shareholder. Although each shareholder has more shares of stock after the stock dividend, his proportionate interest in the corporation is unchanged. Furthermore, with more shares of the corporation outstanding, one would expect the market price of the stock to adjust downward proportionately. Under these circumstances, the only accounting recognition that need be given to a stock dividend would be to reflect the increased "legal capital" (additional shares times the par or stated value) and to reduce the balance in retained earnings by the same amount.

However, following many stock dividends, the market price does not appear to adjust proportionately, and the shareholders are in a real sense "better off." Because of this seeming paradox (which many attribute to the expectations that dividends per share will remain the same, making each share worth as much as before), some accountants have proposed a different treatment for recognizing stock dividends. They contend that the value of the stock dividend should be measured by the current fair market value of the shares outstanding, and retained earnings decreased by this amount. The corresponding increase in paid-in capital is allocated between "legal capital" (in an amount equal to the par or stated value of the new shares issued) and "amount received in excess of par value of stock issued" (the remaining amount). One rationale supporting this treatment is that when a corporation substitutes a stock dividend for a cash dividend, it is analogous to having the corporation pay out cash dividends and then having the owners reinvest the proceeds in new shares of the corporation's stock—which is what the accounting for stock dividends simulates. Under current accounting policy, this second treatment (valuing stock dividends at the fair market value of the shares) is used when the stock dividend is 25 percent or less. Presumably, a stock dividend larger than 25 percent does not justify the assumption that the market price will not adjust proportionately to reflect the new number of shares outstanding.

A stock dividend has the effect of "capitalizing" some portion of the firm's retained earnings. The amount to be capitalized depends of course upon the size of the stock dividend and either the market or par value per share at the time. The practical significance of this capitalization action is to reduce the total amount that the board of directors could declare as a cash dividend if it wanted in the future to distribute the maximum dividend to shareholders. The specific amount of the reduction in potentially declarable dividends depends upon the statutory provisions of the state in which the corporation is chartered.

Stock Splits

Stock dividends are used to increase the number of shares outstanding. An alternative method of achieving this objective, without the "capitalization of retained earnings" that accompanies a stock dividend, is the *stock split*. In a stock split, the old shares of stock are called in by the corporation, and new (generally more) shares of stock with a different par value (generally less than the old par value) are issued to the shareholders. The total amount of legal capital is maintained unchanged by a stock split. Therefore, the par value of the new shares must be adjusted in accordance with the number of new shares that the board of directors wishes to issue.

Example 13-9   Archer Corporation has 100,000 shares of $10 par-value stock outstanding. The board of directors wishes to double the number of shares outstanding in order to reduce the market price *per share* (presumably making the company's stock more easily purchased by the average investor), but it does not want to capitalize retained earnings (as would be necessary if a 100 percent stock dividend were declared). Therefore, the board declares a two-for-one stock split. As a consequence of this action, each shareholder will receive 2 new shares of $5 par-value stock of Archer Corporation for each old share of $10 par-value stock held.

Before the stock split illustrated in Example 13-9, the total legal capital of Archer Corporation was $1 million (100,000 shares with a par value of $10 per share). After the split, Archer's legal capital still remains at $1 million

(200,000 shares with a par value of $5 per share). Because the legal capital is unchanged (as are all other elements of owners' equity), no accounting recognition is required for a stock split—that is, the financial position of the firm has not changed.

Treasury Stock

From time to time, corporations decide to repurchase some of their outstanding shares of stock in the open market or directly from shareholders. This action is taken for a number of reasons, including the need for shares to be issued to executives under stock option plans or perhaps because management believes the stock is undervalued in the market. If the stock is not legally retired or canceled following reacquisition, but rather is held by the corporation for possible reissue in the future, the stock is called *treasury stock*.

In accounting for treasury stock, the first question we must deal with relates to the nature of the treasury stock. Is it an asset or is it a reduction of owners' equity? Although some arguments can be developed in support of treating treasury stock as an asset (for example, it can be resold in the marketplace for cash like any other security), the settled position under present-day reporting practice is to treat treasury stock as a reduction of owners' equity. Several minor variations on this treatment are available. A common method of reporting treasury stock, however, is to show the total cost of the reacquired shares as an "unallocated deduction" from total owners' equity before considering treasury stock. Whatever other variation may be employed, the effect on *total* owners' equity will be the same—the amount of total owners' equity prior to reacquisition of the shares is reduced by the total cost of the treasury shares.

If the treasury shares are subsequently sold, any difference between the proceeds of sale and the cost of the treasury stock is generally reflected in paid-in capital. Irrespective of any specific alternative selected to account for this "sale" transaction, *no* income or loss is recognized because the sale of treasury shares is not considered substantively different from merely issuing the same number of previously unissued shares of the corporation's stock.

Stock Options

A popular form of executive compensation used by corporations in recent years is the stock option. A *stock option* is a legal instrument permitting the holder to acquire a specified number of shares of stock of the issuing corporation at a specified price. The options are typically valid for a limited period of time (usually up to five years), and they are generally not transferable. Among the reasons for the use of stock options as a form of compensation are potential tax benefits to the executive (although current tax rules severely restrict this benefit) and the linking of the executive's compensation to the fortunes of the company.

The important accounting issues related to the existence of a stock option plan are (1) the need for disclosure of the potential number of new shares of stock that may be issued if options are granted and exercised (so that present shareholders are apprised of how their *proportionate* shares may change if the options are exercised), and (2) to the extent that a *measurable* amount of compensation (to the executives) accompanies the issuance of the stock options, the compensation should be recognized as an expense of the period, or periods, benefiting.

The disclosure issue is handled by adding supplementary information to the financial statements which reflects the general provisions of the stock option plan, the number of options granted and exercised during the period, and the number of options outstanding at the end of the period.

Measuring compensation associated with the issuance of stock options is a more controversial issue. Although it is generally conceded that granting options conveys something of value to the recipient (as part of a compensation package), determination of that value is not an easy task. Since the options are generally not transferable, no market price can be used to assess this value. Accordingly, some other basis for measuring the value of the options must be found. For "simple" stock option plans not involving a variable number of shares or a variable option price depending upon future conditions (for which more complex measurement rules are prescribed), current accounting policy calls for measurement of the value of the compensation as the amount of the difference between the price that the holder must pay for the shares if he exercises the options and the fair market value of the stock *on the date the options are granted*.

Example 13-10   Continental Corporation issues stock options on December 15, 1974, to its senior executives, which, if exercised, will allow them to purchase 10,000 shares of the company's stock at $30 per share. On this date, the fair market value of Continental's stock is $40 per share. Accordingly, the amount of compensation imputed to the issuance of the options is $100,000—10,000 shares at $10 per share ($40 − $30).

Other milestone dates over the life of a stock option that have been proposed as more appropriate than the date of grant for the comparison of fair market value and exercise price in measuring the compensation that has been granted include (1) the date on which the grantee has satisfied all conditions necessary to be entitled to exercise the option, (2) the date on which the grantee may first exercise the option, and (3) the date on which the option is exercised. All of these potential comparison dates (including the date of grant) are, however, only alternative approaches to the fundamental measurement objective—measuring the value of the benefit at the time of its award, and none of the approaches are considered completely suitable as a general measurement methodology. Therefore, as more research is completed on this problem, a new and different measurement technique may evolve.

The compensation cost, however measured, is then recognized as an expense of the period, or periods, in which the employee performs the services for which the options were granted. Since options are generally assumed to be issued for future rather than past services, the cost will generally be recognized as an expense of several periods in the future. Therefore, using the data of Example 13-10, at the date of grant an expense (compensation expense) and/or an asset (deferred compensation expense) is recognized in the amount of $100,000, and since payment will be made (if exercised) through the issuance of stock, paid-in capital is also increased by the same amount.

Summary

We have briefly summarized some of the major components of owners' equity that appear in the financial reports of many publicly held corporations. An illustrative owners' equity section of the statement of financial position is shown in Exhibit 13-6.

Exhibit 13-6   ILLUSTRATIVE OWNERS' EQUITY SECTION
CORPORATION STATEMENT OF FINANCIAL POSITION

Shareholders' Equity

Capital stock			
Preferred stock:			
6% cumulative, convertible, $100 par value; 100,000 shares authorized, 50,000 shares issued	$5,000,000		
Amount received in excess of par value of stock	300,000	$5,300,000	
Common stock:			
Common stock, without par value, stated at $5 per share; shares authorized and issued—100,000	500,000		
Amount received in excess of stated value of stock	8,300,000	8,800,000	
Total contributed capital			$14,100,000
Retained earnings			9,200,000
			$23,300,000
Less—Treasury stock, at cost:			
Preferred—1,100 shares		91,000	
Common—1,455 shares		369,000	460,000
Total shareholders' equity			$22,840,000

As we noted at the outset of this section, the classification scheme used in the owners' equity section seeks to report the *sources* of the owners' equity of the corporation. Whether this classification, which in large part originated in old state corporation codes, has any substantive decision relevance is open to question. A case can certainly be made for reporting information that is relevant for dividend distribution decisions. But, in reality, when the legality of possible dividends becomes a major issue, it is doubtful that the general classification scheme used in present reports provides useful and accurate information.

Additionally, several important classes of transactions between the corporation and its shareholders (or potential shareholders in the case of stock options) have been briefly reviewed. While the specific treatment of the transactions within the conventional owners' equity classification system may not be highly significant, the expense or income recognition issues flowing from certain types of transactions (e.g., issuance of stock options and sale of treasury shares) are important questions.

Questions for Review and Discussion

13-1.   Define:

a. Liability

b. Bond premium and discount

c. Face value of a bond

d. Maturity date of a bond

e. Stated and market rates of interest

f. Paid-in capital

g. Retained earnings

h. Common and preferred stock

i. Cumulative and noncumulative preferred stock

j. Convertible preferred stock

k. Par value

l. Stated value (on no-par stock)

m. Stock dividend

n. Stock split

o. Treasury stock

p. Stock option

13-2.   What two attributes are generally common to all liabilities?

13-3.   How are liabilities typically created? How are liabilities typically discharged?

13-4.   The total cost that a firm will incur from using nonowner provided money capital may be measured using two elements from our transaction-based accounting system. State this fundamental relationship.

13-5.   What two measurement problems are associated with liabilities?

13-6.   State the basic relationship that exists between the value of a liability and the flows between parties to the borrowing transaction.

13-7.   How is interest expense calculated, using the implicit interest approach?

13-8.   Explain the difference between the value that is assigned to a liability under the conventional accounting model and the value that would be calculated using the current market-value model.

13-9.   Enumerate the three dates that are important for cash dividends. How do you think the market price of a publicly traded stock would react at each of these dates?

13-10.   Explain the two alternative ways of accounting for a stock dividend, and indicate the circumstances when each is appropriate under current accounting policy.

13-11.   Explain the similarities and differences (including the accounting treatment) between a stock dividend and a stock split.

13-12.   Explain the relationship between (1) the stated and market rates of interest and (2) the face amount of bonds and the proceeds that will be received when the bonds are issued.

13-13.   The financial statements in the 1972 annual report of the Times Mirror Company included the following information on the company's stock option plans:

> The executive stock option plans adopted prior to 1971 are qualified plans and provide that options may be granted to key executive employees to purchase shares of the Company's Common Stock at a price at least equal to the fair market value of the stock at date of grant. The 1971 Executive Stock Option Plan (a non-qualified plan) provides that options may be granted to key executive employees to purchase shares of the Company's Common Stock at a price at least equal to 75 percent of the fair market value at the date of grant. In general, the options under all plans are not exercisable until one year after date of grant and thereafter are exercisable in whole or in increments over a period not to exceed five years, dependent upon the terms of each option.
>
> Accounting entries are made only when options are exercised under the qualified plans. At the time options are granted under the 1971 Plan, the difference between the market price and the option price is . . . [added] to the additional paid-in capital account. That amount is deferred and is charged to operations over the period from the date of grant until the option becomes exercisable. Operations were charged $191,133 and $178,914 in 1972 and 1971 for such grants. At December 31, 1972, $33,694 was deferred and will be charged to operations in subsequent years. At the time the options are exercised under the plans, the cash proceeds are . . . [added] to the common stock and additional paid-in capital accounts.

Why do you suppose accounting entries are made only when options are exercised under the "qualified" plans? Under current accounting policy, is there any compensation expense associated with "qualified" plans? Why or why not? Does the treatment of the measured compensation on the "non-qualified" plans seem reasonable? Why or why not?

13-14.   The following news story appeared in the *Wall Street Journal* in May 1973:

> . . . [the] senior vice president of giant Gulf Oil Corp. doesn't like what he calls "glib criticism."
>
> And when the criticism is directed at Gulf's repurchase in March of 13 million of its own common shares—for which it paid a whopping $338 million—he gets downright annoyed.
>
> "It was a good decision then," he insists, "and we still feel that way now. We didn't borrow any funds for the purchase, our debt is low and we have tremendous borrowing power."

It's a cogent argument. A company has what it considers excess cash lying around, its capital spending requirements have been amply taken care of—what better way to use the money than by purchasing its own stock? The case becomes even stronger when, as in Gulf's case, the stock is selling at a relatively low multiple of earnings and has a relatively high dividend yield. Not only will a large repurchase of shares save the company money in dividends it no longer has to pay out, but shrinkage of the total number of shares outstanding will drive up earnings a few cents a share and might, the theory goes, increase investors' confidence in the company, perhaps driving up the price of its shares.

"Purchase of our own shares appears to be an attractive outlet for surplus funds at this time," is the way . . . [the senior vice president] put it when the March buy-back was completed.

Trouble is, the decision has cost Gulf a bundle, on paper at least. Since March, the price of a share of Gulf stock has tumbled from $25.375 to $23.125. That means the company has sustained a paper loss of around $30 million on its own shares.

And, predictably, the criticism is coming. Gulf isn't the only target (though its size and the size of its buy-back make it, in the words of one critic, "symbolically . . . the kickoff player"). A small but growing number of analysts and economists are beginning to question the logic behind moves by hundreds of companies recently to buy back their own stock at a record clip.

They're suggesting . . . that "buying back shares for reasons other than standard treasury requirements doesn't accomplish any really worthwhile corporate objective, and there may be more risks in it than management is willing to recognize." *

How would the "paper loss of around $30 million" on the treasury shares be recognized under the conventional accounting model? What would be the difference if the treasury shares were resold for $23.125? How does the Gulf situation differ from the early retirement of debt on which income or loss is recognized? Do you think that retirement of long-term debt and reacquisition of common shares should be treated differently in measuring income? Do you see any potential conflicts of interest in a management decision to reacquire its own stock?

13-15.   You are walking along a high-suspension bridge in Queen City enjoying the view when you spot a well-dressed, middle-aged man poised on the railing, apparently about to jump to his death. You yell "Stop!" He hesitates, giving you a chance to move closer and ask him why he wants to "end it all." In a sobbing voice the despondent man explains that he is the president of a medium-size corporation and just this afternoon he was informed by the chief accountant that the head bookkeeper ran off to Argentina with all the company's stockholders' equities. As president he had conscientiously insured all of the company's assets but had never thought of providing for this kind of loss. He is sure that the stockholders

---

* *Wall Street Journal*, May 22, 1973. Reprinted with the permission of The Wall Street Journal, © Dow Jones & Company, Inc., 1973.

would sue him for everything he has. Without his XX-7 sportscar, life is not worth living. With those few words he turns away to jump. Is there anything you can say about his problem that might make him change his mind?

13-1. Calculation of Interest Expense and Liability Value. Gammon Corporation issued on January 1, 1974, five-year bonds with a face value of $10,000 and a stated interest rate of 10 percent. Cash interest payments to holders of the bonds are to be made annually on December 31. The market rate of interest at the date of issue was 12 percent. Based upon the market determination of the value of the bonds at the prevailing interest rate of 12 percent, Gammon Corporation received $9,275 for the bonds.

Required:

Using the implicit interest method for accounting for liabilities, calculate the interest expense for 1975 and the carrying value of the bonds (the amount at which they will be valued in the financial statements) at December 31, 1975. (Note that calculations are for the *second year* the bonds are outstanding.)

13-2. Financial Position Worksheet Treatment of Bond Liability. Bonds with a face value of $100,000 were issued on January 1, 1974, for $92,420. The stated interest rate is 8 percent, and the market rate of interest at date of issue was 10 percent.

Required:

1. Calculate the following values for 1974 and 1975:

   (a) Cash interest payment for the year

   (b) Interest expense for the year

   (c) Carrying value of the liability at the end of the year

2. Set up a partial financial worksheet with column headings for Effect on Cash, Bonds Payable, and Effect on Owners' Equity, and record the transactions and adjustments for 1974 and 1975 that are required to properly account for the bond liability. (Note: The only beginning and ending balances that are needed are for the Bonds Payable column.)

13-3. Cash Dividends, Stock Dividends, and Stock Splits. The owners' equity section of Miller Corporation's statement of financial position on December 31, 1974, follows:

Common stock:		
$10 par value stock;		
500,000 shares authorized,		
100,000 shares issued	$1,000,000	
Amount received in excess		
of par value of stock	1,500,000	$2,500,000
Retained earnings		4,500,000
Total shareholders' equity		$7,000,000

Required:

Determine the balances of each of the components of Miller Corporation's owners' equity at the end of 1975 and 1976, taking into account the following events:

(a) On March 15, 1975, Miller Corporation paid a cash dividend of $10 per share.

(b) On September 15, 1975, Miller Corporation paid a 50 percent stock dividend. The fair market value of Miller Corporation's stock on this date was $150 per share.

(c) Net income for 1975 was $1,600,000.

(d) On March 15, 1976, Miller Corporation paid a cash dividend of $8 per share.

(e) On June 30, 1976, Miller Corporation paid a 20 percent stock dividend. The fair market value of Miller Corporation's stock on this date was $100 per share.

(f) On December 15, 1976, Miller Corporation split its stock four for one.

(g) Net income for 1976 was $2 million.

13-4. Interest Measurement and Liability Valuation. On January 1, 1973, the Acme Manufacturing Company issued five-year bonds with a face value of $100,000 and a stated interest rate of 10 percent. On that date the market rate of interest was 9 percent, and the bonds were sold at a price equal to the present value of future payments discounted at 9 percent. Interest is payable on December 31 of each year.

Required:

1. Prepare a schedule to support the calculation of the amount that Acme received on January 1, 1973.

2. Calculate the annual interest expense and the carrying value of the liability at the end of each year over the life of the bonds.

13-5. Interest Measurement and Liability Valuation. Bonds with a face value of $50,000 were issued by a company on January 1, 1974. The stated interest rate was 7 percent. However, the market rate of interest on January 1, 1974, was 10 percent, and the bonds sold for $46,269. Interest is paid annually on December 31.

Required:

1. Prepare a schedule that shows the annual interest expense, beginning and ending liability valuation, and annual cash payments for each year over the life of the bonds.

2. When will the bonds mature?

13-6. Calculation of Selling Price of Bonds—Present Value Method. A company plans to sell $100,000 worth of bonds immediately. The stated interest rate of the bonds is 8 percent, and the bonds will mature in four years. Interest will be paid annually.

Required:

1. Calculate the selling price of the bonds, using the present value method for each of the following market rates of interest:

   (a) 6 percent

   (b) 8 percent

   (c) 10 percent

2. What is the relationship (greater than, equal to, or less than) between the market rate of interest and the stated rate of interest for each of the following situations?

   (a) Bonds are sold at a discount.

   (b) Bonds are sold at a premium.

   (c) Bonds are sold for face value.

13-7. Interest Measurement and Liability Valuation.   On December 31, 1973, a company issued six-year bonds with a face value of $50,000. The stated interest rate was 9 percent; interest is payable on December 31 of each year. The market rate of interest was 10 percent, and the bonds were sold at a price equal to the present value of future payments discounted at the market rate of interest.

Required:

1. Calculate the selling price of the bonds.

2. Calculate the annual interest expense and carrying value of the liability at the end of each year over the life of the bonds.

13-8. Cash Dividends on Preferred and Common Stock.   The Acorn Company was incorporated in 1973. The company was authorized to issue 100,000 shares of $10 par-value common stock and 10,000 shares of 8 percent, cumulative preferred stock (par value $100).

In December 1973 the company sold 10,000 shares of the common stock at a price of $15 per share and 1,000 shares of the preferred stock at par. Operations began in January 1974.

Net income for 1974, 1975, and 1976 was $30,000, $2,000, and $40,000, respectively.

The board of directors adopted the general dividend policy of paying out 50 percent of the net income for the year in dividends on December 31. This policy was followed in 1974 and 1976, but because of the low earnings in 1975, dividends were not paid in that year.

Required:

1. Prepare a schedule that shows the following for each year of the three-year period:

   (a) Net income

   (b) Total dividends paid on preferred stock

   (c) Total dividends paid on common stock

(d) Dividends paid per common share

(e) Total owners' equity

2. Prepare the owners' equity section of the statement of financial position as of December 31, 1976.

13-9. Owners' Equity—Statement Presentation. Prepare the owners' equity section of the statement of financial position from the following information:

Retained earnings at beginning of year	$1,209,000
Number of 8% cumulative $100 par-value preferred shares authorized	100,000
Premium on bonds payable	$27,000
Total proceeds received from original issue of 100,000 common shares	$4,000,000
Net income for the year	$600,000
6% bonds payable, due at end of 1980	$500,000
Number of no-par common shares authorized	1,000,000
Dividends in arrears at the beginning of the year	$100,000
Cost of treasury stock (1,000 common shares)	$35/share
Number of preferred shares issued (all at par)	20,000
Total amount of dividends on common shares declared on December 31 ($1/share)	$99,000
Stated value of no-par stock	$10/share

13-10. Retiring Debt before Maturity. Debtor Corporation issued bonds with an aggregate par value of $10,000,000 on January 1, 1971. The bonds pay 9 percent interest, or $900,000 each year on December 31. At the time the bonds were issued the market rate for bonds of equal risk was slightly above 9 percent, but after the costs of issuing the bonds the proceeds were only $9,150,000, giving an effective interest rate of 10 percent.

By December 1974 the market rate of interest was about 7 percent on bonds of equivalent risk to Debtor Corporation's bonds. A provision in the original bond indenture agreement provided that at any time after January 1, 1974, but before maturity the original bonds could be retired at 105 percent of par value. Management of Debtor Corporation is considering retiring the original bonds on January 1, 1975, and reissuing on the same date $10,000,000 in bonds paying 7 percent, or $700,000 annually (on December 31). The administrative costs of the retirement of the old bonds are expected to be about $300,000.

The management of Debtor Corporation has asked you to provide it with advice on this matter.

Required:

1. Assuming that Debtor Corporation can earn an average 12 percent return on assets employed in the business, should management retire the bonds? Support your position with appropriate calculations.

2. At what amount will the present bonds be recognized on the corporation's December 31, 1974, balance sheet? How much expense will be recognized with respect to long-term debt in 1974?

3. Assuming that the corporation *does not* retire and reissue the bonds, how much expense will be recognized with respect to the long-term debt in 1975 and 1976?

4. Assuming that the corporation *does* retire the old bonds and reissue new ones on January 1, 1975, what amounts of expense with respect to long-term debt will be recognized in 1974, 1975, and 1976? Assume (*a*) that the new bonds are issued for net proceeds (after costs of issuing) equal to the par value of $10,000,000, and (*b*) that the cost of retiring the old bonds was $300,000, as expected. Is the contrast between this pattern of expense and the expense amounts called for in numbers 2 and 3 consistent with your answer to number 1?

13-11. Recognizing Changes in Owners' Equity.   Below is the stockholders' equity section of the consolidated balance sheet presented in the 1972 annual report of American Airlines, Inc., and Consolidated Subsidiary. However, the 1972 balances in the stockholders' equity accounts have been removed. Following the statement segment is some additional information. Based on the 1971 balances and the additional information, determine the end-of-1972 stockholders' equity account balances.

Stockholders' Equity (in thousands)	*1972*	*1971*
Preferred stock—no par value		
5,000,000 shares authorized; none issued		—0—
Common stock—$1 par value		
60,000,000 shares authorized		
28,486,000 shares issued and outstanding		
(1971—28,311,000)		28,311
Additional paid-in capital		311,188
Retained earnings		238,599
Total Stockholders' Equity		578,098
Total Liabilities and Stockholders' Equity		$1,662,614

Additional information:

a. $1,020,632 in subordinated convertible debentures was converted into 32,632 newly issued shares of $1 par-value common stock during 1972.

b. Employees purchased 5,313 shares of $1 par-value common stock during 1972 under employee stock purchase plans. Proceeds to the company were $232,313.

c. Holders of various stock options purchased 137,265 shares of $1 par-value common stock during 1972 for $4,402,265.

d. No dividends were issued during 1972.

e. The net income for 1972 was $5,635,000.

13-12. Recognizing Effects of Changes in Owners' Equity.   Below is the 1971 column of the stockholders' equity section from the balance sheet appearing in the 1972 annual report of Fuqua Industries, Inc., and Subsidiaries. Following the statement segment is a list of supplemental information.

Required:

1. Based on the information given, estimate the amounts that would appear as the 1972 balances in the stockholders' equity accounts.

2. In satisfying number 1, how did you treat the stock dividends issued during the year? What justification is there for the treatment accorded stock dividends in practice?

3. How would you have treated a stock split of, say, five shares for every four outstanding? Does the treatment differ from the stock dividend? If so, what is the justification for the difference? Do you believe that there is a difference between stock splits and stock dividends?

Stockholders' Equity (*in thousands*)	*1971*
Preferred Stock (represented by shares which entitle the holders to certain preferences not available to holders of common stock)	3,479
Common Stock (represented by shares which entitle the holder to the remaining ownership of the company after all liabilities and preferred stock claims are paid)	8,533
Additional capital (amounts received in excess of par value of shares and other accumulated capital transactions)	43,316
Retained earnings (accumulated profits retained for use in the business)	64,431
Total Stockholders' Equity	119,759
Total Liabilities and Stockholders' Equity	$315,011

Additional information:

a. During 1972 approximately 6,970 preferred shares recorded at their par value of $100 each were converted into 82,000 common shares with a par value of $1 each.

b. Approximately 850 $100 par-value preferred shares were redeemed during 1972 at par.

c. Approximately 375,000 $1 par-value common shares with a total fair market value of approximately $8,160,000 were issued as a stock dividend.

d. The $7,706,000 (approximately) of 7⅝ percent convertible subordinated debentures (bonds) outstanding at the end of 1971 were converted to 617,000 $1 par-value common shares during 1972.

e. 173,000 $1 par-value common shares were issued in connection with acquisitions of other companies. The shares had an aggregate value of $2,926,000.

f. A net amount of 35,000 $1 par-value common shares were sold under stock option plans—the net value being $555,000.

g. 114,000 $1 par-value common shares were purchased to be held as treasury shares. The cost was $1,481,000.

h. Miscellaneous other common stock transactions resulted (effectively) in the issuance of 39,000 shares of $1 par-value common stock for $89,000 in total proceeds.

i. Net income for the year was $18,069,000.

j. Cash dividends (on preferred stock only) amounted to $469,000.

k. There was an adjustment to retained earnings in 1972 to change an acquired company to a calendar year basis consistent with Fuqua Industries, Inc. The adjustment decreased retained earnings by $265,000.

14

Valuation and Income:
Some Further Issues

In the preceding three chapters the discussion focused on broadening the reader's awareness of actual situations with which an accounting model or policy must effectively deal. In contrast to earlier chapters, the discussion did not focus on applying an overall accounting model to business enterprises in general. Rather, we concentrated on applying the principles of a given model (mainly conventional accounting) to the acknowledged varieties of situations within broad classes of transactions or elements of financial position; for example, in Chapter 11 the realization principle was applied to situations involving widely varying lags between productive activity and sale and between sale and cash collection. In this chapter still another alteration in the focus of discussion will be employed to further broaden the reader's awareness of the present-day corporate reporting environment. We will consider several significant and/or generally controversial issues concerning corporate financial statements: (1) accounting for income taxes, (2) accounting for long-term noncancellable leases, and (3) accounting for related companies.

Although these few additional issues are not the only significant issues not covered earlier, in two important respects they give excellent representation to the issues that have confronted policy makers in recent years. First, they are among the issues affecting the largest number of publicly owned companies. Second, they are among the most widely studied and debated—and in some cases the most difficult to resolve—of recent corporate reporting problems.

ACCOUNTING FOR INCOME TAXES

Accountants generally agree that income taxes are genuine expenses of doing business for any enterprise whose income is subject to tax. But income tax expense is incurred or levied in a way that is unique among all of the expenses incurred by business enterprises. As a result, there is some ambiguity as to how income tax expense ought to be matched against revenues (i.e., in what periods and in what amounts).

Income Tax Assessments: Some Basics

In the United States the federal income tax is levied on taxable income *as defined by the Internal Revenue Code*. The corporate rate structure is much simpler than the rate structure for individuals. The first $25,000 of taxable income is taxed at a rate of 22 percent, while the rate on taxable income in excess of $25,000 is 48 percent.

• *Conventional accounting basis.* Taxable income, as defined by the Internal Revenue Code, is largely based on conventional accounting principles. As a general rule, taxable income is based on the difference between revenue realized and the original cost of resources used to produce the revenue of the period. However, certain kinds of revenue (e.g., interest from tax-exempt municipal bonds) and certain kinds of expenses (e.g., "excessive" business entertainment expenses) are not included in taxable income as a matter of national policy (but not because they are not genuine items of revenue and expense in an accounting sense).

Thus, with the exception of certain kinds of revenue and expense that are systematically (and permanently) excluded from the calculation of taxable income, taxable income will tend to be approximately equal to before-tax conventional accounting income *over the whole life of the enterprise*. However, the emphasis on the "whole-life" equality of taxable income and before-tax conventional accounting income is important. Differences in measurement rules selected for accounting and tax assessment purposes mean that in any given period, taxable income will probably differ from before-tax accounting income—often by a substantial amount.

• *Differences in measurement rules and timing.* Although both before-tax conventional accounting income and taxable income are based on the same general principles (i.e., realization, matching, and original transaction cost valuation), they both allow some latitude in selection of the measurement rules used to implement those principles in a given situation. Furthermore, with few exceptions an enterprise need not select the same measurement rule for tax accounting purposes that is selected for financial accounting purposes. Exhibit 14-1 shows some of the alternative measurement rules possible under the Internal Revenue Code. Chapters 11–13 have already acquainted the

Exhibit 14-1
SOME SELECTED CATEGORIES
OF ALTERNATE MEASUREMENT RULES
PERMISSIBLE UNDER THE INTERNAL REVENUE CODE

Revenue Recognition

Installment sales method
Recognition in period of sale

Inventory (Cost of Sales) Valuation	*Depreciation Expense*
Specific identification	Straight-line
Fifo	Sum-of-years-digits
Lifo*	Declining-balance

* Lifo is an exception to the general rule that different measurement rules may be selected for tax and financial accounting purposes. Only those enterprises that adopt Lifo for financial accounting purposes may use Lifo for determining their taxable income.

reader with the various alternatives that may be employed in conventional financial accounting.

Except in those cases where the Internal Revenue Code does not allow a measurement rule that is permissible under conventional accounting, *there is no reason why taxable income must necessarily be different from before-tax conventional accounting income* (allowing for the items permanently excluded from taxable income). Indeed, if the same measurement rules are adopted for both purposes, the numbers will be the same (again, allowing for permanently excluded items in the tax calculations). However, as a general rule, the measurement rules selected for financial accounting and tax purposes will not necessarily be the same. The reason is that two different purposes dominate their selection. For financial accounting purposes, the selection of measurement rules is dominated by the desire to best represent the financial status and activities of the enterprise within the framework of conventional accounting. For tax purposes, wherever a choice is available, the objective in selecting a measurement rule is to optimize the financial effects (the amount and timing) of the taxes that the enterprise will have to pay.

Example 14-1   Vending Machine Company owns and operates a large number of vending machines. The company buys a completely new supply of machines every three years from the manufacturer who allows 40 percent of the original cost of three-year-old machines as a trade-in allowance on new machines. The company purchased its first set of machines in 19X1 for $1 million. All of its sales are for cash, and all expenses incurred other than depreciation are cash expenditures at the time incurred (for both tax purposes and accounting purposes). The supplies in the company's vending machines are the property of the suppliers who bill the company only for the supplies sold. The company's sales for *each* of its first three years of operations were $1 million for both financial accounting and tax purposes. Expenses other than depreciation for both purposes were $600,000 each year. However, the company determined its depreciation on a straight-line basis for financial accounting purposes and on a sum-of-years-digits basis for tax purposes. Thus the company's before-tax financial accounting income and taxable income for 19X1–X3 were as shown in Exhibit 14-2.

Exhibit 14-2
VENDING MACHINE COMPANY
Comparative Income Statements
19X1–19X3

Before-Tax Financial Accounting Income

	19X1	19X2	19X3	Total
Revenues	$1,000,000	$1,000,000	$1,000,000	$3,000,000
Less expenses:				
Depreciation	200,000	200,000	200,000	600,000
Other expense	600,000	600,000	600,000	1,800,000
Before-tax income	$ 200,000	$ 200,000	$ 200,000	$ 600,000

Taxable Income

	19X1	19X2	19X3	Total
Revenues	$1,000,000	$1,000,000	$1,000,000	$3,000,000
Less expenses:				
Depreciation	300,000	200,000	100,000	600,000
Other expense	600,000	600,000	600,000	1,800,000
Taxable income	$ 100,000	$ 200,000	$ 300,000	$ 600,000

- *Two sets of books?* Several aspects of Exhibit 14-2 are worth noting. For one thing, the before-tax financial accounting income and the taxable income calculations agree *in total* for the three years. This will usually be the case except for (allowing for) items permanently excluded from the tax calculations. The two income calculations differ only in the amounts of expense (depreciation) and income recognized *in the individual years*.

Another important observation is that Exhibit 14-2 illustrates the phenomenon of having "two sets of books" for the same set of facts. Although this phenomenon is often thought of by laymen as being "shady" or dishonest, there is nothing illegal, immoral, or unethical in having separate records for financial and tax purposes—as long as all of the revenue and expenses recognized under the Internal Revenue Code are accounted for according to permissible measurement rules in the enterprise's tax calculations.

In fact, the management of an enterprise has an obligation to act in its shareholders' interests. With respect to income taxes, this generally means payment of no more taxes than necessary and no sooner than necessary.

Example 14-2   In the case of Vending Machine Company, management had a choice between using straight-line or sum-of-years-digits depreciation for tax purposes. Tax calculations under the two methods (assuming a tax rate of 50 percent for simplicity) are shown in Exhibit 14-3. Notice that the sum of the three-year tax bill is the same under each alternative. However, under the S-Y-D depreciation alternative less tax is paid initially and more is paid later. Because money has a time value, such postponement is in the interest of the enterprise and therefore its owners.

Income Taxes and Matching

As noted above, selection of the best measurement rules for financial accounting and tax purposes, respectively, often means that before-tax financial

Exhibit 14-3   VENDING MACHINE COMPANY
Comparative Income Tax Calculations

S-L Depreciation:	19X1	19X2	19X3
Taxable income (see before-tax financial accounting income in Exhibit 14-2)	$200,000	$200,000	$200,000
Income tax at 50% of taxable income	100,000	100,000	100,000
S-Y-D Depreciation:			
Taxable income (from Exhibit 14-2)	$100,000	$200,000	$300,000
Income tax at 50%	50,000	100,000	150,000

accounting income will differ from taxable income. Although there is nothing morally wrong with this divergence (and, indeed, it may be the only way to serve the interests to which management is responsible), it creates a certain ambiguity as to how income tax expense ought to be recognized.

• *Income taxes as period costs.* Some accountants argue that income taxes are assessed and payable according to the taxable income of a given period (as defined by the set of permissible measurement rules adopted by the enterprise). As such they are inherently period costs. Under this interpretation, the income tax expense recognized in a given period is equal to the amount of tax calculated on the taxable income of that period (though it may be paid in part after the start of the next period). However, many accountants object in principle to the effect on after-tax accounting income of this interpretation. To illustrate, Exhibit 14-4 shows the after-tax financial accounting net income for Vending Machine Company based on the facts originally given in Example 14-1.

Exhibit 14-4   VENDING MACHINE COMPANY
After-Tax Income
19X1–19X3

	19X1	19X2	19X3
Before-tax accounting income (based on S-L depreciation)	$200,000	$200,000	$200,000
Income tax expense (based on S-Y-D depreciation)	50,000	100,000	150,000
After-tax accounting income	$150,000	$100,000	$ 50,000

• *Income taxes matched against related revenue and expense.* Critics of the period-cost interpretation of income taxes are uneasy with the disparity in the pattern between before-tax and after-tax income that can occur under the period-cost approach illustrated by Exhibit 14-4. They argue that income taxes are a function of the revenues and expenses of the enterprise. Income tax expense should therefore be recognized (for financial accounting purposes) in the period in which the revenues and expenses giving rise to the taxes are recognized (for financial accounting purposes). *The timing of recognition of those same revenues and expenses for tax purposes is relevant only insofar as it determines when income taxes actually become payable.* Most accountants today agree with this position. However, implementation of the matching of income tax expense with the related revenues and expenses requires a (minor) complication in accounting for the enterprise called "interperiod tax allocation."

• *Interperiod tax allocation illustrated.* Perhaps the most straightforward approach to introducing the reader to interperiod income tax allocation is by means of an illustration. That is the approach we will take, using the example below. However, we will restrict ourselves to the one method (the deferral method) for tax allocation that is supported by the authority of the APB (which is no longer in operation but whose opinions carry the weight of authority until the FASB supersedes them). There are other methods, but a discussion of their advantages and disadvantages relative to the deferred method is best left to more advanced texts.

Example 14-3   In earlier examples and exhibits we noted that for Vending Machine Company, before-tax income based on straight-line depreciation was $200,000 in 19X1, 19X2, and 19X3 (Exhibit 14-2). Also, the assumed income tax rate was 50 percent (Example 14-2). This implies that to be matched properly with related revenue and expense of the period, the company's income tax expense should be $100,000 in each of the years (i.e., 50 percent of $200,000). But, on the other hand, we noted that with taxable income based on sum-of-years-digits depreciation, the actual assessed taxes (taxes payable) for the three years was $50,000, $100,000, and $150,000, respectively. The financial position worksheet in Exhibit 14-5 shows how we handle the seemingly divergent schedule of taxes payable and the desired schedule of income tax expense in a consistent manner for all three years. It is based on the additional assumptions that (1) the company started 19X1 with $1 million of vending machines as the only assets, and (2) each year's taxes payable are paid at the beginning of the following year. (In actual practice, taxes payable would be estimated and paid quarterly.)

The key feature of Exhibit 14-5 is the use of the account "deferred income tax liability." It is used to coordinate the desired level of income tax expense determined by the level of before-tax accounting income with the level of currently payable taxes determined by taxable income. For instance, in 19X1, with $200,000 before-tax income, the income tax expense recognized is $100,000. However, the then-current tax liability is only $50,000 because the S-Y-D depreciation used to calculate taxable income is $100,000 greater than the S-L depreciation used for before-tax accounting income in that year. But it is known that in some future period (in this case 19X3) the relationship will reverse because the lifetime depreciation of the assets (and hence, lifetime income) must be equal under the two depreciation methods. Thus the difference between the income tax expense recognized in 19X1 and the tax that must be paid for 19X1 *will presumably be paid in some future period* (in this case 19X3). For 19X1 the reduction in owners' equity of $100,-000 for income tax expense is therefore offset by an increase in the current liability "taxes payable" of $50,000 and an increase of $50,000 in "deferred income tax liability."

Exhibit 14-5

VENDING MACHINE COMPANY
Financial Position Worksheet
19X1, 19X2, and 19X3

Description	Cash	Vending Machines	Accumulated Depreciation	Taxes Payable	Deferred Income Tax Liability	Owners' Equity
Beginning Position		1,000,000				1,000,000
19X1						
Sales	1,000,000					1,000,000 (R)
Other expenses	(600,000)					(600,000) (E)
Depreciation			(200,000)			(200,000) (E)
Income tax expense				50,000	50,000	(100,000) (E)
Ending (Beginning) Position	400,000	1,000,000	(200,000)	50,000	50,000	1,100,000
19X2						
Paid taxes	(50,000)			(50,000)		
Sales	1,000,000					1,000,000 (R)
Other expenses	(600,000)					(600,000) (E)
Depreciation			(200,000)			(200,000) (E)
Income tax expense				100,000		(100,000) (E)
Ending (Beginning) Position	750,000	1,000,000	(400,000)	100,000	50,000	1,200,000
19X3						
Paid taxes	(100,000)			(100,000)		
Sales	1,000,000					1,000,000 (R)
Other expenses	(600,000)					(600,000) (E)
Depreciation			(200,000)			(200,000) (E)
Income tax expense				150,000	(50,000)	(100,000) (E)
Ending (Beginning) Position	1,050,000	1,000,000	(600,000)	150,000	—0—	1,300,000

In 19X2, before-tax accounting income and taxable income are equal by coincidence, meaning no further deferral is necessary in that year. The recognition of income tax expense in the owners' equity account is offset by an equal increase in taxes (currently) payable. In 19X3, when the reversal in the relationship between accounting and tax depreciation takes place, the $150,000 taxes payable exceeds the appropriate expense of $100,000 by precisely the $50,000 that was deferred in 19X1. Thus in recognizing the 19X3 current tax liability and expense, the deferral is reversed.

As a result of the strong stand taken by the APB favoring income tax allocation according to the deferral method, the method is widely adopted in practice. A reader of financial statements will frequently see deferred tax liabilities in published financial statements. Furthermore, the treatment of income tax expense will often resemble the treatment shown in Exhibit 14-6 based on the Vending Machine Company example.

Exhibit 14-6

VENDING MACHINE COMPANY
After-Tax Income Calculations
For the Years 19X1, 19X2, and 19X3

	19X1	*19X2*	*19X3*
Before-tax income	$200,000	$200,000	$200,000
Less income tax expense:			
Currently payable	50,000	100,000	150,000
Increase (decrease) in			
deferred tax liability	50,000	—0—	(50,000)
Income tax expense	$100,000	$100,000	$100,000
After-tax income	$100,000	$100,000	$100,000

ACCOUNTING FOR LONG-TERM NONCANCELLABLE LEASES

A business enterprise requiring certain long-lived assets for its operations can usually acquire and finance their acquisition in a number of different ways. One way is to rent available assets on a period-by-period basis. A great advantage of such short-term rental arrangements is that at any one time the enterprise only has to pay for a fraction of the service potential of an essentially large, indivisible resource. A major disadvantage is the possible lack of availability of suitable assets or the abrupt withdrawal by the owner of assets presently in use. Furthermore, assets rented on a short-term basis may have a higher cost due to the owner's risk that the renter may also abruptly discontinue renting.

Another way to acquire resources, of course, is by outright purchase. Through ownership, the enterprise ensures itself of an ample and relatively more certain supply. But ownership of long-lived assets also requires the commitment of considerably more of the enterprise's money capital or greater risk to owners due to financing the purchase through additional debt. Ownership also carries with it the additional risk that the economic life (usefulness) of the assets may end abruptly due to obsolescence, malfunction, or excessive maintenance costs.

In between the extremes of acquiring long-lived assets by outright purchase and acquiring their use on a strictly period-by-period basis is a spectrum of arrangements that we will refer to as long-term noncancellable leases. A long-term noncancellable lease is a contract between a lessor (owner) who agrees to provide use of the assets for a specified number of periods and a lessee (renter) who agrees to pay a specified schedule of rent payments in exchange. To the lessor a long-term noncancellable lease represents insurance against lack of demand; to the lessee it is insurance against lack of supply. This is so because neither party can unilaterally fail to perform without being held liable for damages to the other. On the other hand, a long-term noncancellable lease is usually an *executory contract,* meaning that although neither party is free to withdraw, if one party does fail to perform its contractual obligation, the other party need not continue to perform as agreed.

Most accountants would concur, in principle at least, as to the recognition to be given to the various expenses, revenues, assets, and liabilities involved in an outright purchase or in short-term rental of assets by one entity from another. Such arrangements for acquiring and using long-lived assets have not usually presented controversial problems to accounting policy makers. Long-term noncancellable leases, on the other hand, present a perplexing problem due to uncertainty (and resultant disagreement) about their nature—particularly relative to other means of acquiring the services of long-lived assets. Those who see long-term noncancellable leases as more similar to outright purchases (sales) of assets advocate one kind of accounting treatment. And those who see long-term noncancellable lease agreements as more similar to period-by-period rental of assets advocate another kind of treatment.

The Capitalization-Financing (Purchase-Sale) Treatment of Leases

- *The lessee.* In a sense, a long-term noncancellable lease may be likened to the purchase of an asset by the lessee (the asset being *the rights* to a number of periods of service). The seller (lessor) extends credit to the buyer, with the purchased asset as security (meaning, if the buyer defaults on the payments, the seller may repossess the asset and resell or rerent it to satisfy the uncollected balance of the original lease agreement). In cases where the above analogy applies, the long-term noncancellable lease agreements should be recognized by the lessee as liabilities in a manner consistent with other long-term debt. As described in Chapter 13, this involves recognizing the discounted value of the contractual lease payments as a liability at the time the lease agreement is entered upon. It also involves recognizing at the same time the related asset received in exchange for that liability, that is, the rights to use the leased assets for the full term of the lease—also at the discounted present value of the lease payments. Thereafter, the expense to the lessee of using the leasehold assets is recognized in the form of amortization (depreciation) of the initial asset value over the term of the lease. In addition, but independent of the actual consumption of the inherent service potential of the leased assets, interest expense is recognized each period on the discounted value of the remaining lease payments. Accountants commonly refer to this total treatment of leases by the lessee under the single term *capitalization* because it requires that the lease payments be discounted or "capitalized" in order to initially value the lease liability and related asset.

• *The lessor.* If a particular lease is judged essentially an installment sale, it should be recognized by the lessor as such, that is, in the manner described in Chapter 11. This means that in the period that the lease agreement is consummated, the present value of the lease payments is recognized as revenue, and the unexpired cost (adjusted for any expected salvage or residual market value at the end of the lease term) of the leased asset is recognized as expense (cost of sales). In implementing such recognition of revenue and expense at the consummation of the lease, the lessor recognizes a new asset, "lease contract payments receivable," valued at the present value of the lease payments, in place of the cost of the leased assets that is expensed (cost of sales). During the term of the lease, the "lease receivable" balance is reduced in each accounting period by any payments received from the lessee and increased by interest on the present value of the remaining payments, the interest being recognized as additional (financing type) income from the lease in that period. This method of handling the financial effects of the lease by the lessor is referred to as the *financing method* because it follows from the conclusion that the lessor has in effect sold the assets to the lessee and "financed" the purchase for the lessee by extending long-term credit.

• *The capitalization-financing treatment illustrated.* Since the capitalization approach for the lessee and the financing approach for the lessor are basically the same approach, they can be illustrated by a single example.

Example 14-4   Slammer Stamping Company has just entered into a six-year lease agreement with Elipse Equipment Company. According to the lease agreement, Elipse will provide Slammer with certain heavy equipment that it manufactures for a six-year period. Slammer in turn has agreed to an immediate payment of $500,000, and a schedule of additional payments of $400,000 at the beginning of each of the second and third years, $200,000 at the beginning of each of the fourth and fifth years, and $120,000 at the beginning of the sixth year. Neither party may cancel or fail to perform any of the terms of the lease without the consent of the other. The retail price of the rights to use of the equipment acquired by Slammer is *approximately* $1,600,000. Based on this price, the effective interest rate (the rate at which the present value of the set of lease payments approximates the value received) is about 8 percent, which is also equal to the market rate of interest for secured loans of risk equal to the lease agreement.

Assuming that Slammer recognized the lease rights as an asset and the lease obligation as a liability at the time of signing the lease, and assuming that the company felt that straight-line amortization (depreciation) of the asset was appropriate, all of the financial accounting effects of capitalizing the lease agreement over its six-year life may be summarized as in Exhibit 14-7.

Assume also that the lease is judged to be an installment sale (in effect) from the point of view of Elipse. Suppose further that Elipse's cost to manufacture the leased assets had been $1,200,000 and that they were recognized at that cost in Elipse's financial position at the time the lease agreement was

Exhibit 14-7

SLAMMER STAMPING COMPANY
Lease-Related Asset, Liability, and Expense Capitalization Treatment

	Asset and Related Expense		Liability and Related Expense				
Year	Amortization Expense	Year-end Balance	Beg. of Year Lease Payment	Discounted Unpaid Balance	8% Interest Expense	Discounted Year-end Balance	Total Expense
Lease signed		$1,600,720				$1,600,720	
1	$ 266,787	1,333,933	$ 500,000	$1,100,720	$ 88,058	1,188,778	$ 354,845
2	266,787	1,067,146	400,000	788,778	63,102	851,880	329,889
3	266,787	800,359	400,000	451,880	36,150	488,030	302,937
4	266,787	533,572	200,000	288,030	23,042	311,072	289,829
5	266,786	266,786	200,000	111,072	8,886	119,958	275,672
6	266,786	0	120,000	(42)*	0	0	266,786
	$1,600,720		$1,820,000*		$219,238		$1,819,958*

* $42 difference due to rounding error in present value factors.

463

consummated. Elipse would recognize a lease receivable from Slammer equal to the discounted value of the lease payments, $1,600,720, and include that amount in its revenue immediately. At the same time the cost of the leased assets, $1,200,000, will be expensed, and the assets themselves will no longer appear in the company's financial position. The difference between the present value of the lease payments and the cost of the leased assets, $400,720, is recognized in full as income in the period of inception of the lease. In addition, interest income would be recognized each year. For convenience, it may be assumed that Elipse would recognize the same balance of lease receivable and interest income that Slammer recognized as its liability balance and interest expense, respectively. Thus, from the Interest Expense column of Exhibit 14-7 we see that Elipse would recognize interest income of $88,058 in year one, $63,102 in year two, and so forth. A schedule showing the lease receivable balance, interest income, and so forth, that would be recognized by Elipse according to the financing method appears in Exhibit 14-8.

Exhibit 14-8

ELIPSE EQUIPMENT COMPANY
Lease-Related Asset and Income
Financing Treatment

Year	Beg. of Year Payment Received	Discounted Outstanding Balance	8% Interest Income	Discounted Year-end Balance
Lease signed				$1,600,720
1	$ 500,000	$1,100,720	$ 88,058	1,188,778
2	400,000	788,788	63,102	851,880
3	400,000	451,880	36,150	488,030
4	200,000	288,030	23,042	311,072
5	200,000	111,072	8,886	119,958
6	120,000	(42)*	—0—	—0—
Total	$1,820,000		$219,238	
Income recognized at time lease is signed			400,720	
Total income			$619,958	

* $42 difference due to rounding error in present value factors.

Looking at Exhibit 14-7, several important relationships are worth noting. First, the initial value of both the liability and the asset recognized, $1,600,-720, is equal to the discounted value of the lease payments, including the initial payment, at the implicit interest rate (with $720 error due to approximation of the actual implicit rate with the more convenient 8 percent rate). Second, during the term of the lease while (1) substantial assets are in use in the business, and (2) Slammer Company is under a substantial obligation to Elipse Company, these conditions will be represented in the financial position (balance sheet) of the company as an asset and a liability, respectively. Furthermore, they will appear in magnitudes approximating those that would appear if Slammer had acquired the same rights by purchase and financed the purchase with a secured loan involving an identical schedule of payments. Third, the sum of the amortization plus interest expense recognized over the six-year term equals (with minor rounding error) the total of the lease payments. But, as is customary in financial accounting, the portion related to the use of the resource in operations (amortization) is separated from the portion related to financing the acquisition of the resource (interest) through an extended schedule of payments.

Looking at Exhibit 14-8, there are two more important points to note in connection with the financing treatment of leases by the lessor. First, the financing method for the lessor is analogous to the capitalization treatment for the lessee. Second, the total income from the lease recognized over its entire term is equal to the sum of the income recognized in the period of inception plus all of the interest on the lease receivable recognized period by period. In the above example, this total is equal to $400,720 "income recognized at time lease is signed" plus the $219,238 sum of the Interest Income column of Exhibit 14-8.

The Short-Term Rental or "Operating" Treatment of Leases

Most accountants would agree that when a lease is in substance an installment sale for a lessor or an installment purchase for a lessee, the financing-capitalization treatment is appropriate. If the lease is not in substance a sale (purchase), the appropriate accounting method is called the "operating method" (traditionally, the term has been applied only to the lessor, but we will use it for both). Under the operating method, the rent paid by the lessee is recognized as expense by the lessee and revenue by the lessor in the period for which it covers occupancy or use of the assets by the lessee according to the rental agreement. The leased assets continue to be recognized in the financial position of the lessor at their unexpired cost, reduced each period by the depreciation charges that are matched against the recognized rental revenue. No assets (except perhaps some prepaid rent) or liabilities are recognized in connection with the lease by the lessee.

Example 14-5   Suppose that the Slammer-Elipse lease was judged not to be a sale (purchase). Suppose further that it was considered appropriate for Elipse to depreciate the leased assets on a sum-of-years-digits basis over the six-year term of the lease and that no salvage value was expected. The schedule of rent expense for Slammer and the schedules of (1) the declining unexpired leased asset balance, (2) the depreciation expense, (3) the rental revenue, and (4) the rental income that would be recognized by Elipse over the term of the lease, according to the operating method, appear in Exhibit 14-9.

Two important observations about the contrast between the schedules in Exhibit 14-9 and those appearing in Exhibits 14-7 and 14-8 should be noted. First, the total income recognized by the lessor (Elipse) over the term of the lease is the same (except for minor rounding errors) under both the financing and the operating treatment. But the timing and nature of the amounts recognized in each period differ. Second, the nature and the amount of the lease-related asset recognized under the two methods differ. Under the financing method the leased assets are considered to have been exchanged by the lessor for another asset, "rent receivable," in a *bona fide* exchange transaction.

Exhibit 14-9   THE SLAMMER STAMPING–ELIPSE EQUIPMENT LEASE
                                     OPERATING METHOD

| | Slammer Stamping (Lessee) | Elipse Equipment (Lessor) | | |
Year	Rent Expense	Year-end Balance Leased Assets	S-Y-D Depreci-ation	Rental Revenue	Rental Income
Lease signed		$1,200,000			
1	$ 500,000	857,142	$ 342,858	$ 500,000	$157,142
2	400,000	571,427	285,715	400,000	114,285
3	400,000	342,855	228,572	400,000	171,428
4	200,000	171,426	171,429	200,000	28,571
5	200,000	57,140	114,286	200,000	85,714
6	120,000	—0—	57,140	120,000	62,860
Total	$1,820,000		$1,200,000	$1,820,000	$620,000

In the case of the lessee (Slammer) the schedule of rent expense (paid) is all that is necessary under the operating method, whereas the financing method required the recognition of the leasehold asset and related amortization expense along with the lease liability and related interest expense. Again it is important to recognize that the sum of the periodic amortization and interest expenses recognized by the lessee under the capitalization treatment is equal to the sum of the periodic rent expense that would be recognized under the operating method.

Accounting for Leases: Positions and Controversies

For the sake of the illustration above, we have simply assumed that it was appropriate to apply either the capitalization-financing method or the operating method to a given situation. However, the two alternative accounting methods (when applied to a given situation) can produce substantially different revenue, expense, asset, and liability recognition period by period for both the lessor and the lessee. This naturally poses the question, Which of the two methods is better? Unfortunately, opinions differ. In present-day practice a view that we will characterize as the "situational" view predominates. However, present-day accounting for leases by both lessors and lessees has often been under fire in recent years from virtually all quarters where there is a substantial interest in financial reporting practice.

• *The situational point of view.* The situational point of view is oriented toward deciding which treatment ought to be accorded a given lease based on the facts in the individual case. The selection of method depends both on the terms of the lease and whether the choice of accounting method is being made for a lessor or a lessee. (The treatment of a given lease can differ for the lessor and the lessee under the situational point of view.)

• *Sale or "no sale."* Since the choice of the financing method or operating method on the part of the lessor determines whether or not revenue will be recognized immediately or postponed to the periods of collection of the lease payments, *the appropriate criterion is the realization principle.* Applying the situational point of view means that if the lease payments can be considered "realized" at the inception of a given lease, the financing method is appropriate. If the lease payments cannot be considered "realized" at the outset, the operating method is appropriate.

Basically, the same conditions are necessary for realization in the case of leases as in the case of any other transaction. The agreed-to payments (1) must be reasonably certain with respect to ultimate collection, and (2) further efforts (costs) required to "earn" the payments must be relatively minor and must be reasonably predictable at the inception of the lease. The second condition will not ordinarily hold for lease agreements under which the lessor agrees to cover highly uncertain future costs (i.e., unspecified as to amount) associated with the leased assets, such as maintenance costs. The first condition will not ordinarily hold for lease agreements under which the lessor continues to bear most of the risk of ownership of the leased assets, for example, if the lessor agrees to guarantee that the assets will not become obsolete during the term of the lease.

Critics of accounting practices of lessors generally do not take exception to the situational point of view in principle. Instead they point out that too frequently lessors interpret their situations with unwarranted optimism, with the result that many lease agreements are treated as "sales" which do not seem to warrant such treatment when subjected to close scrutiny. Understandably, then, recent pronouncements of accounting policy makers (until June 1973 the Accounting Principles Board) have tended to be very detailed and explicit as to the terms and characteristics of lease agreements that do and do not qualify them for treatment as sale transactions.

• *The situational point of view applied to lessees.* The situational view is the view represented by the past authoritative pronouncements emanating from the accounting profession on accounting for long-term leases by lessees. For instance, the Accounting Principles Board expressed the view that long-term noncancellable leases do not constitute liabilities (or assets) *per se.* If circumstances indicate that a given lease *is in substance an installment purchase* of assets, capitalization is warranted. Otherwise, no long-term liability or related asset is recognized in connection with the lease. Instead, the basic condition of any significant lease agreement, including information about the required future payments, is to be disclosed in a footnote to the financial statements. Rent payments (the only effects of such leases that actually appear in the financial statements themselves) are recognized as expenses in the periods for which they cover occupancy according to the lease.

Naturally, the question of when a lease is "in substance a purchase" is open to judgment, but the APB did indicate that if certain features are present in the lease arrangement, they usually mean that the lease is basically an installment purchase. One such condition, for instance, is that (1) the initial term of the lease is less than the economic life of the assets, *and* (2) the lessee has the contractual option to extend the lease for an additional term at a rent level substantially below the expected market rent of the assets. Presumably, such a condition implies that payments required in the lease agreement tend to buy more rights than just the service of the leased assets period by period during the initial term of the lease and therefore warrant capitalization and recognition as an asset from the inception of the lease.

Critics of the situational point of view for lessee accounting typically disagree that such conditions are necessary in order for capitalization of leases by lessees to be warranted. They argue that under a long-term noncancellable lease, the lessee is obligated to a greater extent than in a short-term rental arrangement, since upon failure to pay the contractual rent payment (as opposed to not renewing a short-term rental arrangement) the lessee would not only give up the use of the leased assets but also be liable for damages (possibly up to or exceeding the unpaid rent). It is in this respect that all long-term noncancellable leases are similar to long-term liabilities incurred to finance the purchase of assets. Hence, accountants who take this view conclude that all long-term noncancellable leases should be treated in a manner consistent with other long-term liabilities (i.e., capitalized).

Not surprisingly, defenders of the situational view do not share the view expressed above that any noncancellable lease that specifies a contractual set of payments over a number of future periods ought to be treated by the lessee as a long-term liability. Many focus on the executory nature of the lease contract in differentiating leases from long-term debt, that is, if the lessor ever fails to provide assets in usable condition during the term of the lease, the lessee is not obligated to pay. Others focus on the fact that many leases require that the *lessor* continue to incur most of the risks as well as the ultimate rights of ownership of the assets; for example, the lessor often is required to maintain the assets and pay the taxes, and, of course, the owner may retain the right (or obligation) to sell or otherwise dispose of the asset when the lease term expires. It is felt that such reservation of the rights and risks of ownership on the part of the lessor argues against recognition of the assets as assets of the lessee. Still others focus on the notion that portions of scheduled lease payments are not for use of the leased assets themselves but are often really reimbursements to the lessor for services rendered period by period, such as the payment of taxes and utilities, and the handling of maintenance. To the extent that a purchaser of equivalent assets would not recognize such future routine expenditures as assets and liabilities at the time of purchase, it is argued that they should not become recognized as assets and liabilities at the inception of a long-term lease.

Critics often concede that such arguments have merit. However, they are quick to point out that on balance many long-term noncancellable leases presently in effect ought to be treated as long-term liabilities even under the situational point of view. But in fact relatively few of the many leases presently in existence have been capitalized and appear as liabilities and related assets in the financial statements of the lessees. Until recently, most have received only footnote disclosure of future rent payments and recognition of rent expense as it is incurred. Thus the possibility that there could be substantial amounts of genuine long-term debt unrecorded on the balance sheets of U.S. corporations, because of a permissive policy (the situational view), has fueled the controversy and stimulated the continued concern of accounting policy makers over accounting for long-term leases. In response to the perceived deficiency in the policy based on the situational view, the SEC recently amended its reporting rules to require *footnote* disclosure of the present values and interest and amortization expenses related to long-term noncancellable leases that meet certain minimum size (materiality) tests.

ACCOUNTING FOR INTERCORPORATE INVESTMENTS

It is unusual to examine a set of recent financial statements of any significant public corporation without seeing a reference to one or more consolidated or unconsolidated subsidiaries. Thus a thorough treatment of present-day accounting reporting issues, even at the introductory level, must include some discussion of accounting for enterprises that are related through intercorporate investments (stock ownership).

Degrees of Intercorporate Investment

The degree of investment in (ownership of) one corporation by another can range from zero to 100 percent. At either extreme there is not much doubt as to the relationship between the corporation owning stock (the investor corporation) and the corporation whose stock is owned (the investee corporation).

• *Investments in marketable shares.* When a corporation buys only a relatively small percentage of the outstanding stock of one or more other corporations, it is usually for purely speculative or temporary investment purposes —that is, to make the best use of surplus cash presently available (possibly for several years) until it is needed for acquisition of assets related to the corporation's primary earning activity. For such purposes it is usually unsound policy to invest in more than a small percentage ownership in any one company. Furthermore, it is usually wise to invest only in shares of large companies whose shares are traded on major securities exchanges, so that the shares can be sold with little difficulty when funds are needed for other purposes. Thus, no special or extraordinary relationship necessarily develops between the corporation owning shares and the corporation whose shares are owned, when the percentage owned is quite small.

Such investments in the marketable securities of other corporations are given the same general treatment in practice by accountants as are investments in government securities and corporate bonds. Marketable shares of stock in corporations are valued at their acquisition cost unless their market value is significantly lower (in which case they are valued at market value, and a loss is recognized). Dividends are recognized as income at the time they are "declared" by the corporations whose shares are owned (i.e., when they are legally "receivable" and therefore realized). When the shares are ultimately sold, the difference between their original cost and the proceeds of sale is recognized as a gain or a loss.

The above treatment—called the *cost method* (or *lower of cost or market* where applicable)—contrasts sharply with the alternative of recognizing all changes in market values of marketable securities (and related gains and losses) from one reporting date to the next. We have, of course, illustrated the contrast between the alternatives earlier (Chapter 8).

Although the official sanction of accounting policy-making authorities (the APB) has favored the cost method, the question of possible recognition of market values comes up from time to time as proponents of market value recognition rekindle the controversy. It should be noted, too, that many corporations presently report as supplemental information the aggregate market values of securities held, either parenthetically on their balance sheets or in footnotes to their financial statements.

• *One hundred percent intercorporate ownership.* When one corporation owns 100 percent of the outstanding stock of another corporation, the "owned" corporation is hardly a separate entity except in a narrow legal sense. Exceptions to this commonsense rule, however, are those cases in which the "owned" corporation is set up (or acquired) and maintained as a separate legal entity because its activities are distinctly different from the owner company and perhaps require a separate identity to be pursued. Examples are insurance, finance, and banking subsidiaries of industrial corporations. On the other hand, where the owner and 100 percent-owned corporations are not economically or legally incompatible (merely legally separate), they are viewed by accountants as one economic entity. In such cases financial statements showing the combined financial position and results of operations of the several related corporations (known as *consolidated financial statements*) are considered essential in order to satisfy the purposes for which published financial statements are intended. (Consolidated financial statements are discussed later in this section.)

• *Three recognized gradations in intercorporate ownership and control.* We have now established that a case of minimal ownership interest in one corporation by another merely calls for recognition of the investment by the latter as an asset (usually called "marketable securities") valued at its cost, with recognition of dividend income as realized. We have also established that if one corporation is 100 percent-owned by another, the financial position and results of operations of the owned corporation should be combined with those of the owner corporation into a single set of financial statements unless there is significant economic or legal reason for not combining them. The question is how to account for the many degrees of ownership in between the extremes.

As one would expect, cases close to the extremes of near-zero and near-100 percent ownership are generally agreed to be best handled as described above for the extremes. Naturally, though, the farther ownership departs from either zero or 100 percent, the less agreement there will be as to the appropriateness of treatment of the investment as just another investment in securities, or treatment of the companies involved as a single accounting entity, respectively. As a result, certain "reasonable, but arbitrary," ownership-percentage cutoffs have been prescribed by accounting policy-making authorities, along with the appropriate treatment of cases falling between the cutoffs. The ownership percentage cutoffs that have been deemed significant are 20 percent and 50 percent.

Ownership of less than 20 percent of the stock of a corporation is considered insufficient to justify any special treatment beyond recognition of the investment as an investment in the marketable securities of the other corporation. If, on the other hand, one corporation owns more than 20 percent of the ownership shares of another corporation, there is assumed to be a relationship in which the investor corporation exerts a significant influence on the investee corporation. When one corporation exerts such a significant ownership influence on another, it is considered appropriate to account for its investment according to the *equity method* (to be described later in this section), which differs significantly from the cost method. If the degree of ownership extends beyond 50 percent and therefore to majority status, not only is there a significant relationship, it is usually considered to be that of "parent and subsidiary." In such cases consolidation of financial statements is usually considered warranted (except where reason dictates that the entities should not be combined, as mentioned above).

The 20 percent cutoff which determines whether a given investment is deemed to be a "significantly influential" investment in an investee corporation is arbitrary, of course. But it is clear that as a given ownership interest in any corporation increases from negligible to successively larger percentages, the given owner (whether an individual or another corporation) at some percentage becomes more than an ordinary shareholder. For instance, since the individual owner can vote its (their) shares in a block, it (they) may be able to ensure the election of one or more selected individuals to the board of directors. The percentage at which a given owner becomes "influential" varies from case to case with such conditions as the number of other shareholders and the size of their respective shareholdings. Thus an established, reasonable (though arbitrary) cutoff like the 20 percent cutoff is useful in the sense that it overcomes the necessity of an in-depth case-by-case analysis of the very nebulous notion of "influence" over the corporation whose shares are owned. As a practical matter, the 20 percent cutoff probably embraces few actual cases in which no substantial influence is present but excludes some (perhaps only a few) cases in which ownership is less than 20 percent but where a substantial degree of influence is nevertheless present.

The 50 percent cutoff is less arbitrary—or so it seems intuitively. Since it is already above the first cutoff, a greater than 50 percent ownership interest carries with it the presumption of extraordinary influence. But, since greater than 50 percent ownership also constitutes a majority interest, it means that the influence actually extends to *de jure* control of the investee by the investor corporation. This means that the two corporations may be operated (except for organizational and legal convenience) as one entity and should be recognized as such by accountants. Of course, many corporations can be controlled *de facto* with less than 50 percent ownership. In the absence of the legal reinforcement that comes with majority ownership, however, accountants are reluctant to recognize such investee corporations as "one" with the parent. One troublesome question arises when the financial statements of an investee corporation that is more than 50 percent owned, but not "wholly" owned, are consolidated with the investor corporation's statements. The question is what to do about the interests of the minority shareholders. As will be illustrated in later discussion, that problem is solved by recognition of "minority interests" in the consolidated financial statements themselves.

Accounting for Investments in Other Corporations

In the discussion above we have noted that accountants recognize three distinct classes of intercorporate relationship that result from investment by one corporation in the shares of another. The three classes of relationship dictate three levels of accounting recognition, as summarized in Exhibit 14-10.

Exhibit 14-10   INTERCORPORATE OWNERSHIP
                                AND ACCOUNTING TREATMENTS

Degree of Ownership	*Accounting Treatment*
0%– 20%	Cost Method
20%– 50%	Equity Method
50%–100%	Equity Method plus Consolidation
	(except where consolidation is unreasonable)

The basic features of the first level of recognition have been covered earlier. The other two levels are covered in the remainder of this section.

• *Accounting for 20 percent to 50 percent ownership interests.* We noted earlier that when the ownership interest in one corporation is greater than 20 percent but does not exceed 50 percent, an accounting treatment is accorded the investment that departs significantly from the cost method (for accounting for marketable securities). Specifically, the accounting treatment of 20 percent to 50 percent ownership interests consists of the following:

1. At the time of acquisition, the investment in the stock of the investee corporation is valued at the cost to the investor corporation of acquiring the shares.

2. Thereafter, the value of the investment is altered periodically in the following ways:

   a. Each period, the investment account is increased by an amount equal to the investor's percentage (of ownership) interest in the recognized net income of the investee. The increase in the investment account is considered income to the investor, that is, reflected by an increase in owners' equity (retained earnings) equal to the increase in the investment account.

   b. Concurrently, the investment account and owners' equity (retained earnings) are reduced through amortization of any excess of (1) the cost of the stock of the investee over (2) the investor's share in the net assets of the investee at the time of acquisition. This reduction of the investment account is considered an expense of the investor associated with its share in the earnings of the investee.

   c. As dividends are declared by the investee and therefore become legally receivable (or actually received) by the investor, the investment account is reduced by the amount of the dividends while the dividend receivable (or cash) account is increased concurrently.

The contrast between the above method, called the *equity method,* and the cost method is readily apparent. Under the cost method, items 2*a* and 2*b* are ignored altogether. Income is recognized by the investor corporation only to the extent that dividends become legally receivable (or received) from the investee corporation (item 2*c*). To make the above features of the equity method clearer, it is helpful to apply them to an example.

Example 14-6   On January 1, 19X1, Investor Company purchased 40 percent of the ownership shares of Investee Company from Investee's then-present shareholders for $2,500,000. Immediately after the investment by Investor, the balance sheets of the two companies appeared as shown in Exhibit 14-11. The 19X1 income statement and December 31, 19X1, balance sheet for Investee Company appear in Exhibit 14-12. (Note that all amounts shown in the exhibits are in thousands of dollars.) Notice that the only effect of the initial investment that is evident in any of the statements is the recognition of the investment account (at cost) on Investor Company's January 1, 19X1, balance sheet. No effect appears in the balance sheets of Investee Company because Investor Company purchased its interest from former shareholders, that is, the transaction took place between parties outside Investee Company. If Investor Company had acquired its interest by purchasing new shares issued by Investee, there would have been an infusion of assets and an increase in paid-in capital beyond the levels previously recognized by Investee Company. However, in either case the 19X1 income statement of Investee Company would be as shown in Exhibit 14-12 (since the distribution of ownership interests in a company is extraneous to the determination of its income).

Exhibit 14-11

INVESTOR COMPANY
Balance Sheet
As of January 1, 19X1
(amounts in thousands)

Assets:		Liabilities and Owners' Equity:	
Cash	$ 4,000	Accounts payable	$ 1,200
Accounts receivable	500		
Inventory	2,500		
Net plant and equipment	7,200		
Investment in stock of		Paid-in capital	10,000
Investee Co.	2,500	Retained earnings	5,500
Total	$16,700	Total	$16,700

INVESTEE COMPANY
Balance Sheet
As of January 1, 19X1
(amounts in thousands)

Assets:		Liabilities and Owners' Equity:	
Cash	$ 100	Accounts payable	$ 200
Accounts receivable	100	Bonds payable	1,000
Inventory	1,200	Paid-in capital	4,000
Net plant and equipment	4,800	Retained earnings	1,000
Total	$6,200	Total	$6,200

The transactions and events affecting the financial position of Investor Company during 19X1 are given recognition in worksheet form in Exhibit 14-13. Lines 1–7 represent routine recognition of the individual operations of Investor Company. Lines 8–10 give recognition to the 19X1 effects on Investor's financial position of its investment in Investee Company.

Exhibit 14-12 indicates that Investee Company's net income for 19X1 is $1,250,000. Since Investor Company owns 40 percent of Investee Company's stock, it is presumed that its equitable interest in the company is increased by

Exhibit 14-12

INVESTEE COMPANY
Income Statement
For 19X1
(amounts in thousands)

Revenue (all from sales)		$5,500
Less expenses:		
Cost of sales	$3,100	
Interest	50	
Depreciation	600	
Other expense	500	4,250
Net income		$1,250

INVESTEE COMPANY
Balance Sheet
As of December 31, 19X1
(amounts in thousands)

Assets:		Liabilities and Owners' Equity:	
Cash	$1,450	Accounts payable	$ 300
Accounts receivable	300	Bonds payable	1,000
Inventory	1,100	Paid-in capital	4,000
Net plant and equipment	4,200	Retained earnings	1,750*
Total	$7,050	Total	$7,050

* Retained earnings were increased by income of $1,250,000 and reduced by dividends of $500,000 during 19X1.

40 percent of any advance in the net assets of the company (e.g., net income) from sources other than contributions by other owners. Thus on line 8 of Exhibit 14-13 an increase is recognized in Investor Company's "investment in Investee Co." account equal to $500,000 (40 percent of $1,250,000). The increase in the investment asset is offset by an equal increase in retained earnings (owners' equity), which is a manifestation of the central theme of the equity method, that is, that an investor company recognizes, as income, its equitable share of any earnings recognized by its investee companies.

Line 9 of Exhibit 14-13 represents somewhat of a complication—a complication that frequently occurs in practice. When Investor Company acquired 40 percent of the ownership shares of Investee Company on January 1, it paid $2,500,000. That amount is $500,000 more than 40 percent of Investee's recognized net assets of $5,000,000 at January 1, 19X1 (paid-in capital of $4,000,000 plus retained earnings of $1,000,000—see Exhibit 14-11). In essence, what this means is that Investor Company paid more than 40 percent of the unexpired cost of the net assets of Investee Company in order to obtain the rights to a 40 percent equitable share in the benefits to be generated by those assets. This is not surprising, since the unexpired costs of assets are not purported to represent their value (in generating future benefits) to an outside investor. However, in representing *the income to Investor Company resulting from its equitable interest in the revenue of Investee Company,* it is not sufficient to recognize as expense only the original cost of the assets of Investee Company consumed in producing its revenues (the expense recognized by Investee). Some recognition should also be given to the additional

Exhibit 14-13

INVESTOR COMPANY
Financial Position Worksheet
19X1
(amounts in thousands)

Description	Cash	Accounts Receivable	Inventory	Net Plant and Equipment	Investment in Investee Co.	Accounts Payable	Paid-in Capital	Retained Earnings
Beginning Position	4,000	500	2,500	7,200	2,500	1,200	10,000	5,500
1. Sales		15,500						15,500 (R)
2. Purchases			9,000			9,000		
3. Receipts	15,250	(15,250)						
4. Payments	(9,250)					(9,250)		
5. Cost of sales			(9,500)					(9,500) (E)
6. Other expenses	(2,100)							(2,100) (E)
7. Depreciation				(900)				(900) (E)
8. Earnings of Investee					500			500 (R)
9. Amortization					(50)			(50) (E)
10. Dividends from Investee	200				(200)			
Ending (Beginning) Position	8,100	750	2,000	6,300	2,750	950	10,000	8,950

cost incurred by Investor Company to acquire (produce for Investor Company) its equitable interest in the revenues of Investee.

On line 9 of Exhibit 14-13 we have reduced Investor Company's investment account and retained earnings by one-tenth ($50,000) of the original excess of the cost of the investment over 40 percent of the net asset value of Investee Company at the time of acquisition. Thus we have "matched" a portion of that excess against the related benefits (Investor Company's share of Investee's earnings) realized in year one. Our use of one-tenth, implying a ten-year total expiration period, was selected for illustrative purposes only. In practice the period selected for amortization of the differential cost would depend on the individual circumstances (but in no case may it exceed forty years, according to present accounting policy).

The final feature of the equity method is represented on line 10 of Exhibit 14-13. It is apparent from Exhibits 14-11 and 14-12 that Investee Company declared and paid $500,000 in total dividends during 19X1 (its income was $1,250,000 for 19X1, but retained earnings went up by a net amount of only $750,000 for the year). Rather than being income to Investor Company, its share of the total dividends, $200,000, merely represents the severance and transfer of cash from Investee to Investor Company. Thus on line 10 we recognize a $200,000 increase in Investor Company's cash and a concurrent decrease in its investment in Investee Company, reflecting Investor's equitable share of the total decrease in Investee's cash (i.e., 40 percent of $500,000).

With recognition of the dividends received from Investee Company, all events and transactions affecting Investor Company's financial position are recognized in Exhibit 14-13. Investor Company's balance sheet would be drawn from the balances on the last line of Exhibit 14-13. Its income statement appears in Exhibit 14-14. Notice that Investor's interest in Investee's earnings and the additional amortization are recognized in the income statement, but the dividends received are not.

Exhibit 14-14

INVESTOR COMPANY
Income Statement
For 19X1
(amounts in thousands)

Revenue		$15,500
Less expenses:		
Cost of sales	$9,500	
Depreciation	900	
Other expense	2,100	12,500
Investor Co. operating income		$ 3,000
Income from Investee Co.:		
Equity in earnings of Investee Co.	$ 500	
Less amortization of excess of cost of investment over net assets of Investee Co. at acquisition	(50)	450
Net income		$ 3,450

As a final note about the equity method, it should be added that there has been some disagreement in the past as to whether unconsolidated investees (or even consolidated investees) should be accounted for in the investor company's (separate) financial position according to the equity or the cost method. Arguments can be made for both positions. However, the APB strongly favored the equity method for cases in which the investor influences the operating and financial policies (including dividend distribution policy) of the investees—which is the presumption, according to the APB, when ownership exceeds the 20 percent cutoff.

• *Accounting for greater than 50 percent ownership interests.* Accounting for more than 50 percent ownership interests in investee companies (usually called *subsidiaries* if more than 50 percent owned) is an extended version of the accounting treatment prescribed for investments in the 20 percent to 50 percent range. The reason is that separate financial statements are often prepared for the subsidiary (investee) and parent (investor) corporations as well as consolidated financial statements for the combined entities. Primary among the reasons for separate financial statements is that creditor and other interests (including minority shareowners of the subsidiaries) do not usually transcend the separate, individual legal entities.

According to present accounting policy, the *statements of the parent corporation* are prepared according to the equity method whether or not the subsidiary or subsidiaries are to be consolidated. The only difference, then, in accounting for consolidated subsidiaries versus unconsolidated investee companies (including certain subsidiaries) is the eventual consolidation of the separate statements. Again, an example will serve to bring out the similarities and the important difference between the two treatments.

Example 14-7   Reconsider the Investor Company–Investee Company example introduced above (Example 14-6). Let us take two companies identical to Investor and Investee Company on January 1, 19X1, and name them Parent Company and Subsidiary Company, respectively. We will then suppose that Parent and Subsidiary continued to be identical to Investor and Investee Companies *except that* on January 1, 19X1, Parent Company did two things differently than Investor Company. First, suppose that it acquired 80 percent (instead of 40 percent) of the outstanding ownership interest in Subsidiary Company for $5,000,000 (instead of $2,500,000). (Note that the $5,000,000 exceeds 80 percent of the net assets of Subsidiary as of January 1, 19X1, by $1,000,000, i.e., all of the figures relating to Parent Company's stock ownership of Subsidiary are doubled relative to Investor Company's ownership of Investee.) Second, suppose that Parent also acquired all of the outstanding bonds of Subsidiary Company from the former bondholders at their face value of $1,000,000 (the bonds require interest to be paid annually at 5 percent of face value). All other facts remain as assumed in the earlier example. The effects of these facts on the financial position of Parent Company during 19X1 are depicted in Exhibit 14-15.

The beginning position of Parent Company in Exhibit 14-15 includes the effects of the acquisition of the stock and bonds of Subsidiary Company. Lines 1–7 again represent effects of the separate events and transactions of Parent Company. Line 8 represents the receipt of interest from Subsidiary Company and its recognition as income. Lines 9–11 correspond to lines 8–10 of Exhibit 14-13, with all of the amounts doubled. Lines 9–11 represent the

Exhibit 14-15

PARENT COMPANY
Financial Position Worksheet
19X1
(amounts in thousands)

Description	Cash	Accounts Receivable	Inventory	Net Plant and Equipment	Investment in Subsidiary Bonds	Investment in Subsidiary Stock	Accounts Payable	Paid-in Capital	Retained Earnings
Beginning Position	500	500	2,500	7,200	1,000	5,000	1,200	10,000	5,500
1. Sales		15,500							15,500 (R)
2. Purchases			9,000				9,000		
3. Receipts	15,250	(15,250)							
4. Payments	(9,250)						(9,250)		
5. Cost of sales			(9,500)						(9,500) (E)
6. Other expenses	(2,100)								(2,100) (E)
7. Depreciation				(900)					(900) (E)
8. Interest received	50								50 (R)
9. Earnings of Subsidiary						1,000			1,000 (R)
10. Amortization						(100)			(100) (E)
11. Dividends received	400					(400)			
Ending (Beginning) Position	4,850	750	2,000	6,300	1,000	5,500	950	10,000	9,450

application of the equity method to the revised set of facts in Example 14-6. The 19X1 income statement for Parent Company under the revised set of facts is shown in Exhibit 14-16.

Notice that down to the "Parent Co. operating income" figure of $3,000,-000, Exhibit 14-16 is identical to the income statement illustrating the earlier example of 40 percent stock ownership (Exhibit 14-14). The only differences are the $50,000 interest income received on the investment in Subsidiary Company bonds, the doubling of Parent Company's equity in Subsidiary's earnings, and the amount of additional cost amortization—in accordance with the new assumption of 80 percent ownership. Incidentally, it should also be noted that the assumed increase in the ownership share in Subsidiary Company owned by Parent Company has no effect whatever on Subsidiary's separate financial statements for 19X1. They would be identical to Investee Company's statements illustrated in Exhibits 14-11 and 14-12.

Exhibit 14-16

PARENT COMPANY
Income Statement
For 19X1
(amounts in thousands)

Revenue		$15,500
Less expenses:		
Cost of sales	$9,500	
Depreciation	900	
Other expense	2,100	12,500
Parent Co. operating income		$ 3,000
Income from Subsidiary Co.		
Interest received	$ 50	
Equity in earnings of Subsidiary Co.	1,000	
Less amortization of excess of cost of investment over net assets of Subsidiary Co. at acquisition	(100)	950
Net income		$ 3,950

• *Consolidation of financial statements.* Having given due consideration to the recognition of the effects of investments in consolidated subsidiaries in the *separate* financial statements of the parent, our attention now turns to the consolidation of parent and subsidiary statements. Essentially, the process of consolidating balance sheets consists of adding together the balance sheets of the parent and subsidiary companies after (1) substituting the subsidiary's balance sheet for the parent's investment account (allowing for recognition of minority interests), and (2) making certain eliminations. The eliminations are necessitated by the need to avoid double counting of assets, liabilities, expenses, and revenues within the corporate group when combining statements. To see why double counting is a potential problem, consider the following example:

Example 14-8   Suppose that a group of owners founded Holding Company with a $100,000 combined contribution of cash in exchange for 100 percent of the authorized common stock of the company. Suppose further that Holding Company engaged in no activities of its own, but rather invested its full $100,000 cash endowment in all of the shares of another newly formed company, Held Company. Immediately thereafter, each company has $100,000 in assets (cash in the case of Held Company; an investment in Held Company's stock in the case of Holding Company) and $100,000 in owners' equity. Does that mean that in combination the two companies command $200,000 in total assets? Certainly not! Holding Company is a mere legal shell through which the single set of owners controls the single set of assets (equal to $100,000) which is legally owned by Held Company.

The extremity of the above example makes quite obvious the motivation for making certain eliminations in the process of consolidating the financial statements of parent corporations and subsidiaries that are more than 50 percent owned. Our preceding example, however, provides a more realistic setting for illustrating the consolidation process. We will proceed by first illustrating the combined status (consolidated balance sheet) of Parent and Subsidiary Companies immediately after Parent Company acquired all of the bonds and 80 percent of the stock of Subsidiary Company on January 1, 19X1. We will then consolidate the balance sheets as of December 31, 19X1, and the income statements for the year 19X1.

• *Consolidated balance sheet at acquisition.* Exhibit 14-17 depicts the consolidation of the January 1, 19X1, balance sheets of Parent and Subsidiary Companies. In the data columns, note that the first two columns contain the separate balance sheets of the two companies. (The amounts are traceable back to the beginning position line of Exhibit 14-15 for Parent Company and back to the balance sheet in Exhibit 14-11 for Investee Company.) The most significant features of Exhibit 14-17 are the third and fourth columns. They contain sets of related positive and negative adjustments to the combined figures of the first two columns.

The third column is necessary to avoid the kind of nonsense double counting of assets and ownership interests pointed out in Example 14-8. The separate balance sheet of Parent Company (the first column) already includes an asset, "investment in subsidiary stock," that represents the equitable interest of Parent Company in Subsidiary Company's assets and liabilities. Furthermore, Parent Company's owners' equity accounts represent the equitable interests of its shareholders in all assets and liabilities held by Parent Company (including its interest in Subsidiary Company). Hence, before adding Subsidiary Company's balance sheet to Parent Company's balance sheet, we eliminate (in the third column) Parent's equitable share (80 percent) of Subsidiary's paid-in capital ($3,200,000) and retained earnings ($800,000), along with a corresponding portion ($4,000,000) of Parent's "investment in subsidiary stock." Thus, in effect, in consolidating the two companies we are not adding their balance sheets *per se* but, rather, substituting in Parent Company's balance sheet the specific assets and liabilities of Subsidiary Company for the nonspecific asset, the *Investment in Subsidiary Co. Stock.*

The rationale of the two adjustments labeled "(1)" in the fourth column is similar to the rationale for the eliminations in the third column. Since the purpose of the consolidation is to look at the parent and subsidiary as one entity (controlled by Parent Company's shareholders), it is nonsense to portray as assets and liabilities the bonds of Subsidiary Company owned by Parent Company. The combined, single entity cannot "owe" itself. Thus, the $1,000,000 in bonds is eliminated from the assets as well as the liabilities of

Exhibit 14-17

PARENT COMPANY–SUBSIDIARY COMPANY
Consolidation of Balance Sheets
As of January 1, 19X1
(amounts in thousands)

Accounts:	Parent Company	Subsidiary Company	Ownership Elimination	Other Eliminations and Reclassifications	Consolidated
Assets:					
Cash	$ 500	$ 100			$ 600
Accounts receivable	500	100			600
Inventory	2,500	1,200			3,700
Net plant and equipment	7,200	4,800			12,000
Investment in Subsidiary Co.:					
Bonds	1,000			$(1,000) (1)	
Stock	5,000		$(4,000)	(1,000) (2)	
Excess of investment cost over interest acquired in net assets of Subsidiary Co.				1,000 (2)	1,000
Total assets	$16,700	$6,200	$(4,000)	$(1,000)	$17,900
Liabilities and Owners' Equity:					
Accounts payable	$ 1,200	$ 200			$ 1,400
Bonds of Subsidiary Co.		1,000		$(1,000) (1)	
Paid-in capital:					
Parent Co.	10,000				10,000
Subsidiary Co.		4,000	$(3,200)	(800) (3)	
Retained earnings:					
Parent Co.	5,500				5,500
Subsidiary Co.		1,000	(800)	(200) (3)	
Minority interest				1,000 (3)	1,000
Total liabilities and owners' equity	$16,700	$6,200	$(4,000)	$(1,000)	$17,900

the combined entity by the respective (1,000) eliminations labeled "(1)."

Now consider the column four adjustments labeled "(2)" and recall that in eliminating (in the third column) Parent's equity in the paid-in capital of Subsidiary (80 percent of $4,000,000, or $3,200,000) plus its equity in the retained earnings (80 percent of $1,000,000, or $800,000), only $4,000,000 of Parent's investment in Subsidiary's stock was eliminated. This again points up the fact that Parent Company paid $1,000,000 more for its ownership interest in Subsidiary Company (total $5,000,000) than its 80 percent share of Subsidiary's net assets at acquisition ($4,000,000). Instead of eliminating this excess by offset against Parent's share of the paid-in capital and retained earnings of Subsidiary, the $1,000,000 excess is reclassified in the assets section by deducting it from the investment in subsidiary stock and adding it back opposite the descriptive "Excess of investment cost over interest acquired in net assets of Subsidiary Co." This is completely justified under the "one entity" philosophy underlying consolidation, since the $1,000,000 was an expenditure made to entities outside the corporate group (the former Subsidiary Company shareholders) in order to bring the net assets of Subsidiary Company under the control of the single entity. Thus we *do not fail* to eliminate double counting by eliminating only $4,000,000 of Parent's investment account and reclassifying $1,000,000 into the "excess of investment cost" account.

On the liability and owners' equity side, the balances in the paid-in capital and retained earnings accounts are eliminated in full by the eliminations labeled "(3)" opposite those accounts. Only $4,000,000 of the combined totals were eliminated altogether from the consolidated statements in the column three adjustments—the amount necessary to offset the $4,000,000 net amount of the "investment" eliminated from the assets. The other $1,000,000 is reclassified by deducting $800,000 from the paid-in capital and $200,000 from the retained earnings and adding back the total $1,000,000 opposite the caption "minority interest." The $1,000.000 represents the minority interest in retained earnings (20 percent of $1,000,000, or $200,000) plus the minority interest in paid-in capital (20 percent of $4,000,000, or $800,000) of Subsidiary Company. The two minority interests amounts are combined into one amount in practice because (*a*) the detail of the minority interests in each equity account of each subsidiary is largely superfluous (except for meeting certain SEC requirements) in depicting the single combined entity in consolidated statements, and (*b*) such detail would be burdensome if there were several subsidiaries, each with several equity accounts.

After all appropriate eliminations have been recognized in the elimination and reclassification columns, the first four columns are summed across to arrive at the balances in the consolidated balance sheet of the combined entity. Those amounts appear in the Consolidated column of Exhibit 14-17. Note that (*a*) the consolidated total assets figure is less than the sum of the assets totals from the separate balance sheets, and (*b*) the same is true of the total liabilities and owners' equity—as must be the case, since the equality between assets and liabilities-plus-owners' equity is preserved in all four prior columns.

• *Consolidation of balance sheets and income statements subsequent to acquisition.* Consolidation of balance sheets subsequent to the date of acquisition does not differ in principle from consolidation at acquisition. Hence Exhibit 14-18, which shows the consolidation of balance sheets for Parent

Exhibit 14-18

PARENT COMPANY-SUBSIDIARY COMPANY
Consolidation of Balance Sheets
As of December 31, 19X1
(amounts in thousands)

Accounts:	Parent Company	Subsidiary Company	Ownership Elimination	Other Eliminations and Reclassifications	Consolidated
Assets:					
Cash	$ 4,850	$1,450			$ 6,300
Accounts receivable	750	300			1,050
Inventory	2,000	1,100			3,100
Net plant and equipment	6,300	4,200			10,500
Investment in Subsidiary Co.:					
Bonds	1,000			$(1,000) (1)	
Stock	5,500		$(4,600)	(900) (2)	
Unamortized excess of investment cost over interest in net assets of Subsidiary Co.				900 (2)	900
Total assets	$20,400	$7,050	$(4,600)	$(1,000)	$21,850
Liabilities and Owners' Equity:					
Accounts payable	$ 950	$ 300			$ 1,250
Bonds of Subsidiary Co.		1,000		$(1,000) (1)	
Paid-in capital:					
Parent Co.	10,000				10,000
Subsidiary Co.		4,000	$(3,200)	(800) (3)	
Retained earnings:					
Parent Co.	9,450				9,450
Subsidiary Co.		1,750	(1,400)	(350) (3)	
Minority interest				1,150 (3)	1,150
Total liabilities and owners' equity	$20,400	$7,050	$(4,600)	$(1,000)	$21,850

and Subsidiary companies as of December 31, 19X1, needs no great elaboration. In fact, the same eliminations and reclassifications are made, with only the amounts differing appropriately. We might note, however, that the Parent Company equity in the net assets of Subsidiary Company, which is eliminated in the third column, is now $4,600,000, an increase of $600,000 over the beginning-of-the-year figure of $4,000,000. This is due to recognition in the course of the year of (a) Parent's equity in the earnings of Subsidiary (80 percent of $1,250,000, or $1,000,000), (b) less dividends received of $400,-000. Notice too that the unamortized excess of Parent's investment cost over its equity in the net assets of Subsidiary, which is reclassified in column four, is $100,000 less than at the beginning of the year ($900,000 instead of $1,000,000) due to amortization of $100,000 during the year.

Since a year has passed from the date of acquisition and the companies have therefore operated for a period *as related companies,* it is necessary also to consolidate their income statements for 19X1. Again the process is one of summing the amounts in the separate statements after some appropriate eliminations and adjustments. The process is illustrated for the 19X1 income statements of Parent and Subsidiary companies in Exhibit 14-19. Notice that, as in the consolidation of balance sheets, we first array the separate income statements of Parent and Subsidiary companies (in the first two columns). However, in consolidating the income statements, the first two columns do the work of the first three columns in the balance sheet consolidation. Other eliminations and reclassifications then follow. Again the eliminations and reclassifications are numbered for convenient reference.

Column one of Exhibit 14-19 is simply the separate 19X1 income statement of Parent Company—traceable item for item back to Exhibit 14-16. Looking at column two we observe that (a) the top portion consists of the 19X1 income statement of Subsidiary Company (traceable item for item to the identical Investee Company statement in Exhibit 14-12), and (b) the lower portion of the column consists of some adjustments that are necessary to eliminate double counting and overstatement in arriving at consolidated net income.

The first adjustment, labeled "(1)," eliminates double counting. Since all of Subsidiary's revenue and expenses are brought into the consolidated statements through its separate statement (the top portion of column two), Parent's equity in Subsidiary's earnings appearing in Parent Company's separate statement (column one) is redundant. Hence the elimination labeled "(1)" offsets and eliminates the redundancy.

Then, too, it must be recognized that the earning ability of the combined entities would be overstated by simply aggregating the separate income statements of the companies (after elimination of Parent's equity in Subsidiary's earnings), without giving recognition to the minority shareholders' interest in the separate earnings of Subsidiary Company. Thus we have inserted in the second column a $250,000 reduction (item 2) representing a segregation of the minority interest of 20 percent in the separate 19X1 earnings ($1,250,-000) of Subsidiary from the combined income attributable to the interests of Parent's shareholders.

Turning now to the third column, the first elimination set rids the consolidated statement of some additional double counting. Since the Parent Company statement shows $50,000 interest income and the Subsidiary Com-

Exhibit 14-19

PARENT COMPANY–SUBSIDIARY COMPANY
Consolidation of Income Statements
For 19X1
(amounts in thousands)

Description:	Parent Company	Subsidiary Company	Eliminations and Reclassifications	Consoli-dated
Revenue	$15,500	$5,500		$21,000
Less expenses:				
Cost of sales	$ 9,500	$3,100		$12,600
Interest		50	$(50)(1)	
Depreciation (and amortization)	900	600	100 (2)	1,600
Other expense	2,100	500		2,600
Total expense	$12,500	$4,250	$ 50	$16,800
Operating income	$ 3,000	$1,250	$(50)	$ 4,200
Income from Subsidiary Co.:				
Interest	50		(50)(1)	
Equity on earnings	1,000	(1,000)(1)		
Less amortization of excess of cost of investment over interest in net assets of subsidiary	(100)		100 (2)	
Less minority interest in subsidiary net income		(250)(2)		(250)
Net income	$ 3,950	—0—	—0—	$ 3,950

pany statement shows the same $50,000 as an interest expense, the two amounts are eliminated. Taken as a whole, the combined entities did not pay or receive interest to or from any other entity. Furthermore, the total income is not changed by the offsetting reductions of income and expense.

On the other hand, the second elimination set in column three is really just a reclassification. The $100,000 *amortization* of Parent's excess of cost over its interest in Subsidiary's net assets should *not* be eliminated from the consolidated income statement for the same reason that the unamortized portion of the "excess" is not eliminated from the consolidated balance sheet. However, with the elimination of Parent's equity in Subsidiary's earnings (the first elimination in column two), the amortization is best lumped together (or classified with) the depreciation and amortization of other assets of the combined companies. This is accomplished by the adjustments labeled "(2)" in column three.

With all appropriate eliminations, reclassifications, and adjustments, the consolidated income statement results from summing across the first three columns of Exhibit 14-19. An important feature of the consolidated net income figure arrived at in this way ($3,950,000) is that it equals the separate net income figure arrived at earlier for Parent Company under the equity method (see Exhibit 14-16).

This will always be the case, assuming that consistent measurement rules are used for both the consolidation eliminations and the application of the equity method to separate accounting for the parent company. Furthermore, it makes intuitive sense. Under the equity method the income of the parent is combined with *only* its equitable share of subsidiary earnings. In consolidated statements an attempt is made to portray the earnings of all assets under the control of the parent company shareholders (the same ownership group in both cases) by combining the net income of parent and subsidiaries (eliminating double counting) *and then* deducting from the total the equitable interests in subsidiary earnings *not attributable* to the parent shareholder group (the minority interests). The final figure ought to be the same in either situation.

• *Elimination of intercompany profits.* It should be pointed out that we have not been able to illustrate all types of possible intercompany eliminations in our simple example. One particularly significant omission from the example is intercorporate profits in inventories. When one company sells goods to a related company at a markup, but the related company has not sold those goods to an outside entity by the end of the period, the gross profit on the goods will not have been *realized* (through sale to an outside entity) by the companies as a single entity. Such unrealized profits must be eliminated from the cost of the inventory (on the balance sheet of the buyer) and owners' equity and income for the period (of the related seller) in consolidating the companies' financial statements.

The Purchase versus Pooling Controversy

We should not leave the total topic of accounting for related companies without brief mention of perhaps the most heated recent controversy in financial reporting practice. The controversy centers around the application of the "pooling-of-interests" method of accounting for parent companies and subsidiaries whose stock is acquired from former shareholders by issuing stock of the parent company in exchange—rather than with cash or other consideration.

The controversy arises because such stock-for-stock transactions can be interpreted two different ways. One way is that if the parent company's stock was readily marketable, the transaction may be considered to be a purchase in substance. That is, it is presumed that the parent company could have issued the stock for cash and then traded the cash to the former shareholders of the subsidiary for their stockholdings. Under this interpretation, a stock-for-stock acquisition is accounted for as described above for a cash purchase of subsidiary stock (i.e., under the equity method with consolidation of subsidiaries more than 50 percent owned)—with the "investment in subsidiary stock" valued at the *market value* of the parent stock issued in exchange for it. An important thing to note is that any excess of the value of the stock issued over the equity in the net assets of the acquired subsidiary is amortized or matched against the parent's equity in the postacquisition earnings of the subsidiary (or the combined earnings in the case of consolidation).

The other interpretation of a stock-for-stock acquisition is that it represents a mere coming together (i.e., a pooling) of the interests of (1) the original parent corporation shareholders and (2) the shareholders who give up their shares in the subsidiary to become shareholders of the parent corporation and bring with them in exchange control over the subsidiary. The pooling-of-interests method of accounting implements this reasoning. The investment is assigned a value equal to the equity acquired by the parent in the subsidiary's net assets. Thus even though the acquisition price exceeds the value of the acquired equity, no additional amortization expense need be offset against the postacquisition combined income of the parent and subsidiary—meaning that recognized combined income will be higher subsequent to acquisition than under the "purchase" interpretation.

It is this latter feature that critics of the pooling-of-interest interpretation feel has led to widespread abuses of the method—particularly during the so-called merger movement of the 1960s. They (the critics) assert that the pooling philosophy really only applies to those cases where the new combined ownership group of the parent is composed of two former ownership groups who both retain substantial influence over the combined entity. However, the critics hasten to point out that pooling accounting has been used for many very small subsidiaries that have been literally swallowed by giant parent companies. There is no pooling of interests in such cases, since the parent corporation buys out the *controlling* interest that the shareholders of the subsidiary once had, and their new ownership interest in the parent represents an infinitesimal rather than an influential interest. But, in pooling-of-interests accounting for the combined entities, no recognition is given to the value of the parent's stock given up to acquire control of the subsidiary and its (the subsidiary's) future earning power. As indicated above, this means that higher combined income may be recognized (no additional amortization) subsequent to acquisition (which, of course, makes parent company management look better) than if the acquisition is recognized as an effective purchase.

The increasing frequency of such abuses and the ensuing public criticism of pooling accounting as a possible encouragement for managements to pursue otherwise undesirable acquisitions led to action by the APB. The action came in the form of an opinion clearly prescribing the conditions that must be satisfied by a stock-for-stock acquisition to be considered a genuine pooling of interests for accounting purposes. All acquisitions not meeting the conditions are to be treated as purchase acquisitions. It should be noted that if many of the "pooling" acquisitions of the sixties had been consummated after the effective date of the opinion, they would probably not be considered poolings of interests under the guidelines of the recent opinion.

Questions for Review and Discussion	**14-1.** Define or describe:
	a. Before-tax accounting income
	b. Taxable income
	c. Long-term noncancellable lease
	d. Executory contract
	e. Subsidiary company
	f. Consolidated financial statements

14-2.   Explain why income taxes present problems in asset and liability valuation and expense recognition.

14-3.   In what ways are conventional financial accounting and taxable income calculations similar? In what ways do they differ?

14-4.   It is basically deceptive and immoral for a company (or an individual) to keep two sets of books, one for financial accounting purposes and one for tax purposes. Do you agree or disagree? Defend your position.

14-5.   Explain the nature of the account "deferred taxes" that appears on many corporate balance sheets year after year.

14-6.   In what sense (if any) may a long-term noncancellable lease be considered equivalent to long-term debt? In what sense (if any) do they differ?

14-7.   Describe the two kinds of accounting treatment that may be used by lessors and lessees for valuing the assets and liabilities and recognizing the expenses and revenues associated with leases.

14-8.   Under the financing-capitalization method of accounting for leases, what assets, liabilities, expenses, and revenues (if any) are recognized by (*a*) lessors and (*b*) lessees?

14-9.   Under the operating method of accounting for leases, what assets, liabilities, expenses, and revenues are recognized by (*a*) lessors and (*b*) lessees?

14-10.   Describe the situational approach to selecting accounting methods for the treatment of leases by lessors and lessees.

14-11.   According to accounting policy-makers, there are three significant gradations in degree of ownership of one corporation by another for purposes of accounting for the investor corporation's investment. Describe the gradations and the reasoning behind the distinction drawn between them. Name the accounting treatment accorded each.

14-12.   Describe the cost method of accounting for an investment by one corporation in the stock of another. Contrast it to the market value method. Include such things as (1) how the investment is originally valued, (2) what increases and decreases are recognized, and (3) what is recognized as income periodically.

14-13.   Describe the equity method of accounting for intercorporate investments. Include in the description the items listed in 14-12 above.

14-14.   Explain in words what is involved (in principle) in consolidating the financial statements of parent and subsidiary companies.

14-15.   Discuss the reasoning behind offsetting (as an expense) a portion of the excess of cost to an investor company over its equity in net assets of an investee company against the investor company's equitable share in the earnings of the investee.

Exercises   **14-1.   Selecting Tax Accounting Measurement Rules and Interperiod Tax Allocation.**   Computer Services Company began business on January 1, 19X1. Its balance sheet on that date follows:

COMPUTER SERVICES COMPANY
Balance Sheet
As of January 1, 19X1

Assets:		Liabilities and Owners' Equity:	
Cash	$ 100,000	Accounts payable	$ 50,000
Supplies inventory	50,000	Long-term debt	1,000,000
Computer equipment	2,000,000	Owners' equity	1,100,000
	$2,150,000		$2,150,000

The company is in the business of supplying small businesses with computer assistance for their inventory control, payroll accounting systems, and so forth. The computer equipment on the balance sheet is new. It is expected to be traded in four years later. The manufacturer has agreed to take it back at $400,000 cash or trade-in allowance at that time.

With the exception of depreciation on the computer equipment, the company recognizes all revenues and expenses on the same basis for financial accounting and tax purposes. The company has selected straight-line depreciation for financial accounting purposes but has not yet selected a method for tax purposes. Its options for tax purposes are straight-line, sum-of-years-digits, and declining balance at double the straight-line rate.

Required:

1. Assuming that the sum-of-years-digits method is selected for tax purposes, give the year-end balance, if any, in the deferred tax liability account for each of the years 19X1–X4. Assume that the tax rate is 50 percent.

2. Assuming that (1) the company has an after-tax opportunity rate of 8 percent, (2) taxes will be paid at the end of the year for which they are assessed, and (3) the tax rate is 50 percent, which depreciation method should be used for tax purposes? Defend your choice. (Hint: Consider the differential effects of the methods on the tax bill in each year, assuming all other things are constant and that there is sufficient revenue that taxable income will be positive in every year regardless of the method selected.)

14-2. Some Tax Allocation Inferences from Partial Information.   An excerpt from the income statement of Taxpayer Corporation follows.

Before-tax income		$150,000
Income tax expense:		
Taxes currently paid or payable	$100,000	
Decrease in deferred tax liability	(25,000)	75,000
After-tax income		$75,000

Which of the following conditions could definitely be true of Taxpayer Corporation based on the statement excerpt? Which are not necessarily true but might be true? *Assume that the tax rate is 50 percent.* Explain your answers.

a. Taxpayer Corporation uses straight-line depreciation for tax purposes.

b. Taxpayer Corporation's taxable income is less than $150,000.

c. Taxpayer Corporation uses S-L depreciation for accounting purposes and S-Y-D depreciation for tax purposes, and its depreciable assets are generally all past the midpoint in their useful lives.

d. Same as *c*, only S-L depreciation is used for tax purposes and S-Y-D for accounting purposes.

e. Taxpayer Corporation taxable income is greater than $150,000.

f. Taxpayer Corporation uses S-L depreciation for tax purposes and double-declining-balance depreciation for accounting purposes.

14-3. Some Tax Allocation Inferences from Income Statement Data.   Below is the statement of earnings from the 1973 annual report of Evans Products Company and Consolidated Subsidiaries. In the summary of accounting policies included in the annual report as an integral part of the financial statements, the company noted that it recognizes deferred taxes on earnings to provide for the tax effect of timing differences between components of financial accounting income and taxable income—primarily arising from use of accelerated depreciation methods for tax purposes (straight-line for financial reporting purposes).

EVANS PRODUCTS COMPANY
AND CONSOLIDATED SUBSIDIARIES
Statement of Earnings
Years Ended December 31
(Dollar amounts in thousands)

	1973	1972
Revenues:		
Sales	$1,113,614	$955,616
Other income	4,848	3,960
Earnings before taxes of unconsolidated subsidiaries	8,007	6,609
	$1,126,469	$966,185
Costs and expenses		
Costs of operations	960,462	828,912
Selling and administrative	71,082	58,129
Depreciation and amortization	16,891	13,964
Interest expense	23,981	14,925
	$1,072,416	$915,930
Earnings before taxes	$ 54,053	$ 50,255
Taxes on earnings:		
Current	9,600	8,353
Deferred	13,400	13,284
Net earnings	$ 31,053	$ 28,618

Required:

1. Based on what you observe in Evans's 1973 statement of earnings, approximately in what stage of their useful lives were Evans's fixed assets (on the average) during 1972 and 1973?

2. Estimate the amount of depreciation and amortization expense recognized for tax purposes in 1973 by Evans. (Assume that depreciation and amortization ex-

pense accounted for virtually the total difference between financial accounting and taxable income and that "costs of operations" contained no depreciation costs.)

3. Within the concepts and principles of the conventional accounting model, what justification (if any) is there for allocation (deferral in this case) of income tax expense?

14-4. Effects of Income Tax Allocation. Because of differences in timing of recognition of certain items of expense, Longhorn Corporation reported the following for 1971–73:

	1971	1972	1973
Taxable income per tax return	$30,000	$55,000	$65,000
Financial accounting net income before taxes	50,000	50,000	50,000

Assuming that the company's income is taxed at a 50 percent rate and that interperiod tax allocation is applied, answer the questions below for each of the three years.

1. What is the income tax payable for the year?
2. What is the income tax expense for the year?
3. What is the net income for the year?
4. What is the *balance* of the deferred tax liability account at the end of each year?

14-5. Effects of Income Tax Allocation. Because of differences in timing of recognition of certain items of income, Finegan Corporation reported the following for the fiscal years 19X1 through 19X3:

	19X1	19X2	19X3
Taxable income per tax return	$90,000	$45,000	$30,000
Financial accounting net income before taxes	40,000	65,000	60,000

Assuming that the company's taxable income is taxed at 50 percent, answer the questions below for each of the three years.

1. What is the income tax payable for the year?
2. What is the income tax expense for the year?
3. What is the net income for the year?
4. What is the *balance* of the deferred tax liability account at the end of each year?

14-6. Accounting for a Lease by the Lessor. Central Property Company purchased a building for $100,000 on January 1, 19X0. The building was immediately leased to a highly credit worthy former customer for twenty years at $12,265 per year, payable January 1 of each year. The company expects that the building will have a zero salvage value at the end of the lease period. The company is trying to decide whether to use the financing method or the operating method to account for the lease. The interest rate implicit in the lease payments is 8 percent. The present value of the lease payments is therefore approximately $130,000. If the company uses the operating method, it will use straight-line depreciation on the building.

Required:

1. How much income will be recognized in connection with the lease under each of the two methods of accounting—
   (a) For 19X0?
   (b) Over the whole duration of the lease?
   Discuss any significant differences and similarities in the amounts.

2. What assets and liabilities will be recognized by Central (if any) in connection with the lease under each of the two accounting methods—
   (a) Immediately after the inception of the lease?
   (b) At December 31, 19X0?
   (c) At January 2, 19X1?

3. What considerations should enter into the selection of an accounting method for the lease?

14-7. Accounting for a Lease by the Lessee.   Assume the same facts as in Exercise 14-6.

Required:

1. How much expense (of each kind) will be recognized by a lessee under the operating and financing methods—
   (a) In 19X0?
   (b) Over the life of the lease?

2. What assets and liabilities will be recognized, if any, under each of the two methods—
   (a) Immediately after inception of the lease?
   (b) At December 31, 19X0?
   (c) At January 2, 19X1?

3. Which method should be used by the lessee? Defend your position.

14-8. Lessor and Lessee Accounting for the Same Lease.   At the beginning of 19X5 Shipping Company leased a large warehouse on Pier 67 in Port City from the owner of the warehouse, Storage Company. The lease agreement extends for five years and calls for payments as follows:

Initial Payment	Payment at the Beginning of:			
	19X6	19X7	19X8	19X9
$100,000	$50,000	$50,000	$30,000	$30,000

Storage Company would have accepted a lump sum payment of $225,000 at the outset for the same five-year occupancy. The lease payments therefore include a 12 percent implicit interest charge.

Shipping Company accounted for the lease over its duration according to the capitalization method, using straight-line amortization of the leasehold asset. Storage Company, on the other hand, has accounted for the lease according to the operating method. The unexpired cost at the time the lease was signed was $150,000. The warehouse was then expected to be demolished at the end of the five years. Its salvage value was expected to equal the cost of demolition and removal. Storage Company depreciated the warehouse on a sum-of-years-digits basis.

Required:

1. Prepare a schedule showing the annual expense to Shipping Company recognized in connection with the use and financing of the warehouse, along with the year-end balances in the related asset and liability accounts, for the years 19X5–X9.

2. Prepare a schedule for Storage Company of the lease-related revenue and expense recognized and contribution to net income, along with the year-end asset balances, for 19X5–X9.

3. At the 19X6 annual meetings of both Shipping Company and Storage Company, a representative of the Stockholders Protection Association accused both companies' managements and auditors of fraud and deception. In support of his charge he pointed out that both companies recognized the warehouse facility as an asset. Since it was impossible for the same building to belong to both companies, the companies were obviously misleading their stockholders. Can you defend the practices of the two companies? What explanations of the situation, if any, can you give that might counter the criticism?

14-9. Inferring Financial Statement Effects of Lease Accounting. Following is an excerpt from footnote 6 (entitled "Commitments and Contingencies") to the financial statements contained in the 1973 annual report of Wien Air Alaska, Inc. In the same statements the reported 1973 and 1972 income figures were $643,788 and $62,952, respectively. Other significant totals from the 1973 financial statements were:

	1973	1972
Total assets	$29,745,114	$28,912,965
Long-term debt	10,257,365	12,463,737
Stockholders' equity	13,742,614	11,923,837

Excerpt from Note

Certain of the Company's leases meet the criteria of a "financing lease," as defined by the Securities and Exchange Commission to be a lease which, during the noncancellable period, either 1) covers 75% or more of the economic life of the property, or 2) has terms which assure the lessor of a full recovery of the fair market value of the property at the inception of the lease plus a reasonable return. The present value of aggregate minimum rental commitments of SEC-defined financing leases at December 31, 1973 and 1972 was as follows:

	1973	1972
Aircraft	$3,418,970	$3,676,162
Ground facilities	356,966	371,610
	$3,775,936	$4,047,772

Interest rates implicit in the terms of SEC-defined financing leases ranged from 8.1% to 11.2% with a weighted average interest rate of approximately 9.4%. On the assumption that SEC-defined financing leases had been capitalized, and the related property rights amortized on a straight-line basis and interest expense computed on the basis of the present value of the declining outstanding balance of the lease commitment, net income would have been decreased approximately $76,800 in 1973 and $95,400 in 1972. Under such assumptions, amortization of the property rights would have amounted to approximately $378,000 in each year and interest expense would have amounted to approximately $372,900 and $397,400 in 1973 and 1972, respectively.

Required:

1. Is the difference material in either 1972 or 1973 (or both) between (*a*) income as reported and (*b*) income as it would have been reported had Air Alaska "capitalized" its financing leases?

2. Estimate the amount of rent that was paid by Air Alaska in connection with its financing leases during 1972 and 1973.

3. What items in the 1973 balance sheet and income statement would have been increased, decreased, added, or deleted if Air Alaska had capitalized its financing leases? List the items and the approximate amounts (if possible) for each statement.

14-10. Inferring Implications of Alternative Lease Accounting.   Below are several figures excerpted from footnote 6 (entitled "Leases and Related Guarantees") that appeared as an integral part of the financial statements in the 1973 annual report of Trans World Airlines, Inc., and Subsidiaries. In the same statements 1973 consolidated net income was reported to be $46,476,000, and total assets, long-term liabilities, and stockholders' equity were reported to be $1,919,816,000, $979,598,000, and $414,170,000, respectively.

The effect on net income if all leases identified as non-capitalized financing leases were capitalized is as follows:

	1973	1972
	(Amounts in Thousands)	
Increase in amortization expense	$52,668	$49,764
Increase in interest expense	43,723	44,611
Total increase in expense	$96,391	$94,375
Decrease in lease rental expense	85,889	81,733
Net increase in expense	$10,502	$12,642
Decrease in income tax provision	2,521	3,034
Decrease in net income	$ 7,981	$ 9,608

Required:

1. Assuming that new financing leases entered into in 1973 had present values of approximately $4,960,000 and the present value of all financing leases in force

at December 31, 1972, was $850,151,000, estimate the present value of leases in force as of December 31, 1973.

2. In your opinion, would capitalization of the financing leases have made a material difference in TWA's 1973 consolidated financial statements? Defend your position.

3. What items in the TWA 1973 income statement and balance sheet would have been increased, decreased, added, or deleted if TWA had capitalized its financing leases? List the items and the approximate amounts (if possible) for each statement.

14-11.   Some Inferences Based on Partial Consolidation Information.   Below are some excerpts from the December 31, 1973, balance sheets of Big and Small Corporations plus some supplemental information. Based on these items, answer the questions that appear after them.

Assets of Big Corporation:	
Cash	$ 1,500,000
Accounts receivable	2,500,000
Inventory	3,500,000
Net plant and equipment	4,500,000
Investment in Small Corporation:	
Loans	1,500,000
75% stock ownership	3,500,000
Total assets	$17,000,000
Liabilities and Owners' Equity	
of Small Corporation:	
Accounts payable	$ 500,000
Loans from parent company	1,500,000
Paid-in capital	3,000,000
Retained earnings	1,000,000
Total liabilities and owners' equity	$ 6,000,000

Supplemental information:

a. None of the inventory on hand at December 31, 1973, of either company had been purchased from the other company.

b. Of the total December 31, 1973, accounts payable of Big Corporation (not shown), $100,000 was owed to Small Corporation.

Required:

1. What amount should appear in the consolidated financial statements to represent the minority interests? Support your answer.

2. Will any amount show up on the consolidated financial statements opposite the caption "Unamortized excess of cost of investment over equity in net assets of subsidiary"? If so, what amount? Support your answer.

3. What will be the total amount of consolidated assets as of December 31, 1973?

14-12.   Income Statement Consolidation.   Following are the separate 1973 income statements of Giant Sales and its subsidiary (70 percent owned), Pee Wee

Products, along with some supplemental information. Prepare a consolidated income statement for 1973.

GIANT SALES COMPANY
Income Statement
For 1973

Revenue		$35,000,000
Less expenses:		
Cost of sales	$20,000,000	
Interest expense	400,000	
Wages and salaries	10,000,000	
Depreciation expenses	1,000,000	
Other expense	500,000	31,900,000
Operating income		$ 3,100,000
Income from subsidiary:		
Interest	$ 100,000	
Equity in earnings	700,000	
Amortization of excess of cost over equity in net assets	(50,000)	750,000
Net income		$ 3,850,000

PEE WEE PRODUCTS COMPANY
Income Statement
For 1973

Revenue		$10,900,000
Less expenses:		
Cost of sales	$5,380,000	
Interest expense	120,000	
Wages and salaries	3,700,000	
Depreciation expense	500,000	
Other expense	200,000	9,900,000
Net income		$ 1,000,000

Supplemental information:

During the year, Pee Wee sold $1,000,000 worth of its products to Giant. Giant in turn sold all of the goods purchased from Pee Wee. At year-end Pee Wee had been paid by Giant for all past purchases, and none of Pee Wee's products remained in Giant's inventory.

14-13. Effects of Alternate Methods of Accounting for Intercorporate Investments. Following is a supplemental table included in the notes to Corning Glass Works' financial statements for the fiscal year ended January 2, 1972 (fiscal 1971). Corning accounted for its unconsolidated associated companies (unconsolidated subsidiaries) according to the cost method. Corning owned 50 percent interests in both Pittsburgh Corning and Dow Corning and a 27.3 percent interest in Owens-Corning Fiberglas.

1. What other alternative is *now* required for accounting for these three associated companies?

2. What total income before taxes from the associates would Corning have recognized for fiscal 1971 under (*a*) the cost method (the method used) and (*b*) the alternative method? Show your calculations where appropriate.

3. Evidence is available that Corning Glass Works did not consider itself to have an effective "significant influence" over Owens-Corning Fiberglas with only 27.3 percent ownership. Assuming that Corning Glass Works is correct in that assertion, what alternative (not necessarily acceptable under present accounting policy) exists to the cost method for accounting for Owens-Corning? What items in Corning's fiscal 1971 income statement and the January 2, 1972, and January 3, 1971, balance sheets would differ from the amounts reported under this alternative? Estimate the amounts. Ignore income taxes.

Investments in associated companies not consolidated

	Pittsburgh Corning Corporation and Dow Corning Corporation	Owens- Corning Fiberglas Corporation	Foreign Associated Companies	Total
Year ended January 2, 1972				
Investment	$11,244,563	$ 2,282,155	$ 6,629,354	$ 20,156,072
Equity in Net Assets	$55,417,500	$74,395,238	$14,385,028	$144,197,766
Dividends received	$ 4,375,000	$ 3,023,443	$ 803,269	$ 8,201,712
Equity in Undistributed Income for the year	$ 674,120	$ 3,857,379	$ 559,173	$ 5,090,672
Year ended January 3, 1971				
Investment	$11,244,563	$ 2,302,691	$ 6,741,911	$ 20,289,165
Equity in Net Assets	$53,333,110	$71,012,475	$15,298,752	$139,644,337
Dividends received	$ 4,500,000	$ 2,897,090	$ 898,532	$ 8,295,622
Equity in Undistributed Income for the year	$ 3,279,132	$ 2,807,343	$ 1,057,056	$ 7,143,531

The aggregate quoted market of Owens-Corning Fiberglas Corporation shares was approximately $209,496,000 in excess of the investment at the end of 1971 and $173,659,000 in excess of the investment at the end of 1970.

14-14. Equity Method Accounting.   On January 1, 1973, Ranger, Inc., purchased 8,000 shares of San Juan, Inc., common stock on the open market for $180,000. The shareholders' equity accounts of San Juan, Inc., as of January 1, 1973, were: common stock ($10 par), $100,000; retained earnings, $50,000.

In reviewing the assets of San Juan in order to determine the source of the excess of Ranger's cost over the equity acquired in San Juan's net assets, it was determined that $20,000 is applicable to a building with five years of remaining life. (Such "assignable" differences are amortized over the lives of the related assets.) The remainder of the differential could not be identified with any *specific* tangible or intangible asset, and Ranger elects to amortize it over the maximum period of time permissible under current accounting policy (i.e., forty years).

For the year 1973, the following information on operations and dividends is available:

	Ranger	*San Juan*
Net income	$15,000*	$15,000
Dividends paid	5,000	8,000

*Not including any effects of subsidiary operations or dividends for 1973.

Ranger uses the *equity method* of accounting for its investment in San Juan.

1. What was the balance of Ranger's investment in San Juan account at December 31, 1973?

2. What income did Ranger report for 1973?

14-15. Consolidation of Financial Statements.   Following are the 1974 balance sheets and income statements (before consolidation) of Super Sales, Inc., and its 80 percent-owned subsidiary, Tiny Toys, Inc., along with certain supplemental information. (Super Sales' financial statements are not published separately, but Tiny Toys' statements are.)

Required:

1. Prepare a consolidated balance sheet as of December 31, 1974.

2. Prepare a consolidated income statement for 1974.

3. What was the balance in Super Sales' investment (account) in Tiny Toys at December 31, *1973?* (The equity method is used by Super Sales.)

Supplemental information:

a. Super Sales purchased its share of Tiny Toys on January 1, 1973, at which time it was decided that the excess of its cost over its equity in the net assets of Tiny Toys should be amortized over the maximum period allowed under accounting policy (forty years).

b. Tiny Toys paid total dividends to its stockholders of $500,000 in 1974.

c. During 1974 Tiny Toys sold toys to Super Sales at a markup of 50 percent. The toys cost Tiny Toys $4,000,000. None of those toys were still in Super's inventory at December 31, 1974. However, as of December 31, 1974, Super Sales still owed Tiny Toys $1,000,000 on its past toy purchases.

SUPER SALES, INC.
Balance Sheet
As of December 31, 1974

Assets:		Liabilities and Stockholders' Equity:	
Cash	$ 5,000,000	Accounts payable	$ 3,000,000
Accounts receivable	4,000,000	Wages payable	1,000,000
Inventory	5,000,000	Taxes payable	1,000,000
Prepaid expenses	1,000,000		
Property, plant, and equipment (net)	18,200,000	Paid-in capital	25,000,000
Investment in Tiny Toys, Inc.	11,800,000	Retained earnings	15,000,000
	$45,000,000		$45,000,000

SUPER SALES, INC.
Income Statement
For the Year Ended December 31, 1974

Revenue		$20,000,000
Less expenses:		
Cost of sales	$12,000,000	
Depreciation and amortization	3,000,000	
Other expense (including taxes)	3,000,000	18,000,000
Income from Super Sales' operations		$ 2,000,000
Add equity in earnings of Tiny Toys less amortization of excess of cost over equity in net assets		700,000
Net income		$ 2,700,000

TINY TOYS, INC.
Balance Sheet
As of December 31, 1974

Assets:		Liabilities and Stockholders' Equity:	
Cash	$ 500,000	Accounts payable	$ 2,000,000
Accounts receivable	2,000,000	Wages payable	750,000
Inventory	2,000,000	Taxes payable	250,000
Prepaid expenses	500,000		
Property, plant, and		Paid-in capital	8,000,000
equipment (net)	8,000,000	Retained earnings	2,000,000
	$13,000,000		$13,000,000

TINY TOYS, INC.
Income Statement
For the Year Ended December 31, 1974

Revenue		$10,000,000
Less expenses:		
Cost of sales	$6,000,000	
Depreciation	1,000,000	
Other expense (including taxes)	2,000,000	9,000,000
Net income		$ 1,000,000

15

Resource Flows: Income, Cash, and Working Capital

Income as a Measure of Resource Flows

In earlier chapters we have examined a number of possible valuation bases and the related enterprise income measures. The income measures for a given set of facts differ under the various valuation bases, but they all purport to measure the *change due to operations in the net assets* (net resources) of the enterprise between two points in time. The importance of these measures to decisions dealing with investments in or distribution of benefits of the enterprise has been emphasized earlier. We do not at this time wish to suggest any lessening of this importance.

Yet, while measures of income are useful for informed decisions of the types indicated, they may not adequately serve all other purposes as well. For example, we have previously alluded to the possibility that sufficient cash may not be on hand to make distributions to the owners in an amount equal to net income. Similarly, net operating income supposedly gives some key to the long-run cash-generating ability of the firm. But exclusive reliance on this long-run indicator could presumably cause the investor to overlook short-run deficiencies in the actual flow of cash through the business.

Example 15-1   The Dynamic Growth Company was formed at the beginning of 1972 for the purpose of selling "do-it-yourself" wine-making kits. The formation of the company was coincident with a countrywide spurt in demand for wine products, and business was very brisk and apparently quite profitable. Indeed, abbreviated income statements for 1972–73 (Exhibit 15-1) reflected rapidly growing profits. *Yet the company went into bankruptcy at the end of 1973 for want of cash to meet its December payroll!*

Exhibit 15-1

DYNAMIC GROWTH COMPANY
Comparative Income Statements

	1972	1973
Sales	$200,000	$400,000
Expenses:		
Cost of sales	$100,000	$200,000
Operating expenses	50,000	76,500
	$150,000	$276,500
Net profit	$ 50,000	$123,500

How could such a situation develop in light of the very encouraging results reflected in the income statements? Is it perhaps that accounting measures of income are unreliable? Not necessarily! While income statements may on occasion be unreliable, that is not a complete answer. The business was in fact operating profitably. But net income measures the change due to operations in net assets for the period, *giving equal weight to changes in assets and liabilities of all kinds*. As a result, income statements alone do not reveal certain potentially relevant changes in the enterprise's "mix" of assets and liabilities.

Consider, for instance, the abbreviated statements of the financial position of Dynamic Growth Company at three points in its short and abruptly terminated life—as reflected in Exhibit 15-2. From these comparative statements of financial position, we can see that Dynamic Growth Company's good fortunes stimulated the owners to expand their capacity to operate. Warehouse and office facilities were apparently purchased, the stock of inventory was substantially increased to provide a better selection of products, and, as a consequence of expanding sales to a broader spectrum of customers, the amount of open (uncollected) accounts receivable increased. Assuming that the company could have continued to operate as it had, this capacity to provide greater service would have been converted into additional profits, and the inflow of funds in the *long run* would have been substantial. But, unfortunately, the cash position of the firm at the end of 1973 did become seriously low, and the firm's inability to meet the December payroll stimulated bankruptcy proceedings.

Example 15-1 demonstrates that there are several facets to a company's operating history, not all of which are encompassed by the income statement. Furthermore, this information deficiency is not remedied by choosing a valuation model other than conventional accounting. Whether viewed as a measure of enterprise performance or as an indicator of the amount that

Exhibit 15-2   DYNAMIC GROWTH COMPANY
                                  Comparative Statements of Financial Position

	January 1, 1972	December 31, 1972	December 31, 1973
Cash	$40,000	$ 20,000	$ 1,000
Accounts receivable	—0—	40,000	110,000
Inventory	—0—	50,000	150,000
Office and warehouse (net of accumulated depreciation)	—0—	—0—	112,500
Total assets	$40,000	$110,000	$373,500
Accounts payable	—0—	$ 20,000	$ 60,000
Mortgage payable	—0—	—0—	75,000
	—0—	$ 20,000	$135,000
Owners' equity	$40,000	$ 90,000	$238,500
Total liabilities and owners' equity	$40,000	$110,000	$373,500

could be distributed without reducing wealth (whatever the value base) below what it was at the beginning of the period, income is essentially a long-run
concept. This point of view necessarily abstracts from many important short-
run considerations. And, as was pointed out above, one of the important
short-run considerations not revealed by the income measure is the change
in the composition, or "mix," of the assets of the enterprise. We therefore
turn our attention in this chapter to some other statements, complementary
to the income statement, that depict the flows to and from selected categories
within the net assets of the enterprise.

Selecting Additional Resource Bases for Analysis

At first glance, however, it would appear that comparative statements of
financial position provide adequate information on changes in asset mix. In
our example, the comparative statements of financial position at three points
in time did reveal a continually deteriorating cash position. But, unfortunately,
the changes in financial position communicated by the beginning and ending
balance sheets reveal only the *cumulative effects* of all forces that tended to re-
structure the composition of net assets during the period. While this information may indicate an imminent crisis at times, it does not convey the dynamics
of the changes that took place during a period. Nor do comparative balance
sheets alone provide as clear an indication of potentially serious financial
situations (which may be avoided by appropriate planning) as when they
are accompanied by a well-constructed statement of resource flows designed
to explain changes in the levels of certain categories within net assets in
terms of the causes of those changes. (Forecast statements of resource flows
would provide still earlier warning. But for external use they are subject to
the limitations discussed in Chapter 4.)

If the limitations of income statements are to be avoided, the initial step in constructing other (complementary) statements of resource flows select for analysis some relevant subsets of net assets (the set to which income statement is oriented). The two subsets of net assets that accountant most often select for analysis are (1) cash and (2) working capital.

> **Working Capital.** Working capital is the combined (or net) amount of current assets and current liabilities of the enterprise. It is measured by the difference between the sum of the values assigned to current assets and the sum of the values assigned to current liabilities.
>
> **Current Assets.** Current assets include cash and those other assets whose benefits are expected to be realized in the relative short run (usually less than one year).
>
> **Current Liabilities.** Current liabilities are those liabilities, usually incurred in connection with recurring operations, that will require liquidation (payment) in the short run (usually less than one year).

We will initially examine statements of resource flows that explain changes in a firm's cash position—that is, its cash flows. This focal point, we will see, provides perhaps the most comprehensive analysis of changes in the composition, or "mix," of the net assets of the enterprise (particularly if one takes a broad view of certain resource-consuming transactions). Next, we will move to an analysis of resource flows explaining changes in the enterprise's working capital position.

THE CASH FLOW STATEMENT

In outlining the structure of the cash flow statement, we will for illustration purposes rely on the set of circumstances encountered by the Dynamic Growth Company during its second year of operations, 1973. The transactions for the company for 1973 are reflected in the financial position worksheet in Exhibit 15-3. Since we are interested in explaining the dynamics of the change in the cash position produced by 1973 activities, we will begin our analysis by preparing a statement of cash receipts and disbursements (Exhibit 15-4). The categories of cash inflows and outflows included in the statement are based simply on the descriptions of the transactions (enumerated in the financial position worksheet) that had an effect on the cash account during the period.

The cash receipts and disbursements statement, prepared from a simple enumeration of the increases and decreases in the cash account, shows an excess of disbursements over receipts in the amount of $19,000, thus confirming the observed decrease in the cash balance from the beginning to the end of the period. But, unfortunately, it does not highlight the reasons why a profitably operating company should find itself bankrupt. To produce a statement that affords more insight, we must modify and rearrange the categories of cash inflows and outflows—roughly based on (1) the causes (sources) of the cash inflows and (2) the purposes (uses) for which cash outflows were expended. Such a statement, based on the facts of the Dynamic Growth example, appears in Exhibit 15-5. The statement in Exhibit 15-5 is

Exhibit 15-3

DYNAMIC GROWTH COMPANY
Financial Position Worksheet
Second Year of Operations

Description	Cash	Accounts Receivable	Inventory	Office-Warehouse Facilities Asset Cost	Office-Warehouse Facilities Accumulated Depreciation	Accounts Payable	Mortgage Payable	Owners' Equity Capital Stock	Owners' Equity Retained Earnings
Beginning Position	20,000	40,000	50,000	—0—	—0—	20,000	—0—	40,000	50,000
1. Additional investment by owners (new capital stock issued)	25,000							25,000	
2. Purchase of office-warehouse facilities for $125,000—$50,000 cash and $75,000 mortgage	(50,000)			125,000			75,000		
3. Purchase of inventory on account			300,000			300,000			
4. Sales of wine-making kits on account		400,000							400,000 (R)
5. Collections of accounts receivable	330,000	(330,000)							
6. Payments on accounts payable	(260,000)					(260,000)			
7. Payment of wages and salaries	(40,000)								(40,000) (E)
8. Payment of interest on mortgage	(6,000)								(6,000) (E)
9. Payment of miscellaneous expenses	(18,000)								(18,000) (E)
10. Recognition of cost of wine-making kits sold			(200,000)						(200,000) (E)
11. Recognition of depreciation on office-warehouse facilities					(12,500)				(12,500) (E)
Ending Position	1,000	110,000	150,000	125,000	(12,500)	60,000	75,000	65,000	173,500

Exhibit 15-4

DYNAMIC GROWTH COMPANY
Statement of Cash Receipts and Disbursements
For Year Ended December 31, 1973

Cash receipts:		
Collections of accounts receivable	$330,000	
Additional investment by owners	25,000	$355,000
Cash disbursements:		
Cash payment on purchase of office-warehouse facilities	$ 50,000	
Payments on accounts payable	260,000	
Payment of wages and salaries	40,000	
Payment of interest on mortgage	6,000	
Payment of miscellaneous expenses	18,000	374,000
Excess of disbursements over receipts		($ 19,000)

Exhibit 15-5

DYNAMIC GROWTH COMPANY
Cash Flow Statement
For Year Ended December 31, 1973

Sources of cash:		
From operations:		
Cash inflows:		
Collections of accounts receivable		$330,000
Cash outflows:		
Payments on accounts payable	$260,000	
Payment of wages and salaries	40,000	
Payment of interest on mortgage	6,000	
Payment of miscellaneous expenses	18,000	324,000
Net cash inflow from operations		$ 6,000
Investment by owner		25,000
Proceeds of mortgage loan		75,000
Total sources of cash		$106,000
Uses of cash:		
Purchase of office-warehouse facilities		125,000
Net decrease in cash for 1973		($ 19,000)

characteristic of the statement format traditionally referred to by accountants as a "cash flow statement"—though a recent accounting policy release recommends that the title be changed to "statement of changes in financial position."

The cash flow statement (Exhibit 15-5) contrasts sharply in two respects with the cash receipts and disbursements statement (Exhibit 15-4). First, though cash inflows and outflows are still divided into two major categories, the two categories are "sources of cash" and "uses of cash" rather than "cash receipts" and "cash disbursements." Second, all cash flows resulting from the operations of the enterprise, whether positive or negative, are placed together so that *"operations" is shown as a single net source or use of cash during the period.* The rationale for the "source and use" classification scheme is that it provides greater insight into why the cash balance changed in the amount that it did during the period. The rationale for the treatment of "operations" as a single net source or use of cash is developed below.

Net Cash Flow from Operations

Recall that earlier we described a simple operating sequence for an enterprise in the following terms:

1. The enterprise acquires control or possession of the factors of production necessary to provide a particular product or service in exchange for immediate cash payments or promises to pay at some future date.
2. The factors of production are committed as needed to the process or processes used to generate the enterprise's product or service.
3. Finally, finished products or services are provided as demanded by customers, in exchange for cash or promises to pay cash to the enterprise at some future date.

Two important types of activities are identifiable in the above description of enterprise activity: (1) operating activities and (2) financing activities. Each of the two activities occurs in two distinct patterns: (1) recurring and (2) nonrecurring, or intermittent. Based upon this two-way classification, enterprise activity is graphically depicted in Exhibit 15-6.

The accounting notion of cash flow from operations focuses on the net cash inflow, or outflow, that is generated by the *regularly recurring operating and financing activities of the firm*—those activities depicted in the upper half of Exhibit 15-6. One reason for grouping together in the cash flow statement all cash inflows and outflows due to "operations" is that presumably they are all the result of a single cause—the ongoing productive activities of the enterprise. For instance, it would be nonsense to show receipts of accounts receivable as a separate source of cash and payments of wages and salaries as a separate use of cash. Both are a result of operations, and therefore neither can be managed independently of the other (or, for that matter, independently of the payments on account, the payment of interest, and the payment of miscellaneous expenses).

Another reason for grouping all cash inflows and outflows due to operations together and representing operations as a single net source or use of cash is that the constant recirculation of capital from cash through operations and back to cash is the primary long-run source of the net *cash inflow required to provide for replenishment and expansion of productive capacity and to discharge any long-term obligations* of the enterprise. *In essence, the cash generated by operations is the lifeblood of the enterprise.* Without a positive cash flow from recurring activities in the long run, continuation of the business is generally not justified.

Measuring Cash Flow from Operations

Consider again the data of our illustration and the computation of cash flow from operations reflected in Exhibit 15-5. It should be noted that the categories in the computation parallel directly the activities outlined in our graphical depiction of the recurring operating and financing activities of the enterprise (Exhibit 15-6).

Exhibit 15-6 Enterprise Operating and Financing Activities

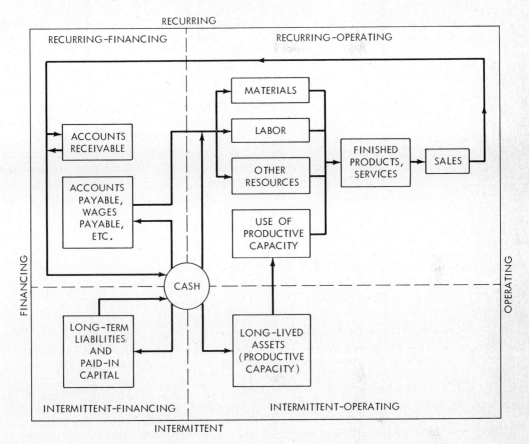

The only recurring cash inflow from the operating activities in the Dynamic Growth case is the collection of accounts receivable. Of course, if the firm had cash sales, these sales would be added to the collections of accounts receivable in the computation of total cash inflows from operations.

On the other hand, there are four kinds of cash outflows from recurring operations. However, the four items can be identified with two activities depicted in Exhibit 15-6. The payments on accounts payable represent one recurring type of outflow of cash, and the remaining three cash outflows are types of cash payments for current operating expenses (wages and salaries, interest, and other operating expenses). In our example, the acquisition of inventory is all financed through purchases on account, and thus we have no direct cash outflows specifically to acquire inventory. If we did have any cash purchases, the amount of cash disbursed in such transactions would obviously be included in the statement along with the other cash outflows from operations.

Combining the cash inflows and outflows from operations, we observe that there is a positive *net* cash inflow from operations of $6,000. This amount is in stark contrast to the net income for the period of $123,500. As will become clear later in the chapter, this difference between cash flow from operations and net income (from operations) is explainable (1) in terms of the effects of short-run financing of the firm's operations and sales through changes in the balances of such items as accounts receivable, inventory, and accounts payable, and (2) in terms of such expenses as depreciation, which are deducted from revenue in measuring income but for which there is no recurring cash expenditure pattern.

Other Sources and Uses of Cash

The explanation of the cash flow statement can now be completed by adding to our analysis of the cash flow from operations all other transactions that generated (or involved) cash flows, that is, the provision of productive capacity, long-term financing activities, payments of dividends, if any, to the owner(s), and so forth. In our example, the following transactions fall into this essentially long-term, intermittent category of transactions:

1. An investment by the owner(s)—$25,000
2. Purchase of office-warehouse facilities ($125,000)——cash ($50,000) and a mortgage loan ($75,000)

By including these two transactions (the former as a source of cash, the latter as both a source and a use of cash) along with the analysis of cash inflows and outflows from operations, the cash flow statement is completed (as shown in Exhibit 15-5).

One item of particular importance in Exhibit 15-5 is the splitting of the purchase of the office-warehouse into two components, even though the purchase for cash and a mortgage note was probably executed in one transaction. First, we impute to the transaction the receipt of cash in the amount of $75,000 from the issuance of the mortgage note *as if* it had actually been borrowed in advance. Then, the purchase of the productive facilities at a total price of $125,000 is treated *as if* it involved the payment of cash in the full amount. That is to say, we disclose the single transaction involving the acquisition of the office-warehouse for cash and a mortgage note as if both an inflow and an outflow of cash had taken place. Notice, however, that the net outflow of cash of $50,000 is equal to the amount actually paid in the single purchase transaction. By analyzing transactions in this manner, *the cash flow statement discloses* the full extent of all purchase and financing transactions of a long-term nature, independent of whether long-term financing is first secured and then productive capacity is acquired, or whether these two separate activities are combined in one transaction.

As a final observation we should return to the point that the cash flow statement hopefully conveys information about alterations in the mix of enterprise net assets that took place during the period. It should be obvious by now that this is the case. For instance, from Exhibit 15-5 it is quite clear that there was a shift from cash to long-lived assets of $125,000 during the period, with part of the cash provided (at least figuratively) by an increase in still another element of net assets, the long-term mortgage note of $75,000.

WORKING CAPITAL FLOW STATEMENT

As was pointed out earlier, several alternative bases can be selected for analyzing the resource flows of a business. We have examined above in considerable detail the nature and form of the resource flow statement that is produced using the cash flows of the firm as the focal point. We now turn our attention to the statement of resource flows that results when our focus is on the *working capital* of the firm. (Recall that *working capital* is defined as the combined current assets and current liabilities of the enterprise.)

Working Capital as a Resource Base

A major reason why working capital is often chosen as a focal point for resource flow statements in current financial reports is that working capital combines all of the assets and liabilities that arise out of the short-run, routine financing activities that are used to support operations. Yet it still provides most of the additional information sought from the resource flow statement. In particular, when our point of focus is working capital, all of the short-run, recurring financing transactions (including inventory buildups or drawdowns) that serve only as short-run buffers between physical operations and cash flows are ignored in the calculation of net "resources" provided from operations. They are ignored because accounts receivable, accounts payable, and inventory are all elements of the same resource group (working capital). *Intragroup* fluctuations in these accounts (such as the acquisition of merchandise, either for cash or for credit) do not change the amount of working capital, and thus they do not influence the working capital flow statement. Only those activities that increase (or decrease) the amount of the composite group of accounts are reflected in the statement. This is in sharp contrast to the cash flow statement in which shifts between cash (one element of working capital) and other working capital accounts are used in measuring cash flow from operations (for example, collection of accounts receivable).

It is for the above reason that working capital flows from operations and operating income are much more similar than are operating income and cash flow from operations. For example, such distinctions as whether sales are made on account or for cash, or whether collections on accounts receivable are more or less than sales, are not important in the calculation of either income or working capital provided by operations because both cash (from cash sales) and accounts receivable (from credit sales) are positive elements of the working capital group. An increase in either cash or accounts receivable is an increase in working capital. However, the same distinctions are significant in measuring cash flow provided by operations.

The Working Capital Flow Statement Illustrated

These general observations about the working capital flow statement are now illustrated by again looking at the second-year activities of the Dynamic Growth Company. Exhibit 15-7 reflects a financial position worksheet containing the same accounts and transactions included in Exhibit 15-3, but with the column headings for the accounts rearranged to group the elements of working capital in one section and all other accounts in another section. This arrangement of accounts allows us to observe the effects of each transaction on the firm's working capital position.

Generally, if a transaction does not affect any of the accounts included in working capital (for example, transaction 11), it is not included in the working capital flow statement. Additionally, transactions changing two or more components (accounts) of working capital such that the *net effect* on the working capital position is zero (for example, transactions 3, 5, and 6) are also excluded from the working capital flow statement. Such transactions do not augment or diminish the firm's working capital, but only alter the form in which the working capital is held. We can readily observe from Exhibit 15-7 that four transactions in all (numbers 3, 5, 6, and 11) had no (net) effect on the level of working capital of the firm.

Transactions 5 and 6 illustrate differences in the calculation of *resources provided from operations* as a result of the change in our focal point for resources from cash to working capital. We recognized these transactions earlier in calculating cash flow from operations; we do not use them now in the determination of working capital flow from operations. The transaction involving the recognition of depreciation expense (transaction 11) is the same in the analysis of working capital flows as it was in the analysis of cash flows. Recognizing depreciation expense does not affect either resource base (cash or working capital).

The working capital flow statement for this example is shown in Exhibit 15-8. The individual items are numbered parenthetically to indicate the corresponding transaction number in Exhibit 15-7. Notice that by contrast to the calculation of cash flow from operations (see Exhibit 15-5), the working capital flow from operations includes the following:

1. Sales revenue (or the increases in accounts receivable due to operations) *rather than* collections of accounts receivable (the decreases in the same account during the period)
2. Cost of goods sold *rather than* payments (on accounts payable) for goods purchased for eventual sale

On the other hand, the financing and operating activities of a long-term character are disclosed in exactly the same manner in Exhibit 15-8 as they were in the cash flow statement (Exhibit 15-5), because (1) all such activities affecting cash affect working capital, a resource group that includes cash, and (2) because there were no long-term or intermittent operating or financing activities that affected a working capital account other than cash. Had there been any of the latter type activities, they would have been included in the working capital flow statement but omitted from the cash flow statement.

Notice also that along with the working capital flows the changes in the balances of cash, inventory, accounts receivable, and accounts payable are disclosed in an accompanying supportive schedule so that the reader can determine what effect(s) the net change in working capital reported in the working capital flow statement had on the individual elements of working capital. (The

Exhibit 15-7

DYNAMIC GROWTH COMPANY
Financial Position Worksheet (Rearranged to Group Working Capital Elements Together)
Second Year of Operations

| Description | Working Capital | | | | All Other Accounts | | | Owners' Equity | |
| | Cash | Accounts Receivable | Inventory | Accounts Payable | Office-Warehouse Facilities | | Mortgage Payable | Capital Stock | Retained Earnings |
					Asset Cost	Accumulated Depreciation			
Beginning Position	20,000	40,000	50,000	20,000	–0–	–0–	–0–	40,000	50,000
1. Additional investment by owners (new capital stock issued)	25,000							25,000	
2. Purchase of office-warehouse facilities for $125,000—$50,000 cash and $75,000 mortgage	(50,000)				125,000		75,000		
3. Purchase of inventory on account			300,000	300,000					
4. Sales of wine-making kits on account		400,000							400,000 (R)
5. Collections of accounts receivable	330,000	(330,000)							
6. Payments on accounts payable	(260,000)			(260,000)					
7. Payment of wages and salaries	(40,000)								(40,000) (E)
8. Payment of interest on mortgage	(6,000)								(6,000) (E)
9. Payment of miscellaneous expenses	(18,000)								(18,000) (E)
10. Recognition of cost of wine-making kits sold			(200,000)						(200,000) (E)
11. Recognition of depreciation on office-warehouse facilities						(12,500)			(12,500) (E)
Ending Position	1,000	110,000	150,000	60,000	125,000	(12,500)	75,000	65,000	173,500

Exhibit 15-8

DYNAMIC GROWTH COMPANY
Working Capital Flow Statement
For Year Ended December 31, 1973

Sources of working capital:			
From operations:			
Sales revenue			$400,000 (4)
Less expenditures of working capital:			
Cost of goods sold	$200,000 (10)		
Payment of wages and salaries	40,000 (7)		
Payment of interest	6,000 (8)		
Miscellaneous expenditures	18,000 (9)	264,000	
Net working capital flow from operations		$136,000	
Investment by owner		25,000 (1)	
Proceeds of mortgage loan		75,000 (2)	
Total sources of working capital		$236,000	
Uses of working capital:			
Purchase of office-warehouse facilities		125,000 (2)	
Increase in working capital for 1973		$111,000	

Schedule of Changes in Working Capital Accounts:

	December 31, 1972	December 31, 1973	Increase (Decrease)
Cash	$ 20,000	$ 1,000	$(19,000)
Accounts receivable	40,000	110,000	70,000
Inventory	50,000	150,000	100,000
Current assets subtotal	$110,000	$261,000	$151,000
Accounts payable	$ 20,000	$ 60,000	$ 40,000
Working capital	$ 90,000	$201,000	$111,000

same information can be obtained by comparing the beginning and ending balance sheets.) In our example, we observe from both the statement of working capital flows and the schedule of changes in working capital accounts that working capital increased by $111,000 over the period. From the latter we observe further that this increase was primarily concentrated in working capital elements other than cash.

Therefore, with a supplementary analysis of the working capital accounts, we can derive essentially the same information from the working capital flow statement as we did from the cash flow statement. In fact, as will be evident in the next section, the relationship between cash and working capital flows from operations is such that, given a statement prepared on one basis, conversion to the other basis can usually be made fairly accurately with little additional information or effort. Thus we need not be overly concerned with choosing (between cash and working capital) the one correct basis for preparing resource flow statements.

RELATIONSHIP BETWEEN INCOME AND RESOURCE FLOWS FROM OPERATIONS

By dealing exclusively with selected transaction elements in the financial position worksheet (i.e., those affecting the resource base of interest), we have been able to construct resource flow statements that indicate the effects on the firm's resource position of its various operating and financing activities during the period. In these statements of cash and working capital flows, we have grouped the regularly recurring activities of the firm to produce a single measure of "net resources provided from operations." From this section of the statement, we may gain some insight into why the resource base selected has fluctuated in the manner it has vis-à-vis the history of wealth generation reflected in the income statement. But the relationship between income and "net resources provided from operations" is only implicitly disclosed using the statement format developed earlier.

In current financial reporting, however, the customary format for resource flow statements is to begin the calculation of resource flows *from operations* with the income figure disclosed in the income statement. Then, by adding and deducting appropriate adjustments, the net resource flow from operations is determined. By relying explicitly on the relationship between elements of income determination (revenues and expenses) and elements of resource flows from operations, this approach always leads to the same conclusion as an analysis of transactions affecting the resource base of interest. At the same time, by making it possible to avoid transaction analysis, a real savings in statement preparation effort is possible. (Of course, the magnitude of this benefit is not as evident in our examples—where transactions are already highly summarized—as it is in practice.)

One corollary benefit of the approach to be described more fully below is that it may be utilized by the financial statement user to construct a resource flow statement from the income statement and comparative statements of financial position when the reporting company does not supply such a statement. While a statement constructed by an outsider may be lacking in some respects, it is often a good approximation of the missing statement. A second corollary benefit, primarily instructional, is that the approach provides an excellent exercise in financial statement interrelationships for the student.

Income and Working Capital Flows from Operations

For purposes of analysis, Exhibit 15-9 shows comparative statements of resource flows from operations for 1973. The resource basis for the statement on the left-hand side of Exhibit 15-9 is net assets—meaning that the statement shows the net flow of net assets due to operations for the period, *that is, net operating income.* The resource base of the statement on the right is working capital. Related sources of positive and negative resource flows are numbered alike (parenthetically) in the statements.

Exhibit 15-9

DYNAMIC GROWTH COMPANY
Comparative Statements of
Resource Flows from Operations
For Year Ended December 31, 1973

Net Assets Provided by Operations:		Working Capital Provided by Operations:	
(1) Revenue	$400,000	(1) Revenue	$400,000
Less:		Less:	
(2) Cost of merchandise sold	$200,000	(2) Cost of merchandise sold	$200,000
(3) Wages and salaries	40,000	(3) Wages and salaries	40,000
(4) Interest expense	6,000	(4) Interest expense	6,000
(5) Miscellaneous expense	18,000	(5) Miscellaneous expense	18,000
(6) Depreciation expense	12,500	(6)	
Total expense	$276,500	Total outflows	$264,000
Net operating income	$123,500	Net flow from operations	$136,000

Exhibit 15-9 again emphasizes the similarity between net income and net working capital flow from operations. In the income statement the major positive component is revenue (item 1)—the increase in accounts receivable (and/or cash) due to operations. Since accounts receivable (and cash) is a working capital asset, revenue is also the measure of the major positive component of working capital flows from operations. Similar reasoning applies to all but one of the decreases in net assets due to operations, that is, the expenses of the period. The cost of merchandise sold (item 2) represents a decrease in a working capital asset (inventory), as does the payment of wages and salaries (item 3), interest (item 4), and miscellaneous expenses (item 5)—all decreases in cash. (In other cases these items could just as well have been the result of decreases in other working capital assets like prepaid insurance or increases in working capital liabilities like wages payable.)

The one exception, in this case, to the correspondence between revenue and expenses recognized and working capital flows from operations is depreciation expense. Depreciation is an expense because an asset has decreased due to operations. *But since the assets involved are long-lived, that is, non-current, no decrease in working capital corresponds to depreciation expense.*

Deriving Working Capital Flow
from Net Operating Income

This leads us to an obvious generalization that working capital flow from operations, in general, would equal net operating income *except for* the effect of depreciation and other similar expenses representing decreases in noncurrent assets or increases in noncurrent liabilities. From this generalization, a shortcut method of arriving at working capital flow from operations suggests itself. Scan the income statement and *add back to net operating income* depreciation and other expenses related to non-working capital sacrifices (also deduct revenue or income, if any, corresponding to increases in non-working capital items). Some examples of non-working capital related expenses other than depreciation are amortization of intangible assets and the portion of income tax expense that represents an increase in deferred taxes payable. An example of a non-working capital income item is a parent company's un-realized equity in the earnings of an unconsolidated subsidiary. This method is illustrated in Exhibit 15-10, a revised working capital flow statement, with the working capital flow from operations derived as suggested above. Notice that the $136,000 working capital flow from operations is the same as was derived earlier (see Exhibits 15-8 and 15-9).

Exhibit 15-10

DYNAMIC GROWTH COMPANY
Working Capital Flow Statement
For Year Ended December 31, 1973
(Usual Format in Current Financial Reporting)

Sources of working capital:	
From operations:	
Net income	$123,500
Add: Depreciation expense	12,500
Net working capital flow from operations	$136,000
Investment by owner	25,000
Proceeds of mortgage loan	75,000
Total sources of working capital	$236,000
Uses of working capital:	
Purchase of office-warehouse facilities	125,000
Increase in working capital for 1973	$111,000

Income and Cash Flow from Operations

Working out the relationships between elements of income and elements of cash flow from operations is more difficult than experienced above for working capital flow from operations. The reason, perhaps now familiar, is that cash is much more restrictive than working capital *relative* to net assets, the basis underlying net operating income. However, by proceeding as we did above for working capital, the relationships can be made evident and a general shortcut procedure for measuring cash flow from operations worked out.

Exhibit 15-11 shows side-by-side income and cash flow from operations statements with related components of income and cash flow from operations again numbered alike. We will proceed from the bottom of the statement to the top in our analysis.

The treatment of depreciation expense (item 6) in deriving cash flow from operations from the operating income figure is identical to its treatment in deriving working capital flow from operations from the income figure. Since *depreciation is a noncash expenditure of resources* in support of operations, it is added back to net operating income in the process of arriving at cash flow from operations.

Now again referring to Exhibit 15-11, notice that the amounts of expense and cash expenditure are equal for items 3, 4, and 5. We know from the 1973 financial position worksheet for the Dynamic Growth example (Exhibit 15-3) that this is not a result of coincidence. All 1973 wages, salaries, inter-est, and miscellaneous expenses were the result of 1973 cash expenditures. Furthermore, there were no 1973 payments on items that were accrued as

Exhibit 15-11

DYNAMIC GROWTH COMPANY
Comparative Statements of
Resource Flows from Operations
For Year Ended December 31, 1973

Net Assets Provided by Operations:		Cash Provided by Operations:	
(1) Revenue	$400,000	(1) Collections of accounts receivable	$330,000
Less:		Less:	
(2) Cost of merchandise sold	$200,000	(2) Payments on accounts payable	$260,000
(3) Wages and salaries	40,000	(3) Wages and salaries paid	40,000
(4) Interest expense	6,000	(4) Interest paid	6,000
(5) Miscellaneous expense	18,000	(5) Miscellaneous expenditures	18,000
(6) Depreciation expense	12,500	(6)	
Total expense	$276,500	Total outflows	$324,000
Net operating income	$123,500	Net cash flow from operations	$6,000

liabilities at the beginning of the period (i.e., unpaid in 1972). In general, however, we would expect the relationship depicted in Exhibit 15-12 to hold for such expenditure categories as represented by items 3, 4, and 5. By examining the relationships depicted in Exhibit 15-12, we can derive the following generalizations:

1. To the extent that accrued liabilities decrease and/or prepaid expenses increase over a period, expenditures (of cash) in support of operations will exceed expenses (i.e., more resources paid for than used).

2. To the extent that accrued liabilities increase and/or prepaid expenses decrease over a period, expenditures in support of operations will be exceeded by expenses (i.e., less resources paid for than used).

Exhibit 15-12   **Relationships between Expenses, Expenditures, Prepaid Expenses, and Accrued Liabilities**

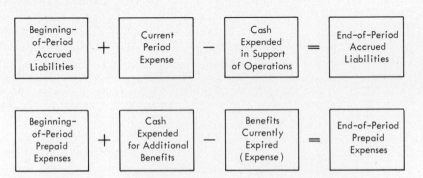

These generalizations intuitively make good sense in that to the extent that prepaid expenses are allowed to expire more (less) rapidly than they are replenished, resource acquisition (and related cash expenditure) requirements for operations will be less (more) than the cost of resources used (expense). Similarly, to the extent that the enterprise increases (decreases) its short-term accrued liabilities, payments actually required are less (more) than the amounts of resources acquired. From these generalizations come logical rules for adjusting expenses to get cash expenditures in support of operations. To adjust expenses to get expenditures in support of operations, start with the expense figure and—

Add:
a. Increases in prepaid expenses
b. Decreases in accrued liabilities

Subtract:
a. Decreases in prepaid expenses
b. Increases in accrued liabilities

Since expenses enter negatively into the calculation of net operating income, the adjustments for the same items to net operating income in arriving at net cash flow from operations should take on the opposite sign as follows:

Add:
a. Decreases in prepaid expenses
b. Increases in accrued liabilities

Subtract:
a. Increases in prepaid expenses
b. Decreases in accrued liabilities

Similar reasoning applies to the adjustments required to convert cost of goods sold to cash expended on inventory purchases (item 2 in Exhibit 15-11). Exhibit 15-13 describes the two basic relationships involved. The first is the relationship between cash payments, purchases, and the balance of accounts payable. The second is the relationship between cost of goods sold, purchases, and the balance of inventory. When the second relationship is solved for "purchases," we get the third relationship, one that expresses purchases in terms of cost of goods sold and the beginning and ending inventory balances. When we substitute the right-hand side of the third relationship for purchases in the first relationship, we get an expression as depicted at the top of Exhibit 15-14 in which appear (a) "payments for inventory purchases" (the amount we wish to know) and (b) "cost of goods sold" (the corresponding amount included under expenses in the income statement). Algebraically solving for "payments for inventory purchases" gives the second expression in Exhibit 15-14, which indicates that to determine the payments for inventory purchases from cost of goods sold, start with the latter figure and adjust as follows:

Add:
a. Any increase in inventory
b. Any decrease in accounts payable

Subtract:
a. Any decrease in inventory
b. Any increase in accounts payable

Exhibit 15-13   **Relationships between Payments, Purchases, Cost of Goods Sold, Accounts Payable, and Inventory**

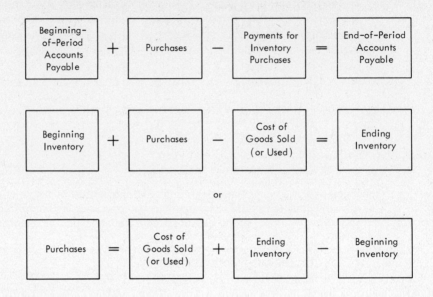

Exhibit 15-14   **Payments for Inventory Purchased Expressed as a Function of Cost of Goods Sold, Inventory, and Accounts Payable**

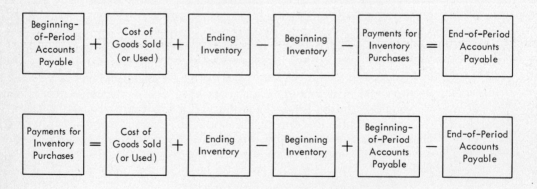

Exhibit 15-15

DYNAMIC GROWTH COMPANY
Calculation of Payments for Inventory Purchases
From Cost of Merchandise Sold

Cost of merchandise sold (from Exhibit 15-11)	$200,000
Add increase in inventory (from Exhibit 15-8)	100,000
Less increase in accounts payable (from Exhibit 15-8)	(40,000)
Payments on accounts payable (see Exhibit 15-11)	$260,000

Exhibit 15-15 applies this rule of thumb to the Dynamic Growth example. Note that Exhibit 15-15 starts with the $200,000 cost of merchandise sold from Exhibit 15-11 and ends with the $260,000 payments on accounts payable. This set of adjustments, of course, makes the same kind of intuitive good sense as the adjustments noted earlier to other expenses to determine related cash expenditures in support of operations. To the extent that inventories are increased (decreased) during the period, more (less) purchases will be required than the amount of inventory used as measured by cost of goods sold (or used). But, to the extent that the accounts payable are greater (less) at the end of the period than at the beginning, less (more) cash was paid to suppliers than the amount of purchases during the period. So we can think of the adjustments for the change in inventory and for the change in accounts payable as taking us, in succession, from cost of goods sold (or used) to purchases to cash payments for purchases. Of course, since cost of goods sold enters negatively into the calculation of operating income, the sign of the adjustments must be changed as shown below in working from operating income to net cash flow from operations:

Add:

a. Any decrease in inventory

b. Any increase in accounts payable

Subtract:

a. Any increase in inventory

b. Any decrease in accounts payable

Having covered all of the items of expense and corresponding cash expenditure from Exhibit 15-11, we can now turn our attention to item 1, revenue and the corresponding cash flow from operations (in this case strictly collections of accounts receivable). The relationship of interest is depicted in Exhibit 15-16. From Exhibit 15-16 it can be seen that when the balance of accounts receivable increases (decreases) over the period, that is, credit sales are greater (less) than collections, cash received from operations will be less

Exhibit 15-16   Relationship between Revenue and Cash Inflows from Operations

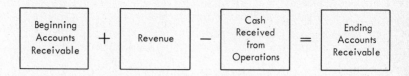

(more) than revenue for the period. This immediately suggests that to adjust revenue to get cash received from operations, start with the revenue figure and:

Add the decrease in accounts receivable, or

Subtract the increase in accounts receivable.

Since revenue enters positively into the calculation of income, the same adjustments apply in going from operating income to net cash flow from operations.

From Income to Cash Flow from
Operations—Summary

We can now summarize all of the above reasoning into a simple procedure for adjusting net operating income to get cash flow from operations:

1. Start with net operating income.
2. Add back such noncash expenses as depreciation and subtract noncash related revenue or income.
3. Add decreases and subtract increases in current assets other than cash, e.g., accounts receivable, inventory, and prepaid expenses.
4. Add increases and subtract decreases in current liabilities, e.g., accounts payable, wages payable, etc.

Exhibit 15-17

DYNAMIC GROWTH COMPANY
Cash Flow Statement
For Year Ended December 31, 1973
(Usual Format in Current Financial Reporting)

Sources of cash:		
From operations:		
Net income	$123,500	
Add: Depreciation expense	12,500	
	$136,000	
Add: Increase in accounts payable	40,000	
Deduct: Increase in accounts receivable	(70,000)	
Deduct: Increase in inventory	(100,000)	
Net cash flow from operations		$ 6,000
Investment by owner		25,000
Proceeds of mortgage loan		75,000
Total sources of cash		$106,000
Uses of cash:		
Purchases of office-warehouse facilities		125,000
Net decrease in cash for 1973		$(19,000)

Exhibit 15-17 illustrates the overall procedure for the Dynamic Growth Company example. The reader should note that the calculation of cash flow from operations begins with the net operating income figure from the left-hand column of Exhibit 15-11 and ends with the net cash flow from operations figure appearing in the right-hand column. The amounts of the various adjustments for increases and decreases in working capital accounts may be confirmed by reference either to the original worksheet (Exhibit 15-3) or to the schedule of changes in working capital accounts in Exhibit 15-8. Notice too that the other sources and uses of cash are treated in the same way under this statement format as under the earlier transactions-based format.

As a final note, it is recognized that the reader may have trouble remembering whether to add to, or subtract from, net operating income a given change in a particular working capital account. One way to avoid using "rote" is to think of the effect of each item *as if* it were increased or decreased directly in relationship to the cash account rather than through the operations of the enterprise. Thus, increases in current liabilities (which should be added to net operating income) may be thought of as additional loans by creditors supplying cash to the enterprise. Decreases in liabilities are the opposite, requiring extra cash expenditures to pay them off. Increases in such current assets as inventory and prepaid expenses are additional acquisitions requiring cash, whereas decreases are like sources of cash savings, since cash expenditures are avoided to the extent that stocks of such assets are used up without replenishment. Similarly, increases in accounts receivable are like loans to customers, which would require outlays of cash; decreases are like repayments of such loans, which would provide additional cash.

Using these *as if* relationships is a handy way of remembering how to treat a given change in a working capital item on the cash-flow statement. However, it should always be remembered that the working capital items are not necessarily independent sources and uses of cash *per se*. Generally, they serve as financial buffers between cash flows and physical operations. When their levels increase or decrease it means only that there are disparities between revenues and expenses and cash receipts and disbursements from operations which must be taken into account in deducing net cash flow from operations from the net operating income figure.

A Note on the Treatment of Depreciation Expense

Because of the manner in which depreciation expense is disclosed in the shortcut resource flow from operations calculations, some users of financial statements often form a misconception about the nature of depreciation. Because depreciation expense is added to net income in the calculation of cash and/or working capital provided from operations, it is often concluded that depreciation is a *resource-providing* "item." This conclusion is, of course, erroneous. Returning to our original statement format in which net income was not explicitly included as a separate item in the resource flow statements (Exhibits 15-5 and 15-8), we see that depreciation *is not* indicated as a source of either cash or working capital. Depreciation does appear in the revised statement format (Exhibits 15-10 and 15-17), not because it has changed its character and become a source of resources, but because it was deducted from revenue in determining net income and did not (in the form of depreciation) involve the outflow of cash or working capital. To arrive at the net cash or working capital inflows from operations when we begin the computation with net income, depreciation (and any other non-resource-consuming expenses) must be added back. While this adjustment is required in the cash or working capital flow calculation, *it does not gainsay the character of depreciation as a valid expense, nor suggest that depreciation is a source of funds.* Indeed, funds were expended for the resources whose consumption is reflected in our measure of depreciation. However, these acquisitions are reflected in the resource flow statements in the enumeration of long-run financing and operating transactions—in our example, we have the purchase of the office-warehouse facilities for $125,000. The total amount expended for the warehouse is reflected in the year of acquisition, but the related expense is allocated over the life of the asset as it is used to generate revenue.

RESOURCE FLOW STATEMENTS —SOME ELABORATION

Treatment of Additional Accounts and Transactions

The number of accounts and transactions considered in our illustration in this chapter was intentionally small so that the complexity of the example data would not obscure the basic concepts we were introducing. Notwithstanding this limitation on the scope of the illustration, it does reveal the basic set of principles that is needed to analyze any particular problem. Little would be gained by going through a long enumeration of different types of accounts and special transactions, in terms of their special effects on the resource flow statement. We will, however, mention a few additional items that are commonly found in resource flow statements to illustrate the application of the basic principles to these particular items.

● *Dividends.* We illustrated in our example a flow of cash from the owners to the business. This investment by owners was reflected in both statements as a source of resources (cash or working capital) during the period. Obviously, there could also be a flow of resources in the other direction, that is, the payment of dividends to owners, and indeed this is a use of funds commonly found in resource flow statements. Resource flows to and from the owners of the business enterprise are not netted. New investments of capital are reflected in the resource flow statement as a source of funds; payments to the owners in the form of dividends are reflected as a use of funds.

● *Sale of fixed assets.* Transactions involving the acquisition and use of long-lived assets have been covered in our illustration. We have seen that the acquisition of new productive capacity in the form of long-lived assets represents the use of resources during the period and is so reflected in the resource flow statement. On the other hand, the use of the facilities, as reflected through the recognition of depreciation expense, does not affect cash or working capital, and thus it is not a source or use of funds. But how would we treat the disposition of a fixed asset? In measuring net income for the period, we calculate a gain or loss on the disposition of the asset as the difference between the proceeds of sale and the unexpired cost of the asset at the time of sale. For purposes of preparing a resource flow statement, however, the effect on cash (and working capital) is determined by the proceeds of sale; the amount of gain or loss calculated for income measurement purposes is generally not relevant. Therefore, the resource flow statement will reflect as a source of resources during a period the total proceeds received on the disposition (sale) of any long-lived asset, and net income must be adjusted to exclude the effect of the gain or loss.

Preparation of Resource Flow Statements from the Statement of Financial Position and the Income Statement

Throughout our discussion of the construction of a resource flow statement, the financial position worksheet (and thus the details of each individual transaction) was always in the background as a reinforcing source of information. While we did not draw heavily on the information contained in this worksheet in the latter part of our development, it did provide some data that we were looking for. But it is possible to construct a reasonably accurate resource flow statement from the information contained in the other two major financial statements. How is this done? Primarily, it is accomplished by examining each account in the statement of financial position other than those included in the resource base that is our focal point (i.e., cash or working capital), determining the change in the balance of the account over the period, and then inferring the broad class, or classes, of activity that would generate such a change.

We can illustrate this notion by considering a few of the accounts and the manner in which they would be analyzed. For example, if the resource flow statement that we are attempting to construct is based on working capital, we would exclude all of the current assets and current liabilities from our analysis. That is, we would look at each of the noncurrent accounts (fixed assets, long-term liabilities, and owners' equity) and try to explain the source of the change in each of the account balances. In our example, we would have observed that office-warehouse facilities increased over the period from a zero balance to a balance of $125,000. In the absence of any additional information, we would infer that this change represented acquisitions of new long-lived assets. Of course, we would be wrong in our inference to the extent that there were some dispositions of long-lived assets during the period. One way that our initial inference can be further tested is to analyze the change in the accumulated depreciation account. Since the amount of depreciation expense is generally reflected in the income statement, one can determine whether or not this account was reduced during the period as the result of dispositions of assets. But, as with all inferences, it is not always possible to be certain. Thus, to the extent that there were dispositions of long-lived assets during the period, that fact would not be reflected in the resource flow statement and the amount of new acquisitions would be understated by the same amount.

The mortgage payable account provides yet another example. The change in this account from the beginning to the end of the period was $75,000. One would, therefore, infer that a new source of funds in the amount of $75,000 was derived from the issuance of a mortgage, which in this case is correct. However, if there were activity in the account during the period of both a positive and a negative type, this activity would not be detected by examining only beginning and ending balances. In general, one analyzes each of the accounts of a noncurrent type, and after the reason for the change in the balance has been explained satisfactorily, a reasonably accurate resource flow statement may be prepared.

Status of Resource Flow Statements in Present Corporate Financial Reporting

Although the resource flow statement has long been recognized as a source of potentially useful information for external decision makers, until recently its inclusion in the set of financial statements regularly presented to investors was at the option of management. However, current accounting policy requires that a resource flow statement be presented along with the statement of financial position and the income statement.

The terminology employed in resource flow statements has, in the past, varied widely among companies and among accountants. One term frequently used in the past for the statement itself was "funds statement," which was based upon the notion that the statement analyzed the flow of funds, where "funds" had the same meaning that we attribute to "resources." Funds were interpreted as cash, working capital, or some other resource base. However, as noted earlier, current accounting policy recommends that this statement be titled "statement of changes in financial position." This recommendation is based, in part, upon the broad concept that is attributed to the statement— certain noncash or non-working capital transactions (such as the acquisition of the stock of one company for the stock of the acquiring company) should have resource flows imputed to them. This is, of course, the same reasoning that we used in our example in imputing equal two-way resource flows in the situation where office-warehouse facilities were acquired for both cash and a mortgage note.

Although the accounting policy-setting body (in this case the APB) did recommend specifically on the title of the statement, it recognized the need for flexibility in form, content, and terminology of the statement. Thus, you will encounter in current practice resource flow statements that vary in their appearance as well as in the resource base selected for analyzing the resource flows. But the substance of the statements will be congruent with the basic principles developed in this chapter.

Questions for Review and Discussion

15-1. Define:

a. Current assets

b. Current liabilities

c. Working capital

15-2. Explain briefly how a company earning a substantial annual income can become financially "embarrassed," that is, not be able to pay its obligations when due. Does this mean that income is really not a useful index of performance?

15-3. The APB recently recommended that the resource flow statement be titled "statement of changes in financial position." In what sense does a cash flow statement depict changes in financial position other than changes in the cash account? What kinds of changes in other elements of financial position are ignored altogether in a cash flow statement?

15-4. Both cash and working capital are often chosen as the basis for resource flow statements. What advantage(s) does each basis offer, if any?

15-5. Describe the steps that you would follow in constructing (1) a cash flow statement and (2) a working capital flow statement based on the enterprise's transactions for a period (using a financial position worksheet as a source of data).

15-6. Describe the steps that you would follow in constructing (1) a cash flow statement and (2) a working capital flow statement based on the relationship between income and resource flows.

15-7. Contrast the cash flow statement with the cash receipts and disbursements statement.

15-8. In depicting flows of resources *other than from operations,* resource flows are often imputed where no physical flow of resources (cash or working capital) actually took place. Explain why this is done.

15-9. An increase in merchandise inventory (usually considered a working capital account) is also an increase in working capital. However, "increase in merchandise" would never appear as a source of working capital on the working capital flow statement. Explain.

15-10. Working capital flow from operations is much more similar to operating income than is cash flow from operations. Do you agree or disagree? Explain your position.

15-11. Early in the chapter, depreciation expense was ignored in arriving at cash and working capital flows from operations. Later, depreciation expense was explicitly used to derive cash and working flows from operations. Is this a fundamental inconsistency in our presentation? Why or why not?

15-12. What advantages, if any, are there to determining resource flows from operations starting with operating income rather than reviewing the transactions of the enterprise for the period?

15-13. Working capital flows from operations would equal net operating income were it not for certain items entering into the calculation of net operating income. Name some typical items of this sort. Explain their treatment in deriving working capital flow from operations from the operating income figure.

15-14. In general, would you expect working capital provided by operations to tend to be greater than, equal to, or less than net operating income? Defend your position. Can you take the same kind of position with respect to the relative sizes of operating income and cash flow from operations?

15-15. In deriving cash flow from operations from the net operating income figure, changes in current assets and liabilities are added to, or subtracted from, operating income. Are such changes therefore sources or uses of cash *per se?* In what sense can such items be considered sources or uses of cash? Give examples and explain.

Exercises

15-1. Preparing Resource Flow Statements from a Financial Position Worksheet. A worksheet describing the first year of operations of a new business is shown in Exhibit 15-18.

Required:

1. Prepare a cash receipts and disbursements statement for 1974.

2. Prepare a 1974 income statement.

3. Prepare a 1974 cash flow statement based on an analysis of transactions.

4. Prepare a 1974 working capital flow statement based on an analysis of transactions.

15-2. Calculating Resource Flows from Operations.   The following information was taken from the financial statements of Calendar Company for 1971–74.

	December 31, 1971	December 31, 1972	December 31, 1973	December 31, 1974
Cash	$ 5,000	$12,000	$14,000	$ 6,000
Accounts receivable	8,000	10,000	6,000	14,000
Inventory	12,000	9,000	12,000	16,000
Prepaid insurance	—0—	—0—	2,000	1,000
	$25,000	$31,000	$34,000	$37,000
Accounts payable	$ 5,000	$ 7,000	$12,000	$ 8,000
Accrued wages payable	—0—	—0—	3,000	2,000
	$ 5,000	$ 7,000	$15,000	$10,000
Working capital	$20,000	$24,000	$19,000	$27,000
Net income for year ending on indicated date	$10,000	$15,000	$18,000	$20,000
Depreciation expense for year ending on indicated date	$ 3,000	$ 4,000	$ 4,000	$ 5,000

Required:

For each of the years 1972, 1973, and 1974, and for the three-year period ended December 31, 1974, prepare a computation of the following:

(a) Working capital flow from operations

(b) Cash flow from operations

15-3. Transaction Analysis and Resource Flow Statements.   Using the worksheet shown in Exhibit 15-19, satisfy the following requirements:

1. Prepare a cash flow statement for the period based on an analysis of transactions affecting the cash account.

2. Prepare a working capital flow statement based on an analysis of transactions affecting the working capital accounts.

Exhibit 15-18

HOBIE'S BUS COMPANY
Financial Position Worksheet—1974

Description	Cash	Bus	Accumulated Depreciation	Accounts Receivable	Supplies Inventory	Accounts Payable	Notes Payable	Owners' Equity
Initial investment by owners	6,000							6,000
Purchased bus for $2,500 cash and $5,000 note	(2,500)	7,500					5,000	
Cash fares	12,000							12,000 (R)
Credit fares				5,000				5,000 (R)
Payment of one-year insurance premium	(1,000)							(1,000)(E)
Wages paid	(7,500)							(7,500)(E)
Customer payments	2,000			(2,000)				
Supplies purchased					2,000	2,000		
Payments to suppliers	(500)					(500)		
Payment of principal and interest on note	(1,300)						(1,000)	(300)(E)
Supplies used					(1,600)			(1,600)(E)
Repairs and maintenance paid	(1,800)							(1,800)(E)
Depreciation expense			(1,200)					(1,200)(E)
Withdrawal	(3,600)							(3,600)(W)
Balances, Dec. 31, 1974	1,800	7,500	(1,200)	3,000	400	1,500	4,000	6,000

15-4. Preparing Resource Flow Statements from Other Financial Statements.
The financial statements for Umunhum Corporation for 1974 are as follows:

	December 31, 1973	December 31, 1974
Cash	$ 100,000	$ 200,000
Accounts receivable	350,000	600,000
Inventory	800,000	1,200,000
Land	750,000	1,000,000
Buildings and equipment	2,500,000	3,000,000
Accumulated depreciation—		
Buildings and equipment	(500,000)	(700,000)
	$4,000,000	$5,300,000
Accounts payable	$ 500,000	$ 800,000
Bonds payable	1,000,000	500,000
Owners' equity:		
Capital stock	1,000,000	2,000,000
Retained earnings	1,500,000	2,000,000
	$4,000,000	$5,300,000
Sales		$8,000,000
Expenses:		
Cost of sales	$4,800,000	
Depreciation expense	200,000	
Other operating expenses	2,300,000	7,300,000
Net income for 1974		$ 700,000

Required:

From the information contained in these statements, and making any assumptions
that are necessary, prepare the following:

(a) A working capital flow statement

(b) A cash flow statement

15-5. Calculating Resource Flows from Operations.   The financial statements
of the Greenstone Company contained the following information for 1972, 1973,
and 1974.

	December 31, 1974	December 31, 1973	December 31, 1972
Cash	$15,000	$20,000	$10,000
Accounts receivable	30,000	20,000	25,000
Inventory	40,000	35,000	30,000
	$85,000	$75,000	$65,000
Accounts payable	30,000	20,000	25,000
Working capital	$55,000	$55,000	$40,000
Net income for year	$45,000	$50,000	$40,000
Depreciation expense for year	$15,000	$12,000	$10,000

Exhibit 15-19

BUENA VISTA ENTERPRISES
Financial Position Worksheet—1974

Description	Cash	Accounts Receivable	Mer-chandise	Prepaid Rent	Equip-ment	Accumulated Depre-ciation—Equipment	Accounts Payable	Wages Payable	Interest Payable	Mortgage Payable	Owners' Equity
Beginning Position	1,500	1,000	2,500	200	6,000	(1,500)	1,750	—0—	100	3,000	4,850
Cash sales	1,300										1,300 (R)
Purchased merchandise on credit			500				500				
Credit sales		2,000									2,000 (R)
Paid rent in advance	(100)			100							
Receipts from customers	2,500	(2,500)									
Payments to suppliers	(1,000)						(1,000)				
Purchased equipment	(500)				1,000					500	
Credit sales		1,500									1,500 (R)
Paid wages	(700)										(700)(E)
Paid advertising	(300)										(300)(E)
Paid interest owing	(100)								(100)		
Purchased merchandise with cash	(200)		200								
Depreciation of equip-ment						(800)					(800)(E)
Merchandise used			(900)								(900)(E)
Rent expense for period				(150)							(150)(E)
Accrued wages								200			(200)(E)
Interest expense for period (not paid)									80		(80)(E)
Contribution by owner	2,000										2,000
Ending Position	4,400	2,000	2,300	150	7,000	(2,300)	1,250	200	80	3,500	8,520

Required:

1. Prepare a schedule of working capital flow from operations for each of the years 1973 and 1974 and for the two-year period ended December 31, 1974.

2. Prepare a schedule of cash flow from operations for the same periods as in number 1 above.

15-6. Resource Flow Concepts and Relationships.   The statement of changes in financial position from the 1972 annual report of the National Cash Register Company and its subsidiaries is shown in Exhibit 15-20.   The statement is based on the working capital concept of financial resources. With reference to the statement, where appropriate, satisfy the following requirements:

1. Is depreciation a source of working capital? Explain why depreciation appears in the statement under the section headed "Working capital was provided by."

2. From the information in the statement, estimate the amount of cash flow *from operations* experienced by NCR in 1972. Show your work.

3. Explain *in words* the significance in deriving cash flow from operations of the increase in the working capital liability entitled "Customers' deposits and service prepayments."

15-7. Transaction Analysis and Resource Flow Statements.   Based on an analysis of the transactions and events appearing in the financial position worksheet shown in Exhibit 15-21, satisfy the following requirements:

1. Prepare an income statement for the period.

2. Prepare a statement of cash receipts and disbursements.

3. Prepare a cash flow statement.

4. Prepare a working capital flow statement.

15-8. Preparing a Statement of Resource Flows from Other Statements.   Following is the financial position of the Hebert Medical Clinic at December 31, 1973 and 1974.

	December 31, 1973	December 31, 1974
Cash	$ 40,000	$ 45,000
Accounts receivable	80,000	70,000
Inventory	20,000	25,000
Equipment and furnishings	100,000	125,000
Accumulated depreciation— Equipment and furnishings	(40,000)	(55,000)
	$200,000	$210,000
Accounts payable	$ 15,000	$ 18,000
Accrued wages payable	5,000	2,000
8% notes payable, due 6/30/78	50,000	—0—
Owners' equity:		
Capital stock	100,000	140,000
Retained earnings	30,000	50,000
	$200,000	$210,000

During 1974 the clinic reported a net income of $110,000. (*Problem 15-8 continues on p. 533.*)

Exhibit 15-20

THE NATIONAL CASH REGISTER COMPANY
AND SUBSIDIARY COMPANIES

Changes in Financial Position

	1972	*1971* *
Working capital was provided by:		
Net income (loss) for the year	$(59,612,000)	$ 2,131,000
Depreciation:		
Property, plant, and equipment	52,466,000	54,584,000
Rental equipment	89,473,000	89,036,000
	$141,939,000	$143,620,000
Sale of property, plant, and equipment	23,939,000	4,246,000
Sale of rental equipment	22,528,000	13,230,000
Write-down of tooling, machinery, and equipment	22,205,000	—
Sale of common stock	13,568,000	12,383,000
Proceeds from debentures and mortgages	30,898,000	40,502,000
Increase in minority interests	4,643,000	3,521,000
	$200,108,000	$219,633,000
Working capital was used for:		
Cash dividends to stockholders	$ 9,456,000	$ 16,299,000
Expenditures for:		
Property, plant, and equipment	59,784,000	58,538,000
Rental equipment	93,019,000	108,013,000
	$152,803,000	$166,551,000
Future income tax benefits	76,068,000	—
Investment in Computer Peripherals, Inc.	31,494,000	—
Reduction of long-term debt	29,111,000	16,681,000
Other	583,000	(1,007,000)
	$299,515,000	$198,524,000
Net increase (decrease) in working capital	$(99,407,000)	$ 21,109,000
Analysis of changes in working capital:		
Increase (decrease) in current assets		
Cash and short-term investments	$(51,234,000)	$102,116,000
Accounts receivable	48,735,000	(73,703,000)
Inventories	(73,265,000)	(47,135,000)
Future tax benefits (current portion)	6,372,000	37,808,000
Prepaid expenses	(4,300,000)	1,360,000
	$(73,692,000)	$ 20,446,000
Increase (decrease) in current liabilities		
Notes payable	$(13,631,000)	$(26,696,000)
Payables and accruals	36,909,000	6,661,000
Accrued taxes	(4,616,000)	2,062,000
Customers' deposits and service prepayments	7,053,000	17,310,000
	$ 25,715,000	$ (663,000)
Net increase (decrease) in working capital	$(99,407,000)	$ 21,109,000

* Restated principally for a change in inventory valuation from a LIFO to a FIFO method.

Exhibit 15-21

BAINBRIDGE DISTRIBUTING COMPANY, INCORPORATED
Financial Position Worksheet——1974

Description	Cash	Accounts Receivable	Merchandise Inventory	Machinery and Equipment*	Buildings*	Land	Accounts Payable	Mortgage Notes Payable	Owners' Equity
Beginning Position	20,000	63,000	56,000	79,000	93,000	35,000	47,000	25,000	274,000
Purchase of inventory for sale			121,000				121,000		
Revenue from sales	26,000	265,000							291,000 (R)
Wages paid	(86,000)								(86,000) (E)
Collections of accounts receivable	256,000	(256,000)							
Payments of accounts payable	(136,000)						(136,000)		
Dividends paid	(10,000)								(10,000) (D)
Miscellaneous expenses (heat, light, taxes, etc.)	(29,000)								(29,000) (E)
Equipment purchased	(10,000)			30,000				20,000	
Equipment depreciation				(14,000)					(14,000) (E)
Buildings depreciation					(7,000)				(7,000) (E)
Advertising	(18,000)								(18,000) (E)
Cost of goods sold			(116,000)						(116,000) (E)
Paid interest on note payable	(1,500)								(1,500) (E)
Ending Position	11,500	72,000	61,000	95,000	86,000	35,000	32,000	45,000	283,500

* Balances are net of accumulated depreciation.

(Problem 15-8 cont.)

Required:

From the information contained in these statements, and making any assumptions that are logical and necessary, prepare a *working capital* flow statement *and* the supporting schedule of changes in working capital elements for the year 1974.

15-9. Resource Flow Concepts and Relationships.   Exhibit 15-22 shows the statement of source and use of funds from the 1970 annual report of Armco Steel Corporation. For purposes of this statement, Armco has used the term *funds* (resources) as a synonym for *cash plus marketable securities*. Referring to the statement, complete the following requirements:

1. Explain how each of the following items appearing in the statement may be considered a "source" or a "use" of cash:

   (a) Increase in accounts payable and accruals

   (b) Increase in accounts and notes receivable

2. Do you agree with Armco that the $140,193,000 shown on the statement as

Exhibit 15-22   ARMCO STEEL CORPORATION
Source and Use of Funds
For the years ended December 31, 1970 and 1969 (Dollars in thousands)

	1970	1969
Source of Funds		
Operations		
Net income for the year	$ 56,153	$ 95,674
Depreciation	66,033	64,693
Lease right amortization	13,981	9,691
Deferred income taxes	7,955	13,666
Equity in net income of unconsolidated subsidiaries	(3,929)	(437)
Total	$140,193	$183,287
Proceeds from debentures and long-term notes payable	233,848	56,068
Increase in current notes payable	25,888	24,729
Increase in accounts payable and accruals	5,088	24,950
Increase in other liabilities	3,921	2,722
Decrease (increase) in investments	1,318	(29,883)
Other—net	4,443	(788)
Total	$414,699	$261,085
Use of Funds		
Capital expenditures	$182,899	$122,883
Payments on long-term debt	149,597	7,196
Cash dividends	54,889	46,476
Increase in inventories	25,379	45,806
Increase in accounts and notes receivable	20,154	36,161
Payments on long-term lease obligations	5,900	4,825
Purchase of common stock for treasury	—	9,511
Total	$438,818	$272,858
Decrease in Cash and Marketable Securities for Year	$ 24,119	$ 11,773
Cash and Marketable Securities		
Beginning of year	53,365	65,138
End of year	$ 29,246	$ 53,365

the total "funds" provided by operations is indeed the amount of current cash (plus marketable securities) generated by operations during 1970? If so, why? If not, what amount should be shown? Show your work.

3. What items, if any, appearing on Armco's 1970 statement would have been omitted if Armco had prepared a statement of funds based on the working capital concept of funds instead of the cash (plus marketable securities) concept? If you indicate that any items would be omitted, explain why.

4. Explain why in the given statement "Net income for the year" is increased by the amount of "Deferred income taxes" and decreased by the amount of "Equity in net income of unconsolidated subsidiaries" in arriving at the $140,-193,000 figure for funds provided by operations.

15-10. Resource Flows from Operations.   The financial position of Teton Village Restaurant, Inc., at December 31, 1973 and 1974, is as follows.

	December 31, 1973	December 31, 1974
Cash	$ 4,000	$ 2,000
Inventory	8,000	7,000
Land	20,000	20,000
Building and equipment	40,000	50,000
Accumulated depreciation—		
Building and equipment	(12,000)	(15,000)
	$60,000	$64,000
Accounts payable	$ 6,000	$ 2,000
Mortgage payable	25,000	30,000
Owners' equity:		
Capital stock	20,000	25,000
Retained earnings	9,000	7,000
	$60,000	$64,000

During 1974 Teton Village Restaurant, Inc., reported a net income of $12,000.

Required:

1. Prepare a schedule of the changes in working capital elements during 1974 (*not a working capital flow statement*).

2. Prepare a computation of estimated working capital flow from operations for 1974. (Make necessary assumptions explicit.)

3. Prepare a computation of estimated cash flow from operations for 1974.

4. In addition to the cash flow from operations, indicate the nature *and* amount of—

   (a) *One* additional source of cash during 1974.

   (b) *One* additional use of cash during 1974.

15-11. Preparing Resource Flow Statements from Other Financial Statements and Supplemental Information.   The financial statements for the Whitten Manufacturing Company are as follows (000s omitted).

	12/31/74	12/31/73
Current assets:		
Cash	$ 15	$ 20
Accounts receivable	30	25
Inventory	60	50
Prepaid expenses	5	10
	$110	$105
Property, plant, and equipment (net)	330	295
	$440	$400
Current liabilities:		
Accounts payable	$ 20	$ 25
Accrued expenses	15	10
Estimated income taxes payable	30	25
	$ 65	$ 60
Owners' equity:		
Capital stock	$240	$220
Retained earnings	135	120
	$375	$340
	$440	$400

Income Statement for 1974

Net Sales	$480
Cost of sales	330
Gross profit	$150
Operating expenses (including depreciation of 10)	75
Net income before taxes	$ 75
Provision for federal income taxes	35
Net income	$ 40

Required:

1. Compute the amount of dividends that were declared and paid during the year, the value of equipment purchased during the year, and the value at which capital stock was sold during the year.

2. Prepare a working capital flow statement.

3. Prepare a cash flow statement.

15-12. Preparing a Statement of Resource Flows from Other Statements.
The financial position of Bulloch Wine and Spirits, Inc., at December 31, 1973 and 1974 follows.

	December 31, 1973	December 31, 1974
Cash	$ 25,000	$ 21,000
Accounts receivable	15,000	12,000
Inventory	40,000	50,000
Display equipment	25,000	40,000
Accumulated depreciation—		
Display equipment	(5,000)	(8,000)
Delivery truck		6,000
Accumulated depreciation—		
Delivery truck		(1,000)
	$100,000	$120,000
Accounts payable	$ 30,000	$ 25,000
10% notes payable, due 9/30/77		10,000
Owners' equity:		
Capital stock	50,000	60,000
Retained earnings	20,000	25,000
	$100,000	$120,000

Required:

The corporation reported a net income of $25,000 for 1974. From the information presented and making any assumptions that are logical and necessary, prepare a *cash flow statement* for the year 1974.

15-13. Resource Flow Concepts and Relationships. Exhibit 15-23 shows the statement of changes in financial position from the 1972 annual report of United Brands Company and Subsidiary Companies.

Required:

1. The 1972 statement of changes in financial position is based on the working capital concept of "resources." Recast this statement based on the "cash" concept of resources, that is, prepare a cash flow statement. Isolate the cash flow from operations in the recast statement.

2. Did the changes in "marketable securities" and "long-term debt due within one year" enter into your calculation of cash flow from operations? Explain why or why not.

3. "Extraordinary items" appear on the 1972 income statement at $6,971, but on the given 1972 statement of changes in financial position at $28,906. Give a *probable, general* explanation.

Exhibit 15-23   UNITED BRANDS COMPANY AND SUBSIDIARY COMPANIES
Consolidated Statement of Changes in Financial Position
(In thousands)

Year Ended December 31,
1972

Working capital provided by:
Income before extraordinary items	$ 10,737
Add depreciation ($31,135) and other charges not requiring working capital	31,960
Total from operations	$ 42,697
Extraordinary items of $6,971 in 1972	28,906
Proceeds from long-term borrowings	44,819
Other sources	14,413
	$130,835

Working capital applied to:
Additions of property, plant, and equipment	$ 58,690
Retirement of long-term debt	18,379
Investment in Foster Grant Co., Inc.	24,849
Additions of intangible assets	677
Dividends	2,142
Other uses	41
	$104,778
Increase in working capital	26,057
Working capital at beginning of year	157,795
Working capital at end of year	$183,852

Increases (decreases) in *working capital* are as follows:
Cash	$ (2,620)
Due from banks	—
Marketable securities	15,143
Receivables	27,558
Inventories, growing crops, materials, and supplies	5,399
Prepaid expenses	(596)
Total	$ 44,884
Notes and loans payable to banks	(14,486)
Accounts payable and accrued liabilities	5,114
Long-term debt due within one year	(7,063)
U.S. and foreign income taxes	(2,392`)
Total	$(18,827)
Increase in working capital	$ 26,057

16

Dissemination and Content of
Corporate Financial Reports

Corporate financial reports are the end product of the accounting data accumulation process (the accounting information system) and the set of accounting measurement rules selected from the alternatives examined in previous chapters. These reports are distributed to many external decision makers with an interest in the corporation through a variety of communication channels. The purpose of this chapter is to describe the nature of this public dissemination process for corporate financial information, and to review briefly some general considerations relating to use of the information.

INFORMATION DISSEMINATION
(THE REPORTING PROCESS)

The ultimate objective of financial accounting is the dissemination of relevant financial information on a timely basis to interested external parties. The reporting process is a complex one, involving a variety of reporting formats and numerous legal requirements. While the financial statements *per se* contain the core information that is transmitted, they are not the sole vehicles. The financial statements included in the annual (and often quarterly) reports of corporations are, when issued, usually accompanied by a large amount of supporting statistics and explanatory information. In addition, selected pieces of information that are eventually included in the financial statements (for example, sales and net income) are often communicated on a more timely basis through media other than the annual reports. In this section, we will try first to provide some perspective on the various types of information that are made available and contrast some of the important properties of this information. Next, we will move to consider ways in which this package of financial information can presumably be used by the decision maker.

Some Typical Reports to External Parties

• *Annual financial reports.* A corporation receives a charter to do business from a state, and one of the responsibilities often imposed by law on that corporation is to report at least annually to the shareholders. This accountability obligation often includes the distribution of copies of the corporation's annual financial report to each of the shareholders. Besides this general statutory responsibility, if the corporation's shares are listed and traded on an organized stock exchange, such as the New York Stock Exchange (NYSE), additional requirements may be imposed. For example, a corporation listed on the New York Stock Exchange must submit its annual financial report to shareholders not later than 120 days following the end of its fiscal year, or 30 days prior to the annual stockholders' meeting, whichever comes first.

The content of the annual financial report will vary among corporations, but for corporations that are "publicly held," certain inclusions have evolved as a matter of law, listing requirements and/or accounting policy. The corporate financial report will typically include three primary statements: (1) a statement of financial position, (2) an income statement, and (3) a statement of changes in financial position (resource flows). As an integral part of these financial reports, there will be a number of "notes" appended to the statements. The notes contain important explanatory information that enables the reader to understand the underlying economic circumstances and the related accounting policy choices that have been made in arriving at certain monetary representations in the financial statements. Corporations will also often include five- or ten-year summaries of selected financial statistics so that the reader will have a time-based perspective on the current figures (NYSE-listed companies are required to provide at least a five-year summary). If the financial statements are attested to (audited) by an independent certified public accountant (as are most of the financial reports of large publicly held corporations), the auditor's opinion will be included in the annual report. This audit opinion normally covers most of the accounting representations of the corporation described above. (Chapter 17 is an introduction to the attest function as it applies to present-day financial reporting.)

The corporation's annual report often includes not only financial statement information but also descriptive information about its activities and product lines, as well as some summary comments and prognostications by the chief executive officer of the corporation. Frequently, a summary of the financial information included in the financial statements will be presented in the form of an unaudited "financial review."

As an illustration, the financial statement information included in the 1973 annual report of Burroughs Corporation is reproduced in the Appendix to this chapter.

• *Interim financial reports.* The information contained in the annual financial report is probably the most complete package of financial data that is given to the shareholder and other interested external parties. Thus, annually, the decision maker can use this information to evaluate that particular business enterprise and reconsider his objectives. It may be useful, however, to have more current readings on the financial progress of a corporation. Such readings are provided by *interim financial statements.*

Typically, interim financial statements are submitted to shareholders quarterly (a requirement for most corporations listed on major securities exchanges) and are restricted to financial statement information only—they do not include the more elaborate discussion of the corporation's activities that is included in the annual report. Because the time period involved is shorter, additional measurement problems exist (for example, the impact of seasonal activity), and as a result the reports are generally considered somewhat less reliable (less objective) than the annual reports. While improvements have recently been made in the methods of adapting the conventional accounting model to these quarterly time periods, the inevitable consequence of the shortened time period on the reliability of the reports means that the decision maker may find it advantageous to make additional adjustments in using the information to predict the future cash-generating ability of the business. Yet, the trade-off between timeliness and reliability seems increasingly in favor of more frequent reporting.

• *SEC reporting.* Besides the annual financial reports that are sent to shareholders and certain other interested parties, such as security analysts, the Securities and Exchange Commission also requires that all corporations subject to its jurisdiction file audited annual reports with the commission. These annual reports are filed on Form 10-K (and are usually referred to in the financial community as 10-Ks). The SEC 10-K report includes financial information that is similar to that included in the annual financial report to shareholders, but it also includes some additional information. In general, the additional information expands upon the amount of detail included in a typical annual report. For example, the corporation may report sales and expenses by certain "product lines" in its 10-K, while the same information is usually reported in aggregated form in the annual financial report. Thus, if the external investor wishes to probe more deeply into the diverse activities of a corporation, it may be useful for him to obtain a copy of the 10-K annual report. The 10-K report is a document of public record and may be obtained at SEC offices (as well as at selected quasi-public repositories, such as the NYSE library). At least one commercial financial service makes available, on a subscription basis, copies of 10-Ks and other filings with the SEC.

In addition to the 10-K report that corporations file annually with the SEC, there are several other types of filings of financial information that are triggered by specified corporation activities. For example, if a corporation (under SEC jurisdiction) plans to make a public offering of a new stock issue, it must file on a registration statement (Form S-1) an extensive description of its financial and economic affairs (including the prospectus it plans to issue offering the shares to the public). The SEC explicitly disclaims any endorsement of the value of the stock issue, leaving this assessment of the company's future prospects to the prospective investor; but the commission does attempt to monitor the accuracy of the factual representations included in the prospectus and other promotional material. Another SEC filing that is made by "widely held" public companies is the unaudited quarterly financial report (Form 10-Q). Thus, for the investor who is prepared and able to seek out and obtain the reports on file with the commission, a considerable amount of information is publicly available.

● *News announcements.* Along with the formal financial statements included in the annual and interim financial reports sent to shareholders, and the annual 10-K report and other reports filed with the SEC, corporations also release selected financial information at various times throughout the year through the financial press. The large publicly held corporations whose securities are listed on national exchanges are actually required to release certain financial information to the press and newswire services as soon as it is accurately measured. In this sense such information is always assumed to have significant newsworthiness. Typically, this information consists of data on sales and earnings for the quarter or the year. An example of this type of information dissemination is presented in Exhibit 16-1. While these news announce-

Exhibit 16-1   ILLUSTRATIVE CORPORATION NEWS RELEASE

From
BURROUGHS CORPORATION
Detroit, Michigan 48232

FOR IMMEDIATE RELEASE
April 10, 1974

BURROUGHS REPORTS 31 PERCENT INCREASE IN
EARNINGS ON AN 18 PERCENT INCREASE IN REVENUE.
ORDERS CONTINUE VERY STRONG IN FIRST QUARTER.

Ray W. Macdonald, Chairman of the Board of Burroughs Corporation, today reported record earnings and revenue for the first quarter of 1974.

Net operating earnings for the quarter were $21,376,000, a 31 percent increase over the 1973 quarter operating earnings of $16,346,000. Net earnings per share were 55 cents on 38,961,516 average shares outstanding. Operating earnings for the first quarter of 1973 were 43 cents on 38,004,880 average shares outstanding. Earnings per share reflect the 2-for-1 stock split effective March 29, 1974.

Last year's first quarter earnings also had an additional 6 cents per share capital gain which was realized from the sale of securities.

Estimated U.S. and foreign income taxes for the 1974 first quarter were $17,490,000, compared with $14,415,000 in the 1973 first quarter.

Operating revenue for the first quarter reached $322,797,000, an 18 percent increase compared with $274,435,000 in the 1973 quarter.

Macdonald stated that incoming orders for the first quarter continued last year's strong performance, both Overseas and in the United States, registering a 28 percent increase over the 1973 first quarter. Worldwide backlogs continued to build and were 11 percent higher than the beginning of the year position.

# # #

Corporate Public Relations

Exhibit 16-2   ILLUSTRATIVE COMMERCIAL FINANCIAL SERVICE REPORT

BURROUGHS CORPORATION

LISTED	SYMBOL	INDICATED DIV.	RECENT PRICE	PRICE RANGE (1973)	YIELD
NYSE	BGH	$0.50	89	126 - 92	0.6%

AN EXPANDING PRODUCT RANGE AND BROADENING RENTAL BASE HAVE CONTRIBUTED A TO STRONG EARNINGS UPTREND. STOCK IS INVESTMENT GRADE.

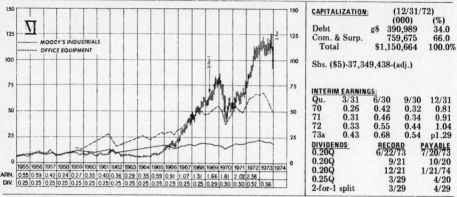

MOODY'S INDUSTRIALS
OFFICE EQUIPMENT

	1955	1956	1957	1958	1959	1960	1961	1962	1963	1964	1965	1966	1967	1968	1969	1970	1971	1972	1973	1974
EARN.	0.55	0.59	0.42	0.24	0.27	0.35	0.40	0.36	0.29	0.35	0.59	0.91	1.07	1.31	1.66	1.81	2.02	2.36		
DIV.	0.25	0.25	0.25	0.25	0.25	0.25	0.25	0.25	0.25	0.25	0.25	0.25	0.25	0.29	0.30	0.30	0.32	0.36		

CAPITALIZATION: (12/31/72)

		(000)	(%)
Debt	g$	390,989	34.0
Com. & Surp.		759,675	66.0
Total		$1,150,664	100.0%

Shs. ($5)-37,349,438-(adj.)

INTERIM EARNINGS:

Qu.	3/31	6/30	9/30	12/31
70	0.26	0.42	0.32	0.81
71	0.31	0.46	0.34	0.91
72	0.33	0.55	0.44	1.04
73a	0.43	0.68	0.54	p1.29

DIVIDENDS

	RECORD	PAYABLE
0.20Q	6/22/73	7/20/73
0.20Q	9/21	10/20
0.20Q	12/21	1/21/74
0.25Q	3/29	4/20
2-for-1 split	3/29	4/29

BACKGROUND:

Company is a leading producer of business equipment with a broad line which covers most major sectors of the data processing market. Products range from very small to giant systems. In addition, the Company offers a full range of peripherals, terminals and data entry equipment. Computer products are supported by an extensive library of application programs which are sold primarily to small users who do not have their own programming capability. Products are designed so that customers can easily move up to larger equipment as their needs expand. The business machines group accounted for 46% of 1972 revenues, international, 37%, defense, space and special systems, 9%, and business forms and supplies, 8%.

RECENT DEVELOPMENTS:

The Company extended its long uptrend in earnings in 1973. On a 22% rise in revenues to $1.28 bill., net income increased 30% to $113.4 mill. The Company's order rate was strong and trended upward throughout the year. All product groups participated in the improvement. Orders for large and medium size electronic data processing systems rose 28%; orders for small EDP systems, business mini-computers and small application machines were up 32% over 1972. Total worldwide backlogs were up 30% year-to-year.

PROSPECTS:

Burroughs is expected to continue to show good progress. Company objectives call for revenue growth of 15% annually which seems a realistic expectation. This represents a long term average, however, rather than a minimum expectation in a given year. An expanding product line combined with an effective research and development program should help achieve this goal. Earnings should rise somewhat faster than sales as the Company benefits increasingly from the economies of higher volume. The growing rental base adds a degree of stability.

STATISTICS:

YEAR	GROSS REVS. ($ MILL.)	OPER. PROFIT MARGIN %	NET INCOME ($ 000)	WORK CAP. ($ MILL.)	SENIOR CAPITAL ($ MILL.)	NO. SHS OUT (000)	EARN. PER SH. $	DIV. PER SH. $	DIV PAY %	PRICE RANGE	PRICE X EARN.	AVG YIELD %
64	390.2	6.5	10,212	136.1	95.3	29,568	0.35	0.25	70	$7^2 - 5^4$	18.5	3.9
65	456.7	8.9	17,528	130.0	91.8	29,540	0.59	0.25	42	$12^2 - 6^2$	16.1	2.6
66	489.7	13.2	a29,607	174.1	114.4	32,696	a0.91	0.25	28	$23^7 - 12^3$	19.7	1.4
67	550.6	13.2	34,831	175.6	116.9	32,800	1.07	0.25	24	$48 - 20^2$	32.1	0.7
68	650.8	15.3	43,301	210.0	212.5	33,038	1.31	0.25	19	$64^2 - 39^2$	39.4	0.5
69	751.8	16.6	55,199	196.0	236.2	34,464	1.66	0.29	17	$83^6 - 55^1$	41.8	0.4
70	884.6	19.1	66,542	283.9	352.1	36,716	1.81	0.30	17	$86^3 - 39^3$	34.7	0.5
71	932.7	17.8	74,151	338.2	383.4	36,990	2.02	0.30	15	$80^6 - 52^2$	32.8	0.5
72	1,040.8	16.5	87,541	410.3	391.0	37,349	2.36	0.32	13	$114^6 - 73$	39.9	0.3
p73	1,284.2		a113,415				2.94	0.36	12	$126^3 - 92$	37.1	0.3

Note: Adjusted for 2-for-1 stock splits 4/69, and 4/74. a-Excl. $1.3 mill. (4c a share) capital gain in 1966 and $2.5 mill. (7c a share) in 1973. g-Incl. $100.0 mill. debentures convertible into common at $79.50 a share.

TAX FREE IN PENNA.

INCORPORATED: Jan. 16, 1905—Michigan	**TRANSFER AGENT:**	Bankers Trust Co., New York National Bank, Detroit, Mich.	**OFFICERS**
PRINCIPAL OFFICE: Detroit, Mich. 48232			**CHAIRMAN:** R.W. MacDonald
ANNUAL MEETING: Fourth Wed. in March	**REGISTRAR:**	Morgan Guaranty Trust Co., N.Y. Detroit Bank & Tr. Co., Detroit, Mich.	**PRESIDENT:** P.S. Mirabito **SECRETARY:** K.L. Miller
NUMBER OF STOCKHOLDERS: 52,416	**INSTIT. HOLDINGS:**	NO.: 329 SHS.: 9,407,044	**TREASURER:** L.W. Bowen

Source: Moody's *Handbook of Common Stocks,* First Quarterly 1974 Edition.

ments contain highly aggregated data and primarily focus on revenue and earnings for the year, they are generally available up to thirty days prior to the release of the annual or interim reports and thus represent a more timely source of information for the external investor.

• *Financial services.* In addition to the information that is made publicly available by the corporation, the interested external investor may also have recourse to one or more of the several commercial financial services that tabulate information for a large number of corporations and compile it in an easily usable form. Such digests will normally include more detail than is contained in the news announcements released by the corporation, but less information than will be found in the quarterly and annual reports. An example of commercial financial service information is presented in Exhibit 16-2.

Comparative Summary of Characteristics of Reports

In this brief survey of the various types and forms of financial information available to the external investor, we have implicitly noted certain properties or characteristics of each of the reports. We have specifically commented on the timing of the release of the report, the scope of distribution, the comprehensiveness of the information contained in the report, and the formality of the report requirements. In Exhibit 16-3 these properties are summarized for each of the reports discussed. Although necessarily abbreviated, this comparative summary should provide a good introductory perspective on the corporate reporting process now in existence. We should note here that there is an abundant amount of other "nonaccounting" information about most listed corporations' activities and plans that is publicly available, and the external investor will often find this information relevant to his investment decision.

SOME CUSTOMARY WAYS OF RELATING CONTENT OF FINANCIAL REPORTS TO RESOURCE ALLOCATION DECISIONS

Now that we have briefly reviewed the types and sources of financial information that is made available to external decision makers through the corporate reporting process, we will consider the manner in which this total package of information might be used by the decision maker. In our brief examination of this matter, we will focus on the investment decision. This choice of emphasis is motivated by two factors. First, the investment decision is an important, pervasive, yet relatively definable kind of decision problem. And second, the information used in the analysis of investment alternatives typically includes a variety of measurements from the publicly available corporate annual report. As a result, the investment decision problem illustrates the decision relevance of the interrelated set of information included in the financial statements. In contrast to this use of publicly available information, the distribution of benefits decisions are more often specified by some legal or regulatory authority such that the information is specifically designed in accordance with the objectives of the particular distributional process.

COMPARATIVE SUMMARY OF
CHARACTERISTICS OF REPORTS

Exhibit 16-3

Reports / Characteristics	Annual Financial Reports	Interim Financial Reports	SEC Reports	News Announcements	Commercial Financial Services
Timing of release	Annually	Quarterly for larger corporations	10-K annually, 10-Q quarterly; other reports (e.g., Form S-1) when specified economic activities occur	At intervals throughout year (usually at least quarterly)	Usually monthly or quarterly, plus special reports
Scope of distribution	Shareholders (generally available to public on request)	Shareholders	SEC offices (available to public on request)	Newswire services; financial press	Available by subscription (and in many libraries)
Comprehensiveness of information	Extensive	Somewhat summarized	Most comprehensive source of information	Highly abbreviated	Somewhat summarized
Formality of report requirements	Relatively formal (compliance with generally accepted accounting principles)	Less formal than annual report	Highly formal (requirements imposed by SEC)	Few formal requirements	Based on source data formality

The Investment Decision Problem in Review

Prospective owners and creditors who supply capital to a business do so in return for expected future cash inflows. A creditor (e.g., the owner of a corporate bond) acquires contractual rights to specified future payments of interest and principal amounts. A purchaser of shares of corporate stock, on the other hand, acquires the right to share proportionately with all other shareholders in the residual cash flows generated by the corporation. To choose to invest in a particular business, both the creditor and the owner will presumably want to assess the present value (adjusted appropriately for risk) of the rights that come from the investment and compare that present value with the amount they will have to pay to receive those rights. They will then compare the net present values of investments in various businesses in determining the investment or set of investments they will undertake.

The nature of the decision to invest in a business is simple in principle. In practice, however, it is a formidable challenge. The process of arriving at present values, as described in Chapter 3, begins with the task of specifying the cash flows expected from an investment in future periods. Of course, other elements, such as selection of the appropriate time preference rate, are necessary as well. But the valuation of a particular investment opportunity cannot proceed without a projected stream of future cash flows on which to operate.

For the prospective owner, the task of projecting or forecasting future cash flows is quite open-ended. For the prospective creditor, the task is simplified somewhat, as the maximum cash flows from his investment are usually specified in a contract. On the other hand, in a world of uncertainty, both the creditor and the owner will want to assess the risk associated with expected future cash flows, because the greater the risk associated with a given expected future cash flow, the less it will be valued by either a creditor or an owner, other things equal. The necessity for risk assessment means that in addition to forecasting various potential future cash flows, thought must also be given to the likelihood that the forecast flows will or will not materialize. Thus investors face the task of looking into the future and making some fairly complex predictions or forecasts about the amounts and probabilities of the cash payments the enterprise will be able to make to them in fulfillment of their rights as owners or creditors.

The ultimate objective for the investor of this forecasting-analysis process is the selection of a portfolio of securities that has the optimum return to risk trade-off. A representative decision model for the investor therefore includes parameters (generally numerical measures) dealing with two major elements: (1) *expected return* (future cash flows), and (2) *expected risk*.

Estimating Investment Decision Parameters from Financial Statement Information

Use of information from corporate financial statements to estimate the two parameters of the investment decision is dependent upon the assumption that historical data are relevant to a meaningful formation of expectations. We have addressed this issue previously in developing the rationale for the conventional accounting model, but its importance to the investment decision problem justifies repetition here.

The notion that information about events and activities already experienced by an enterprise can be relevant to expectation formation is based upon an assumed continuity of events and activities engaged in by the enterprise. That is, although many aspects of an enterprise's activities (like its product lines, production processes, etc.) may change over time, many important aspects remain constant or change slowly. The immediate past provides a context in which to consider future possibilities. The farther various future possibilities depart from the immediate past, the less credible or probable they will seem.

This idea of continuity of events was then applied to the enterprise as a generator of cash flows. Assuming that there is some continuity in the cash-generating process, a portrayal of the enterprise's present "performance" in that process will presumably be relevant to investors who are interested in future cash flows. Thus, the conventional accounting performance measurement was developed in the context of representing the enterprise's long-run cash-generating ability. To the extent that these assumptions are valid, the financial statements obviously contain information relevant to the estimation of the expected return parameter. The estimation of the expected risk parameter is similarly dependent upon the assumption of the relevance of historical data. The particular data that are presumably useful to this estimation process will be discussed later in this section.

Before leaving the subject of using historical data as a basis for estimating the relevant decision parameters for the investment decision problem, we should briefly note recent developments in the finance literature suggesting possible limitations on this approach for the individual investor. In particular, the analysis of financial statements for an individual company is a manifestation of what is labeled "intrinsic value" analysis of investment opportunities. This same intrinsic value concept is also implicit in our categorization of the investment decision problem. A company that appears to be a good investment on the basis of an analysis of the information included in the financial statement is one whose intrinsic value is relatively high in relation to its current stock price, and a company that does not appear to be a desirable investment is one whose intrinsic value is low in relation to its current stock price. However, recent research on the efficiency of the capital markets suggests the possibility that the average individual investor *cannot* systematically identify investment opportunities that will enable him to earn consistently above-normal returns. That is, the research suggests that the prices established in the capital markets are already based on all available public information (which includes all publicly available financial statements), and the individual investor can do no better than to invest in a diversified portfolio with an appropriate (to him) risk level (as defined by market indicators of risk) and earn the market return for that level of risk. In this context, the investor accepts market prices as reasonable estimates of value and abstains from analysis of individual investments for purposes of seeking "bargain purchases."

Whether this "price-taking" posture is actually optimal for a given investor, however, depends upon a number of factors, including the market in which the investment is traded and the individual's personal assessment of his ability to evaluate information vis-à-vis the aggregate class of investors in that market (i.e., whether he has a comparative advantage in this type of activity). It seems reasonable to conclude, therefore, that though intrinsic value analysis is not an activity that should be engaged in by everyone, those who have (or believe they have) superior skills in estimating the intrinsic values of securities will act accordingly.

Developing Financial Statistics
from Financial Statements

Before considering the specific financial statistics that may be helpful in assessing the risk and return parameters for an investment alternative, we first need to consider some general properties of these financial statistics. The values (measurements in dollar terms) reflected in corporate financial reports represent in one sense merely "numbers" that have limited meaning and significance in and of themselves. Meaning and significance come from and depend upon an understanding of (1) the environmental context from which the numbers were drawn, (2) the relationship between the numbers and the underlying economic phenomena that are the real items of interest, (3) the relationship of any particular number or set of numbers to other numbers included in the statements, and (4) the relationships between the real economic phenomena that underlie the numerical relationships expressed in the statements.

Example 16-1   The High Profit Corporation reported net income for 1974 of $100,000. This measure in itself does provide some information to the investor in that it suggests a potential level of cash-generating ability that is relevant to his investment decision. However, the investor is interested in a broader, more comprehensive, measure of the corporation's performance as a basis for predicting future performance. In particular, given the amount of investment that the High Profit Corporation had in its productive facilities for the period, does the $100,000 represent good or bad performance? Additionally, how does the $100,000 reported profit stand compared with previous profits that the firm has generated or with profits or productivity by other firms in the same industry?

The unanswered questions raised in Example 16-1 suggest two important requirements of the investor's interpretive process: (1) the need for some type of *scaling* of the reported, unadjusted "numbers," and (2) the need for base figures, or *standards,* indicating performance over time and by similar companies (industry standards).

• *Need for scaling.* The process of "scaling" the numbers reported in the financial statements is a process of relating one number to another number based upon a presumably important relationship between the numbers. In Example 16-1 the implicit relationship alluded to in the first question is the relationship, or ratio, between the net income for the year and the investment required to generate this return. By combining these two measures in the form of a ratio, the investor generates a new measure indicating an important relationship—return on investment. More will be said about this particular ratio and others later.

• *Need for standards: time and industry.* In addition to developing the ratios alluded to above, the investor engaging in intrinsic analysis is interested in the relationship between numbers (or ratios) and some standard. Two standards are of general interest to investors—*time standards* and *industry standards*. Time standards merely call for the provision of the numbers (or ratios) from preceding time periods so that the investor can assess the progress of the firm in relationship to prior performance.

Example 16-2   Assuming investment is constant, if the High Profit Corporation had reported profits of $60,000 and $80,000 in 1972 and 1973, respectively, the $100,000 profit reported in 1974 suggests a continued improvement in the performance of the corporation *relative to its past performance*. On the other hand, if the reported profits for the preceding years had been $140,000 and $120,000, the investor would probably assess the desirability of an investment in High Profit Corporation in a much different light.

Because time standards are important in evaluating the reported numbers for any particular time period, present accounting policy calls for the inclusion of data from the immediately prior period in corporate financial reports. In many instances a corporation also reports selected numbers from prior financial statements for a period of five or ten years. (Recall that NYSE listing requirements call for inclusion of a five-year summary in the annual report.)

The other class of standards that is frequently useful in evaluating the overall attractiveness of an investment alternative is based on the performance of other business enterprises. In some cases, the standards are developed from the financial representations of all other corporations. More frequently, the standards represent norms developed from other corporations within the same industry.

Example 16-3   If the scaling alluded to earlier produced a measure of return on investment of 10 percent ($100,000 net income divided by $1 million investment in production facilities), the investor still needs additional information regarding the level of performance implicit in this measure. If the average performance in this industry were an 8 percent return on investment, the investor might conclude that the management of High Profit Corporation was performing better than the industry norm. On the other hand, if the average return on investment in the industry were 12 percent, the particular investment alternative might not seem as desirable.

Because of the importance of industry norms, commercial financial services make them available (at a price) to interested investors.

**Customary Statistical Measures (Indicators)
for Decision Parameters**

In analyzing the information provided in corporate financial reports, analysts have developed a number of statistical measures, or indicators, that they presumably use as a basis for reaching general estimates of the expected risk and return parameters. Rather than attempt to cover all of these various measures, which is better left to a more advanced course in accounting or finance, we will briefly consider a few of the more important indicators to illustrate the analysis procedure. These indicators will be grouped under the two decision parameters, risk and return, for purposes of exposition. However, the reader should be aware that some of the indicators often have implications for both of the decision parameters, and the specific way in which the various pieces of information are assembled and processed to arrive at estimates of the parameters is a complex and somewhat individualistic information-processing problem. The more competent the investor is in this processing of information, the more likely it is that intrinsic analysis of investment alternatives will represent a profitable use of his resources.

The various statistical measures will be illustrated using the data included in the simple financial statements reflected in Exhibit 16-4. Although these statements do not include data for preceding years, or draw upon the information contained in the resource-flow statement, they suffice for our exposition at this point. Selected exercises at the end of the chapter call for similar types of analyses to be applied to the more complete information contained in the actual financial statements for Burroughs Corporation included in the Appendix to this chapter.

• *Indicators of return.* The investor's principal interest in analyzing the returns of various investment alternatives is the comparative return efficiency of the alternatives. Hence investors are interested in several different indicators of return efficiency. The set of general statistical measures of return efficiency to be reviewed are (1) earnings per share and earnings yield, (2) net income to equity and/or assets, and (3) net income to sales.

EARNINGS PER SHARE (EPS) AND EARNINGS YIELD. One indication of potential return is the earnings that will accrue to the investor's benefit. Since the investor's interest in the corporation is typically reflected in terms of the number of shares he possesses relative to the total number of shares outstanding, an important measure of the performance of the company in terms of his interest, or potential interest, is provided by scaling the income in terms of total number of shares outstanding.

$$\text{Earnings per share} = \frac{\text{Net income}}{\text{Total shares outstanding}}$$

$$= \frac{\$390,000}{400,000}$$

$$= 97.5 \text{ cents per share}$$

EPS is the earnings attributable to each share of common stock, with the dividend requirements on any preferred stock (which does not share to any greater extent than the amount to which it has preference) deducted from net income in arriving at the income available to common stockholders.

To relate EPS more directly to the decision parameter of interest—expected return, EPS may be divided by the price of a share of stock. The resulting statistical measure represents the current "earnings yield" on the required monetary investment. Whether this potential yield needs to be further adjusted depends upon the dividend policy of the corporation and the investor's attitude toward the relative desirability of "paid out" and "retained" earnings.

NET INCOME TO EQUITY AND/OR ASSETS. As suggested in Example 16-1,

Exhibit 16-4

A MERCHANDISING COMPANY
Statement of Financial Position
As of December 31, 1974

Assets

Current assets:

Cash		$ 350,000	
Marketable securities at cost (market value, $542,000)		460,000	
Accounts receivable	$1,410,000		
Less allowance for bad debts	(70,000)	1,340,000	
Inventory (at lower of Fifo cost or market)		2,300,000	$4,450,000

Property, plant, and equipment:

Land		$ 300,000	
Buildings	$ 750,000		
Store equipment	375,000		
	$1,125,000		
Less accumulated depreciation	(200,000)	925,000	1,225,000
Total assets			$5,675,000

Liabilities and Shareholders' Equity

Current liabilities:

Accounts payable	$1,400,000	
Accrued expenses payable	420,000	
Federal income taxes payable	140,000	$1,960,000

Long-term liabilities:

Long-term notes, 8% interest, due 1978	1,500,000
Total liabilities	$3,460,000

Shareholders' equity:

Common stock, $1 par value; authorized 1,000,000 shares, issued and outstanding 400,000 shares	$ 400,000	
Paid-in capital in excess of par value of common stock	900,000	
Retained earnings	915,000	
Total shareholders' equity		2,215,000
Total liabilities and shareholders' equity		$5,675,000

A MERCHANDISING COMPANY
Income Statement
For Year Ended December 31, 1974

Sales		$11,500,000
Expenses:		
Cost of merchandise sold	$6,800,000	
Depreciation expense	80,000	
Selling and administrative expenses	3,700,000	
Interest expense	120,000	10,700,000
Net income before federal income tax		$ 800,000
Federal income tax expense		410,000
Net income		$ 390,000

the performance of a corporation is often judged in terms of the investment required to generate a particular return. Performance in this sense is an indicator of the average efficiency of capital employed by the firm.

This type of return indicator is calculated by dividing income for the period by the firm's capital investment. Two possible investment bases are customarily used: (1) total assets and (2) owners' equity (net assets). (Note: Since the purpose of return indicators is to depict the efficiency of capital utilized *during* the period, the average levels of total assets or owners' equity may be preferred as bases. However, recognizing this possible preference, we will use the end-of-period figures from Exhibit 16-4 for simplicity of exposition.) When the total value of assets deployed is used as the investment base, the return measure presumably reflects the percentage return that the corporation is able to generate on its total asset commitment, *regardless of the source of the investment* (i.e., whether from creditors or owners). This general measure of earning power is important in assessing the performance of two or more companies that have different mixes of debt and owners' equity.

The ratio of return to total assets is calculated below:

$$\text{Return on assets} = \frac{\text{Net income} + \text{Interest expense}}{\text{Total assets}}$$

$$= \frac{\$390,000 + \$120,000}{\$5,675,000}$$

$$= 9\%$$

Since return on assets is a measure that is intended to be independent of the source of funds, the relevant measure of return should be independent of the cost of the various types of financing. The interest expense of $120,000 on the long-term notes is therefore added back to the net income for the year of $390,000 to arrive at the return figure included in the numerator. We have not attempted here to adjust for the income tax effect of interest expense, although a more precise calculation would do so.

In addition to the firm's ability to generate a return on its total asset base, the investor is also interested in the return residual (after payments to creditors) accruing to him as a holder of common stock. In this case, the denominator of our return on investment ratio is the value of owners' equity (net assets), and the return in the numerator accruing to this group is net income for the year. Note that in contrast to the return on assets ratio, we essentially exclude the value of assets supplied (in the past) by creditors from the denominator and the interest paid to the creditors from the numerator.

The ratio of return to owners' equity is calculated for our illustrative data as follows:

$$\text{Return on owners' equity} = \frac{\text{Net income}}{\text{Owners' equity}}$$

$$= \frac{\$390,000}{\$2,215,000}$$

$$= 17.6\%$$

This measure of return reflects the scaled return accruing to shareholders on their contributed capital, after payments to other sources of funds. It is larger than the return on assets because the return on total assets (9 percent) s larger than the cost of borrowed capital. This phenomenon is known as the *leverage effect*.

NET INCOME TO SALES. Another indicator of a firm's return efficiency is the ratio of net income for the year to total sales. This indicates the amount of profit that is generated from each dollar of sales. In our example, this is calculated as follows:

$$\text{Net income to sales} = \frac{\text{Net income}}{\text{Sales}}$$

$$= \frac{\$390,000}{\$11,500,000}$$

$$= 3.4\%$$

For every dollar of sales, the expenses of producing this revenue amount to approximately 96.6 cents, and the residual return accruing to the owners of the business is 3.4 cents.

Whether a particular return for a dollar of sales is good or bad depends, of course, upon the total volume of sales that a firm generates, and also the investment required to generate this level of sales. This particular statistic, net income to sales, can be related to the return on investment (say, investment by owners) through the following relationship:

$$\text{Return on owners' equity} = \frac{\text{Net income}}{\text{Sales}} \times \frac{\text{Sales}}{\text{Owners' equity}}$$

$$= \frac{\$390,000}{\$11,500,000} \times \frac{\$11,500,000}{\$2,215,000}$$

$$= 3.4\% \quad \times 5.19$$

$$= 17.6\%$$

The reasoning behind this expanded equation is that the second of the two ratios on the right-hand side of the equation indicates the number of times that the total owners' investment "turns over" during the year. Thus, if the firm earns 3.4 percent on each dollar of sales, and the total investment of the owners is in a sense "realized," or turned over, approximately five times per year, the total return on owners' equity is roughly five times the return on sales. Obviously, for firms that turn over total investment frequently (such as the grocery-chain industry), a lower profit per dollar of sales can be sustained while generating a reasonably good return on total investment. On the other hand, a firm that has a slow turnover of investment (such as a jewelry retailer) may require a higher return on each dollar of sales in order to maintain a reasonable return on investment.

• *Indicators of risk.* The set of general statistical measures used to estimate expected risk that will be reviewed are (1) current and acid-test ratios, (2) debt-equity ratio, and (3) times interest earned.

CURRENT AND ACID-TEST RATIOS. An obviously important indicator of the potential riskiness of a particular investment is the company's short-term solvency, or ability to meet its financial obligations in the immediate future. Two different ratios are often used as indicators of an enterprise's short-term solvency: (1) the current ratio and (2) the acid-test (or quick assets) ratio. The current ratio is determined in the following manner:

$$\text{Current ratio} = \frac{\text{Current assets}}{\text{Current liabilities}}$$

$$= \frac{\$4,450,000}{\$1,960,000}$$

$$= 2.27:1$$

This ratio suggests that for each $1.00 of current liabilities, there are $2.27 in current assets to "back it up." Presumably, the larger this ratio is, the less the risk of default and bankruptcy or takeover by the creditors (other things being equal).

The current assets in the numerator of the current ratio include, of course, the total value of inventories. And, in many cases, inventories are not readily available for settlement of liabilities. Therefore, a more stringent indicator of the short-term solvency of a corporation is determined by including only cash, marketable securities, and accounts receivable in the assets available to satisfy the current liabilities. This group of assets is often referred to as quick assets, that is, they are susceptible to fairly quick conversion into cash without any substantial loss in value. The acid-test ratio is determined as follows:

$$\text{Acid-test ratio} = \frac{\text{Quick assets}}{\text{Current liabilities}}$$

$$= \frac{\$2,150,000}{\$1,960,000}$$

$$= 1.10:1$$

This ratio suggests that for each $1.00 of current liabilities, there are $1.10 in quick assets available to satisfy it.

DEBT-EQUITY RATIO. Another indication of the relative riskiness of a corporation is provided by the relationship between funds provided by creditors and funds provided by owners. Obviously, the higher the percentage of assets provided by creditors, the potentially more risky the investment is in terms of susceptibility to insolvency. For our example, the debt-equity ratio is computed as follows:

$$\text{Debt-equity ratio} = \frac{\text{Total liabilities}}{\text{Total liabilities and owners' equity}}$$

$$= \frac{\$3,460,000}{\$5,675,000}$$

$$= 61\%$$

Creditors of all types therefore supply approximately 61 percent of the assets for this corporation, and the owners supply approximately 39 percent.

Since the current liabilities may fluctuate in amount and may not represent, in a sense, a permanent capitalization, we may choose to exclude them from creditor-supplied funds. In this case, we obtain a measure of the firm's *long-term capitalization:*

Long-term notes	$1,500,000	40%
Common equity	$2,215,000	60%
	$3,715,000	100%

The debt-equity ratio, or alternatively the long-term capitalization of the firm, may be important in an overall assessment of the riskiness of the particular investment to shareholders (or additional creditors whose claims would be subordinated to present creditors). It is also an indicator of potential return on investment. The larger the amount of funds supplied by creditors, the potentially larger the return that will accrue to the owners (in good times) from the leverage effect. Thus, in assessing a firm's debt-equity ratio, the investor is confronted with a trade-off between the risk of having too much debt and the potentially high return on a small investment by the owners.

TIMES INTEREST EARNED. A final indicator of the risk of a particular investment that we will examine is the extent to which interest requirements are covered by net income. Presumably, the larger the net income (before interest expense) in relationship to contractual interest requirements, the smaller the possibility that the firm will be unable to meet its legal obligation to make interest payments as they come due. On the other hand, if net income (before interest expense) is not much larger (if as large) than its interest obligations, there is a greater chance of insolvency, and thus a higher degree of general riskiness.

This measure is determined as follows:

$$\text{Times interest earned} = \frac{\text{Net income} + \text{Interest expense}}{\text{Interest expense}}$$

$$= \frac{\$390,000 + \$120,000}{\$120,000}$$

$$= 4.25$$

Thus the required interest payments are covered by earnings amounting to roughly four times the dollar amount of the interest requirement.

SOME LIMITATIONS OF FINANCIAL RATIOS. We could continue to develop other relationships between measures included in the financial statements, but the ratios covered illustrate the way in which the total package of financial information can be used to develop estimates of the required decision parameters. One point of importance that should be kept firmly in mind is that each of the measures is essentially evaluated in a *ceteris paribus* mode. That is, the interpretation of any single statistic in terms of evaluating its desirability or lack of desirability is based upon the assumption that all other measures are held constant. In point of fact, whether a higher or a lower value is desirable for any single statistic is a function of the values for all other financial statistics and all other sources of information about the enterprise as well.

Another point of extreme importance is the effect of conventional valuation policy on the degree of fidelity between financial ratios and the underlying economic relationships of interest. Present-day financial reports contain mixtures of unexpired (or undischarged) original transaction values of assets and liabilities. Such values impose additional limitations on the usefulness of ratios in at least two respects: (1) current exchange values may better relate to the intended information of a particular ratio, for example, the average efficiency of capital employed in a business might be measured better by the ratio of market-value-based net income to total assets than by the ratio of the counterpart conventional measures, and (2) the dollars of various original transaction values (established in exchanges at various times in the past) do not represent the same economic sacrifice as time passes and the general level of prices changes.

These and other limitations on the use of statistics based on present-day financial reports (brought out in the next section) serve to emphasize again the complex information-processing problem faced by investors in arriving at assessments of the expected returns and risk associated with investments in business enterprises.

THE COMPARABILITY QUESTION

An implicit issue in the analysis of the financial statements (and financial statistics or ratios) of several investment alternatives is the comparability of the data over time and between firms. Comparisons with both the past and with other firms are presumably used in analyzing any particular company's data. (Of course, between-firm comparisons are presumably at the heart of assessing the relative values of alternative investment opportunities.) Whether or not actual comparisons are useful, however, is another matter—depending on the comparability of the accounting methods used by each firm and the particular situation.

Comparability over Time

Comparability *over time* (i.e., stability in whatever relationship exists between accounting data and economic phenomena of interest) is enhanced through the application of the same accounting policies each year. Accordingly, present accounting policy includes a principle, referred to as the *consistency principle,* that urges the use of the same accounting policies by a given firm from one time period to the next (assuming circumstances have not changed). In those instances when an accounting method is changed, the consistency principle calls for prominent disclosure in the financial statements of the existence of the change and the dollar impact on affected items in the statements. Thus, although the corporation may choose among the alternative accounting policies available for valuing its resources and obligations, one can assume that the choices have been consistently applied over time unless a specific indication of a change is noted. And when such a change is made, some (if not always totally adequate) data are provided to facilitate the modifications necessary for the investor to reconstruct time comparability standards.

Comparability between Firms

The question of comparability between firms is unfortunately not as well settled as that of comparability over time. Different firms in different industries, and in many cases within the same industries, use different accounting methods to value similar resources. The resulting mixture of valuation bases and measurement rules creates a serious problem for the investor in comparing the financial status and operating performance of different companies. One obvious solution to this problem is for appropriate policy makers (FASB or SEC) to require the uniform application of one approved set of accounting methods—either by all companies or within particular industries.

Notwithstanding its intuitive appeal, this solution also has its drawbacks. Although many measurement problems and situations appear to be similar, they are not in most cases identical. Hence there may be merit in allowing management some flexibility in choosing the accounting policies to be used in best representing the financial status of the firm. At present, the trade-off between the advantages and disadvantages of uniformity and flexibility has been resolved in favor of substantial, albeit not unlimited, flexibility for management. Accordingly, the external decision maker must adapt to this situation when making cross-sectional (between companies) comparisons.

Present Adaptations to Absence of Cross-Sectional Comparability

In seeking comparability across companies (cross-sectional comparability), the external decision maker or financial analyst may wish to make some types of adjustments to the data included in the various financial reports. To facilitate this adjustment process, certain actions have been taken by accounting policy-making bodies. First, "full disclosure" of all material facts has long been a tenet of accounting and, not unimportantly, a legal requirement embodied in the Securities Acts of 1933 and 1934. Recently, the interpretation of what constitutes material, relevant information has been increasingly broadened by the APB (superseded in 1973 by the FASB) and the SEC, and the investor now receives a larger amount of supplementary information which may be helpful in reconciling differences in accounting methods between firms.

A second adaptation to the need for cross-sectional comparability is the elimination of some alternative accounting policies. While the accounting profession, and the business community, do not seem prepared at this time to accept *uniform* accounting methods, there is considerable consensus that the number of acceptable alternatives should be reduced. This reduction process is now going on and will probably continue over the next few years. To the extent that it is successful, the investor's adjustment process is obviously simplified, as there will be fewer discrepancies in accounting policies between firms.

As long as management continues to have some flexibility in choosing the accounting policies to be used in preparing financial reports, however, it seems reasonable that investors will want some type of independent review of management's choices. This independent review is provided by the independent certified public accountant. The manner in which the review is undertaken, and some of the standards employed by the auditor, are the subject of the next chapter. Suffice it to say at this point that the auditing process is an important and integral part of the corporate financial reporting process.

APPENDIX: ILLUSTRATIVE FINANCIAL STATEMENTS FROM BURROUGHS CORPORATION 1973 ANNUAL REPORT

BURROUGHS CORPORATION AND
SUBSIDIARY COMPANIES
Summary of Significant Accounting Policies

Principles of Consolidation

All subsidiary companies are wholly owned and are included in the consolidated financial statements.

Foreign Currency Translation

Inventories, properties, and other noncurrent assets of subsidiaries outside the U.S. and long-term debt owed in foreign currencies are translated into U.S. dollars at historical rates of exchange. Current maturities of long-term debt and other balance sheet accounts of subsidiary companies outside the U.S. are translated at current rates of exchange. Revenue and expense amounts are translated at average exchange rates prevailing during the year except that inventories charged to cost of sales and depreciation are translated at historical rates. Exchange adjustments are charged or credited to the reserve for international operations.

Inventories

Inventories are valued at the lower of cost or market, less progress billings on U.S. Government contracts. Cost is determined mainly on the first-in, first-out method.

Depreciation

Plant, rental equipment, and other property is depreciated over the estimated lives of such assets using the straight-line method, except for tools, dies, and fixtures which are depreciated by the declining-balance method. Depreciation rates are as follows:

	Rate per Annum (%)
Buildings	2– 5
Machinery and equipment	5–25
Tools, dies, and fixtures	10–33⅓
Rental equipment	25

Revenue Recognition

Revenue from rental agreements is recorded as earned over the life of the contracts. Revenue from installment contracts is recognized at the time of sale.

Research and Development

Research and development expenditures are charged to income as incurred.

Income Taxes

Income taxes are provided on worldwide income at the appropriate statutory rates applicable to such income. In addition, United States and Overseas taxes are provided for taxable dividends to be received out of each year's Overseas earnings. No additional taxes have been provided for cumulative undistributed Overseas earnings which have been or are planned to be reinvested in rental equipment, plant and other properties.

Investment tax credit is accounted for on the flow-through method which reduces the provision for estimated income taxes in the year in which the related assets are placed in service.

Consolidated Statement of Income and Retained Earnings

	Year Ended December 31, 1973	Year Ended December 31, 1972
Revenue		
Income from sales, rentals, and services	$1,263,631,562	$1,040,188,421
Other income	20,610,343	12,594,925
	$1,284,241,905	$1,052,783,346
Costs and expenses		
Cost of sales, rentals, and services	$ 660,174,885	$ 544,892,313
Selling, general and administrative	324,793,504	270,305,405
Research and development	65,603,767	53,491,462
Interest	25,979,364	32,103,325
	$1,076,551,520	$ 900,792,505
Income before Income Taxes	$ 207,690,385	$ 151,990,841
Estimated Income Taxes	91,800,000	64,450,000
Net Income for the Year (per share: 1973—$6.01; 1972—$4.71)	$ 115,890,385	$ 87,540,841
Dividends declared to shareholders (per share: 1973—$.76; 1972—$.63)	(14,732,077)	(11,715,552)
Retained earnings at beginning of year	415,966,351	340,141,062
Retained earnings at end of year	$ 517,124,659	$ 415,966,351

Consolidated Balance Sheet

Assets	December 31, 1973	December 31, 1972
Current assets		
Cash	$ 30,934,834	$ 22,842,843
Marketable securities, at cost which approximates market	66,059,577	5,335,993
Accounts and notes receivable, less allowance for doubtful accounts of $6,810,000 and $5,117,000	369,016,838	304,086,785
Inventories	363,807,517	357,796,926
Prepaid taxes and other expenses	29,971,787	24,890,050
	$ 859,790,553	$ 714,952,597
Plant, rental equipment, and other property, at cost		
Land	$ 8,808,298	$ 8,608,752
Buildings	112,144,720	106,006,783
Machinery and equipment	216,424,727	201,795,080
Tools, dies, and fixtures	129,360,026	121,000,666
	$ 466,737,771	$ 437,411,281
Less—Accumulated depreciation	233,347,342	205,397,586
	$ 233,390,429	$ 232,013,695
Rental equipment and related inventories	$ 789,253,596	$ 710,242,432
Less—Accumulated depreciation	320,194,313	268,324,945
	$ 469,059,283	$ 441,917,487
	$ 702,449,712	$ 673,931,182
Installment accounts due after one year and other assets	$ 133,955,674	$ 101,459,959
	$1,696,195,939	$1,490,343,738

Liabilities	December 31, 1973	December 31, 1972
Current liabilities		
Notes payable within one year	$ 81,508,391	$ 86,797,428
Current maturities of long-term liabilities	14,062,063	84,467
Accounts payable and accrued expenses	157,789,728	122,033,588
Customers' deposits and prepayments	75,688,707	53,652,488
Dividend payable	3,886,872	2,983,503
Estimated income taxes	67,400,000	39,100,000
	$ 400,335,761	$ 304,651,474
Deferred income taxes	$ 41,674,518	$ 29,029,065
Long-term liabilities	$ 261,484,762	$ 390,988,614
Reserve for international operations	$ 6,000,000	$ 6,000,000

Consolidated Balance Sheet continues on p. 560.

Consolidated Balance Sheet (*cont.*)
Shareholders' Equity

Common stock—$5 par value	$ 97,469,490	$ 93,490,295
Paid-in capital	372,582,473	250,693,663
Retained earnings	517,124,659	415,966,351
	$ 987,176,622	$ 760,150,309
Less—Treasury stock	475,724	475,724
	$ 986,700,898	$ 759,674,585
	$1,696,195,939	$1,490,343,738

Consolidated Statement of Changes
in Financial Position

	Year Ended December 31, 1973	Year Ended December 31, 1972
Working capital was provided by		
Net income	$115,890,385	$ 87,540,841
Charges (credits) not affecting working capital—		
Depreciation	133,540,152	115,662,381
Installment accounts due after one year	(30,784,637)	(33,603,503)
Other	32,136,370	33,004,036
Working capital provided from operations	$250,782,270	$202,603,755
Increase in long-term liabilities	3,166,782	19,801,698
Proceeds from sale of common stock and conversion of convertible debt	125,868,005	19,412,023
	$379,817,057	$241,817,476
Working capital was used for		
Dividends declared to shareholders	$ 14,732,077	$ 11,715,552
Capital additions—rental equipment	146,398,800	115,046,974
—other	34,450,321	32,062,936
Reduction of long-term liabilities	132,670,634	12,247,797
Other	2,411,556	(1,345,039)
	$330,663,388	$169,728,220
Increase in working capital	$ 49,153,669	$ 72,089,256
Changes in working capital		
Cash and marketable securities	$ 68,815,575	$ (2,347,825)
Accounts and notes receivable	64,930,053	1,831,975
Inventories	6,010,591	(44,487,806)
Notes and current maturities payable	(8,688,559)	117,341,208
Accounts payable and accrued expenses	(35,756,140)	(14,317,424)
Estimated income taxes	(28,300,000)	21,500,000
Other	(17,857,851)	(7,430,872)
Increase in working capital	$ 49,153,669	$ 72,089,256

Notes to Consolidated Financial Statements

Accounting Policies

The accounting policies of the Corporation described on pp. 557–58 are an integral part of the consolidated financial statements.

1. Inventories

Inventories, as of the balance sheet dates, comprised the following:

	1973	*1972*
Machines, supplies, and accessories	$219,862,691	$224,310,220
Work in process, raw materials, and factory supplies	133,442,224	123,738,551
Cost of uncompleted government contracts, less progress billings	10,502,602	9,748,155
Total	$363,807,517	$357,796,926

2. Notes Payable within One Year

Notes payable within one year of the balance sheet dates were as follows:

	1973	*1972*
Borrowings of subsidiaries outside the United States	$ 81,508,391	$ 46,247,428
Commercial paper		35,550,000
Revolving credit agreements		5,000,000
Total	$ 81,508,391	$ 86,797,428

In 1973, the Company's $75,000,000 revolving credit agreement negotiated in 1971 with Overseas branches of U.S. banks was amended to reduce the maximum available amount to $65,000,000. Under this amended agreement, the Company or a designated subsidiary may borrow Eurodollars or other Eurocurrencies at maturities from one to 12 months. The agreement provides that the Company maintain consolidated working capital at not less than $200,000,000. The Company agrees to guarantee repayment of principal and interest due from a borrowing subsidiary. A commitment fee is payable on the average unused portion of the credit, and the interest rate is determined by the London Interbank Rate.

The Company has agreements with 31 U.S. banks whereby it may borrow up to $90,000,000 under open lines of credit. The Company has agreed to maintain with the banks as compensating cash balances an average of 10% of the line extended as well as an additional 10% on any borrowings. The lines of credit were not used in 1973.

In 1973, a $75,000,000 three-year Eurocurrency revolving credit agreement with nine European banks was terminated.

3. Common Stock and Paid-In Capital

The Company has 30,000,000 shares of authorized common stock. Changes in issued common stock and paid-in capital are summarized as follows:

	Common Stock		Paid-In
	Shares	Amount	Capital
Balance at December 31, 1971	18,518,463	$92,592,315	$232,179,620
Sale of stock under the stock option and purchase plans	169,103	845,515	17,067,836
Conversion of convertible debt	10,493	52,465	1,446,207
Balance at December 31, 1972	18,698,059	$93,490,295	$250,693,663
Sale of stock under the stock option and purchase plans	117,166	585,830	19,733,877
Conversion of convertible debt	678,673	3,393,365	102,154,933
Balance at December 31, 1973	19,493,898	$97,469,490	$372,582,473

Treasury stock consists of 23,340 shares valued at cost. At December 31, 1973, 1,238,740 shares of unissued common stock of the Company were reserved for conversion of convertible debt, and the stock option and purchase plans.

4. Stock Purchase and Stock Option Plans

a. Employees' Payroll Deduction Stock Purchase Plan—Under this plan, approved by the shareholders in 1972, employees (except directors and officers) may contribute up to 10% of their pay toward purchase of the Company's common stock at 85% of the lower of the market prices on the first or last day of each purchase period. During 1973 and 1972, 65,688 and 70,804 shares, respectively, were sold to employees and at December 31, 1973, 507,686 shares were reserved for future purchases.

b. Stock Option Plans—In 1971, the shareholders approved a new stock option plan and the Board of Directors terminated the 1967 qualified stock option plan except as to options then outstanding. Under the 1971 plan, awards consisting of qualified, non-qualified, or simultaneously granted options for the purchase of up to 600,000 shares of common stock, at the market price at date of grant, may be granted prior to April 1, 1976, to officers and other key employees. Qualified options will expire no later than five years from date of grant and non-qualified options will expire no later than 10 years after grant. All outstanding options granted prior to 1973 become exercisable in annual installments of 25% beginning one year after date of grant. Options granted in 1973 become exercisable in annual installments of 20% beginning two years after date of grant.

The following summarizes the changes in options under both plans during 1972 and 1973:

	Shares under Option	Price Range
Outstanding at December 31, 1971	440,894	$ 61–163
Granted	5,900	$148–207
Exercised	(98,299)	$ 61–163
Terminated	(9,151)	
Outstanding at December 31, 1972	339,344	$ 95–207
Granted	254,250	$219–241
Exercised	(51,478)	$104–206
Terminated	(3,363)	
Outstanding at December 31, 1973	538,753	$ 95–241
Exercisable at December 31, 1973	151,551	

Options granted in 1972 were simultaneously granted options under the 1971 plan, including non-qualified options expiring in seven years. All options granted in 1973 were non-qualified options expiring in seven years.

The amount of shares available for granting of options was 329,226 and 78,164 at December 31, 1972, and 1973, respectively.

5. Dividend Restrictions

Under the terms of the revolving credit agreement and the various indentures underlying the Company's debenture issues, there are certain restrictions on the amounts of retained earnings available for cash dividends. As of December 31, 1973, approximately $300,000,000 was free of any such restrictions.

6. Pension Plans

Retirement income plans cover substantially all of the employees of the Company and its subsidiaries. The Company and its domestic subsidiaries have retirement plans under which funds are deposited with trustees. All major subsidiaries outside the United States provide pension plans for their employees which conform to the practice of the country in which they do business. Some of these plans are trusteed, some are insured, others are government plans or industry-group plans. Pension costs charged to operations in 1973 amounted to $13,900,000 compared to $12,900,000 for 1972, including amortization of prior service costs over periods up to 30 years. It is the Company's practice to fund pension costs as accrued. As of the latest valuation date, December 31, 1972, the actuarially computed value of vested benefits of all plans exceeded the total of their funds (at cost value which is below market) by approximately $61,000,000.

7. Foreign Exchange

The exchange losses in 1973 were insignificant. Such losses in 1972 aggregated $1,400,000 net of $1,000,000 income taxes. The Company translates long-term liabilities owed in foreign currencies at the rate of exchange in effect when the obligation was incurred. Translated at rates of exchange in effect at the end of 1973, consolidated long-term liabilities would be $17,000,000 greater than the amount included in the accompanying consolidated balance sheet. This difference will vary in the future with the U.S. dollar valuation of the currencies in which long-term debt of the Company and its subsidiaries is denominated. The long-term liabilities affected mature principally in 1975, 1976, 1983, and 1985.

8. Estimated Income Taxes

Provisions for estimated income taxes were as follows:

	1973	1972
Income taxes currently payable	$78,200,000	$44,470,000
Tax effects of timing differences	13,600,000	19,980,000
Total	$91,800,000	$64,450,000

The provisions for estimated income taxes for 1973 and 1972 are 44.2% and 42.4%, respectively, of income before income taxes. The principal reason for the difference between these rates and the 48% U.S. income tax rate is the lower effective tax rate on earnings of Overseas subsidiaries. Investment tax credit was $750,000 in both 1973 and 1972. Tax effects of timing differences result primarily from installment receivables and depreciation.

Cumulative undistributed Overseas earnings, for which no additional U.S. and Overseas taxes have been provided, approximate $120,000,000 at the end of 1973. The additional taxes payable if these earnings were distributed would be at a rate less than the U.S. income tax rate since taxes already paid in each country could be credited against such taxes.

9. Net Income Per Share

Net income per share is based on the average number of shares of common stock outstanding. The common stock reserved under employee stock options granted and outstanding during each year and the convertible debentures outstanding during each year are considered to be common stock equivalents. These securities, however, have not been included in the computation of net income per share because the aggregate potential dilution resulting therefrom is less than two percent.

10. Lease Commitments

The minimum annual lease rentals paid by the Company and subsidiary companies in 1973 and 1972 amounted to $9,600,000 and $9,500,000, respectively. The leases are primarily for marketing quarters and are for the most part renewable. Certain of the leases provide that the Company pay insurance and taxes. These leases require minimum annual rentals as follows:

Period	Minimum Annual Rentals
1974	$ 9,600,000
1975	8,600,000
1976	7,700,000
1977	7,200,000
1978	6,700,000
1979–1983	25,400,000
1984–1988	16,500,000
1989–1993	6,400,000
1994–2007	1,300,000

Noncapitalized financing leases (as defined by the Securities and Exchange Commission) are not significant.

11. Litigation

In 1972, the Company settled litigation with Trans World Airlines, Inc. which arose out of a contract for the sale of an electronic data processing system and related equipment. Earnings for 1972 were reduced by $4,813,000 net of taxes ($.26 per share) as a result of this settlement.

REPORT OF INDEPENDENT ACCOUNTANTS

To the Shareholders   Detroit, Michigan
of Burroughs Corporation: January 14, 1974

In our opinion, the accompanying consolidated balance sheet and the related consolidated statements of income and retained earnings and of changes in financial position present fairly the financial position of Burroughs Corporation and subsidiary companies at December 31, 1973 and 1972, the results of their operations and the changes in financial position for the years then ended, in conformity with generally accepted accounting principles consistently applied. Our examinations of these statements were made in accordance with generally accepted auditing standards and accordingly included such tests of the accounting records and such other auditing procedures as we considered necessary in the circumstances.

Price Waterhouse & Co.

16-1.   Define or explain:

a. Annual financial report

b. "Notes" to financial statements

c. Interim financial report

d. Forms 10-K, 10-Q, and S-1

e. News announcements

f. Commercial financial services

g. Expected return

h. Expected risk

i. Intrinsic value analysis

j. Scaling

k. Industry standards

l. Consistency principle

16-2.   Interim financial reports are typically considered less reliable and more abbreviated than annual financial reports. Why then might the investor find interim reports useful in evaluating investment alternatives?

16-3.   What is the usual relationship between a company's annual report and the company's 10-K report which it files with the SEC?

16-4.   Rank the financial information reports provided by a company (annual report, etc.) according to the following criteria:

a. Level of detail (comprehensiveness)

b. Scope of distribution

c. Formality or rigidity of reporting requirements

d. Frequency of release

16-5.   What are the major elements in a representative decision model for an investor?

16-6.   "*Expected* return is a crucial parameter of the investment decision. Accounting reports are historical in nature. Therefore, accounting reports are useless in the investment decision." Comment.

16-7.   "Since it is impossible for the average investor to earn an above-average return on investments, brokerage houses can provide no useful financial information to the potential investor." Comment.

16-8.   The meaning and significance of "numbers" reflected in corporate financial reports depend upon an understanding of several different variables and relationships. Enumerate these critical factors.

16-9.   Why is it important to "scale" the reported numbers in corporate financial reports?

16-10.   What are the two main classes of "standards" used in interpreting financial statements, and how are they useful?

16-11. What is an accountant or financial analyst attempting to measure or describe when he calculates various financial statistics? Are the financial statistics sufficient for this task, or is additional information necessary?

16-12. What usually is the *minimum* number of years for which financial data are included in a company's annual report? Why is this a minimum (i.e., why not include data only for the current year)?

16-13. What are the major classifications of financial statistics? Are these sets mutually exclusive? Why or why not?

16-14. The naive interpretation of many financial statistics implies that "higher is better, lower is worse." However, such a sweeping generalization is incorrect. For example, a high current ratio may imply an unwarranted buildup in inventory, and the buildup in inventory may be a sign of an unfavorable situation in the future.

For each of the following statistics, give an example, if possible, of a high value that might *not* be interpreted favorably (or might have *unfavorable* connotations as well as a favorable interpretation):

a. EPS

b. Return on assets

c. Return on owners' equity

d. Net income to sales

e. Current ratio

f. Acid-test ratio

g. Debt-equity ratio

h. Times interest earned

16-15. "The problem of comparability between firms would be settled if a national uniform set of accounts were required for all industrial corporations (similar to the set of accounts prescribed by the Federal Power Commission for utilities under its jurisdiction)." Comment.

Exercises

16-1. Analyzing Financial Statements. Using the financial statements from the Burroughs Corporation 1973 Annual Report included in the Appendix:

1. Calculate the statistical indicators of return and risk for 1972 and 1973.

2. What major decisions or actions by Burroughs Corporation during 1973 are highlighted by the statement of changes in financial position (the working capital flow statement)?

3. Based upon the numerical measures developed in 1, and any other background information on the company or the industry you might be familiar with, evaluate the company's financial status and prospects.

4. Comment briefly on any accounting policies chosen by the company that you feel are, or may be, important to take into account when evaluating the company as an investment opportunity.

16-2. Computing Financial Statistics. Condensed financial statements for Standard Corporation follow.

	(000s omitted)	
	1974	1975
Cash	$ 20	$ 15
Marketable securities	10	5
Accounts receivable	30	40
Inventory	50	70
Plant and equipment (net of depreciation)	290	370
	$400	$500
Current liabilities	$ 60	80
Long-term debt	100	170
Owners' equity (10,000 shares outstanding)	240	250
	$400	$500
Sales		$480
Expenses		
Cost of sales		320
Selling and administrative		70
Depreciation		20
Interest		10
Federal income taxes		30
		450
Net income for 1975		$ 30

Compute the financial statistics that may be used to evaluate the expected return and risk parameters for Standard Corporation. Where the measures refer only to balance sheet relationships, calculate the statistics for both 1974 and 1975.

16-3. Relationship between Return on Owners' Equity and Net Income to Sales. For each independent case below, calculate the amount or percentage for each item with a question mark.

Case	Sales	Net Income	Owners' Equity	Net Income to Sales (Percent)	"Investment" Turnover	Percent Return on Owners' Equity
1	$20,000	$ 2,000	$10,000	?	?	?
2	40,000	?	30,000	25	?	?
3	50,000	?	?	1	10	?
4	?	15,000	?	?	0.8	15
5	?	8,000	?	5	?	40
6	30,000	6,000	?	?	0.5	?
7	?	?	50,000	?	2	10
8	?	?	25,000	4	?	20
9	60,000	?	20,000	?	?	10
10	?	5,000	?	5	4	?

16-4. Effect of Financial Leverage.   Conservative Appliances, Inc., and Highly Leveraged Appliances Company both manufacture and distribute home appliances. Each company has total assets of $1 million, but Highly Leveraged Appliances Company has outstanding debt (current and long-term) of $700,000, while Conservative Appliances, Inc., has no outstanding debt. The annual interest cost incurred by Highly Leveraged Appliances Company amounts to $50,000. For two consecutive years, the two companies earned the following rates of return on total assets (before considering interest expense):

Year	Return on Assets
19X1	10%
19X2	6

Required:

1. Determine the net income for each company for each of the two years.

2. Determine the return on owners' equity for each company for each of the two years.

3. Explain the reason for the variation in performance (as measured by return on owners' equity) over the two years for the two companies, given that both earned the same return on assets deployed.

4. What factor(s) would be critical in choosing between the two companies as investment alternatives (assuming the price was the same)?

16-5. Effect of Transactions on Current and Acid-Test Ratios. The current asset and liability sections from a corporate balance sheet follow.

Current assets:	
Cash	$ 150,000
Marketable securities	125,000
Accounts receivable	175,000
Inventory	500,000
Prepaid expenses	50,000
	$1,000,000

Current liabilities:	
Accounts payable	300,000
Estimated federal income taxes payable	60,000
Accrued liabilities	40,000
	$ 400,000

For each of the following *independent* transactions, indicate whether the current ratio and the acid-test ratio would be *increased, decreased,* or *unaffected* after the transaction.

a. Collected $75,000 from customers on account.

b. Paid $80,000 to suppliers on account.

c. Borrowed $100,000 on a 90-day note.

d. Paid the federal income tax liability.

e. Sold the marketable securities for $125,000.

f. Purchased new equipment for the plant costing $200,000, and signed a 180-day installment contract with the seller.

g. Purchased inventory of $100,000 on account.

h. Purchased inventory of $100,000 for cash.

i. Purchased $50,000 marketable securities for cash.

j. Recognized expense of $20,000 from the prepaid expense account.

16-6. Evaluating Long-Term Capitalization Structures.   C. Madelyn Panozzo, chief executive officer of the Madpan Corporation, is studying alternative means of financing a new 100 percent-owned subsidiary that is being set up to market a new soft drink. The total investment required is $2 million, and the return on assets (before interest costs) is expected to range between 5 percent and 15 percent.

Three alternative financing plans are under consideration:

	Long-Term Debt	Common Stock
Plan I	80%	20%
Plan II	50	50
Plan III	20	80

The interest rate on long-term debt issued by the subsidiary will be 10 percent. Whichever plan is selected, Madpan Corporation will furnish the total funds for the common stock and will therefore be a 100 percent owner of the equity interest in the subsidiary.

Required:

1. To evaluate these financing alternatives, Ms. Panozzo asks you to prepare a schedule that depicts net income, return on owners' equity, and times interest earned for each plan, assuming a return on assets (before interest) of:

   (a) 5 percent

   (b) 10 percent

   (c) 15 percent

   Ignore the effect of income taxes in your solution.

2. Comment on the risk-return trade-off in the alternative financing plans.

16-7. Interpreting Changes in Accounting Methods.   In the 1972 annual report of the National Cash Register Company, the following note dealing with changes in accounting methods appeared:

> Since 1950 the Company had used the LIFO (last-in, first-out) basis for valuing most domestic inventories. Effective January 1, 1972, the FIFO (first-in, first-out) method of inventory valuation was adopted for inventories previously valued on the LIFO basis. This results in a more uniform valuation method throughout the Company and makes the financial statements with respect to inventory valuation comparable with those of the other major United States business equipment manufacturers. As a result of adopting the FIFO method, the net loss for 1972 is approximately $4,565,000 ($.20 per share) less than it would have been on a LIFO basis. The financial statements for prior years have been retroactively restated for this change and, as a result, earnings retained for use in the business have been increased by $25,297,000 as of January 1, 1971. Also, the 1971 income statement has been restated resulting in an increase in net income

of $847,000 ($.04 per share). Inventories at December 31, 1971 are stated higher by $50,276,000 than they would have been had the LIFO method been continued.

Beginning with 1972 additions, the Company changed its method of computing depreciation on rental equipment and on property, plant and equipment in the United States from the sum-of-the-years digits method to the straight-line method while continuing the former method for assets acquired prior to 1972. This change in depreciation method was made to bring the company in line with general accounting practices in the business equipment industry. Concurrent with the change in depreciation method, for additions after January 1, 1972 the Company reduced the estimated useful life of rental equipment from 6 to 5 years and changed the estimated useful lives of certain other fixed assets. The effect of the change in depreciation method was to reduce the net loss after tax for the year 1972 by approximately $2,400,000 ($.11 per share), while the effect of the change in useful lives was not significant.

Required:

1. What reason(s) does NCR give to support the changes in accounting methods? Are there any other reasons you think might have motivated the changes?
2. What effect do the changes have on the comparability over time of the NCR statements? Is there sufficient information provided to allow the statement user to reconstruct this comparability element?
3. What effect do the changes have on cross-sectional comparability?
4. With respect to the change in inventory method:
   (a) Was income (loss) higher or lower in 1972 as a result of the change? How much?
   (b) Was there any effect on income of prior years? How much?
   (c) What do you suppose was the reason for the rather large difference in the amount of the effects of the change on income (loss) in 1971 and 1972?
   (d) What do you think the effect of the change will be on future years' income?
   (e) What was the effect of the change on the value of the inventory in the balance sheet?
   (f) What effect would the change have on the financial statistics used to estimate NCR's risk and return parameters?
5. With respect to the changes in depreciation method:
   (a) What two distinct changes were made?
   (b) Was income (loss) higher or lower in 1972 as a result of the changes? How much? Did both changes contribute to this effect?
   (c) Was there any effect on income of prior years? How much?
   (d) What was the effect of the changes on the value of the rental equipment and the property, plant, and equipment in the 1972 balance sheet? What will be the effect in the future?

16-8. Reporting "Lines of Business." One of the controversial financial reporting issues is whether or not companies should disaggregate reported data to reflect the operating performance of separate divisions, segments, or lines of business. Present SEC regulations require information of this type under certain conditions in SEC filings, but it is at present strictly optional in corporate annual reports.

The following example of this type of expanded reporting is taken from the 1972 annual report of National Distillers and Chemical Corporation.

DIVISIONAL OPERATING PROFIT
AND RETURN ON INVESTMENT (000 omitted)

Divisions	Operating Profit		Investment		% Return on Investment	
	1972	1971	1972	1971	1972	1971
Liquor	$36,188	$43,072	$290,000	$289,000	12%	15%
Chemical	27,896	17,427	205,000	209,000	14	8
Bridgeport Brass	16,789	11,138	118,000	112,000	14	10
Almaden Vineyards	12,135	8,380	56,000	42,000	22	20
Textiles	(5,728)	4,043	65,000	58,000	—	7
Totals	$87,280	$84,060	$734,000	$710,000	12%	12%

Note: Divisional investment includes only those assets and liabilities directly applicable to divisional operations.

Required:

1. Do you believe that this additional information on the performance of divisions (or lines of business) would aid the investor in evaluating the risk and return parameters for the corporation? How?

2. National Distillers and Chemical Corporation reported net income for 1972 of approximately $35 million in its income statement. What do you think accounts for the difference between this reported income and the total operating profit reflected in the above schedule of divisional operating profit?

3. Do the return on investment measures in the above schedule reflect return on assets or return on owners' equity? Explain your reasoning. (Note: The total assets reported in the 12/31/72 balance sheet amounted to approximately $966 million, and the shareholders' equity was approximately $494 million.)

4. Enumerate some potential accounting problems that you think would have to be resolved if line-of-business, or segmental, reporting became a standard inclusion in corporate annual reports.

16-9. Comparative Financial Ratios under Alternate Valuation Bases. Following are the Statement of Income, the Statement of Assets, and the Statement of Capital (the last two together making up the traditional balance sheet) from the 1971 annual report of Indiana Telephone Company. The column B figures are based on the column A figures *adjusted* for changes in the general price level.

Required:

1. Calculate the statistical indicators of risk and return described in the chapter, based on the 1971 column A and B figures.

INDIANA TELEPHONE CORPORATION
Statement of Income

	Column A Historical Cost		Column B Historical Cost Restated for Changes in Purchasing Power of Dollar	
	1971	1970	1971	1970
Operating Revenues:				
Local service	$ 5,744,356	$5,384,154	$ 5,788,990	$ 5,695,270
Toll service	4,852,156	4,350,496	4,889,858	4,601,883
Miscellaneous	304,522	234,979	306,888	248,557
Total operating revenues	**10,901,034**	**9,969,629**	**10,985,736**	**10,545,710**
Operating Expenses:				
Depreciation provision	1,943,551	1,541,560	2,497,078	2,026,211
Maintenance	1,486,495	1,427,487	1,505,457	1,523,311
Traffic	1,226,906	1,157,565	1,237,139	1,224,453
Commercial	511,661	449,104	515,637	475,054
General and administrative	1,055,318	1,170,198	1,068,682	1,278,407
State, local, and miscellaneous federal taxes	912,601	648,996	919,692	686,497
Federal income taxes				
Currently payable	1,132,500	1,127,087	1,141,300	1,192,215
Deferred until future years	315,800	295,000	318,254	312,047
Deferred investment tax credit (net)	9,708	(14,997)	3,262	(21,018)
Total operating expenses	**8,594,540**	**7,802,000**	**9,206,501**	**8,697,177**
Operating Income	**2,306,494**	**2,167,629**	**1,779,235**	**1,848,533**

Statement of Income continues on p. 574.

INDIANA TELEPHONE CORPORATION
Statement of Income (cont.)

	Column A Historical Cost		Column B Historical Cost Restated for Changes in Purchasing Power of Dollar	
	1971	1970	1971	1970
Income Deductions:				
Interest on funded debt	651,195	659,567	656,255	697,679
Other deductions	36,828	21,355	40,229	24,573
Interest charged to construction (credit)	(63,905)	(30,442)	(64,402)	(32,271)
Other income (credit)	(95,974)	(98,759)	(96,720)	(104,456)
Gain from retirement of long-term debt through operation of sinking fund (credit)	(15,192)	(15,865)	(15,310)	(16,731)
Price level gain from retirement of long-term debt (credit)	—	—	(61,137)	(55,175)
Gain from retirement of preferred stock through operation of sinking fund (credit)	(5,055)	(5,515)	(5,094)	(5,834)
Price level gain from retirement of preferred stock (credit)	—	—	(12,908)	(12,029)
Price level loss from other monetary items	—	—	87,508	118,125
Total income deductions	507,897	530,341	528,421	613,901
Net Income	1,798,597	1,637,288	1,250,814	1,234,662
Preferred stock dividends applicable to the period	96,209	97,541	96,957	103,178
Earnings Applicable to Common Stock	$ 1,702,388	$1,539,747	$ 1,153,857	$ 1,131,554
Earnings per Common Share	$ 3.49	$ 3.16	$ 2.37	$ 2.32
Book Value per Share	$ 21.45	$ 18.29	$ 20.19	$ 18.14
Stations in service at end of year	75,015	72,569	75,015	72,569

2. Are there any significant differences between the column A and column B indicators? Are the differences in predictable directions, that is, would they be the same (or tend to be) for all businesses?

3. Indiana Telephone is a regulated company. Its rates are set by the Public Service Commission of Indiana at a level expected to ensure that the com-

Statement of Assets—December 31, 1971

	Column A Historical Cost	Column B Historical Cost Restated for Changes in Purchasing Power of Dollar
Telephone Plant, at original cost		
In service	$32,681,923	$41,791,787
Less—Accumulated depreciation	10,598,883	14,354,244
	22,083,040	27,437,543
Plant under construction	1,568,243	1,580,428
	23,651,283	29,017,971
Working Capital:		
Current assets—		
Cash	679,475	679,475
Temporary cash investments accumulated for construction—at cost, which approximates market	3,074,351	3,074,351
Accounts receivable, less reserve	1,220,555	1,220,555
Materials and supplies	531,855	536,583
Prepayments	71,059	71,611
	5,577,295	5,582,575
Current liabilities—		
Sinking fund obligations	162,000	162,000
Accounts payable	635,552	635,552
Advance billings	315,647	315,647
Dividends payable	23,886	23,886
Federal income taxes	242,393	242,393
Other accrued taxes	600,190	600,190
Other current liabilities	713,455	713,455
	2,693,123	2,693,123
Net working capital	2,884,172	2,889,452
Other:		
Debt expense being amortized	201,810	260,266
Other deferred charges	49,616	57,566
Deferred federal income taxes	(1,273,254)	(1,390,176)
Unamortized investment tax credit being amortized over the useful lives of related property	(391,778)	(472,321)
	(1,413,606)	(1,544,665)
Total Investment in Telephone Business	$25,121,849	$30,362,758

Statement of Capital—December 31, 1971

	Column A Historical Cost		Column B Historical Cost Restated for Changes in Purchasing Power of Dollar	
	Amount	Ratio	Amount	Ratio
First Mortgage Sinking Fund Bonds:				
Series 1, 3% due June 1, 1977	$ 770,000		$ 770,000	
Series 2, 3⅜% due June 1, 1977	390,000		390,000	
Series 3, 3⅞% due June 1, 1977	410,000		410,000	
Series 4, 3¾% due June 1, 1984	935,000		935,000	
Series 5, 4¼% due September 1, 1986	870,000		870,000	
Series 6, 5⅜% due September 1, 1991	1,840,000		1,840,000	
Series 7, 4¾% due May 1, 1994	1,995,000		1,995,000	
Series 8, 4¾% due July 1, 2005	2,910,000		2,910,000	
Series 9, 6½% due October 1, 2007	2,940,000		2,940,000	
Less—Current sinking funds	(142,000)		(142,000)	
Total first mortgage sinking fund bonds	12,918,000	51%	12,918,000	43%
Preferred Stock (no maturity):				
Cumulative, sinking fund, par value $100 per share, 30,000 shares authorized of which 10,000 are unissued:				
1950 Series 4.80%	240,000		240,000	
1951 Series 4.80%	242,900		242,900	
1954 Series 5¼%	333,400		333,400	
1956 Series 5%	256,900		256,900	
1967 Series 6⅛%	686,000		686,000	
Less—Current sinking funds	(20,000)		(20,000)	
Total preferred stock	1,739,200	7%	1,739,200	6%
Common Shareholders' Interest:				
Common stock, no par value, authorized 500,000 shares, issued 492,086 shares	4,251,785		6,474,592	
Retained earnings	6,295,365		3,500,069	
	10,547,150		9,974,661	
Less—Treasury stock, 4,336 shares, at cost	(5,192)		(7,882)	
Stock discount and expense	(77,309)		(121,103)	
Total common shareholders' interest	10,464,649	42%	9,845,676	32%
Unrealized Effects of Price Level Changes	—	—	5,859,882	19%
Total Investment in Telephone Business	$25,121,849	100%	$30,362,758	100%

pany recovers its investment plus a fair return on that investment. In petition-
ing the commission for rate changes, would the company prefer to use the
column A or column B based indicators of the return on investment earned
in the past? Explain your answer.

16-10. Using Risk and Return Indicators.   Based on (1) the partial information appearing in the balance sheet below, (2) the additional information that
follows it, and (3) the definitions of the various return and risk indicators described in the chapter, determine the amounts of the missing numbers.

PARTIAL INFORMATION, INCORPORATED
Balance Sheet
As of February 9, 1977

Assets

Cash	$ 2,000,000
Accounts receivable	2,000,000
Marketable securities	?
Prepaid expenses	1,000,000
Inventory	?
Total current assets	$?
Plant and equipment (net)	?
Total assets	$?

Liabilities and Stockholders' Equity

Accounts payable	$?
Wages payable	1,500,000
Taxes payable	1,000,000
Total current liabilities	$?
6% Bonds payable	10,000,000
Total liabilities	$?
Stockholders' equity:	
Common stock, $1 stated value 10,000,000	
shares authorized; ? outstanding	$?
Paid in excess over stated value	8,000,000
Retained earnings	?
Total stockholders' equity	$?
Total liabilities and stockholders' equity	$?

Additional Information:

Expenses	$16,000,000
Times interest earned	7⅔
Current ratio	2:1
Debt to equity ratio	2:3
Acid-test ratio	1.2:1
Earnings per share	.50

Permanent capital: ¼ long-term debt;
              ¾ stockholders' equity

17

The Attest Function in Financial Reporting

Most of the discussion in the earlier chapters of this book is built on the premise that accounting is an information specialization. This point was established in Chapter 2. Subsequent chapters have demonstrated how decision-relevant accounting information might be produced within different financial accounting models and how it is in fact produced within the contemporary corporate financial reporting environment. Now we must address the question of the general reliability of reported accounting information. In so doing, our focus shifts from aspects of quantity and types of information to quality of information.

Quality of information is presumably improved when completely independent and competent outside experts review it and attest to its reliability, fairness, and other aspects of quality. Investors have a big stake in such attestation, since they can make decisions with better expected outcomes if they have relatively better information available. The public interest is also involved. If incomplete, unreliable, or even misleading financial information is furnished to investors so that they enter into (sell off) investments that they would not otherwise have undertaken (disposed of), the public interest is affected in the sense that the level of capital formation in the economy may decrease (as was described in Chapter 10). Moreover, scarce resources may be misdirected into socially less desirable channels or inefficient processes.

Example 17-1   Three brothers have invested all of their resources in the purchase of a parcel of land suitable for a shopping center development. They have borrowed from banks for purposes of surveying the land, acquiring architectural layouts, and installing streets, utilities, and parking lots.

To secure building construction loans, they have approached Jack Ehrlich to invest $75,000 in their venture. In return, Mr. Ehrlich would receive a one-third equity interest in Brothers Three, Ltd., a company to be formed if the additional investment is made.

Before Mr. Ehrlich is willing to invest, he would like to know the full investment history of the venture. Financial statements attested to by competent outside experts would be relatively more reliable than any furnished by the three brothers themselves, since they have a direct self-interest in having Mr. Ehrlich make the investment.

Striving for a high degree of financial information reliability is, of course, not limited to the information needs of investors. Enterprise managements likewise require reliable financial information for managerial decision making. For instance, decisions about lines of credit extended to customers depend on good data about accounts receivable collections. Product line profitability must be measured in part by reliable costing procedures.

Internal Revenue agents examine financial information provided by taxpayers with a view to detecting errors and omissions (intentional and unintentional) and, therefore, increasing its reliability for federal income tax collection purposes. The General Accounting Office of the federal government helps to ensure the reliability of financial information compiled and furnished by federal government departments and agencies.

The Soviet system uses financial reviewers (i.e., auditors) as extensively as do market-based systems, even though its reviewers are government employees and not independent professionals as in the case of, let us say, the Anglo-Saxon countries. Moreover, financial review activities are as old as accounting itself. They were present in the ancient tax collection systems of Babylonia and Egypt as well as in the extensive trading systems of the Middle Ages. In the Western countries, independent auditors established themselves as separately recognized professionals in Scotland during the 1860s.

Auditing today is as complex as the financial systems of the enterprises that it serves. Due to this complexity and in keeping with the emphasis adopted for this book, the remaining discussion in this chapter is limited to the branch of auditing concerned with financial reporting to third parties by private enterprises.

Role of Auditing

Independent auditors (CPAs) perform an attest function aimed primarily at establishing and maintaining the integrity of financial information. As review specialists, they can presumably accomplish this function in an economically efficient manner. The objective of their ordinary examinations (audits) of financial statements is the expression of an opinion (attestation) on the fairness with which the financial statements present financial position and results of operations of an enterprise. The auditors' reports are the medium through which they express their opinions or, if circumstances require, disclaim professional opinions.

● *Audit reports.* In an audit report, the auditor states whether his examination has been made in accordance with generally accepted auditing standards. In turn, these standards require him to attest whether, in his opinion, the financial statements are presented in conformity with generally accepted accounting principles and whether such principles have been consistently applied in the preparation of the financial statements of the current period in relation to those of the preceding period.

The CPA profession, with concurrence from the SEC, has adopted the following standard form of an independent auditor's report which would be used when the examination reveals no reservations about the adequacy of the financial statements under audit:

> We have examined the balance sheet of X Company as of December 31, 19—, and the related statements of income and retained earnings and changes in financial position for the year then ended. Our examination was made in accordance with generally accepted auditing standards, and accordingly included such tests of the accounting records and such other auditing procedures as we considered necessary in the circumstances.
>
> In our opinion, the aforementioned financial statements present fairly the financial position of X Company at December 31, 19—, and the results of its operations and the changes in its financial position for the year then ended, in conformity with generally accepted accounting principles applied on a basis consistent with that of the preceding year.

● *Responsibility for financial statements.* While professional literature establishes the unequivocal responsibility of the independent auditor for his report on the financial statements, it is equally emphatic in pointing out that enterprise management has the responsibility for the production and preparation of proper financial statements. Thus it is management's responsibility to adopt sound accounting policies, to maintain adequate and effective systems of accounts, to safeguard enterprise assets, and to devise control systems that will accomplish these imperatives.

At all times the financial statements remain representations of enterprise management and as such are an implicit and integral part of management's responsibility. No one should know an enterprise better than its management. Consequently, management is usually in the best position to choose procedures and policies and ultimately financial statement formats that will most fairly report a company's financial position and results of operations to third parties.

The auditor's responsibility with respect to financial statements is therefore secondary. He cannot issue an unqualified audit report on a set of financial statements unless these statements represent actual business transactions and events and conform to established accounting policy. The London *Economist* once called the auditor's responsibility a "watchdog function." Later on in the chapter we describe how this function is performed.

• *Effects of independent audits.* Many treatises have been written on behavioral effects produced when auditors perform audit activities in a client's office. Company accounting personnel often feel uneasy when the independent auditors are around. Thus auditing produces what might be called a "report card" effect. Jobs get done with fewer errors, and systems improvements are constantly sought because of the periodic report card prepared by the independent auditors. Some observers feel that this effect may even prevent some contemplated frauds or lesser irregularities by employees. However, the typical financial audit review is not intended to guarantee fraud detection. This is discussed at greater length in a later section.

Another consequence of auditing relates to producing valid and reliable financial information efficiently. As pointed out in earlier paragraphs of this chapter, management clearly knows the most about the business enterprise and understands its strengths and weaknesses best. Therefore, management usually is and should be most efficient in preparing financial representations about the firm.

Unfortunately, however, management also has a direct interest in the representations made. If things are not going well, then management, in its own interest, might make biased representations. Such biases might even shade into misrepresentations or dishonesty. From the point of view of management, occasional presentation of biased financial information may be a perfectly logical step to take in terms of survival of the company, availability of ready borrowing capacity, or a strong product image with consumers. Knowing that independent audit procedures will eventually test their financial representations, managements are probably less prone to make deliberately or intentionally biased judgments and estimates than would otherwise be the case.

• *Efficiency provided by independent audits.* Despite report card effects within enterprises, outside users of financial information want additional assurances about its validity and reliability. Here is where the full impact of the economics of auditing enters the picture. If users of financial information had to obtain and verify this information item by item and user by user, an immensely costly process would unnecessarily be repeated over and over.

As it stands, division of responsibilities produces significant efficiencies. Management is most efficient in preparing and offering financial representations needed by outsiders. The independent auditing function helps to ensure that these representations are by and large free of bias and "present fairly . . . in conformity with generally accepted accounting principles applied on a basis consistent with the preceding year." Thus presumably we have an economically more efficient information process both for the providers and for the users of the information.

Moreover, independent auditing has spawned many techniques and procedures that might be described as self-auditing devices. Internal control, defined later in this chapter, is a good illustration. To some degree all modern business enterprises operate systems of checks and balances and exception reports. Also, many companies have sizable internal audit staffs. Internal auditors not only audit many aspects of enterprise operations on a continuous basis for the information of top management, but their work is often utilized by independent auditors. Internal audit results thus become part of the evidence needed in forming evaluative judgments about the integrity of the system and the records on which the financial statements are based.

Auditing in a Changing World

We mentioned earlier that professional auditing had its genesis in Scotland during the middle of the nineteenth century. As British railroad, insurance, and other investments moved to North America, independent auditors moved with them initially to protect large British investor interests. The antecedents of North American professional accounting are therefore British.

Until the late 1940s, auditing was viewed as a process of examining the documentation supporting recorded transactions and verifying their classification in financial statements. This approach to auditing has been characterized as "auditing the books."

• *Internal control emphasis.* In 1949 a committee of the AICPA issued a special report containing a comprehensive statement on the significance of internal control to the auditing process. In this statement internal control is defined as follows:

> Internal control comprises the plan of organization and all of the coordinated methods and measures adopted within a business to safeguard its assets, check the accuracy and reliability of its accounting data, promote operational efficiency, and encourage adherence to prescribed managerial policies. This definition possibly is broader than the meaning sometimes attributed to the term. It recognizes that a system of internal control extends beyond those matters which relate directly to the functions of the accounting and financial departments.

Soon after the special report, independent auditors began to place greater reliance on internal control considerations. Prior to the start of an audit process, they now carefully evaluate a company's internal control system. If internal controls operate well, the system is likely to produce reasonably complete and accurate financial data. In turn, such data are a good starting point for reliable financial statements. On the other hand, the financial data base of an enterprise is not very dependable when internal controls are either weak or absent altogether.

Example 17-2   After the Brothers Three, Ltd., Shopping Center is built, rents and fees are collected from different occupants according to a wide variety of individual contracts. The controller's department of the Shopping Center has established the following internal control procedures, among others, to correspond to recognized internal control principles.

Procedure	Why Done	Principle
1. The receptionist prepares and mails all bank deposits. The bookkeeper reconciles each monthly bank statement to the company's cash records.	To avoid misuse of funds received (as can occur when the same individual who receives funds also controls the records) and ensure timely bank deposits.	A plan of organization that provides appropriate segregation of functional responsibilities among employees.
2. Each advertising allowance made to tenant stores is individually authorized by the controller.	To control total amount of allowances granted and prevent kickbacks.	A system of authorization and recording procedures adequate to provide reasonable accounting control over assets, liabilities, revenues, and expenses.
3. New construction activities are recorded in accounts clearly separated from repair and maintenance accounts.	To ensure appropriate accounting classifications and control repair and maintenance operation.	Sound practices to be followed in the performance of duties and functions of each of the organizational departments.
4. The job description for the controller's position requires that appointees hold a CPA certificate.	To seek best possible job performance within budgeted salary range.	A degree of quality of personnel commensurate with responsibilities.

If an internal control system is found to be highly effective, independent audit procedures can be curtailed. With a well-functioning internal control system, relatively less extensive tests or samples may be required to supply the auditor with needed evidential matter because he can rely more readily on the quality of the data produced by the system. On the other hand, a weak system of internal control generally dictates more extensive auditing procedures to satisfy the need for sufficient evidence for an adequate evaluation of data quality and opinion formulation on the financial statements under audit.

• *Business approach to auditing.* The business approach to auditing recognizes that the fairness of presentation of financial statements can be evaluated more effectively if the independent auditor is aware of and understands the environmental conditions in which an enterprise operates. Hence at present the audit process is being extended to include many types of management controls and environmental conditions which are likely to have financial statement effects.

Auditing Framework

When the independent auditor begins an audit assignment, he assumes that (1) the internal control system of the enterprise is appropriate and effective; (2) generally accepted accounting principles have been applied in all accounting processes underlying the financial statements; (3) the generally accepted accounting principles utilized have been applied consistently between the current and the prior periods; and (4) there is an adequate amount of informative financial disclosure in the financial statements and footnotes. Evidence gathering and its evaluation enable the auditors to reject or confirm these *a priori* assumptions. We are thus in a position to define auditing.

> **Auditing.** The analytical process of gathering sufficient evidential matter on a test or sampling basis to enable a competent professional to express an opinion as to whether a given set of financial statements meets established standards of financial reporting.

Now we can enumerate the major steps of the auditing process: (1) become acquainted with the firm—its environment and its accounting, personnel, production, marketing, and other systems; (2) review and evaluate the management and the accounting control system in operation; (3) gather evidential matter on the integrity of the system; (4) gather further evidence related to the representations made in the financial statements; and (5) formulate a judgment opinion on the basis of the evidence available.

• *Getting acquainted.* Auditing is an analytical process applied to everyday business situations. Hence it is closely related to existing business practices. Without first-hand knowledge of the nature of these practices and their larger setting, the auditor would have to rely exclusively on available financial data. This would jeopardize both audit efficiency and effectiveness. It would also preclude the business approach to auditing. Therefore a getting-acquainted phase (often in the form of a visit to a client's facilities) initiates the typical audit process. The likely activities of this phase are described later in Example 17-6.

• *Control system review.* We have already described the nature of internal control and its relationship to the auditing process. As was pointed out earlier, the auditor's evaluation of the control systems operating within the enterprise has a direct influence on the scope of the examination he undertakes and the nature of the tests he conducts. However, even though preliminary evaluation of control systems is an essential ingredient of planning the audit scope, we must remember that eventually *both the system and the data* it produces are covered by the audit process.

Example 17-3

The Brothers Three Shopping Center has leased space to Mr. Hines who operates a quality restaurant named The Duncan Inn located within it. Lease payments are based on a minimum monthly amount sufficient to cover taxes and insurance on the building plus a graduated percentage of the restaurant's gross sales to diners and bar patrons. No percentage payments are due on catering services.

Bar and restaurant receipts of The Duncan Inn are collected in cash and from credit card billings. A select few patrons have the privilege of open credit with monthly billings.

In planning the initial audit of The Duncan Inn's financial statements, a CPA finds that virtually no internal control exists over cash bar receipts.

Hence tests covering bar cash revenues are scheduled more comprehensively than those extending to credit card sales.

• *Evidential matter.* Evidential matter supporting financial statements consists of the underlying accounting data and all corroborating information available to the auditor. The auditor tests underlying accounting data by analysis and review, retracing some of the procedural steps followed in the original accounting process and reconciling the events with the information reported.

The auditor's evidential material is the result of tests, selected observations, and statistical sampling where large compilations of data are involved. The auditor must always balance the natural desire for more evidential matter to support an opinion against the costliness and social usefulness of completely reconstructing the underlying data and processes that produced the financial statements. One key justification for independent audits, as we have seen, is the economy that results from producing expert opinion-based judgments from limited but reliable evidential matter.

Example 17-4   Among tests covering cash bar receipts of The Duncan Inn, the CPA determined what the expected average ratios should be between liquor used up, average number of individual drinks per bottle of liquor, and the price structure of drinks served. Making appropriate allowances for credit card sales, the CPA was then able to make a reasonable estimate of cash bar receipts for the period under audit. The estimate of the cash bar receipts constitutes evidential matter for purposes of the audit. (Note that the foregoing test has physical and financial dimensions. A purely financial test could have subtracted cash restaurant receipts from total bank deposits to arrive at cash bar receipts. In a real-world situation, an auditor might have undertaken both types of tests.)

• *Professional judgment.* The object of an independent audit, as we have noted, is to express a professional opinion on a set of financial statements. Rendering such an opinion is a matter of judgment. Professional evaluation of audit evidence gathered is therefore a key function of the independent auditor. The AICPA's *Statement on Auditing Standards No. 1* (paragraph 330.02), 1973, puts it into the following context:

> Most of the independent auditor's work in formulating his opinion on financial statements consists of obtaining and examining evidential matter. The measure of the validity of such evidence for audit purposes lies in the judgment of the auditor.

The foregoing statement can be rephrased to say that judgment of *what* evidential matter should be obtained and *how* it is to be interpreted permits confirmation or rejection of the assumption that the financial statements examined are in conformity with established financial reporting standards. There is no way in which the individual auditor's judgment can be completely eliminated from the attest function—despite a concerted effort by the profession to evolve more quantitative standards for the types of evidence that will support a given audit opinion.

• *Standards and procedures.* AICPA literature carefully distinguishes between auditing standards and auditing procedures:

> Auditing standards differ from auditing procedures in that procedures relate to acts to be performed, whereas standards deal with measures of the quality of performance of those acts and the objective to be obtained by the use of the procedures undertaken.

Exhibit 17-1 lists the ten generally accepted auditing standards which are binding upon each CPA performing an independent audit. The binding force of these standards is established by (1) AICPA membership and the corresponding requirement to observe its Code of Professional Ethics, or (2) state CPA licensing requirements, which might have built these standards into a state accountancy statute, or (3) regulatory enforcement of these standards by administrative agencies like the SEC.

Exhibit 17-1   GENERALLY ACCEPTED AUDITING STANDARDS

General Standards

1. The examination is to be performed by a person or persons having adequate technical training and proficiency as an auditor.
2. In all matters relating to the assignment an independence in mental attitude is to be maintained by the auditor or auditors.
3. Due professional care is to be exercised in the performance of the examination and the preparation of the report.

Standards of Field Work

1. The work is to be adequately planned and assistants, if any, are to be properly supervised.
2. There is to be a proper study and evaluation of the existing internal control as a basis for reliance thereon and for the determination of the resultant extent of the tests to which auditing procedures are to be restricted.
3. Sufficient competent evidential matter is to be obtained through inspection, observation, inquiries, and confirmations to afford a reasonable basis for an opinion regarding the financial statements under examination.

Standards of Reporting

1. The report shall state whether the financial statements are presented in accordance with generally accepted principles of accounting.
2. The report shall state whether such principles have been consistently observed in the current period in relation to the preceding period.
3. Informative disclosures in the financial statements are to be regarded as reasonably adequate unless otherwise stated in the report.

4. The report shall either contain an expression of opinion regarding the financial statements, taken as a whole, or an assertion to the effect that an opinion cannot be expressed. When an over-all opinion cannot be expressed, the reasons therefore should be stated. In all cases where an auditor's name is associated with financial statements the report should contain a clear-cut indication of the character of the auditor's examination, if any, and the degree of responsibility he is taking.

Auditing procedures are less clearly established, because the nature, substance, and importance of any single procedure varies with the circumstances. No two companies or no two transactions are completely alike. Consequently, few auditing procedures have been officially established, as the following AICPA statement indicates (from *Audits by Certified Public Accountants*):

Each audit discloses circumstances which require differences to a greater or lesser degree in the auditing procedures that should be employed, the manner in which they should be used, and the extent to which they should be applied. Among the reasons for their differences in requirements are that (1) significant variations exist in the nature and scope of the operations of companies in different industrial or commercial groups, or even of companies within the same group or classification; (2) the degree of effectiveness of the internal control varies among companies; (3) even within a single company the operating and accounting problems frequently change from year to year; and (4) the amount of detail to be included in the financial statements varies. In new engagements, there may be the additional problem of making an appropriate review of the important transactions of prior years and determining the nature and extent of the accounting procedures and internal control in effect.

These differences make it apparent that it is impossible to lay down specific procedures which could be applied satisfactorily in all cases. Often there is a choice of procedures, any of which would be satisfactory in a given situation. Here, as elsewhere in accounting and auditing, there must be an exercise of judgment based upon experience and upon a clear view of the objective of providing a sound basis for an informed, professional opinion.

From time to time the AICPA issues formal *Statements on Auditing Standards* (formerly known as *Statements on Auditing Procedure*). These standards serve as guidelines for the work of independent auditors. In the words of the AICPA's Auditing Standards Executive Committee (*Statement on Auditing Standards No. 1*, p. 205):

Such statements [on auditing standards], covering recommended auditing procedures, represent the opinion of the Committee on the particular matters recited therein. While it is true that circumstances alter cases . . . such pronouncements point the general direction in which conclusions might be expected to lie under circumstances not radically different; while they [the standards] do not preempt the independent auditor's judgment, they do guide his judgment.

An Audit Engagement

Some audit engagements are so large that the CPA firm responsible for the audit may assign one or more of its partners full time to the particular client. In turn, each partner would be working with several audit managers, each of whom would be responsible for a number of supervising accountants and staff accountants working under supervision. In contrast, the independent audit needed by the local university YWCA for purposes of continued allocations from the United Good Neighbor Fund may require no more than two hours of a supervising accountant's time. The vast majority of independent audit engagements fall between these two extremes. Auditors typically visit company offices for relatively short periods of time. Usually, small teams of auditors perform an engagement.

- *Start of an engagement.* Most independent audit engagements begin as a consequence of (1) legal requirements, (2) referrals by head offices of companies or home offices of large international CPA firms, or (3) suggestions from attorneys, bankers, or other businessmen.

Example 17-5

When Mr. Hines, owner of The Duncan Inn, realized that his restaurant was highly profitable, he discussed with his banker the possibility of a large loan for the purpose of building The Second Duncan Inn. The banker suggested an independent audit of the Hines Company's financial statements as a condition for the loan. Furthermore, three to five years hence the Hines Company, which owns The Duncan Inn and would be the owner of The Second Duncan Inn, might offer some of its stock for sale to the public which might require registration with the SEC and therefore audited financial statements. To explore the possibility of an independent audit for his company, Mr. Hines makes an appointment with Jonathan Lee, a partner in the CPA firm of MacLean & Co.

Mr. Hines comes to the meeting with two sets of financial statements prepared by his bookkeeper—one for the year just ended and one for the preceding year. After short introductory amenities, Mr. Hines comes right to the point by asking how much it will cost to have the two sets of financial statements audited by MacLean & Co. Mr. Lee explains that his firm has an hourly billing rate for each staff classification and that Mr. Hines's company would be billed for the exact number of hours spent on the audit at an appropriate billing rate for each auditor. Mr. Lee then estimates a range for the probable cost of an annual audit for Mr. Hines's company.

The estimate satisfies Mr. Hines and he agrees to appoint MacLean & Co. as his company's auditors. (This is possible, since Mr. Hines is at present the sole stockholder.) In further discussion it is agreed that retroactive audits are difficult and costly to undertake and that therefore the engagement will begin now so that the first audited financial statements can be produced a year from now.

- *Planning audit activities.* Once an engagement is agreed upon, many different planning procedures take place. Within a CPA firm, appropriate staff assignments are necessary. At the client's level, dates for the auditors' visit must be agreed upon and needed documents and information made available.

Personal introductions and tours of facilities are another type of essential preliminary.

As established earlier in this chapter, a comprehensive evaluation of a company's internal control system is the main determinant of the types and amounts of evidential matter needed for a given audit. The effectiveness of other organizational and operational controls must also be considered.

Example 17-6   Continuing the case of Example 17-5, an initial visit from two MacLean & Co. auditors is scheduled almost immediately. The purpose of the initial visit is to gather facts about the Hines Company in general and collect data concerning its various control systems.

During the visit, the auditors acquaint themselves with all management personnel of the company, its physical facilities, and a long list of such relevant information as membership on the board of directors, name and address of the company's attorneys, and copies of governmental and tax reports filed. Some desk space is arranged for the auditors, and they begin their first assignment. The task is finished in two days. Evidence gathered is recorded in audit working papers and completed standard format questionnaires which MacLean & Co. uses.

• *Setting a regular audit examination.* Independent auditors always keep in mind that their primary purpose is the expression of an opinion on the fairness of representations in financial statements. Hence it is not surprising to find that each audit step and each audit test is a building block toward the final expression of a professional opinion.

For example, what are some things an auditor would wish to know about sales revenues appearing in the financial statements of the Hines Company? A partial list might include the following:

1. Have actual revenues been recorded *properly* and *completely?* Tests like the one described in Example 17-4 help to answer this question. Unrecorded revenues understate, *ceteris paribus,* reported net income. Revenue overstatements may arise from misclassified bank loans and the like.

2. Were reported revenues earned in the *period* for which they are reported? In this connection the auditor will perform so-called cutoff tests, making sure that all December sales, for instance, are recorded in December and not carried forward to January. Improper cutoffs of revenues and/or expenses allow manipulation of reported net income between different periods.

3. Do accounts receivable shown at year-end reflect *bona fide receivables* and are they *collectible?* Correctness is tested by direct correspondence with debtors to confirm outstanding balances. Analysis of subsequent actual payments received helps to establish whether any bad accounts were among the receivables listed. Overstatement of receivables may again overstate reported period net income (because of insufficient provision for uncollectibles) as well as financial position amounts and ratios.

With an appreciation of what is needed to achieve fair presentation in financial statements, an auditor can evaluate an individual company situation and the state of its control systems for purposes of setting scope and depth of needed audit examinations. In determining which aspects of an accounting system should be tested and in what fashion, the auditor typically relies on guidelines available in the professional literature. These help him to arrive at his own judgments in given circumstances. Exhibit 17-2 contains a "Guide to Audit Programs and Procedures" for sales and receivables of a larger company. Similar guides are available for other financial statement categories. Evidential matter produced by following such guides provides at least a minimum basis for the eventual expression of a professional opinion on the financial statements under audit.

Exhibit 17-2   GUIDE TO AUDIT PROGRAMS AND PROCEDURES—
                               SALES AND RECEIVABLES

Review, test, and record explanations for significant fluctuations in sales and sales-related accounts noted in comparing current results with budgets, forecasts, prior periods, industry data

Evaluate overall reasonableness of recorded sales and related amounts by reviewing available marketing data:
- Reconcile volume, activity, statistical or dollar reports to regulatory agencies or others with recorded amounts
- Reconcile internal sales and shipping reports with recorded amounts
- Compute an estimate of sales using production or shipping data and average sales prices, known gross profit margins
- Summarize sales by major contracts and reconcile to control account balances (consider confirming major transactions with customers)

Evaluate and test internal accounting controls over sales and receivables—sales order entry, credit, shipping, billing, accounts receivable ledger controls, general ledger controls

Review and test general ledger accounts for entries to sales, receivables and related control accounts from controlled accounting journals—investigate entries from other sources

Summarize observations and conclusions on types and levels of management controls over granting and monitoring of credit

Circularize receivables

Evaluate and test adequacy of provisions for doubtful accounts, returns and allowances, warranties and guaranties, discounts and renegotiation liabilities

Evaluate and test period cutoffs of sales and sales-related transactions

Review and test all nontrade receivables

On initial examinations, determine work required to substantiate balances at beginning of period

Review appropriateness and consistency of accounting principles and methods for recording sales and receivables

Determine existence and appropriate accounting treatment or disclosure of:
- Sales recognized under percentage-of completion method
- Consignment sales
- Sales to affiliates
- Long-term sales contracts or other delayed billing arrangements
- Unusual or adverse sales commitments

Review appropriateness of proposed disclosure of:
- Revenues by operating, nonoperating, and nonrecurring categories
- Receivables by type (trade, instalment, affiliate, employee, officer, other) and by due date (current vs. noncurrent)
- Revenue recognition basis
- Pledged or discounted receivables

Summarize conclusions as to whether all material elements of sales, receivables, and related accounts have met the financial statement objectives

• *Audit completion and reporting.* The tests and other necessary procedures that are included in an audit are documented in a set of audit working papers. The AICPA recommends that audit working papers include or show the following:

1. Data sufficient to demonstrate that the financial statements or other information upon which the auditor is reporting were in agreement with (or reconciled with) the client's records.

2. That the engagement had been planned, such as by use of work programs, and that the work of any assistants had been supervised and reviewed, indicating observance of the first standard of fieldwork. (See Exhibit 17-1.)

3. That the client's system of internal control had been reviewed and evaluated in determining the extent of the tests to which auditing procedures were restricted, indicating observance of the second standard of fieldwork.

4. The auditing procedures followed and testing performed in obtaining evidential matter, indicating observance of the third standard of fieldwork. The record in these respects may take various forms, including memoranda, checklists, work programs, and schedules and would generally permit reasonable identification of the work done by the auditor.

5. How exceptions and unusual matters, if any, disclosed by the independent auditor's procedures were resolved or treated.

6. Appropriate commentaries prepared by the auditor indicating his conclusions concerning significant aspects of the engagement.

Working papers are reviewed by managers and partners of the CPA firm conducting the audit. Eventually, a partner signs an appropriate auditor's report on behalf of his firm.

Example 17-7   Let us assume that all necessary fieldwork is now completed on the first annual audit of Hines Company. The supervising accountant on the engagement completes the working papers and sends them to his manager for review. Thereafter, a number of accounting adjustments are suggested to Mr. Hines and his bookkeeper so that the financial statements will be brought into conformity with generally accepted accounting principles. The representatives of the Hines Company agree, and the financial statements are adjusted accordingly.

At this point, Mr. Lee reviews all of the working papers that have been prepared, as well as the drafted financial statements and footnotes. Mr. Lee asks quite a few questions of the audit manager and receives satisfactory answers so that he feels justified in signing the auditor's opinion on the Hines Company financial statements. Copies of the statements and the opinion are then mailed to Mr. Hines as the sole shareholder. A statement (bill) for professional auditing services rendered by MacLean & Co. is sent to the company as well.

Special Auditing Tools and Techniques

The case just described is highly simplified to acquaint the reader with the essential steps in conducting an audit. Engagements for large clients are enormously more complicated and often involve large-scale coordination between client locations and subsidiaries not only across North America but in many overseas countries as well. In addition, auditors rely on some rather sophisticated techniques in conducting large-scale engagements. Three of these techniques are described briefly in the following paragraphs.

• *Flowcharts.* A quick and comprehensive way of understanding, but more importantly reviewing, the information system of a client company is to flowchart all or parts of it. Flows of documents and document storage are quickly apparent from flowcharts, and weaknesses in information systems can be fairly readily analyzed by an expert. A flowchart used to typify an auditor's summary of a client's payroll procedures by Robert M. Rennie in an article appearing in the March 1965 edition of *The Quarterly* (a publication of Touche Ross & Co.) is reproduced in Exhibit 17-3.

• *Statistical sampling.* Where populations of evidential matter are relatively large and homogeneous, statistical sampling can be applied to good advantage. This is most likely to apply to auditing procedures involving invoices payable to creditors, accounts receivable from customers, inventories, and payroll applications. By using statistical sampling in these areas, the auditor is able to reduce the amount of evidence actually examined and at the same time control the reliability, and therefore the confidence level, of the evidence. As a result, statistical sampling may reduce audit costs to clients.

• *Computer-assisted auditing procedures.* The latest and probably most sophisticated auditing technique is the use of computers in the auditing process. Among the more simple tests in this connection is deliberate processing of nonsensical or impossible transactions to determine the client company's computer system's reaction. For instance, if a payroll program would process a monthly payroll check exceeding, let us say, $500,000, then the internal control of the system is weak. It should reject processing orders exceeding reasonable maximum amounts.

Computer audit software packages are increasingly efficient in expediting audit tests and procedures. The larger CPA firms have developed such software packages, which use the client's own computing equipment to perform predetermined test and check functions on the client's computerized information systems and records. These packages have enabled auditors to audit "with the computer" rather than "around" the computer.

Detection of Fraud

In the course of an ordinary examination, the independent auditor is aware that the possibility of fraud may exist. Financial statements may be misstated as a result of defalcations or deliberate misrepresentations by management. The auditor recognizes that fraud, if sufficiently material, will affect his opinion about the financial statements. Therefore his examination, made in accordance with generally accepted auditing standards, considers this possibility.

Exhibit 17-3   FLOWCHART OF WEEKLY FACTORY PAYROLL PROCEDURES

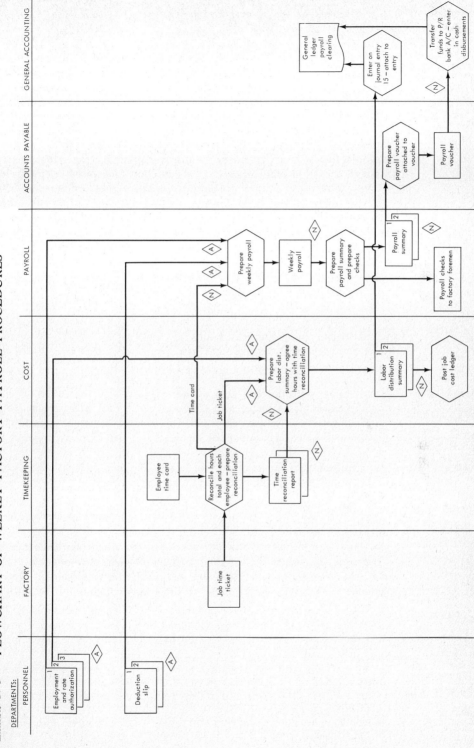

Source: Robert M. Rennie, *The Quarterly* (Touche Ross & Co.), March 1965, p. 17.

However, the ordinary examination for the purpose of expressing an opinion on financial statements is *not primarily* designed to disclose defalcations or fraud, although their discovery may result. Thus, although the discovery of deliberate misrepresentations by management is closely associated with the objectives of an ordinary examination, such an examination cannot be relied upon to guarantee their discovery. The responsibility of the independent auditor for failure to detect fraud arises primarily when such failure clearly results from failure on his part to comply with generally accepted auditing standards.

If an objective of an independent auditor's examination were the discovery of all fraud, the audit would have to be extended to a point where its cost might be prohibitive. Even then the auditor could probably not give assurance that all types of fraud had been detected or that none existed, because items such as unrecorded transactions, forgeries, and collusive fraud would not necessarily be uncovered. Therefore, reliance for the prevention and detection of fraud is placed principally upon an adequate accounting system with appropriate built-in controls.

In the course of an ordinary examination, the independent auditor may find specific circumstances that lead him to suspect that fraud may exist. He must then decide whether the possible fraud might be of such magnitude as to affect his opinion on the financial statements. If the opinion would be affected, a special investigation becomes necessary. If not, disclosure is made to proper representatives of the enterprise (probably the board of directors or one of its members) together with a recommendation for further action.

Example 17-8   Lisa Young is a third-year staff auditor in a large public accounting firm. As a member of an audit team, she was performing examinations of the financial records of a large pulp mill. Her specific assignment was to check truck-weighing tickets so that the recorded amounts of trucked-in raw material (logs) could be established as a reliable basis for the cost of the pulp manufactured. No log inventory was kept at the pulp mill; all logs were fed directly into the shredding machinery as delivered.

Checking weighing tickets was not a particularly exciting task for Lisa. They all seemed to be in order, with serial numbers properly accounted for and authorization initials appearing on each. After she had established the totals for the month she was checking, she wondered what the daily usage rate was. After she had computed that amount, she was struck by the fact that the plant's superintendent had quoted a total capacity for the shredding machinery which was below the actual volume she had calculated.

Lisa then checked her findings with the auditor in charge of the team. They both went over the calculations and found that indeed the reported amount of logs delivered could not have been used by the available shredding capacity. Since the most important cost item of the pulp mill was affected, the partner in charge of the audit was contacted and brought into the picture immediately.

Since there existed the possibility of fraud at the plant superintendent's level, top production management at corporate headquarters was informed of the suspected irregularity. The corporate vice-president in charge of production then confronted the plant superintendent, who was both surprised and embarrassed. An unobtrusive surveillance system was then put into effect over the scale master. Long-distance scale reading was compared with imprinted weighing tickets. Over the course of several days, it was discovered that the scale master was in collusion with three driver-operators. He advanced his scales from actual readings by as much as 10 to 20 percent on individual loads being delivered. The copies of weighing tickets which remained with the truck operators even had the fictitious weight differential noted!

Over a three-year period, the company had paid for approximately 20 percent more than it should have on the logs it had purchased from those operators. If better internal control over the scale master had been in effect (job rotation, required vacations, direct observation by supervisor), the defalcation could not have occurred. Lisa Young's role in discovering it was not a part of her routine obligations as an independent auditor. Also, Lisa would not have become suspicious if the plant superintendent had not quoted the plant's shredding capacity. Had the superintendent been in collusion with the scale master, the defalcation might not have been discovered.

Professional Independence

Ideally, CPAs must be completely independent when they perform attest functions related to financial statements. The reliability of an auditor's report is directly related to his independence. The auditor must be without bias with respect to the financial statements under audit, since otherwise he lacks the impartiality necessary for the dependability of his findings. Auditor independence implies a judicial impartiality that recognizes an obligation for fairness not only to management and owners (shareholders) of a business enterprise but also to creditors and others who may rely (in part at least) upon the auditor's report, as in the case of prospective owners or creditors.

Public confidence in independent auditors' reports would be impaired if there were evidence that independence was actually lacking. It might also be impaired by the existence of circumstances that reasonable people would believe likely to influence independence. To be independent, the auditor must be intellectually honest. To be recognized as independent, he must be free from any obligation to or interest in the client, its management, or its owners. Through the AICPA's *Code of Professional Ethics* (which has been written into local law by many state legislatures), the profession guards itself against public presumption of a loss of independence. The code requires that CPAs acting as independent auditors must avoid situations that may lead outsiders to doubt their independence.

The requirement for complete independence creates several dilemmas for the CPA. One dilemma is *economic*. Since managements directly pay auditors' fees, an economic relationship necessarily exists between the auditor and "the audited." The creation of audit committees among corporate boards of directors as the boards' conduits to their independent auditors has alleviated but not eliminated the dilemma. When board audit committees exist, auditors have an opportunity to become more independent of a company's top operating management.

Another dilemma is *behavioral*. Mental attitudes are difficult to change through laws and codes of ethics. Despite all outward appearances of independence, the behavioral makeup of some persons simply precludes a consistent and pervasive mental attitude of independence on their part. Some CPA licensing rules and continuing professional education requirements for license renewals again mitigate this dilemma without eliminating it.

• *SEC influence.* We pointed out earlier that the SEC administers the Securities Acts which provide for the adequate and accurate disclosure of all material facts relating to financial information filed by companies with the agency. The SEC believes that an auditor's independence is fundamental in implementing the purposes of the Securities Acts. Most filings of financial statements with the SEC must include an independent auditor's report on such statements.

On July 5, 1972, the SEC issued Accounting Series Release No. 126 entitled "Guidelines and Examples of Situations Involving the Independence of Accountants." The following examples are taken directly from this SEC release. Examples 1 and 2 deal with family relationships, while example 3 addresses the question of an outside interest. Other situations, like performing EDP or bookkeeping services for a client, becoming a client's creditor, or having other business or occupational conflicting interests, may affect independence as well.

1. An accountant has a sister-in-law whose husband is a 40 percent stockholder of a company. There is no other business connection between the company, the stockholder, the accountant, or his wife. Conclusion: *Independence is adversely affected because of the family relationship between the accountant and a major stockholder in a client company.*

2. The father of a partner in a public accounting firm was the chairman of the board and chief executive officer of a client's company. The accounting firm had approximately 400 general partners and had offices throughout the U.S. The client was a large and diverse company with many consolidated subsidiaries. The partner's office was located over 500 miles from the client's home offices and the partner was totally isolated from the audit engagement. This situation and the independence issue involved were presented to and reviewed by the company's board of directors. This body, which performs the functions typically delegated to an audit committee of directors, decided that, if the son would not be involved in the audit in any way, his association with the accounting firm would not be incompatible with the independence relationship. Conclusion: *No question of independence was raised under these circumstances.*

3. A partner in an accounting firm is a member of an investment club. The club owns stock in a company which is a client of the accounting firm. Neither the number nor the value of the shares purchased is material to the club or the company. Conclusion: *The firm's independence would be adversely affected as a result of the partner's interest in the investment club. In this regard, an investment club does not stand on the same footing as the mutual fund, because the former is comprised of relatively few members, and each member plays an active part in the selection of investments.*

• *Changing nature.* Professional independence is really a system of various trade-offs. The appropriate balance changes as social patterns change. For instance, British auditors may still serve on boards of directors of companies they audit. German and Swiss audit companies are in many cases owned by large banks (which affects independence when audit clients are also bank customers). Thus economic, social, legal, and behavioral forces must be balanced against each other at a given point in time and space to arrive at a workable construct of professional independence. Obviously, such a construct (or equilibrium point) must necessarily shift in response to changing conditions if the social usefulness of professional independence is to be maintained.

Social Setting of the Attest Function

Recent court cases have extended the professional liability of independent auditors to third parties. Growing economic complexity of industrialized society has brought in its wake a clearly discernible extension of the traditional boundaries of the attest function. Auditing of public sector agencies and programs has become a steadily growing activity.

• *Third-party liabilities.* With regard to potential auditor liabilities to third parties, several hundred well-publicized legal actions have been brought during the last decade. Bar Chris Construction Corporation (1968), Memorex Corporation (1970), Penn Central Company (1970), and Four Seasons Nursing Homes (1971) are among the more widely noted. Legal entanglements are still pending on more recently brought cases.

In the Bar Chris action, the suing bondholders did not accuse the underwriters, auditors, or outside directors of trying to *deceive* them or anyone else *intentionally*. But were the auditors nevertheless liable for the demonstrably incorrect information that management had distributed? *Yes,* ruled U.S. District Court Judge Edward C. McLean, because they had *not* made a *reasonable effort* to check the facts.

Civil negligence charges by stockholders against independent auditors characterize the suit involving the Yale Express System, Inc. A failing internal control system led to a reported net income for 1963 of $1.1 million, which upon later review resulted in a change to a loss approximating $1.9 million. In the Westec Corporation case, certain accounting procedures were drawn into question. Nine months after reporting 1965 earnings of $4.9 million and assets of $56 million, Westec Corporation went into bankruptcy.

The Continental Vending Machine Corporation case produced criminal convictions against some auditors. Illegal funds transfers and other irregularities involving Continental's president were not properly reported in the audited financial statements, which had shown $250,000 cash as an asset when in fact a cash deficit of more than $1 million should have been reported. Continental went into receivership in 1963.

Most observers seem to agree that the trend toward greater third-party responsibility for auditors will continue and possibly accelerate.

• *Broader applications of auditing.* Aside from naming independent auditors as codefendants in suits brought by the SEC (under the U.S. Securities

Acts), other administrative agencies, individual business enterprises, or class actions by stockholders and creditors, new developments are likely with regard to using the auditor's professional expertise more broadly. This appears certain to occur in such matters as greater emphasis on the auditing function prior to proposed business combinations or mergers, audit coverage of business forecasts by enterprise managements, and heavier audit requirements in regulatory activities like direct foreign investment control or domestic price and wage control. Also, the field of the so-called social audit can be expected to open up in the next decade or two. Social auditing concerns the social impact of business enterprises in such areas as work environment, noise and air pollution, inefficient use of natural resources, and minimum performance and safety standards for consumer products.

• *Public sector developments.* Auditing can also be expected to extend its traditional boundaries in the public sector. The General Accounting Office, which is the auditing watchdog of the U.S. Congress, increasingly engages in "performance" audits—an audit function addressed more to the effectiveness of a particular agency or program management than to its financial affairs and conditions. It is noteworthy that in 1972 the GAO published a body of audit standards applicable to all forms of governmental organizations and activities.* These standards are intended to apply to government and private auditors alike when audit work is performed in the public sector.

Aside from the GAO, most large federal cabinet-level departments and state governments maintain growing audit agencies of their own. These auditors, while internal to the respective organizations, typically have the power to publish their findings without jeopardy and are able to deliver their reports and recommendations to the highest management levels of the organizations they serve. Large audit organizations of this type are found in the Department of Defense and the Department of Health, Education, and Welfare. State auditors and their staffs are similarly organized, even though in some states the state auditor is publicly elected and therefore subject to at least some influence from political pressures.

The CPA Profession

Performance of the independent attest function on financial statements is limited to CPAs. In Chapter 1 we pointed out that professionalization is one of the cornerstones of the accounting discipline. According to Professor Howard Stettler of the University of Kansas, the annual growth rate of the number of CPAs in the United States has been around 6 percent since 1930. This compares with growth rates of less than 2 percent per year for the United States population as a whole and for the professional groups of physicians and surgeons, and lawyers.

CPA certificates, which are state licenses to practice as independent auditors, are issued by the individual states and territories. The issuing agency is normally a State Board of Accountancy. Typical prerequisites for a CPA certificate include (1) a baccalaureate degree from an accredited college or

---

* U.S. General Accounting Office, *Standards for Audit of Governmental Organizations, Programs, Activities & Functions* (Washington, D.C.: The Comptroller General of the United States, 1972).

university, (2) passing of the Uniform CPA Examination, which is a rigorous two-and-a-half-day examination covering accounting practice, accounting theory, auditing, and commercial law, (3) practical experience under the supervision of a CPA, (4) demonstrated knowledge of local professional ethics statutes, and (5) satisfactory personal references. A number of jurisdictions now require specified periodic amounts of postgraduate education as a condition for renewal of the license to practice as a CPA.

Professional CPA organizations include the AICPA and the State Societies of CPAs. However, membership in these two types of organizations is not compulsory for practicing CPAs. The AICPA acts as spokesman for the profession vis-à-vis government, industry, and the financial community. In connection with the attest function, it establishes guidelines and standards for "generally accepted" auditing. It also conducts research and professional development activities on a wide scale. Furthermore, it prepares and administers the Uniform CPA Examination twice each year.

State Societies of CPAs are predominantly concerned with local or regional matters. They seek to safeguard professional interests in state legislatures, support state boards of accountancy in their various activities, and conduct scores of professional seminars and continuing education programs. Quite often they also operate speakers' bureaus, assist local social programs and charitable organizations, and encourage public professional involvement.

Questions for Review and Discussion

17-1. Define the following:

a. Audit reports

b. Internal control

c. Auditing

d. Auditing standards

17-2. What is the objective of audits of financial statements of enterprises by independent professional accountants?

17-3. Who has primary responsibility for the preparation of financial statements? Why?

17-4. Explain how independent audits presumably provide economies in the production of reasonably reliable corporate financial reports.

17-5. What is the relationship between an internal control system of an enterprise and the scope of an audit of financial statements performed by independent auditors?

17-6. What are the typical prerequisites for obtaining a CPA certificate?

17-7. The standard audit report makes a number of representations about audit performance and financial statement characteristics. List and explain briefly three additional items that a standard audit report might refer to.

17-8. Differentiate between a transactions approach and a business approach to auditing corporate financial statements.

17-9. Why do auditing procedures that independent auditors actually use differ from year to year and from company to company?

17-10.   What kinds of things do independent auditors typically want to accomplish on an initial visit to the offices of a new client?

17-11.   List three things that independent auditors might want to know in forming an opinion about the liabilities listed in a company's statement of financial position.

17-12.   What is the relationship between detection of fraud and an audit of financial statements for the purpose of expressing an independent opinion thereon?

17-13.   Why is the SEC concerned with professional auditor independence?

17-14.   Find the description of a recent third-party liability suit involving independent auditors (from the *Wall Street Journal* or another financial newspaper) and explain concisely the charge against the auditors.

17-15.   Is the professional audit function limited to private enterprises? If not, how and where else does it operate?

Exercises

17-1.   Flowchart Preparation.   Enrollment in and ultimate completion of a course of study at a college or university involve a series of actions constituting a system, which may be better understood when represented in flowchart form. Design a flowchart of the system for enrolling in and completing the course for which you are studying this chapter. Restrict your flowchart to fifteen stages or less and include only those stages in which you are personally involved.

17-2.   Internal Control System Design.   Jerry Mander is chairman of the "Committee to Reelect Stan the Man as State Governor." The committee has its own offices and a large number of workers. Like Stan the Man, the campaign workers are regarded as the ultimate in dedication and integrity by Jerry. Nevertheless, Jerry is concerned about the control over the handling of donations.

Potential donors are listed in a directory kept at the committee's offices. Each day Phil E. Buster (Jerry's second-in-command) allocates several names from the list to each of his campaign workers. They then visit the prospective donors and, if possible, collect a check or cash from them. No donations are ever received by mail. At the end of the day they return to the offices and hand Phil their collections, which he places in a safe. Periodically, the contents of the safe are deposited in the committee's checking account by Griselda Grassroots. Devise an effective but simple internal control system for the solicitation and receipt of donations.

17-3.   Professional Independence Case Analysis.   For each of the following cases, state whether the independence of the auditor concerned is adversely affected, and give brief reasons for your answer:

a. A partner in an accounting firm is the trustee of the estate of a deceased friend and administers the estate on behalf of the friend's children. A material portion of the value of the estate lies in stocks of a company that is a client of his accounting firm.

b. A partner in a public accounting firm is a member of a tennis club of which his brother is president. The club has raised a relatively large amount of funds to finance the eventual construction of additional courts and social facilities. Most of these funds have been invested temporarily in common stocks. Half the total investment has been made in a company that is a client of the accounting firm.

c. A manufacturing company employs a small firm to handle most of its advertising activities. Without the revenue generated by this association, the advertising firm could not remain in business. The owner of the advertising firm has a son who is a partner in an accounting firm. The manufacturing company is a client of the accounting firm.

d. A partner in an accounting firm has not completed repayment of a large loan made by a bank. The money had been borrowed to enable payment of damages resulting from a car accident involving a member of the partner's family. The bank has now appointed his firm as its auditors. The partner will not be involved in the audit of the bank, and he now resides in a state in which the bank has no branches.

17-4. Conflict of Interest Resolution. Some have claimed that a reasonable degree of independence is rarely maintained by CPAs, chiefly because remuneration of the CPA comes from clients. However, there is little evidence of agreement on possible alternatives to the present practices. Two possible alternatives may be—

(a) Performance of the attest function by a governmental body, or

(b) A requirement that companies change their auditors fairly frequently, for example, every three years.

Required:

Critically evaluate both of the above alternatives.

17-5. Physical Inventory Program. You are an audit manager in a large accounting firm. One of the clients for whose audit you are responsible is the Diaper Distributors Company. The company purchases fully completed and packaged diapers from major suppliers and arranges their distribution throughout the state. You are now developing an audit program for the verification of inventories. The company's inventories will be counted on December 31, 19X5, and you intend that your staff auditors will be present on that day at all locations where inventory counting is to be undertaken. From past experience you know that a substantial quantity of inventories will be in transit between locations on that day. For example, inventory from the head office warehouse will leave by truck on December 30 and will not reach the company's regional warehouse until January 2, 19X6.

Required:

Draw up an audit program that will ensure that no inventories on hand or in transit are counted twice or omitted altogether from the inventory records compiled in the count.

17-6. Marketable Securities Audit. A large company holds a substantial number of bonds and stocks in other companies. The stocks and bonds are kept in a safe at the company's offices, with the exception of some that are kept at the bank. Ignoring the problems of valuation of the stocks and bonds, how would you verify their existence? That they are actually owned by the company? How would you ensure that dividends and interest have been recorded properly?

17-7. Leased Equipment Audit. Hubert's Hirings specializes in the leasing of construction equipment—compressors, welders, pneumatic drills, and bull-dozers. On any given day, approximately 75 percent of its lease equipment will not be in the company's yards, but out on lease to customers of Hubert's Hirings. Design an audit program to verify the existence of the equipment shown on the company's records at any given time.

17-8. Accounts Receivable Analysis. Debts due from customers, that is, ac-counts receivable, normally constitute a significant portion of an enterprise's total assets. How would you audit accounts receivable? What steps would you take to ensure that they have not been overstated due to inadequacies in the recog-nition of doubtful debts?

17-9. Contingent Liability Procedure. When an individual is being sued, or guarantees repayment of loans made to others by his local bank, he has a con-tingent liability, that is, he must pay out money if a certain future event occurs. Likewise companies may have contingent liabilities which should be disclosed to stockholders. How would you approach the problem of satisfying yourself that the company you are auditing has no undisclosed contingent liabilities?

17-10. Reasons for Internal Control Weaknesses. After their interim audit of a small company, the auditors sent their client a letter, listing weaknesses in the client's system of internal control. Among the weaknesses were the following:

a. Checks and cash are accumulated for three or four days before being de-posited.

b. The cashier (who handles all cash receipts) has access to the accounts re-ceivable ledger from which monthly statements are prepared.

c. The person responsible for preparing the bank deposit and depositing funds at the bank also prepares the bank reconciliation.

d. Persons who are authorized to sign checks for payment of accounts payable do not cancel the supporting documentary evidence (e.g., invoices).

e. There is no rotation of employees' duties, nor are annual vacations compulsory.

Required:

Give a brief explanation of why each of these facts involves an internal control weakness.

17-11. Fraud Discovery. Yecch Breakfast Foods Company is a small family business which specializes in breakfast cereals. Its financial statements have never been audited by a CPA. To the owner's chagrin, he eventually finds that—

a. Bags of spices which ostensibly filled a large portion of his warehouse were arranged in hollow stacks. In some cases, bags were found to be filled with sand. In addition, the quality (and hence the cost) of many of the spices ac-tually in stock was inferior to the quality specified in the company records.

b. The company accountant occasionally pocketed receipts from customers which had arrived by mail. He would then sign a credit note for the amount, so that the balance of the statement eventually mailed to the customer would be in accordance with the customer's records. To Yecch Breakfast Foods Company, the credit note indicated that the client had received a reduction in the amount due because goods delivered to him were spoiled on arrival.

c. The company accountant had also sold some of the company's marketable securities for $10,000. When the stock market price of these securities subsequently dropped, he replaced them at a cost of $4,000. No records of the transactions were made in the company's books, and the accountant retained the $6,000 net proceeds for himself.

Although examinations by independent auditors are not specifically designed to discover fraud, it is possible that their presence and their procedures may have prevented or more quickly disclosed these defalcations. For each of the above examples of fraud, indicate how the independent auditor may have detected it during the course of a normal audit examination.

Appendix

**FINANCIAL ACCOUNTING DATA-GATHERING
AND PROCESSING REQUIREMENTS**

All accounting processes and all accounting policy applications depend upon the availability of relevant data. Such data must reflect financial events and transactions affecting the unit to be accounted for and must be collected, analyzed, organized, summarized, and stored in some form of data-processing system. In a small organization, this system would be a simple bookkeeping function carried out by one or more clerks either manually or with the aid of bookkeeping machines. In a larger, more complex organization, the system might be referred to as a *financial information system* and is often based upon a network of computers and related peripheral equipment. Because the design and operation of an accounting system, whatever its level of complexity, is an important aspect of accounting practice, the basic elements of such a system are examined briefly in this appendix.

We will restrict our attention to a simplified, manual accounting system for two reasons. First, one can easily generalize one's understanding of these simple elements to a more complex, computer-based system without becoming involved in the technical characteristics of computer systems. Second, it is possible to draw upon the methodology developed in this simplified analysis to serve the purposes of other business and accounting courses. Occasionally, personal or business situations can be covered adequately on the basis of this simplified analysis as well.

The Financial Position Worksheet as a System

When the financial position framework was introduced in Chapter 5, it was pointed out that the new financial position of the firm could be computed after analyzing the effects of each transaction. Indeed, following such a procedure illustrated that the fundamental equation—assets equal liabilities plus owners' equity—remained in balance at all times. A closer approximation of actual accounting data gathering and processing was then achieved through the introduction of the financial position worksheet. This device enabled us to defer the computation of financial position until the end of a chosen interval of time—whether a month, a quarter, or a year. The financial position worksheet is therefore a means of analyzing, organizing, and storing the transactions of the firm in a form that allows us to apply appropriate accounting policy and generate financial statements at periodic intervals. It is thus an accounting system, albeit a simple one.

What then are the limitations of the financial position worksheet as a practical accounting system, even for a small firm? Two limitations are readily apparent. First, a principal purpose of an actual financial information system is to organize and summarize raw economic data into a form that makes the preparation of financial statements more convenient. However, even for a firm with a relatively small number of transactions, it would be tedious to go back through the single owners' equity column of the financial position worksheet to determine the items and amounts that would be used in the construction of the income statement. One would essentially have to reanalyze every item included in this column and prepare independent summary totals for all similar items (e.g., the total of all salary and wage payments to be included under the single "salary expense" classification in the income statement). It would be useful, therefore, if the system could be modified to perform this accumulation function as individual events were analyzed and recorded.

A second limitation stems from the physical configuration of the worksheet. The average business, even a small one, has a larger variety of resources and obligations than we have used in our intentionally simplified examples. To use the worksheet format for a firm with, say, twenty-five different types of assets and liabilities, the accountant would be confronted with a "wall-to-wall worksheet." Furthermore, if the owners' equity "column" of the worksheet were expanded into a number of component columns for various revenue and expense categories in response to the first limitation described above, this physical size problem would only be compounded.

Because of these limitations, the accountant would seldom if ever attempt to use a financial position worksheet for comprehensive record-keeping purposes. Rather, he or she would employ two components of the conventional bookkeeping system—the general journal and the general ledger—as a means of avoiding the limitations. Essentially, this involves (1) breaking up the columns (accounts) of the worksheet and collecting them into a general ledger (book), and (2) coordinating the general ledger accounts affected by the balanced transaction lines or rows in the worksheet by means of a general accounting journal.

The General Accounting Journal

A general journal in an accounting system is a chronological record of transactions. Each entry in the general journal contains the date, the accounts affected, the dollar amount of these effects, and occasionally an explanation of additional details of the transaction.

General journals used in accounting practice come in many different forms and designs. Most, however, use specialized bookkeeping conventions that are not yet needed for our purposes. Accordingly, we have designed and will use a special format (see Exhibit A-1) that incorporates the main ideas of the general accounting journal without requiring new specialized knowledge.

Exhibit A-1   AN ILLUSTRATIVE GENERAL ACCOUNTING JOURNAL

Date	Accounts Affected	Amounts	
		Assets	Liabilities and Owners' Equity
May 1	Cash	(1,200)	
	Owners' equity		(1,200)
	To record cash payment for monthly rent.		
May 3	Merchandise inventory	10,000	
	Accounts payable		10,000
	To record purchase of merchandise on account.		
May 4	Cash	2,500	
	Accounts receivable	(2,500)	
	To record collection of accounts from customers.		

The first two columns of the general journal in Exhibit A-1 are fairly self-descriptive. The first column contains the date of the transaction. The second column includes the accounts that are affected by the transaction, and an explanation of the nature of the transaction. After one achieves a certain degree of proficiency in analyzing transactions, explanations of the type shown in this example are generally unnecessary because the nature of the transaction is fairly obvious from the accounts affected. Thus, in practice, explanations are usually restricted to more specific types of information (e.g., the interest rate and the due date on a promissory note a firm gives to the bank).

The last two columns of the general journal contain the dollar effects of the transaction on the accounts. One column labeled "Amount" would be sufficient to record the transactions. However, since we wish to be certain that our analysis of each transaction maintains the equality between the sum of the assets and the sum of the liabilities and owners' equity, the general journal is designed in a way to provide a visual check on this relationship. Specifically, the first column of "amounts" includes changes in asset accounts, and the second column reflects changes in liabilities and owners' equity. Thus, after each transaction has been recorded, the dollar change in assets should be equal to the dollar change in liabilities and owners' equity. We continue our convention of showing decreases in accounts by enclosing these figures in parentheses.

Three sample transactions are included in the illustrative general journal. A brief review of these transactions follows:

Transaction 1. On May 1 the monthly rent of $1,200 was paid in cash (or by check). The effect of this transaction is to decrease the asset account, cash, and to decrease the owners' equity for rent expense. Accordingly, the affected accounts are identified in the second column, and the amount of the decreases in their balances placed in the appropriate amount columns. Cash is an asset, and thus its decrease is placed in the assets column; the decrease in owners' equity is of course itemized in the last column. After the transaction is recorded, it is immediately apparent that we have decreased total assets by $1,200 and also decreased the sum of liabilities and owners' equity by $1,200. Therefore, the fundamental accounting equation remains in balance; that is, total assets remain equal to the sum of liabilities and owners' equity.

Transaction 2. On May 3 our hypothetical firm purchased inventory items at a cost of $10,000 and charged the purchase to its account with the supplier. The effect of this transaction is to increase the balance of the asset account, merchandise inventory, and to also increase the liability, accounts payable. Again after this transaction is recorded, the fundamental accounting equation remains in balance. Total assets increased by $10,000, and the sum of liabilities and owners' equity also increased by $10,000.

Transaction 3. In this last transaction in our illustration, $2,500 is collected from a customer, or customers, to whom the firm had previously sold merchandise on account. The effect of this transaction is to increase the firm's cash balance, and to decrease the total amount due from customers, accounts receivable. The transaction does not affect any liability or owners' equity accounts. Therefore nothing is entered in the last column. Since the net effect of the transaction on total assets is zero, and similarly the total of liabilities and owners' equity is unchanged, the fundamental equation again remains in balance.

The process of analyzing transactions and recording them in a general journal differs only in form, not substance, from the line-by-line analysis in the financial position worksheet. What advantage then does the general journal offer? The answer may already be apparent. We previously alluded to the size limitation imposed by the physical configuration of the financial position worksheet. As more and more accounts must be given recognition, the financial position worksheet becomes increasingly impractical as a data accumulation device.

However, the general journal has no such limitation. The physical dimensions of the general journal need not be varied, regardless of the number of accounts. The illustrated four-column format is sufficient, because each account that is affected by a transaction is entered in the general journal at the time the transaction is recorded. All accounts whose balances are unaffected by a particular transaction are not needed to complete the recording of that transaction. The complete general journal for any period of time thus consists of a chronological series of entries (transactions) on as many pages as are required by the firm's volume of transactions.

Using the general journal, we have a manageable technique for recording all transactions. But how do we then periodically prepare a statement of financial position and an income statement from this unorganized record of transactions? This is accomplished through the use of a general accounting ledger.

The General Accounting Ledger

The general ledger is a collection of the accounts of the firm. Each account is normally placed on a separate page. After transactions have been recorded in the general journal, respective amounts are transferred (or posted) to the affected accounts in the general ledger. This posting process can be carried out immediately after each transaction is recorded in the general journal, or it may be done for a group of transactions at periodic intervals (e.g., weekly or monthly).

Exhibit A-2 illustrates a form of general ledger account that is consistent with the general journal format we have used. Note that each account in the general ledger corresponds to a column in the financial position worksheet. The collection of all such accounts for a firm constitutes the firm's general ledger.

Exhibit A-2

AN ILLUSTRATIVE ACCOUNT
FROM A GENERAL ACCOUNTING LEDGER

Cash

Date	Explanation (if any)	Journal Page	Transaction Amount	Balance
April 30	Brought forward	—		8,400
May 1	Daily activity	GJ-1	(1,200)	
May 4	Daily activity	GJ-1	2,500	9,700

The cash account illustrated in Exhibit A-2 is assumed to have a balance on April 30 of $8,400. This should correspond to the amount of cash the firm has on hand and in the bank on that date. Below this beginning balance, the two cash receipts or disbursements transactions recorded in the general journal in Exhibit A-1 are entered and a new balance is calculated. A new balance could be entered after each transaction was recorded, or it could be calculated only at convenient intervals (such as the end of a month). The effects of the transactions on the other accounts identified in each transaction entry in Exhibit A-1 are transferred to the appropriate ledger accounts in a similar manner.

The other columns of the account format shown in Exhibit A-2 provide a means of indicating the date the transaction occurred, explanatory comments if any are desired, and the page of the general journal on which the particular transaction is recorded. The latter reference enables one to refer back to the details of the total transaction for any particular entry (increase or decrease) in an account.

Thus we see that the general journal and the general ledger taken together constitute an integrated system for recording and summarizing all the transactions of the firm. The general journal is a chronological record of the individual transactions, and the general ledger shows the effects of all transactions on the financial position—categorized by accounts. At any point in time at which all entries in the general journal have been posted to the general ledger, financial statements may be prepared using the balances indicated for each account in the general ledger.

This system is clearly more redundant than the financial position worksheet, because each transaction is necessarily recorded twice. It is first recorded in the general journal, and then the components of the journal entry are recorded again in the general ledger. However, the system is a feasible one (whereas the financial position worksheet is not), and it also facilitates such management objectives as a degree of internal control. In Chapter 17 we note that a division of work functions (for example, recording in the general journal *and* recording in the general ledger) between two separate employees may yield certain protection against error and possibly against fraud or misuse of resources.

Use of Temporary (Period-Related) Accounts

We have not yet indicated how to resolve the other limitation of the financial position worksheet, that is, the need to reanalyze and summarize each of the entries in the owners' equity column whenever one wishes to prepare an income statement. As the system has been explained to this point, *one* owners' equity account contains the many different types of revenues and expenses for the period, as well as any contributions or withdrawals of capital by the owner. What we seek is some means of summarizing the revenue and expense transactions into desired categories during the journal-ledger recording process.

This objective is accomplished by introducing a new set of accounts for certain classes of revenue and expense items into our accounting system. These accounts are called *temporary accounts* (or nominal accounts). They are subdivisions of owners' equity and maintain balances only for specified periods of time (usually one month or one year). At the end of the selected time interval, the balances of the temporary accounts are transferred back (closed) to the owners' equity account.

Because the temporary accounts are subdivisions of owners' equity, we will maintain "owners' equity" in the title of each such account with the particular revenue or expense type indicated parenthetically (although in actual practice, "owners' equity" does not explicitly appear in the titles of temporary accounts). For example, in our first sample transaction (May 1) in Exhibit A-1, the payment of rent for the month was recognized as a decrease in owners' equity. Using the temporary accounts, however, it would be recorded as a decrease to the account "owners' equity (rent expense)." Thus the entry in the general journal would show:

Date	Accounts Affected	Amounts	
		Assets	Liabilities and Owners' Equity
May 1	Cash	(1,200)	
	Owners' equity (rent expense)		(1,200)

Since the incurring of any expense necessarily reduces owners' equity, all expenses are recorded parenthetically, indicating negative amounts. Revenue, on the other hand, increases owners' equity, and thus the temporary accounts for revenue items (e.g., sales) would normally have positive balances. The comprehensive example illustrated in Exhibits A-3 through A-7 shows the integrated use of temporary accounts within our simplified hypothetical accounting system.

We want to reemphasize that the temporary accounts are merely *"change" components of the owners' equity account*. Selected categories of revenue and expense items are accumulated separately for a period of time rather than recorded directly in the owners' equity (master) account. By expanding owners' equity with the temporary revenue and expense accounts in this manner, we have immediately available in the temporary account balances in the general ledger the information needed to prepare an income statement for the period. When the balances of the temporary accounts are transferred (closed) as net increases or decreases in owners' equity for a given period, the accumulation of the amounts of expenses and revenues for that period terminates. Then we begin a new accumulation for the next period in new temporary accounts.

Illustration of an Accounting System

The general journal and the general ledger (including the set of temporary accounts, as well as the permanent accounts for assets, liabilities, and owners' equity), form the basis for a simple accounting system. We present in Exhibits A-4 and A-5 the system as it would appear after handling one month's transactions.

The data for this illustration are taken from the financial position worksheet for the Ice Cream Parlor in Chapter 5 which is reproduced as Exhibit A-3. Although our choice of data demonstrates the congruence of the journal-ledger system with the financial position worksheet used earlier in the text, a comparative evaluation of the efficiency of the two systems from this illustration would be misleading. As pointed out earlier, the financial position worksheet breaks down as a viable system when the volume of transactions and/or the number of accounts increases. However, for ease of exposition, our illustration does not encompass either of these two conditions.

The general journal for the Ice Cream Parlor is presented in Exhibit A-4. To clarify unique elements of the accounting-processing function, the entries

Exhibit A-3

ICE CREAM PARLOR
Financial Position Worksheet
For Month of August 19XX

Description	Cash	Accounts Receivable	Prepaid Rent	Ice Cream	Supplies	Equipment	Accumulated Depreciation	Wages and Accounts Payable	Owner's Equity
Original Position	7,500								7,500
1. Purchase of equipment	(6,000)					6,000			
2. Prepayment of rent	(600)		600						
3. Purchase of supplies	(200)				200				
4. Purchase of ice cream				300				300	
5. Additional ice cream purchases				1,350				1,350	
6. Payments for ice cream purchased	(1,300)							(1,300)	
7. Additional supplies purchased					100			100	
8. Sales	4,000	500							4,500 (R)
9. Miscellaneous expenses paid	(100)								(100) (E)
10. Payment of salaries and wages	(1,200)							300	(1,500) (E)
11. Cost of ice cream sold				(1,450)					(1,450) (E)
12. Cost of supplies used					(150)				(150) (E)
13. Recognition of expired rent			(200)						(200) (E)
14. Recognition of equipment depreciation							(100)		(100) (E)
New Position	2,100	500	400	200	150	6,000	(100)	750	8,500

611

Exhibit A-4   ICE CREAM PARLOR
                                   General Journal for August 19XX

Date (Entry #)	Accounts Affected	Assets	Liabilities and Owner's Equity
	TRANSACTIONS		
(1)	Equipment	6,000	
	Cash	(6,000)	
	To record purchases of equipment.		
(2)	Prepaid rent	600	
	Cash	(600)	
	To record prepayment of three months' rent.		
(3)	Supplies inventory	200	
	Cash	(200)	
	To record purchase of supplies.		
(4)	Ice cream inventory	300	
	Accounts payable		300
	To record purchase of ice cream on account.		
(5)	Ice cream inventory	1,350	
	Accounts payable		1,350
	To record additional purchases of ice cream on account.		
(6)	Cash	(1,300)	
	Accounts payable		(1,300)
	To record payment (partial) to the ice cream supplier.		
(7)	Supplies inventory	100	
	Accounts payable		100
	To record purchase of additional supplies on account.		
(8)	Cash	4,000	
	Accounts receivable	500	
	Owner's equity (sales)		4,500
	To record cash and credit sales.		
(9)	Cash	(100)	
	Owner's equity (miscellaneous expense)		(100)
	To record payment for miscellaneous services received during the month (e.g., cleaning services).		
(10)	Cash	(1,200)	
	Wages and accounts payable		300
	Owner's equity (salary and wage expense)		(1,500)
	To record payment of salaries and wages.		

Amounts

Date (Entry #)	Accounts Affected	Amounts	
		Assets	Liabilities and Owner's Equity
	END-OF-PERIOD ADJUSTMENTS		
(11)	Ice cream inventory	(1,450)	
	Owner's equity (cost of ice cream sold)		(1,450)
	To adjust the ice cream inventory balance to the cost of ice cream on hand at the end of the month and recognize the cost of ice cream sold.		
(12)	Supplies inventory	(150)	
	Owner's equity (cost of supplies used)		(150)
	To adjust the supplies inventory balance to the cost of supplies on hand at the end of the month and recognize the cost of supplies used.		
(13)	Prepaid rent	(200)	
	Owner's equity (rent expense)		(200)
	To recognize the portion of the rent prepayment that was for the month of August as an expense.		
(14)	Accumulated depreciation—equipment	(100)	
	Owner's equity (depreciation expense)		(100)
	To recognize the depreciation of equipment applicable to August 19XX.		
	CLOSING ENTRY		
(15)	Owner's equity (sales)		(4,500)
	Owner's equity (salary and wages expense)		1,500
	Owner's equity (miscellaneous expense)		100
	Owner's equity (cost of ice cream sold)		1,450
	Owner's equity (cost of supplies used)		150
	Owner's equity (rent expense)		200
	Owner's equity (depreciation expense)		100
	Owner's equity		1,000
	To close the temporary revenue and expense accounts to owner's equity.		

in the journal are divided into three categories: (1) entries to record transactions (external events), (2) entries to give recognition to needed end-of-period adjustments (typically called adjusting entries), and (3) an entry to terminate (close) the temporary accounts to owner's equity (typically called closing entry or entries).

From the general journal Exhibit A-4, we proceed directly to an illustration of the corresponding general ledger in Exhibit A-5. Explanations of the journal-ledger accounting system follow after Exhibit A-5. Such explanations benefit from simultaneous references to all elements of the system.

ICE CREAM PARLOR
General Ledger
CASH

Date (Entry #)	Explanation	Transaction Amount	Balance
Aug. 1	Initial balance		7,500
(1)		(6,000)	
(2)		(600)	
(3)		(200)	
(6)		(1,300)	
(8)		4,000	
(9)		(100)	
(10)		(1,200)	2,100

ACCOUNTS RECEIVABLE

Date (Entry #)	Explanation	Transaction Amount	Balance
Aug. 1	Initial balance		—0—
(8)		500	500

PREPAID RENT

Date (Entry #)	Explanation	Transaction Amount	Balance
Aug. 1	Initial balance		—0—
(2)		600	
(13)	To adjust	(200)	400

ICE CREAM INVENTORY

Date (Entry #)	Explanation	Transaction Amount	Balance
Aug. 1	Initial balance		—0—
(4)		300	
(5)		1,350	1,650
(11)	To adjust	(1,450)	200

SUPPLIES INVENTORY

Date (Entry #)	Explanation	Transaction Amount	Balance
Aug. 1	Initial balance		—0—
(3)		200	
(7)		100	300
(12)	To adjust	(150)	150

EQUIPMENT

Date (Entry #)	Explanation	Transaction Amount	Balance
Aug. 1 (1)	Initial balance	6,000	—0— 6,000

ACCUMULATED DEPRECIATION—EQUIPMENT

Date (Entry #)	Explanation	Transaction Amount	Balance
Aug. 1 (14)	Initial balance To adjust	(100)	—0— (100)

WAGES AND ACCOUNTS PAYABLE

Date (Entry #)	Explanation	Transaction Amount	Balance
Aug. 1 (4) (5) (6) (7) (10)	Initial balance	300 1,350 (1,300) 100 300	—0— 750

OWNER'S EQUITY

Date (Entry #)	Explanation	Transaction Amount	Balance
Aug. 1 (15)	Initial balance To close temporary accounts and recognize net income for the month	1,000	7,500 8,500

OWNER'S EQUITY (SALES)

Date (Entry #)	Explanation	Transaction Amount	Balance
(8) (15)	To close	4,500 (4,500)	4,500 —0—

OWNER'S EQUITY (SALARY AND WAGES EXPENSE)

Date (Entry #)	Explanation	Transaction Amount	Balance
(10)		(1,500)	(1,500)
(15)	To close	1,500	—0—

OWNER'S EQUITY (MISCELLANEOUS EXPENSE)

Date (Entry #)	Explanation	Transaction Amount	Balance
(9)		(100)	(100)
(15)	To close	100	—0—

OWNER'S EQUITY (COST OF ICE CREAM SOLD)

Date (Entry #)	Explanation	Transaction Amount	Balance
(11)	To adjust	(1,450)	(1,450)
(15)	To close	1,450	—0—

OWNER'S EQUITY (COST OF SUPPLIES USED)

Date (Entry #)	Explanation	Transaction Amount	Balance
(12)	To adjust	(150)	(150)
(15)	To close	150	—0—

OWNER'S EQUITY (RENT EXPENSE)

Date (Entry #)	Explanation	Transaction Amount	Balance
(13)	To adjust	(200)	(200)
(15)	To close	200	—0—

OWNER'S EQUITY (DEPRECIATION EXPENSE)

Date (Entry #)	Explanation	Transaction Amount	Balance
(14)	To adjust	(100)	(100)
(15)	To close	100	—0—

Recording and Posting Transactions

Each transaction journal entry (entries 1–10 in Exhibit A-4) shows the financial effects of an exchange transaction between the Ice Cream Parlor and an individual (e.g., an employee) or another business organization (e.g., the supplier of ice cream). As indicated before, recording these transactions in the general journal and then posting them to the general ledger produces results substantially equivalent to those produced in the financial position worksheet. For example, transaction (1) in the financial position worksheet (Exhibit A-3) reflects a $6,000 purchase of equipment by decreasing cash $6,000 and increasing equipment $6,000. The same effect is achieved within our simple accounting system in Exhibits A-4 and A-5. The transaction is recorded in the general journal (Exhibit A-4) wherein it is indicated that equipment increases $6,000 and cash decreases $6,000.

Following entry of the transaction in the general journal, it is transferred (posted) to the general ledger. Thus, referring to the general ledger in Exhibit A-5, we note that the cash account reflects a decrease of $6,000 (referenced back to entry number 1 in the general journal), and the equipment account contains an increase of $6,000 (similarly referenced). In like manner, the other nine transactions are recorded in the general journal and posted to the appropriate general ledger accounts with the same substantive effects as were achieved in the financial position worksheet.

As was pointed out in Chapter 5, we have in most of the entries aggregated the effects of a large number of individual exchanges. Our entries are, in effect, summary transactions. For example, entry (8) records the total effect of all of the individual sales transactions during the month. While this degree of aggregation prior to recording in the general journal would be unlikely in most practical systems, it should be recognized that some prior summarization may not be unusual. In the case of an ice cream parlor, for example, the accounting system might be designed to record in the general journal the total sales each week—this figure to be obtained from the cash register tapes for that period of time.

The foregoing brief consideration of the nature of transaction entries in the general journal reveals an important new dimension of the accounting system. Not only must accounting processing be a mechanism for recording, organizing, and summarizing identified events that have financial effects, it also must encompass the design of procedures and methods that identify and collect these events as they occur. At times the system must even achieve some degree of summarization before entry into the general journal takes place. It may be of interest to note that for the complex organization (e.g., General Motors or an agency of the federal government), the general journal and general ledger activities consume a trivially small portion of the time, equipment, and creativity devoted to the accounting system. This is not to say that these elements (journal and ledger) are unimportant in such an organization. Indeed, they represent for these entities, as for a small business, the culmination and in a sense the objective of all financial accounting processing. We only raise this point to hint at the scope and challenge of a facet of accounting—systems design, or the accounting-processing function—which is perhaps obscured by the discussion of our simplified system.

Recognizing End-of-Period Adjustments

Merely recording transactions with outside parties in the manner indicated does not complete the entire accounting cycle as described in Chapter 5 as necessary for the preparation of financial reports. That is, we have not yet recorded all of the changes in financial position that took place during the period. We need a set of entries (entries 11–14 in Exhibit A-4) at the end of the accounting period to bring the balances in the accounts into agreement with the objectives of the conventional accounting model. This set of entries is referred to as *end-of-period adjustments,* or *adjusting entries.* Adjusting entries may be thought of as recognition of "internal events" in the business operations of the firm.

The end-of-period adjustments are of two basic types: (1) cost allocations and (2) accruals. The *cost allocation process* is one of examining balances of asset accounts at the end of the period (e.g., in our illustration, the prepaid rent account) and determining the portion that should be allocated as an expense to the period. The balance in the asset account may have been recorded in this or in some prior period. In either case, it is the result of an exchange transaction in which the firm acquired resources that were expected to be of benefit in the future. The decision as to how much of these resources (benefits) was consumed in the period is in many cases a product of specific accounting measurement rules, which are discussed in some detail in Chapters 11–14.

In our illustration, entries (11) and (12) both cause decreases in the inventory accounts such that the remaining balances reflect the cost of items (or quantities) still on hand. At the same time, the decreases constitute recognition of the cost of items consumed (used or sold) as an expense of the period. For example, the ice-cream inventory account had a balance of $1,650 after all transactions were recorded (see the general ledger, Exhibit A-5). The balance reflects the cost of all ice cream purchased during the period. However, at the end of the period, the asset we hold is the ice cream still on hand from which we can benefit (through sale) in the next period. The ice-cream inventory account, therefore, needs to be adjusted to a balance that is equal to the cost of the ice cream still on hand. In our example, it is assumed that the cost of ice cream on hand is $200. The ice-cream inventory account must therefore be decreased by $1,450, an amount that presumably reflects the cost of ice cream sold during the period. Thus our adjusting entry (11) records the decrease to the inventory account, and the decrease to owner's equity through the temporary (expense) account, owner's equity (cost of ice cream sold).

The same reasoning is applied in entry (12), in which the cost of supplies on hand at the end of the period is assumed to be $150. It should be pointed out that estimates of the cost of inventory on hand at the end of the period for a business such as the Ice Cream Parlor would be determined in practice by counting, measuring, or otherwise physically establishing the quantity on hand and then assigning the appropriate cost to this quantity. In larger businesses with more elaborate accounting systems, reasonable estimates of the inventory on hand can usually be made throughout a year without any physical survey. However, even these firms normally make a physical count of their inventory at least once each year. Accounting for inventories is discussed at some length in Chapter 12.

Entry (13) deducts the (expired) cost of renting the building space for August from the asset, prepaid rent. The concurrent decrease occurs to owner's equity via the account, owner's equity (rent expense). The underlying transaction—entry (2)—recorded the prepayment of three months' rent. Thus, after recognizing the $200 rent expense for August, the $400 balance of the prepaid rent account at the end of the month reflects the cost of occupancy for September and October to which the Ice Cream Parlor is still entitled.

Entry (14) allocates $\frac{1}{60}$ of the cost of the equipment, which is assumed to have a five-year useful life, to depreciation expense for August. This amount is determined under the assumption that the services inherent in this equipment are realized equally during each month of its useful life. Other possible methods of recognizing depreciation are discussed in Chapter 12.

Accruals are end-of-period adjustments which give recognition to expenses incurred or revenues earned for which there have been no exchange transactions during the period. There are no accruals in our illustrative set of four adjusting entries, but accrued wages payable are recognized among the transactions in entry (10) in the general journal. An adjusting entry to recognize an accrual is only necessary if it is not recognized in connection with the transactions of the period.

Preparing the Income Statement

After appropriate adjusting entries have been recorded in the general journal and the amounts posted to the general ledger, the financial statements for August can be prepared directly from the balances in the general ledger accounts. This process is analogous to using the balances on a financial position worksheet, with the new benefit that even though numerous transactions may have affected selected revenue and expense accounts, their effects will already be summarized (in the temporary accounts) for use in preparing the income statement.

The income statement in Exhibit A-6 reflects the process of matching the

Exhibit A-6

ICE CREAM PARLOR
Income Statement
For the Month of August 19XX

Sales		$4,500
Expenses:		
Salary and wages expense	$1,500	
Miscellaneous expense	100	
Cost of ice cream sold	1,450	
Cost of supplies used	150	
Rent expense	200	
Depreciation expense	100	
Total expense		3,500
Net income		$1,000

efforts (expenses) and accomplishments (revenue) for the period as recorded in the various temporary accounts shown in Exhibit A-5.

Terminating (Closing) the Revenue and Expense Accounts

The revenue and expense accounts are, as we have stated before, temporary subdivisions of the owner's equity account. They are established merely to aggregate the effects of operations for the period into categories that facilitate the preparation of an income statement. At the end of the period, these accounts are terminated (closed) by transferring their balances to the owner's equity account. Thus the amount of owner's equity at the end of the period can be determined and the statement of financial position prepared.

Within Exhibits A-4 and A-5, the one revenue account, owner's equity (sales), accumulates the effects of operating transactions that increase owner's equity. Therefore, the balance of the account, $4,500, is positive. The entry to close this account, entry (15), records a decrease to owner's equity (sales) so as to produce a zero balance in the sales account. In a similar manner, the other elements of entry (15), except the last, close the various expense accounts. The expense accounts summarize transactions or adjustments that decrease owner's equity. They therefore carry negative balances before closing and are closed to zero balances by increases.

The net effect of the recognized revenue and expenses of the period is an increase in owner's equity, corresponding to the net income for the period of $1,000. This is given recognition in the accounts by the increase in the owner's equity account indicated on the last line of entry (15). Had the net effect of the closing entry been a decrease in owner's equity, it would imply that a net loss was incurred. After the closing entry (15) is recorded in the general journal and transferred (posted) to the general ledger accounts, all of the temporary accounts have zero balances.

A special closing account, revenue and expense summary, is sometimes used so that individual revenue and expense accounts are first closed to the summary account with only the net effect of operations for the period (net income or loss) being transferred from the summary account to owner's equity. As its title implies, this account is merely a summarizing account. It always has a zero balance before and after the closing entries are made. Since its use is merely a procedural convenience, it is not illustrated in our simplified example.

Preparing the Statement of Financial Position

The final step of periodic activity in a manual accounting system is the preparation of the end-of-the-month statement of financial position. For this purpose we use general ledger account balances *after* all appropriate adjusting and closing entries have been posted.

The statement of financial position in Exhibit A-7 reflects the balances (unexpired costs in the cases of nonmonetary assets) of resources on hand and obligations due at the end of the month as indicated by the *balances in the permanent ledger accounts* shown in Exhibit A-5. The balance of the owner's equity account shown in Exhibit A-5 as of month-end equals the

Exhibit A-7

ICE CREAM PARLOR
Statement of Financial Position
As of August 31, 19XX

Assets:		
Cash		$2,100
Accounts receivable		500
Prepaid rent		400
Ice cream inventory		200
Supplies inventory		150
Equipment	$6,000	
Less: Accumulated depreciation	(100)	5,900
Total assets		$9,250
Liabilities and Owner's Equity:		
Wages and accounts payable		$ 750
Owner's equity		8,500
Total liabilities and owner's equity		$9,250

beginning balance plus the income (in some cases the loss) for the period. This is so because entry (15), the closing entry in this case, effectively adds (algebraically) the balances in all temporary accounts (revenue and expense accounts) to the beginning balance in the owner's equity account. The effect, again, is to add an amount equal to net income for the period to beginning owner's equity.

Recap of the Process—The Accounting Cycle

The set of steps we have followed in the foregoing illustration is sometimes referred to as the *accounting cycle* because it is followed in the same sequence period after period. The accounting cycle was first introduced in Chapter 5 in connection with the financial position worksheet. To that earlier discussion we have now added some new terminology and have introduced some new processes uniquely related to the simplified accounting system postulated in this appendix. But the substance of the cycle discussed in Chapter 5 remains unchanged. To summarize, the essential steps of the accounting cycle are as follows:

1. Systematically collect data associated with transactions having a financial effect on the firm as they take place.
2. Record transactions (external events) with individuals or other business firms in the general journal, and transfer (post) the amounts recorded to the general ledger accounts.
3. Record and post end-of-period adjustments, giving recognition to the cost allocations and accruals necessary to reflect efforts and accomplishments of the period.
4. Prepare an income statement for the period.
5. Record and post closing entries to transfer the balances of the temporary accounts to owner's equity.
6. Prepare a statement of financial position as of the end of the period.

After the sequence of steps is completed for one period (in our case, a month), the cycle is resumed at step 1 at the start of the next period, and so on.

The major task of accumulating the financial data base for the firm is accomplished in steps 1 and 2 of the cycle. It is in this activity that the mass of individual transactions are identified and assimilated into the system. The systems design requirements mentioned earlier are principally concerned with this function. Steps 4, 5, and 6 are fairly mechanical, albeit necessary, operations. It is in step 3, however, that many of the major issues involving financial reporting under the conventional accounting model surface. The cost allocations and accruals that are necessary before financial statements can be prepared are largely the product of the measurement rules discussed in Chapters 11–14.

Summary Transactions and Subsidiary Records

We noted previously that several of the transactions illustrated in this appendix summarize, or aggregate, many individual transactions of the same type. For example, we observed that the sales transaction recorded for the Ice Cream Parlor summarized all of the individual sales transactions during the month—perhaps from a collection of cash register tapes. While source documents such as cash register tapes might be informally collected and summarized for a weekly or monthly entry in the general journal, complex accounting systems often employ more formal record-keeping devices. These additional records are often referred to as *subsidiary records* because they support the summary entries or balances reflected in the general journal and general ledger. For example, one such record might be a special sales journal into which sales transactions were recorded more frequently than they would be recorded in the general journal described in this appendix. In the sales journal only sales transactions are recorded, and at periodic intervals (e.g., monthly) the totals from the sales journal would be recorded in the general journal. Subsidiary journals like the sales journal might also be used for cash receipts, cash disbursements, and purchases of merchandise on account.

Additionally, subsidiary ledgers are frequently established to maintain details not reflected in the general ledger (for example, individual customers' accounts in support of the balance in accounts receivable). The larger the volume of transactions a firm experiences, the more likely it is that subsidiary records will be used in the firm's accounting system. Elaboration of these matters, as well as many others related to the design and implementation of a financial information system, is the subject of more-advanced accounting courses.

The Traditional Bookkeeping Model

The traditional bookkeeping model has been used by bookkeepers and accountants for many years as the manual (and sometimes automated) accounting system for business firms. Although not differing in substance from the accounting system described in the prior section of this appendix, it does draw on some special conventions and notational devices. Since these additional features tend to distract attention from the more important basic characteristics of a manual accounting system, we elected not to use them in our earlier exposition. However, for the reader who plans to be involved with the mechanics of a traditional bookkeeping model, we now present an overview of its essential details.

Increases and decreases to accounts are not represented algebraically in the traditional bookkeeping model. Rather, notational designations of "Debit" and "Credit" are used. These designations are typically abbreviated as "Dr" and "Cr." They have a Latin origin, since they were evolved during the genesis of formal bookkeeping (so-called double-entry bookkeeping) in medieval Italy. However, the Dr and Cr expressions no longer have any intrinsic language meaning—they are strictly notations.

Changes in accounts are changes in financial position and, therefore, can be expressed in terms of the accounting equation. Recall that based on the agreed-upon residual nature of the measurement of owners' equity, the following financial position relationship should always hold at any point in time:

$$A = L + OE \qquad (1)$$

But in order for relationship (1) to continue to hold as new transactions and events are recognized, the successive changes in financial position must also obey the relationship depicted in (2) below (where "Δ" denotes "the change in"):

$$\Delta A = \Delta L + \Delta OE \qquad (2)$$

This condition says that the change in assets (recognized in connection with a given event or transaction) must equal the recognized change (if any) in liabilities plus the recognized change (if any) in owners' equity.

Now if we simply expand condition (2) so that increases (Δ^+) in elements of financial position are distinguished from decreases (Δ^-), we get the more detailed expression (3) for condition (2):

$$[\Delta^+A - \Delta^-A] = [\Delta^+L - \Delta^-L] + [\Delta^+OE - \Delta^-OE] \qquad (3)$$

Then by rearranging terms (so as to eliminate minus signs from the expression), we obtain:

$$\Delta^+A + \Delta^-L + \Delta^-OE = \Delta^+L + \Delta^+OE + \Delta^-A \qquad (4)$$

$$\text{Debits} = \text{Credits} \qquad (5)$$

As expression (5) indicates, all left-hand elements in (4) are designated as debits, and all right-hand elements as credits. Therefore, a *Dr* to an account signifies—

1. An increase if the account is an asset account, or
2. A decrease if the account is a liability or an owners' equity account.

In contrast, a *Cr* to an account signifies—

1. An increase if the account is a liability or an owners' equity account, or
2. A decrease if the account is an asset account.

The importance of expressions (4) and (5) is that together they indicate that *if in processing transactions the debits equal the credits,* condition (3) and, therefore, condition (1) will be satisfied.

Before we illustrate the use of the Dr-Cr convention in processing transactions, we might note certain of its advantages and disadvantages. One advantage is that it simplifies notations in that it eliminates negative numbers from the system and avoids some possible clerical error sources (e.g., failure to put parentheses on numbers to specify decreases). It also affords a numerical self-checking device, since the accounting equation implies that sums of debits equal sums of credits and conversely. This self-checking property makes it easier to ensure that all the effects of transactions on financial position are in fact recorded.

One disadvantage of the Dr-Cr convention perhaps is its potential to obscure misclassifications. For instance, if an asset decrease is erroneously recorded as a liability increase, total debits still equal total credits, and a false sense of system accuracy is conveyed simply because of the debits = credits condition. Of course, the most serious disadvantage is that it constitutes a rather special notational scheme which has to be learned and remembered (at a cost) before it can be applied.

The General Journal for the Traditional Bookkeeping Model

The general journal for the traditional bookkeeping model is organized just like our earlier examples in Exhibits A-1 and A-4 except that amounts are recorded in terms of Dr and Cr. To illustrate this difference, Exhibit A-1 is now presented in traditional bookkeeping fashion as Exhibit A-8.

Exhibit A-8   AN ILLUSTRATIVE GENERAL ACCOUNTING JOURNAL IN TRADITIONAL BOOKKEEPING FORMAT

Date	Description	Dr	Cr
May 1	Owners' Equity (Rent Expense) Cash (To record cash payment for monthly rent)	1,200	1,200
May 3	Merchandise Inventory Accounts Payable (To record purchase of merchandise on account)	10,000	10,000
May 4	Cash Accounts Receivable (To record collection of accounts from customers)	2,500	2,500

We note from Exhibit A-8 that (1) the defined equality in amount between debits and credits applies not only to the aggregate of all bookkeeping entries made during a period but to *each individual recorded transaction* as well, (2) by convention, the *Dr* portion of an entry precedes the *Cr* portion, (3)

Cr portions of entries are customarily indented toward the right, and (4) left-hand amount columns are devoted to *Dr* portions of entries and right-hand amount columns to *Cr* portions. These procedures are universally used and therefore have some bookkeeping meaning in and of themselves.

The General Ledger for the Traditional Bookkeeping Model

Based on the first general ledger account appearing in Exhibit A-5 (the cash account), Exhibit A-9 shows how such an account would appear in a manually operated traditional bookkeeping system.

Exhibit A-9

ICE CREAM PARLOR
General Ledger
Traditional Bookkeeping Format

Acct. No.: XXX			Acct. Name: Cash		Year: 19XX
Date (Entry #)	Reference	Amount	Date (Entry #)	Reference	Amount
Aug. 1 (8)	Initial Balance GJ	7,500 4,000	(1) (2) (3) (6) (9) (10)	GJ GJ GJ GJ GJ GJ	6,000 600 200 1,300 100 1,200
Aug. 31	Ending Balance	2,100			

In Exhibit A-9, again by convention, Dr entries are posted on the *left* side of a general ledger account and Cr entries on the *right* side. This convention has become so deeply entrenched that the respective account sides are not even labeled "Dr" or "Cr." In fact, although the format shown in Exhibit A-9 is representative of an actual traditional ledger account, accounting educators have for years used an even simpler representation known as the *T-account* for purposes of exposition. A T-account representation of the same information as contained in Exhibit A-9 is shown in Exhibit A-10. Notice that

Exhibit A-10

ICE CREAM PARLOR
T-account

CASH

Aug. 1 (8)	7,500 4,000	6,000 600 200 1,300 100 1,200	(1) (2) (3) (6) (9) (10)
Aug. 31	2,100		

all that is really needed is an account name and two columns, with convention specifying that the left column contains the debit entries and balances and the right column the credit entries and balances.

The *balance* of any account is the difference between the sums of the amounts recorded on its two sides. Because of the way that debits and credits relate to assets, liabilities, and owners' equity, one would normally expect assets to have debit balances, and liabilities and owners' equity to have credit balances.

When temporary accounts are taken into consideration, we must recall that these accounts are components of owners' equity. Therefore they will reflect Dr-Cr characteristics congruent with their ultimate absorption back into owners' equity. Hence revenue accounts, which record ultimate increases to owners' equity, normally have credit balances. Expense accounts, which record ultimate decreases to owners' equity, normally carry debit balances.

Other Features

With the exception of the aforementioned special conventions, all other aspects of the traditional bookkeeping model are the same as those illustrated for the simplified accounting system described earlier in this appendix. After entries are recorded in the general journal (after summary in whatever special journals are used), the entries are posted to the general ledger. Adjustments are made at the end of each accounting period, income statements are prepared, the temporary revenue and expense accounts are closed to owners' equity, and finally statements of financial position are drawn up. No substantive differences result from the application of the traditional bookkeeping model—only the forms in which entries are recorded and accounts maintained.

Since the traditional bookkeeping model has found universal acceptance, its power as a unifying and simplifying force in actual financial accounting processes warrants recognition. Still we did not wish to leave readers confused between the procedures of traditional bookkeeping and the essential financial accounting data-processing requirements. Thus we separated the two.

Questions for Review and Discussion

A-1.   Define:

a. General journal

b. General ledger

c. Posting

d. Temporary account

e. Adjusting entry

f. Closing entry

g. Accruals

h. Accounting cycle

i. Special journal

j. Dr-Cr convention

A-2. State concisely the objectives of a financial accounting system. How does such a system differ from other data-processing systems, for example, traffic tickets, university course grades, social security payments, and so forth?

A-3. What three elements does a typical accounting journal entry consist of?

A-4. List twenty general ledger account titles that might be found in the accounting system of a large department store.

A-5. Distinguish between a regular general ledger account and a temporary account.

A-6. For any given period would one be likely to find a greater number of entries in the general journal or in the general ledger of a business firm? Why?

A-7. Make a typical adjusting entry in general journal form and explain why it would be made in a given situation.

A-8. Why are closing entries required? What accounts are normally the objects of closing entries?

A-9. Give at least one reason for each of the six steps that comprise the accounting cycle.

A-10. What distinguishes a special journal from a general journal?

A-11. List the advantages and disadvantages of the Dr-Cr convention in traditional bookkeeping.

A-12. Explain the reason behind the often quoted bookkeepers' maxim that debits must equal credits.

Exercises

A-1. Making Dr-Cr Transaction Entries. Using the data given in Exhibit A-4, record the ten transactions described in terms of Dr-Cr entries. In your solution, employ the general journal format illustrated in Exhibit A-8.

A-2. Making Dr-Cr Transaction Entries. Refer to the external transactions listed in Exercise 5-8. Set up a general journal as illustrated in Exhibit A-8 and record these transactions in Dr-Cr fashion.

A-3. Making Dr-Cr Transaction and Adjusting Entries. Several transactions and events are described in Exercise 5-15. Set up a general journal as illustrated in Exhibit A-8 and analyze and record the transactions described. Also make appropriate adjusting entries, distinguishing them from transaction entries. Employ the Dr-Cr convention in this exercise.

A-4. Dr-Cr Analysis. Since the accounting equation has only three elements, there can be no more than nine possible pairwise changes of equation elements. For each of the following changes, specify a corresponding business event or transaction that could give use to it:

1. Dr Asset = Cr Liability
2. Dr Asset = Cr Asset
3. Dr Asset = Cr Owners' equity

4. Dr Liability = Cr Asset

5. Dr Liability = Cr Liability

6. Dr Liability = Cr Owners' equity

7. Dr Owners' equity = Cr Asset

8. Dr Owners' equity = Cr Liability

9. Dr Owners' equity = Cr Owners' equity

A-5. Partial Applications of Dr-Cr Accounting Cycle. Refer to Exercise 5-6. Set up a general journal format like the one in Exhibit A-8 and several general ledger accounts as illustrated in Exhibit A-10.

Required:

1. Record the listed transactions in Dr-Cr fashion.

2. Make any necessary adjusting entries.

3. Post all entries to individual general ledger accounts, using T-account format.

4. Prepare an income statement for the Record Center for the month of July 1974.

5. Prepare an entry to close the temporary accounts.

A-6. Account Analysis. The inventory account of Schilthorn Enterprises has a Dr balance of $32,000 at 12/31/74. During the 1974 accounting cycle, *a closing entry* was made crediting $142,000 to owners' equity (cost of goods sold). Inventory transactions during 1974 included:

1. Purchases of $145,000 of inventory

2. A Cr of $6,000 to the inventory account because some unacceptable items were returned to a supplier

3. A Dr entry of $12,000 to the account because some inventories were discovered in a warehouse which had not been included in the 12/31/73 inventory count

Required:

Determine the 1/1/74 beginning balance in the inventory account of Schilthorn Enterprises. Support your calculations.

A-7. Account Analysis and Closing Entry. The owners' equity account of Luft Corporation had credit balances of $830,000 on 1/1/74 and of $785,000 on 12/31/74 after closing entries had been made. Net sales revenue for the year 1974 was $1.85 million, and $25,000 in dividends was paid. Except for operating expenses and the forgoing events, no other items affected owners' equity during 1974.

Required:

1. Calculate total operating expenses of Luft Corporation for 1974.

2. On a Dr-Cr basis, make the appropriate closing entry as of 12/31/74, using the information available to you. (Hint: Assume that only one temporary account was used to accumulate all expenses of the period.)

A-8. Applying the Dr-Cr Accounting Cycle.   The financial statements of the
NJW Art Shop at November 30, 1974, follow.

NJW ART SHOP
Statement of Financial Position
As of November 30, 1974

Cash	$ 4,200			
Accounts receivable	2,000	Accounts payable		$ 1,800
Merchandise inventory	4,000	Accrued salaries payable		200
Fixtures	3,500	Owners' equity:		
Accumulated depreciation—		Balance, January 1	$2,000	
Fixtures	(1,000)	Net income for		
Prepaid rent	300	eleven months	9,000	11,000
	$13,000			$13,000

NJW ART SHOP
Income Statement
For November 1974 and Eleven Months Ended November 30, 1974

	Month of November 1974	*Eleven Months Ended November 30, 1974*
Sales	$4,500	$51,000
Expenses:		
Cost of merchandise sold	$2,300	$26,000
Salaries expense	900	10,450
Rent expense	300	3,300
Advertising expense	150	1,700
Depreciation expense	50	550
	$3,700	$42,000
Net income	$ 800	$ 9,000

The NJW Art Shop engaged in the following transactions in December:

Dec. 2 Purchased frames (inventory) on account for $1,500.
Dec. 5 Paid salaries (including those accrued at the end of November) of $350.
Dec. 7 Paid $200 for a special Christmas advertising supplement put out by the local Junior Achievement.
Dec. 10 Collected $1,500 on account.
Dec. 15 Recorded sales for the first half of the month: cash sales, $4,000; credit sales, $1,000.
Dec. 15 Paid salaries of $500.
Dec. 17 Paid $2,200 to suppliers.
Dec. 18 Purchased art supplies (inventory) for $1,000 cash.
Dec. 24 Paid salaries of $800.
Dec. 28 Collected $1,200 on account.

Dec. 30 Paid $150 for advertising in the local newspaper for the month.

Dec. 31 Paid rent in advance for the first six months of 1975, $1,800.

Dec. 31 Recorded sales for the last half of the month: cash sales, $5,000; credit sales, $800.

The information for the end-of-period adjustments follows:

a. When the fixtures were purchased, it was estimated that they would have a five-year life and a salvage value at the end of the five years of $500.

b. The prepaid rent at the end of November was for the month of December.

c. The cost of merchandise (frames and other art supplies) on hand at the end of December was $1,500.

d. As of December 31, the total earned but unpaid wages amounted to $100.

Required:

1. Employ the Dr-Cr convention throughout.

2. Assuming the temporary (revenue and expense) accounts are only closed to owners' equity at the end of the calendar year, construct a general ledger (set of accounts) for NJW Art Shop with appropriate balances as of November 30, 1974. (Note: The balance of the owners' equity account will be $2,000, since the temporary accounts have not yet been closed to it.)

3. Record the transactions for December in a general journal, and post them to the general ledger.

4. Record the end-of-period adjustments in the general journal, and post them to the general ledger.

5. Prepare an income statement for the month of December 1974 and for the year ended December 31, 1974.

6. Record a closing entry in the general journal, and post it to the general ledger.

7. Prepare a statement of financial position as of December 31, 1974.

A-9. Applying the Dr-Cr Accounting Cycle.   The financial statements of the Modern Sound Shop at November 30, 1975, follow.

MODERN SOUND SHOP
Statement of Financial Position
As of November 30, 1975

Cash	$ 1,200			
Accounts receivable	500	Accounts payable		$ 1,000
Records and tapes	6,500	Accrued salaries payable		500
Furniture and fixtures	3,000	Owners' equity:		
Accumulated depreciation—		Balance, January 1	$4,000	
Furniture and fixtures	(600)	Net income for		
Prepaid rent	800	eleven months	5,900	9,900
	$11,400			$11,400

MODERN SOUND SHOP
Income Statement
For November 1975 and Eleven Months Ended November 30, 1975

	Month of November 1975	Eleven Months Ended November 30, 1975
Sales	$6,000	$72,000
Expenses:		
Cost of sales	$4,000	$48,000
Salaries expense	1,000	12,600
Rent expense	400	4,400
Advertising expense	100	825
Depreciation expense	25	275
	$5,525	$66,100
Net income	$ 475	$ 5,900

The Modern Sound Shop engaged in the following transactions in December:

Dec. 3 Paid $200 for advertising in the local paper for the month.

Dec. 4 Received a special order of records and tapes for the Christmas season. The total cost was $3,200 (purchased on account).

Dec. 5 Paid salaries accrued at the end of November. (The pay period is semi-monthly; however, the salaries are not paid until five days after the end of the pay period.)

Dec. 12 Collected $450 on account.

Dec. 15 Recorded sales for the first half of the month—cash sales, $4,000; credit sales, $200.

Dec. 20 Paid salaries of $600 for the 12/1–12/15 pay period.

Dec. 20 Paid $1,000 to suppliers.

Dec. 21 Paid $100 for spot advertising over a local radio station.

Dec. 31 Recorded sales for the last half of the month—cash sales, $4,400; credit sales, $400.

The information for the end-of-period adjustments follows.

a. The cost of records and tapes on hand at 12/31/75 was $3,600.

b. Salaries for the 12/16–12/31 pay period totaled $650.

c. The prepaid rent at the end of November was for December and January.

d. The original estimated life of the furniture and fixtures was ten years; the salvage value was estimated to be zero.

Required:

1. Employ the Dr-Cr convention throughout.

2. Construct a general ledger (set of accounts) for the Modern Sound Shop with appropriate balances as of November 30, 1975. Assume that the revenue and expense accounts are closed to owners' equity only at the end of the calendar year.

3. Record the transactions for December 1975 in a general journal, and post them to the general ledger.

4. Record the end-of-period adjustments in the general journal, and post them to the general ledger.

5. Prepare an income statement for the month of December 1975 and the year ended December 31, 1975.

6. Record a closing entry in the general journal, and post it to the general ledger.

7. Prepare a statement of financial position as of December 31, 1975.

A-10. Making Adjusting Entries.   For each of the following *independent* situations, prepare a journal entry or entries to record appropriate end-of-period adjustments. Record all entries, using the Dr-Cr general journal format. Select descriptive account titles; however, it is not necessary to precede all temporary owners' equity accounts with the caption "Owners' Equity." Assume that December 31 is the end of the accounting period and that no previous adjustments have been made during the year unless otherwise specified.

1. The inventory on January 1 totaled $35,000. Purchases of inventory during the year totaled $200,000. The inventory on hand at December 31 totaled $25,000.

2. A company is using the present value method to value an account receivable. The company's time preference rate for money is 12 percent. The account balance on January 1 was $6,340. A payment of $1,500 was received on December 30.

3. Rent was prepaid for four months on November 1. The total amount of the prepayment was $2,000. Rent payments for months prior to November have already been deducted from the appropriate owners' equity temporary account.

4. Equipment costing $10,000 and having an estimated life of five years with $1,000 salvage value was purchased on January 1. The company uses the double-declining-balance method for calculating depreciation.

5. The supplies inventory on January 1 totaled $4,000. Purchases of supplies during the year totaled $8,000. Calculations at year-end showed that $7,000 of supplies were consumed during the year.

6. A company is working on a long-term construction project. *Work began in the current year.* The total contract price is $2,000,000. The estimated remaining costs to complete on December 31 are $1,050,000. Costs in the current year totaled $450,000.

7. A monthly magazine publisher received 10,000 annual subscriptions totaling $120,000 during the year. For 5,000 of the subscriptions, eight issues were mailed during the year. For the remaining 5,000 subscriptions, six issues were mailed during the year.

Index